The Americanization of Europe

By the same editor

*Americanization and Anti-Americanism: The German Encounter
with American Culture after 1945*
     Edited by Alexander Stephan

THE AMERICANIZATION OF EUROPE

Culture, Diplomacy, and Anti-Americanism
after 1945

Edited by

Alexander Stephan

Berghahn Books
New York • Oxford

First published in 2006 by

Berghahn Books

© 2006, 2007 Alexander Stephan
First paperback edition published in 2007

Library of Congress Cataloging-in-Publication Data

The Americanization of Europe: culture, diplomacy, and anti-Americanism after 1945
/ edited by Alexander Stephan.
    p. cm.
Includes bibliographical references and index.
Contents: Cold war alliances and the emergence of transatlantic competition / Alexander
Stephan -- Britain / Hugh Wilford -- From French anti-Americanism and Americanization
to the "American enemy"? / Richard J. Golsan -- A special German case of cultural
Americanization / Alexander Stephan -- Television, education, and the Vietnam War / Dag
Blanck -- Ameri-Danes and pro-American anti-Americanization -- Two sides of the coin /
G-unter Bischof -- From cold war to wary peace / Marsha Siefert -- Polish transmissions
and translations / Andrzcj Antoszek and Kate Delaney -- Containing modernity / David W.
Ellwood -- The interface between politics and culture in Greece / Konstantina E. Botsiou --
Waiting for Mr. Marshall / Dorothy Noyes -- Imaginary Americas in Europe's public
space / Rob Kroees.
  ISBN 1-84545-085-X
   1. Europe--Civilization--American influences. 2. Popular culture--Europe--American
influences. 3. Europe--Relations--United States. 4. United States--Relations--Europe. 5.
Anti-Americanism--Europe. I. Stephan, Alexander, 1946-

CB205.A45 2005
303.48'24073'09045--dc22

2005047335

British Library Cataloguing in Publication Data
A catalogue record for this book is available
from the British Library

Printed in the United States on acid-free paper

ISBN 978-1-84545-085-4 hardback
ISBN 978-1-84545-486-9 paperback

For Halina, Michael, and Argus
My fellow wanderers between two worlds

CONTENTS

Part III: USSR/Russia, Poland

Part IV: Italy, Greece, Spain

Conclusion

ACKNOWLEDGMENTS

This book received generous support from the following institutions and organizations:

Mershon Center for the Study of International Security, The Ohio State University
Rothermere American Institute, University of Oxford, Great Britain
Alexander von Humboldt Foundation, Bonn, Germany

My sincere thanks go to Anna Goben who coordinated the preparation of the manuscript, to Jaime Taber for her meticulous work as copy editor, to Jan van Heurck for her reliable translations, and to Michael Dempsey at Berghahn Books who proved to be a patient and attentive editor.

COLD WAR ALLIANCES AND THE EMERGENCE OF TRANSATLANTIC COMPETITION: AN INTRODUCTION

◆   ◆   ◆

Alexander Stephan

The history of American culture in Europe after 1945 has not been written. The same is true of the story of European resistance against the spread of U.S. culture, often labeled anti-Americanism.

This lack of interest in the transfer of culture "Made in the USA" across the Atlantic is surprising, because postwar Europe would not be the same without the ubiquitous presence of America—in television, movie houses and music clubs, fast food and matters of lifestyle, popular literature and musicals, education and the style of political campaigning. In a sharp reversal of its withdrawal from Europe after 1918, after the end of World War II Washington employed all available tools of public and cultural diplomacy to influence the hearts and minds of Europeans. Simultaneously, and with much more success, American popular culture, which had already established firm footholds in the Old World during the Golden Twenties, invaded Europe with new intensity in the second half of the twentieth century, first by winning over the young and then by gradually eroding the resistance put up by elites eager to protect traditional high culture. The anti-Americanism that had been expressed in different forms and in varying intensity since the 1940s in most European countries by the political right and left alike seemed to have largely vanished by 1990. Yet only a decade later, in the wake of the events of 11 September 2001, it was revived in reaction to U.S. exceptionalism and Washington's worldwide war against terrorism.

Looking back at the period since 1945, it is clear that the Cold War was the driving force of U.S.-European relations in the second half of the twen-

---

tieth century.[1] Indeed, between the end of World War II and the fall of the Berlin Wall the real or perceived threat from the Soviet Union was the glue that held the Old and the New World together. In order to contain communism the United States maintained not only a continuous and wide-ranging military, economic, and political commitment in Europe, but also a strong cultural presence. A dense network of American military bases and cultural facilities extended—and still extends today, in streamlined form—from Turkey to Great Britain and from Spain to the borders of the former Warsaw Pact countries. Initiatives like the Marshall Plan and the creation of NATO served both to contain the Soviet Union and to cement the transatlantic alliance under American control. After World War II, the U.S. supported the creation and development of a European community designed to counter any threat from Germany and at the same time to mobilize the economically and politically destabilized Western Europe against the adversary in the East. On the ideological and cultural front, groups like the CIA-sponsored Congress for Cultural Freedom (CCF) organized a battle of minds against communism that replaced the reeducation of Nazis and Fascists before it gained any momentum, enabling countries like Germany, Austria, Italy, and Spain to avoid confronting their recent history, or to pass on the task to later generations.

Once politicians pledged themselves to a transatlantic community of values, words like freedom, democracy and market economy became empty slogans. Intellectuals and artists in Europe and the United States have cooperated in expanding the canon of a common Western culture, for the most part taking the legitimacy of this project for granted. Under American leadership, a model of mass culture has spread from New York and Los Angeles to Paris, Berlin, Rome, and Copenhagen, and since 1990 to Warsaw, Budapest, Prague, and Moscow. It is driven by commercial interests more than by tradition or inherited demands for form and quality, and at the same time it has set off a process of democratization that makes cultural products accessible to a broader public than ever before. Rob Kroes, a leading expert on American culture and cultural anti-Americanism in Europe, claims in this volume that it was the presence of America that helped Europeans to find a common identity.

Attempts to examine the assumptions behind the so-called transatlantic community, or to draft alternative models, have been doomed by the fact that both the United States and Western Europe profited by the arrangement they reached in the Cold War. Europe's inability, and later its unwillingness, to open the Iron Curtain on its own was used by Washington to establish itself as the leading military, political, economic, and cultural power in Europe and to consolidate its position internationally as one of two superpowers. American cultural centers and exchange programs, Hollywood and the novels of Ernest Hemingway, Abstract Expressionism in painting, jazz and rock music, and a multitude of conferences, magazines, lecture tours, exhibitions, and events staged by the Congress for Cultural Freedom insured that Europe, which formerly had held a mythic notion of America, was flooded with images—concrete if not always realistic—of the American way of life and the American model of democracy. The growing economic stability of Europe and the changing role of art in the "age of mechanical reproduction,"[2] driven by innovations like audio cassette players, television, CD players, video recorders, and computers, opened up Europe to American pop culture, which since the nineteenth century had been determined by economic factors. The form of anti-Americanism based on antagonism to U.S. mass culture was driven into retreat, now that in Europe as well the boundaries between high and popular culture had turned porous, generational differences in the consumption of culture were on the wane, and the traditional links that tied specific forms of culture to class, social background, or education had begun to dissolve. When the European workers' movement and the socialist parties moved more overtly to the political center at the end of the 1950s, Washington declared victory in the battle of minds in Europe and turned its attention to other parts of the world.

But in quite a different way, Europe too profited from the waging of the Cold War. Weakened by two disastrous wars, Germany, and a little later Britain and France as well, had to abandon the costly quest for *Lebensraum* and ambitions for foreign empire. The centuries-old train of wars and conflicts between neighboring states thus seems to have ended for the foreseeable future. Because the United States insisted on its role as the military power that fended off the "red menace," Europe was free to devote resources, that would otherwise have gone into armaments, to the building of welfare states and the subsidy of high culture. Much of the European public benefited from the fact that the U.S. culture industry, driven by the need to open new markets for its products, offered a wide variety of entertainment and Made-in-the-USA lifestyle. Moreover, during the Cold War Europeans of all ages and socioeconomic backgrounds were willing and able to commit more time and energy than their American contemporaries to protection of the environment and a humane form of globalization. They participate in a wealth of regional cultural activities, generally prefer peaceful forms of conflict resolution to military confrontations, and have shown themselves willing to cede a good part of their sovereignty and national identity to multinational organizations like the EU, the UN, and the International Criminal Court.

Yet by 1990, the stability that the Cold War had provided seemed to have come undone. Even before the collapse of the Soviet Union, Georgi Arbatov, director of the Institute of the United States and Canada in the Soviet Academy of Sciences, wrote a *New York Times* piece on the policy of the Gorbachev government in which he warned his American readers that one day they would miss the Soviet Union because it was the glue that had held the transatlantic alliance together for half a century.[3] Today, some fifteen years later, Arbatov's prediction appears to have come true.

Since 1990, U.S. wars, police actions, and sanctions against Iraq, Serbia, the Sudan, and Afghanistan have made clear that military conflict, pacifism, and international law are not accorded the same value in the New World as in the Old. A militarily irrelevant and politically marginalized Europe urges the strengthening of organizations like the UN and the International Criminal Court, while the majority of Americans regard these institutions with distrust because they would limit American sovereignty. Since 1990 the United States has stepped up the pace of withdrawal from international treaties and agreements that are important to Europeans, including the Kyoto accords, the ban on landmines, and the elimination of stores of long-range missiles. The polar oppositions Washington's neoconservatives rely on in establishing their "second American Century"—European paradise vs. American power, Jihad vs. McWorld, evil vs. good, Venus vs. Mars, "the West against the rest"—awaken in the Old World unpleasant memories of the centuries-old spiral of violence that was laid to rest, with America's help, only at the end of the Cold War. Not only politicians and intellectuals but the wider public in Europe are concerned by the "go it alone" policy of the United States, which now seems less reluctant than ever to ground its actions in concepts like "new world order," "empire," and "American exceptionalism." Complaints can be heard that Washington has set the United States outside international law by allowing America privileges that are not granted to other states.

At the same time, Americans reproach Europe for constructing a post-modern Eden while living under American military protection since 1945, and for failing to respond to crises like those in the Balkans, not to mention what Washington calls the "war on international terrorism." Europeans who hoped for a peace dividend after the fall of the Iron Curtain are accused by the United States of being unwilling to make sacrifices for freedom, democracy, and globalization of the economy, or to defend these if necessary by force of arms throughout the world. Because in the economic sphere America swears by growth, "deregulation," and free-trade zones, it resents Europe's greater reliance on the regulatory powers of the state, its socialized market economy, and its pursuit of a capitalism "with a human face." As for Europe's active role in international organizations, preference for negotiation over military operations, and commitment to ecology, humanitarian issues, and development aid, American analysts often attribute these to Europe's loss, after World War II, of the ability to engage in power politics.

In short, the relationship between the United States and Europe since the elimination of their common enemy the Soviet Union has deteriorated beyond the predictions of Georgi Arbatov. Many elements in the seemingly solid canon of shared Western values have come unstuck since 1990, and more so since 2001. Terms like "hegemony," "geopolitics," and "Eurotrash" are tossed about, while the law of the powerful threatens to crowd out the power of law. Egalité and fraternité, it appears, are not identical with the inalienable right to the "pursuit of happiness," and international humanitarian law, born out of the wars of religion in the sixteenth and seventeenth centuries and the Treaty of Westphalia, is not consistent with the nationalist religious attitudes reflected in George W. Bush's proclamation: "May God *continue* to bless the United States of America."[4] And even a basic concept like "freedom" tends to be interpreted in one way in the United States and another in Europe, not to mention other parts of the world.

This continental drift that is pulling apart the United States and Europe has relatively little in common with the traditional forms of anti-Americanism or America-criticism on the one side and "Europe-bashing" on the other, even though both sides, in the wake of 11 September 2001 continue to trot out the familiar clichés about an ungrateful Europe and an uncivilized and trigger-happy America. Instead, the current discord between the Old and New worlds is more likely to be the manifestation of a conflict between rival systems grounded in fundamental differences in politics and economics, social organization and the conduct of everyday life, human relations and the function of culture. Or to put it a little differently, the term "anti-Americanism," defined as a wholesale emotion-based rejection of American culture and lifestyle, is clearly outdated, and even the more politically correct "America-criticism," meaning disquiet at specific decisions by a current U.S. administration, inadequately reflects the differences in intellectual traditions that have shaped the United States and Europe and become more prominent since the end of the Soviet Union.

Topics and Issues

This volume, consisting of eleven studies of individual European countries covering the period from 1945 to the present, sets out to trace the influence of American culture on Europe, the reception or hybridization of U.S. cultural imports, and the phenomenon of anti-Americanism. As far as possible, it also examines the shifts occurring since 1990 in U.S.-European relations, which in future may be shaped less by the unchallenged values of a shared transatlantic community than by the conflict between systems that arises out of the differences in historical background and principles that have formed the two regions. Each essay looks at one country in the light of four different themes: first, the role of U.S. cultural diplomacy, sometimes defined as a form of "soft power;" second, the transfer and influence of American high culture, which is often facilitated by governmental or quasigovernmental bodies; third, the spread of American popular or mass culture, regulated for the most part by supply and demand; and fourth, the rejection of American cultural products and their modes of distribution that we associate with the term anti-Americanism.

Culture is here understood as a broad and flexible concept ranging from Abstract Expressionism in painting and the plays of Thornton Wilder to Hollywood films, youth culture, and lifestyle features like wearing jeans and eating fast food. Differences in the definition of culture—i.e. how it is distinct from civilization—and disparities in the ranking of high and popular culture between America and Europe are integrated into the discussion. The same holds for terms like Americanization, anti-Americanism, counter-Americanism, Westernization, modernization, and globalization, all phenomena that have been explored and defined in a host of publications, many of which have appeared since 1990. A bibliography at the end of the book lists some of the most important of these.

The abundant material and limited space available for each essay made it necessary to restrict the studies to the period after 1945, although this date does not have the same resonance in all the countries of Europe as a Zero Hour or point of a new beginning. Where possible and essential, pre–World War II conditions are outlined to show certain constant and variable features in the European response to America. The choice of countries to be studied was guided by the wish to include small as well as large nations, a variety of different regions within Europe, and countries that were on opposite sides of the Iron Curtain as well as those that remained neutral during the Cold War.

The existing literature on the impact of American culture on Europe and European anti-Americanism is surprisingly uneven. It ranges from an abundance of general and specialized studies of Germany, which for obvious reasons has been a main focus of scholarly attention, to relatively sparse treatments of Spain, Denmark, and Poland, where the influence of U.S. culture has been less publicized. Whereas French scholars and journalists have shown a long-standing interest in the theme of anti-Americanism—an interest that has been renewed and intensified since the United States mobilized for its second war against Iraq—in Uppsala an interdisciplinary research group is looking more broadly at "American Influences in Sweden." For Austria we have Reinhold Wagnleitner's classic volume *Coca-Colonization and the Cold War,* and a book on "Americanization/Westernization" just appeared. For Great Britain, there is the online project "Americanisation and the Teaching of American Studies" (AMATAS)[5] and a series of specialized studies on the Congress for Cultural Freedom, popular culture, and art. Italy recently produced an analysis of mass culture, Stephen Gundle's *Between Hollywood and Moscow.* Propaganda, high culture, rock music, and anti-Americanism have been central to a number of studies of the Soviet Union, just as popular culture, film, and television have been to research on the Russian Federation.

Generally speaking, U.S. cultural or public diplomacy is especially prominent as a central theme in the so-called eastern bloc and in countries like Germany and Austria that were occupied and controlled by the United States, although the CIA-sponsored Congress for Cultural Freedom has left its mark on the reports from other countries as well. The influence of American high culture, most visible up to the end of the 1950s, is closely linked with the cultural operations of American diplomatic agencies, the United States Information Agency (USIA), which has been defunct since 1999, and other Washington bureaus. Attempts have been made, with limited success, to examine the influence of Hemingway's writing style and the dramas of Thornton Wilder and Eugene O'Neill on European literature, or of American Abstract Expressionism on European painting. All essays in this volume trace the victory march of American popular culture and ascribe varying degrees of importance to the influence of Hollywood, rock music, youth culture, and lifestyle issues. Several authors had to digest a flood of academic, essayistic, journalistic, literary, and artistic contributions to the themes of anti-Americanism and anti–anti-Americanism, especially in France, Greece, the Soviet Union, Germany, and Italy. Central to all the essays are the years immediately after World War II, the American war against Vietnam, the arms race during the administration of Ronald Reagan in the 1980s, the New World Order after the collapse of the Soviet Union, and the so-called international "war on terror" declared by Washington after 11 September 2001.

At the same time, we see indications that the traditional concepts of anti-Americanism have been on the wane since the end of the Soviet Union and are being replaced by discussions of the clash of cultures or civilizations that is developing, or already exists, between the Old World and the New. Envy of the American standard of living as a motive for anti-Americanism has been out of date since Europe's achievement of a universally high quality of life. Few Europeans today will explain the confrontation between America and Europe using the traditional arguments that American society is materialistic, shallow, and lacking in spiritual depth and that its mass culture leads to mediocrity and standardization. American secularism and social leveling are no longer seen as grounds for criticism by Western European welfare states that are themselves secular and egalitarian. European artists and intellectuals no longer resist the erosion of boundaries between high and popular culture. Criticism of America by Germans can hardly be attributed to an attempt to avoid confronting the Nazi past, or to a Freudian urge to rebel against the U.S. as a paternal authority figure, now that this criticism is coming from the second and third generations after the war. The theory of some European conservatives that the systems of the United States and the Soviet Union could be equated under the general rubric of totalitarianism disappeared long before the death of communism. And it seems certain that after the loss of two world wars, no one in Germany is about to reawaken the anti-American vision of a "special way" in politics, economics, or culture.

The Countries

Although they played differing roles in World War II, the Big Three in Europe—Great Britain, France, and Germany—were all among the losers of the American Century. After the devastating war of 1914–18, all three were overtaken economically by the United States. Great Britain and France gradually had to cede their leadership in various parts of the world to the United States. The U.S. intervened twice in military conflicts in Europe and in the process eliminated competition from Germany and its ambitions for regional hegemony. In the Cold War, Western Europe became dependent on the United States militarily and for its security policy, while Eastern Europe became the target of a long, all-out ideological war ending in the collapse of the Soviet Union. And from the Golden Twenties to the present day, the nonstop importation of a democratic, Made-in-the-USA pop culture that was formed by commercial interests began to change the inherited high culture that had been shaped by social class, education, and the Western classical tradition.

But these factors affecting Britain, France, and Germany, for the most part negatively, cannot conceal their differences with regard to the importation of American culture and the phenomenon of anti-Americanism. Hugh Wilford, author of this volume's essay on **Great Britain,** considers Britain "relatively unresistant to American cultural influences." For some time Britain has held a "special relationship" with the United States, both politically and militarily, that can be revived when needed, as evidenced by the recent wars against Iraq. The high percentage of English immigrants to the U.S. over a period of several centuries has created strong cultural ties that have blotted out negative memories of British colonial rule. And the shared language smoothes the way for Britain's importation of American films, TV programs, popular music, and best-selling books. Moreover, both the elites and the public in the U.K. feel a longstanding distrust of continental Europe and have so far not clearly decided whether Britain should work more closely with the European Union, with Washington, with both, or with neither. Anti-Americanism, detectable among both conservatives and the British Left, consequently plays a subordinate role in Britain. Meanwhile, the U.K. is a leader in the transfer of American culture to Europe, and sometimes even succeeds in transferring its own cultural products back across the Atlantic, as has happened with the Beatles and the Rolling Stones.

A less straightforward case is **France,** as described by Richard Golsan. Anti-Americanism, often with strong emotional undercurrents, has been a central theme here, starting with France's criticism of Washington's support for the Vichy regime and continuing through the Vietnam War to the current conflict over America's second engagement against Iraq. As in Italy, left-wing intellectuals, at least until 1990, looked not to the United States but to forms of communism or democratic socialism as models for the improvement of society. Charles de Gaulle, who like German chancellor Konrad Adenauer was poorly informed about the United States, encouraged formation of the Force de Frappe, France's independent military strike force, and an exit from the integrated command structure of NATO to gain independence from what he viewed as U.S. domination, yet at critical junctures he remained tied to the Western alliance. French journalists today warn against America's overweening power (*hyperpuissance*) and contrast France's "civilizing mission" (*mission civilisatrice*) with America's "cowboyism"—yet cannot change the fact that U.S. imports like Disneyland, McDonald's, and Pizza Hut, however much they are opposed at the outset, are able to achieve commercial success in France. And while the government in Paris talks about import quotas on Hollywood films and the Académie Française discusses how to keep the French language pure of foreign phrases, the French public has consumed American ideas and cultural products with keen enthusiasm—if less so during the 1960s, then more during the period of Reaganomics.

A very different case, in some respects perhaps even a "special case," is the history of the postwar Americanization of **Germany,** described by Alexander Stephan. Militarily defeated, its national identity profoundly damaged by National Socialism and the Holocaust, West Germany was occupied and remained dependent on the United States for half a century, even after it had largely regained its autonomy. Its geographical location on the front lines of the Cold War, along with the division of the country into East and West, enabled the American occupiers to adapt their reeducation and denazification programs for the ideological and cultural war against communism. Exiles returning from the United States, German POWs, and hundreds of thousands of GIs stationed in Germany brought the starving and distraught population into direct contact with American culture. Cultural officers and attachés had a free hand in German libraries, universities, publishing houses, and radio stations. So-called *Amerikahäuser* transported selected U.S. high culture across the Atlantic, until the German "economic miracle" at the end of the 1950s brought Germans enough extra buying power to afford the products of popular culture; a market that was dominated by the U.S. Exchange programs recruited influential Germans and educators, while the Congress for Cultural Freedom courted left-wing anticommunists.

But what began as a far-ranging cultural disenfranchisement for the compatriots of Goethe and Beethoven eventually turned into a series of unique opportunities for the disempowered and occupied state. Washington's containment policy led Germany, earlier than other countries, to commit to a united Europe. Germans born after 1945 were educated not for war and violence but for multilateral relationships. Cultural work in Germany focused on analysis of the terror regime of the Nazis, and on devotion to peace and the environment. Allowed little scope for power politics, the German state concentrated on provision of a broad range of public services and subsidized cultural products of every kind. Alongside the traditional anti-Americanism from the political right and left that is found in other countries, West Germany developed its own brand of America-criticism based on pacifist motives. This criticism was expressed in the Easter marches of the 1950s, in the antiwar and anticorporate movement of the so-called Generation of '68, by the Greens and others who opposed the deployment of U.S. missiles in the 1980s, and in the broad-based resistance to German participation in the American attacks on Iraq. Meanwhile, the German Democratic Republic, i.e. East Germany, which is only briefly treated in this volume, became a state that was both firmly embedded in the communist eastern bloc and at the same time infiltrated by a youth and pop culture that followed Western models transmitted through West Germany.[6]

Britain, France, and Germany each evolved its own relationship with the United States and with American culture after World War II. At the same time, certain constant elements can be found in the cultural Americanization and anti-Americanism of the Big Three that in turn reflect the experiences of the other countries discussed in this volume, along with clear variations and sometimes pronounced regional differences. (Exceptions to the pattern are the eastern-bloc countries Poland and the Soviet Union, which are looked at separately.) **Sweden** and **Greece,** for example, as the chapters by Dag Blanck and Konstantina E. Botsiou respectively show, is connected to the United States by sizeable émigré communities and thus is less prone to America-criticism. The end of World War II did not mark the same kind of turning point for Sweden as for some countries because it had not been an active belligerent in the war, as was the case for **Spain** (Dorothy Noyes), where views of the United States are overshadowed by longstanding relations with Latin America. In **Italy** (David W. Ellwood) and, to a lesser degree, in **Austria** (Günter Bischof), the arrival of American troops was viewed more as a liberation than an occupation. Austria, which like Germany was divided after 1945 into an American and a Soviet zone, denazified, reeducated, and then unified again in 1955, belongs with Sweden in the group of states that were politically neutral but remained open to the entry of American culture. **Denmark** (Niels Arne Sørensen and Klaus Petersen), which was liberated by British troops in 1945, like Austria and Germany became a target of the American battle for hearts and minds because of its geographical position and its membership in the transatlantic alliance during the Cold War, but in its popular culture has been more receptive to the influence of Britain. Austria and Sweden, once again, share a factor in that both countries have tried to build cultural bridges between the enemy camps in Western and Eastern Europe.

For obvious reasons, the Americanization of Eastern Europe took a very different course than in the West, both during the period of communist rule (1945–1990) and subsequently. For example, in the **Soviet Union** (Marsha Siefert) a clash ensued between the government-sponsored image of America as a capitalist and imperialist class enemy, and the image born in the 1920s when Henry Ford and American mass-production methods were admired as the model for a new socialist society. Official campaigns against "cosmopolitanism" and Americanization, which were especially heated during the 1930s and then again around 1950, were mitigated by the World War II alliance between the United States and the Soviet Union, and by efforts beginning in the thaw of the 1950s to reduce East-West tensions through cultural exchange programs. Among the Soviet public, who were suspicious of any form of propaganda, negative images of a brutal, racist America presented to them by their own Soviet government collided with the equally exaggerated promises of freedom, individualism, and wealth spread by Radio Free Europe, Radio Liberty, and the occasional imported Hollywood film.

Yet, the Warsaw Pact nations too are far from being as monolithic as they may appear at first glance with respect to American culture and anti-Americanism. Whereas **Poland** (Andrzej Antoszek and Kate Delaney) since 1956 has been quite receptive to cultural imports from the West, East Germany tried in every way to shield itself from jazz, rock, and blue jeans into the 1960s and 70s. Periods of cultural détente brought a flourishing exchange of artists and magazines, alternating with periods of chill when authors like Jack London and Theodore Dreiser were acclaimed for their "un-American" qualities, and dissidents and defectors challenged or left their countries. While Poland, like Greece, is directly tied to the United States through a large colony of immigrants, American culture penetrated the GDR mainly through television and radio across its West German border. And Yugoslavia, which is not discussed in this volume, as a nonaligned country had a different relationship with the United States than did Hungary and Czechoslovakia, which were occupied by Soviet troops in 1956 and 1968 respectively.

The spread of American culture east of the Iron Curtain was limited or prevented by two factors: state censorship and the lack of hard currency to pay for imported films and royalties to the West. Both restrictions vanished overnight with the fall of the communist bloc in 1990. Cultural Americanization, which in Western Europe had unfolded relatively slowly after 1945, was now repeated in Eastern Europe at an accelerated pace. State-controlled media were commercialized overnight and flooded with American products.

The deeply rooted readers' culture in the East was replaced in a flash by the film and music industries, which generate better profits. High culture, which in communist countries was regarded as part of the cultural heritage and consequently was state-promoted and subsidized, was crowded out by violent videos, pornography, and a riot of self-help books. The new-won freedom and diversity of expression that were welcomed with such enthusiasm are now under threat from the concentration of media in the hands of just a few investors, often foreign, who show no scruples about setting profit above quality. Meanwhile, the relatively desolate condition of many postcommunist economies means that most people lack the hard cash to buy cultural goods imported from the U.S. or Western Europe, just as they did before 1990.

It is difficult to predict when and how the situation in Eastern Europe will stabilize. Entrepreneurs will no doubt welcome the commercialization of the cultural market in line with the American model, as will the younger generation, whose principal concern is to gain access to the broad spectrum of pop culture as quickly and cheaply as possible. Others who cannot embrace the harsh competition of the global marketplace are beginning to long for the more settled conditions that held sway before 1990, not only in the Soviet Union and Poland but also in the so-called new German states of eastern Germany, where Berlin's welfare system is devoting substantial sums to easing the transition of artists and other cultural workers to the new conditions. Nationalists in Eastern Europe are calling on people to remember their traditional local values, while the more internationally minded figures, such as Gorbachev and Putin, appear to prefer the Western European model to the American. And just as in Western Europe after 1945, anti-American voices can be heard throughout the East: in the Catholic and Russian Orthodox churches, among ex-communists and Slavophiles, and from all who have no taste for the commercialization and globalization of their culture.

In the concluding essay of this volume, Rob Kroes examines many of these issues, playing down Europe's significance as a counterweight to the United States but at the same time tracing signs of a common cultural identity that sets Europe apart from the New World, while from Istanbul to Stockholm and Spanish-Basque Bilbao to Dutch Haarlem indigenous cultural forms are blended with American imports to create something new. For Kroes, public space is the place where this mélange can be seen most clearly, where "Europe's exposure to American imagery" is being used "to Europeanize Europe." Or as Kroes puts it, paraphrasing a line from Henry James, "it is for Americans rather than Europeans to conceive of Europe as a whole, and to transcend Europe's patterns of cultural particularism [and] to conceive it as one cultural canvas of a scale commensurate with that of America—as one large continental culture."[7]

Across Europe: Similarities and Differences

The history of American culture in Europe has not yet been written, perhaps because it is so difficult to disentangle key themes from the confused mass of shared experiences and national differences. This volume sets out to trace such themes, taking eleven countries as examples.

For instance, we find in the majority of countries a series of key dates relating to the admission and rejection of American culture. Among these is the year 1945, which in varying degrees marked the start of U.S. dominance over Europe. In 1990, nearly half a century later, the collapse of the Soviet empire ended the automatic functioning of the transatlantic community and at the same time, for better or worse, opened up Eastern Europe to cultural imports from the West. After 11 September 2001, when the United States launched wars against Afghanistan and Iraq independently of NATO and the UN, a negative image of the United States developed in Europe and around the world. Certain populist features of this negative image reflect traditional forms of anti-Americanism. At the same time, after 1990 and 11 September 2001 an awareness seemed to emerge among the majority of intellectuals, the general public, and the circles of government that it is possible for the Old World to differ from the United States in the interpretation of basic values and ideas: freedom, democracy, the sovereignty of the individual and of the state, preventive military strikes, economic and social justice, the importance of history and culture, multilateral agreements, international organizations, and so on.

On the other hand, key dates of this kind clearly do not have the same meaning to all the countries of Europe. The year 1945, for example, is less important to Spain and Sweden than to Germany and Austria, where terms like "zero hour" witnessed the hope for a radically new beginning with the support of the United States. France and Greece associate 1945 with the arrival of American troops and the restoration of their sovereignty, while Poland remembers being transferred from one occupying power to another. Whereas the overwhelming majority of Poles and East Germans experienced the year 1990 as a liberation from a foreign culture, many Russians see the same date as the end of their country's status as a superpower and the beginning of a threat to their cultural identity. For Austria, the withdrawal of the occupation forces in 1955 is a decisive moment, whereas in Spain the death of General Franco in 1975 plays a special role and in Greece the image of the United States is strongly influenced by the rise and fall of the military dictatorship of 1967–1974, which many Greeks believe was backed by America. And in the wake of 11 September 2001, European governments do not always seem to be speaking the same language as their populations when it comes to the United States—or, more accurately, to the political line, rhetoric, and manners of the administration of George W. Bush.

The history of European cultures, while reliant on key dates such as the beginning and end of the Cold War, is marked by another landmark development that took place at different times throughout Europe in the second half of the twentieth century and was closely associated with U.S. influence: the rapid erosion of the boundary between traditional high culture, which was state-sponsored and linked to class, education, and elite groups, and a popular culture powered by commercial interests and consumed by the broad public. In Europe, as in other regions of the world, a nation's youth devouring American products and indulging in new forms of lifestyle functioned as the gateway for these changes. Young people were the first to visit rock concerts, wear jeans, or patronize McDonald's, Pizza Hut, and Starbucks, and as a rule they regarded these activities not as a move to Americanize their societies but as a liberation from rules and customs they grew up with. Teenagers, preteens and even pre-preteens turned first to radios and record players, and later to Walkmans, DVDs, and computers, to create private spaces for themselves in which they could consume music and films without interference—music and films that often, though by no means always, originate in the U.S. The modernization and commercialization of culture and leisure time, which by now has engulfed young and old alike and often continues, rightly or wrongly, to be attributed to the United States, is associated with the victory march of Hollywood and of commercial television through Europe since 1945. The economic boom that began in the north and west, which later moved on to include the south of Europe and since 1990 has been impatiently awaited in the east, provided the "kids," as Germans like to say, with the financial resources and leisure time to enjoy the revolutions of the entertainment industry.

And, finally, anti-Americanism must enter the discussion as a common element that can be detected across Europe. Entrenched conservatives, whether in Italy, Germany, France, or Greece, have long complained that traditional values and traits of their national high culture are being eradicated by short-lived commercialized U.S. imports. Quality is replaced by quantity, and people are deluded by images of wealth, pleasure, and Happy Ends that have little to do with real life in the United States. American pop culture, conservatives claim, accelerates the spread of mass consumerism and a loss of standards; it leads to domination by a soulless technology, and threatens decency by its sexual license. Especially in the 1950s, government agencies, teachers, and parents warned that Westerns, rock music, and public dancing undermined the morals of the young. In Southern Europe, the Catholic and, in Greece, the Orthodox churches resisted the alleged godlessness and sinfulness of American influences, while at the same time they collaborated with Washington to combat the greater evil of communism. In the aesthetic domain, conservatives complained of the tastelessness, and the dominance of content over form, in American popular music, *Reader's Digest* books, and TV soap operas. Those concerned for the purity of language—the Académie in France or the journalist Dieter Zimmer in Germany—tried to raise barriers against the invasion of American English into advertising, academia, and everyday life.

Opposition from the European left was equally virulent but had different causes. Liberals, social democrats, and even communists from Italy to Scandinavia and from Germany to Britain began in the 1920s to welcome the ideas of progress, technology, and modernism coming from the U.S. and viewed them as the way to the future—but at the same time they sharply criticized America as the stronghold of capitalism and imperialist interventions around the world. In many parts of Europe, first in the 1950s, and again in the 1980s, intellectuals and peace activists demonstrated against the deployment of American atom bombs and Pershing missiles. In France, Germany, and Italy, and less avidly in Britain, Scandinavia, and Austria, the so-called Generation of '68 waged intensive ideological and political campaigns against the stale middle-class society of their own countries, combined with protests against the American war in Vietnam, the imperialist policies of the United States in the Third World, and America's colonization of the European subconscious. Meanwhile protest in Spain focused less on the Vietnam war than on the presence of U.S. military bases and on the U.S. overthrow of Salvador Allende's government in Chile.

At the same time, Europeans looked to the American civil rights movement and the student movement as models for their protest, and imitated American sit-ins and teach-ins as effective ways to put ideas into practice. Since then, environmental campaigners who learned from the experiences of the Generation of '68 have criticized globalization, which they see as generated by Washington and Wall Street, and its effects on the lives, economies, and cultures of developing countries. At times they find they are joined by groups on the right, which oppose globalization for other reasons. And since 1990 in the states of the former Soviet empire, people have had to learn almost overnight how to live with an American culture that had been officially demonized in their societies and that they had been able to experience only in private or through the underground, or in the form of more or less blatant propaganda over the airwaves from the West.

All contributors to this volume agree that although "Made in the U.S.A." culture has played a strong and sometimes negative role in Europe, so far it has not proved dominant in any country. Until the 1960s and 70s, when revolutions in communications, media, and transportation got fully underway, the United States was a country almost as unknown as it had been in the nineteenth and early twentieth centuries; it was more the locus of wishes, dreams, and fears than a place of real experiences. American cultural imports were unable to stifle home-grown products except, to some degree, in the film industry, and even here there were wide local variations. Denmark continued to look to its neighbor Germany in the field of entertainment and received American culture second-hand, through Britain. In Germany, where curry sausages and doner kebabs are still today the number-one fast food, anxiety-ridden postwar youth took French Existentialism as a guide—but they listened to American jazz. Between the erection of the Berlin Wall in 1961 and its destruction in 1989, East Germans, although ideologically cut off from the West, absorbed American cultural products through West German TV and radio stations like RIAS (Radio in the American Sector), and by meeting visitors from the West or going to rock concerts along the Wall. Spain continued to be oriented mainly toward Latin America, not North America. In Britain, the Beatles and Stones blended American rhythms so skillfully into native themes that some of their fans on the Continent took them for American bands. And in Berlin, Amsterdam, and Zurich, the children of Turkish guest-workers developed their own variety of rap, creating a space of freedom from their parents and from the culture they lived in.

Moreover, American cultural products were never adopted wholesale in any country of Europe. Pick and choose, shopping mall, mélange, network, and hybridization are the terms used by cultural anthropologists to describe how the porous boundaries between cultures are crisscrossed as they borrow, process, adapt, and reject imported goods. Throughout Europe we find a blend of traditional and newly evolved regionalisms that resist cultural globalization by the United States. Slogans like *Leitkultur* (prevailing culture) mark the resistance to the cultural imperialism, real or perceived, of the U.S. Soap operas and film thrillers like the successful German TV series *Tatort* get high ratings precisely because of their specific national and regional features. And when a new American ideology emerged after the Cold War and Washington politicians began to talk about a U.S.–dominated world order, hegemony, and global culture and gained broad support for these ideas from the American public, Europeans resisted by launching, in the summer of 2003, an intensive debate about the need for a pan-European identity. This debate, initiated by the German Jürgen Habermas and the Frenchman Jacques Derrida and joined by the Swiss Adolf Muschg, the Italians Umberto Eco and Gianni Vattimo, and the Spaniard Fernando Savater, has since been debated by historians and intellectuals on both sides of the Atlantic.[8]

The authors of this volume were asked to discuss the cultural Americanization of Europe, focusing on the areas of cultural diplomacy, high and popular culture, and anti-Americanism. This opened up so many areas of investigation that the manuscript could easily have gone beyond its permitted length if each author had given equal attention to every possible theme. For example, the Americanization of education plays a role in the discussions of

Sweden, Denmark, and Greece, but not of Germany and Austria, which for a long time resisted restructuring of their traditional school and university systems. There is scant mention (e.g. in the discussion of the Salzburg Seminar in the Austria essay) of the development of American Studies programs promoted by Washington, which have already been the subject of several specialized studies. An equally important omission is the U.S. influence on disciplines like sociology and political science, the transatlantic history of feminism and gender studies, and concepts like interdisciplinary and area studies. Separate volumes could be filled with essays on the influence of American English in school instruction, advertising, pop music, and youth slang, along with the defensive maneuvers by regional linguistic purists. The activities of philanthropic organizations based in the United States also get short shrift in these essays, and only the piece on Austria gives any space to the effect of exchange programs and programs for visiting students and scholars. And it proved impossible to evaluate in detail the U.S. influence on Europe via the Internet and e-mail, or to gauge the effect of the somewhat older information revolution that led from the record player in the 1950s to today's DVD players.

U.S. cultural imports like jazz and rock, or the various youth rebellions in the 1950s and 1960s, ought ideally to be viewed not only in their effects on the receiver country but also in the context of their origins within the United States. It would be equally interesting to compare the movements toward Americanization in Western Europe with the Sovietization of the eastern-bloc countries. No one yet has seriously broached the counterfactual question of what form the modernization of European culture might have taken if the United States had not been present as a cultural superpower. And the current international situation seems to call for an in-depth examination of Washington's notion that its liberation of Germany, Austria, and Japan from totalitarian regimes offers a model for change in Eastern Europe, or for U.S. nation-building in Afghanistan and Iraq.

After the End of the Cold War: A Transatlantic Rift?

Europeans have typically responded with anger or irony to the Bush administration's suggestion that Europe's experiences of Americanization are transferable to developing countries in the Third World, but in doing so, they may be missing out on an opportunity to exert influence themselves. If Rob Kroes is right in his thesis that after 1945 the United States helped to Europeanize Europe, then it may also be true that the hybrid Western European culture, with its blend of tradition and modernism, government subsidies and market competition, may offer a more useful model for Eastern Europe and other regions of the world that are going through radical change than the American example, which is more focused on innovation and market forces. As the essay on Russia suggests, in this scenario traditional cultural values that have evolved over millennia could play an important role in the new societies, alongside the concepts of permanent growth and technological innovation that America, as a nation "without history," embraces at home and abroad. The use of public funds to subsidize high culture, familiar throughout Europe, could work in cooperation with the market forces of supply and demand. High culture, which has always been produced and consumed by a small minority, would then not be marginalized to the point of invisibility by the products of mass entertainment, as is happening in the United States. Local and regional forms of culture could survive, or even expand their market as is now the case all over Europe, by offering something different from the standardized global culture, which manufactures products without social, ethnic, and historical features because only in such a form can they be easily marketed worldwide to produce the maximum profit. In short, if a clash of systems really has evolved between the United States and Europe since the end of the Cold War, the Old World could suddenly have an advantage over the New. First, because the traditional cultural elites of Europe can reference experiences and values that the far younger United States has been unable or unwilling to develop. And second, because in their process of Americanization these elites have had to open up to the general public's demand for new kinds of entertainment and to market forces geared to meet these demands.

As a result, the values of the "transatlantic community" that appeared fixed for half a century now seem on the point of being replaced by a rivalry between systems that requires both sides to redefine their positions. The United States has pulled away from "old Europe," partly because of the changed strategic situation in which the Old World lost its privileged position on the front lines of the Cold War, but also, it appears, because America has made a definitive cultural break from Europe. Theories partly originated by European thinkers—including the somewhat abstract notions of an end of ideology[9] or the end of history[10]—became practice in 2002 in the *National Security Strategy of the United States of America* and the policies of the administration of George W. Bush. Whereas the idea of an "American Century" was born back in 1941 from a single mind, namely that of Henry Luce, the editor of *Time* and *Life* magazines, today the government in Washington collaborates with well-endowed think tanks on the project of a "second American century." Concepts like "manifest destiny," "city upon a hill," and "entangling alliances," which belonged to the foundation myths of the United States, are being resurrected as if the world were largely unchanged since the day the Puritans landed in New England. Instead of reflecting cautiously on the theme of "Our Country and Our Culture" as was done in the early 1950s,[11] both conservative and liberal intellectuals from New York to Los Angeles are demanding the right to a military first strike, thus crossing the fine line between "unilateralism" and "exceptionalism."

Culturally and politically loaded code names and phrases like "crusade," "Infinite Justice," "Enduring Freedom," and "axis of evil" are interpreted differently on opposite sides of the Atlantic. The United States, with its postmodern ideology and a democratic mass culture that almost totally permeates the society, is exporting to the world cultural models that claim to realize the unfulfilled dreams of the European Enlightenment and of European modernism. And while European culture, affected by American imports, is forced to remain adaptable and to learn new things, U.S. culture, which is shaped by the American internal market and by its mission as the leading global culture, has less and less reason to open itself up to the classical cultural tradition and—notwithstanding discussion of the canon and debates over political correctness—to learn from cultural models from elsewhere in the world.

Europe, meanwhile, seems to have developed a new self-confidence since the fall of the Berlin Wall, based on its own historical memories blended with past influences from the United States. At least for the moment, its experiences in the twentieth century have left Europe less interested in armaments and preventive wars than in multilateral agreements as a tool to make the world safe for democracy. Recollections of the negative consequences of "imperialism" and "colonial overstretch" are still fresh in France, Britain, Germany, and somewhat older in Portugal and Spain, making international military operations less appealing than "soft globalization" through development aid, the promotion of human rights, and the buildup of international aid organizations. Europe believes that it offers an alternative model to the social and cultural overstretch of American postmodernism, and is able to create a hybrid cultural landscape where regionalism remains free of fundamentalism. Instead of the American reliance on a popular culture regulated by supply and demand, Europe pursues its own multilateral blend of entertainment and publicly subsidized high culture.

In February 2003 the magazine *The Nation* carried a lead article on "How Europeans See America" and headlined it "USA Oui! Bush Non!"[12] Clearly, such simple distinctions are no longer adequate in the wake of the Cold War and 11 September 2001. Instead, indications are that in future there needs to be reflection on both sides of the Atlantic about fundamental cultural differences between the United States and Europe—or, should this "Europe" not yet exist, between the U.S. and France, Germany, Great Britain, Italy, and other countries. Such reflections would go beyond anti-Americanism, "Europe-bashing," or mere criticism of the policies of this or that particular government by examining the disparities between the Old and the New World over such basic concepts as freedom and democracy, the relations between the state and the individual, the importance of religion, the organization of society, and the status of culture. If the current and still rather unproductive clash of cultures or civilizations were to develop into a healthy transatlantic competition between systems from which *both* sides were capable of learning, we would be better off—the Old World, the New, and everyone else.

Notes

1. Detlef Junker, ed., *The United States and Germany in the Era of the Cold War, 1945–1990: A Handbook* (Cambridge: Cambridge University Press, 2004); published first in German as *Die USA und Deutschland im Zeitalter des Kaltes Krieges 1945–1968: Ein Handbuch,* 2 vols. (Stuttgart: Deutsche Verlags-Anstalt, 2001).
2. Walter Benjamin, "The Work of Art in the Age of Mechanical Reproduction," in William McNeill and Karen S. Feldman, eds., *Continental Philosophy: An Anthology* (Malden: Blackwell, 1998) 244–252.
3. Georgi Arbatov, "It Takes Two to Make a Cold War," *New York Times*, 8 December 1987, A38.
4. George W. Bush, "State of the Union (January 2003)," http://www.whitehouse.gov/news/releases/2003/01/20030128-19.html (last accessed: 24 July 2004). [Emphasis mine]
5. http://www.uclan.ac.uk/amatas (last accessed: 24 July 2004); see also Neil Campbell, *Landscapes of Americanisation* (Derby: University of Derby, 2003).
6. Therese Hörnigk and Alexander Stephan, eds., *Rot = Braun? Brecht Dialog 2000: Nationalsozialismus und Stalinismus bei Brecht und Zeitgenossen* (Berlin: Theater der Zeit, 2000).
7. See the essay by Rob Kroes in this volume, pages 346 and 348.
8. For a brief discussion of the Habermas/Derrida initiative, see my talk "Der große Freund-Feind: Das gespannte Verhältnis zwischen Deutschland und den USA." Südwestrundfunk 2. 11 July 2004. http://www.swr.de/swr2/sendungen/wissen-aula/archiv/2004/07/11 (last accessed: 28 February 2005), and article "Der wiedererwachte Systemkonflikt: Der 'neue' Bruch zwischen den USA und Deutschland ist eigentlich ein 'alter.'" In Hermann Strasser and Gerd Nollman, eds. *Endstation Amerika? Sozialwissenschaftliche Innen- und Außenansichten* (forthcoming, 2005).
9. Daniel Bell, *The End of Ideology: On the Exhaustion of Political Ideas in the Fifties* (New York: Collier Books, 1962 [second, revised edition]).
10. Francis Fukuyama, *The End of History and the Last Man* (New York: HarperCollins, 1992).
11. "Our Country and Our Culture," *Partisan Review* 19 (1952).
12. Eric Alterman, "USA Oui! Bush Non! How Europeans See America," *The Nation* 10 February 2003: 11–18.

Part I

GREAT BRITAIN, FRANCE, (WEST) GERMANY

BRITAIN: IN BETWEEN

◆   ◆   ◆

Hugh Wilford

Historic bonds between American and British culture, the most obvious being a shared language, have made Americanization and anti-Americanism less
emotive issues in the United Kingdom than in many continental European
countries. Just as the UK has tended to be the U.S.'s most supportive ally in
the realm of foreign policy, so the British have been relatively unresistant to
American cultural influences, both highbrow and popular. This does not
mean, however, that Britain has been spared bouts of anxiety about and opposition to Americanization in the period since World War II. As in other
European countries, cultural elites were already concerned about such effects
of modernization as the rise of "mass culture," a phenomenon with which the
U.S. was particularly associated. Conservative intellectuals feared the threat
to their own "minority culture" presented by the democratization of cultural
consumption; socialists fretted about the apparent susceptibility of young,
working-class Britons to mass-produced U.S. cultural artifacts, a tendency
they saw as a danger to the survival of both local folk traditions and proletarian political consciousness. Such anxieties were aggravated by the painful necessity of having to adjust to a greatly reduced role in world affairs and
troubling questions about British identity thrown to the fore by the passing
of empire. This helps explain why there were outbursts of anti-Americanism
in postwar Britain and corresponding official attempts (all, it has to be said,
unsuccessful) to curb U.S. cultural influence. It also explains why the U.S.
government, while confident of Britain as a firm ally, did nonetheless feel the
need to make some effort to promote positive images of American culture in
that country.

Notes for this section begin on page 40.

U.S. Government Programs

The years of World War II saw the U.S. engaging in a number of information activities on British soil. In 1942, for example, the newly created Office of War Information (OWI) set up a reference library in the London embassy and launched a series of traveling exhibitions about American life. Establishing a pattern of governmental cooperation that would run throughout the postwar period, these initiatives were complemented by similar measures carried out by the British Ministry of Information, such as film presentations, lectures, and magazine publishing.[1] With the end of the war and dismantling of the OWI, United States Information Service (USIS) operations came to an almost complete standstill in Britain.

The continuation of the Anglo-American alliance into peacetime and the relative weakness of the British communist movement meant that the UK ranked low on the U.S.'s list of information targets. That said, in official American circles there was some concern about the Cold War political allegiance of the left wing of the governing Labour Party and an uncomfortable awareness that even among the U.S.'s staunchest political allies on the British right there were reservations about American *cultural* influence over Europe. Such anxieties increased after 1950 when a series of strains in Anglo-American relations (such as the diplomatic fallout from the UK's botched attempt to regain control of the Suez Canal in 1956) prompted a corresponding surge in British cultural anti-Americanism. The result was the stepping up of the U.S. cultural diplomacy effort in Britain, a development accompanied by a similar escalation of informational activities by pro-Americans within the British government and various civil institutions. Even when at its height, however, the U.S. publicity campaign in the UK lacked the intensity it possessed in many continental countries, with information officers typically adopting a low-key, "soft-sell" approach.

Reflecting this preference (and restrictions on the dollar allowance, which made travel to the U.S. impossible for all but the wealthiest Britons), the most important tool of cultural diplomacy in postwar Britain was the citizen exchange. As in other countries, it was the Fulbright program, created in 1946, that dominated the field. In 1949 alone (its first year of operation in the UK), it was responsible for sending 257 American professors, teachers, and students to Britain, and 237 Britons to the U.S.[2] But just as the Fulbright was not the only university exchange scheme operating between the two countries—it was predated by the Rhodes and Commonwealth Fund scholarships[3]—so academics were not the only citizen group targeted for exchange. The Anglo-American Council on Productivity, a Marshall Plan initiative intended to spread modern working practices in postwar Europe, dispatched U.S. productivity "experts" to help modernize UK industry, while hundreds of British managers and workers traveled in the other direction.[4] "Leader-specialist" awards, established under the Smith-Mundt Act of January 1948, were available to politicians, journalists, and other opinion-formers of all political persuasions, but tended in practice to go disproportionately to pro-Americans on the British left, who were perceived as Washington's most valuable allies in the Cold War battle for hearts and minds.[5] Typifying the behind-the-scenes collaboration between government officers and private citizens that underpinned much of the U.S. diplomatic effort in the UK, the Current Affairs Unit of the English-Speaking Union launched a "Workers' Travel Grants Scheme" in late 1954 with the aim of sending British trade unionists on month-long tours of the U.S.[6] An official helping hand was discreetly extended to other civil institutions promoting transatlantic exchanges, such as the American and British Council of Churches, which in 1955 sent nine British ministers to the U.S.[7]

These exchangees' experiences appear generally to have been extremely positive. Used to the austerity and drabness of postwar Britain, many were overwhelmed by the affluence and generosity they encountered in America. Penurious young scholars such as literary critic and novelist Malcolm Bradbury discovered a "paradise of consumer splendours," including a kitchen waste-disposal unit into which his host gratuitously fed a cooked chicken: "I stared at the gurgling hole as it slowly ate the entire chicken and flushed it away; and then I knew I had seen America, and it worked."[8] Up-and-coming politicians, especially social-democratic intellectuals on the right wing of the Labour movement, developed an enduring fascination with and admiration for things American. For example, writing in 1991, Roy Jenkins recalled his two-month tour of America in 1953 on a Smith-Mundt grant as "a brilliant piece of unforced propaganda" and "a fairly sound investment of not much more than $3,000."[9] (The program would later have a similar effect on young Thatcherites within the Conservative Party: the Iron Lady herself, who crossed the Atlantic in 1967, experienced an "excitement" on arriving in the U.S. that "never really subsided.")[10]

There were some hitches: while many workers and bosses were converted to the "productivity gospel," British industrial relations generally changed surprisingly little as a result of the Marshall Plan, remaining as class-bound and conflict-prone as ever. Other exchanges had unintended consequences, as when the pro-American Labour MP Woodrow Wyatt returned home "resentful and scornful" about the "patronizing" attitudes he had encountered toward Britain and other nations receiving U.S. aid;[11] funding shortages and the effects of McCarthyism, which prevented some Labour grantees from receiving visas, also posed problems. Overall, though, the various exchange programs proved highly effective conductors of American influence to postwar Britain, sometimes in unexpected ways. In 1956, for example, Morlais

Summers, a Cardiff funeral director, returned from the U.S. "with certain concepts of undertaking," including the building of "a funeral home and chapel in American style," which won him a reputation as "the most progressive undertaker" in South Wales.[12]

Another "one of the major aims of the cultural affairs program" in Cold War Britain (according to a 1959 London embassy "Annual Assessment Report") was "the introduction of American studies into the British university curriculum."[13] Although there were chairs of American history at the universities of Oxford, Cambridge, and London (those at Oxbridge being occupied by visiting American professors), the U.S. had otherwise been ignored as an object of academic study in Britain. This situation, the consequence of a combination of cultural snobbery and academic traditionalism, was to change during the 1950s, as U.S. officials, motivated partly by Cold War concerns, quietly assisted the founding of the British American Studies movement. In July 1952, the Fulbright Commission funded a conference at Cambridge attended by sixty-five British academics and ten American professors, among them Henry Steele Commager, Alfred Kazin, and Merle Curti.[14] Three years later, following some gentle nudging from the U.S. Cultural Attaché, Dick Taylor, a meeting at Oxford launched the British Association for American Studies (BAAS). A Rockefeller Foundation grant of $150,000 secured in 1956 (perhaps not coincidentally, in the wake of the Suez crisis) ensured the young organization's survival and growth.[15] By 1959, the budding new discipline had, so a U.S. embassy official concluded, "turned a corner."[16] The stage was set for a period of steady if not spectacular growth, with the creation of a number of new American Studies posts and departments at provincial British universities.

Clearly, then, U.S. government prompting played an important part in the birth of British American Studies. Still, it would not do to see the movement merely as a creature of the Cold War. The British academics involved—individuals such as Harry Allen, Frank Thistlethwaite, and Marcus Cunliffe—had their own reasons for wanting to found a new discipline, including a preexisting interest in America (often engendered during World War II), entrepreneurial ambition, and youthful rebelliousness (many hailed from working- or lower-middle–class, provincial backgrounds and were therefore predisposed to question the intellectual prejudices of more patrician colleagues, as well as finding relatively classless America itself a congenial environment).[17] Firsthand accounts of the period recall the "*élan* and intimacy" of "a pioneering band" that believed it was "riding the wave of the future."[18] Moreover, American cultural diplomats, having helped create American Studies in Britain, found that they could not always control its development. As in other European countries, antinomian currents unleashed during the 1960s helped transform the discipline into a critical interrogation of American identity and international influence, so that some U.S. observers began to complain about "anti-American Studies." This critical impulse helps explain a recent self-reflexive turn among younger British American Studies scholars to uncover the previously hidden power relations in their discipline's origins.[19]

A similar tendency lies behind the recent interest shown in the CIA's efforts in the so-called "cultural Cold War"—the superpower struggle for the "hearts and minds" of the world's intellectuals—and, in particular, the Agency's principal weapon in this conflict, the Congress for Cultural Freedom (CCF). Although the CCF did not get off to a good start in Britain—its 1950 founding conference in West Berlin was disrupted by mischievous interventions by two Oxford dons, A. J. Ayer and Hugh Trevor-Roper—it eventually succeeded in establishing a formidable presence in Cold War British intellectual life. A national affiliate, the British Society for Cultural Freedom, was set up in January 1951 under the leadership of such distinguished literary intellectuals as Stephen Spender, Malcolm Muggeridge, and Fredric Warburg. Links were also established with the sort of Atlanticist Labour intellectuals who were already being targeted for exchange grants. Anthony Crosland, the recipient of a Smith-Mundt award in 1954 (and a future Labour Foreign Secretary), performed a number of tasks on the CCF's behalf, for example, touring and reporting on its Scandinavian sections. He was also present at the organization's conference on the "Future of Freedom," held in Milan in 1955, along with a number of other prominent British intellectuals, including the Labour Party leader, Hugh Gaitskell.[20]

Most spectacular of all was the success of the CCF's London-based magazine, *Encounter.* Launched in 1953 under the editorship of Spender and the New York intellectual Irving Kristol, *Encounter* quickly overcame early apprehensions that it was a Cold War "Trojan Horse" and gained a reputation as the foremost journal of "serious" political opinion and cultural expression in the English language, securing contributions from a remarkably wide cross-section of British writers, again including young Labourites such as Crosland and Jenkins. When Labour achieved election under Harold Wilson in 1964, Kristol's successor as U.S. editor, Melvin J. Lasky, was able to boast: "We are all pleased to have so many of our friends in the new government."[21]

The impact on Britain of the CIA's cultural campaign is hard to measure. It would be simplistic to say that British intellectuals were brainwashed by the CCF. Many remained mistrustful of the organization: Bertrand Russell, for example, resigned from one of its honorary chairs in 1957 following a series of noisy rows over McCarthyism with its American affiliate, the American Committee for Cultural Freedom. Talk of hoodwinking also seems inappropriate given that many of the CCF's most prominent collaborators later confessed that they had either known or strongly suspected that it was secretly funded by the CIA. Indeed, it now seems that several were principally interested in spending the Agency's clandestine patronage on pet cultural projects that had little or nothing to do with the Cold War. These considerations notwithstanding, it would be unwise to underestimate the long-term effect of covert American subsidies on postwar Britain. The secret support given the "Gaitskellite" intellectuals of the Labour Party, for example, arguably helped make the political culture of the British left more Atlanticist and less social-ist, thereby preparing the ground for the "modernizing," pro-American poli-cies of Tony Blair's New Labour.

Highbrow Culture

Fear of the potentially corrupting effects of American cultural influence had long been a feature of British intellectual life, a tradition traceable from Matthew Arnold's *Culture and Anarchy* to F. R. Leavis's *Mass Civilisation and Minority Culture.* If anything, this impulse was strengthened after World War II, in response to anxieties about a perceived "invasion" by U.S.-produced mass culture and Britain's relative decline as a world power. Combined with other factors peculiar to the period, such as the expansion and (again relative) democratization of the British higher education system, these developments helped generate a set of new literary tendencies—the Movement, the Angry Young Men, and Leavisite literary criticism—that rejected modern, "foreign" influences in favor of more traditional, "English" themes and forms. Although by no means identical in their origins or modes of expression, these groups also shared a provincial, working, or lower-middle class background and a suspicion of the London literary establishment, "Bloomsbury," which as well as being definitely modernist in its tastes was identified with America. Witness, for example, the constant transatlantic to-ing and fro-ing of "MacSpaunDay" poets such as Stephen Spender (Movement poet Philip Larkin barely ever left the country).

Although heavily publicized during the 1950s (indeed, it has been argued that the Angry Young Men were in part a media fabrication), the literary re-volt of the provinces did not last. By the early 1960s, metropolitan taste-makers such as Spender—supported by the apparatus of the U.S. effort in the cultural Cold War—had succeeded in (to use a phrase of cultural historian Alan Sinfield) "reinventing" modernism.[22] The canonical status of T. S. Eliot and Ezra Pound was reasserted; William Faulkner was added to the pantheon of great moderns; critical theories and methods borrowed from "New Crit-ics" such as John Crowe Ransom aided in the institutionalization of English studies in the newly expanded universities. "It was as a U.S. construct, often recognised explicitly as such," writes Sinfield, "that Modernism was recen-tered in Britain from the end of the 1950s."[23] Aiding in this process were several writers and critics who had previously belonged to the antimodernist camp, such as ex-Movement poet Donald Davie and the former Leavisite Al Alvarez. This reflected the fact that, to quote Sinfield again, "while U.S. influence obviously undermined the autonomy of British culture, it also promised release from more traditional mores and local structures of wealth, class and cultural capital."[24] It is perhaps suggestive in this regard that such self-consciously "English" Movement writers as Larkin and Kingsley Amis were also ardent fans of American jazz (the traditional, Dixieland variety, that is; they were resolutely opposed to "modern" bebop).

Since the 1950s, then, there has been a pronounced trend in British literary culture toward American-influenced internationalism and experimentalism. In the world of theater, for example, the gritty social realism and deliberate formal simplicity of *Look Back in Anger* by John Osborne (the archetypal Angry Young Man) was overtaken in the 1960s by the dramatic innovations of Americans like Jim Haynes, Charles Marowitz, and Ed Berman.[25] Indeed, by the end of the century, the popular British and American theaters seemed to be merging into each other, as U.S. film stars appeared on the West End stage and Kenneth Branagh shuttled between London and Hollywood. Meanwhile, American "postmodern" fiction, especially the novels of Donald Barthelme, Kurt Vonnegut, and Thomas Pynchon, exerted a growing transatlantic influence, so that a "deconstructive seepage of separate worlds into each other" has become commonplace in recent British writing.[26]

Postmodernism has not swamped Britain altogether: its influence did not begin to tell until late, that is, during the 1970s, and the formalistic excesses of American fiction have been tempered by a continuing deference to the realist conventions of the English novel tradition. Nor, of course, is American literature the only "foreign" influence working on British literature: quite apart from the influence of South American Magical Realism on such authors as Angela Carter, new postcolonial voices have been raised, within as well as outside the British Isles, so that the legacy of empire is now expressed in ways very different from the imperial nostalgia of the 1950s. This, however, is not to deny the continuing pull of America, as shown by the cosmopolitan, mid-Atlantic accent of perhaps the most prominent of contemporary British novelists, Martin Amis (the son of Movement novelist Kingsley Amis).

Visual and material culture in postwar Britain tells a similarly complex story of repulsion, attraction, and (heavily mediated) influence. As was the case with literary intellectuals, British art and architectural critics had long tended to identify the U.S. with obnoxious modern values—the commercial, technological, and urban—extolling instead the humanist, organic, and pastoral. The design principle of "streamlining" was an early object of British denunciation, standing for all that was thought superficial and meretricious in mass culture.[27] Suburban housing was another target; the *Architectural Review* dismissed much of the contemporary American built environment as "a visually scrofulous wasteland."[28] The prevailing viewpoint was that these design and architectural styles threatened to colonize the British landscape. Tellingly associating signs of cultural Americanization with the U.S. military presence in Britain, critic W. G. Hoskins wrote of an English countryside disfigured by "the nissen hut, the 'pre-fab' and the electric fence," and hovering over it "the obscene shape of the atom-bomber, laying a trail like a filthy slug upon Constable's and Gainsborough's sky."[29] Confronted by this horrid spectacle, many British artists sought refuge in an idealized vision of the national past, a neoromantic aesthetic embodied in several of the exhibitions staged during the Festival of Britain in 1951.

Not all artists and architects shared this impulse. Indeed, several strongly objected to what they perceived as neoromanticism's insularity and amateurishness, "the Moore-ish yokelry of British sculpture or the affected Piperish gloom of British painting," as sculptor Eduardo Paolozzi put it.[30] In 1952, Paolozzi began meeting with other disgruntled artists and intellectuals, among them painter Richard Hamilton, architects Peter and Alison Smithson, and critics Reyner Banham and Lawrence Alloway, at the recently created Institute of Contemporary Arts (ICA) in London. The Independent Group, as it became known, was drawn to precisely the mass-produced American artifacts that their contemporaries so detested: Detroit-styled cars, magazine advertising, industrial architecture. Transgressing traditional boundaries between high art and popular culture, Paolozzi and the others produced American-style collages, sculptures, and architectural plans that embodied what Alloway called an "aesthetics of plenty."[31] As they did so, a series of exhibitions, the most important of which were "Modern Art in the United States" and "The New American Painting," staged at the Tate Gallery in, respectively, 1956 and 1959, introduced British artists to the massive canvases of the American Abstract Expressionists. The influence of U.S. abstractionism was very much in evidence at the "Situation" show of young British painters, mounted by the RBA Galleries in 1960. As with the transmission of U.S. literary influences to Cold War Britain, this was not an entirely spontaneous process. The official support given to the exhibition of Abstract Expressionism overseas is already well documented; recently, British scholars have pointed out links between the ICA and successive cultural affairs officers at the American embassy in London.[32] There is also evidence suggesting CIA involvement in funding a worldwide competition to design a Monument to the Unknown Political Prisoner organized by the ICA in the early 1950s.[33]

Since the 1960s, many British painters, designers, and architects have found "explicit inspiration" in the work of their American counterparts.[34] However, this was not a simple case of cultural imperialism, with the metropolis New York holding sway over the colony London. Despite the undoubted influence of Abstract Expressionism, there was so little demand among British collectors for homegrown abstractionists that Pop artists such as David Hockney typically resorted to representation. What is more, the influence was not one-way, but filtered back across the Atlantic, with, for example, the "New Brutalist" architecture of the Smithsons inspiring the work of Denise Scott Brown and, through her, Robert Venturi.[35] U.S.–produced Minimal and Conceptual art did have a considerable impact on British art during the 1970s, but again this was far from Coca-colonization: the Tate's purchase of Carl Andre's *Equivalent VIII* (120 American firebricks) in 1976 famously provoked a storm of protest in the British tabloid press, while tensions within the Anglo-American Conceptual art group "Art and Language" led eventually to the disbanding of its U.S. wing. During the 1980s, the focus of cultural power seemed to move back across the Atlantic, with influential taste-makers like critic Robert Hughes and collector Charles Saatchi preferring British to American art. The celebrity artists of the 1990s BritArt movement—Damien Hirst, Jake and Dinos Chapman, Tracey Emin—displayed the kind of brash confidence previously associated with British punk. However, even here a closer inspection reveals a more complex picture: for instance, the highly publicized survey show that toured the U.S. in 1995 and 1996, "Brilliant! New Art from London," featured American styles of exhibition.[36]

Popular Culture

If many conservative British intellectuals perceived American influence as profoundly threatening to high cultural standards, an equally strong socialist tradition was to see it as fatally damaging to homegrown working-class culture. Mass-produced cultural imports, it was believed, were destroying long-established folk-ways and enervating British workers intellectually, morally, and politically. Writing just prior to the period under discussion, George Orwell lamented "how deep the American influence has already gone," singling out the popularity of the U.S. crime novel as both symptom and cause of moral decay in British society.[37] J. B. Priestley, who denied he was anti-American but admitted that he had a reputation as "the man who does not like America," coined the term "Admass" to describe a new kind of culture dominated by "mass communications, showmanship, [and] ballyhoo" that had originated in the U.S. and was now colonizing the minds of the British, which were "wide open as well as being empty."[38]

The most important expression of leftist unease about American influence in the postwar period is to be found in Richard Hoggart's much-discussed treatise on working-class culture in the North of England, *The Uses of Literacy* (1957), a founding text of the British "Cultural Studies" movement. Like

Orwell, Hoggart despised "gangster-fiction," seeing it as a particularly vicious form of pornography, a "new style in sex-novels spreading from America."[39] The best-known passage on Americanization in the book concerns the lifestyle of the "juke-box boys," newly affluent teenagers "who spend their evening listening in harshly-lighted milk-bars to the 'nickleodeons,'" sporting "drape-suits, picture ties and an American slouch.... Many of the customers—their clothes, their hair-styles, their facial expressions all indicate—are living to a large extent in a myth-world compounded of a few simple elements which they take to be those of American life."[40] Here, in Hoggart's powerful word-picture, is the Americanized working-class youth, cut adrift from the folk traditions that would once have given his life meaning and now mindlessly consuming the debased forms of mass culture.

While continuing to command respect for having opened up previously unexplored areas of popular culture to serious critical inquiry, Hoggart's views on Americanization have largely been refuted by later British practitioners of Cultural Studies. Research based on surveys of reader responses, for example, has shown how working-class British consumers of American crime fiction found in the genre representations of urban experience and a democratic, demotic style that were missing from the more genteel "whodunits" produced at home.[41] Similarly, studies of the teenage lifestyle so pilloried by Hoggart have shown not only that it was more complex in origin than he supposed—the drape suits, for example, originated in an upper-class fashion for "Edwardian" clothing that was then appropriated by gangs of working-class "Teddy Boys" in South London—but that it also carried an oppositional political meaning he failed to detect. According to Dick Hebdige, 1950s working-class youths deployed American cultural artifacts in a deliberate "attribution of meaning," "an attempt at imposition and control" in defiance of a dominant culture that otherwise paid them scant regard.[42] Combined with teenagers' sometimes riotous behavior (young audiences greeted scenes of Bill Haley performing "Rock Around the Clock" in the film *Blackboard Jungle* by tearing out cinema seats and dancing in the aisles), this active creation of a youth subculture made (in the words of Alan Sinfield) "the first significant dent in the postwar settlement."[43] (The fact that this juvenile threat arose around the same time that the Suez debacle demonstrated Britain's enfeeblement as an imperial power made it appear all the more menacing.) It is worth mentioning again the fact that another subcultural formation of the 1950s—the group of working- and lower-middle–class, provincial "scholarship boys" to which Hoggart himself belonged—also listened to a form of American popular music, trad jazz.

However, the most convincing refutation of Hoggart came not from later practitioners of Cultural Studies (some of whom perhaps overstated the elements of subcultural resistance in popular consumption of American culture) but from four mop-haired Liverpudlians. Rather than being passive imbibers of prepackaged mass culture, the Beatles (who as the "Skiffle" group the Quarry Men had sported a Teddy Boy–influenced look during the 1950s), actively appropriated American musical influences from a variety of sources: U.S. servicemen in Liverpool, the Armed Forces Network, Radio Luxembourg (as is discussed below, the BBC deliberately rationed the broadcast of rock'n'roll). These they skillfully synthesized with a variety of other traditions, including that of the British Music Hall, to produce a hybridized form of American popular music that was then, in a momentous cultural transaction replete with irony, reexported to the U.S.[44] As well as helping to Europeanize American culture, the Beatles and successor acts in the so-called British Invasion played a crucial role in conveying U.S. influences to continental Europe. "In countries like the Netherlands and Italy," writes Richard Pells, "much of what passed ... for 'American' rock and roll was really a British mutation."[45]

This blurring of British and American traditions during the 1960s and 1970s has led some critics to talk of a single, distinct musical culture, "Anglo-America."[46] There are, however, problems with this concept. First, it ignores the ways in which the British pop scene has been influenced by continental European styles. While listening to American soul, for example, the Mods of the 1960s dressed in Italian-designed suits, rode on Italian-made scooters, and drank Italian-style coffee (indeed, many of the "milk-bars" that Hoggart so deplored were in fact coffee houses run by Italian immigrants). Similarly, British dance music of the 1980s and 1990s—Hi-NRG, Balearic beat, and acid house—drew as much on the European club scene as on American musical influences. For that matter, the Beatles themselves had survived the lean years before they broke into the U.S. market by playing Hamburg. Second, immigration from former colonies has brought with it to Britain a number of other influences, most importantly Caribbean-derived musics such as reggae, ska (which enjoyed a major revival in the early 1980s), and, most recently, the house-reggae fusion, drum'n'bass. Indian and Pakistani communities in British cities are also producing new hybridized musical forms such as Bhangra, a combination of North Indian folk song and European dance music. This is not to say that American influence has disappeared—rap, of course, has proven immensely popular in Britain, as elsewhere—but it needs to be seen in the context of an increasingly diffuse, global musical culture.[47]

Finally, it is important to acknowledge a strong element of resistance to Americanization in British popular music. BritPop, the 1990s musical equivalent of BritArt, was, as its name implies, a self-consciously nationalistic movement. Several of its exponents engaged in gestures that might be interpreted as anti-American, some playful and witty, others less so: the satirizing of American artist Jeff Koons in Damien Hirst's video for Blur's single "Country House," Jarvis Cocker (lead singer of the Sheffield band Pulp) mooning Michael Jack-

son during an awards ceremony, Oasis abusing and spitting at American audiences.[48] Moreover, in Britain there has long been an association between popular music and explicitly political criticism of the U.S. During the late 1950s,
protest actions by the Campaign for Nuclear Disarmament (CND), such as
its famous march on the weapons research establishment at Aldermaston, were
accompanied by live jazz, just as jazz events often featured CND badges, leaf-
lets, and posters. In British jazz there has always been a marked ambivalence
about the U.S.: with his West-Country burr and Edwardian dandy attire, trad-
band leader and clarinetist Acker Bilk struck fellow jazz-man George Melly as
embodying "some kind of chauvinistic revolt against American domination";[49]
in 1973 trumpeter Ian Carr voiced his hopes for "the emancipation of British
jazz from American slavery."[50] Much the same was true of British punk, which,
although partly inspired by the New York music scene of the early 1970s, was
highly antagonistic to American influence. Hence, when CND enjoyed a period of renewed activism during the early 1980s, it was bands like the anarchist collective Crass who supplied the soundtrack, with songs like "Smash
the Mac," which features the immortal couplet: "ET go home, Mickey Mouse
fuck off!"[51] This mobilization of American cultural forms to protest against U.S.
political power has been a characteristic strategy of the postwar British left.

Turning from music to America's other major cultural export item, film,
one encounters a similar set of responses. British elites perceived the glam-
orous products of Hollywood as threatening to swamp indigenous traditions
of realist cinema and colonize the consciousness of the country's film-going
public (government measures to prevent American films from entering Britain
are discussed below). While no one would seriously dispute the U.S. film industry's commercial dominance over the British—in 1950, for example, only
seventy-two of the four hundred films distributed in the UK had been made
there[52]—film historians have recently challenged the notions of passive spectatorship implied in earlier discourses about Americanization, suggesting that
working-class Britons found in American movies ways of countering the privations and inequalities of postwar British society. Jacky Stacey, for example,
has documented how young female film-goers enjoyed "the pleasure of temporary participation in the abundant femininity of their favourite Hollywood
stars."[53] Not only did imitating the appearance of American starlets enable
British women to mitigate the effects of rationing, it also helped them produce new and, to a certain extent, transgressive modes of femininity. This is
particularly pertinent given that the rhetoric of Americanization often constructed the British consumer of American culture as not only pacified but
also feminized by the experience. Studies of British women's consumption of
U.S.–produced television soap opera have reached similar conclusions.[54]

Recent scholarship has also interrogated the binary opposition between British and American styles of film-making implied in earlier commentary on the

subject, for example, a 1944 pamphlet by Michael Balcon, head of the Ealing Studios, that distinguished between a cinema of "tinsel" (spectacle, the star system, individualistic values) and one of "realism" (documentary, social engagement, communitarian values).[55] The realistic impulse was clearly important in the New Wave and "social problem" films of the late 1950s and early 1960s, but the critical success of these genres has obscured the popularity of other homegrown British cinema, such as Hammer horror and the *Carry On* series. Just as British directors and stars have constituted a powerful presence in Hollywood, so it is possible to detect American influence on even the most realistic of New Wave films: for instance, the resemblance of Richard Burton and Richard Harris, cast as the (anti-)heroes of, respectively, *Look Back in Anger* and *This Sporting Life*, to Marlon Brando. As with pop music, however, notions of an "Anglo-American" cinema are complicated by European influences: the formal traces of German Expressionism in the films of Michael Powell and Emeric Pressburger, "quotations" from Truffaut's *400 Blows* in *The Loneliness of the Long Distance Runner*, the prominence of such continental directors as Antonioni and Polanski in 1960s London. For many British Asians, "Bollywood" is a more important provider of film entertainment than the U.S., while new immigrant voices are being heard in productions such as *My Beautiful Laundrette, Handsworth Songs,* and *Bhaji on the Beach*. Finally, contrary to notions that British cinema eschews visual pleasure, "New New Wave" directors such as Peter Greenaway, Derek Jarman, and John Maybury have created films of sumptuous spectacle.[56]

This is not to deny that Hollywood has continued to crowd out Britain's film industry commercially: even during the 1990s, supposedly a decade of revival in the British cinema, when new sources of subsidy became available in the form of grants from the European Union and National Lottery, American movies counted for over 90 percent of UK box office revenues.[57] Rather, it is to suggest that the best of postwar British cinema has taken advantage of its unique location between America and Europe to produce films that combine native traditions of realism with continental formal devices and an ironized version of the Hollywood "classical style."[58] Paradigmatic of this approach was one of the most successful "British" films of the 1990s, *Trainspotting*, which ingeniously synthesized the grittiest of subject matter (heroin addiction in Edinburgh slums) with constant references to America and passages of what one critic has called "black magical realism" to make a truly transnational entertainment.[59]

Anti-Americanism

As already noted, cultural anti-Americanism spanned the political spectrum in postwar Britain, uniting conservatives appalled by the threat U.S. mass culture posed to "civilized" values with socialist intellectuals who feared the destruction of working-class communities. The creation of new cultural institutions such as the National Theatre and BBC Third Programme in this period might be interpreted as, in part, attempts to preserve the "best" of British culture in the face of Americanization. "Let every part of England be merry in its own way," proclaimed Lord Keynes, first Chairman of the Arts Council, before declaring, "Death to Hollywood."[60] This helps explain why British communists seized on anti-Americanism as one of the best ways out of their traditional political obscurity, conducting an "America Go Home" campaign and holding conferences with titles like "The American Threat to British Culture."[61] It also illuminates what Martin Barker has called the "strange history" of a campaign against horror comics that took place during the first half of the 1950s.[62] Kick-started by the communists, who referred to the publications in question as "American" or "American-style," this moral crusade culminated in the passage of the Children and Young Persons (Harmful Publications) Act in 1955 (a measure that fell short of the outright ban called for by Labour MP Horace King, who complained that the comics were "not even comparatively decent pagan pornography").[63] As Duncan Webster has pointed out, the public controversy about "video nasties" that took place in Britain during the 1980s echoed many of the points made in this earlier debate, including the references to a baleful American influence.[64]

The success of the horror comics campaign attests to the fact that anti-Americanism had ceased being merely an elite pursuit and become truly popular in postwar Britain. A residue of (mainly male) resentment at the wartime presence of American GIs on British soil ("overpaid, oversexed, and over here," as the popular saying has it), envy of American affluence, and deliberate fanning of the issue by elements of the tabloid press all contributed to the rise of working-class anti-American sentiment during the 1950s. That said, there were also powerful counterforces at work: the positive effects of the kind of cultural diplomacy discussed above, the pro-Americanism of some well-placed political groups (such as the right wing of the Labour Party), and the continuing susceptibility of working-class youth to American cultural (as opposed to political) influence. Taken together, these factors help explain why it was that, while the comics campaign succeeded, other official attempts to curb U.S. penetration of British culture failed.

The most conspicuous of these failures was in the area of film. In 1947, the Attlee government, concerned about the ideological influence of U.S. cinema on Labour Britain (with some reason—Washington viewed Hollywood as an extremely powerful unofficial propaganda weapon) and the commercial threat it posed to the domestic film industry, attempted to impose a 75 percent customs tax on all new films entering the country. The British people wanted "bacon but not Bogart," explained Chancellor of the Exchequer Hugh

Dalton.[65] In fact, they wanted both. When the State Department–backed Motion Picture Export Association responded to the tax by boycotting the British market altogether, there was a popular outcry that forced a humiliating backing off by Dalton. Other protectionist measures backfired badly. Attempts to keep the bulk of Hollywood's UK earnings in the country resulted in American film companies using the unconverted currency to buy up British studios, thus jeopardizing rather than protecting the independence of the domestic industry.[66] The National Film Finance Corporation (NFFC), set up in 1949 to subsidize British film production, sank over £3 million in Alexander Korda's British Lion Production Company. Korda used these funds to launch an assault on the U.S. market by mimicking Hollywood gangster movies.[67] The result was the mini-genre of "spiv" films. Whether one sees these developments as a victory for popular taste over paternalistic regulation or as the death knell of an independent British cinema is a matter of individual interpretation.

The paternalistic impulse was even stronger in the realm of broadcasting. "It is occasionally represented to us that we are setting out to give the public what we think they need, and not what they want, but few know what they want, and very few what they need," stated John Reith, the first director-general of the BBC, in 1924.[68] Such principles still held sway in the BBC during the late 1940s. Added to lobbying by British musicians' unions, racist objections to black-influenced musical forms such as rock'n'roll ("It has something of the African tom-tom and voodoo dance," editorialized the *Daily Mail* in 1956),[69] and elite concerns about the potentially destabilizing effect of American popular culture in a country that still had to endure rationing, Reithian values made British radio deeply inhospitable to U.S. popular music. Throughout the late 1940s and early 1950s, the BBC laid down strict guidelines governing how much American material was to be broadcast and how it should be presented. When U.S. subject matter was aired, it was usually filtered through the commentary of British experts, such as Alistair Cooke. Similarly, even after austerity receded, the BBC avoided broadcasting American performers, so that in 1956, the year that Elvis Presley's *Heartbreak Hotel* was released, not one rock'n'roll record was featured in the BBC's annual review of popular songs.[70] None of these measures, though, prevented the likes of John Lennon from surfing the airwaves until they encountered snatches of Buddy Holly or Chuck Berry; indeed, the BBC's policies probably only helped to enhance rock'n'roll's subcultural appeal.

Anxieties about Americanization also dominated the early history of British TV. When the period began, the BBC enjoyed a monopoly on televisual broadcasting. During the early 1950s, however, pressure began to grow for the licensing of a new, commercial TV station. Opponents of this proposal cited the example of American television as proof that commercial sponsorship drove down broadcasting standards. The debate intensified in 1953 when reports reached Britain that U.S. coverage of Queen Elizabeth II's coronation had been interrupted by advertisements for shampoo and an interview with a chimpanzee called J. Fred Muggs, who was asked, "Do you have a Coronation where you come from?"[71] Loyal British subjects contrasted these antics with the BBC's dignified broadcasting of the same event, failing to note that BBC executives had spent the previous year in the U.S. studying American coverage of President Eisenhower's inauguration. A National Television Council was formed by such eminent personalities as William Beveridge, E. M. Forster, and Bertrand Russell, who distributed a manifesto, "Britain Unites Against Commercial TV." Labour MP Christopher Mayhew issued a similar pamphlet, "Dear Viewer," which sold 60,000 copies, and spoke in Parliament of "the menace of the impact of Americanism."[72] (The fact that Mayhew was, politically, a keen Atlanticist serves as further proof that pro-American views and enthusiasm for U.S. popular culture did not necessarily go hand in hand.) Lord Reith himself compared commercial TV with "Smallpox, Bubonic Plague and the Black Death."[73] All to no avail: a Television Act authorizing the creation of an "independent" TV service was passed in July 1954, with the proviso that there should be "proper proportions" of matter of British "origin and performance."[74] In fact, the new ITV network relied heavily on American imports, including *I Love Lucy, Dragnet,* and *Gunsmoke,* while home-produced programs often imitated U.S.–invented formats, such as the quiz show (although with much smaller prizes). By 1957, commercial TV in Britain commanded 72 percent of the national audience share.[75] Once again, cultural elites raising the specter of Americanization had failed to dampen the popular appetite for American-style entertainments.

Conclusion

Cultural anti-Americanism did not disappear from the British scene following the protectionist failures of the 1950s. Elite concerns continue to be expressed about the threat posed to an ancient, organic national culture by American-style homogenization and leveling-down—witness Prince Charles's tirades against U.S.–influenced "modern" architecture—just as the various recent cultural movements with the prefix "Brit" have, to greater and lesser degrees, expressed Orwellian or Hoggartian objections to Americanization. Such tendencies have, if anything, become stronger since 2001, when the mood of sympathy that prevailed in the wake of 11 September soon evaporated— "however tactfully you dress it up, the United States had it coming," wrote one Cambridge academic in the *London Review of Books* in October 2001, provoking another contributor to complain of the "knee-jerk anti-Americanism posing as thought in your letter pages"[76]—to be replaced by a widespread unease about American power in the post–Cold War world. Nonetheless, the threat of Americanization does not appear to be as frightening to the British as it once was. For the political right, it is the prospect of a European "super-state" that, combined with the internal devolution of power from Westminster to new regional assemblies, presents the more urgent threat to national sovereignty and the British "character." Meanwhile, the left (such as it is) seems increasingly preoccupied with checking the excesses—the environmental irresponsibility, exploitation of third-world workers, and disregard for consumer welfare—of transnational corporate power. Although often viewed as a campaign directed specifically at Americanization, the international protest movement against McDonald's, in which British activists such as Helen Steel and David Morris (the "McLibel" two) have played a leading role, might equally well be interpreted as an attempt to remedy the evils of "globalization."[77] As historian David W. Ellwood has observed, it is somewhat surprising, given the ubiquity of American culture in the UK today, how few protests Americanization has elicited from contemporary British intellectuals. Indeed, there now seems to be—in stark contrast to the situation that prevailed in the early postwar period—a political consensus positively in favor of American influence, with elites of both left and right engaging in a process of top-down Americanization.[78]

Reviewing the history of Americanization and anti-Americanism in postwar Britain, some generalizations do seem possible. First, preexisting concerns about the cultural effects of modernization combined with anxieties about national identity caused by imperial decline to produce a determination, among both conservative and leftist elites, to combat the importation of U.S. mass culture. Second, British cultural protectionism was defeated by American cultural diplomacy, both overt and covert (a factor perhaps neglected in much of the Cultural Studies literature on Americanization), by the pro-Americanism of certain powerful elements within British society, such as the Gaitskellite (later Blairite) wing of the Labour movement and the Thatcherites of the Conservative Party, and by the hunger for American cultural artifacts expressed by certain popular elements, in particular, working-class youth. Third, British consumption of American popular culture was far more complex than the intellectuals of the right and left first thought: it was creative, with subcultural groups appropriating elements and combining them with locally-produced artifacts to create new, hybrid cultural forms; and it could be oppositional, that is, resistant to British cultural hierarchies and even, in certain instances, associated with protest against American political power itself. Fourth, similar effects were observable in the realm of high culture, with American-influenced modernism, then postmodernism, overcoming various forms of postimperial, neoromantic nostalgia. This, however, was not a complete takeover: native traditions of representation, realism, and social engagement survived—and, in some cases, fused with formal American innovations to create truly new works of art. Fifth, the resulting Anglo-American cultural forms proved extremely powerful, helping mediate American influences on continental Europe and, ironically, Europeanize U.S. culture. Finally, it is necessary to take into account the influence of other "foreign" cultures on Britain, especially in the present day, when immigration from the former colonies and the rise of new, global communication technologies has rendered British society increasingly multicultural and transnational.

Acknowledgment

Many thanks to the following for offering comments on earlier drafts of this essay: Robert Cook, Dominic Sandbrook, Duco van Oostrum, Rosie Wild, and David Wilford.

Notes

1. Giora Goodman, "'Who is Anti-American?': The British Left and the United States, 1945–56," (Ph.D. diss., University College London, 1996), 19–26.
2. Ibid., 322.
3. Richard Pells, *Not Like Us: How Europeans Have Loved, Hated, and Transformed American Culture Since World War II* (New York: BasicBooks, 1997), 99.
4. Anthony Carew, *Labour under the Marshall Plan: The Politics of Productivity and the Marketing of Management Science* (Manchester: Manchester University Press, 1987), 131–57.
5. Hugh Wilford, *The CIA, the British Left and the Cold War: Calling the Tune?* (London: Frank Cass, 2003), 173–74.
6. Ibid., 175–76.
7. Goodman, "'Who is Anti-American?'," 302.
8. Malcolm Bradbury, "How I Invented America," *Journal of American Studies* 14, no. 1 (1980): 130.
9. Roy Jenkins, *A Life at the Centre* (London: Macmillan, 1991), 101.
10. Quoted in Giles Scott-Smith, "'Her Rather Ambitious Washington Program': Margaret Thatcher's International Visitor Program Visit to the United States in 1967," *Contemporary British History* 17, no. 4 (2003): 66.
11. Wilford, *CIA, British Left and Cold War,* 174.
12. Ibid., 189.
13. F. Bowen Evans to United States Information Agency (USIA), "USIS/United Kingdom Annual Assessment Report—October 1, 1957 through September 30, 1958," 19 January 1959, Records of the USIA (Record Group 306), National Archives, Washington, D.C.
14. Pells, *Not Like Us,* 118.

15. See Ali Fisher and Scott Lucas, "Master and Servant? The U.S. Government and the Founding of the British Association for American Studies," *European Journal of American Culture* 21, no. 1 (2002): 16–25.

16. F. Bowen Evans to USIA, "Educational Exchange: The 1959 Conference of the British Association for American Studies," 27 April 1959, RG 306, National Archives, Washington, D.C.

17. Pells, *Not Like Us,* 116–18.

18. Herbert Nicholas, "The Education of an Americanist," *Journal of American Studies* 14, no. 1 (1980): 24.

19. See, for example, Fisher and Lucas, "Master and Servant?"

20. Wilford, *CIA, British Left and Cold War,* 193–224.

21. Quoted in ibid., 288.

22. Alan Sinfield, *Literature, Politics and Culture in Postwar Britain* (Oxford: Blackwell, 1989), 182.

23. Ibid., 191.

24. Ibid., 192.

25. Michael Woolf, "Lifting the Lid: Theatre, 1956–99," in Clive Bloom and Gary Day, eds., *Literature and Culture in Modern Britain, Volume Three: 1956–99* (Harlow: Pearson, 2000), 104.

26. Steven Earnshaw, "Novel Voices," in Bloom and Day, *Literature and Culture,* 66.

27. Dick Hebdige, "Towards a Cartography of Taste, 1935–62," in Dick Hebdige, ed., *Hiding in the Light: On Images and Things* (London: Routledge, 1988), 58–66.

28. Quoted in Neil Campbell, *Landscapes of Americanisation* (Derby: University of Derby Press, 2003), 61.

29. Quoted in ibid., 44.

30. Quoted in John A. Walker, *Cultural Offensive: America's Impact on British Art Since 1945* (London: Pluto, 1998), 42.

31. Quoted in David Masters, "Going Modern and Being British: Art in Britain, 1930–55," in Gary Day, ed., *Literature and Culture in Modern Britain, Volume Two: 1930–55* (Harlow: Longman, 1997), 212.

32. Anna Massey, *The Independent Group: Modernism and Mass Culture in Britain, 1945–59* (Manchester: Manchester University Press, 1995), 62–71.

33. Robin Burstow, "The Limits of Modernist Art as a 'Weapon of the Cold War': Reassessing the Unknown Patron of the Monument to the Unknown Political Prisoner," *Oxford Art Journal* 20, no. 1 (1997): 68–80.

34. Alistair Davies and Alan Sinfield, eds., *British Culture of the Postwar: An Introduction to Literature and Society, 1945–99* (London: Routledge, 2000), 105.

35. Campbell, *Landscapes of Americanisation,* 81–86.

36. Walker, *Cultural Offensive,* 244.

37. Quoted in Duncan Webster, *Looka Yonder! The Imaginary America of Populist Culture* (London: Routledge, 1988), 188.

38. Quoted in Lawrence Black, *The Political Culture of the Left in Affluent Britain, 1951–64: Old Labour, New Britain?* (Basingstoke: Palgrave Macmillan, 2003), 88.

39. Richard Hoggart, *The Uses of Literacy: Aspects of Working Class Life with Special Reference to Publications and Entertainments* (London: Chatto & Windus, 1957), 212.

40. Ibid., 203–4.

41. Ken Worpole, *Dockers and Detectives: Popular Reading, Popular Writing* (London: Verso, 1983).

42. Hebdige, "Towards a Cartography of Taste," 74.

43. Sinfield, *Literature, Politics and Culture,* 155.

44. Laura E. Cooper and B. Lee Cooper, "The Pendulum of Cultural Imperialism: Popular Music Interchanges Between the United States and Britain, 1943–67," *Journal of Popular Culture* 27, no. 3 (1993): 61–78.

45. Pells, *Not Like Us,* 206. See also Mel van Elteren, "Sounds from America in Holland: The Counter-Culture of the Sixties," in Rob Kroes, Robert Rydell, and Doeko F. J. Bosscher, eds., *Cultural Transmissions and Receptions: American Mass Culture in Europe* (Amsterdam: VU University Press, 1993), 171–97; and Franco Minganti, "Rock'n'Roll in Italy: Was It True Americanization?," in ibid., 138–51.

46. Simon Frith, "Anglo-America and Its Discontents," *Cultural Studies* 5, no. 3 (1991): 263–69.

47. See Andrew Blake, "Popular Music since the 1950s," in Bloom and Day, *Literature and Culture,* 51–75.

48. Clive Bloom, "Epilogue and Overture," in Bloom and Day, *Literature and Culture,* 261.

49. George Melly, *Revolt into Style: The Pop Arts in Britain* (Harmondsworth: Penguin, 1970), 70.

50. Quoted in George McKay, "Anti-Americanism, Youth and Popular Music, and the Campaign for Nuclear Disarmament," in AMATAS, http://www.uclan.ac.uk/amatas (last accessed: 28 February 2005).

51. Ibid.

52. Richard Weight, *Patriots: National Identity in Britain, 1940–2000* (London: Macmillan, 2002), 181.

53. Jacky Stacey, *Star-Gazing: Hollywood Cinema and Female Spectatorship* (London: Routledge, 1994), 111.

54. See Christine Geraghty, *Women and Soap Opera: A Study of Prime Time Soaps* (Cambridge: Polity Press, 1991). While often functioning as a derogatory rhetorical device, this equation of British consumption of American popular culture with femininity does bear examination. For example, mass spectator sports in Britain, traditionally a masculine preserve, have been relatively immune to American influence (although recently, there have been some signs of Americanization). This remains, however, a surprisingly underresearched subject.

55. Quoted in Alistair Davies, "A Cinema in Between: Postwar British Cinema," in Davies and Sinfield, *British Culture of the Postwar,* 112.

56. Ibid., 110–24.

57. John Hill, "Cinema," in Jane Stokes and Anna Reading, eds., *The Media in Britain: Current Debates and Developments* (Basingstoke: Macmillan, 1999), 75.

58. Davies, "Cinema in Between," 120.

59. Murray Smith, "Transnational Trainspotting," in Stokes and Reading, eds., *Media in Britain,* 219–27.

60. Quoted in Goodman, "'Who is Anti-American?,'" 123.

61. Robert Hewison, *Culture and Consensus: England, Art and Politics since 1940* (London: Methuen, 1995), 131.

62. Martin Barker, *A Haunt of Fears* (London: Pluto, 1984), 5.

63. Weight, *Patriots,* 243.

64. Webster, *Looka Yonder!,* 197–99.

65. Weight, *Patriots,* 178.

66. Pells, *Not Like Us,* 218.

67. Weight, *Patriots,* 179–80.

68. Quoted in Lez Cooke, "Television," in Bloom and Day, *Literature and Culture,* 179.

69. Quoted in Weight, *Patriots,* 304.

70. Hebdige, "Towards a Cartography of Taste," 54–56.

71. Quoted in Valeria Camporesi, "There Are No Kangaroos in Kent: The American 'Model' and the Introduction of Commercial Television in Britain, 1940–54," in David W. Ellwood and Rob Kroes, eds., *Hollywood in Europe: Experiences of a Cultural Hegemony* (Amsterdam: VU University Press, 1994), 280.

72. Weight, *Patriots,* 242.

73. Ibid., 245.

74. Camporesi, "There Are No Kangaroos in Kent," 280.

75. Weight, *Patriots,* 251. See also Black, *Political Culture of the Left,* 94–104.

76. Quoted in Richard Crockatt, *America Embattled: 9/11: Why America Fascinates and Infuriates the World* (London: Routledge, 2002), 39–41.

77. See John Vidal, *McLibel: Burger Culture on Trial* (London: Pan Books, 1997).

78. See David W. Ellwood, "American Myth, American Model and the Quest for a British Modernity," in R. Laurence Moore and Mauruizio Vaudagnda, eds., *The American Century in Europe* (Ithaca: Cornell University Press, 2003), 131–50. This would certainly help explain why Britain is now the leading opponent within the European Union of protectionist quotas designed to curb the importation of American audio-visual products. C. Anthony Gifford, "Culture versus Commerce: Europe Strives to Keep Hollywood at Bay," in Sabrina P. Ramet and Gordana P. Crnković, eds., *Kazaaam! Splat! Ploof! The American Impact on European Popular Culture since 1945* (Lanham: Rowman and Littlefield, 2003), 45.

From French Anti-Americanism and Americanization to the "American Enemy"?

◆ ◆ ◆

Richard J. Golsan

In his masterful—and massive—recent study of French anti-Americanism, *L'ennemi américain,* Philippe Roger observes that of all the Western European nations, France is the only country not to have gone to war with the United States. And yet, as Roger also observes, among these same European nations France is also the country where anti-American sentiment is the most powerful and heartfelt. It is a "tradition" dating back to the very inception of the younger country and has been fueled by the writings of France's greatest poets, novelists, historians, and philosophers. Roger discusses its presence in the works of Tocqueville, Stendhal, Valéry, Sartre, and many, many others, and yet does not exhaust a list that, most recently, includes figures like novelists Annie Ernaux, Tahar Ben Jaloun, and Michel Houellebecq.[1] Indeed, so heartfelt is French anti-Americanism that it has often served as a model or even inspiration for other European anti-Americanism. Moreover, as is the case perhaps to a lesser degree in those countries, it is inextricably linked to the various cultural and economic processes of Americanization itself. For this reason, anti-Americanism and Americanization will be discussed together here, with anti-Americanism providing the *fil conducteur* or "guiding thread" of the discussions.

In emphasizing the persistence, depth, and uniqueness of French anti-Americanism, Philippe Roger, as noted, traces its roots back to the eighteenth century and examines its manifestations in politics, diplomacy, and literature. He stresses too, as a kind of linguistic *pièce de résistance,* that in current dictionaries of the French language "American" is the only adjective represent-

---

ing a nationality that can have the prefix "anti" attached to it.[2] Apparently, despite several devastating wars with Germany over the last century and a half, the word *"antiallemandisme"* is not recognized in the French language.

Although the long tradition of French anti-Americanism seems contradictory and even paradoxical in light of the equally long history of peaceful and indeed friendly relations between the two countries, Roger argues that this is not the only paradoxical feature of French anti-Americanism. One would think, Roger states, that if anti-Americanism persists, it is a reaction against a French *américanisme*. But according to Roger, the latter is nothing more than the string of clichés concerning the U.S. generated by *antiaméricanisme*. Roger concludes therefore, borrowing an old formula from existentialism, that "the existence of anti-Americanism precedes the essence of America" to the degree that the latter is misconstrued by *américanisme*.[3] Stated more simply, French anti-Americanism is not based on any real knowledge or understanding of what America *is*, but rather a prejudicial misinterpretation, indeed a string of misleading clichés, concerning America's nature. In essence, then, French *antiaméricanisme* feeds on itself: it is a vicious circle or even a self-fulfilling prophecy. Although Roger does not go this far, the individual French *antiaméricain* appears in this light to be a little like the anti-Semite as defined by Jean-Paul Sartre (Sartre was himself a fervent *antiaméricain*, as we shall see). According to Sartre, the anti-Semite's need to despise "the Jew" is so intense that, if the Jew did not exist, the anti-Semite would have to invent him. Similarly, for the visceral *antiaméricain*, if "America" did not exist, the *antiaméricain* would have to invent it.

Employing a comparable logic in a broader social and national context, one could argue from a Girardian perspective that French hostility toward the American scapegoat—portrayed as the embodiment of multiple cultural and social ills and the principal source of global disorder—serves as a glue binding French of the right and left together.[4] This would explain why *antiaméricanisme* is a common attitude among individuals along the full range of the political spectrum, including both extremes. It would also account for the fundamental irrationality or contradictoriness that often characterizes the phenomenon. Case in point, in his own recent essay on French anti-Americanism, *L'Obsession anti-américaine*, Jean-François Revel underscores the fact that the U.S. is frequently blamed for one particular sin or transgression as well as for its opposite, often sequentially but on occasion even simultaneously.[5] For example, as Revel notes, throughout its history the U.S. has been excoriated for excessive interventionism as well as for extreme isolationism, often within the same geographical or historical context. In a similar vein, Roger observes that at the time of the NATO bombings in Kosovo, American interventionism was widely approved by French public opinion at the same time that a more generalized *antiaméricanisme* was on the rise.[6] For Revel, contradictory attitudes such as these can be attributed to a generalized ignorance on the part of the French public as to what America is and what its motives really are. Moreover, he continues, one of the more peculiar and troubling traits of this ignorance is that it is deliberate. Indeed, he argues, an abiding "mystery" of *antiaméricanisme* is precisely that it is characterized by a will "not to know," a desire to be "deliberately misinformed."[7]

While both Roger's *L'ennemi américain* and Revel's *L'obsession anti-américaine* offer intriguing—if perhaps simplistic—psychological and theoretical insights into French *antiaméricanisme,* they also highlight other aspects of the phenomenon that are similarly crucial. As Roger demonstrates, *antiaméricanisme* in France is very much a phenomenon that has fluctuated over time. It has flared up and faded out over the last two centuries, and has been stoked periodically by a variety of concerns ranging from geopolitical crises (war, colonialism, occupation, etc.), to economic issues and policies (tariffs, trade agreements, export and import disparities, foreign aid), to questions relating to cultural identity and hegemony.

Equally important, the recent—and proximate—publication of the two books, which appeared a month apart in fall 2002, constitutes only a very small part of a steady and copious stream of books, articles, editorials, television programs, and radio broadcasts dealing with "America" and French, European, and even global attitudes toward it. Clearly, "America" was—and is—very much at the heart of French debate and—as Roger's and Revel's books confirm—so, too, is *antiaméricanisme.*

Given the events of the last several years, neither a fascination with the U.S. nor a resurgence of anti-American sentiment in France is surprising. The terrorist attacks of 11 September 2001, for example, provoked an extraordinarily powerful—and mixed—response in France, as they did in much of the world. An initially strong, largely sympathetic, and indeed solidary response to the trauma Americans were facing—summed up best, perhaps, in a 12 September editorial by *Le monde's* Jean-Marie Colombani entitled "We are all Americans"—was quickly tempered in many quarters by George W. Bush's declaration of a "War on Terror" and the American attack on Afghanistan. The March 2003 invasion of Iraq, which took place over vehement French and international opposition spearheaded by French President Jacques Chirac, unleashed in France and throughout much of Europe a powerful backlash against U.S. interventionism and "unilateralism." Reflecting both tendencies, an Alsatian told me in July 2003 that whereas after 11 September he considered himself to be "an American," after the invasion of Iraq he considered himself to be "an Iraqi." In addition to stimulating feelings of solidarity with the Iraqi people, the American invasion kindled a more gut-level emotion: fear. According to the Swiss television journalist Malik Melihi, many Swiss he had interviewed for a program on current Franco-American relations feared that if Europe did not "toe the line" or if America needed European resources, the U.S. would not hesitate to invade Europe as well.[8] As Philippe Roger points out in *L'ennemi américain,* such European fears of an American invasion date back at least to the U.S. invasions of Cuba and the Philippines at the turn of the twentieth century, when many Europeans feared Spain—and Europe—would be the next American targets.

Much of this is merely anecdotal evidence of a new wave of *antiaméricanisme* in France and in French-speaking Switzerland. Taken at face value, such evidence tends, among other things, to oversimplify or schematize the phenomena and then to "freeze frame" it within the limited confines of the current geopolitical context. Where the current wave of French *antiaméricanisme* is concerned, it is important to stress that French attitudes toward America were neither uniformly positive at the time of the attacks on 11 September 2001 (hereafter 9/11) nor uniformly negative when Coalition forces crossed into Iraq. In a shocking essay appearing in *Le monde* in November 2001 entitled "The Spirit of Terrorism," the philosopher Jean Baudrillard argued that the United States had brought the attacks on itself due to its "unbearable power" and that, while it was the terrorists who carried out the attacks, "it was we," Baudrillard claimed, "who longed for them."[9] Since *Le monde*'s readership is first and foremost French, one would assume that the philosopher was addressing his fellow countrymen, at least in the first instance.

Baudrillard was not alone in expressing such sentiments. Annette Lévy-Willard, a journalist for the Parisian daily *Libération,* reports that on the day of the attacks the newspaper's switchboard was lit up by anonymous callers, a number of whom applauded the catastrophe and claimed that the Americans "had deserved it."[10] In *L'obsession anti-américaine,* Jean-François Revel notes that in the days following 9/11 delegate members of the leftist Confédération Générale du Travail (CGT) as well as officials of Jean-Marie Le Pen's far right Front National refused to honor the French government's call for three minutes of silence for the World Trade Center victims.[11] More nuanced but still fundamentally anti-American views were also expressed by the likes of the novelist Tahar Ben Jelloun, who saw the event not as a moment to rally round Uncle Sam, but as a terrible crisis in Islamic civilization: the fanatical hatred that produced the attacks was also poisoning and endangering Arab societies and cultures; meanwhile, the realities that fueled that hatred—the bombing of Iraqi civilians by American and allied planes and the killing of Palestinians by the Israeli military—were real, terrible, and totally unjustified.[12]

Conversely, when American forces entered Iraq, leading public intellectuals including André Glucksmann, as well as the novelist Pascal Bruckner and the filmmaker Romain Goupil, signed a petition in support of the Bush administration's effort to rid the world of the tyrant Saddam Hussein.[13] In a recent article in the *New Yorker,* Glucksmann (who has recently written a book on Euro-American animosities entitled *Ouest contre Ouest*) is quoted as praising George W. Bush's vision and actions and as describing him as "a nearly Shakespearean figure, a man who has met tragedy and recognized it as such."[14]

While these remarks point to the complexity of French responses to America and the storm of recent events at whose vortex the U.S. has found itself, they should also suggest that to a certain extent 9/11 and the invasion of Iraq merely reinvigorated or reactivated attitudes and sentiments already present. For example, the CGT delegates' apparent callous indifference to the victims of the World Trade Center collapse certainly derives at least partially from the visceral anti-Americanism on the French far left that dates from the Cold War, and indeed earlier. Similarly, Front National callousness derives from a longstanding distaste on the French right for American democracy and power, and certainly for its traditional support of Israel as well. For the broader, and more politically centrist French public, anti-American sentiment had been stoked in recent years—even before 9/11 and Iraq—by, among other things, the U.S. refusal to ratify the Kyoto accords or to support the creation of an international criminal tribunal. As if these transgressions were not enough, U.S. import-export policies have recently infuriated many in France. American bans on unprocessed cheeses, for example, have offended French sensibilities. Cheese is, after all, a source of French national pride. Similarly, efforts to export genetically engineered crops to Europe strike many in France as dangerous and indeed sinister. Finally, the "invasion" of American fast food in the form of McDonald's, and of American culture in the form of Hollywood films and other exports, have been a burr under the French saddle for decades.

The hostility to American fast food has in fact lately produced a "folk hero" in the person of José Bové, the leader of the "anti-*McDo*" forces. For those who celebrate Bové it doesn't seem to matter that many French still frequent McDonald's (which has been in France for several decades). And on at least one other issue mentioned, if Revel is correct it also seems not to matter to anti-Americanists that other countries, including France, have themselves failed to implement many of the toughest measures stipulated in the Kyoto accords. In his book, Revel takes obvious pleasure in pointing out the failure of the Socialist government of Lionel Jospin (1997–2002) in tackling the difficult issues of imposing an "ecotax" and of eliminating nitrates—and this, Revel crows, with Green Party members among Jospin's ministers.[15]

If, then, the current wave of *antiaméricanisme,* along with its paradoxes, preceded the terrible events of the last few years, and if its roots extend well into the past and touch not only on geopolitical concerns but on economic and cultural issues associated with "Americanization" as well, it is important to look briefly at the recent past and the *péripéties,* or twists and turns, of

Franco-American relations. This should help not only to better contextualize French attitudes and especially *antiaméricanisme* today, but also to more precisely identify the most salient features of these current attitudes. As a number of commentators have suggested, French *antiaméricanisme* now is unique in a number of ways, and that uniqueness appears in sharpest relief when cast against the broader backdrop of the postwar years.

A Brief Look at Americanization and Anti-Americanism since 1945

In order to understand French attitudes towards America in the postwar period, several factors need to be taken into account. First, looking back briefly at the war years themselves, relations between the United States and de Gaulle's Free French were troubled from the outset. Despite the efforts of many French living in the United States to forward the cause of the Free French in this country through the creation of organizations like "France For Ever,"[16] Free French lobbying was vexed early on by poor and even counterproductive lobbying by some of its representatives. Moreover, Roosevelt's faith in France had been seriously undermined by the catastrophic French defeat of May-June 1940. As a result, he regarded France as a second-class and ineffectual nation. To make matters worse, Washington cultivated the collaborationist Vichy regime until 1942 because it believed that good relations with the Pétain government would forward the cause of defeating Germany by keeping the French fleet out of Nazi hands.

After the Japanese bombed Pearl Harbor, relations between Washington and the Free French assumed a formally friendly status because America had now entered the war on the side of the Allies. But for quite some time, this did not entail the Americans breaking off relations with Vichy or recognizing the Free French officially as representatives of the French nation. So, in effect, Washington found itself maintaining some form of diplomatic relations with two conflicting French governments for a brief period.

Despite their new status as allies, serious tensions between Washington and the Free French under de Gaulle remained, and were periodically exacerbated by the actions of one side or the other. American authorities were outraged by De Gaulle's decision to take control of the French possessions of Saint-Pierre and the Miquelon Islands in December 1941. De Gaulle had not informed American authorities of his intentions. Later, with the Allied invasion of North Africa, the U.S. sided with General Giraud over de Gaulle, and enraged the Free French (as well as the British), by nominating the former Vichyite and Nazi ally Admiral Darlan as High Commissioner of France in North Africa. De Gaulle's eventual displacement of Giraud in Algiers still did not earn him official recognition, nor did Washington's breaking off of relations with Vichy in 1943. Only several months after de Gaulle's triumphal welcome at Bayeux in June 1944 did Washington officially recognize him and his provisional government. According to Raoul Aglion, Washington's hostility toward the Free French derived in large part from Roosevelt's dislike of de Gaulle, who, he was told, harbored dictatorial ambitions.[17]

Owing again to American friendliness with Vichy early in the war, relations between Washington and the internal Resistance were also poor. This was especially the case among *résistants* on the left and the Communists in particular, who by the war's end constituted the other major political force dominating the Resistance along with the Free French. To the degree that attitudes and sentiments created by wartime relations between France and the U.S. affected postwar relations, the two sides were in for a rocky ride.

It is important to stress that French grievances against the United States stemming from the war were not only diplomatic and political in nature. In *Past Imperfect* Tony Judt notes that the French also resented American bombing of French towns and cities, especially Royan and le Havre, but other locations as well.[18] Even before the Liberation, collaborationist publications in Paris such as *La Gerbe* carped constantly on Allied and especially American bombing of Paris's industrial suburbs, and in his personal journal *La Gerbe* founder Alphonse de Châteaubriant likened the bomber pilots to the biblical Beast.[19]

In postwar literary representations of the conflict by writers such as Marcel Aymé and Louis-Ferdinand Céline, death and destruction are rained down upon the French not by the Germans but by American and Allied bomber squadrons. In Celine's novel *Nord,* the narrator witnesses the suffering of defenseless civilians caused by these bombings as he flees across northern Europe while the Reich collapses. In Aymé's acerbic postwar novel *Uranus,* the village of Blémont is largely destroyed by American bombs, and the Liberation itself does nothing but cause renewed suffering and privations and bring old—and new—animosities to the surface. The tyranny of the Communists and the hypocrisy and cowardice of former Vichyites dominate postwar life in the village, and American and Allied sacrifices have obviously in no way improved the lot of the French themselves. Yet in both novels, the murderousness of German dive-bombing of civilians during France's catastrophic 1940 defeat and German abuses of French citizens during the Occupation are neatly forgotten.

During the Liberation, French resentment towards America also seethed over the presence of U.S. forces on French soil. Although individual experiences with GIs were often (although not always) recollected as positive, many in France resented the presence of another "occupational force," likened in some quarters to the recently departed Germans. And although U.S. troops departed soon after the Liberation, they returned in 1949 with the advent of

NATO. Especially in this context, they seemed—at least to some—the bodily (and military) incarnation of the "culture in soda cans" that many French feared was engulfing France.

As Judt observes, comparing the American military presence to the earlier German one seems incredible, but it was fed by several factors that made it seem plausible to a significant number at the time, especially among intellectuals. As an example of the latter, Judt sites the case of Julien Benda, the renowned author of *La Trahison des clercs,* whose lifelong animosity toward Germany and fear of the "German menace" were not assuaged by Hitler's defeat. German ideas, Benda feared, "might yet triumph in other hands,"[20] especially those of the Americans, who were also at the moment consciously and visibly promoting a restoration of German power and sovereignty in their sector so that Germany might serve as a bulwark against a feared Communist incursion from the East. Indeed, Richard Kuisel asserts that the American support of a German resurgence was the most painful thorn in the side of Franco-American relations, exacerbated especially in 1950 when America strongly backed German rearmament.[21]

While American support for Germany was part of the much larger picture of the Cold War geopolitical situation, America's role and status in that broader context were irritants to French sensibilities on a number of other levels as well. The U.S.'s complete domination of the Western Alliance, especially in military terms, was vexing, not to say genuinely painful, to many French who were still wounded and humiliated by four years of "accommodating" Nazism's absolute authority and living with their own terrible military defeat of 1940. On that score, the historian René Rémond, who had witnessed the debacle of May-June 1940, observed:

> There is probably no more terrible trial for a people than the defeat of its armies: in the scale of crises, this is the supreme catastrophe. It scarcely matters whether one was formally a pacifist or a militarist, whether one hated war or resigned oneself to it . . . defeat creates a deep and lasting trauma in everyone. It wounds something essential in each of us: a certain confidence in life, a pride in oneself, an indispensable self-respect.[22]

Also, America's obvious wealth only reminded the French of their own poverty during the Occupation and following the Liberation, and the influx of funds through the Marshall Plan beginning in the late 1940s did not rectify the situation. As Kuisel points out, the French were convinced that whatever benefits they were receiving, the British—"perfidious Albions" that they were in French eyes—were getting a better deal. Moreover, where the administration of the funds in France was concerned, officials in Washington disagreed with the French Fourth Republic's rush to modernization, and in 1949 officials of the Economic Cooperation Administration (ECA), which managed

Marshall Plan funding, threatened to withhold certain monies from French administrators as a result of these disagreements.[23]

But if American political and economic clout and the ECA's efforts to impose American solutions on French economic difficulties generally chafed, the left-wing intelligentsia, which dominated French intellectual life in the postwar years, despised America chiefly as the philosophical opponent of Marxism, which, as Sartre had famously asserted, was "the unsurpassable philosophy of the times."[24] America was also obviously the major opponent and obstacle to Soviet power and hegemony. Stalin's Soviet Union was admired and even worshiped, at first, as the embodiment of revolutionary idealism. As François Furet's *The Past of an Illusion,* among a number of other recent works, points out, the tendency of the French left to view the October Revolution as a continuation of 1789 casts the Soviet experiment in an almost exclusively positive light.[25] Moreover, the Soviet victory at Stalingrad made Stalin appear to be the real victor over Nazism. All of this, and other factors as well, garnered passionate support for the Soviets, a support supplemented by an equally visceral hatred of Americans. Simone de Beauvoir wrote in *Force of Circumstance* that even the likes of Sartre, who had reservations about Stalinism, would have allied himself without reservation with the Soviet Union against the U.S. if war came, and the moderate and generally pro-Western Raymond Aron referred to unconditional apologists of America as the "new collaborators."[26]

The intertwined passions of unbridled support for the Soviet Union and hatred of America led, on important occasions, to willful distortions of historical realities, and worse. Nowhere was this disturbing tendency more evident than during the Kravchenko Affair of 1947–1949. Victor Kravchenko was a Soviet official who, on a purchasing mission in Washington, D.C. in 1944, chose to defect and demand asylum. In 1946, he published an autobiographical book describing the horrors of Soviet life and of totalitarianism entitled *I Chose Freedom.* A year later, the book appeared in French translation and immediately became the target of the pro-Soviet literary review, *Les lettres françaises.* Attacks on the author characterized Kravchenko as a traitor, a liar, and a puppet whose strings were "made in USA." The book itself was described as the worst form of propaganda, identical in its aims to Nazi propaganda. Indeed, in an editorial in *Les lettres françaises* appearing in April 1948, André Wurmser stated: "In the past these pissers of pages came to us from Germany. Now they are imported from America. But whether it is Hitler or Truman who inspires them, as long as there are Kravchenkos there will be free men to answer them."[27]

Eventually, Kravchenko sued *Les lettres françaises* for defamation, and in January 1949 came to Paris to testify at the trial, which lasted for two tension-filled months. As Michel Winock explains, in the first instance the Kravchenko trial became an occasion for *Les lettres françaises* to present itself as a bastion of French "thinking" fighting the massive and "shameless dumping"

of a mindless American culture through the dissemination of "infantile" publications like *Reader's Digest* and movie magazines. For Claude Morgan, this
pro-American "propaganda was much more skillful than Hitler's crude propaganda,"[28] but it nevertheless took up many of the latter's themes.

As Winock stresses as well, the Kravchenko trial also became the trial of
the Soviet system itself. The most ferocious of the USSR's defenders denied
the existence of Soviet concentration camps and denounced the numerous
witnesses who had actually experienced them. Some, like André Wurmser, went
so far as to equate anti-Sovietness with anti-Frenchness: "Whoever says anti-
Soviet says anti-French in the same breath."[29] For those who shared Wurmser's
perspective, it is easy to see why America appeared doubly diabolical.

As the testimony of Claude Morgan suggests, the American menace was
conceived and perceived at least as much in cultural terms as it was in geopolitical ones. Figures like Sartre denounced American culture and ideology,
which, he wrote in 1949, came to France "with screws, manufactured goods,
and canned fruit juices." He generally declined any intellectual exchange with
Americans, according to Philippe Roger, because he did not believe Franco-
American cultural exchange was possible. Moreover, as a popular literary figure in postwar America whose works were read and plays performed, Sartre
was outraged by adaptations of his works such as *Dirty Hands,* whose plot and
meaning, he believed, had been grossly distorted in its American production.
(Given the extremely negative and stereotypical view of America presented in
some of Sartre's plays, especially *The Respectful Prostitute,* it is surprising in
some ways that he enjoyed the following in the United States that he did.)
The surrealist André Breton also believed no true cultural, or perhaps even
human exchange, was possible. As Roger notes, Breton, who had spent the war
years in New York, proudly announced once back in Paris that he had made
no American friends.[30]

Breton's comment suggest that trips or even prolonged stays in the U.S.
did not generally produce positive results. Following a visit in 1946, Albert
Camus lamented the overwhelming presence of commercialization. He observed, for example, that even the Salvation Army advertised. For Sartre, the
problem was still larger. Walking down streets filled with billboard advertisements, huge shop windows, and neon signs, he observed that one could never
"get away" in America: "The nation walks about with you, giving you advice
and orders."[31] Simone de Beauvoir wrote of her lecture tour of American universities and her visits to America's cities in *America by the Day.* Among other
things, she lamented the commercialization of artistic and intellectual cre-
ations and especially the isolation and loneliness of American writers and intellectuals.[32] Some three decades later, during the Vietnam war, Sartre would
criticize the same isolation of American (left-wing) writers and intellectuals,
whom he included among "the wretched of the earth."

On a broader scale, cultural anti-Americanism in France in the postwar years was also exacerbated in the mid to late 1940s by agreements such as the 1946 Blum-Byrnes agreement, which canceled France's debt to the U.S. but also facilitated the influx of American products and especially American films, which were not necessarily of the best quality. As Tony Judt notes, the number of these films increased precipitously from 1946 to 1947. In the first half of 1946, 38 American films were released in France. In the same period in 1947, 338 American films were released.[33] Over the next decade, half the films released in France were American, and these films garnered fully 43 percent of the viewing public. No wonder that the French film industry, eager to compete with Hollywood productions while celebrating not American but the French national heritage in film, sought to imitate Hollywood's grandiose studio productions in bringing French literary classics such as Stendhal's *Red and Black* to the screen. Essentially derivative in nature, these films, characterized as belonging to the so-called "Tradition of Quality," would later be denounced in the 1950s as the "Cinema of Papa" by the French New Wave filmmakers. To the degree that the "Tradition of Quality" films reflected American studio production values and commercialism, it is possible to see the New Wave itself as a revolt against a particular form of American—or "Hollywoodian"—cultural hegemony, although many New Wave directors greatly admired such American movie makers as Howard Hawks, among others.

It is important to stress at this juncture that not all aspects of American culture were viewed entirely negatively by the postwar French intelligentsia, and not all postwar intellectuals were unequivocally anti-American. On the first score, Philippe Roger notes that among the intellectuals as well as France's educated classes, certain features of and figures from American culture were admired and even adored in France. Writers like William Faulkner and John Dos Passos were greatly esteemed after the war by the likes of Sartre (some in France claim—faultily, needless to say—that Sartre and other French writers made these American writers famous in the U.S. as well), and jazz was immensely popular among the existentialists. Hollywood Westerns, certain actors, including Jerry Lewis, and more recently Mickey Rourke and rap have enjoyed the same prestige. But as Philippe Roger points out, all of these American "imports" were admired in France largely because they were perceived as part of a "rebel" or subversive culture within the U.S. itself. Hence, they reinforced the generally negative stereotype of the dominant American culture.[34]

As for postwar intellectuals in France who were not anti-American, many were motivated primarily by a staunch anticommunism and a more "Atlanticist perspective." Figuring most prominently among these was the Swiss writer Denis de Rougemont, who was most famous for his study of romantic love in Western literature and culture, *L'amour et l'occident* (*Love in the West-*

ern World). Rougemont edited the review *Preuves*, which was published "under the auspices" of the Congress for Cultural Freedom and which was itself funded by the AFL-CIO and the American government (in part and indirectly by the CIA, as it turned out). The review attracted writers of international standing, including Karl Jaspers, Ignazio Silone, Bertrand Russell, Arthur Koestler, and Jacques Maritain. These figures were known less for pro-American views than for their vehement opposition to Marxism and the Soviet Union. In fact, as Jean-Philippe Mathy states, many of these authors wrote disparagingly of America and American culture in the pages of *Preuves* and feared an American hegemony that would cast Europe in the role of Greece and America in that of Rome.[35]

To a significant degree, attitudes toward America and *antiaméricanisme* took a different turn in the 1960s following the return to power of de Gaulle in 1958. Especially where strategic issues were concerned the contrast was striking. Richard Kuisel explains:

> De Gaulle charted a different course for France than his predecessors did. Whereas the Fourth Republic, for example saw a unified supranational Europe as the way to independence, the Fifth Republic saw it as a pawn in America's game. Where the pre-1958 regime found security in an integrated American-led defense system, the post-1958 regime saw NATO as undependable, perhaps dangerous, and possibly expendable protection. Whereas the Fourth Republic welcomed the United States because it provided security for Western Europe, de Gaulle thought it was exploiting its excess of power.[36]

Given these attitudes, de Gaulle's actions over the next decade were predictable. Not wishing to rely on American might, the French president inaugurated France's own nuclear arms program in order to develop its so-called *force de frappe*, or "strike force." In 1966, France withdrew from NATO. By 1967, Kuisel observes, "it was evident that France was the principal obstacle to American policy,"[37] and anti-French sentiment in the United States ran high as a result. French products were boycotted, and there were even demands to bring home the remains of American soldiers killed in European wars and buried in France. And yet, despite these political tensions, de Gaulle remained a staunch ally in times of crisis, including during U.S. showdowns with the Soviets over Berlin and Cuba.

In economic matters as well, the Fifth Republic's policies could be viewed as oppositional, although de Gaulle was aware of the need to chart a careful course between encouraging needed American investments and a comparable need to encourage greater French financial independence. The result was often policies, decisions, and economic moves on both sides that further strained Franco-American relations. In 1963, the Chrysler Corporation purchased controlling shares of Simca, France's third largest automobile maker, a move that Kuisel affirms "irritated and alarmed the [French] government."[38] At the height of the Simca controversy, news of Libby McNeil's plan to build a large vegetable and fruit processing plant in the Languedoc became public. The plan had quietly been approved by the Ministry of Agriculture; this, when it was leaked to the French press, provoked a strong backlash. The irony was that the processing plant would in all likelihood have proved beneficial to farmers in the region. Another venture that stirred fear of an American invasion and takeover of French business occurred subsequently when General Electric offered to buy twenty percent of *Machines Bull*'s shares and help the ailing French company with its "technology gap." The French government's flip-flops over the proposed deal only underscored French insecurity in the face of the American economic juggernaut. Given these examples of the American economic challenge (there were many others as well), it is no wonder that Jean Jacques Servan-Schreiber's book dealing with that very challenge, *Le Défi américain,* was an instant bestseller upon publication in 1967.

By the end of the 1960s, de Gaulle had stepped down as French President, ushered out in part by the "events" of May 1968, which were themselves characterized by their own form of anti-Americanism. But before leaving the subject of de Gaulle, it is important to underscore his own overriding attitudes towards the United States as well as American culture. In a number of ways, they are suggestive of the salient features of *antiaméricanisme* discussed so far, and also of attitudes that have enjoyed a vogue in many quarters in France in the last decade.

In *L'obsession anti-américaine,* Jean-François Revel underscores the fact that on at least one occasion, de Gaulle indulged in the same contradictory logic that characterizes many expressions and outbursts of *antiaméricanisme.* Upon withdrawing France from NATO's integrated command in 1966, de Gaulle argued that he was doing so because on two occasions in the recent past—1914 and 1940—America had come to France's aid only belatedly. Presumably, France could not allow this to happen again. But as Revel points out, the principal purpose of NATO was precisely to provide immediate Allied military support should one of its member nations be invaded.[39] As contradictory as de Gaulle's logic apparently was in this context, however, it is perhaps less evidence of illogic on his part than proof of a deep mistrust of American motives and reliability. Given his own experience with the American leadership during World War II and at the time of the Occupation, this is not entirely surprising.

Like many other French, de Gaulle also disliked what he considered an excessive American superficiality, materialism, and consumerism, a soulless obsession with gadgets, and a "rootlessness" that offended a man of traditions and heritage like the General. Moreover, in the 1960s, it should be recalled, American popular culture was increasingly making inroads in France, from the popularity among France's youth of figures like Al Capone to the invasion of rock and roll. Although the "ye-ye girls" Francoise Hardy, Sylvie Vartan, and Sheila were a response to the "British invasion" led by the Beatles and the Rolling Stones, France's major rock icon of the period, Johnny Hallyday—still very popular today—was a deliberate imitator of American rockers, Elvis Presley in particular.

In essence, as Kuisel observes, for de Gaulle America was "a society without history and therefore without an identity."[40] But the truth was that de Gaulle was ill-informed about that history, or at least failed to grasp its wellsprings. According to his friend and Gaullist minister René Pleven, de Gaulle's dealings with the U.S. were strained primarily because he proved unable to discover its historical keys, something he did well with Britain, Germany, and China, among others. Under any circumstances the latter were "real" nations while America, at least to him, was not.

In the main, the student revolts and subsequent workers' strikes of May 1968 were directed, at least initially, against French government policy on education, the stultifying effects of bourgeois culture, and the *vieux jeu,* anachronistic French leadership embodied in the person of the General. But they were also inspired by *marxisant* philosophies as well as deep animosities toward American imperialism represented by the American war effort in Vietnam and its policies in Latin America. In fact, in both areas American imperialism for many in France was an echo and a "ghost" of France's own imperialist past, still traumatic and chronologically proximate: the crisis in Algeria was, after all, less than a decade old. Moreover, especially where Vietnam was concerned, the Vietnamese FNL owed its leftist support in France not only to its struggle against U.S. hegemony, but also to the fact that it represented a new type of revolution that French intellectuals could identify with, one that fell outside the Soviet paradigm.[41] Later, of course, Vietnam's victory over the U.S. seemed for many a happy indication of the decline of American global influence.

In 1968, Maoism enjoyed a heyday among youthful intellectual leaders like André Glucksmann, who would later, of course, change course. Che Guevara was a hero of mythical dimensions, and in 1968 Régis Debray was in a Bolivian jail after having crossed the Atlantic to join the struggle of the Cuban leader against American imperialism in Latin America. Guy Debord's influential *situationnisme* denounced the "society of the spectacle," with its emphasis on technology, image, and rootlessness, that was so closely linked in the French mind with an American-inspired modernity.

If, intellectually speaking, May '68 was born on the revolutionary left and drew its primary inspiration from Marxist philosophies, it also eventually brought to prominence figures who would react against both it and the pro-Soviet, pro-Communist or fellow-traveling politics of the French intellectual left. Among the more visible, if intellectually lightweight, of these were the self-styled *nouveaux philosophes*—figures like Bernard-Henri Lévy and André Glucksmann. Their anti-totalitarian, anti-Soviet views, expressed in the mid 1970s in works like Lévy's *Barbarie à visage humain* (1977), broke violently with Marxist and Soviet orthodoxies and paved the way—eventually—for their own generally pro-American positions and those of others, for instance Pascal Bruckner. This has been the case especially in the 1990s and indeed up to the present.

Visible as they were, the *nouveaux philosophes* were not the only leftist intellectuals to break with a pro-Soviet and unproblematically revolutionary stance. Following the publication of Alexandr Solzhenitsyn's *Gulag Archipelago* in France in 1974, other prominent and better-established intellectuals, including Claude Lefort and Cornelius Castoriadis, articulated strident critiques of Soviet totalitarianism. According to Sunil Khilnani, in France it was only in the 1970s that a leftist but anti-Soviet position "became intellectually and politically sustainable."[42]

This did not, however, translate immediately (if at all, for some of these figures) into an intellectual, political, and cultural pro-American position. As Richard Kuisel points out, even as late as 1976 intellectual leaders such as the historian Pierre Nora—like many other postwar intellectuals before him, as we have seen—argued that there could be no real common ground, no possible "dialogue" between French and American intellectuals. Despite the Gulag, the Prague Spring, and other disappointments with Soviet totalitarianism, French intellectuals were still wedded to the idea of revolution as "the eternal future of a country with a long memory." In America, by contrast, revolution "is the eternal past of a nation that has no memory."[43] Where the U.S. was concerned, Nora's views complement de Gaulle's. If the U.S. had a history—something de Gaulle rejected—it would not, according to Nora, remember it anyway.

In some ways, Nora's comparisons of the two countries and their different outlooks seem to presage the political and cultural divergences that marked France and America in the 1980s. In France the decade was ushered in by the presidential victory of François Mitterrand, which for the left encouraged the dream of a Socialist and "revolutionary" future at last. The first few years of Mitterrand's mandate were indeed marked by major efforts at industrial and economic reform through, among other means, plans to nationalize important industries. But many of the most ambitious of these efforts would fail. By contrast, in the U.S. 1980 brought the election of Ronald Reagan, the victory of wholesale economic liberalism, and a return of "morning in America" following the supposed *malaise* of the Carter years. The new combination of the flexing of American muscle and Reagan's "trickle-down economics" was hardly geared, at least in the abstract, to building affinities with a Socialist France.

Moreover, where the 1980s are concerned, it should be stressed that even as Reagan's emphasis on American pride and power was apparently putting the ghosts of Vietnam and the recent past behind, France, by contrast, was increasingly preoccupied with its recent past and other, non–U.S.-related dilemmas such as adjusting to the "identity crisis" provoked by immigration and the efforts involved in "Europeanization." As for France's past, the nation found itself faced with a growing obsession with Nazism and the Vichy period in particular. Fueled by an increasing public awareness of French complicity in the Holocaust, many in France felt that coming to terms with the nation's past and fulfilling a "duty" to the memory of its victims was necessary before the nation could move forward with confidence. So absorbed was the nation with its "criminality" during World War II that the major literary and cinematic works of the period reflected this historical and geographical "insularity" to a remarkable degree. One need only think of Louis Malle's extraordinary film *Au Revoir les enfants* or Marguerite Duras's novel *La Douleur* to appreciate this tendency. In addition, this "duty to memory" expanded in the 1990s to include the victims of French abuses during the Algerian War as well as, toward the end of the decade, the ravages of Communism. Clearly, France's continuing meditation on its own—and Europe's—past was not in sync with a forward-looking America that displayed no apparent interest in focusing on its own past misdeeds. Perhaps de Gaulle and Nora had been right about the essential difference between their country and America after all.

Despite France's preoccupation with its past, which as noted extended well into the 1990s, European and global crises, and the role America played in these crises, would strongly affect and indeed largely determine French attitudes toward American hegemony in the new decade and especially the new millennium. These crises, including the Gulf War, the breakup of the former Yugoslavia, the bombing of Kosovo, and later 9/11 and Iraq, would eventually help to place America—and *antiaméricanisme*—squarely in the middle of the French radar screen. But before concluding this chapter with an examination of these European and global political crises and conflicts, it is important to stress as well the impact of cultural developments and exchanges that also strongly influenced French attitudes towards the U.S. The most appropriate point of departure for these discussions is, perhaps, the creation of Eurodisney outside of Paris.

As Carolyn Durham points out, given that Eurodisney now has its own Michelin guide—which lists, by the way, Versailles and Fontainebleau among other national monuments as nearby "tourist attractions"—it is sometimes difficult to remember the horror and outbursts of anti-American sentiment Eurodisney provoked among the French upon its creation.[44] The theater director Ariane Mnouchkine's famous attack on it as a "cultural Chernobyl" poisoning French and European culture was echoed in other diatribes by numerous individuals in the arts and other areas. The film critic Serge Toubiana depicted it as an invasion and conquest of French and European space that would drain off millions of tourists throughout Europe from what he clearly considered more worthwhile and enlightening touristic pursuits.[45] Jean-Marie Rouart, the literary critic of *Le Figaro,* cited it as proof that France had to defend "universal cultural values" against such abominations.[46] In fact, the outrage produced by Eurodisney was comparable to that generated more than a decade earlier by the construction of the Pompidou Center—ironically a very "French" project.

Despite these outbursts by artists and intellectuals claiming French cultural superiority, Shanny Peer suggests that the French government's extraordinarily generous support of the Eurodisney project probably reflected deep-seated social and economic insecurities that were much less flattering to France's exalted self-image. She suggests, for example, that the arrival of Eurodisney demonstrated in all probability a growing fatigue on the part of the French with their own *étatisme* as well as a wish to imitate the dynamic liberalism of Reaganism, despite the official Socialism of the Mitterrand presidency. Moreover, according to Peer, the ease with which American popular culture was successfully invading France at this time again pointed to a very evident French cultural anemia along the same lines.[47] One need only think of the success in France of the television show *Dallas,* which may well be better remembered there than in the U.S.

Despite the French desire to emulate Reaganite liberalism that was reflected in the government support for Eurodisney, once the amusement park came into existence the "downside" of that liberalism became evident as well. American corporate labor practices provoked controversy after controversy in Eurodisney's reported efforts to exploit and intimidate French workers.[48]

If Eurodisney was (and, to a certain degree, still is) a sore spot inspiring familiar denunciations of American cultural vacuousness and resentments concerning American economic hegemony, Hollywood's domination of the movie industry generated similar attitudes in the early 1990s and up to the present. Durham notes that in 1993, "American movies accounted for 60 percent of box office receipts in France and an even higher percentage of video sales."[49] That many of these movies were also Hollywood dross provoked still more contempt for American culture in many quarters, despite box office successes. Finally, as Durham observes, the fact that Hollywood was producing remakes of classic (or successful) French films by Godard (*Breathless*) and Clouzot (*Diabolique*), among others, not only struck many as cultural cannibalism but served as well to guarantee that French originals would neither do well nor even necessarily make it to American box offices.[50] This was, for anti-Americanists, yet another sign of an absolutist American economic colonialism.

But it is important to recall that not *all* Franco-American intellectual artistic and cultural transmissions were completely one-sided. For example, any academic working in the humanities and especially in literary studies and critical theory is well aware of the extraordinarily profound influence of French intellectuals and critics in American universities. The "first wave" to arrive were the structuralist critics in the 1960s and 1970s—Roland Barthes, Tzvetan Todorov, and René Girard among them—to be followed in the 1980s and 1990s by poststructuralists, including especially Michel Foucault and Jacques Derrida. More recently, Jean Baudrillard and especially Pierre Bourdieu have been very influential on the American scene. In academic and intellectual terms, at least, there has been, and continues to be, a remarkable and positive flow of French ideas "imported" into the U.S., although many of the figures responsible for these "imported ideas" were (and are) occasionally given to voicing expressions of *antiaméricanisme*. Yet it must be noted that some of the French intellectuals who are admired and even worshipped in some quarters in the U.S. are dismissed by their compatriots. Therefore, American admiration of these figures constitutes less of an "intellectual bridge" between the two countries than an additional source of misunderstanding.

To return to European and especially global conflicts of the 1990s and the new millennium and their impact on French attitudes toward America, the first of these, the Gulf War of 1991, produced official support for America as well as a fair amount of intellectual dissent. Despite the widespread disappearance on the left of hard-line procommunist and even Stalinist *nostalgiques* after the collapse of the Berlin Wall, there remained viscerally anti-American intellectuals as well as government ministers whose fear of American military might and "imperialism" reappeared during the fighting in Kuwait. These included Ignacio Ramonet, editor of the profoundly anti-American *Le monde diplomatique,* and Jean Baudrillard, who offered an apocalyptic assessment of the Gulf War and America's amazing technological skill at sanitizing its own destructiveness in *La Guerre du Golfe n'a pas eu lieu.* On the political level, François Mitterrand's support of the Gulf War did not necessarily reflect all of French public opinion; Jean-Pierre Chevènement, for one, then Minister of Defense, resigned in protest over Mitterrand's policy. (Of course, it is also true that Chevènement was chairman of the Franco-Iraqi Friendship Society and preferred not to give up his position there in order to maintain his ministerial portfolio.[51])

Whereas French support of the American-led Gulf War was not wholehearted or unqualified, American intervention in the former Yugoslavia, by the time it occurred, was generally welcomed. Had it occurred earlier, however, this might not have been the case. According to James Gow, "the French position moved from an étatiste-cum-Bonapartist attachment to the Yugoslav state and the Serbian cause at the outset, through various fluctuations, to being the principal advocate of air strikes against the Bosnian Serbs around Sarajevo in early 1994."[52] So when the Clinton administration decided, finally, to intervene, and when the Dayton Accords were signed in 1995, few stepped forward in France to speak out against American interventionism or the American role in the peace process.

With the beginning of the NATO bombardment of Kosovo in the spring of 1999, many of those who had earlier supported Croatian and especially Bosnian independence immediately expressed their support for NATO's intervention on behalf of the Kosovar Albanians. Rallies led by intellectuals lauded the NATO effort and condemned Serb brutalities and the policies of Slobodan Milosevic. But despite widespread support of the American-dominated NATO coalition, anti-NATO—and anti-American—voices on both the right and left were quick to surface. In many cases, those who protested the NATO bombing of Serbia characterized it as an example of NATO/American imperialism, as well as a naked and deliberate display of American military might. In the magazine *L'Événement du jeudi* of 1–6 April 1999, Serge Faubert gave voice to these sentiments in language reminiscent of the Cold War's cynical anti-Americanism paranoia. According to Faubert, America actually cared little for the fate of the Kosovar Albanians. Instead,

> Clinton intends to remind Europe, economic giant but military midget, that America remains the sole [global] military power. A demonstration of force that should make Paris, London, Rome and Bonn think. Henceforth, Washington will intervene in the heart of Europe with the same ease that characterized its expeditions to Grenada and Panama. The World Company has expanded its back yard to include the entire world.[53]

Faubert was by no means alone in expressing these views, and many other commentators on the right and left also denounced the "Imperial state's" administering of a "spanking" to those who did not follow its wishes. In many quarters, these denunciations of the American-led coalition were accompanied by condemnations of the weakness and cowardice of French President Jacques Chirac for meekly going along with American wishes. The philosopher Régis Debray chastised Chirac on the front page of *Le monde* for toadying to American might and participating in the unjust persecution of Slobadon Milosevic. Moreover, in a bizarre and perhaps telling reference to France's recent history, Debray compared Milosevic to Charles de Gaulle, thereby not only casting Milosevic in an unwarranted heroic light but, more tellingly, linking NATO and U.S. efforts in the region to Nazi aggression. Debray's rhetoric in this instance was obviously not far removed from much of the rhetoric of Cold War *antiaméricanisme* discussed earlier.

It is important to stress that the fear of and hostility toward American hegemony that emerged in these and other expressions of opposition to the

NATO intervention in Kosovo did not derive solely from old animosities dating back to the immediate postwar period as well as the 1960s and 1970s. They also date back more recently, to 1989 and its aftermath. The fading of the generalized European euphoria over the end of Communism and the Cold War—over the end of the "end of history" itself—was accompanied by a growing, and uncomfortable, awareness of a now unique and unchecked American might. Indeed, in 1998, even before the demonstration of devastating American military power in Kosovo, Hubert Védrine, then Minister of Foreign Affairs under Prime Minister Lionel Jospin, coined the term *hyper-puissance*—"hyper-power"—to characterize the "new America" and its position in the world.

By way of turning, finally, to what might best be described as a new and, in many ways, more profound *antiaméricanisme* in the wake of 9/11 and above all the war in Iraq, it is instructive to look more closely at Védrine's conception of the American *hyperpuissance,* the global Incredible Hulk the U.S. has become for many French, not just Védrine. To a significant degree, Védrine's definition connects the dots, so to speak, with the postwar past, while at the same time integrating new elements in a French perception—or misperception—of America. It also offers a sort of chronology of how this so-called *hyperpuissance* developed and finally emerged.

Already in the early postwar years, Védrine argues, the three constituent elements of this new American *hyperpuissance* were developing. The first was reactionary religiosity, with its born-again Christianity and its antiabortion politics. Although Védrine does not insist on it, it is clear that for him, this was and is essentially a Protestant religiosity since, he claims, it was shocked by the election of the Catholic John Kennedy as President in 1960. The other two constituent elements were a "unilateral" and "increasingly imperialist mind set," and finally, a visceral support for Israel coupled with strong anti-Palestinian, anti-Arab, and anti-Muslim sentiments.[54]

But for this new America to fully emerge and come to power, two events were necessary. The election of George W. Bush was the first of these events, but the "detonator," to use Védrine's expression, was 11 September 2001. The choice of the term "detonator" is apposite here, not simply because it graphically captures the events of 9/11, but because for Védrine, clearly, it evokes the new and explosive adventurism of American foreign policy.[55]

Védrine's vision of an essentially Bible-thumping, pro-Israeli U.S., bent on going its own way and intervening wherever and whenever it pleases, captures, in effect, the most essential features of the French understanding of Bush's America. Others besides Védrine, such as the Harvard-based French historian Patrice Higonnet, have been more precise in localizing the source of this new America. In an editorial in *Libération* published in 2003, Higonnet characterized the recent turn in American politics as an invasion from

Texas, the South, and the Midwest that has taken over all but the remaining bastions of liberalism on the East and West coasts. But whatever its source, for Higonnet the image of America is essentially the same.[56]

If America has emerged, especially over the last several years, as a kind of menacing Behemoth distinct, in important ways, from what it had been before, why have the French—and presumably other Europeans—been unable to detect its emergence until very recently? To this question, Védrine offers some interesting answers. First, he argues, the French are incapable of understanding religious fundamentalism, and they certainly are incapable of comprehending its political dimension. Second, he believes, the French have failed to grasp the new "populism" of the Republican Party. Finally, and perhaps most interestingly, he argues that there has been little or no critical analysis of the U.S. and what is actually happening in America. *Antiaméricanisme* has dominated and continues to dominate the discourse. Presumably, the resulting image, or myth, of America that is "analyzed" is actually the cluster of negative stereotypes *antiaméricanisme* fosters. On this score, Védrine's analysis dovetails with Philippe Roger's assessment, presented at the outset of the present chapter.

It is ironic, of course, that Védrine's perception of American *hyperpuissance* is itself subject to a few misperceptions or distorting stereotypes. For example, the new religious and Protestant right is not as neatly fused with antiabortion politics as Védrine suggests, nor can the supposed "populist turn" in the Republican Party account for the extraordinarily close ties between the Bush administration and corporate America, or the tax cuts aimed at the very rich. Be that as it may, he is not far off base in suggesting that the French did not see the new *hyperpuissance* coming because even now, analyses of America are often slanted by powerful, and in some instances apparently willful misperceptions about not only its nature but its role and status in the world. The best example of the phenomenon is Emmanuel Todd's best-selling *Après l'empire*.

Todd's main thesis—that American power is *not* on the rise but in fact on the decline, and for largely demographic reasons—clearly runs counter to many current perceptions in France of America's global status. Tony Judt, for one, has dismissed the demographic arguments as the products of the mind of a "mad scientist," and they are not particularly interesting for our purposes here. The rest of the argument, however, confirms Védrine's perspective, and is worth rehearsing briefly.

From his opening sentence, Todd demonstrates that he shares the view of America as a reckless global power by asserting baldly that "[t]he United States is in the process of becoming a problem for the world." Once the guarantor of political liberty and economic order, it has now become a source of global disorder, uncertainty, and conflict. Moreover, if Star Wars finally comes on line, America could well "reign over the world by terror." In the meantime, the U.S. threatens countries like North Korea, which Todd argues will collapse of its own accord if left well enough alone, and Iran, which Todd asserts is only interested in "internal and external pacification"—whatever that means. Clearly, he concludes, America is subject to a "feverish militarism" with no end in sight.[57]

But just when things are looking particularly dire, Todd insists that ultimately, the American threat should not be feared because it will die off on its own. In an increasingly democratized world, military power—American power—will become superfluous. Moreover, the increasing futility of its military might will be matched by its growing economic dependency on the outside world. In order to sustain the illusion that its hegemony is undiminished, the United States will increasingly engage in acts of what Todd calls "theatrical militarism," picking on weaker adversaries, prolonging indefinitely the conflicts in which it engages, and maintaining at all costs a massive weapons superiority. But in the end all of this will be to no avail. As American dominance declines, Todd claims, it will be the role of Europe to oversee its decline for the benefit of all.[58]

To be sure, Todd is not a "conventional anti-American," for he ultimately dismisses the effective threat of American military power and hegemony. But to make his case, Todd has to resort to a number of dubious truisms. Is the world in fact becoming more democratic? Will North Korea collapse of its own accord? Is Iran interested only in pacification? Todd assumes so, but these are assumptions that, when taken together, serve to justify his claim that America has become a "predator" in the world. They are also so constraining as to suggest that Todd's reading is profoundly *ideological*. Moreover, in its essential Manichaeanism, Todd's analysis constitutes a kind of mirror image of the analysis of Robert Kagan, so controversial in contemporary France. In *Of Paradise and Power*, Kagan describes a Hobbesian America obliged to protect a Kantian Europe from the harsh realities of the brutal world. For Kagan, Europeans mistakenly believe that they can offer the world not power but the "transcendence of power." And it is "America's power and its willingness to exercise that power—unilaterally if necessary—that constitute a threat to Europe's new sense of mission."[59] The results are deep-seated tensions and animosities that, for Kagan at least, cast America in the heroic and tragic role of manning the walls but never being able to walk through the gates into a European-style paradise. And this situation, Kagan implies, is not likely to change.

If Emmanuel Todd's *Après l'empire* seems to confirm Védrine's claim that the American *hyperpuissance* is poorly understood because the analysis of it is prejudicial from the outset, when placed alongside works like Kagan's it also helps to illuminate what is perhaps truly *new* in Franco-American relations after 9/11 and the American invasion of Iraq. In essence, it casts the United

States and France not as grudging allies bent on the same or even similar global missions, but as *opponents* offering very different values and visions to the world. Shortly after the invasion of Iraq began, Denis Jeambar articulated this new and disturbing reality in a column in *L'Express* entitled, suitably, "The Logic of Rupture." In transatlantic relations, he argued, "the distinction between ally and enemy has been erased." And as for French sentiments toward the United States, Jeambar continued, "We no longer aspire to work with them. We are even ready to work against them."[60]

Given France's traditional view of its *mission civilisatrice* and the fact that it finds no echo in the Bush administration's jingoistic "cowboyism," relations between the two countries are likely to remain unchanged in the short run and perhaps even longer. Unlike virtually all other postwar American Presidents, Bush has inspired neither sympathy, nor affection, nor respect in France, except among a few figures like André Glucksmann. It is no surprise, therefore, that the Iraqi quagmire has provoked muted, but nevertheless gleeful, comparisons with Vietnam.

Yet it is not clear that *antiaméricanisme* would subside in France even if what Michael Hirsch describes as the current "Michael Corleone foreign policy" of "just killing everybody" of the Bush administration disappeared.[61] A front-page story in the *New York Times* of 11 September 2003 stresses that a generally favorable attitude on the part of the French toward America has declined from 62 percent in 1999/2000 to just 43 percent in 2003. And that figure might well worsen because, as Eric Conan points out, *antiaméricanisme* is weakest among the generation that lived through World War II, that is, the generation that is dying out.[62] Finally, if the brief postwar history of Franco-American relations sketched out here confirms anything, it is that *antiaméricanisme* is a constant in postwar France, that it is inextricably linked to the processes of economic and cultural Americanization, that it is triggered by an unforeseeable variety of circumstances, and that it is inspired as much by myths and distortions as it is by realities. Whether the current antipathy toward the United States will ultimately conform to this pattern or mutate into something much more deep-seated and permanent, only time will tell.

Notes

1. Philippe Roger, *L'Ennemi américain: Généalogie de l'antiaméricanisme français* (Paris: Seuil, 2002), 9.
2. Roger, *L'Ennemi américain*, 16.

3. Roger, *L'Ennemi américain,* 15.
4. See René Girard, *Violence and the Sacred* (Baltimore: Johns Hopkins University Press, 1977).
5. Jean-François Revel, *L'Obsession anti-américaine* (Paris: Plon, 2002), 21.
6. Roger, *L'Ennemi américain,* 10.
7. Revel, *L'Obsession anti-américaine,* 20.
8. Conversation with the author. At the time Melihi made this remark, he was in Texas filming a program on deteriorating Euro-American relations for the Swiss television program *Temps présent.* The program, entitled "Our Dear American Enemies," aired on the international French language station TV5 on 13 September 2003.
9. Jean Baudrillard, "L'Esprit du terrorisme," *Le monde,* 2 November, 2001.
10. Annette Lévy-Willard, "Paris, le 11 septembre, 2001," *South Central Review* 19, nos. 2–3 (2002): 73.
11. Revel, *L'Obsession anti-américaine,* 23.
12. Tahar Ben Jelloun, "Pour sortir de la malediction," *Le Monde,* 3 November 2001.
13. Pascal Bruckner, André Glucksmann, and Romain Goupil, "Saddam doit partir, de gré ou de force!"*Le Monde,* 3 March 2003.
14. Adam Gopnick, "The Anti–Anti-Americans," *The New Yorker,* 1 August 2003, 5.
15. Revel, *L'Obsession anti-américaine,* 56.
16. Raoul Aglion, "The Free French and the United States from 1940 to 1944," in Robert Paxton and Nicholas Wahl, eds., *De Gaulle and the United States: A Centienial Appraisal* (Oxford: Berg, 1994), 34.
17. Aglion, "The Free French," 48.
18. Tony Judt, *Past Imperfect: French Intellectuals 1944–1956* (Berkeley: University of California Press, 1992), 195.
19. Alphonse de Châteaubriant, *Cahiers 1906–1951* (Paris: Grasset, 1955), 222.
20. Quoted in Judt, *Past Imperfect,* 200.
21. Richard Kuisel, *Seducing the French: The Dilemma of Americanization* (Berkeley: University of California Press, 1993), 20.
22. Quoted in Julian Jackson, *The Fall of France: The Nazi Invasion of 1940* (Oxford: Oxford University Press, 2003), 2.
23. For a detailed discussion of the Marshall Plan in France, see chapter 4 in Kuisel, *Seducing the French.*
24. Quoted in Jean Philippe Mathy, *Extrême Occident: French Intellectuals and America* (Chicago: University of Chicago Press, 1993), 137.
25. François Furet, *The Past of an Illusion: The Idea of Communism in the Twentieth Century* (Chicago: University of Chicago Press, 1999).
26. Quoted in Mathy, *Extreme Occident,* 139.
27. Quoted in Michel Winock, *Le Siècle des intellectuels* (Paris: Seuil, 1997), 460.
28. Winock, *Le Siècle des intellectuels,* 461.
29. Quoted in Winock, *Le Siècle des intellectuels,* 462.
30. Roger, *L'Ennemi américain,* 570–571.
31. Quoted in Mathy, *Extrême Occident,* 142.
32. Mathy, *Extrême Occident,* 148–159.
33. Judt, *Past Imperfect,* 201.
34. Roger, *L'Ennemi américain,* 572.
35. Mathy, *Extrême Occident,* 140.
36. Kuisel, *Seducing the French,* 136.
37. Kuisel, *Seducing the French,* 140.
38. Kuisel, *Seducing the French,* 156.

39. Revel, *L'Obsession anti-américaine*, 22.
40. Kuisel, *Seducing the French*, 146.
41. Sunil Khilnani, *Arguing Revolution: The Intellectual Left in Postwar France* (New Haven: Yale University Press, 1993), 140.
42. Sunil Khilnani, *Arguing Revolution*, 129.
43. Pierre Nora quoted in Kuisel, *Seducing the French*, 220.
44. Carolyn Durham, *Double Take: Culture and Gender in French Films and their American Remakes* (Hanover: Dartmouth/UPNE, 1998), 2.
45. Durham, *Double Take*, 1.
46. Durham, *Double Take*, 4.
47. Shanny Peer, "Marketing Mickey: Disney goes to France," *The Tocqueville Review* 13, no. 2 (1992): 130.
48. On these issues, see Marianne Debouzy, "Does Mickey Mouse threaten French Culture? The French Debate over Eurodisneyland," in Sabrina P. Ramet and Gordana P. Crnkovič, eds., *Kazaam! Splat! Ploof! The American Impact on European Popular Culture since 1945* (Lanham: Rowman and Littlefield, 2003), 15–36.
49. Durham, *Double Take*, 6.
50. Durham, *Double Take*, 7.
51. John Laughland, *The Death of Politics: France under Mitterrand* (London: Michael Joseph, 1994), 232.
52. James Gow, *Triumph of the Lack of Will: International Diplomacy and the Yugoslav War* (New York: Columbia University Press, 1997), 158.
53. Serge Faubert, "Rendez-nous de Gaulle," *L'événement du jeudi*, 1–6 April 1999, 16.
54. Hubert Védrine, "Que faire avec l'hyperpuissance?" *Le débat* 125 (2003): 4–5.
55. Védrine, "Que faire avec l'hperpuissance?" 4.
56. Patrice Higonnet, "La résistible ascendance du nouvel empire américain," *Libération* 3 January 2003.
57. Emmanuel Todd, *Après l'empire: Essai sur la décomposition du système américain* (Paris: Gallimard, 2002), 9–10.
58. Todd, *Après l'empire*, 32.
59. Robert Kagan, *Of Paradise and Power: Europe and America in the New World Order* (New York: Knopf, 2003), 61.
60. Denis Jeambar, "La logique de rupture," *L'express*, 27 March–2 April 2003.
61. Interview with Michael Hirsh as a press release for his book, *At War with Ourselves: Why America Is Squandering Its Chance to Build a Better World* (New York: Oxford University Press, 2003).
62. Éric Conan, "L'antiaméricanisme: un mal français," *L'express*, 10 April 2003, 49.

A SPECIAL GERMAN CASE
OF CULTURAL AMERICANIZATION

❖   ❖   ❖

Alexander Stephan

Prefatory Remarks

When in the late afternoon of 11 September 1944 Staff Sergeant Werner L. Holzinger of the 85th Reconnaissance Squadron, 5th Armored Division, became the first American GI to cross the German border near the Luxemburg village of Stolzenbourg,[1] few could have predicted that the United States would remain a political and military presence in Germany for half a century. And surely in those autumn days no one guessed that in just fifty years, the U.S., once again on German soil, would complete its evolution into the world's only superpower when the Berlin Wall collapsed, heralding the downfall of the Soviet Union.

But what quickly did become clear was that Germany[2] was going to be a special case in the Americanization of Europe, not only politically and economically but culturally, too. The reasons are obvious. Germany had lost its sovereignty with its unconditional surrender and, like Japan, was dependent on the United States to a far greater extent, and for a much longer period, than any other nation in Europe, including Italy and Austria. The disparity in power increased because the divided and demilitarized Germany remained on the front lines of the Cold War until 1990 and West Germany had to rely on the military protection of the United States. The economic reconstruction of the devastated land, split into zones of occupation and destabilized by its millions of refugees, depended, at least in the beginning, on the support of the U.S., which in 1945 had eliminated its strongest competitors in Europe and Asia and economically and politically, if not yet ideologically, become the world's premier power. Moreover, no country in Europe had so great a need

Notes for this section begin on page 87.

as Germany—its history discredited, its culture distorted and language contaminated by the Nazis—to find a replacement for its lost national identity. In this morally disoriented land, few had the strength or the courage to evolve their own alternatives to the ideals and values that had been lost. Terms like "the zero hour" and *Kahlschlag* ("clear-cutting") were widely used, showing not only the depth of Germans' insecurity but also their hope that they could start over.

Historians later downplayed the notion of a "zero hour" because it tended to mask the social and cultural continuity of German life that went on more or less intact after 1945 despite the denazification programs. This view overlooks the fact that Germany (albeit against its will) was given the opportunity to fundamentally change direction, to turn away from its brief and unhappy history as an expanding nation-state, its disastrous project to "go it alone," and a social structure that was deeply rooted in the nineteenth century—and what was even more important, to move toward integration into Europe as it began coming together, first economically, then politically, and now perhaps culturally as well. By a remarkable twist of fate, the total political, military, moral, and cultural disenfranchisement of Germany put it in a position to commit earlier and more intensively than other countries to a united Europe, to promote construction of a model welfare state, and, in the cultural sphere, to develop a pronounced antinationalism and pacifism. After World War II, realistic German politicians, economic leaders, and intellectuals all agreed on one thing: the traditional instruments of power politics, to which postwar Britain and France tried to cling with ever-diminishing success, would not be available to Germany in the foreseeable future, nor could Germany follow a third path between the two major camps in the Cold War. It is true that a sizeable number of the German elite, including the cultural elite, were reluctant at first to adopt the role of pacifist pan-Europeans. But the United States needed a Western Europe that was as strong, homogeneous, and united as possible, as a bulwark against communism, which the U.S. perceived as a threat both externally and internally, leaving Germany no choice but to opt for Europe. Eventually Germany's neighbors, suspicious of its power after their experiences with the Third Reich, also came to realize that their own economic and security interests could best be served by a Germany that internally was stable and externally was solidly integrated into the context of Europe as a whole.

American Cultural Policy

The American cultural officers who started to reconstruct cultural life in Germany in the spring of 1945 were no doubt surprised by the scale of the physical and intellectual destruction of the country, by the unbroken power of the conservative elites, and by the hunger of Germans for culture of every kind. But they had not come to Europe unprepared. Agencies like the Foreign Nationalities Branch of the Office of Strategic Services, which in 1947 became the CIA, had for years been reading analyses of the future of Europe, prepared for them by a small army of German and Austrian exiles. The State Department interviewed refugees from the Nazis, trying to form a picture of conditions in postwar Germany and of the role the Soviet Union might play in the territories it had occupied.[3] The Office of War Information had an *Operational Plan for Germany* that listed films that were to be shown in the postwar country. German-born GI's like Klaus Mann, Stefan Heym, and Hans Habe were assigned to sound out the mood in their homeland or to help reorganize newspapers according to an American model. The German Erich Pommer and the Austrian Billy Wilder were sent to Berlin to gear up the film industry. Robert M. W. Kempner, who until 1933 had been a midlevel bureaucrat in the Prussian Ministry of the Interior, participated in the Nuremberg trials as America's deputy chief prosecutor.

These American or German-American postwar pioneers proved clearly successful. Most political and intellectual leaders of the Third Reich were quickly stripped of their power, denazified, and reeducated. Under Allied supervision, the press, radio, theaters, and publishing houses began immediately after the war to supply Germans with a surprisingly wide-ranging cultural program. National Socialist publications in libraries and schools were replaced by a flood of American books that had been banned between 1933 and 1945 or were being made available for the first time via an extensive translation program administered by the occupation authorities. Many of the almost 400,000 German POWs returning from the U.S. had been exposed to the basic values of democracy and could tell of hands-on experiences with the American way of life. Twenty-seven America Houses established in heavily populated areas by 1950, supplemented by well over one hundred reading rooms and mobile information centers, served more than one million visitors per month. When in 1948 the U.S. government permitted the newly issued German mark to be exchanged for dollars at profitable rates, Hollywood began to flood the German market with films of every description. The soldiers' radio station American Forces Network (AFN) brought not only jazz and swing but American radio dramas into German households. Contacts between American soldiers and the German population, especially the female population, who quickly circumvented the ban on fraternization, became a gateway for American popular culture, lifestyle, and manners.

Compared to all the other countries of Europe, with the temporary exception of Austria, Germany, ravaged morally by the National Socialists and physically by Allied bombs, was wide open to the American cultural officers. But

this does not mean that the traditionally anti-American right and left political camps put up no resistance to the work of the Office of Military Government United States (known as OMGUS), its Information Control Division,
the U.S. information centers, and the United States Information Agency. And
Soviet officials quickly put an end to American activities in East Germany,
just as in the Western zones the U.S. banned organizations labeled as communist or run by so-called fellow travelers.

Foremost among this opposition were the traditional conservative elites
who, undisturbed by revolutions and uninterested in reforms, clung until
well into the second half of the twentieth century to their time-honored cultural values and to an outdated educational system. Indeed, it can be argued
that the conservative tradition of German culture reaped certain benefits from
the period of the Third Reich to the extent that it had not been too overtly
identified with National Socialist values. They had taken advantage of the
power vacuum created in 1933 when the Nazis had brutally eliminated the
conservatives' most significant opponents, namely the modernist movement
in art, the avant-garde intellectuals of the 1920s, and the so-called proletarian-
revolutionary culture. And after the war the conservatives gained power because,
although they had always despised the American brand of "civilization" and
now sought to circumvent the American reeducation programs wherever possible, the U.S. occupation forces turned out to be their new allies in the struggle against communism.

Nevertheless, German conservatives today still complain that German postwar culture was overwhelmed by outside forces.[4] They claim that Anglo-Saxon
mercantilism, with its utilitarian model of civilization, has triumphed over
German values and traditions, while washing machines, refrigerators, and
electric shavers have usurped the place of humanism, intellect, and insight.[5]
Technology, the big cities, and tourism are described, without mincing words,
as "extermination camps for the individual."[6] Konrad Adenauer chose Bonn
over Frankfurt as West Germany's capital because it was not yet "totally Americanized."[7] According to the conservative elite, the final decline of the West
was now at hand under the joint onslaught of Americanism and Bolshevism.

Left-wing support for a grassroots cultural revolution, on the other hand,
caused relatively little problem for U.S. cultural policymakers in Germany,
unlike the Socialist and Communist movements in such countries as France,
Italy, and Greece. Members of the artistic avant-garde who had escaped Nazi
persecution by going into exile were scattered all over the world, and either
had no interest in returning to Germany or were denied travel permits by the
Allies. Many had been so repelled by the brutal policies of Stalinism that they
had abandoned their leftist principles as early as the 1930s and started supplying the Americans with handy theories of totalitarianism that put Nazis
and Communists on the same level.[8] Others had discredited themselves by

their wholesale adoption of the dogmatic aesthetic of socialist realism. The U.S., waging a worldwide propaganda war financed through the CIA and the Congress for Cultural Freedom (CCF), succeeded in integrating some members of the democratic, liberal German left into the anti-Soviet phalanx in the Cold War. An ideological "crusade" against communism fused the old theory of consensus liberalism with the new idea of the "end of ideology," while a war of words, which blazed from 1947/48 until the 1960s and was stoked again by Ronald Reagan two decades later, drew a line in the sand between American and Soviet culture.

When neither persuasion nor cash sufficed to ensure the victory of the Americanization campaigns, the U.S. occupation authorities did not hesitate to resort to tried-and-true methods like censorship and outright bans. For example, when Hans Werner Richter and Alfred Andersch propagated a social-democratic, European third way between East and West, the Americans withdrew the license for their magazine *Der Ruf* in 1947. In the Western zones, the Kulturbund zur demokratischen Erneuerung Deutschlands (Cultural League for the Democratic Renewal of Germany), which had been founded in East Berlin, was banned. To the horror and derision of Germans who had just been freed from the Nazis, libraries in the America Houses were not spared from purges and book-burning raids in the early 1950s, when cohorts of the communist-hunter Joseph McCarthy traveled through Germany searching for un-American, that is, left-wing literature, including the novels of John Dos Passos and Thomas Mann and books by Frank Lloyd Wright. Skeptics who railed against the contradictions that ensue when a military occupation force tries to spread freedom, democracy, and culture by diktat saw their views confirmed when the U.S. censors hesitated to allow Schiller's *Wilhelm Tell* or the MGM film *The Seventh Cross* to be seen in Germany because the protest against state power in these works might supply Germans with arguments against the occupation forces. Nor did a German need to be a communist to feel offended that the Americans exported to Germany not only democracy and a free market economy but also the racial segregation practiced in the U.S., which made black GI's into second-class citizens on an even lower plane than the defeated Germans.

The official U.S. operation to control Germany's culture peaked in the early 1950s. A decade later, it became clear that the "battle for the hearts and minds" of West Germans had for the most part been won despite occasional setbacks, and American cultural policy began to relax its grip. German authorities were taking over more and more of the costs of running American organizations like RIAS (Radio in the American Sector), which had become an effective propaganda weapon directed against East Germany, and the Fulbright program, which promoted the exchange of scholars. In the mid-1960s, the Congress for Cultural Freedom ceased operating after the revelation of its

ties to the CIA caused a minor scandal that rebounded against German intellectuals who had been CCF protégés. The America Houses either were closed,
passed into German hands, or, after the collapse of the Berlin Wall, were re-
located to the provinces of the former East Germany. At German universities, programs in American Studies that had been sponsored by American
money and know-how began to take on a life of their own. Enterprises like
Radio Free Europe and academic exchange programs like the International
Research and Exchanges Board (IREX), which had been active in the East
German Democratic Republic, had to be redefined after the breakup of the
Soviet Union. And the gradual withdrawal of American soldiers and the rising standard of living in West Germany reduced the contacts between the
troops and the German population.

At the same time, beginning in the 1950s, the U.S. government's cultural
programs increasingly were replaced by the free market system that had long
dominated public culture in the United States. Concentrated on the profitable area of pop culture, this system more or less ignored the niche audience
for high culture, which offered little commercial reward. Hollywood raked in
profits from the German market, while at the same time it spread images of
the American way of life that spoke to people more directly than the reeducation programs of OMGUS. More recently, a rapidly growing number of
private German broadcasters who, like their American models, depend on
advertising income and therefore on the number of people tuning in, have
crowded out the more intellectually demanding news, documentary, and cultural programs of the state-run channels. Well-financed publishers speed American novels and self-help books onto German best-seller lists. MTV, portable
mp3 players, and websites on the Internet, which was originally developed to
serve the American military, dominate the future-oriented youth market,
while the recreational activities and consumption patterns of the young have
become more and more identical to those of their contemporaries in other
Western European nations and in the U.S. In short, the cultural reeducation
and Americanization of the Germans has been so successful, from an American point of view, that Washington today is citing it (somewhat prematurely)
as a model for the reconstruction of other defeated nations like Afghanistan
and Iraq.

High Culture

The cultural officers and America Houses assigned to spread American high
culture in Germany after 1945 had to battle on several fronts simultaneously.
The traditionally strong isolationist political faction in the U.S. Congress were
urging the country to pull out of Europe as quickly as possible after the war.

The field of cultural diplomacy, at the time a recent discovery by Washington, has been chronically undervalued, apart from the period of the Cold War, with its current budget in the administration of George W. Bush only a small fraction of one percent of that for armaments. After World War II, few U.S. cultural diplomats had extensive experience working with foreign cultural affairs. Moreover, conservative politicians from outside the beltway repeatedly intervened in cultural matters. Much like today, they attacked real or imagined liberals, accusing them of engaging in un-American activities. Conservatives portrayed the counterculture of the beatniks as controlled by godless homosexuals. And the artists of Abstract Expressionism were told that they were a "deviation from the standard of 'Americanism'"[9]—all at a time when Europeans showed great interest in the American counterculture and people in Paris and Munich admired Abstract Expressionist art as authentically American.

For many people, these and other divisive factors were part of a broader clash of cultures between America and Europe. For instance, in the United States, unlike Germany, the boundary between high and popular culture had been blurred since the nineteenth century, making it difficult to define what constituted high culture in America. And since high culture in the United States, like popular culture, is subject to the laws of the marketplace, Americans had a hard time communicating with Germans who were used to a system of state-subsidized culture. Many among the occupation forces struggled to find the right balance between their role as victors and a latent feeling of inferiority with regard to European traditions, which still dominated the cultural life of the American elites after World War II. As U.S. cultural policy abroad increasingly promoted popular culture during the 1950s, it became evident that Europeans were putting up a strong resistance to the merging of high and low culture. Both in the educated middle class and among German intellectuals, deeply rooted prejudices closed minds to cultural expressions from the United States, on the grounds that they were poor copies of European originals or that they compromised the standards of high culture by their commercialism and the fact that they were geared to appeal to a mass market.

The occupation authorities' attempts to avoid these culture clashes were not always successful. For example, the directors of many America Houses during the first years after the war believed that they could best reach the German public by inviting American symphony orchestras on tour through Germany to play pieces by Beethoven and Mozart, or by sending German intellectuals who had been driven out by the Nazis to lecture on such topics as "Music in the USA" (Paul Hindemith) and "Nietzsche in America" (Ludwig Marcuse). American writings based on ideas derived from the European Enlightenment, including those of Benjamin Franklin and Thomas Jefferson, were distributed in vast quantities to introduce German readers to American thought. Magazines like *Amerikanische Rundschau* lost readers although their articles were of high quality, because they were originally written for an American public. And even Abstract Expressionism, which was presented as an American art from the 1950s onward and came to be increasingly admired by Germans, had been strongly influenced by European émigrés and was built on terms, concepts, and forms that had evolved in Europe fifty years earlier.

High culture with a Made-in-the-USA label found a better response when the cultural diplomats relied on typically American products and forms of distribution: the short story, a more accessible form than the German novella; novels by Ernest Hemingway, whose terse, laconic style made him stand out from the convoluted, philosophy-laden texts of German authors; books by Mark Twain and William Faulkner that described life in the American West and South. Plays like Thornton Wilder's *Our Town* and *By the Skin of Our Teeth* (whose title, translated into German, was "We Got Out Alive," which struck a chord with the population in postwar Germany) were viewed not only as a commentary on people's own postwar experiences but also as a soft and positive variation on German and French existentialism. German soldiers were able to see their own lives reflected in American war literature by Hemingway, Norman Mailer, and Irwin Shaw.[10] Novels printed in newspaper format, paperbacks, and abridged versions modeled on America's *Reader's Digest* condensed books ensured that a broad public had access to literary texts. Younger readers, looking for alternatives to the depressing German literature set in the ruins of the war, and wanting to be different from their conservative and only superficially denazified parents and teachers, were attracted to the easy-to-read style of American literature, its suspensefully told stories, its generally optimistic view of the future, and its freedom from a weighty cultural past.

Nevertheless, literary historians find few signs that the widely distributed American prose and drama had any enduring influence on the form and style of German literature until the 1970s and 1980s, when postmodern authors and filmmakers like Peter Handke, Rolf Dieter Brinkmann, and Wim Wenders arrived on the scene with new ways of writing and seeing.[11] Another divisive factor was that the transmission of American high culture, intended to spread a positive image of an open, diverse and democratic America, quickly got caught up in the Cold War in a Germany divided between East and West. Thus when Melvin J. Lasky was an American guest speaker at the First German Writers' Congress in October 1947, he asked his audience to discuss not so much the new beginning for German literature as the control of Russian and East German culture by Stalinism. That same year OMGUS announced "Operation Talkback"[12] and shifted its efforts from the reeducation of the Germans to the ideological conflict with communism. A group of U.S. senators demanded "a worldwide Marshall plan in the field of ideas,"[13] and Dwight D. Eisenhower ordered the deployment of "T-bombs,"[14] that is, Truth bombs. Art exhibitions like "Non-Representational Painting in America" and musicals like *Porgy and Bess* were sent to tour Europe, not only to show the achievements of contemporary American artists but also to counterbalance the socialist realism propagated on the other side of the Iron Curtain. Millions of anticommunist brochures and books like Victor Kravchenko's *I Chose Freedom* (1946) and the anthology *The God That Failed* (1949) were issued to help Americans gain the victory in their culture war against communism in general and the government of Walter Ulbricht in East Germany in particular. On another tack, Senator McCarthy wanted a list drawn up of 30,000 titles that were no longer to be circulated abroad because of their un-American form or content, or because they had been used in Eastern Europe to promote the image of another, self-critical America.

From 1950 on, the leader in the "battle for the mind of Europe"[15] was the Congress for Cultural Freedom (CCF), financed in part by European contributions to the Marshall Plan fund and supported by philanthropic organizations like the Ford Foundation, which had promoted American high culture domestically as well as abroad well before World War II, when the government in Washington had no interest in pursuing cultural diplomacy nor indeed had any theory of how it could be done. The CCF conceived of its operations as a form of "psychological warfare"[16] against the Soviet Union with special attention paid to the dissemination of American high culture and to winning over a stable of highly regarded writers, artists, and intellectuals from the liberal-left anticommunist bloc in Europe. For West Berlin, the CCF organized an "intellectual airlift" and a reorientation program that, like the Free University of Berlin founded in 1948, was aimed primarily at youth. In 1950, President Harry Truman announced a "total mobilization" in the Campaign of Truth, that is, the culture and propaganda war against communism, and identified West Germany as an "area of concern."[17] Between 1948 and 1953, some 10,000 influential Germans were given the opportunity to travel to the United States with the support of the CCF, government programs, and private foundations. A much smaller number of American specialists crossed the Atlantic in the other direction.

The fact that the CIA, a body designed for foreign espionage and intelligence-gathering, played a leading role in the spread of American high culture overseas, makes clear the degree to which U.S. cultural diplomacy was governed by ideological and power-political considerations in the first two decades after the war.[18] In the 1950s, the so-called New York Intellectuals abandoned the social criticism that they had derived from European models before World War II, and traded it for the consensus-building myth of American exceptionalism. By 1960, Daniel Bell was proclaiming the end of ideology and the victory of the American social and economic system. And theoreticians like Marshall McLuhan ("The Medium Is the Message"), Susan Sontag, and Leslie Fiedler conjured images of a media-created global village and a classless culture where—rather like the ideal presented by socialist realism on the other side of the Iron Curtain—the European Enlightenment's dream of an independent, emancipated people had been largely achieved.

At about the same time, strategic motives—including the elimination of the German threat by integrating West Germany into the European community, and a shift in the conflict with communism from Europe to Asia—led to Washington's withdrawal from efforts to propagate American high culture, an enterprise for which it had never felt any enthusiasm, leaving both high and popular culture to the culture industry. The art scene, following the laws of the marketplace, shifted from Paris and Munich to New York and San Francisco, and Guggenheim, Getty, and other private foundations began to contribute to the Americanization of European museum culture. Ailing German theaters and opera companies tried to attract new audiences with American comedies and musicals. Films like *Schindler's List* and the television series *Holocaust* popularized and, in the view of many European critics, trivialized the central theme of postwar German high culture, the Holocaust.

In other words, by the beginning of the 1960s the active Americanization of German culture by the occupation forces and the Congress for Cultural Freedom began to be replaced by a self-Americanization that was part of the U.S.–led worldwide blend of art, commerce, modernization, and globalization. Increasingly, supply and demand, not abstract definitions of style and quality, began to determine the production and distribution of culture. Galleries and auction houses, advertising agencies and box-office success, best-seller lists and the mass media gradually took over the role of the state, whose means to promote culture and education have steadily diminished. In the Communist East Germany people made a statement against the official anti-American propaganda of their government by wearing jeans, listening to rock and roll, and sporting long hair. During the 1980s, while the U.S. government exported "Reaganomics"—that is, deregulation, an aggressive opening-up of markets, and the globalization of competition—to Western Europe, new fields like culture studies and postmodernism were plotted at American universities, supplying the theoretical framework to eliminate the boundaries between intellectual disciplines, the established formal styles, and the distinction between high and popular culture that had been inherited from European class society.

Popular Culture

Eyewitnesses who saw the march of the Americans into Germany in spring 1945 almost all reported the same images: gangling GIs with cigarettes casually drooping from the corners of their mouths, handing out chewing gum and chocolate to the population. Jazz and swing—music that could only be heard underground during the Third Reich—now resounded from the bars. German women, many of whom had lost their husbands or sweethearts in the war, were attracted by the prosperity and open manners of the occupation troops, who quickly found ways to get around the ban on fraternization. African-American GIs, whom Germans feared most at the beginning, bonded with the impoverished population, who like them were treated as people of a lower order. Young Germans quickly identified with the unauthoritarian behavior of the victors.

Of course, the middle-aged and older generations of Germans were by no means unfamiliar with much of the popular culture that crossed the Atlantic with the baggage of the U.S. army. American music and dances, from the shimmy to the one-step and the Charleston, had been part of the standard repertoire of the entertainment industry in the Weimar Republic. Black jazz musicians and show celebrities like Josephine Baker and her American Revue Nègre were hugely popular in Berlin in the Golden Twenties. Women remembered the cult of the American Girl, which had brought them social and sexual freedom earlier in the century, or advertisements that addressed them as shoppers. Coca-Cola, which came to Germany in 1929, was sold in bars in the Third Reich until the United States entered the war. Until deep into the Nazi period, Hollywood films showed images of American prosperity and the American lifestyle. The German media, along with writers like Bertolt Brecht, revered Chicago, New York, and Las Vegas as icons of a futuristic world, or were familiar enough with American modernism to condemn it as a threat to European culture. There were similarly divided views about Henry Ford, whose ideas of a society based on economic growth and consumerism were regarded by some as a liberation from the hierarchically ordered world of Europe, and by others as a plunge into an undifferentiated, standardized mass society.

Initially, because of the bleak economic situation in their country, Germans after 1945 were more onlookers than consumers of American pop culture. But that was to change quickly in the mid 1950s, when the West German economic miracle, the growth of the German advertising industry (under strong American influence), and technological innovations like television, portable radios, and audio-cassette players began to fundamentally and permanently change lifestyles and recreational behavior.

German youth were the gate of entry for American popular culture, whose triumphal march into the country has been going on ever since. In jazz cellars and at jam sessions, high-school and university students in black turtleneck sweaters discussed the newest plays of Thornton Wilder and Tennessee Williams along with the books of Jean-Paul Sartre and French existentialism. Young people from working-class neighborhoods in the big cities danced to jitterbug and boogie-woogie music, organized themselves into fan clubs, and raced through the industrial landscape on motorbikes with their girlfriends riding behind them. On both sides of the Atlantic, American entertainment culture stood for liberation from the narrow confines of the parental home and the childhood dependency maintained by school and by society at large. Films like *Rebel Without a Cause, Jailhouse Rock,* and *The Wild One,* along with their German imitations, *Die Halbstarken* or *Wenn die Conny mit dem Peter,* gave the young generation models of uncensored leisure behavior, mobility, and consumption. When in 1958, during the rearmament of Germany, Elvis Presley was sent as a GI to Friedberg near Bad Nauheim, many Germans saw him as the symbol of a soldier free of authoritarian drilling and blind obedience. Concerts by Bill Haley and films starring James Dean, Marlon Brando, and Elvis Presley not infrequently resulted in riots. To be "cool," West and East German[19] youth had to wear authentic blue jeans and throw as many Americanisms as possible into everything said or written, from "manager," "sex," "investment," and "recycling" to "shooting star" and "kids," all of which are popular terms today. And a whole generation of young people at matinee showings in stuffy little suburban movie theaters, or watching late-afternoon TV lineups, became familiar with the open American landscape and with the American ideals of freedom, justice, and democracy through the characters of Lassie and Fury, the never-ending Western series with Tom Mix, Lash LaRue, and Zorro, and the Western films of John Ford.

Wim Wenders, famed for making German road movies like *Kings of the Road* and the culture-clash feature *The American Friend,* said in looking back at his youth in the 1950s, "Rock saved my life." For Peter Handke it was the Wurlitzer jukebox that freed him from the stale air of provincial Austria. Other authors like Günter Kunert and Yaak Karsunke recall their first encounter with the music of Glenn Miller.[20]

But Wenders also made another remark that is quoted far more often because it describes another image of America held by the postwar generation, who were dubbed the "children of Coca-Cola and Marx": "The Yanks colonized our subconscious." What separates the two comments is the break between the 1950s and the 1960s, a crack that runs not so much between the generations as through the middle of the age cohort that grew up with the GIs and the forms of American pop culture that they brought across the Atlantic after 1945.

Several quite distinct Americas thus came into conflict within Germans. First, there was the memory, which was still very fresh, of America's soft occupation of West Germany, and the confusing mix of the Cold War and economic growth that were both tied up with the United States. On the other side stood the superpower U.S. whose imperialistic and savagely criticized war against Vietnam, along with its extreme capitalism, gambled away the credit it had earned right after 1945 as a model for democracy and freedom among young Germans who by now had grown into adults. And finally, the generation of students who took to the streets in 1968 in Berlin, Paris, and Rome to protest against Washington's policies, although they did not derive their ideological foundation from the United States, did take many of the forms of their protest against war, materialism, and the middle-class establishment directly from America, from the sit-ins and teach-ins on American university campuses, from the passive resistance of the flower children and the hippies all the way to the militant program of the Black Panthers.

What today has become the norm for anti-American demonstrations all over the world began in the late 1960s, not just in Germany but everywhere. German students who demonstrated outside American bases or institutions chanting "USA—SS—SA" (alluding to the Nazi SS and to the Nazi storm troopers, the SA) wore jeans and parkas left over from the American army occupation. Protesters who burned American flags outside an America House might have just finished picking up brochures there about exchange programs with U.S. colleges, and later might go to a late-night Hollywood movie or to a disco to listen to the music of Jimi Hendrix. And during their semester breaks, when they hitched rides or traveled on Greyhound buses through the United States to escape the geographical and social limitations of Germany, they would carry in their backpacks a copy of their Mao-Bible, a text by Lenin against capitalism, or, today, Naomi Klein's *No Logo*.

The 1960s also saw the beginning of another change in which the model of American culture played a central role: the separation between the generations and classes, which had still been clearly evident in Germany a decade earlier, began slowly but continuously to erode as prosperity and technological advances brought new patterns of recreational behavior. Prep-school students and working-class children now listened side by side to soul, rock, and the pop music of the Beatles and the Stones, which some Germans mistakenly regarded as coming from America. Today, intellectuals no longer feel embarrassed to be caught enjoying an American crime film. People who tend to watch TV channels like ARTE and 3SAT will occasionally take a look at the entertainment-based RTL Plus or CNN news as well. And Germans from every age group and level of society, all wearing jeans, patronize the fast-food restaurants of McDonald's, Burger King, and Pizza Hut that have sprouted up everywhere across the German landscape.

A flood of studies has established that to date the triumphal march of American pop culture into German society in unabated. In 1990, three quarters of films shown in German movie houses were imported from North America;[21] in 1996, forty-one percent of the top fifteen best sellers listed in *Der Spiegel* came from the U.S. and only twenty-six percent from Germany;[22] McDonald's, which opened its first German branch in Munich in 1971, added sixty-nine new outlets in 2002, bringing the total number of its restaurants in Germany to over 1,200. On the other hand, homemade products clearly can hold their own against overseas imports, with varying degrees of success, as is evident from New German Film, from German "Schlager" (hit songs) and folk music, and from television series like "Tatort," "Schwarz-waldklinik" and "Lindenstraße," in which social and political context are emphasized more than in their American counterparts. U.S. products like talk, reality, and court TV shows are "creolized" for German audiences. Punk music and heavy metal turn up in German incarnations as Nina Hagen or 'Kraut-rock' bands and rap is transformed into a German-Turkish blend. Among members of the peace movement, the Greens, and the opponents of global-ization, the culture of protest that has developed since the 1980s, unlike the demonstrations against the Vietnam war, has evolved its own themes and forms independent of American models. It often, as in the debate over Amer-ica's second war against Iraq in spring 2003, has considerably more support among the population and the media than do comparable groups in the United States. Also, there are no indications that popular culture in Germany has succeeded in sweeping high culture from public view, as has been the case in the United States for many decades past.

Anti-Americanism

"Unlike the 1920s and 1930s, anti-Americanism in . . . the postwar period has been an important but not a crucial factor in shaping the political culture in West Germany."[23] This statement, referring to the period of the Cold War, is unreservedly true insofar as it applies to politics, security, and economics, in which the United States left West Germany little scope to set its own path. Things were different in the more wide-open field of culture, where opinions are hard to control and there is little need to reach compromises. In this area, criticism of specific aspects of American cultural policy in Germany and of the Americanization of German culture could quickly turn into open anti-Americanism. Arguments and stereotypes that had circulated through Europe at the turn of the last century blended with a new, at times specifically Ger-man critique of America that initially came from the right-wing camp, then was carried on by students of the so-called Generation of '68, and briefly ac-quired terrorist traits in the Red Army Faction. The German Democratic Re-public waged official campaigns against a "cosmopolitanism" that in large part was equated with the United States, against the "barbaric poison of . . . boogie-woogie,"[24] and against the moral decline associated with "open dancing."

Since the 1980s, West German peace and environmental groups, which include a sizeable part of the German population, have distanced themselves from the policies of the United States. East Germans who had been grateful for the U.S. support provided for the reunification of Germany quickly began to realize that there were disadvantages to the "elbow-society" imported from the West. And when the U.S. bombed Afghanistan in October 2001 and waged war against Iraq in 2003, a wide range of political groups, including both the right-wing neonationalist NPD and the postcommunist PDS, made statements opposing U.S.–controlled globalization.

After the end of World War II, the conservative critics who were firm allies of the United States in the Cold War resurrected the old notion that American culture is soulless and demythologized because America has no historical experience and Americans lack the will to endure pain and loss. In this view, Americans' strong urge to form a mass society has led to a leveling of all distinctions and to the loss of quality for the sake of quantity. What is presented on the surface as a democratization of culture, the conservatives say, is really just standardization, driven by pragmatism and profit and ending in total monotony. Moreover, imports from the U.S. like jazz, rock music, Hollywood films, and from the mid 1950s onward, American television programs, have led to the undermining of manners and morals in Germany, to a coarsening of youth and a rise in violence, habits of passive reception, and ultimately, the creeping death of traditional German high culture.

The German left did not enter the debate over the rapid spread of American popular culture until the 1960s, after the end of the Konrad Adenauer era, the first economic crisis, the clear shift of the Social Democrats toward accord with the United States, and the victory of American-style consensus liberalism in the Great Coalition between the conservative Christian Democrats (CDU) and the Social Democrats (SPD). This period brought a radical confrontation with U.S. policy and the American presence in Europe, led by students who emerged from the Vietnam War protests critical of American society, which they viewed as aggressively capitalistic, and critical of their own homegrown materialism and their society's failure to deal more swiftly with the Nazi past. Among the Red Army Faction, the conflict with U.S. policy resulted in open violence, including numerous attacks on American facilities. But German youth at that time had no cause to reject Made in the USA culture along with the military-industrial complex. Quite the contrary: in the 1960s and 1970s—unlike today after the U.S. attacks on Sudan, Afghanistan, and Iraq—German protesters knew that the majority of American intellectuals and artists and a sizeable part of the U.S. media were on their side. Moreover, Europeans saw the Americans who shared their views as pioneers and models in the struggle against the imperialist aggression of a superpower that militarily and economically, if not ideologically and culturally, was too strong for everybody's good.

Attempts were and still are made to dismiss the Generation of '68's critique of America as a maneuver to evade dealing with Germany's past, the

Third Reich, and the Holocaust. This dismissal fails for at least three reasons. First, the Germans of '68 were at least as sharp in their charges against their own parents and teachers as against the American superpower. Second, virtually all leading German intellectuals directly linked their critique of capitalism with their analyses of the origins and the bases of National Socialism. Finally, cultural anti-Americanism in Germany ran along exactly the same lines as in other European countries that had not experienced a fascist past.

Thus Germans had a double vision of the U.S., expressed by Wim Wenders in handy sentences and prize-winning films, which identified America with all the evils of the modern world and at the same time borrowed forms and themes for its critique from the United States. But this was not the end of the story.

The Old World and the New seem to have been drifting apart in many spheres since the 1970s and 1980s. In the United States, the "Me"-generation of yuppies, made uneasy by the oil crisis and the economic downturn, looked on passively as American power politics were promoted by Ronald Reagan, practiced by George Bush, and after 11 September 2001, declared an official policy by his son, George W. Bush. During this same period, Germans who had been young in '68 grew up to join the Green Party, found new tasks in environmental protection, Third World concerns, and the anti-globalization movement. Some, like Joschka Fischer and Gerhard Schröder, set off on a long march through the institutions to gain power in parliament and government and to change policy.

While writers and artists in Germany and elsewhere in Europe protested against the deployment of American Pershing and Soviet SS-20 missiles, the Reagan administration's Star Wars program, and the U.S. wars against Iraq, the American antiwar movement was marginalized after the end of the Vietnam War because many of its supporters had been driven less by ideological views than by the tangible fear of the draft. Both European and American Greens concerned with the issues of peace, anticapitalism, the world's ecological future, and the inequities of the North-South divide were painted as fringe socialists by the American right and abandoned by centrists like Bill Clinton, in whom they had hoped to find an ally. Open conflict broke out between German and American intellectuals in the wake of 9/11 over such issues as preemptive strikes and just wars against so-called rogue states.[25] Germans reacted with subdued irony when the administration of George W. Bush propagandized abroad by publishing an anthology of selections from American writers that combined hymns of praise to "American values" with the self-assured claim that Americans possess a "powerful sense of the universal" that links them directly with "all humankind."[26] Meanwhile, Jürgen Habermas, Jacques Derrida, Adolf Muschg, Umberto Eco, and other European intellectuals, along with the American Richard Rorty, have written simultaneous essays examining the differences between the Old and the New World and what international role a united Europe should play after the second Iraq war.[27] And now that the United States is the world's only superpower, Europe's citizens as well as its leading thinkers suspect that Washington is no longer willing to solve conflicts at the negotiating table and is thus supplying other states that have little experience of democracy with arguments and vocabulary to justify the swift resort to military force as the means to control their own regional conflicts.[28]

Summary

On that late summer day when Staff Sergeant Werner L. Holzinger was the first GI to be sent over the border into the Third Reich because he spoke German, he no doubt had other things on his mind than world history. But the veritable army of American cultural officers, U.S. Information Agency employees, diplomats, ordinary soldiers, and tourists who followed Holzinger in the coming months, years, and decades cannot have failed to notice that Germany after 1945, admittedly against its will, came to play a special role in the Americanization of Europe. This role, which can be divided into two distinct phases, resulted from the vast scale of Germany's defeat, from the lengthy occupation that ended only in 1990, from the division of the country that reflected the geopolitical interests of the United States and the Soviet Union, from the West German economic miracle of the 1950s, from the slow but undeviating integration of the Federal Republic into the transatlantic alliance and the European Union, and finally, from Germany's unexpected unification in 1989/90.

Phase One of the Americanization process lasted from the end of World War II to the late 1950s and was shaped by three factors: first, the cultural policies of the occupation forces, which achieved only limited success in their reeducation of the Germans and their dissemination of American high culture; second, the direct contact with American popular culture through German POWs and encounters with U.S. soldiers, contacts that were limited at first by the financial constraints on the German population; and third, the tendency of the German elites to hold on to traditional values and forms of German high culture. Phase Two, extending from the late 1950s to the present, is characterized by increasing internationalization and, more recently, a clash of values between Europe and the U.S. That is, the specifically German confrontation with American culture was progressively swallowed up in the larger international context of economic and technological changes. These developments, although they often emanated from or were dominated by the United States, evolved features that increasingly were global rather than national.

Central to this second phase in the cultural Americanization of Germany is the ever more pervasive triumph of a popular culture that, while initially American, later became more and more internationalized, thus allowing the border of high culture to be permeated while at the same time democratizing and commercializing the consumption of culture and leveling distinctions between classes and generations.

This development, which is ongoing today, is rooted mainly in two factors: the steadily rising prosperity, along with its accompanying changes in consumer behavior, that followed the German economic miracle of the 1950s; and the growing array of technological capabilities, which can make cultural goods of all kinds available to the German population any time, anywhere, along with the means to store and reproduce them at low cost. In the course of this development, which was deliberately intensified by the United States during its engagement in the Cold War and which changed the definition, production, distribution, and consumption of culture at breakneck speed, the one thing that has tended to remain constant are the concepts and slogans in the critique of modern culture, which often enough is equated with American culture: its mass appeal, its lack of standards, its reduction of everything to the lowest common denominator, its commercialization.

Despite this no doubt justified criticism, the overall sum of the encounter between German and American culture since World War II has been rather positive—although admittedly, not quite in the way the United States intended. The democratization of access to culture, which was imported from America, has not led in Germany to the disappearance of high culture from public consciousness or to its concentration in two or three high population centers. State subsidies, which are frowned upon in the U.S., in Germany continue to promote the production of high-quality films, exhibitions, and a wide selection of museums, theaters, opera companies, and musical performances in urban centers and in areas outside the big cities. Whereas in the United States the media, and especially television, have reduced their interest in the international scene and are governed to a large extent by the advertising industry, Europe offers a broad range of local and international programming: entertainment plus high culture, tabloid press along with—but separate from—hard news and critical analysis. And so far at least, the commercialization of culture in Germany has not advanced to the point where classical texts and the experiments of young artists are shunted into the equivalent of off–off-Broadway while multiplex cinemas show blockbuster films and in the megamalls museum shops, Disney outlets, and Planet Hollywood take over the work of local culture. In short, Europe, including Germany, seems at the moment to have an attractive form of culture in which high and popular culture nourish each other, state support and the free market exist side by side, and much of the population have learned to compose their own cultural program, depending on their needs and education, from the wide range of entertainment, knowledge, and information on offer.

Notes

1. My thanks go to Allan Millett from the Mershon Center for the Study of International Security at Ohio State University, who provided this information to me.
2. This essay does not address the special situation of American culture and anti-Americanism in the German Democratic Republic. For more information on this little researched topic see in the bibliography at the end of the volume, among others, the books by Hörnigk and Stephan, Giovanopoulos, Große, Jarausch and Siegrist, Poiger, Schnoor, and Weßel.
3. Alexander Stephan, *"Communazis:" FBI Surveillance of German Emigré Writers* (New Haven: Yale University Press, 2000).
4. Hans Egon Holthusen, quoted in Klaus Lubbers, "Zur Rezeption der amerikanischen Kurzgeschichte in Deutschland nach 1945," in Horst Frenz and Hans-Joachim Lang, eds., *Nordamerikanische Literatur im deutschen Sprachraum seit 1945: Beiträge zu ihrer Rezeption* (Munich: Winkler, 1973), 47.
5. Erich von Kahler, quoted in Axel Schildt, *Zwischen Abendland und Amerika: Studien zur westdeutschen Ideenlandschaft der 50er Jahre* (Munich: Oldenbourg, 1999), 91.
6. Erich Kuby, quoted in ibid., 93.
7. Hans-Jürgen Grabbe, "Das Amerikabild Konrad Adenauers," *Amerikastudien: American Studies* 31, no. 3 (1986), 319.
8. Therese Hörnigk and Alexander Stephan, eds., *Rot = Braun? Brecht Dialog 2000: Nationalsozialismus und Stalinismus bei Brecht und Zeitgenossen* (Berlin: Theater der Zeit, 2000).
9. Lisa Phillips, *The American Century: Art and Culture, 1950–2000* (New York: Whitney Museum of American Art, 1999), 35.
10. Lubbers, "Zur Rezeption der amerikanischen Kurzgeschichte," 28.
11. Gerd Gemünden, *Framed Visions: Popular Culture, Americanization, and the Contemporary German and Austrian Imagination* (Ann Arbor: University of Michigan Press, 1998).
12. Ralph Willett, *The Americanization of Germany, 1945–1949* (London: Routledge, 1989), 22.
13. Quoted by Phillips, *The American Century*, 35.
14. Frank Schumacher, *Kalter Krieg und Propaganda: Die USA, der Kampf um die Weltmeinung und die ideelle Westbindung der Bundesrepublik Deutschland, 1945–1955* (Trier: Wissenschaftlicher Verlag, 2000), 110.
15. Stephen Spender, "We Can Win the Battle for the Mind of Europe," *New York Times Magazine*, 25 April 1948, quoted in Willett, *The Americanization of Germany, 1945–1949*, 48.
16. Frances Stonor Saunders, *The Cultural Cold War: The CIA and the World of Arts and Letters* (New York: New Press, 2000), 148.
17. Schumacher, *Kalter Krieg und Propaganda*, 83–84.
18. See also Shawn J. Parry-Giles, *The Rhetorical Presidency, Propaganda, and the Cold War, 1945–1955* (London: Praeger, 2002).

19. Therese Hörnigk and Alexander Stephan, eds., *The New Sufferings of Young W. and Other Stories from the German Democratic Republic* (New York: Continuum, 1997).

20. "Günter Kunert und Yaak Karsunke im Gespräch," Therese Hörnigk and Alexander Stephan, eds. *Jeans, Rock und Vietnam: Amerikanische Kultur in der DDR* (Berlin: Theater der Zeit, 2002), 17.

21. Thomas Koebner, "Hollywood in Deutschland," in Detlef Junker, ed., *Die USA und Deutschland im Zeitalter des Kalten Krieges, 1945–1990: Ein Handbuch*, vol. 2 (Stuttgart: Deutsche Verlags-Anstalt, 2001), 531.

22. Harald Wenzel, "Einleitung," in *Die Amerikanisierung des Medienalltags*, ed. Harald Wenzel (New York: Campus, 1998), 7.

23. Philipp Gassert, "Gegen Ost und West: Antiamerikanismus in der Bundesrepublik," in Junker, *Die USA und Deutschland im Zeitalter des Kalten Krieges*, vol. 1, 944.

24. Ernst Hermann Meyer, quoted by Peter Wicke, "Rock 'n' Roll im Stadtpark. Von einer unerlaubten Vision in den Grenzen des Erlaubten," in Hörnigk and Stephan, *Jeans, Rock und Vietnam*, 70.

25. This debate involved an exchange of several open letters. It took place in 2002 and is available on the website of the Institute for American Values (www.americanvalues.org, [last accessed: 21 November 2003]). For more information, see my radio talk "Der große Freund-Feind: Das gespannte Verhältnis zwischen Europa und den USA." Südwestrundfunk 2. 11 July 2004. http://swr.de/swr2/sendungen/wissen-aula/archiv/2004/07/11 (last accessed 28 February 2005) and "The Historical Context of the German Reaction to 9/11." In Vladimir Shlapentokh, Joshua Woods, and Eric Shiraev, eds. *America: Sovereign Defender or Cowboy Nation?* (Aldershot: Ashgate, 2005), 15–27.

26. George Clack, "Writers on America" [Introduction]. Available on the website of the U.S. Department of State, Office of International Information Programs (http://usinfo.state .gov/products/pubs/writers/homepage.htm, [last accessed: 21 November 2003]).

27. The initial essay by Jürgen Habermas and Jacques Derrida, "Unsere Erneuerung. Nach dem Krieg: Die Wiedergeburt Europas," appeared in *Frankfurter Allgmeine Zeitung*, 31 May 2003. It was accompanied by similar statements published in *La Repubblica* (Umberto Eco), *Neue Züricher Zeitung* (Adolf Muschg), *El País* (Fernando Savater), and *La Stampa* (Gianni Vartimo). During the following months numerous European and some American intellectuals responded to these essays.

28. See for instance Ernst-Otto Czempiel, *Weltpolitik im Umbruch: Die Pax Americana, der Terrorismus und die Zukunft der internationalen Beziehungen* (Munich: Beck, 2002); Gret Haller, *Die Grenzen der Solidarität: Europa und die USA im Umgang mit Staat, Nation und Religion* (Berlin: Aufbau, 2002); Ziauddin Sardar and Merryl Wyn Davies, *Why Do People Hate America?* (New York: Disinformation, 2002); Richard Crockatt, *America Embattled: September 11, Anti-Americanism, and the Global Order* (London: Routledge, 2003); Ulrich K. Preuß, *Krieg, Verbrechen, Blasphemi: Gedanken aus dem alten Europa* (Berlin: Wagenbach, 2003); Emmanuel Todd, *After the Empire: The Breakdown of the American Order* (New York: Columbia University Press, 2003).

Part II

SWEDEN, DENMARK, AUSTRIA

TELEVISION, EDUCATION, AND THE VIETNAM WAR: SWEDEN AND THE UNITED STATES DURING THE POSTWAR ERA

◆　　◆　　◆

Dag Blanck

Introduction

In the mid 1990s, a group of political scientists in Sweden tried to assess their country's relationship to the outside world. In one survey, those Swedes who said that they had considered moving abroad within the last few years indicated their preferences. Among these potential emigrants, the United States was the most popular destination, named by 20 percent of the respondents. Australia came in second with 15 percent, whereas other Scandinavian and European counties were chosen by between 5 and 10 percent of the Swedes.

The U.S. was also a common answer when the question was posed of where Swedes would move if political upheavals or other circumstances forced them to. The most popular choice given between 1991 and 1995 was, perhaps not surprisingly, Norway, with between 17 and 32 percent of the answers. The U.S., however, was not far behind; between 12 and 32 percent of the respondents preferred the North American republic, well ahead of Denmark in third place, and then Australia and Great Britain.[1] The United States thus must play a significant role in Sweden, and it is not surprising that Swedish author Ludvig Rasmusson has commented that Sweden's American orientation became especially noticeable after World War II, when like "a super tanker with a new destination on the radar ... the entire country turned westwards."[2]

As Erik Åsard has pointed out, the concept of Americanization is contested and often used in political contexts in a pejorative manner.[3] In this

---

article, American influences in Sweden and elsewhere are seen not as a simple one-way communication from the U.S. to the receiving countries, but as a process of adaptation. This means that what could be called the "cultural imperialism" thesis, which assumes a strong U.S. domination and influence in the communication process, is questioned. Instead, as some scholars have argued in recent years, following the early lead of Rob Kroes,[4] the process is a complex one in which certain influences are accepted and others are not. Although as a sending country the U.S. plays an important role, the receiving countries are not merely seen as passive recipients of cultural influences but also take a more active part; furthermore the influences are mediated in different ways.[5]

It is also important to underscore that the American influences that are accepted into Sweden are transformed or domesticated so that they function in a Swedish context—as ethnologist Orvar Löfgren has put it: "if Sweden was Americanized during the post-war era, it happened in a very *Swedish* way."[6] This process of domestication or adaptation is, then, one of the most important aspects of the ways in which American influences are mediated into a Swedish context.

The notion of domestication is linked to a distinction between influences that operate on the surface of Swedish society and those that have a deeper impact. Surface influences are those that are easily noticed in Swedish society, in music, film, slang, or in the appearance and methods of McDonald's or Pizza Hut restaurants. Criticism of the "Americanization" of Sweden is often directed against these manifest influences. Deeper influences, on the other hand, are those influences that have much more successfully, and without storms of criticism, been incorporated into Swedish society; they remain there in a latent way. They have had a longer-lasting effect on Sweden as they have been mediated into a Swedish cultural context through the processes of adaptation and domestication.[7]

James Gilbert has also pointed to this dimension of American influences. He calls the adaptations undergone by the American ideas, products, or institutions "invisible," suggesting that their American origins are not immediately noticeable. In his view, this type of Americanization—which corresponds to what I have called deeper influences—is the most significant as it results in more or less "universal" cultural patterns in certain fields "in which influences from the United States are particularly powerful but largely imperceptible."[8]

Using the terms of domestication and surface and depth as starting points, this article seeks to explore how American influences have reached Sweden during the second half of the twentieth century, and how and in what way Sweden has been affected by the United States and American influences. It draws on empirical evidence from both the cultural and social spheres, focusing on American elite and popular culture as well as on certain political ideas

emanating from the U.S. popular culture. The reactions to American influences in Sweden have at times been strong, so the article will also deal with the
Swedish responses, particularly in the context of anti-Americanism. We will,
however, begin with a discussion of American cultural diplomacy in Sweden.

American Cultural Diplomacy in Sweden

The ways in which the United States has sought to influence Sweden through
official or unofficial programs are largely unknown. The Marshall Plan, launched
in 1947/48, in which Sweden played an initially reluctant and eventually
fairly marginal role,[9] also had a cultural component that became an important aspect of what is often called American cultural diplomacy towards Europe. Besides rebuilding European industries and infrastructure, it was
important to win the "hearts and minds" of the Europeans through the promotion of American culture.[10] This policy did not begin with the Marshall
Plan, but can be traced back to the Office of War Information (OWI), which
President Roosevelt created two months after the attack on Pearl Harbor. It
is interesting to note that as a neutral country, Sweden played an important
role for the OWI.[11]

American cultural diplomacy of this period took different forms, including, for example, the establishment of the Fulbright program and of the U.S.
Information Agency (USIA), the creation of American libraries and support
for the academic study of America in European universities, and the activities of the Congress for Cultural Freedom. The policy of "winning hearts and
minds" clearly played an important role in the transmitting of American influences to Europe.[12]

For Sweden alone, its functioning remains by and large unexplored. An
agreement between the American and Swedish governments in 1952 established a Fulbright Commission in Sweden, which together with other organizations, such as the Sweden-American Foundation, has played an important
role in educational exchange between the two countries. Over the years, about
a thousand Swedish students have participated in the Fulbright program.[13]
The United States Information Service (USIS) has been present via the U.S.
embassy in Stockholm throughout the postwar era, seeking to promote different aspects of American life as well as official American policies. Some
examples of the information distributed include the numerous films about
American society, culture, and politics available free of charge to Swedish
schools, organizations, and institutions from at least the late 1950s to the beginning of the 1970s,[14] and press releases about events in America from the late
1940s to the early 1970s, first in English but soon also in Swedish, obviously
intended for the use of Swedish newspapers.[15] A USIS-sponsored visitors pro-

gram was initiated in the 1950s and is ongoing to this day; through it, Swedish academics, professionals, and politicians are able to visit the United States.

The role of the Congress of Cultural Freedom has received considerable attention in many European countries but has not been studied with regard to Sweden. Ture Nerman, a well-known author and journalist, was present at the 1950 conference in Berlin where the Congress was launched,[16] and in 1952, author Vilhelm Moberg circulated an appeal among his fellow authors, encouraging them to attend a meeting in Stockholm to form a Nordic branch of the Congress.[17] Eventually, a Swedish section called "Svenska kommittén för kulturens frihet" was founded, which between 1954 and 1960 published the journal *Kultur-kontakt*. Its editors and contributors included well-known authors, academics, and intellectuals such as Bengt Alexandersson, Ingemar Hedenius, Ture Nerman, Göran Palm, Birgitta Stenberg, Kurt Salomonson, and Per Wästberg. An examination of *Kultur-kontakt* reveals few references to the U.S. and American culture. It was mainly a cultural and literary magazine, voicing strong criticism of the repression in the Soviet Union and Eastern Europe, but also of the situation in South Africa. *Kultur-kontakt* was thus not primarily a vehicle for American positions and viewpoints.[18]

American Elite Culture in Sweden

Interest in expressions of American high culture is a relatively recent phenomenon in Sweden. American culture was long looked down upon by Swedish and Scandinavian critics. It was seen as materialistic, crude, shallow, and lacking in historical continuity and cohesiveness. Count Axel von Fersen, for example, who had joined the French forces under de Rochambeau during the Revolutionary War and fought at Yorktown, wrote about America and the Americans in a letter to his father in 1781: "Money is the prime mover behind their actions; they think of nothing else than how to acquire it. Everyone is for himself and no one thinks of the public good." Thirty years later, lieutenant Otto Natt och Dag, who for political reasons fled Sweden for the U.S. in the 1810s, characterized the Americans as "sour," counting everything "according to gold and silver." He continued his diatribe, noting that what Swedes called "honor, altruism, integrity, and honesty" were lacking in the U.S., and that the guiding principle for the Americans was "to exploit each and everyone they know."[19]

Similar ideas also came strongly to the fore in the Norwegian Knut Hamsun's highly critical and dystopian view of the U.S. in *Fra det moderne Amerikas aandsliv* (From the Spiritual Life of America). This book, which was first published in 1889, appeared in a 1969 English translation as *The Cultural Life of Modern America*. It painted a very dark picture of America as an over-patriotic country, with no literature or painting, a short history, and strong xenophobic tendencies, concluding that the Americans "have no culture."[20] It had a significant impact in Sweden, where it shaped Swedish opinion of American culture and deterred at least one Swedish author from traveling to the U.S. [21]

During the 1920s and 1930s the situation improved, but it is worth noting that the first American Nobel Laureate in literature in 1930 was Sinclair Lewis, whose negative vision of American life and culture was obviously shared by the Swedish Academy.[22] Following the end of World War II, Swedish opinion of and interest in American literature again improved. For example, the Swedish Academy awarded Nobel Prizes in literature to William Faulkner in 1949, Ernest Hemingway in 1954, John Steinbeck in 1962, Saul Bellow in 1976, Isaac Bashevis Singer in 1978, Joseph Brodsky in 1987, and Toni Morrison in 1993.

According to Rolf Lundén, who has studied the period 1975–1991, some five hundred American literary works were translated into Swedish or performed on stage since 1945.[23] The great majority of these have been works of prose, primarily novels of "a realistic/naturalistic mode of expression." Their authors include a core group, of whose body of work almost all titles have been translated, formed of writers such as Norman Mailer, Philip Roth, John Updike, Kurt Vonnegut, Saul Bellow, E. L. Doctorow, Anne Tyler, John Gardner, John Irving, and Joyce Carol Oates. Joseph Heller has become a Swedish bestseller, selling more than 100,000 copies—a very high number for the Swedish market. The most successful American writer seems to be Isaac Bashevis Singer, who has had fifteen titles translated, and who by 1984 had sold over a million copies in Sweden.

American poetry is much less represented among the translations, and Lundén estimates that only some thirty collections of American poetry appeared between 1975 and 1991, representing such names as Gary Snyder, W. S. Merwin, and John Ashbery. From the field of drama, he notes seventy-five productions either on stage or on television, with three dominant playwrights: Edward Albee, Sam Shepard, and Eugene O'Neill. Albee's *Who's Afraid of Virginia Woolf* and *The Zoo Story* seem particularly popular. In addition, O'Neill's special relationship to Sweden should be noted. His last wish was that the Royal Dramatic Theater produce the first performance of *Long Day's Journey into Night*. It and other plays have since been staged several times in Sweden, and a strong Swedish interest in O'Neill has developed.[24] American literature as it been represented in the Swedish literary market in the last decades thus mainly reflects contemporary American fiction of a realistic nature, with little room for poetry or for representatives of earlier periods.

Some of these larger patterns can be followed in a study by Elisabeth Herion Sarafidis of Bonniers bokklubb, one of the largest book clubs in Sweden. When the club was started in 1970 American literature occupied a rather marginal position, and the texts in the book club magazine were often critical of the U.S. and American society. Following the tendencies of Lundén's results, the American fiction distributed through the club included "mainly elite authors" like Bellow, Roth, and Updike. Herion Sarafidis shows how the presence of American literature has increased in Sweden since the late 1970s in parallel with its coming to play a major part in the book club. Moreover, she argues that the increase in the American literary presence in Sweden seems linked to the growth of American popular fiction. The book club offerings in the 1980s and 1990s showed a strong emphasis on bestsellers like the romantic novels, detective stories, and psychological thrillers by authors such as Ira Levin, Harold Robbins, Sidney Sheldon, and Judith Krantz.[25]

The influx and popularity of American literature in translation has generated a debate among Swedish authors many of whom fear that Swedish literature is in danger. In 1990, Peter Curman, the president of the Swedish Writers' Union, noted the increasing number of translations on the book market, claiming that the "real losers in this battle" were the Swedish authors who were "being crowded out by foreign celebrities like Jackie Collins, Sidney Sheldon, and Stephen King." As Lundén has noted, by specifying American popular writers as the main threat, Curman further strengthened the image of America's literature and culture as a threat to Sweden's.[26]

American Popular Culture in Sweden

As in many other countries, American popular culture has played a powerful, influential role in Sweden since World War II. This is nothing new—during the decades after World War I American films and music had become popular in Sweden, resulting in similar public discussions about the suitability of these developments. The discussions about post–World War II developments are a part of a longer conversation about American popular culture in Sweden that notably displays a remarkable continuity in its arguments.

Media historian Ulf Jonas Björk has identified several debates about American popular culture in the country during the twentieth century.[27] Because they all expressed a fear that Sweden and Swedish culture ran the risk of being overrun by American popular culture, they have been characterized as "moral panics." In most cases, there were also calls for restrictions of different kinds—calls that only rarely were heeded. Around 1910 an intense debate raged over American dime novels—called "gutter literature" by their critics—and in the 1920s the focus was on American films, resulting in a parliamentary proposal to limit their importation as they posed a danger for Swedish culture and the Swedish "psyche."[28]

The debates established many of the patterns for what was to follow during the second half of the twentieth century. In the 1950s, American comic strips became the focus of controversy, and in the words of one of their critics were seen as an "American infection that is spreading around the world."[29] Swedish versions of *Superman* and the *Phantom* that had become great commercial successes were the most common targets of criticism. In the words of teacher and school librarian Lorentz Larson, they promoted "a mentality of violence, gangster romanticism, a brutal cult of success and vulgar eroticism."[30]

American television has been a source of Swedish concern ever since regular broadcasting started in the mid 1950s. From the very beginning Swedish TV depended on foreign programs, and the U.S. share has always been considerable. The inaugural season 1956/57 included *I Love Lucy* as the premier offering on Saturday nights, and American programs directed at children, such as *Jungle Jim, Lassie,* and *Whirlybirds,* were introduced shortly thereafter. Reactions to the American programs for children were quick. Two prominent child psychiatrists argued in favor of Swedish-produced programs for children, worrying that American imports, such as *Lassie,* portrayed "a brutal and rough film reality, where fist fights are always in the air and guns are loose in their holster," and pleading for an end to this "Americanization."[31]

The debate continued during the following years, when Swedish TV began broadcasting American westerns. *Gunsmoke* was introduced in 1959 and immediately became very popular with the Swedish audience. The genre became very common in Sweden during the following decade, with *Bonanza* claiming a special place in the hearts of Swedish viewers. Westerns raised concerns about the effects of dangerous American violence similar to those that had been voiced a few years earlier. A survey on audience reactions to westerns, commissioned by the Swedish Broadcasting Corporation, showed the great popularity of the genre among Swedish viewers but also revealed that many parents were concerned about the effects on their children. The television company recognized these apprehensions but publicly reassured the parents that each episode of *Bonanza* was carefully screened so that "certain forms of violence, pure stupidity, racial and religious persecution and sex with a sensational purpose" would not be present. These concerns are also evident in correspondence between the Swedish Broadcasting Corporation and various U.S. suppliers of programs. "Many of the American series are too 'tough' for Swedish mentality ... [and we] have even ... been forced to exclude some episodes ... because we found them too hard-boiled here in Sweden," wrote the head of program acquisition in 1960.[32]

The Swedish Broadcasting Corporation also actively tried to reduce its American offerings, mostly replacing them with British programs, so that by 1977 British-made shows accounted for 45 percent of the entertainment programs, a share almost twice that of the American-made. Even so, the Swedish

Broadcasting Corporation had to admit that American programs remained popular with the public and were in fact the only foreign imports that could compete successfully with Swedish-made programming.[33]

The advent of rock music in 1956 and 1957 is another example of American popular culture that generated a heated controversy in Sweden. Films like *Blackboard Jungle* and *Rock Around the Clock,* which both included the song "Rock Around the Clock," helped pave the way for the new music form from America. Because *Blackboard Jungle* dealt with juvenile delinquents and violence in a school, the ensuing ardent debate tended to associate rock music with these phenomena. One music magazine bemoaned the ongoing "rock rage," opining that this new form of music ought to be "scorned" and describing it as "raucous" and "exaggerated." The outcome of this moral panic was that rock music was partly banned from regular Swedish radio programming, being instead limited to special times. Many Swedish teenagers responded by tuning their dials to Radio Luxembourg, where the music could be heard without impediment.[34]

The discussion of American cultural influences in Sweden shows strong continuity in arguments throughout the postwar era, indeed stretching even further back in time. In 1988 a Swedish MP from the then Communist Party proposed (unsuccessfully) government funding for an inquiry into the negative effects of "Americanization" on Swedish society.[35] Eight years later the well-known journalist and author Herman Lindqvist claimed that American culture had descended on Sweden like a "heavy and slippery blanket" preventing all "spiritual and intellectual development," and that the "masses" were kept "hypnotized" in front of their TV sets until they fell asleep, "dreaming the American dream, duped by the American myth."[36] In many ways, then, the influx of U.S. cultural products in Sweden has been seen as a threat to Swedish culture, and images of a cultural flood from America characterized by commercialism, shallowness, and sentimentality have been invoked to demonstrate Sweden's need to defend itself against this attack on the national culture.

American Educational Influences in Sweden

Not all American influences in Sweden have been cultural. Political and social ideas have also been of great importance, and one field of particular note has been education. The twentieth century saw a significant influx of American educational ideas in Sweden, and it is interesting to note the different trajectories of these American influences as they work their way into Swedish society.

Alva Myrdal, a leading Social Democratic politician, social scientist, and eventually cabinet minister and Nobel Peace Laureate, played a crucial role in this context. She first visited the United States on a Rockefeller scholarship together with her husband Gunnar in 1929, a year that historian Walter Jackson has called "a turning point" in their lives.[37] Much of what they encountered there shaped their future careers, and Alva devoted her year to studying psychology, family sociology, and developmental psychology. In 1938 the couple visited the U.S. again, staying until 1940; they returned in 1942 for a final visit. Gunnar Myrdal had been commissioned to do a study of American race relations, which became his influential *An American Dilemma*. Alva, for her part, continued to develop her interests in education, particularly the educational philosophies of John Dewey. The Myrdals' son Jan attended a school in New York City based on these educational ideas,[38] which gave his mother ample opportunities to learn more about them.

The U.S. had a deep and long-lasting influence on both Gunnar and Alva. In 1970, Gunnar summarized their feelings: "America—the New World—made an extraordinarily deep impression on us ... We came to identify very deeply with America, and we have never been able to quite shed this sense of identification."[39] Alva Myrdal's role in introducing American educational ideas to Sweden is clear from many of her writings and public addresses in the 1940s.

In 1941, Alva Myrdal wrote that as the Swedish school system was in need of serious reforms, "[i]t is a matter of life and death for our nation that we receive new and powerful stimulances from American education."[40] One important aspect was the American comprehensive or common school, open to all students regardless of social or economic background, which contrasted greatly with the Swedish system's division of students into several tracks of study, resulting in a socially and culturally segmented and non-inclusive school system. In Sweden, only 10 percent of all children received the necessary educational preparation for higher education, whereas under the American system over 50 percent of the students were prepared for higher studies. Alva Myrdal commented ironically that "the passion which Swedes expend in protecting a selected part of the country's youth from sharing its destiny with others for more than four years" could simply not be understood in America.[41] In America, she wrote in 1944, "the [educational] ideology is the open school policy.[42]

Ultimately, Alva Myrdal argued, education was a matter of democracy. A democratic society was both shaped and defended by democratic schools, and such schools were being built in the United States. In a 1940 speech she offered some key concepts that she felt characterized the American educational practice, namely a belief in rationality, and a belief in popular education and in the possibility of changing and improving individuals.[43] The discussion about reforming Swedish schools was fundamentally not a discussion of pedagogical methods, but rather one of the nature of contemporary

Swedish society and its citizens, as she wrote in one of her columns in *Afton-tidningen* in 1943. By establishing a common school with equal access for all, by introducing new pedagogical methods, and by being willing to change the instructional contents, a new democratic school would be created, and with it a new democratic person.[44]

Myrdal played a key role in a parliamentary school commission that was appointed in 1946 to propose reforms for the Swedish schools.[45] Many of the educational ideas that she advocated are reflected in the commission report from 1948, such as her central vision of the elimination of the divided Swedish schools and the establishment of nine-year comprehensive schools for all students.[46] Her advocacy for the role of Swedish schools in shaping a democratic society was also strongly endorsed by the commission, and the report declared that the "main task" for Swedish schools was "to educate democratic persons," developing individual skills and talents to the fullest, while also working together for the common good.[47]

As educational historians Åke Isling and Gunnar Richardson both have pointed out, it does seem clear that many of the ideas advocated by Alva Myrdal became important dimensions of the new Swedish comprehensive school as it emerged in the 1950s and 1960s.[48] American educational ideas, mediated through Alva Myrdal, repeatedly found their way into the discussions of the organization of Swedish public education and, when implemented, became a centerpiece of the Social Democratic reform project in Sweden during the postwar era.

During the following decades American educational influences in Sweden continued to grow, and in 1994, political scientist Olof Ruin noted that the Swedish universities and colleges constitute "the best example of a conscious 'Americanization' of Swedish society."[49] The organizational structure of American higher education, for example, has attracted Swedish attention. When the Swedish Ph.D. degree was reformed in the early 1970s, it was strongly influenced by American models, and a government study from 1977 called it "almost a translation" of the American Ph.D. degree.[50]

American models and practices have also been important for the development of several disciplines in Swedish higher education. American influences have always been strong in the social sciences; education has already been discussed above. Economics and business administration are two other fields where the exchange of persons and ideas has been very lively, and where study trips to America and the use of American textbooks have been very common. Further examples include sociology, which was established in Swedish universities in 1947, and political science. It also seems clear that a period of study in an American university has been beneficial for further academic careers in Sweden.[51]

When Swedish students choose to study in foreign universities, the U.S. is by far the leading country of choice, and during the past half-century thousands of Swedes have been students at various levels and for various lengths of time in American colleges and universities. In 2002 it was estimated that over 4,500 Swedes were enrolled in American colleges or universities, placing Sweden fourth among Western European countries sending undergraduates to the U.S, after Germany, the U.K, and France.[52]

The social sciences have consistently drawn Swedes to American institutions of higher learning, with business administration, economics, and political science as leading subjects. Engineering has been another popular field of study, especially before 1960. To many Swedish engineers, a period in the U.S. seems to have been a natural part of their training, and in the 1930s and 1940s, J. Sigfrid Edström, the head of the electrical engineering company ASEA, actively recruited engineers with American experience. The natural sciences and medicine, finally, have become increasingly important fields of study since World War II. [53] With regard to medicine, the first generation of Swedish anesthesiologists was trained almost entirely in the United States,[54] and it is sometimes jokingly said that there are three kinds of medical researchers in Sweden: those who currently are in the United States, those who have just returned, and those who are planning their trip.

According to the intellectual historian Svante Lindqvist, Sweden's admiration of American higher education and academic research inspired the construction of the Wenner-Gren Center in Stockholm in early 1962.[55] Following a donation of five million Swedish crowns by the Swedish industrialist and millionaire Axel Wenner-Gren in 1955 for an international center in Stockholm to accommodate visiting international scientists, the highly positive attention given the modernistic Wenner-Gren Center project became an illustration of the high esteem that Sweden attached to the world of research. The center was inaugurated by the King in the presence of the Minister of Education, the vice-chancellors of Sweden's universities at the time, and several Swedish and foreign Nobel Laureates. The 23-story, 70-meter skyscraper—the first in Stockholm—stood as a link between Sweden and the international world of science.

Clearly, that international world of science was strongly associated with the United States, as many visitors were Americans and as the Center was discussed in reference to the U.S. The Stockholm daily *Svenska Dagbladet* noted that a "pleasant environment for geniuses and families of geniuses" had been created, and that in the living quarters "everything was even more tip top American than in the United States" itself. The buildings themselves were described as the first offerings of Swedes who had begun to "fully build in the American fashion," and several newspapers covered what may have been the first celebration of Halloween in Sweden, among the families of visiting American scholars. According to Lindqvist, the reporting on the Wenner-Gren Center was characterized by a combination of "an admiration of science, academic life, the United States and modernity," contributing to a Swedish self-image of modernity that had entered into a covenant with the future through the international—American—academic world.[56]

Reacting to America: Anti-Americanism in Sweden?

As we have seen, American influences in Sweden have generated different kinds of reactions in the receiving country. Negative reactions and assessments of America are sometimes seen as a sign of anti-Americanism. Is it possible to speak of anti-Americanism in Sweden during the postwar era? To a large degree, this depends on the definition of anti-Americanism. A survey of the literature shows a variety of definitions, all including some element of criticism of the U.S.; most point to the critique of certain American values as the basis for anti-Americanism. For the present purposes, four dimensions are important.[57] First, many scholars seem to share Marie-France Toinet's assertion that a distinction should be made between "criticism of the United States," such as specific American actions or policies, and "judgement of America,"[58] which implies a denunciation of the entire country. Being critical of a specific U.S. policy does not necessarily imply anti-Americanism. This distinction seems to be reflected in the popular mind as well. Roughly between half and two thirds of the European respondents, in a survey from 2002 by the Pew Research Center for People and the Press on their attitudes towards the U.S., attributed the differences between the U.S. and their own countries to a difference in policies rather than values,[59] suggesting that people do seem to distinguish between criticism and judgement.

A second important point deals with the fact that there are different kinds of anti-Americanism. In almost all European countries in the Pew study, more than half of the respondents were critical of the spread of American customs and ideas. On the other hand, most European countries overwhelmingly approved of American popular culture, with between two thirds and three fourths of the respondents expressing favorable views.[60] As Paul Hollander has made clear, it thus seems important to distinguish between *political anti-Americanism,* which is related to the political role of the United States in the world, *cultural anti-Americanism,* comprising the discussions relating to American cultural influences in the rest of the world, and *ideological anti-Americanism,* which focuses on ideological aspects of the U.S., such as the capitalistic-materialistic nature of the U.S. economy.[61]

Thirdly, the questions of degree and context must also be taken into account. At some point, the line between criticism and judgement is crossed, meaning that the argument changes from being a critique of specific aspects of U.S. policies or society to a condemnation of America as a whole. It seems to be a matter both of degree, i.e., how harsh and comprehensive the criticism is, and of the context in which the critique is articulated. An emotional irrational element is also often inherent in the discussion, and Richard Kuisel suggests that "the nature and range of grievances and the intensity of feeling" are essential in determining anti-Americanism. And as Kuisel notes, the significance of the attitudes does not depend on whether the speaker was well informed about America. "No matter how irrational, emotional, self-serving, or 'false' the images may be, they form part of the phenomenon."[62]

A fourth aspect in the discussion of definitions is the need for a historical perspective. In his exhaustive study of French anti-Americanism, Philippe Roger underscores the continuity or *longue durée* of French anti-Americanism, arguing that once it had been formed, it followed its own "trajectory." In this way, the anti-American discourse transcends the immediate context in which the U.S. is being discussed, making it possible for individual participants in the conversations about America to be part of a longer negative (or positive) discussion and to (re)use the different arguments about America without being aware of them.[63]

Anti-Americanism in Sweden

What, then, can be said about anti-Americanism in Sweden? Clearly, we can find examples of cultural anti-Americanism in the Swedish debate. Many of the reactions and arguments from the above discussion of American culture in Sweden fall in this category. They do seem to focus on American popular culture in its entirety, not just individual films, TV programs, or comic strips, and are judgements of the country and its culture in the sense in which Marie-France Toinet uses the term. Moreover, the intensity of the debate is often great, and the arguments have frequently assumed emotional characteristics.

The question of anti-Americanism in Sweden must also be discussed in the context of the Vietnam War. In 1973 a study showed that a slight majority of Swedes had a negative view of the U.S., an attitude that was no doubt shaped by the public discussion of the U.S. in general and the Vietnam War in particular. According to Birgitta Steene, "[a] whole generation of Swedes lashed out at American society and culture during the Vietnam War and the Civil Rights Movement."[64] In November 1965, for example, journalist Sivar Arnér initiated a debate, in the Social Democratic daily *Stockholms-Tidningen* under the headline "Why We Hate America," that took its starting point as the American war in Vietnam but also became an indictment of American capitalism and imperialism.[65] Around the same time, author Artur Lundkvist talked about the "American problem," saying that the U.S. was responsible for "unbearable injustices, fascist regimes ... [and] economic imperialism" around the globe, and that through "American commercialism" Swedes were becoming subject "to cultural and psychological colonialism through imported entertainment, treacherous advertisements, and biased news reporting."[66]

Social and racial problems in the U.S. also attracted Swedish attention and were reported and discussed fairly widely in the Swedish press from the 1950s onward.[67] In the preface to his 1964 book *Skuggor över USA* (Shadows over the U.S.A.), Sven Öste, the well-known U.S. correspondent for the largest Stockholm daily, *Dagens Nyheter*, wrote of his desolation when he thought of America's "hidden poverty" and of the African-American confrontation "with bludgeons and teargas in the North and burning Klan crosses in the South."[68] When Swedish writer and literary scholar Sven Delblanc spent a year in Berkeley in 1968/69, he encountered a country with an engrained tradition of racial oppression and racism. "I ask myself if the U.S. will ever learn to live with the truth, the whole truth, about its history?" he wrote, characterizing American freedom as a myth and concluding that violence and oppression were endemic in American society.[69]

Sweden and the Vietnam War

With regard to the Vietnam War, Swedish official criticism began in 1965 when Olof Palme, at the time Minister of Education and from 1969 Prime Minister, voiced strong disapproval of the American war in Vietnam.[70] Swedish criticism continued until the mid 1970s, and it is striking to note that owing to the wars in Southeast Asia, the U.S. was the fourth most criticized country in official Swedish pronouncements between 1966 and 1976, behind South Africa, Portugal, and Rhodesia.[71]

As the Swedish critique grew stronger, representatives of the political opposition began characterizing the pronouncements as anti-American. In 1967, for example, the conservative newspaper *Barometen* talked about an ongoing "anti-American campaign," instigated by the Social Democrats, that was both "disheartening and shameful," while in November of the same year the liberal *Upsala Nya Tidning* wrote critically about the "front figures in the anti-American propaganda."[72] Olof Palme, who came to symbolize much of the Swedish critique, said in 1977 that the conservative opposition in Sweden had seen his statements as "irrefutable evidence of my anti-American attitudes."[73]

Among American politicians, who held both negative and positive opinions of Sweden and of its criticism of the American role in the Vietnam War, a feeling also prevailed that "strong anti-American" attitudes existed in Sweden at the time.[74] One of the more visible expressions of this was the protests from parts of the U.S. labor movement that Palme encountered during his 1970 visit to the U.S. The "rank and file" of the International Longshoremen's

Association staged a rally on 10 June at the Waldorf Astoria in New York City. They called the prime minister "pro-communist" and "anti-American," claiming, among other things, that he had "encouraged" and "participated in anti-American demonstrations" and had made "vicious attacks against the U.S.," pronouncing him "not welcome in America," and calling for a boycott of Volvo and Saab cars.[75]

The Swedish government, however, strongly denied any charge of anti-Americanism, as in 1969 when an official government document maintained that "[a]nti-Americanism is not a feature of Swedish policy" and added that "[w]e are well aware of the role the U.S. plays for democracy and freedom in the world." Four years later, the American chargé d'affaires in Stockholm reported to Washington that Sweden's Undersecretary of State Sverker Åström had told him that the Swedish government considered it "important to be understood" that Swedish criticism of U.S. Vietnam policies should not be seen as "hostility to the U.S. as such," and that the Swedish people had the "highest admiration and affection" for the U.S.[76]

Prime Minister Olof Palme was, according to his close collaborator Jan Eliasson, "hurt" by accusations of anti-Americanism, and said that they were plainly "wrong." Palme felt his comments to be "a necessary reaction to the flawed behavior by a superpower" and argued that they had nothing to do with the U.S. or with Americans in general. Palme greatly admired Franklin Roosevelt and John Kennedy, Eliasson notes, and was "fascinated by American politics and the vitality of American democracy," perhaps as a result of his years as a student at Kenyon College in the late 1940s. It was, Eliasson concludes, Palme's "almost emotional ties to the U.S." that made his criticism so harsh.[77]

The diplomatic tensions between Sweden and the United States culminated during the Christmas season of 1972. In a public statement following the American bombings of Hanoi, the prime minister used very strong language in his critique of the American government's actions. He said that the bombings were "crimes," of which there were many in modern history, and that such crimes "are often associated with a name—Guernica, Oradour, Babi Yar, Katyn, Lidice, Sharpeville, Treblinka ... Now there is another name to add to the list—Hanoi, Christmas, 1972." This statement immediately caused a severe diplomatic crisis between Sweden and the United States. American government officials filed an official protest, calling the Swedish comments "outrageous," and were especially incensed by the comparisons with Nazi Germany. The prime minister's statement, the outgoing Swedish ambassador to Washington was informed, "came with singular ill grace" and "assumes the worst motives and the basest of attitudes on the part of the U.S. government."[78] Subsequently, the incoming Swedish ambassador was denied accreditation and the U.S. chargé d'affaires in Stockholm was withdrawn. For a period of eighteen months diplomatic relations between the two countries were frozen.

Was the Swedish policy on the Vietnam War an example of anti-Americanism? Official Swedish government pronouncements were careful to draw a distinction between criticism and judgement, making it difficult to classify the official Swedish position as anti-American. Palme's Christmas statement might be seen in a different light. The comparisons with not only Nazi Germany, which particularly offended Henry Kissinger, but also with South Africa, Franco's Spain, and Stalin's reign of terror, carry with them strong connotations of brutal dictatorial regimes that clearly go beyond the bounds of normal diplomatic discourse between nations. Thus, the context of the pronouncements suggests that they might be considered an example of an anti-American discourse. Moreover, the Christmas statement was obviously intensely emotional, which meets another important criterion of anti-Americanism.

Anti-Americanism has thus been a part of the Swedish public discourse during the second half of the twentieth century. The strongest sentiments have expressed cultural anti-Americanism, which has mainly focused on American cultural expressions. Political anti-Americanism has been less common, and was most noticeable during the debate over the American role in the Vietnam War. With a few exceptions, it does not seem that the official Swedish policy during the 1960s and 1970s can be characterized as anti-American.

Conclusion

What have the American influences in Sweden during the second half of the twentieth century meant? Although the web of causes and effects is notoriously difficult to assess, there is a clear consensus among scholars in the field that some kind of American impact on Sweden has taken place. In her study of American literature for Bonniers bokklubb, for example, Elisabeth Herion Sarafidis suggests that an important dimension of the impact is the "familiarizing of the foreign," meaning that American settings and ways of thinking are, through fiction, "incorporate[d]" into Sweden, so that "to most Swedes today, life on Manhattan actually seems more familiar than life in Torneträsk." In more general terms, James Gilbert has talked about the "importation of cultural products from the United States that bear the clear markings of American origin and accent," suggesting that there is an impact, though that its exact nature is not given.[79]

In an attempt to more precisely ascertain the nature of the American impact, a distinction has been drawn between types of American influences in Sweden, suggesting that some work on and affect the surface of Swedish society, whereas others have a deeper and longer-lasting effect. Surface influences, the easiest to identify, have often generated debates in Sweden about Americanization and its dangers. Discussions about American popular culture and the threat posed by American films, television, music, and comic strips can be seen as examples of such influences, which have often met with resistance in Sweden. Calls have been made for restrictions on the importation of films and comic books, and Swedish television has deliberately tried to control its American programming, in terms of both volume and content.

American literature in Sweden provides an example of both deeper and surface influences. In the 1940s, a group of authors emerged on the Swedish literary scene—the so-called Fortyists—for whom Hemingway played an important role. For some of them—for example Thorsten Jonsson, Peter Nisser, and Mårten Edlund—it seems possible to speak of direct or manifest influences from the writings of Hemingway, as these authors have explicitly adopted both Hemingway's narrative techniques and his outlook on the world. For others—such as Walter Ljungquist, Tage Aurell, Lars Ahlin, and to some degree Eyvind Johnson—Lundén speaks of a Hemingway "apprenticeship." They closely studied Hemingway's work, at times trying to imitate it and often acknowledging his significance. Eventually, however, few of these authors ended up writing like Hemingway, so the influence is thus of a deeper kind.[80]

American educational ideas are an example of influences that have had a deep impact on Sweden, in that they have been transformed into a Swedish cultural context and have become domesticated. Alva Myrdal played a significant role in bringing them to Sweden, and they became an important element in the Social Democratic efforts to reform the Swedish school system after the war. To most Swedes, the building of the welfare state in the 1950s and 1960s was a national project, and the new school system, one of its central aspects, was equally perceived as a Swedish undertaking. The American educational impulses were thus successfully transformed and domesticated, and took on a new, Swedish meaning in their new cultural context.

It is not coincidental that American education found a sounding board in postwar Sweden. The Swedish Social Democrats showed great interest in and sympathy for the various programs associated with the New Deal. In numerous public appearances all over Sweden in 1942, Alva Myrdal spoke on the topic "The New America," saying that while Europe was bleeding to death "a new world is being shaped in America," with ideals "very much like our own [and].... which are of the greatest importance to us."[81] New Dealers, in turn, were also interested in developments in Sweden as the Social Democrats set out to reform Swedish society, a story perhaps best told in Marquis Childs' 1936 book *Sweden—The Middle Way*.[82]

American modernity, with its emphasis on reform and its orientation towards the future, resonated with the modernity it touched on in the welfare project of the Swedish Social Democrats. Ethnologist Orvar Löfgren has pointed out how the emphasis on modernity and rationality in the construction of modern Sweden made it much easier to incorporate American ideas into a Swedish context.[83] In other words, the American impulses that Alva Myrdal encountered during her time in the U.S. were "transplanted" into an already existing Swedish counterpart, where they found fertile ground.

There are also examples of American political influences that have not so easily been domesticated into the Swedish political culture. In the election campaign of 1994, for example, the Social Democrats used American political consultants, a step that was criticized in Sweden as an example of the "Americanization" of Swedish politics. Still, as Erik Åsard has shown, the actual impact of the American consultants and of American trends and ideas on Swedish politics by the mid 1990s had been "minimal." Åsard's explanation is that "Swedish politics is still very much *sui generis*," and that the strong national nature of Swedish political culture creates barriers to American influences.[84] The existence of a political milieu in Sweden that is receptive to American ideas, as was the case with education, is thus crucial for the process of domestication.

During the postwar era, Sweden has undergone a cultural reorientation. Prior to 1945 the U.S. played a relatively small role in terms of Swedish external cultural relations, and the Swedish cultural and political orientation were oriented toward Great Britain, France, and Germany. During the latter half of the twentieth century, however, the United States assumed a much more dominant role and, as noted at the beginning of this chapter, assumed a prominent place on the Swedish mental map, ahead of many European countries.

Systematic data on Swedish opinions of the U.S. are hard to come by. With the possible exception of the Vietnam era during the late 1960s and early 1970s, it still seems reasonable to assume that Swedish public opinion in general has been positive to the U.S. during the postwar era. This positive view of the U.S. fits into a tradition of Swedish admiration of the U.S. that can be traced back to the beginning of the nineteenth century, and is perhaps best expressed by Fredrika Bremer in her well-known *The Homes of the New World* from 1854. "Nowhere on earth," she wrote, has "true human freedom" been expressed as fully as in the United States, a country in which the highest goal was "a free, pious and happy people, with equal rights and equal opportunity to acquire the highest human worth."[85]

Sweden has been quite receptive to American cultural expressions, as in 1994, for example, when a Swedish government commission concluded that the influence of the U.S. with regard to film, TV, and literature in Sweden was very strong.[86] The resistance to American culture has largely come from a cultural or political elite, while rank-and-file Swedes seem to have been eager consumers of American films, television, and music throughout the period—

regardless of the outbursts of moral panic over the danger of American culture that have taken place regularly in the country.

An examination of articles dealing with the U.S., American culture, and Swedish-American cultural and political relations in the leading Swedish newspapers during the postwar era also shows positive views of America and American culture. A shift began around 1965, when critical voices emerged in the Swedish public debate. As noted above, a 1973 study also showed that a slight majority of Swedes had a negative opinion of the U.S. During the following fifteen years there was a noticeable change, and the by the end of the 1980s it was the positive views of America that dominated in Sweden.[87]

Swedish criticism of the U.S. has, as noted above, mainly been couched in cultural terms, and it is possible to speak of a tradition of cultural anti-Americanism in Sweden. Political and ideological anti-Americanism, however, have been short-lived and often connected to specific events, such as the Vietnam War. The mid 1960s marks a clear turning point, introducing the period of sustained critique of American society and culture in Sweden that lasted for about fifteen years. Still, the negative attitudes should not be exaggerated. It is noteworthy that the Swedish interest in studying at American universities and colleges did not diminish during this time.

During the final two decades of the twentieth century, American culture once again came to occupy a prominent position in the Swedish cultural matrix, in spite of Sweden's 1994 membership in the European Union and Swedish criticism of certain aspects of American foreign policy. Sympathy for the United States was especially visible following the terrorist attacks of 11 September 2001, when the leading Swedish newspaper *Dagens Nyheter*, like many other European papers, claimed that "We are all Americans today."[88]

Although they are difficult to measure, it seems possible to advance the hypothesis that expressions of anti-Americanism have been weaker in Sweden than in many other European countries and that the Swedish ties to the United States in general and American culture in particular have been quite strong. Different explanations for this can be advanced. The mass emigration of some 1.3 million Swedes to the United States between 1840 and 1930— in 1910 between one third and one fourth of the Swedish population resided in the U.S.—established an intricate network of personal bonds and channels of communication between the countries.[89] This network has played a major role in maintaining a largely positive awareness of and readiness for the United States and American ideas in Sweden. It is, as author Anders Ehnmark has put it, difficult to hate the U.S. "for historical reasons," as it "still is the country of emigration where aunt Ottilia lives."[90]

Moreover, Sweden's position as a nonaligned and neutral country means that it has remained outside the major military conflicts over the past century and a half. The absence of direct military and political relations with the

United States, such as membership in NATO, means that questions of Swedish dependence on or subservience to the U.S. never have played a very prominent role in the Swedish public debate. Sweden's role as a neutral country during World War II at times put the country in a difficult position vis-à-vis the U.S. This realization meant that concerted efforts were made to improve Sweden's image and position in the U.S., especially in the late 1940s and 1950s, laying the foundations for even closer Swedish-American ties.[91]

A final explanation relates to Sweden's relative remoteness from intellectual developments on the European continent. Although the country has certainly both followed and to some degree participated in larger European trends, the sense of a European identity—which could be contrasted and used against the United States—has been, at best, weakly developed in Sweden. The reasons for this need not be discussed here, but geography, demography, and economics all play a role. It seems prudent, meanwhile, to interpret the country's relations with the U.S. in light of these circumstances.

The processes through which cultural impulses and influences are transferred between different countries are complex and at times quite slippery. One way of better understanding them is to combine theoretical discussions with case studies. By focusing on Sweden, this article has attempted to do so, in order to contribute empirical results that will shed some new light on the larger question of cultural influences between the United States and other countries.

Notes

1. Anna Rönström and Lennart Weibull, "Världen utanför," in Sören Holmberg and Lennart Weibull, eds., *Mitt i nittiotalet* (Göteborg: SOM-Institutet, 1996), 415.
2. Ludvig Rasmusson, *Fyrtiotalisterna* (Stockholm: Norstedt, 1985), 130.
3. Erik Åsard, "Americanization or Globalization? Themes and Topics in a Recurring Debate," in Kerstin Shands, Rolf Lundén, and Dag Blanck, eds., *Notions of America: Swedish Perspectives* (Huddinge: Södertörns högskola, 2004), 18–20.
4. Rob Kroes, "Americanisation: What are We Talking About?" in Rob Kroes, et al., eds., *Cultural Transmissions and Receptions: American Mass Culture in Europe* (Amsterdam: VU University Press, 1993).
5. Some recent examples include Richard Pells, *Not Like Us: How Europeans Have Loved, Hated, and Transformed American Culture Since World War II* (New York: Basic Books, 1997), Jessica C. E. Gienow-Hecht, *Transmission Impossible: American Journalism as Cultural Diplomacy in Postwar Germany, 1945–1955* (Baton Rouge: Louisiana State University Press, 1999), and Reinhold Wagnleitner and Elaine Tyler May, eds., *Here, There, and*

Everywhere: The Foreign Politics of American Popular Culture (Hanover: University Press of New England, 2000).

6. Orvar Löfgren, "En svensk kulturrevolution?" in Orvar Löfgren, ed. *Hej, det är från försäkringskassan* (Stockholm: Natur och kultur, 1988), 192.

7. Rolf Lundén, "America in Sweden: Visible and Invisible Influence," in Rob Kroes, ed., *Within the US Orbit: Small National Cultures vis-à-vis the United States* (Amsterdam: VU University Press, 1991); Erik Åsard, "Influence and Presence, Depth and Surface: Studying the American Impact on Other Countries," *American Studies in Scandinavia* 35 (autumn, 2003).

8. James Gilbert, "The Problem of Americanization," in *Explorations of American Culture*, ed. James Gilbert (Uppsala: Uppsala University Press, 2000), 102.

9. Charles Silva, *Keep Them Strong, Keep Them Friendly: Swedish-American Relations and the Pax Americana, 1948–1952* (Stockholm: Silva, 1999), chap. 2.

10. Pells, *Not Like Us*, 53–54.

11. Harald Runblom, "American Propaganda in Scandinavia During the Second World War," in Rolf Lundén and Erik Åsard, eds., *Networks of Americanization: Aspects of the American Influence in Sweden* (Uppsala: Almqvist & Wiksell, 1992).

12. Pells, *Not Like Us*, chaps. 2–3.

13. Dag Blanck, "The Impact of the American Academy in Sweden," in Lundén and Åsard, *Networks of Americanization*, 80–93.

14. *Livet i Amerika: Upplysnings- och dokumentärfilmer 1957–58. USIS, Stockholm* (Stockholm, 1957); *USA på film 1960/61—1970* (Stockholm, 1959–1970).

15. *News Bulletin: USIS, Stockholm* (Stockholm, 1949–1972); *Ur USA-krönikan: USIS, Stockholm* (Stockholm, 1959–1972).

16. Nils Runeby, "Klerkernas ansvar och frihetens organisation. Kring de intellektuellas mobilisering i 1950-talets Sverige," in Wolfgang Butt and Berhard Glienke, eds., *Der nahe Norden. Otto Oberholzer zum 65. Geburtstag: Eine Festschrift* (Frankfurt: Lang, 1985), 293.

17. "Vilhelm Moberg kallar till frihet," *Arbetarhistoria* 4 (2001), 47.

18. *Kultur-kontakt* (Stockholm, 1954–1960).

19. Harald Elovson, *Amerika i svensk litteratur 1720–1850: En studie i komparativ litteraturhistoria* (Lund: Gleerup, 1930), 89, 271.

20. Knut Hamsun, *The Cultural Life of Modern America* (Cambridge: Harvard University Press, 1969), 145. Orig. published in 1889.

21. Birgitta Steene, "The Swedish Image of America," in Poul Houe & Sven Haakon Rossel, eds., *Images of America in Scandinavia* (Amsterdam: Rodopi, 1998), 170.

22. Rolf Lundén, "Theodore Dreiser and the Nobel Prize," *American Literature* 50, no. 2. (1978): 222–25.

23. The following is based on Rolf Lundén, "The Dual Canon: A Swedish Example," in Huck Gutman, ed., *As Others Read Us: International Perspectives on American Literature* (Amherst: University of Massachusetts Press, 1991), 239–41.

24. Lundén, "The Dual Canon," 242–43.

25. Elisabeth Herion Sarafidis, "The Swedish *Bonniers boklubb* and the Role of Anglo-Saxon Translation Literature," *American Studies in Scandinavia* 35 (autumn, 2003): 36–40.

26. Rolf Lundén, "American Literature in Sweden: A Threat to the Indigenous Culture?" in Lundén and Åsard, eds., *Networks of Americanization*, 108.

27. Ulf Jonas Björk, "American Infection: The Swedish Campaign Against Comic Books, 1952–1957," Paper presented at the Biennial Conference of the Nordic Association for American Studies, Trondheim, 8 August 2003, 1.

28. Martin Alm, *Americanitis. Amerika som sjukdom eller läkemedel. Svenska berättelser om USA åren 1900–1939* (Lund: Studia Historica Lundensia, 2002), 232.

29. Quoted in Björk, "American Infection," 1.
30. Björk, "American Infection," 3.
31. Ulf Jonas Björk, "Swedish Television and American Imports, 1956–1978," in Shands, Lundén, and Blanck, *Notions of America*, 60–1.
32. Björk, "Swedish Television," 64.
33. Björk, "Swedish Television," 67.
34. Dan Malmström, *Härligt, härligt med farligt, farligt: Populärmusik i Sverige under 1900-talet* (Stockholm: Natur och kultur, 1996), 163, 171–72.
35. Dag Blanck, "Inte bara McDonald's. Amerika i Europa- och i Sverige," in Gunilla Gren-Eklund, ed., *Att förstå Europa- mångfald och sammanhang: Humanistdagarna vid Uppsala universitet 1994* (Uppsala: Uppsala Universitet, 1996), 219.
36. Herman Lindqvist, "Hjärntvättade av amerikansk TV," *Aftonbladet*, 18 February 1996, 11.
37. Walter Jackson, "Gunnar Myrdal: America's Swedish Tocqueville," *Swedish-American Historical Quarterly* 50 (October 1999), 209.
38. Sissela Bok, *Alva: Ett kvinnoliv* (Stockholm: Bonnier, 1987), 129.
39. Quoted in Lars Lindskog, *Alva Myrdal: "Förnuftet måste segra"* (Stockholm: Sveriges Radio, 1981), 20.
40. Gunnar Myrdal and Alva Myrdal, *Kontakt med Amerika* (Stockholm: Bonnier, 1941), 30.
41. Myrdal and Myrdal, *Kontakt*, 101.
42. Alva Myrdal, "En studie av skolfördomarna," *Aftontidningen*, 5 May 1943; Alva Myrdal, "Västerlandets skola demokratiseras: Amerikas skola inför efterkrigsvärlden," *Lärarinneförbundet* 31 (8 March 1944), 8.
43. Alva Myrdal, Notes for speech on education in America, 6 August 1940, in Alva Myrdal Archives, Arbetarrörelsens arkiv (Archives of the Swedish Labour Movement), Stockholm.
44. Alva Myrdal, "Bildningsstandarden efter kriget, "*Aftontidningen*, 20 October 1943.
45. Per Thullberg, "Alva Myrdal," in *Svenskt Biografiskt Lexikon*, vol. 26 (Stockholm, 1987–89), 164–65.
46. Statens Offentliga Utredningar (SOU) 1948: 27, *1946 års skolkommissions betänkande med förslag till riktlinjer för det svenska skolväsendets utveckling* (Stockholm, 1948), chaps. 3–4.
47. SOU, 1948: 27, 4.
48. Åke Isling, *Kampen för och mot en demokratisk skola, 1. Samhällsstruktur och organisation* (Stockholm: Sober, 1980), 313–16; Gunnar Richardson, *Svensk skolpolitik 1940–1945: Idéer och realiteter i pedagogisk debatt och politiskt handlande* (Stockholm: Liber, 1978), 249.
49. Olof Ruin, *Amerikabilder: Anteckningar om USA från 50-tal till 90-tal* (Stockholm: Natur och kultur, 1994), 228.
50. Li Bennich-Björkman, *Learning A Passionate Profession: The Failing of Political Reform in Higher Education: A Swedish Example* (Stockholm: Rådet för forskning om universitet och högskolor, 1993), 3–10.
51. Franklin Scott, *The American Experience of Swedish Students: Retrospect and Aftermath* (Minneapolis: University of Minnesota, 1956), 96; Blanck, "The Impact of the American Academy," 89.
52. Wheeler, David, "Boon Times for Border Crossing," *Chronicle of Higher Education* 49 no. 13 (22 November 2002): A62.
53. Blanck, "The Impact of the American Academy," 85–86.
54. Scott, *The American Experience*, 103.
55. The following paragraphs are based on Svante Lindqvist, "Forskningens fasader: Wenner-Gren Center som symbol för svensk vetenskap," *Lychnos: Årsbok för idé- och lärdomshistoria/Annual of the Swedish History of Science Society* (1997): 122–31.
56. Lindqvist, "Forskningens fasader," 131.

57. The following is based on Dag Blanck, "Anti-Americanism in Sweden? A Discussion of Terminology and Examples," *American Studies in Scandinavia* 35 (autumn, 2003): 21–25.

58. Marie-France Toinet, "Does Anti-Americanism Exist?" in Denis Lacorne et al., eds., *The Rise and Fall of Anti-Americanism: A Century of French Perception* (London: St. Martin's, 1990), 220.

59. Pew Research Center for People and the Press, *What the World Thinks in 2002: How Global Publics View Their Lives, Their Countries, The World, America* (4 December 2002), 69, and question 64 in appendix. Available online at http://people-press.org/reports/display .php3?ReportID=165 (last accessed: 3 March 2005).

60. Pew Research Center for People and the Press, *What the World Thinks in 2002*, 63, 66.

61. Paul Hollander, *Anti-Americanism: Critiques at Home and Abroad, 1965–1990* (New York: Oxford University Press, 1992), 444.

62. Richard Kuisel, *Seducing the French: The Dilemma of Americanization* (Berkeley: University of California Press, 1993), 8.

63. Philippe Roger, *L'Ennemi américain: Généalogie de l'antiaméricanisme français* (Paris: Seuil, 2002),16–20.

64. Blanck, "Inte bara McDonald's," 219; Steene, "The Swedish Image of America," 183.

65. Sivar Arnér, "Varför vi hatar USA," *Stockholms-Tidningen,* 4 November 1965.

66. Artur Lundkvist, "Problemet är USA," *Clarté* 38, no. 4 (1965), 2.

67. Steene, 185.

68. Sven Öste, *Skuggor över USA* (Stockholm: Bonnier, 1964), preface.

69. Sven Delblanc, *Åsnebrygga: Dagboksroman* (Stockholm: Bonnier, 1969), 80–87, 76, 155–56, 206–7.

70. Yngve Möller, *Sverige och Vietnamkriget: Ett unikt kapitel i svensk utrikespolitik* (Stockholm: Tiden, 1992), 37–52.

71. Ulf Bjereld, *Kritiker eller medlare? En studie av Sveriges utrikespolitiska roller, 1945–1990* (Stockholm: Nerenius och Santerus, 1992), 46, 52, 57.

72. *Barometen,* 6 July 1967; *Upsala Nya Tidning,* 13 November 1967.

73. Olof Palme, *Med egna ord: Samtal med Serge Richard och Nordal Åkerman* (Uppsala: Bromberg, 1977), 38.

74. Lars-Göran Stenelo, *The International Critic* (Lund: Studentlitteratur, 1984), 146.

75. "Demonstrate Against Olof Palme" [June 1970], flyer in the archives of the American Swedish News Exchange, folder Vietnam War, Swenson Swedish Immigration Research Center, Augustana College, Rock Island, Illinois.

76. Utrikesdepartementet, *Utrikesfrågor: Offentliga dokument m m rörande viktigare svenska utrikesfrågor. 1969* (Stockholm: Utrikesdepartementet, 1969), 125; Leif Leifland, *Frostens år: Om USA's diplomatiska utfrysning av Sverige* (Stockholm: Nerenius och Santérus, 1997), 29.

77. Jan Eliasson, "Olof Palme och utrikespolitiken," in Erik Åsard, ed., *Politikern Olof Palme* (Stockholm: Hjalmarson och Högberg, 2002), 171–72.

78. Leifland, *Frostens år,* 39, 212–13.

79. Sarafidis, "The Swedish *Bonniers boklubb,*" 40; Gilbert, "The Problem of Americanization," 101.

80. Rolf Lundén, "Reception, Influence, and Imitation: Resonances of American Authors in Swedish Literature," *Swedish-American Historical Quarterly* 50, no. 3 (1999): 189–93.

81. Alm, *Americanitis,* 160–62; Alva Myrdal, Notes for speech "Det nya Amerika" (The New America), October, November and December 1942, in Alva Myrdal Archives, Arbetarrörelsens arkiv, (Archives of the Swedish Labour Movement), Stockholm.

82. H. Arnold Barton, "The New Deal and the People's Home: American and Swedish Perspectives from the 1930s," in Dag Blanck et al., eds., *Migration och mångfald: Essäer om*

kulturkontakt och minoritetsfrågor tillägnade Harald Runblom (Uppsala: Centrum för multietnisk forskning, 1999); Marquis W. Childs, *Sweden—The Middle Way* (New Haven: Yale University Press, 1936).

83. Orvar Löfgren, "Nationella arenor," in Billy Ehn, Jonas Frykman & Orvar Löfgren, eds., *Försvenskningen av Sverige: Det nationellas förvandlingar* (Stockholm: Natur och kultur, 1993), 53–65; Jan Ölof Nilsson, *Alva Myrdal—En virvel i den moderna strömmen* (Stockholm: Brutus Ostlings bokförlag Symposion, 1994).

84. Erik Åsard, "The Limits of 'Americanization' in Swedish Politics," *Swedish-American Historical Quarterly* 50, no. 3 (1999): 176–78.

85. Fredrika Bremer, *Hemmen i den nya verlden*, vol. 3 (Stockholm: Norstedt, 1854), 507.

86. Internationella Kulturutredningen, *Vår andes stämma- och andras: Kulturpolitik och internationalisering,* SOU 1994: 35 (Stockholm, 1994), 172.

87. "Sverige och Amerika," series K3b, 1945–1999. In the newspaper clipping collection at the archives of Sigtunastiftelsen, Sigtuna, Sweden; Blanck, "Inte bara McDonald's," 219.

88. *Dagens Nyheter,* 12 September 2001.

89. Sweden had the third highest relative rate of emigration in Europe, after Ireland and Norway.

90. Anders Ehnmark, *Krigsvinter: Dagbok från skogen* (Stockholm: Bokförlaget Atlas, 2002), 26.

91. Per-Axel Hildeman, *Upplysningsvis: Svenska Institutet 1945–1955* (Stockholm: Almqvist and Wiksell, 1995), 7–14.

AMERI-DANES AND PRO-AMERICAN ANTI-AMERICANS: CULTURAL AMERICANIZATION AND ANTI-AMERICANISM IN DENMARK AFTER 1945

❖   ❖   ❖

Nils Arne Sørensen
Klaus Petersen

Looking at the Danish case of Americanization and anti-Americanism in Europe, one can overemphasize the importance of the year 1945 as a dividing line. While the United States had not been very high on the agenda in political discussions and debates in the interwar years, American culture and lifestyle—mediated by Hollywood movies, dime novels, comics, and popular music and dance—were embraced enthusiastically by many Danes, especially the young generations. "We were crazy with jazz music," reminisced an 80-year-old retired nurse in the summer of 2003, thinking back to the jazz music of her late teens, spent in the provincial town of Randers. American words started entering the Danish vocabulary. As early as 1906, Danish readers were introduced to the "hot dog" in a short story by Johannes V. Jensen (one of the few Danish pro-American intellectuals). This was followed by such words as "jazz," "drink," "cocktail," "hot," and "swing" from the late 1910s. Other American phenomena were given more or less proper Danish names, such as "chewing gum" ("tyggegummi," first used in 1922) or the Western films that became known as "cowboyfilm" from 1925 onward. In other cases American imports were substituted for well worn Danish words—as was the case for "sminke," which became more and more widely known as *make-up* as of the 1930s.[1] As the examples show, America was synonymous with a new popular culture focused on entertainment, leisure, and youth. Underlying this was the dream of a problem-free life of material wealth that seemed to eager consumers in Denmark, as elsewhere, to be the essence of the American way of life.

If American cultural imports (and local copies) were highly visible before World War II, so was intellectual Anti-Americanism. This took two forms. One was a sweeping critique of American "civilization"; the other expressed concerns about what impact "Amerikanisering" (another of the new Danish words of the period) would have on Danish culture and society. For instance, the film critic Harald Engberg in 1939 expressed concern that Hollywood movies might give those who saw them, and especially children, "strange notions on how to solve problems, ... inoculate racial prejudice towards 'evil natives' and ... [contribute to misleading] the general public when demands for decent living conditions and hopes for the future [are] lulled to sleep with a couple of hours dreaming about how it could be, if only ..."[2]

For a more sweeping criticism, we can turn to the vice-president of the Conservative Party's youth organization, who in 1935 lamented that the "superficial culture of American movies, jazz idolization and propaganda literature ... is the direct road to cultural degeneration."[3]

This is close to a more general anti-Americanism that was widespread among intellectuals both on the left and to the right. If they disagreed about solutions to the "problem" of American civilization, they approached unanimity on the diagnosis. America was characterized by a vulgar, materialist culture. The conservative critic Harald Nielsen put it this way in 1939:

> Americanisation—that means smartness, the ability to do business and to organise matters in such ways that they can be dealt with speedily. It means lots of cars, lots of refrigerators, lots of radios, lots of telephones, but first and foremost it means lots of money for both the purpose and the precondition of all of these things are money, lots of money.... Everything is put at the service of money and the pursuit of money. Everything is influenced by this, all ideals are fashioned by this.... The pursuit of money is also more and more dominant in the domain of culture. One talks of *bestsellers* and gets used to measuring the importance of a book by its sales figures.... The nurture of cultural life has become the task of idle women. The results are bloodless and facile; what ought to be serious matters have been reduced to dilettantism.[4]

These patterns continued after 1945, as in most other European countries, especially regarding popular culture. But Denmark also did have a special background, an individual experience, that has to be considered when discussing the influence of American culture. Here two things are important. Firstly, Denmark was liberated by the British and not the Americans in 1945. Even though Danes acknowledged the American war effort, the first decades after World War II witnessed a strong Danish partiality for Britain and all things British. To most Danes, Britain was "their" local great power who served as a role model, not least in the realm of culture. The British position was strengthened by the fact that Britain was Denmark's most important trading partner. Secondly, for economic reasons imports from the U.S. were limited until the late 1950s. Because the Danish economy suffered from a lack of U.S. dollars, imports were strictly regulated. Furthermore, because postwar economic growth began later in Denmark than elsewhere, few people could afford to become Americanized.

Overt and Covert Cultural Operations: Official U.S. Programs in Denmark

In the first years after 1945, U.S. interest in Denmark focused on military strategic needs and especially on the U.S. military bases in Greenland. There seems to have been no serious effort to culturally influence the Danes, and in many ways Denmark was seen to be part of the British sphere of interest.[5] Denmark's place in the Western coalition was unquestionable, even though Danish politicians were hesitant to take sides in the emerging rivalry between the two superpowers. One important step was the Danish decision to join the Marshall Plan. Denmark was, considering the size of its population, among the countries receiving the most aid: USD 278 million. This had two chief effects. First, the funds helped to meet the existing dollar gap and made it possible to import both goods and know-how from the U.S. and other Organization for European Economic Cooperation (OEEC) countries. Second, participation in the European Recovery Plan (ERP) integrated Denmark into the Western alliance. As the Cold War became "colder," and with international developments such as the 1948 coup in Prague acting as a major influence, Denmark joined the NATO alliance in 1949.[6]

Parallel to Denmark's political orientation toward the U.S. was a growing American preoccupation with Denmark and Danish attitudes towards the United States. The goals of "psychological warfare" were primarily military and political, but linked to them was also a desire to "Demonstrate the extent and quality of U.S. cultural traditions and achievements," as stated in a June 1953 report from the embassy in Copenhagen.[7]

From 1948 on, the U.S. Embassy in Copenhagen started to work with "information programs." These activities involved a variety of actions such as exchange programs, publications on U.S. policies, establishment of a public library in the U.S. Embassy, and press and media contacts. From the outset, the strategy was to influence Danish opinion makers within the media, politics, and the educational system, as well as arts and culture. But political propaganda, even if presented as a friendly gesture or as culture, is a sensitive issue.

Throughout the 1950s officials at the Copenhagen embassy warned against overdoing these kind of activities. The Danes were firmly anticommunist but at the same time very sensitive toward American propaganda.[8] In the words of the Copenhagen European Cooperation Administration (ECA) mission in 1953, the "only way to sway Danish opinion is through Danish sources, as they thoroughly resent outside comments and criticisms."[9] Initiatives from American agencies in Denmark had to take the form of "objective" information, or more covert support of local Danish activities. Consequently, three types of official programs can be found: those making information about the United States available for Danes, those influencing Danish institutions to adopt and use American propaganda products as their own, and—as evidenced by specific examples—those providing secret support to pro-American Danish operators. Naturally, there is much evidence about the first kind of programs, whereas the other two are much more difficult to trace and evaluate.

The information activities were organized around American institutions and agencies in Denmark, the most important being the U.S. Embassy. Setting up a library and a film distribution program in the Embassy in Copenhagen may have helped the raise Danish awareness of American literature and culture. In 1950, the US Information Agency (USIA) library collection in Copenhagen totaled some 6,500 books and 3,000 pamphlets, as well as a music collection.[10] Starting in the 1950s, the USIA in Copenhagen published two periodicals (entitled *Panorama USA* and *USA Today*) as well as a number of booklets in Danish on contemporary political themes such as presidential elections, the U.S. in international politics, the Vietnam War (e.g., *Why Vietnam* in 1966), and American society and culture. The latter included both controversial themes like *The Negro in the USA* (1961), and more popular themes such as *American Music Life* (1961). It is difficult to evaluate the effects of these kind of activities. In 1953 the Embassy found that along with the published material, the library itself was quite popular among young Danes.[11]

In this respect, the invitation to Danes to go on U.S. study tours was more effective. In all participating countries, the Marshall programs were used to influence attitudes toward the United States among political leaders, trade unionists, and others. The idea was that the "backward" Danes should learn from, and eventually imitate, U.S. industrial organization, management, planning, and marketing—and that the study teams should adopt and present a positive image of the United States.[12] Beginning in the late 1940s, hundreds of Danish technicians, managers, farmers, and trade unionists visited the United States as members of such study teams.

Most participants were pro-American from the outset, and normally their reports, many of which were published, gave very positive pictures of the United States (as expected by the host). There were exceptions, however.

In 1949, a group of Danish trade unionists traveled to the U.S. to study production efficiency and industrial relations. Among the participants was the chairman of the Danish Congress of Trade Unions, Euler Jensen, whom the American representation in Denmark knew to be an anti-Communist hardliner.[13] The delegation visited several cities, trade unions, and factories in the United States. Returning to Denmark, one of the delegates, Jørgen Paldam, worked out a mandatory report entitled *America is different,* which was published in more than 50,000 copies and widely distributed throughout the Danish labor movement.[14] It did not focus only on American productivity and the standard of living (the standard items in such reports given the positive image of the United States) but also included sections on the "Negro Problem" and comparisons between welfare benefits in the two countries. This ambiguous view of the United States caused some disgruntlement at the ECA office in Copenhagen.

After the end of the Marshall Plan, the support for study trips to the U.S. was continued under several other programs in cooperation with private organizations such as "The American-Scandinavian Foundation" and "The Danish-American Society." An official report from the U.S. Embassy estimated that 500 Danish students had visited the U.S. in 1949. The report also pointed out the need to set up a Fulbright program in Denmark—"in the long run the exchange of persons would be our most effective approach to the Danes."[15] As of 1951, Danes were able to participate in the Fulbright program; some 200–300 Danes were sent to the United States annually. Among the more prominent students who visited the United States was Anker Jørgensen, who later was to become Danish Prime Minister (1972–1982). As a young trade unionist in the mid 1950s, Jørgensen received a Fulbright scholarship to visit Harvard University for three weeks of summer school, where he attended lectures by such prominent Americans as Jimmy Hoffa.[16] Returning from United States, Jørgensen brought Elvis Presley records for his children and a fascination for automobiles.

But apart from these formal programs, American officials in Denmark also used other means to create for Danes a positive image of the United States. Once we have entered the "grey zone" of U.S. activities in Denmark, our knowledge is naturally very scarce. We know that U.S. officials tried to influence Danish State Radio and the Danish press, supported Danish books and publications through various channels, and also supported Danish organizations. But we do not know if these examples are part of a larger operation.

When it came to placing American propaganda productions in the Danish public sphere, special attention was given to the press and radio broadcasting. As was stated in a report from the press section at Copenhagen Embassy, "Unlike any other operation of the USIS, the Press Section can bring a direct policy message to a critical or opposition audience without identification of source."[17] The Press Section in Denmark in 1952 produced 239 feature articles used by numerous Danish newspapers and magazines. The top 30 articles, the Section estimated, reached more than 1 million readers each. Although this work focused on political ends, the Press Section also wanted to convince Danes of the "high cultural standards of the United States."

The Embassy staff also managed to get Danish State Radio to broadcast programs produced by U.S. headquarters in Paris, leaving—in the words of the U.S. Embassy—"... the impression with the listener that the State Radio itself had arranged for coverage and financed it."[18] Political news programs dominated, but the Americans also supplied recordings of American orchestras and bands playing music ranging from classical to jazz and features on music and literature. According to an Embassy report from 1953 the following cultural highlights on the Danish State Radio was based on U.S.–produced material:

> Among such programs were during this period, for example, a repeat performance of Thornton Wilder's Our Town, as well as a ninety-minute performance of Saroyan's Don't Go Away Mad; the reading of short stories by Hawthorne, Melville, Bret Harte, Stephen Crane, Irving Shaw, and Truman Capote; recitals by such American artists as Todd Duncan, Dean Dixon, and Andor Foldes; performance of American organ music, Barber's piano sonata Op. 26, Louis Gruenberg's sonata Op. 2 for violin and piano, as well as pieces by more popular U.S. composers (Gershwin, Kern, etc.) ... And further more the Embassy had assisted Danish productions on ... a two-hour musical salute addressed to the city of Denver by the State Radio's symphony orchestra (including an address by Ambassador Anderson); a one-hour program of new American music (Barber, Charles Ives, Norman Dello Joio); a one-hour program devoted to the American composer Roger Sessions; a 45 minutes broadcast on American folk music; and a one-hour broadcast on post-war American literature.[19]

Far from all attempts to influence radio broadcasting were successful. Suspicion was a common feeling toward programs that mixed politics and entertainment. Because of this the Danish State Radio, according to the U.S. Embassy, did not show interest in using programs produced by "Voice of America." But economic considerations in Danish State Radio allowed some room for enterprising Americans:

> Due to its agreements with the commercial manufacturers of gramophone records, the Danish State Radio has always been exceedingly hesitant to use IBS recordings, and as a result USIS has included in its presentation program the presentation of commercially-produced American records to the State Radio (which, due to import restrictions, it has been unable to obtain through other channels).[20]

Apart from establishing a library and delivering cultural "raw material" to the Danish press and radio, U.S. sources also financially supported the publication of books and magazines in Denmark. Except for reports documenting the experiences of the ECA study groups, these books were not so much pro-American as they were anticommunist. A striking example is the translation into Danish of Charles A. Orr's book *Stalin's Slave Camps* in 1952. In this case the Social-Democratic publishing house "Fremad" received generous financial support from the local ECA administration and the book was published in no fewer than 50,000 copies, an enormous number by Danish standards.[21] In this case, the investment did not pay off. Not only did "Fremad" have great difficulty distributing even the free copies of the book, but the whole arrangement was exposed in the media and came to be seen as an example of blunt American propaganda. Much more successful were the anticommunist comic books like *Who Is the Imperialist?* provided by USIS for the national guard magazine, *Hjemmeværnet*, which had a circulation of 50,000.[22] Later *Who Is the Imperialist?* was printed in no fewer than 150,000 copies as a black-and-white pamphlet for use in schools and civic organizations.

The third type of official U.S. programs in Denmark provided covert support to pro-American Danish operators. The extent of this kind of support is not known due to the nature of the work: secret operations do not normally leave many traces behind. There is some evidence that the U.S. has supported political organizations such as the pro-NATO Atlantsammenslutningen, and they might also have supported noncommunist political organizations like the Danish Labor Movement. The best-known example in cultural circles is the Congress for Cultural Freedom (CCF).

In Denmark, as elsewhere, the CCF became a meeting ground for "progressive anticommunists." Denmark was represented at the founding CCF congress in Berlin in 1950 by the prominent Social Democrat and wartime resistance leader, Frode Jacobsen. The initiative to form a Danish branch, however, was taken three years later by the Conservative Arne Sejr.[23] Since 1945, Sejr had been involved in anticommunist activities of various kinds, freelancing for Danish and American intelligence and even creating his own private organization for "grey" operations entitled "the Firm." Especially in its first years, the Danish branch of the CCF did not behave as if it was under any kind of control from the outside. It took a name of its own—The Society for Freedom and Culture—hereby distancing itself from the international (American) mother organization, and in the first years even seems to have claimed economic independence.

Its activities resembled those of a private club more than an organization for political and cultural propaganda. Whereas the purpose of the CCF was to be a voice in the international political and cultural debate, Sejr seems to have been more interested in fighting Communism domestically. This conflict became clear in 1954, when the progressive Danish composer Niels Viggo Bentzon was invited to a CCF festival in Nice. Sejr and some of his Danish associates became very upset about Bentzon's inclusion, claiming that Bentzon was rather shady politically. The CCF in Paris was mainly interested in the public and cultural value of its activities, whereas the Danish were fighting Communists and their fellow-travelers.

In the following years Sejr's control over the organization diminished, and under the auspices of less conspiratorial members such as the young Social Democratic journalist Jørgen Schleimann, the relationship with the CCF was strengthened. In the period 1953–1957 the Society for Freedom and Culture cultivated contacts at the right-wing intellectual journal *Danske Magasin,* and in 1956 the Society started working closely together with the well-established journal *Perspektiv.* This was a broadminded magazine that printed articles on culture, science, and politics by numerous Danish intellectuals, and even though the editorial tone was antitotalitarian and pro-Western it also published articles by well-known Communist writers.[24] The cooperation with the CCF made it possible to publish translated articles from the international CCF journals like *Encounter* and *Preuves,* and with financial support from the CCF it was possible to reduce the selling price.

By 1957, the CCF headquarters in Paris had decided to bring Danish society more into line with its overall strategy, and the Danish autonomy over the Society for Freedom and Culture gradually disappeared. Eventually, by 1960, the Danes had to ask the CCF to take over all financial responsibilities and the contract with *Perspektiv.* In the early 1960s *Perspektiv* became the leading political and cultural magazine in Denmark, attracting prominent local and international intellectuals as editors and writers, but the exposure of the CIA's support of the CCF in 1967 was the beginning of the end of its Danish branch. Tellingly, the last two issues of *Perspektiv,* published in 1967 and 1969, were dedicated to the international student movement and critical evaluations of the Vietnam War.

America for the Cultural Elites: The Reception of American Highbrow Culture in Denmark, 1945–1970.

In 1968, the literary critic Erik Wiedemann contributed a chapter on American literature after 1945 to a major work titled *Foreign Authors in the Twentieth Century.* He lamented that new American literature was little known in Denmark compared to the literature of the interwar years, which had a "prominent position in Denmark."[25]

This assessment of the position of interwar literature is corroborated in the 1950 edition of the bestselling almanac *Hvem Hvad Hvor.* Here the editors published a list of some three hundred books presented as an "*allround* suggestion including the most important books in Danish literature and those of the principal languages." Looking at the recommendations in non-Scandinavian literature from the twentieth century, American literature is the largest single group represented, with twelve titles (closely followed by French and British literature). A closer look is striking. Most of the novelists listed offer critical portraits of American society (Sherwood Anderson, Erskine Caldwell, Dreiser, Sinclair Lewis, Upton Sinclair, and John Steinbeck) while Hemingway is represented by his two most politically engaged "European novels" (*A Farewell to Arms* and *For Whom the Bell Tolls*). Thus it was American writers' self-critical gaze at America that was hailed by the anonymous critic who compiled the list—and devoured by thousands of Danish readers in the postwar decades, when the works of Steinbeck and Hemingway especially were immensely popular.[26]

While no postwar writer has managed to rival the popularity of Steinbeck and Hemingway, there still are several American writers who have had a strong impact in Denmark. In 1950, the Royal Theatre premiered Arthur Miller's *Death of a Salesman* to ecstatic reviews. In a typical example, Erik Seidenfaden of *Information* characterized the play as "a conscious showdown with the American dream of 'unlimited opportunities.'"[27] The theatergoing public in Copenhagen shared the opinion of the reviewers. Measured in the number of performances, the play was by far the most successful produced by the Royal Theatre in the early 1950s. Arthur Miller cemented his reputation with *The Crucible*, which was successfully staged at Copenhagen's Det ny Teater in February 1954 and broadcast as a radio play by Danish State Radio later that year.[28]

By then, *The Catcher in the Rye* (translated in 1953) was already gaining cult status among part of the young generation in Denmark. Both the theme of bewildered, rebellious youth and the novel's linguistic mode probably served as a key source of inspiration for two of the most controversial (and critically acclaimed) Danish novels of the late 1950s: Klaus Rifbjerg's *Den kroniske uskyld* and Leif Panduro's *De uanstændige*.[29]

Rifbjerg had become the modernist *enfant terrible* of Danish literature and cultural debates in the mid 1950s. Strongly influenced by American culture, and following the tradition of left-wing radicals from the 1930s, he fully accepted both film and jazz as bona fide ways of artistic expression. He was instrumental in introducing the beat generation to a Danish readership when in 1959, *Vindrosen*, an influential literary journal that Rifbjerg co-edited, printed translations of "Howl!" and Ferlinghetti's "A Coney Island of the Mind" while another rising star in the Danish intelligentsia, Villy Sørensen, positively reviewed the Danish translation of Kerouac's *The Subterraneans*.[30] *On the Road* was translated into Danish in 1960, a year that also saw the publication of Rifbjerg's immensely influential collection of poetry, *Konfrontation*, where the inspiration from the beat generation was evident.

Wiedemann's lamenting of the lack of impact of post-1945 American literature in Denmark does not quite ring true. If middle-brow Danish readers by the early 1960s still preferred the "classics" from the interwar years, the literary avant-garde were impressed with, and inspired by, their American contemporaries. Thus the status of American contemporary literature was clearly elitist.[31]

The same can be said of jazz music. While most jazz fans in the 1920s and 30s probably primarily saw it as energetic and liberating dance music, a much smaller radical audience ascribed more meaning to jazz. One of their most eloquent members, Sven Møller Kristensen, wrote in 1938, that jazz was "natural," "physical," "primitive," "non-individualistic," "productive," (universally) "human," and "popular" in the sense that it was music for the people by the people.[32] In short, jazz was authentic folk music, rooted in the experiences of the African-American slaves and underclass, and therefore the ideal soundtrack to social and political experiments of a more or less revolutionary nature. However, this authentic music had been bastardized into commercial dance music, much to the chagrin of the real aficionados. So, while the years during and immediately after the German occupation of Denmark in many ways were a golden era for jazz as dance music, the same years saw the making of a much smaller group of jazz fans, generally politically to the left, who worked to promote jazz as a new art form.

This group, supplemented after 1945 by a handful of youthful fiery souls, took jazz very seriously indeed. Erik Wiedemann (whom we met earlier as a literary critic) claimed in a 1952 feature article on contemporary jazz music that "Jazz is an art form that develops at tremendous speed. In 50 years, it has developed from primitive folk music to a music that is comparable to the other artistic forms of contemporary society." He argued that this was an "inevitable" consequence of the position of jazz "in the heart of the modern, intellectual urban culture" and compared "bop" with European expressionist music. However, this magnificent development created problems. Adolescents, who had previously made up the core of jazz fans, did not "possess the mental energy needed" to appreciate modern jazz. "And even if there seems to be a growing appreciation of the values of jazz in progressive cultural circles, the number of jazz supporters here is not large enough to secure a social base."[33]

If this was the case, the mission for jazz lovers was clear. This social base had to be created, and the group worked hard to this end. In 1954 the journal *Musikrevue* was launched, and although it claimed to cover classical music and even pop, the prime focus was on jazz.[34] In 1956, the group created *Den danske Jazzkreds* (The Danish Jazz Circle) to further understanding of the importance of jazz as an art form and to promote Danish jazz. In their struggle, the jazz enthusiasts received crucial support from Danish State Radio, which in late 1945 began airing jazz recordings and programs where jazz connoisseurs played and commented. In 1946/47, a series of programs told the history of jazz, and as of 1948 the biweekly program *Radioens Jazzklub* was a fixture. By the late 1950s it had become a weekly event and was supplemented by a number of other programs. There were regular transmissions of jazz concerts, altogether "several hundreds" over the four decades after 1952. In 1951, the first Radio Jazz Band was established, and in 1964 the State Radio formed a permanent big band, Danmarks Radios Big Band.[35]

These initiatives proved unable to secure a broad social base for modern jazz. Most people probably found the music noisy, and the intellectual jazz-lovers boring. The point we want to make here, however, is that over the first decade or so of the postwar period, modern jazz was established among the young and progressive intellectuals as their preferred music. And although they tried to promote an active Danish jazz scene (by the 1960s they had succeeded, thanks in no small part to the support of the State Radio), American jazz continued to be the real thing. While Louis Armstrong and other jazz stars from the 1930s had gained mainstream status by the mid 1950s, the same cannot be said for the real heroes of the jazz intellectuals. There was nothing middle-of-the-roadish about the stars of bebop. Quite the opposite, this music was the perfect soundtrack to the more adventurous American literature that was enjoyed by the same group. By the early 1960s, then, literary icons such as Hemingway and Steinbeck were well established in bestselling dimensions, whereas more recent, critical voices, such as those of Salinger, Miller, and the beat generation, had won the ear of younger intellectuals especially. What most of these writers had in common was a critical view of middle-class America.

As for the reception of American movies by Danish film critics, we find a similar picture. Since 1948, the Association of Danish film critics has offered awards, one of which, the *Bodil*, is dedicated to the best non-European movie of the year. Comparing this awards ceremony to that of the American Academy Awards for the period 1948–75, we find that only five Oscar winners in the "best picture" category had been awarded a *Bodil*. It was not that the critics did not like American films; they simply did not share the same taste as the Academy. Thus from the late 1950s to the mid 1960s when the Oscar winners were musicals and historical costume dramas, Danish critics preferred socially and politically engaged films such as *The Defiant Ones, Twelve Angry Men, Judgement in Nuremberg, Dr. Strangelove,* and *Seven Days in May.*[36]

To conclude this section on the reception and status of American culture among intellectuals, we will take a look at the development of the teaching of English in the Danish *Gymnasium,* which is the Danish equivalent of the American secondary school catering to students 16–19 years old. The postwar decades saw frequent educational reforms, both to secure the skills for the economic modernization the country was undergoing, and to strengthen democratic structures and values, which was an important political project for the Social Democrats and the social-liberal Radical Party, the two parties that dominated Danish governments from 1945 to the 1970s. In this process the *Gymnasium* changed from being an elitist institution to a school for, at least in terms of numbers, the many. While only 5 percent of an age cohort graduated from the *Gymnasium* in 1945, the number had risen to 10 percent in 1960 and leapt to 32 percent by 1975. Neither the reforms nor the growing number of students changed the fundamental understanding that one of the prime goals of the *Gymnasium* was to secure the *almendannelse*—that is, the very literal Danish translation of Wilhelm von Humboldt's classical concept of *allgemeine Bildung* (general education) with a strong focus on the humanities— of the students. Therefore, the teaching of English in the *Gymnasium* is an excellent way to assess the status of America in Danish highbrow culture.

By 1945, the *Gymnasium* had for decades been divided into a science line and a language line. In the language line, English had by the 1930s established itself as the most popular modern language. In 1945, teaching was regulated by laws and regulations that had been passed in 1935. Here "English" was taken in a very literal sense. Students were required to read Shakespeare, English poetry and prose, and even texts on "English history, political institutions and contemporary social conditions." At no stage, either in the wording of the 1935 law or in the general guidelines for teaching, does "America/n" enter.[37]

American texts at last squeezed their way into the *Gymnasium* in 1953, when a new law for the *Gymnasium* still required students to learn about "English culture"—from Shakespeare to political institutions and contemporary affairs. A new development, however, was that "American texts can, in reasonable proportions, be read instead of English ones."[38]

In the late 1950s, education in Denmark went through a major overhaul. For the *Gymnasium*, the objective was to make the institution "up-to date without diminishing its quality as the foundation for higher education."[39] In its report, the Ministry of Education's Advisory Committee did not suggest major changes in the study of English. However, they noted in their comments that "with the ever-growing cultural importance of the United States, it is deemed natural to make reading of American texts mandatory."[40] Based on this, the draft law stated that "American literature must be represented" in the readings.[41] However, in the committee's proposal for teaching guidelines, it was made clear that this requirement would be fulfilled by reading as little as a poem and a short story.[42]

In 1961, the new law for the *Gymnasium* followed these recommendations closely. However, while one can argue that this reform finally acknowledged American literature (and culture) as a bona fide subject matter, it is also clear that American culture was still seen very much as the junior partner in the English-speaking world. This reflects the opinion of the committee (and maybe even of the politicians who passed the law) probably less than it does that of the English teachers. Like their colleagues in the other Fine Arts disciplines, they saw it as their first duty to give the students an understanding of the "best," culturally speaking, and for English teachers in Denmark this meant English culture.

American and English cultures were finally given equal status in a reform from 1971. Whether this equal footing was realized in the daily teaching practice is doubtful, however. It is telling, at least, that the law is utterly silent as to the provenance of the texts to be used at actual examinations.[43]

America for the Masses—
Americanization of Popular Culture in Denmark

In the decades after 1945 Denmark gradually became a modern industrial society. In this process the U.S. became an icon as well as a model whose ways of life were imitated by Danish consumers and entrepreneurs. The 1950s and 1960s witnessed an Americanization of production and consumption. Danish adoption of "American" ideas was promoted by official U.S. programs such as the ECA. Production was heavily influenced by American ideas on industrial relations, scientific management, and rationalization (piecework).[44]

Product marketing began to rely on American tools such as PR campaigns. Often products were given an American slant, even if the product in question was purely Danish. For instance, a Danish grapefruit soft drink was titled *Majami* ("Miami"). The Danish cigarettes *Holiday* consisted—so an advertisement informed consumers—of an American blend of tobacco produced by American machines under control of American experts exclaiming: *"It's OK, it's a Holiday."*[45] Retail distribution of goods changed dramatically when new concepts such as self service, supermarkets, shopping malls, and drive-in appeared in most Danish cities.[46] The first Danish supermarket opened in 1953, and the variety of drive-ins included banks and book shops. This was openly inspired by the U.S. example and actively supported as part of the official American programs in Denmark as stated by USIS in 1953: "Encouraged by American consultants ... both independent and cooperative retail food outlets have started experimental changeovers to self-service stores and there are indications that this move may gain considerable momentum."[47]

Finally, Danish consumers also started to consume in the American way.[48] First, dedicated youth started drinking *milkshakes* and eating *popcorn* the 1950s. Later, during the 1960s *juice, steaks, yogurt,* and *corn flakes* appeared on Danish dining tables. In the kitchen, food was prepared less "from scratch" as canned and frozen food became more widespread and electric gadgets made their entry. Refrigerators became standard items in the 1950s; freezers, in the 1960s. In the early 1950s the widely read journal *Samvirke* (which arose out of the cooperative movement) stated that "An American kitchen is the dream

of most Danish housewives."[49] In 1957, the first cookbook devoted to barbecue meals was published in Denmark. The blurb informed potential (and
maybe skeptical) readers that "the strange word *barbecue* (pronounced bar-
be-kju) is borrowed from American."[50] Barbecue caught on only in the 1960s.
By then a barbecue had become a "grill" (like in the rest of the Nordic countries and Germany), and barbecue food consequently "grillmad" (grilled food),
one of the many neologisms in Denmark based on creative adaptation of American words.

With shorter working hours and longer vacations, more time was left for
leisure, and in this sphere American influence is also prominent. Besides the
strong influence in areas such as music and movies (this will be discussed below) there was a development in the pursuit of hobbies. Having a *hobby* became very important, and in 1946 the first *hobby* handbook was published.[51]
The suggested hobbies were, apart from lasso throwing, not distinctly American. In sports Danes were similarly reluctant to follow the Americans. In
1946 the first *basketball* game was played in Copenhagen between two teams
from the American occupation forces in Germany.[52] Shortly afterward, a national basketball union was founded, but it remained marginal in comparison to European disciplines such as soccer and the Danish-created sport of
handball. American sports like baseball and American football were, and still
are, considered exotic and odd. A more successful leisure activity was *camping*. Even though camping had been a known concept before 1945, the
growth of the camping scene in post-1945 Denmark clearly based itself on the
American example, especially given the use of automobiles and *caravans*.[53]

This gradual movement toward an affluent society was, of course, not a
product of American economic and cultural imperialism alone. Programs for
the modernization of Europe, American business interests, the Danish fascination with the new superpower, and a growing orientation toward material
wealth worked together in changing the Danish way of life. The complex in-
terplay among these pushing and pulling forces was also influenced by such
factors as economic performance and national market interests. Compared to
other European countries, Denmark witnessed strong economic growth at a
relatively late stage. What has generally been termed the "Silver Fifties" reached
Denmark only in the last years of the decade. Meanwhile, relative economic
backwardness and strong state regulation of trade limited the import of American goods.

Under these conditions, in the first 10–15 years after 1945, Americanization of Danish consumer habits was characterized by inexpensive activities
such as camping, or by an Americanization by proxy. There are several examples of Danish companies producing American "look-alike" products for the
Danish and European markets. *DANDY* (originally started up in 1939) produced chewing gum, and in 1946 Toms started producing a chocolate bar

called *Yankie Bar* (which was also sold to U.S. troops in Germany).[54] Denmark even sports the only example of a national cola drink competing successfully with the American originals: in 1959, Danish breweries started producing *Jolly Cola,* which until the late 1970s was the best selling cola drink on the Danish market.

Import regulations, dollar gaps, and slow economic growth affected the entertainment industry much more than most other sectors. For good reason, movies, records, and comics were not considered to be of vital interest to the nation. Exact figures for imports and restrictions are not available, but a closer look at the importation of records reveals that America played a very limited role. Until 1956, between 80 percent and 95 percent of all imported records came from Britain, and only in 1980 did U.S. imports exceed the British.[55] Naturally, the British exports to Denmark may partly have been a re-exportation of American music, but it is important to stress that American culture had strong and even sometimes overwhelming competition from British popular culture (especially pop and rock music in the 1960s), as well as from homegrown Danish culture and European culture in general.

It is clear that Danish marketers did not distinguish between British and American English but used both. This might have been due to a lack of linguistic skills, but other factors can also be considered, first among them the strong and well-established political and economical links to Britain, Denmark's most important trading partner. Secondly, in many ways Britain served as a cultural entrepôt that received, filtered, and retransmitted American popular culture to Europe. This entrepôt function was used very successfully by the British entertainment and fashion industries in the 1960s, once Britain became "cool" and London was "swinging." In Danish youth magazines from the 1960s and 1970s, British fashion and music are much more prominent than their American counterparts. Hollywood products dominated among movies, but by the 1960s (at the latest) music had become the main component in youth culture.

The influx of American popular culture falls into two categories: conformist and entertaining popular culture for the general public, and popular culture as youth culture. In many ways, the consumption of popular American culture was a continuation of the patterns established in the interwar period when American movies, popular music, and literature started to attract Danish attention. Perhaps the clearest example of this is the Danish edition of *Readers Digest,* published from 1946 under the title *Det Bedste,* i.e. The Best (of *Readers Digest*).[56] It was a direct copy of the American edition in both format and content. Articles were translated from the American original with only minor adjustments. With its mixture of political comment, family-oriented features, novels, and short stories, it was a huge success in Denmark. The publisher claimed sales of between 200,000 and 280,000 copies, an extremely high figure by Danish standards, and a survey in 1951 showed that *Det Bedste* was the most widely read magazine in Denmark, with a national coverage of 23 percent. *Readers Digest* clearly propagandized American political ideals and the American way of life, and it was important in creating a pro-American attitude among the Danish people.[57]

In the book market, the introduction of paperbacks and book clubs in the 1950s was directly inspired by its American counterpart. Furthermore, the number of American books published grew through the 1940s. By 1950 more American than British titles were published, and in 1958, translations of American books even outnumbered Danish titles, comprising 50 percent of all translated titles.[58] No figures exist for the number of books actually sold, but surveys made in the 1950s show that popular writers such as Frank G. Slaughter were among the best known in Denmark, and that many "pulp fiction" crime novels (e.g., the books of Mickey Spillane) were published in large quantities. A similar trend can be found in popular magazines, where Hollywood gossip was an important topic and half the short stories were translations of American originals.

In comics, we find the same picture. Even though American comics such as *Popeye* were already well known in Denmark before 1945, their circulation grew dramatically in the postwar years.[59] Comic classics such as *Donald Duck* (1946), *The Phantom* (1952), and *Superman* (1953) were well established with magazines of their own, and Western comics such as *Black Mask* (1958), *Kit Carson* (1955), and *Roy Rogers—King of the Prairie* (1955) were published on regularly basis. The moral panic of the mid 1950s with its critique of violent comics (see below) caused publishers to cancel the Danish publication of series like *Superman* and *The Phantom* for a period. Less violent series remained immensely popular. Disney's *Donald Duck,* which became a weekly magazine in 1949, was the leading comic magazine for children, selling more than 170,000 copies in the late 1950s. (In 2003 the weekly number of copies was around 65,000.[60])

The American dominance in these markets was not unchallenged. British literature especially maintained a strong position in genres such as thrillers (featuring such attractions as James Bond and Norman Conquest) and detective stories (from the adventures of Sexton Blake to the more genteel heroes of Agatha Christie). In the genre of war comics, Danish readers showed a strong partiality for British sailors, the "Desert Rats," and R.A.F. aces.

Movies are a special case. In 1945, Danish cinema-goers were longing for the return of Hollywood movies to the Danish screens. American movie companies began regaining their prewar position: out of 28 "remarkable" foreign films that premiered in Denmark from May to October 1945, 18 were American, and 14 out of 16 "new movie stars" presented in the *Hvem Hvad Hvor* almanac were from Hollywood.[61] To the Danish authorities this success was proof of the potential for a trade deficit if more American movies were imported. Consequently, an unofficial import embargo on American films was established to save dollars for other more important items.

A recent study shows how Hollywood engaged in an export strategy combining monopolistic trading methods with massive diplomatic support from the State Department and the local Embassy in Copenhagen.[62] The American Motion Picture Association started to put pressure on Denmark to open its markets and accept higher charges for the so-called "super" (i.e. colored, wide screen) movies. Danish authorities were hesitant to open up to America, and cinema owners refused to pay more. As a result, on several occasions during the 1940s and 1950s Danish cinemas were boycotted by the American film industry. The longest of these boycotts lasted from 1955 to 1958 and was only solved after prolonged negotiations between the American Motion Picture Association and Danish cinema owners and intervention by both American and Danish state officials.

Because of this, American movies were not always accessible to Danish cinema-goers and Americanization through Hollywood productions was delayed. Disney productions were not included in the boycott, but otherwise Danes had to go a long way to enjoy the world of Hollywood—and in fact, many did. During the boycott period, people in Copenhagen could take the so-called "Scarlet Ferries" (named after Scarlet O'Hara) to Sweden to watch epics such as *Moby Dick, Young Rebel,* and *All that Heaven Allows.* After 1958, Danish markets were finally opened and American movies soon established a strong position on the Danish market.

The American boycott gave Danish film producers a chance to hang on to, and to develop, the market share won during the war. With a few exceptions, Danish filmmakers did not try to "out-Hollywood" Hollywood, but instead focused on light productions in the genres of drama and comedy with a very high content of "Danishness." The most successful films were adaptations of the pastoral romances of Morten Korch, set in a sunny Danish countryside unmarred by too many tractors or other reminders of the reality of Danish agriculture in the 1950s. Another successful series of the 1950s and 60s was the *Far til fire* comedies. Here too the pressures of modernization are almost absent. Instead, the films give a humorous but utterly sympathetic look at the daily life and core values of a lower-middle–class family (in *Far til fire og onkel Sofus,* from 1957, the main character, the boy Lille Per, even rejects the opportunity to go to America with his rich Danish-American uncle. Per prefers cozy provincial Denmark and his family to the lure of American modernity). In a third series, *Soldaterkammerater,* produced from 1958 to 1968, the audience could follow the adventures of a group of young conscripts in the army without ever being reminded of what armies are for—or, for that matter, that Denmark was an American ally. Danish producers also took stabs at more traditional American genres such as thrillers and youth movies. The Danish thrillers of the 1950s were mainly cheap copies of the originals and disappeared once American films became available. The youth films—for instance, *Bundfald* (Dregs)—were of better quality; it is significant that they at once copied American youth films and pointed toward the potential dangers connected to United States. This can be seen in the movie *Natlogi betalt* (1957), about the so-called "American girls," girls who dated (or prostituted themselves to) American soldiers.[63]

For many Danes, American culture was youth culture. The whole concept of youth as a specific lifespan is captured in the concept *teen-ager*, which became a common word in Denmark in the 1950s. In 1958, the Copenhagen department store Magasin opened a special *teen-age* department—"the meeting place of the young ones"—and in both commercial and public debate on youth, the idea of the teenager as a modern young consumer became common.[64] For young people, American popular culture offered a medium through which to distance themselves from the parent generation and the norms of the establishment. One can speak of rebellion in a series of phases: the rock'n'roll rebellion of the 1950s, followed by the beatnik rebellion of the 1960s, culminating in the flower power revolution of the late 1960s and early 1970s. Likewise, the interest that dates from the 1980s in urban underground cultural media such as rap, hip-hop, and graffiti can also be seen as an example of youth rebellion. In every one of these cases, an American cultural style was imported to Denmark and eventually integrated.

The first rock Danish rock'n'roll concert took place in October 1956, when Ib "Rock" Hansen, accompanied by a band of jazz musicians, set off to rock. In the Danish press, the arrival of rock'n'roll was awaited with anxiety and fear.[65] The newspapers had reported on rebellious rock'n'roll youth and street fights in cities such as London and Oslo. However, these fears proved groundless: Danish teenagers enjoyed the music and dance, but behaved within accepted norms. The only accident happened when a journalist—working for an American news agency—paid of a couple of youngsters to throw "bangers" (firecrackers) into the crowd.

The history of Danish rock still has to be written, but the influence of American rock'n'roll in the 1950s might easily be exaggerated. American music was not easy to obtain. It was, for instance, only in 1958 that Elvis Presley records were officially released in Denmark.[66] This created ample space for Danish copies, and also for British ones. Thus in the late 1950s, Tommy Steele, presented as a nicer and less rebellious version of the pelvis-rotating Elvis Presley, became the key teenage icon in Denmark.[67] Later Steele's position was taken over by the equally unthreatening Cliff Richard, and by the early 1960s Denmark had witnessed its first successful "British invasion." The charts in the youth magazine *Tempo* in 1963 showed a clear dominance of Danish and German pop songs, among them only two American recordings—Elvis Presley's "Good Luck Charm" and "Hawaii Tattoo" by the Waikikis. Throughout the 1950s and 1960s, pop music—Danish, American, German, and others alike—was evenly distributed in the charts.

Until the 1960s, access to rock'n'roll and pop music was also very limited on Danish airwaves. The monopolist State Radio had a very highbrow attitude toward entertainment and pop in general, and rock'n'roll was (unofficially) banned. In 1958 this dearth was challenged by a commercial "radio pirate," Radio Mercur, which broadcast from international waters.[68] The success of Radio Mercur was staggering; contemporary surveys show very high ratings. Danish authorities saw Radio Mercur as a direct challenge and ordered the Danish navy to board the transmitting ship if by accident it should enter Danish territory. When direct attacks proved an inefficient tactic, in 1963 the State Radio followed a line of repressive tolerance by opening its own channel, "Program 3," for youth music. This decision caused some concern among music connoisseurs and also created conflicts within State Radio. Young disc jockeys had to defend their musical choices against an enraged music director, Vagn Kappel, who stated:

> For me, pop is one of the most repulsive, stupid and filthy phenomena—and here filthy is not in a pornographic sense, as pornography is not nearly as cynical as the thoughts behind the manufacturing of pop-products, and I mean to underline, that it would not in any way do harm, on the contrary it would be beneficial, to keep this disgusting industry outside the doors of the National Danish Radio.[69]

But this was already a voice of the past. During the 1960s pop, rock, and beat were widely accepted, and in the late 1960s they even became partly intellectualized—especially experimental rock such as that by Frank Zappa and Captain Beefheart, and politicized rock music. Tellingly, in January 1972 the State Radio was able to set up a program called "Beat—a musical balance sheet."

It was not only American records that were hard to come by in Denmark of the 1950s. The same goes for the iconic garment blue jeans (or *cowboy busker*, i.e. cowboy trousers, as they were called in Denmark). The Copenhagen retailer Troelstrup was the first to import jeans in 1948/49, and by the mid 1950s they were still very rare. A prominent Danish historian has recalled how as a young teenager in 1953/54 he received a pair of Wrangler jeans from his female cousin and wore them with pride—even though they were a girls' style that buttoned on both sides.[70] Thus the slow process of the Americanization of Danish youth culture must be explained in terms of supply rather than demand. This changed when Denmark, in economic terms, entered its Golden Sixties. From the mid 1960s, jeans became ubiquitous. A survey from the mid 1970s showed that Denmark by then was one of the most "jeansified" countries in Europe.[71]

An important part of the new teenage culture was the use of American words. *Pop, rock'n'roll* and *OK* became part of the everyday language of younger people. It was important to be *in*, and in the 1960s Danish youths started *petting* (instead of "kælen," i.e. fondling). Later, words from the American counterculture entered the Danish vocabulary. In a feature article in the Danish newspaper *Politiken* from January 1967, a female Danish exchange student reported from the mind-blowing American hippie culture, presenting expressions such as *psychedelic, grass, stuff, joint, high, stoned, a flash, trip*.[72] In the following years these words (directly or translated) became everyday slang in Danish youth culture. In many cases, the words came from the music scene or the world of advertising. Danish products for the teenage market were often given "American" names like the earlier mentioned *Dandy* chewing gum and the chocolate bar, *Yankie Bar*. Another example is the milkshake bars that became popular under the Danish name "Milk Pops" (*Mælkepops*), evidently referring to both the words pop and pubs. The *Mælkepops* were the commercial incarnation of American teenage culture, according to a newspaper description from 1963: "In the three existing *Mælkepops*, thousands of teenagers suck up tons of milk made unrecognizable with fruit juices, ice cream and other delicacies … , accompanied by the extreme noise of Elvis Presley records."[73]

"We do not want to become Americanized."

In a speech given in London in 1949, the Danish prime minister, the Social Democrat Hans Hedtoft, commented on the postwar reconstruction of Western Europe. Exactly one week after Denmark had signed the North Atlantic Treaty, he stated:

> Western Europe has its own way. We all know it at home. We want to keep it. We do *not* want to be subject to the *enforced collectivisation* of the East but we do not want to become *Americanised* either. We want something that is equally far from both of these extremes…. If we use the Marshall Aid properly, we here have an instrument to reconstruct Western Europe and to maintain our *independence*.[74]

Critics might well point out that by joining the ERP and the Atlantic alliance Danish governments had already accepted a high degree of political and economic Americanization. However, these choices were not easily made. In 1947, the Liberal government sought British advice before accepting Marshall aid, and in 1949, the Danish Social Democratic government opted for the Atlantic alliance only after a failed attempt to form a Scandinavian Defense Alliance. This was done with very little enthusiasm and widespread criticism, not only from Communists but also from social liberals and Social Democrats.[75] With this in mind, one might expect political initiatives in the cultural sphere in an attempt to safeguard Danish culture from the American onslaught after 1945. However, there is very limited evidence for government-sponsored anti-Americanism.

In the press, commentators regularly voiced concern about the American influence on the Danish language. One commentator in 1951 even claimed that Danes were beginning to speak *ameridansk* (i.e. "Ameri-Danish").[76] None of these lamenting voices, however, persuaded Danish governments that a policy of linguistic purity was necessary to save the nation from the Americans.

The government did act, however, in another "American scare" of the early postwar period. The early 1950s saw an upswing in concern over the cultural consumption of children and adolescents. This widespread anxiety was triggered by the expanding market for "trash" novels and comic books, which, according to one commentator, Tørk Haxthausen, were educating children to become monsters.[77] The debate, conducted mainly by teachers and librarians, resulted in the appointment of a government committee "to look into and reflect upon the problems concerning substandard and destructive literature." When it was published in 1960, the report of the committee proved tepid reading. The committee opposed censorship, and while it was accepted that "trash" literature was a problem, this could be solved by producing more books of better quality.[78] The report had no legal consequences, and even though a committee member who favored censorship tried in 1961 to argue his case in a book, it was evident that the comics scare had effectively died down.[79]

Although it is difficult to find strong evidence of anti-Americanism in public policy, it is evident that far from everyone was happy about the growing impact of American culture in the broadest sense of the word. In a U.S. Embassy report from 1950, we find the following assessment:

> One must recognize that two different Danish groups exist so far as receptivity to American culture is concerned. The youth generally, the working classes and the lower middle classes like American popular culture, i.e. jazz, Hollywood, automobiles, speed, informality, gadgets, best-seller novels, detective stories and slick magazines. The older people in the more privileged classes, the Communist intelligentsia, and many intellectuals reject American popular culture, but are receptive to good American aesthetic and academic accomplishments.[80]

Judging from what we have discussed in this chapter's sections on highbrow and popular culture, this seems to be a quite precise assessment. However, it must be acknowledged that for many intellectuals, the rejection of America went well beyond popular culture. To communists, anti-Americanism seems to have been an almost Pavlovian reflex. The U.S. was often compared to Nazi Germany. Prominent politicians were seen to be American versions of Göring or Goebbels, and for the well-known Communist lawyer Carl Madsen, the U.S. was simply "the new power of occupation."[81] However, the

Danish Communist Party remained a loyal puppy to the Kremlin to the bitter end, and thus need not concern us further here.

One of the political consequences of the defeat of Nazism was the disappearance of the criticism of democracy that had been widespread among conservative politicians and intellectuals in the 1930s.[82] This also meant that conservative anti-Americanism was watered down substantially. In 1953, the new cultural journal *Det danske Magasin* dedicated its first issue to "anti-Americanism and the Culture of Europe." The editor wrote of the growing anti-Americanism in Western Europe that was being "nurtured by caring if not always clean hands," stressed that much of it originated in Moscow, and concluded that "in many cases, criticism of America is well founded and therefore useful.… However, the "speaking in tongues" movement called anti-Americanism that is currently spreading across Europe is an intellectual fraud and a political luxury we cannot afford."[83]

It is easy see why the conservative editors and contributors of *Det danske Magasin* came to the defense of America. By 1953, McCarthyism had been making headlines in Denmark as elsewhere for several years. What worried the conservative intellectuals (as well as staff members at the U.S. Embassy) was the harsh criticism of the United States that McCarthyism generated.[84] Looking at the reception of McCarthyism in the Danish press, we encounter an explicit rejection of the methods of McCarthy that is normally set within a strongly anticommunist discourse.

One of the fiercest critiques of McCarthyist America, published in the small, but influential liberal newspaper *Information,* was written by the literary critic Elsa Gress, who, thanks to an American grant, followed the phenomenon at first hand in 1952. In a scathing tone, she argued that the general notion of America as the land of the future was utterly wrong. America was dominated by medieval institutions and values, and "descendants of the Jeffersonian democracy, grandchildren of the Enlightenment and the French Revolution ironically become the victims of authorities that Europe is growing away from." The "medieval institutions" that undermined American democracy were "Big Business" and the churches. Two years later, she went even further and characterized McCarthyism as an expression of "the American form of Neofascism," warning that "the plague over America" might be worse than "the plague whose repercussions we still suffer from in Europe."[85] The editor of *Information,* Erik Seidenfaden, gave an utterly unflattering presentation of McCarthy's career and concluded by expressing the pious hope that somebody would shoot the senator.[86] In early 1953, the Grand Old Man of the liberal left, Poul Henningsen, compared "the purges" in the United States with those taking place in the Soviet Union, stating that those in America were "no less effective … even if the means might seem more humane."[87]

It is, however, crucial for our understanding of these criticisms that Gress, Seidenfaden, and Henningsen did not consider themselves anti-American. Quite the opposite: Seidenfaden stressed that his pro-American credentials were impeccable and that his criticism was rooted in a strong admiration of American political culture. Likewise, Gress characterized herself as a "Pro-American Anti-American." With his usual acumen, Poul Henningsen pinpointed the dilemma of Danish observers:

> The United States is two things that exist side by side—one thing we like and that enriches us and one thing we justly fear. Every time we talk about McCarthy it is probably necessary to add that there is another America, a land of culture from where we get modern literature, jazz, drama and film. Let us stress as strongly as possible that Hemingway, Chaplin, Armstrong, Arthur Miller—to mention just four names—constitute a decisive part of the image of America for us Europeans.[88]

To this Seidenfaden and Gress would probably have added the idea of the American liberal tradition. The central point here is that outside of the Communist camp, it is very hard to find diehard anti-Americans in Denmark. Instead, critics to the left, like Poul Henningsen, saw "two Americas." In politics, "good America" was the liberal Democrats; "bad America" the Republican right. In culture, "bad America" was the dominant middle-class conformism, materialism, and the commercialized popular culture, whereas "good America" was the authentic antiestablishment voices hailed by Henningsen.

After the demise of McCarthy, political criticism of America subsided (although at regular intervals the race issue was brought up as an example of the severe shortcomings of American politics and society). Cultural criticism continued, however. A constant theme in the writings of Poul Henningsen from the 1920s to the 1960s is that commercial interest and "real art" are like fire and water. Whenever commercial interests are dominant, "art" becomes conformist, bland, and socially conservative, and when commercial values dominate, people are reduced from democratic citizens to mere consumers. In the 1950s and 60s, America served as the main illustration of these assertions, and it is in this sense of the word that Poul Henningsen frequently warned against the "Americanization" of Danish culture and society. It is also clear, however, that much of the inspiration for Henningsen's criticism came from American intellectuals, and at one point he lamented that "we are turning into a caricature of the American industrial state, but without its eminent critics." [89]

It was quite typical that some of the strongest criticism of American popular culture was rooted in—American culture. Thus Haxthausen's tirades against the dangers of comics found most of its ammunition in the writings of the American psychiatrist Frederick Wertham (whose work, almost ironically from an anti-American perspective, was first introduced to Danish readers in *Readers Digest*).[90] In 1962, Ernst Bruun Olsen's musical *Teenagerlove*, a vicious satire of Americanized commercial popular culture, was the talk of the town among polite society in Copenhagen. At the same time, the score was written by Finn Savery, who listed Parker, Powell, and Gillespie as his main sources of inspiration.[91]

Anti-Americanism thus was clearly very selective. Yet, this selective anti-Americanism was beginning to retreat at the start of the 1960s just as John F. Kennedy was becoming an icon in Denmark.[92] The Kennedy administration included some of the liberal left's favorite Americans, such as John K. Galbraith, and the civil rights legislation passed by Kennedy's successor, Lyndon B. Johnson, was seen as a sign of an America correcting its "bad habits." Even the hard line against communism was hailed as a demonstration of strong political leadership. A prominent example can be found in a comment on the Tonkin Bay incident in the Social-Democratic daily, *Aktuelt:* "He [LBJ] took his decision with an admirable mixture of resource, diligence and mental strength.... It took both personal courage, sense of responsibility and self-confidence to reach such a decision in so little time."[93]

The tone changed dramatically over the next few years. Criticism of the Vietnam War grew rapidly and was the dominant tenor in the press coverage as of 1968 at the latest. When Danes celebrated the twenty-fifth anniversary of the liberation from German occupation, several commentators paralleled the situation of Europe under the yoke of Nazism with the present plight of the Vietnamese people.[94] By 1972, even the conservative *Berlingske Tidende* called on its readers to join the anti-American demonstrations. In the same year, the Social-Democratic Prime Minister Anker Jørgensen made a major diplomatic *faux pas* when he commented that personally he would have preferred George McGovern as the winner of the presidential elections.[95]

By stating his preference for McGovern, Jørgensen reproduced the notion of the "two Americas" we saw earlier. The vast majority of criticism of U.S. conduct in East Asia was a criticism not of the United States as such but of a United States gone wrong.

This also is true of the key protagonists in the antiwar movement among college students. They too were very selective in their anti-Americanism. Many of the participants in the antiwar demonstrations wore blue jeans and t-shirts. They watched such films as *Dr. Strangelove, Bonnie and Clyde, Soldier Blue*, and from the middle of the 1970s onward, the growing number of American films dealing with the Vietnam War. American counterculture symbols were taken in together with those of classical revolutionaries. Thus, in 1967, an advertisement in the underground magazine *Love* offered posters of Humphrey Bogart, Marlon Brando, Jean Harlow, and Allen Ginsberg side by side with Mao Zedong and Karl Marx.[96] In the concert halls of Copenhagen, radicals enjoyed Jefferson Airplane, the Doors, the Mothers of Invention, Jimi Hendrix, Country Joe MacDonald, and CSNY, to mention some of the main rock attractions of 1969/70. If the preeminent icon, Bob Dylan, was not readily available after 1966, the inspiration from Dylan is almost painfully clear on the first original Danish rock album, recorded by the Steppeulvene in 1967. That the album was called *Hip* was no coincidence. By 1970, the "hip" and "politically engaged" part of Danish youth culture was, to a high degree, simply a copy of the American counterculture. A crucial part of the import was, of course, strong criticism of "official America" and the "materialism" and "conformity" of mainstream American culture.[97] American visitors rooted in the counterculture might have preferred Budweiser to Tuborg or Carlsberg and pot to the Middle Eastern hashish that was to become the dominant "soft" drug in Denmark. This aside, they would have felt very much at home.

Conclusion

American-Danish cultural encounters can be divided into successive phases. In the interwar years, Denmark witnessed the first invasion of American popular culture while intellectuals generally spoke critically of America and Americanization. In the next phase, from about 1945 to 1960, Denmark entered the American sphere in politics and economics, and as a consequence the position of the intellectuals vis-à-vis the United States became much more complex. To most Danes, however, America was synonymous with a good material life. Dollar shortages also meant that it was a quite distant utopia, and the Americanization of the first postwar decades, was to a high degree, one of the imagination. Danish firms and cultural workers successfully catered to this trend with a wide array of *ersatz* American products, from refrigerators to candy bars and homegrown pop stars. In this period the impact of America was also lessened by the high prestige of the United Kingdom. Until the mid 1950s, Danish politicians tried to use Britain as a buffer against American influence, and culturally, British writers and artists unwittingly performed the same role. In the sphere of high culture, the American avant-garde influenced the young generation of Danish writers, and contemporary jazz was lauded as fitting music for urban modernity. Meanwhile, many intellectuals were highly critical of American commercial "popular" culture, and McCarthyism was criticized by influential liberal and left-wing commentators.

The third phase of American-Danish encounters started in the early 1960s. By then, Denmark was finally entering the era of affluence that made American goods affordable for consumers from both the middle and working classes. Although Elvis Presley gained a following in Denmark, the early and middle 1960s saw Danish youth culture being solidly dominated by imports from Swinging London. Only in the late 1960s did American influence become strong, to a high degree through the import of the American counterculture in its entirety, including its outspoken criticism of "official America." In the years following the late 1960s, anti-Americanism too was in vogue, both in popular and elite culture.

The fourth, current phase started in the late 1970s. If the earlier periods had witnessed a progressive Americanization of lifestyle and popular culture, it is also important to stress the limits of the process. First, "Americanization" was part of a broader process of internationalization: to give just one example, in the 1970s Danish pop music still owed much more to German *schlager* than to American popular music. Second, one should not overestimate the penetration of the American lifestyle. The favorite Danish fast food may have been the *hot dog*, but the Danish version (topped with mustard, ketchup, pickles, gherkins, and onions both roasted and raw) was a far cry from the American original. Most families had a barbecue (or rather a *grill*) but seldom used it. The favorite food of most Danes continued to be the traditional heavy dishes originating in the rural culture that was only slowly dying in the 1950s and 1960s, and when pizza arrived in Denmark around 1970, it was the Italian version. Although many American series were shown on the single Danish television channel, local productions were by far the most popular, while British series like "The Forsyte Saga," "A Family at War," and "Upstairs, Downstairs" attracted far more viewers than American shows. According to the American immigrant Ellen Bick Meier, the Denmark she encountered in the late 1960s was a far cry from New York.

However, for Bick Meier, Denmark in the late 1980s was much less of a foreign country. In an article published in the widely read *Samvirke,* she lamented the onslaught of American commercial culture and begged her Danish readers to fight it.[98] However, her appeal fell on deaf ears. By the late 1980s, the Danes no longer "said 'Jolly' to their Cola," to quote a popular advertisement slogan from the 1960s. They had switched to Pepsi and Coke. The *hot dog* stands were pressured by the growing number of McDonald's and Burger Kings (first established in Denmark in 1979), and even up-and-coming young Conservatives were using Bruce Springsteen's "Born in the USA" as an anthem.[99] The trend continued at ever increasing speed in the 1990s. If the Danes have become increasingly reluctant Europeans over the last decade or so, we have in the same period almost turned into enthusiastic Americans.

In this, Denmark is simply following the global trend of economic and cultural globalization. However, two local developments were also important. First, in the early 1980s the left-wing hegemony in the politicized youth culture came to an end. Danish youth turned to the right with a vengeance, and in the youth organizations of the Liberal and Conservative parties, official America, with its Reaganite rhetoric of anticommunism and the Free Market gospel, was idolized. Second, the broadcasting monopoly of the Danish State

Radio came to an end. In 1988, commercial radio was introduced and a second public service television channel was launched. Cable TV—and thus foreign television channels—became available to more and more Danish households from 1985 on, and in the early 1990s commercial television channels began to be established. This liberalization of the airwaves has, in Denmark as elsewhere, led to a massive influx of American programs, from soap operas to talk shows, and even local productions seem to be mere copies of American originals. If the old radical Poul Henningsen, who criticized the Americanization of the State Radio in the 1950s, had been alive, he would have been outraged.

In this process anti-Americanism has also withered. Of course, criticism of the aggressive American foreign policy under the Bush administration has been raised, often echoing the notion of the "two Americas" discussed above. But criticism of the war in Iraq in 2003/04 focused much more on the Danish government's decision to join the "coalition of the willing." At a much more innocent level, some sorts of anti-Americanism still pop up once in a while. When McDonald's sued a *hot dog* stand owner for naming his stand "McAllan," Danes were jubilant when the High Court ruled against the Americans in 1996. And when Disney, which owns the name Tarzan, decreed that the beloved hero of the children's book *Gummi-Tarzan* in the future must be known only as "Gummi-T," we were appalled.[100] However, nobody suggested that the proper response to this example of blatant American cultural imperialism would be a boycott of Disney products. The criticism of McDonald and Disney was ironic, not political. And after all, we would certainly hate to miss the traditional Disney Christmas Show on national public service television.

Notes

1. The examples of American impact on the Danish language have been found in *Ordbog over det danske Sprog*, 28 vols. (Copenhagen: LFL's Bladfon, 1919–1950), and in the archive of Dansk Sprognævn in Copenhagen. For American popular culture in Denmark, see Klaus Bruhn Jensen, ed., *Dansk Mediehistorie*, vol. 2 (Copenhagen: Samleren, 1997), 308–24; for intellectual anti-Americanism, see Hans Hertel, "Armstrong, Bogart, Churchill … Penguin: The Danish Turn to Anglo-American Cultural Values from the 1920s to the 1950s," in Jørgen Sevaldsen et al., eds, *Britain and Denmark. Political, Economic and Cultural Relations in the 19th and 20th Century* (Copenhagen: Museum Tusculanum Press, 2003), 436–38. The retired nurse quoted is Ms. Astrid Christensen-Dalsgaard.
2. Harald Engberg, *Filmen* (Copenhagen: Ferlaget Fremad, 1939), 181, 187.

3. Poul Meyer, quoted in Erik Wiedemann, *Jazz i Danmark—i tyverne, tredvierne og fyrrerne*, vol. 1 (Copenhagen: Gyldendal, 1982), 239.
4. Radio talk on Danish State Radio, 18 January 1939, reprinted in Harald Nielsen, *Uden Traad—og med! Bidrag til Kulturforsvarets Historie* (Copenhagen: Aschehoug dansk forlag, 1941), 37, 41–42.
5. Rasmus Mariager, *I tillid og varm sympati: Dansk-britiske forbindelser og USA 1945–1950–1955* (unpublished Ph.D. diss., University of Copenhagen, 2003).
6. Poul Villaume, *Allieret med forbehold: Danmark: NATO og den kolde krig: En studie i dansk sikkerhedspolitik 1949–1961* (Copenhagen: Eirene, 1995).
7. Embassy Chp. to Dep. State, "USIS country plan—Denmark, 511.59/6-3053," desp. 1239, 30 June 1953, Record Group 59 (State Department), National Archives, Washington, D.C.
8. Embassy Chp. To Dep. State, "Revised Joint USIE/MSA Country Plan for Denmark," 511.56/4-1552, desp. 866, 15 April 1952, Record Group 59 (State Department), National Archives, Washington, D.C. See also Villaume, *Allieret med forbehold*, 772, 783–4, 808–9.
9. Quote from Ole Bech-Petersen, *Encounters: Danish Literary Travel in the United States* (unpublished Ph.D. diss., University of Southern Denmark, 2000), 220.
10. Embassy Chp. to Dep. State, "Revised draft of USIA Country Paper for Denmark," 511.59/5-250, desp. 452, 2 May 1950, Record Group 59 (State Department), National Archives, Washington, D.C.
11. Villaume, *Allieret med forbehold*, 789–90.
12. Bech-Petersen, *Encounters*, 214–17.
13. The following case is based on material in Archive of the Danish Labour Movement (Arbejderbevægelsens Erhvervsråd, box 18, "Amerikarejsen. Efteråret 1950," Copenhagen) and Bech-Petersen, *Encounters*, 220–27.
14. Paldam had when leaving been denied a visa for the United States because it turned out he had been a member of a Communist youth organization in the 1930s. ECA in Copenhagen had to interfere to get him into the United States. See *Note of August 25 1949*, Records of the officer of British Commonwealth and Nothern European Affairs, Subject files 1941–53, box 12, Lot Files, Record Group 59 (State Department), National Archives, Washington, D.C.
15. Embassy Chp. to Dep. State, "Revised draft of USIE Country Paper for Denmark," 511.59/5-250, desp. 452, 2 May 1950, Record Group 59 (State Department), National Archives, Washington, D.C.
16. A. F. Madsen, *Anker* (Copenhagen: Gyldendal, 1999), 141–42.
17. Embassy Chp. to Dep. State, "Survey of USIS/MSA Press Features in 1952," 511.59/2-253, desp. 764, 2 February 1953, Record Group 59 (State Department), National Archives, Washington, D.C.
18. Villaume, *Allieret med forbehold*, 790–92.
19. Embassy Chp. to Dep. State, "USIS Semi-Annual Evaluation Report," 511.59/2-2553, desp. 845, 25 February 1953, Record Group 59 (State Department), National Archives, Washington, D.C.
20. Embassy Chp. to Dep. State, "USIS Semi-Annual Evaluation Report," 511.59/2-2553, desp. 845, 25 February 1953, Record Group 59 (State Department), National Archives, Washington, D.C.
21. Correspondence concerning publications, "Orr, Charles A, udtalelser om 'Stalins slavelejre,'" Fremad Publishers, *Archive of the Danish Labour Movement*. Only 2,000 of the 50,000 books were to be sold on market terms. The rest were handed out for free.

22. Embassy Chp. to Dep. State, "USIS Semi-Annual Evaluation Report," 511.59/2-2553, desp. 845, 25 February 1953, Record Group 59 (State Department), National Archives, Washington, D.C.

23. The following history on the Danish branch of the Congress for Cultural Freedom is based on Ingeborg Philipsen, "Selskabet for Kultur og Frihed: Congress for Cultural Freedom i Danmark 1953–60," *Kritik* 35, no. 158 (2002): 38–51 and Hans Christian Hertel, *Vor tids Reitzel: En pionerforlægger og hans samtid 1949–1999* (Copenhagen: Reitzels, 1999).

24. Hertel, *Vor tids Reitzel*, 17–27.

25. Erik Wiedemann, "Amerikansk roman og novelle efter 1945," in Sven Møller Kristensen, ed., *Fremmed litteratur i det 20. århundrede*, vol. 3 (Copenhagen: GAD, 1968), 493–506, quotes from p. 493.

26. See *Hvem Hvad Hvor: Politikens Årbog 1951* (Copenhagen: Politikens, 1951), 395–98.

27. *Information*, 16 March 1950. See also the reviews in *Politiken*, 16 March 1950, and *Social-Demokraten*, 17 March 1950, and in the journal of the folk high school movement, *Højskolebladet*, 1950, 266–67.

28. Cf. the list of "the greatest successes and failures" of Danish theater, 1949–54, printed in *Hvem Hvad Hvor*, 376. For *The Crucible*, see ibid., 376 and Felix Nørgaard et al., eds., *Radioteater-Musik-TV teater: De musiske udsendelser i DR 1925-1975*, vol. 1 (Copenhagen: Nyt Nordisk Forlag, 1975), 91.

29. Cf. Jens-Emil Nielsen, *Ung i 50'erne* (Frederiksberg: Bogforlaget Her&Nu, 2002), 110–14.

30. See C. Kold Thomsen, *Frihedens hylen: En bog om den amerikanske beat-generation* (unpublished manuscript, Centre for American Studies, University of Southern Denmark, 2003), 29–32.

31. Our argument is not that American avant-garde literature gained a dominant position in intellectual circles. In the 1950s and 60s, the influence of both French existentialism and the British "Angry Young Men" was probably much greater. Thus in his 1968 chapter on American prose, Wiedemann commented that French, German, and English literature had "more eloquent advocates" than American.

32. Sven Møller Kristensen, *Hvad Jazz er* (Copenhagen: Munksgaard, 1938); quoted in Wiedemann, *Jazz i Danmark*, vol. 1, 236–37.

33. Erik Wiedemann, "Bliver også jazzen uforståelig," *Information*, 21 February 1952.

34. The pretense of covering pop music was dropped in 1958, and in 1959 the journal added the fitting subtitle "Journal for Jazz Music."

35. Cf. the biased account of jazz in Danish State Radio (and television) in *Den hemmelige Krystal—en bog om radiojazzgruppen* (Aarhus: Elkaer og Hansen, 2003), written by one of its key protagonists, Erik Moseholm.

36. The five pictures that received both the Oscar and the Bodil were *The Best Years of Our Life, All about Eve, On the Waterfront, Marty*, and *Midnight Cowboy*. If we compare the Danish awards with the Golden Globe Awards instead, we find a slightly bigger overlap: seven films that were awarded Golden Globes also received the Bodil in this period. The information on the awards was found at http://www.filmkritik.dk; http://www.oscars.org and http://hfpa.org (all last accessed: 3 March 2005).

37. Cf. *Lovtidende for Kongeriget Danmark* (Copenhagen: Schultz, 1935), vol. A, 128.

38. *Lovtidende for kongeriget Danmark*, 1953, vol. A, 390.

39. *Det nye Gymnasium. Betænkning afgivet af det af undervisningsministeriet nedsatte læseplansudvalg for gymnasiet*, Report no. 1043 (Copenhagen: Statens Trykningskontor, 1960), 5.

40. Ibid., 36.

41. Ibid., 52.

42. Ibid., 66.

43. "Bekendtgørelse om undervisningen i gymnasiet og om fordringerne ved og eksamensop-givelserne til studentereksamen, par. 5: Engelsk," in *Lovtidende for kongeriget Danmark,* 1971, vol. A, 826–28.

44. Søren Toft Hansen, *Rationaliseringsdebatten i Danmark 1918–1947: Industriledelse, Pro-duktivitet og Social Fred. Jern- og Metalsektoren som eksempel* (unpublished Ph.D. diss., University of Ålborg, 2001), 320–442.

45. *Filmjournalen* (January 1963) 2; Peter Knoop Christensen, ed., *USA og os: En antologi om det danske samfunds påvirkning af impulser fra USA efter 1945* (Herning: Systime, 1984), 99.

46. Dansk Sprognævn Collection: "Selvbetjening," Copenhagen.

47. Embassy Chp. to Dep. State, "USIS Semi-Annual Evaluation Report," 511.59/2-2553, desp. 845, 25 February 1953, Record Group 59 (State Department), National Archives, Washington, D.C.

48. E.-M. Boyhus, "Mad og drikke," in George Nelleman, ed., *Dagligliv i Danmark i vor tid,* vol. 1 (Copenhagen: Nyt Nordisk Forlag A. Busck, 1988), 475–98.

49. *Samvirke* 1953, quoted in Christensen, *USA og os,* 38.

50. B. Poulsen, *Grill-mad: Barbecue og El-grill* (Copenhagen: Politikens Forlag, 1957).

51. *Politikens Hobbybog* (Copenhagen: Politikens Forlag, 1946). The book was extended dur-ing the 1950s (in 1955 it was a three volume book) and published in several editions.

52. V. Bertram, *Basketball* (Copenhagen, 1955), 11.

53. A.N. Hvidt, *Camping og friluftsliv* (Copenhagen: Politikens Forlag, 1953). However, to a high degree camping became adapted to established Danish habits. Many caravans were located more or less permanently in established camps that in many ways came to resem-ble the established tradition of allotments.

54. A. de Waal, ed., *Tæring eller Næring: 1950'erne i Danmark* (Copenhagen: Gyldendal, 1987), 58–60; Jørgen O. Bjerregaard, "Toms fylder 75 år," *Byhornet* 3 (1999): 30–36.

55. Our own calculations on the basis of National Trading Accounts 1945–1985, which also show huge imports of records from Germany and Holland after 1958 that might also consist partly of American music.

56. Peter Knoop Christensen, ed., *Amerikaniseringen af det danske kulturliv i perioden 1945–1958* (Ålborg: Ålborg University Press, 1983), 100–136.

57. See a more detailed analysis in ibid., 132–36.

58. Ibid., 154–78; Hans Hertel, "Kulturens kolde krig: Polarisering, antikommunisme og antiamerikanisme i dansk kulturliv 1946–1960," *Kritik* 35, no. 158 (2002): 9–23; Bruhn Jensen, *Dansk mediehistorie* 2, 248–51.

59. Knoop Christensen, *Amerikaniseringen af det danske kulturliv,* 137–151; Bruhn Jensen, *Dansk mediehistorie,* vol. 2, 175–80, 253–55.

60. Figure, of second half of 2003, from Dansk oplagskontrol [Danish Circulation Control]: www.do.dk (last accessed: 3 March 2005).

61. *Hvem Hvad Hvor Politikens Aarbog 1946* (Copenhagen: Politikens Forlag, 1946), 414–18.

62. Jens Ulff-Møller, "Hollywoods generobring af det danske marked efter 2. Verdenskrig," *Sekvens: Årbog for Film og Medievidenskab* (2000): 243–84.

63. Bruhn Jensen, *Dansk Mediehistorie,* vol. 2, 238–40.

64. See the advertisements in *Filmjournalen,* 1958.

65. Peder Bundgaard, *Lykkens Pamfil* (Copenhagen: Borgen, 1998); Niels W. Jacobsen, et al., *Dansk Rock'n'roll—anderumper, ekstase og opposition* (Ålborg: Mjølner, 1980).

66. *Filmjournalen,* 1958, no. 2.

67. C. Rønn Larsen, "Above All, It's Because He's British. Tommy Steele and the Notion of 'Englishness' as Mediator of Rock'n'Roll," in Sevaldsen et al., *Britain and Denmark,* 493–510.

68. Henrik Nørgaard, *Pirater i æteren: Radio Mercur og Danmarks kommercielle radio: Dansk Reklameradio fra Øresund 1958–1962* (Odense: Syddansk Universitetsforlag, 2003).

69. "Intet er, som det var—og dog." Feature in *Jyllandsposten,* 21 August 2003.

70. Dansk Sprognævn collection, "Cowboybusker," Copenhagen; Karl Christian Lammers to the authors.

71. *Information,* 12 June 1976. According to the survey, less than 3 percent of young people between 12 and 24 years of age had *not* owned a pair of blue jeans.

72. *Politiken,* 23 January 1967.

73. Dansk Sprognævn collection, "Mælkepop," Copenhagen.

74. Speech at the British Import Unions lunch, 11 April 1949. Quoted in Mariager, *I tillid og varm sympati,* 255. The underlining is from the original speech manuscript.

75. Cf. L. Dalgas Jensen, "Denmark and the Marshall Plan, 1947–48: The Decision to Participate," *Scandinavian Journal of History* 14 (1989): 57–83; Nikolaj Petersen, "Atlantpaten eller Norden? Den danske alliancebeslutning 1949," in Carsten Due-Nielsen, ed., *Danmark, NATO og Norden* (Copenhagen: Jurist- og økonomforbundets forlag, 1991), 17–41.

76. See "Our Ameri-Danish Language," in *Ålborg Stiftitidende,* 11 October 1951. The neologism is more elegant in Danish where American is "amerikansk." For more examples, see Henrik Galberg Jacobsen, *Dansk Sprogrøgtslitteratur 1900–1955,* (Copenhagen: Dansk Sprognævns Skrifter, 1974), and J. Lund, "Danskerne og deres sprog 1945–1990: Kritik og tolerance," in Ole Feldbæk, ed., *Dansk Identitetshistorie,* vol. 4 (Copenhagen: Reitzel, 1992), 452–56.

77. See Tørk Haxthausen, *Opdragelse til terror* (Copenhagen: Forlaget Fermad, 1955). For a more representative intervention that also offers a good contemporary summary of the debate, see C. Winther, "Børnene og den 'kulørte' litteratur," *Folkeskolen* (1954): 854–60, 886–91, and 922–24.

78. Cf. the government report *Betænkning afgivet af det af Undervisningsministeriet under 27 januar 1955 nedsatte udvalg vedrørende børns og unges læsning.* Betænkning nr. 260 (Copenhagen 1960).

79. Vagn Jensen, *Stene for brød: de kulørte hefters problem* (Copenhagen: Gad, 1961).

80. Embassy Chp. to Dep. State, May 2 1950, "Revised draft of USIE Country Paper for Denmark," 511.59/5-250, Record Group 59 (State Department), National Archives, Washington, D.C.

81. See T. Hansen, "Den danske presse og McCarthy," in Klaus Petersen and Nils Arne Sørensen, eds., *Den kolde krig på hjemmefronten,* (Odense: Syddansk University Press, forthcoming) and Carl Madsen, *Vi skrev loven* (Copenhagen: Stig Vendelkær, 1968), 193 and passim.

82. See N. A. Sørensen, "Danmarkshistoriens vigtigste parentes," in Joachim Lund, ed., *Partier under pres* (Copenhagen: Gyldendal, 2003), 352–54.

83. T. M. Terkelsen, "'Ami go home'—En studie i Anti-Amerikanisme," *Det danske Magasin* 1, no. 1 (1953): 12–18.

84. For the assessment of Embassy officials, see Mariager, *I tillid og varm sympati,* 340.

85. E. Gress, "Det Middelalderlige Amerika," *Information,* 12 February 1952, and idem, "Massehysteri 1692 og nu," *Dialog* (April 1954): 1–4.

86. E. Seidenfaden, "McCarthyismen, Amerika og os," *Fremtiden* 10 (1953): 14–15, 18–24.

87. P. Henningsen, "Rejs dig menneske," *Social-Demokraten,* 2 January 1953.

88. P. Henningsen, "Amerikas for- og bagside," *Social-Demokraten,* 22 December 1954.

89. P. Henningsen, "Hvad er det" (1965), reprinted in idem, *Kulturkritik,* vol. 4: 1956–1967 (Copenhagen: Rhodos, 1973), 165–72.

90. See Frederic Wertham, "Atompigen & Co," *Det Bedste* (1948): 45–48.

91. Ernst Bruun Olsen, *Teenagerlove* (Copenhagen: Gyldendal, 1962). For Finn Savery, see the interview in *Filmjournalen* 20 (1963): 10–11.

92. A telling example is *John F. Kennedy: 22. November 1965,* a collection of commemorative prose and poetry published by the Danmark Amerika Fonden on the second anniversary of his assassination. Among the contributors was Klaus Rifbjerg, the archetypal left-leaning radical. All the contributions had previously been printed in Danish newspapers spanning the entire the political landscape—with the exception of the Communists.

93. *Aktuelt,* 15 August 1964.

94. Cf. N. A. Sørensen, "En traditions etablering og forfald," *Den jyske Historiker* 71 (1995): 120–21.

95. Jørgensen's comment is quoted in *Avisårbogen 1972* (Copenhagen: GAD, 1973), 160.

96. Advertisement in *Love* (1967–68), nos. 1–3.

97. The antiwar movement in Denmark has been analyzed from a narrow political perspective by Søren Hein Rasmussen in his book *Søre Alliancer: Politiske bevægelser i efterkrigstidens Danmark* (Odense: Odense Universitetsforlag, 1997). We still have no substantial works on the Danish counterculture as such. So far, the best book available is Bente Hansen, ed., *Dengang i tresserne* (Copenhagen: Information, 1976).

98. E. Bick Meier, "Made in the USA," *Samvirke* 60, no. 9 (1987): 15–17.

99. In an interview in "Søndagsmagasinet," *DR1,* broadcast 24 August 2003, Brian Mikkelsen, Denmark's Conservative Minister for Culture, admitted that only much later did he find out that Springsteen's vision of the United States differed dramatically from his own. To his credit it should be added that he still considers "Born in the USA" his favorite song.

100. See "McAllan flygter fra Danmark," *Ekstra Bladet,* 8 October 1998, and "Disney tvinger Gummi Tarzan i knæ," *B.T.,* 29 August 2003.

TWO SIDES OF THE COIN:
THE AMERICANIZATION OF AUSTRIA
AND AUSTRIAN ANTI-AMERICANISM

◆ ◆ ◆

Günter Bischof

*"Yet all this said, it remains true that for the major thinkers who
have made America an object of sustained attention and
reflection, few have viewed American in a positive light."*[1]

Introduction

It is a given among those who study the projection and presence of America
in the world that ever since its discovery America has produced European
projections—images of paradise and barbarian outpost. The corresponding
European views of America as fact and as fiction, utopia and dystopia, of
Traum and *Alptraum*, have always been intimately related. "Thousands have
joined in the European game of deploring, baiting, or praising America over
the last two centuries," noted C. Van Woodward in his authoritative essay
The Old World's New World, yet in the end tended "to influence and repeat
each other" and "perpetuate stereotypes."[2] The people of Austria have not
been different in this regard—Americanization is the twin brother of anti-
Americanism there also, and too much of one perpetuates the other.

Those who have studied European images of America (more precisely
since the foundation of the Republic the United States of America) sooner or
later arrive at the *"German"* Romantics of the old-regime *"Vormärz"* period,
who have shaped ambivalent images of the fledgling United States more than
any other group. Both Nikolaus Lenau in the early 1830s—and before him

---

Notes for this section begin on page 173.

Karl Postl, *alias* Charles Sealsfield, in the late 1820s[3]—and these poets came to America in search of pristine nature and "noble savages." What they discovered instead on the "frontier" were forests cut down and native Americans murdered or chased westward. They found not music or poetry but a complete absence of culture. The Romantics, with their backward-looking ideal of a harmonious society striving for natural beauty, found a soulless new world of shocking materialism and avarice, base utilitarianism, and technological advancement. Lenau quickly wearied of the U.S. and came home to decry America as a soulless material society totally devoid of culture. Based on Lenau's writings and myths, along with the stereotypes accumulating in the growing travel literature, Ferdinand Kürnberger "paraphrased" Lenau in his Americaphobe novel *Der Amerika-Müde* (1855) without ever having visited the U.S. It is an early indictment of American capitalism as dominated by swindlers and worshippers of mammon and an alienating stock exchange. Earlier, Johann Georg Hülsemann (1823) had analyzed American democracy as a profound threat to the monarchical and aristocratic order of things in Europe. Democracy and liberalism needed to be stopped at the gates of Europe.[4]

In his *America in the Eyes of the Germans,* Dan Diner indicts Kürnberger's novel in turn as a "hyper-German and racist anti-American polemic," indicating the growing threat of American decadence and degeneration Europeans feared in mid-century and setting the tone of German anti-Americanism for decades to come. Diner takes Lenau, Hülsemann, and Kürnberger as the most prominent examples of "German" Romantics who produced "lasting anti-American images and metaphors."[5] The problem with Diner is that as a point of fact, all three hailed from the Austrian empire of Prince Metternich's days, Lenau born in the Banat and later to live in Vienna, Hülsemann, born in Hanover though he later became Austria's longtime diplomatic representative in Washington (1838 to 1863), and Kürnberger from Vienna too (Sealsfield, not mentioned by Diner, was from Southern Moravia). What Diner lambasts as the "German" view of America, strictly speaking, is a Central European "Austrian" view.[6]

These nineteenth-century "Austrian" observers, then, were at the forefront in producing the abiding images of America as an uncivilized and crass materialistic society devoid of culture. Political scientist James W. Caesar, in fact, posits in the "German" romantics an important transition from the "degeneracy thesis" of the eighteenth century (where decay in America was tied to physical forces) to a nineteenth-century "idea of disfigurement" (where deformation is attributed to America's political principles and culture).[7] This may be the most important Austrian contribution to European anti-Americanism, since the German Romantics' views diffused beyond Central Europe.

At the end of the nineteenth century an even more prominent Austrian visitor to the United States returned to Vienna with similar images of urban wasteland and social degeneration and corruption. The Habsburg Crown Prince, Archduke Francis Ferdinand (yes, the one assassinated in Sarajevo in 1914), went on a trip around the world in 1892/93 (arranged by the British travel bureau of Thomas Cook). He also visited Canada and the United States for a few weeks in the fall of 1893. Embarking on the *Empress of China* in Yokohama, Japan, to cross the Pacific, the crown prince arrived in Vancouver on 9 September. He went on a sightseeing and hunting tour through the Canadian Rockies and entered the Pacific Northwest of the United States. He visited Yellowstone Park, saw Salt Lake City and Colorado Springs, attended the famous World Exposition in Chicago and Niagara Falls, and departed from New York back to Europe on 7 October 1893.

Not being on an official mission, he acted like a common tourist and regularly jotted down his impressions of America in his diary. Like many an European itinerant, the archduke was impressed by the vast country and the rugged nature of the land (previously only imagined as the home of the trappers and Indians he was familiar with from children's books) but detested the raw and bustling urban landscape and uncouth American society. Francis Ferdinand was not opposed to progress,[8] but he seems to have detested the social consequences that too much rapid progress had produced in America. Yellowstone's beauty and colors left a deep impression on him, yet the wholesale destruction of millions of trees in the West and the missing preservation of forests and natural resources bothered him immensely. Unlike many an educated visitor from the Habsburg monarchy, he had little interest in the industrialization of America, which was pioneering mass production at the time, and was less than impressed by modern mass transport (railways, electric streetcars, and trolleys) and the electrification of America, singling out telephone poles as a perennial eyesore in the American landscape.

In his uncensored diary entries Franz Ferdinand comes across as a haughty, unimaginative, unimpressionable petty bourgeois brimming with traditional European resentments and stereotypes (indeed, Kürnberger's *Der Amerika-Müde* proclaimed that "America *is* a prejudice").[9] Like any traditional Austrian, what he missed above all was *"Gemütlichkeit"* or coziness. Instead he found "cold" American cities full of citizens "in a hurry." To the crown prince all the North American cities looked the same in their lack of taste (*"Geschmacklosigkeit"*). Like so many Legos™ (*"Kinderbaukästen"*) the houses were painted red and green. Like the Hungarian towns of Kecskemet and Szegedin in his own empire, the streets of Spokane, Washington, were full of dirt. Butte City, Idaho, topped Spokane in tastelessness. The houses, sporting ugly advertisements, looked like so many gypsy carts. The town was full of millionaires who amassed wealth but did not allow themselves any conveniences. Only the gardens and trees of Salt Lake City, laid out like an orderly chessboard, managed to garner a bit of praise from the noble diarist. He only spent a few hours at the Chicago World Exposition, being appalled at the "lack of distinguished visitors." Only when the white buildings of the exposition were electrified at night ("White City") was the archduke's interest aroused. In New York City the homesick Francis Ferdinand spent only a few hours being taken to lunch at the fabulous Delmonico's restaurant. He preferred the few hours he then passed on a farm across the river in New Jersey, indulging his bucolic, agricultural interests.

In his final observations, jotted down on his way home across the Atlantic, Francis Ferdinand conceded that the natural beauty of the North American continent, along with the hard work and the technological progress of its people, could not be denied. But he quickly added that the unattractive customs of the inhabitants, along with the absence of "*Gemütlichkeit*" and the higher gifts of poetry, which ran in the bloodstream of Europeans, made the Americans as uncivilized as the Papua New Guineans, whom he had also visited.[10]

Sigmund Freud may be the best-known anti-American Austrian. To his famous statement that America is a "gigantic mistake" can be added many other such uncharitably prejudiced and traditional European bourgeois stereotypes: he saw the Americans as either "saint or moneygrabber"; America as the "anti-Paradise"; the U.S. as "Dollaria," a land governed by the almighty dollar—"what is the use of Americans, if they bring no money?"; Americans as having "unhappily wedded materialism to conformity"; American existence as marked by "haste." Freud feared Americans' "prudery" when traveling to the U.S. and noted that they had "no time for libido." He blamed his trip to the U.S. in the fall of 1909 and bad American food for his dyspepsia and colitis, displacing his rage about these ailments "onto a single convenient target," as his biographer Peter Gay has observed, adding "he never ceased calling them bad names."

Freud's clichés were the projections of nineteenth-century travelers and the traditional views of the educated European classes, and their anti-Americanism was "not really about America at all," as his faithful pupil Ernest Jones remarked. Gay correctly concludes that such condescending pronouncements had been uttered by "cultivated Europeans" for years and adds: "And these in turn were largely echoing the views of their fathers and grandfathers who had been projecting on the Americans certain vices, some of them real and more of them trumped, for a century. It had long been a social game to decry Americans' craze for equality, their no less pronounced craze for the new, and their materialism." Gay wonders how the radical antibourgeois Freud (when it came to sexuality) could display such a musty bourgeois "mixture of tendentious observation and unmitigated cultural arrogance."[11]

Archduke Francis Ferdinand may have been handicapped in his perception of the new land by the traditional and class-conscious "mental map" of European high aristocracy. His observations, however, are quite representative of the longstanding traditional Austrian—which is to say, European—stereotypes about America. They are mirrored in the impressions that one Yankee blueblood (who felt like an American natural aristocrat) had imparted in regular letters to his wife at home twenty years earlier.

In 1873 the Commonwealth of Massachusetts sent Charles Francis Adams, Jr., scion of a family that had produced two American presidents, as head of the state's commission to the Universal Exposition in Vienna. Adams' prejudice easily matched the Austrian archduke's. He was fully convinced of his American "superiority and exceptionalness" (Mayer) vis-à-vis the Viennese. He did not speak German, had "neither an eye for cultural attractions, nor an ear" (Mayer), and had little that was positive to say about the Viennese: "it is, indeed, a city of Jews,—regular German Jews,—and they charge & cheat out of all moderation" (the valet he hired he denounced as "a Hebrew dog"). Himself a major general in the Army of the Republic during the American Civil War, he was impressed by the uniforms sported by the Austrian military and aristocracy and asked his wife to send him his so he would be admitted to the highest circles of Viennese society. He hated not being at the center of attention and deemed it "detestable" to "be in a gay place like this and be one of the third or fourth cut." Like Francis Ferdinand in Chicago, he was not much impressed by the Vienna Exposition, and like the archduke, Adams ignored much of the social and economic dynamics of Austria-Hungary (which was going through a financial meltdown that sparked a great depression in Europe). Adams delighted in the sight of the Tyrolese Alps, just as Francis Ferdinand would later cherish the wild Rockies. "Fresh from the most beautiful mountain scenery in Europe," he detested the Danube capital more than ever after his return. On another trip to Hungary he described the country between Lake Balaton and Graz as "level and not picturesque,—the civilization is low and almost barbarous ... society is made up of a very stiff and proud nobility and of peasantry," adding a sharp barb against his countrymen: "living very much like the people in the South before the civil war."[12]

Here we have it—mirror-image, class-driven views of America and Europe by leading aristocratic members of their respective societies, each ending in damning verdicts that the other lacked "civilization." Both the archduke and the Yankee blueblood are unwilling to abandon their traditional mental maps and open their eyes to probe more deeply. Both tend to see the worst in the places they observe with their blinkered eyes and fail to understand the larger context of these societies (both America and Austria-Hungary were going through extraordinary spurts of industrialization and urbanization, inching towards modernity), or to give "new America" or "old Europe" the benefit of the doubt. Both end up indicting the places they observe and thus adding to the rich repertoires of European "anti-Americanism" and American "anti-Europeanism." While the aristocrats clung to the traditions that guaranteed them their high place in society, the masses of European emigrants could not wait to see the New World for themselves during the nineteenth century; nor did those who stayed on the old continent hesitate to indulge in "Americanization" in the twentieth. Richard Kuisel is surely correct when positing that "as historians or tourists we may prefer the old to the new and protest against the loss of 'tradition,' but those receiving Americanization usually seem to delight in it."[13]

The Americanization of Austria

In the Americanization of what today constitutes Austria, a growing number of personal visits to the United States and the aggressive American occupation regime after World War II played crucial roles in familiarizing Austrians with the U.S. and its political, economic, and cultural system ("Americanism").

The Americanization of Austria began after World War I, yet the subtle roots of it go back into the late nineteenth century, when Austrian industrialists and engineers visited the United States, as did Francis Ferdinand, to attend world expositions in the U.S. (Philadelphia 1876, Chicago 1893, St. Louis 1904). Unlike the condescending successor to the ancient Habsburg throne, they came to America to study mass production methods and were deeply impressed with American machinery and advanced technology. Some came with the intention of spying on American industrial techniques. The iron and steel tycoon Karl Wittgenstein ran away to America for a couple years after the U.S. Civil War and returned twice for intense study tours of American production methods developed during the "Gilded Age." Wittgenstein's critics blamed his reckless business practices on American-style "capitalism." Here too, admiration and rejection of "Americanism" were two sides of the same coin.[14]

After World War I an American-style "productivity craze" swept through Austrian industrial production and management style. *Fordism* and *Taylorism* conquered the continent. In 1920 the Vienna business community started a *Taylor-Zeitschrift*, the *Österreichisches Kuratorium für Wirtschaftlichkeit* was established, and the "Refa movement" began—time studies were done at Alpine-Montan iron foundries, and motion studies at Siemens-Halske in Vienna. Private organizations like the Rotary Clubs began propagating the American efficiency model too.[15] Though National Socialism interrupted the Americanization of Austrian business practices, it was only to be resumed even more furiously after World War II through the Marshall Plan. The European Recovery Program's Austrian Productivity Center (ERP and APC, respectively), established in 1950, played a crucial role in implanting American management styles in Austria. In the 1960s leaders of the APC founded the leading Austrian private management institutes, such as Hernstein, years before the universities began to preach American management practices.[16] Even though American management styles triumphed in Austrian business as elsewhere in Europe, not all sectors of the economy adopted them. In the tourism industry, where hidebound family businesses prevailed until recently, American-style marketing was resisted. Traditional low-cost Austrian tourism has had a difficult time adopting the modern individualistic quality of "destination" tourism offered through an Americanized global tourism industry.[17]

The biggest cohorts of Austrians ending up in the United States during World War II were *émigrés*/exiles and prisoners of war (POWs). Neither group went to the U.S. voluntarily—one was displaced by Hitler's expansionism, the other by his defeats on the battlefield—which shaped their outlook on America profoundly. Some 30,000 Austrians were forced into exile or (in)voluntarily emigrated to the U.S. after the *Anschluß* in 1938.[18] Most of them were Jewish emigrants who had no choice but to leave Austria to save their lives. They did not return after World War II. As film directors, artists, professors, and consummate professionals they influenced American society enormously. Having observed Austrians' rapacity in "aryanizing" their property in 1938, their unwillingness to invite them back after the war, and their unpreparedness to face the Nazi past, these immigrants affected the American view of Austria negatively (thus feeding into latent anti-Europeanism) more than they helped shape Austria's view of America.[19]

Maybe as many as 30,000 Austrian *Wehrmacht* soldiers were shipped to American POW camps between 1943 and 1946 (my own father included). Either shaped by the Nazis' negative images of the United States or guided by stereotypes of America they had garnered as teenagers from Karl May's adventure stories, they expected to encounter either a deformed and plutocratic American society or cowboys and Indians. What they found instead was a vibrant country, teeming cities, and industrial might that outproduced Nazi Germany by leaps and bounds at the height of its wartime productive capacity in 1944. Most of the POWs were employed in agriculture or the logging industry. Finding it hard to cast aside their Nazi mental baggage in the land of the victors, their views about America remained very ambivalent.[20]

Yet a number of educated Austrian officers who spoke English landed in reorientation programs. The well-known Austrian banker Heinrich Treichl stressed how much the lectures and conversations with top-notch American university lecturers at Fort Getty in Rhode Island changed his views about America. His growing appreciation of the philosophical foundations of the American egalitarian system and its constitutional balancing act, shaped by the brilliant, classically educated founding fathers, shaped his positive view of the United States for the rest of his life.[21] The American intention, in influencing educated young Germans and Austrians in their "barbed wire college," was indeed to garner "respect for the American people and their ideological values." The entire reeducation effort, beginning with the almost 400,000 German POWs during the war, rested on Washington's hope that once repatriated they "might form the nucleus of a new German ideology which will reject militarism and totalitarian controls *and will advocate [a] democratic system of government*" (emphasis added). About 20,000 German-speaking POWs (among them numerous Austrians like Treichl) were exposed to courses of intense training and "thus became favorably disposed toward the U.S. and a democratic turn in Germany" (Schmidt)—and in Austria, I hasten to add.[22]

The American occupation of Austria (1945–1955) had an even larger effect. Tens of thousands of American soldiers entered Austria in 1945, and thousands stayed on until the State Treaty was signed in 1955. This presence of a very young, healthy, and wealthy American army impressed the Austrians, especially the *Fräuleins* and the youngsters. The U.S. Army fed the Austrians through the first postwar years. The Marshall Plan revived and rebuilt the country's economy and set Austria on the path toward postwar prosperity. The Education Division was modestly successful in reforming and "democratizing" the authority-prone Austrian school system. New, American-style press and radio programs were sponsored by the occupation army with the goal of building an argumentative, open democratic society. The U.S. Information Services lured hundreds of thousands of Austrians into the thirteen branches of the *"Amerika Houses,"* familiarizing Austrians with American values free of charge through literature, magazines, and films. Jazz and the American musical (re)entered the country. The Congress for Cultural Freedom fought the intellectual Cold War against communism in Austria via the intellectual magazine *Forum,* initiated in 1953 and edited by the "remigré" Friedrich Torberg.[23]

The *Fräuleins* ("Ami whores" in the view of the hidebound) and kids were taken in by the El Dorado of American army PX stores—nylons, jeans, chewing gum, Coca-Cola, and all kinds of canned food fed a population hungry for basic daily calories and consumer goods. The mobile U.S. Army was so wealthy that every GI seemed able to afford a car. In 1952 the U.S. Army spent USD 28.7 million in its occupation zone in Salzburg alone—more revenue than Salzburg made from tourism that year. The Salzburgers forgave the Americans for being cultural barbarians and turning the fabled *Festspielhaus* into the variety-show theater "Roxy." The familiar Austrian highbrow stereotype of the lowbrow American "hillbillies" was reinforced: "Culturally we looked down upon the Americans. We sensed that they were not up to par with our expectations." Still after a long war, when all the young men had left in the *Wehrmacht* and many returned as cripples or not at all, the sex-starved ladies regarded the healthy, cocky young GIs as highly desirable apparitions from another planet. Austrian youth greeted the American presence as a welcome liberation from the stultifying authoritarianism and paternalism of their parents' generation. The Americanization of Austrian consumer habits came quickly with the presence of the American army and the extraordinary largesse of the Marshall Plan.[24]

Arguably the most important and lasting influence in the Americanization of post–World War II Austria came via the various visitor programs. Particularly during the decade of occupation, a trip to the United States not only opened up to poor and starved Austrians visitors a world of new ideas and ways of doing things but also gave the materialists among them a taste of consumerist heaven. Unfortunately, these programs for Austrians have not attracted systematic study in the fashion of Oliver Schmidt, who has analyzed the German visitor programs in a series of case studies (of some 12,000 opinion leaders shipped to the U.S. between 1945 and 1960, 10,000 were Germans[25]). But the American occupation regimes in Austria and Germany were comparatively close enough to merit the application of some of Schmidt's conclusions for the Austrian situation.

Austria, like Germany, participated in a program to help young "leaders and specialists" visit the U.S. for stays of up to three months. As was the case with the POWs, the principal goal was the long-term political democratization and economic liberalization of the war-torn country—"aiding not the physical, but the ideological reorientation of Austria." In the immediate postwar period, the U.S. Army sent only a few individuals to the U.S.; visits by prominent politicians, for instance, Foreign Minister Karl Gruber in the fall of 1946, were of the highest order in reorienting the country towards the West in the early Cold War. Starting in 1948, the flow of Austrian visitors became constant. In 1950, the Austrian leaders' program had a budget of USD 115,000. Some 500 Austrian leaders (politicians, journalists, chamber, union and church leaders, professors, artists, and youth leaders) had visited the U.S. by 1960. The young leaders' program continues today; and it brought another 500-plus young Austrians to the U.S. between 1960 and 2003.[26] What the German historian of Americanization Hermann-Josef Rupieper asserts for postwar Germany also is a persuasive argument for Austria: "The trip to America figured as an educational experience for postwar politicians. For many it was the first trip abroad in their lives."[27]

Starting in 1950, the second big wave of Austrian visitors to the U.S. (and Western Europe) were businessmen and union leaders sent by the "Österreichisches Produktivitätszentrum" (Austrian Productivity Center, *ÖPZ*) mentioned above, financed through the Marshall Plan. The goal was to familiarize Austrians with American production and management methods. Between 1950 and 1960 the *ÖPZ* organized 258 trips with 1,477 participants to the U.S. and 198 trips with 1,054 persons to Western Europe. Fifty percent of the visitors were from management, 30 percent from unions, and 20 percent from agriculture. The political scientist Kurt Tweraser, in his analysis of these programs, is skeptical about the overall success of the Americanization mission of the ÖPZ. He concedes that the introduction of American industrial and management techniques improved the utilization of Austrian resources and dissemination of technical information. But the Austrians picked what they wanted from the American smorgasbord of industrial and technical know-how:

> *Acceptance of new production techniques does not necessarily mean acceptance of the total cultural package in which they are embedded.* The American example may have reinforced rather than weakened the Austrian managers' idea that increases in productivity are primarily management tasks. They have sympathized with the political self-abnegation of the American unions who contributed to the depoliticization of economic problems. But they may have been quite skeptical about the American credo of competitiveness or the possibility of transferring the American model of sharing productivity profits with the workers. The unions, on the other hand, were probably quite impressed with the American hostility towards cartels. They were also enamored of the industrial engineering and science management departments and research institutes of the American unions, which they felt were worth imitating. Yet the unions were quite unimpressed with the American unions' renunciation of "political" codetermination. *It appears that these "America-tourists" adopted only those American methods which fitted into their already existing ideological packages* [emphasis added].[28]

Tweraser's analysis, then, provides a good example of the most recent anthropological and cultural paradigm of Americanization as an encounter between societies. Cultural imports are blended with the indigenous, and mutual influences are being negotiated and/or rejected. German Americanist Wilfried Fluck has called it the "tool-kit argument" of cultural studies where recipients appropriate elements of foreign cultures selectively. In an analysis of the Americanization of Austrian politics in the past thirty years, Austrian political scientist Fritz Plasser terms it the "shopping mall" model—Austrian parties adopted those American campaign strategies that they saw as suitable for the Austrian political arena.[29]

From the long-term perspective it was the various teenager and student exchange programs that had the deepest impact on the Americanization process. High-school exchanges were based on the assumption of public opinion researchers that "the ideological plasticity of the teenage group might single them out as an ideal point of entry for introducing democratic ideas."[30] Shepard Stone, an American cultural diplomat in the German occupation and later a central character in the Ford Foundation's efforts to fuel the rebuilding of Germany's and Western Europe's anticommunist strongholds in the intellectual Cold War, recognized the long-term impact of student exchanges. Students were the "human capital from which the next generation of Germany would draw its leaders."[31] The same is true for Austria or any other country, for that matter.[32]

The oldest and most venerable post–World War II student and faculty exchange program is that of Senator William J. Fulbright. Initiated in 1946, it was financed from the sale of U.S. government surplus goods—and later on, in Austria, from Marshall Plan counterpart funds handed over to the Austrian government in 1961. The first group of 139 Austrian "Fulbrighters" (117 of them students) lived in the U.S. in 1951/52. Between 1951 and 2002, the program selected 3,266 Austrians to study, lecture, and do research in the United States. While an annual average of seventy students and professors went to the U.S. during the Cold War, the numbers declined after the end of the Cold War, indicating the sorry demise of cultural diplomacy in favor of commercial diplomacy during the Clinton years (in 2001/02 awards for study in the U.S. went to twenty-four students, 1 lecturer, and 7 researchers). In those same years 2,126 Americans (among them 1,360 students and 371 researchers) received Fulbright grants to Austria.[33] Only if we add personal testimonials to these raw figures do we begin to understand the enormous impact the Fulbright program had in educating the Austrian elites. Many of the leading politicians, diplomats, journalists, managers, and professionals in all fields studied abroad for the first time with generous Fulbright grants. Not only were these young Austrians internationalized in their outlook, but they tended to return from the U.S. with a positive image of the country.

As teachers they tended to pass it on to their students. If they first encountered American Fulbright lecturers in Austria, the impact was no less profound, as Arno Heller, one of the leading Austrian American Studies scholars, enthusiastically relates:

> I look back with great pleasure to those years and to those marvelous, open-minded, communicative, witty Fulbright professors who shaped my life so profoundly. They were not just servants of American propaganda during the cold war period, as some detractors tried to maintain. For this they were much too sophisticated, liberal and self-critical. They surely were messengers of the best the American way of life could offer, but, on the other hand, they never hesitated to point out its negative side as well. And we on our part mediated to them our European views and perspectives, which they then took back to the States and integrated into their own life-styles, their teaching, and scholarship. To me this mutual exchange of ideas and attitudes, the readiness to accept criticism, the dismantling of prejudices and stereotypical notions—in short, the continuing dialogue emerging from these encounters—has certainly been the most valuable aspect of the Fulbright program.[34]

Thomas Chorherr, one of Austria's leading postwar print journalists and the longtime editor of the conservative daily *Die Presse,* studied at Ohio Wesleyan in the first cohort of Austrian Fulbrighters. An impressionable young man (like the POWs before him), he marveled at the skyscrapers of New York and Chicago, and the endless bands of cars on the highways indicating both American prosperity and mobility. He was infatuated with speech students' ability to speak freely but less impressed with their historical knowledge. The only critique he encountered from his fellow students was grumbling that he raised the curve in his classes. Yet he remained ambivalent over the erstwhile enemies who had endlessly bombed his native Vienna, now becoming friends overnight. He concludes that he was "inoculated with a love for America which he would never abandon."[35] Yet if one would analyze the numerous columns he wrote on America in the course of his long career as a journalist, one would encounter more likely the implicit old bourgeois ambivalence rather than the explicit love. Like the managers in the ÖPZ exchanges, he came with his own mental baggage and was selective about what he would take home.

Another program with similarly profound effects on the long-term Americanization of young Austrians has been the high-school exchange American Field Service (AFS). The first AFS cohort of 5 young Austrians went to the U.S. in 1950/51, a year earlier than the Fulbrighters. By the 1960s an average of 70 Austrians AFSers lived with American families annually. In 1972 the AFSers were first dispatched to continents other than America, and in 1976 an intra-European exchange option was added. Since the mid 1980s a growing number of Austrian AFSers have opted for stays outside the U.S. (in Europe or on any other continent). Since the end of the Cold War the majority of Austrian AFSers have chosen non–U.S. options increasingly, indicating the growing globalization of student exchanges. From 1950 to 1993, the AFS sent 2,322 Austrians to the United States (on the basis of the average of 40 that have gone annually to the U.S. since, one would have to update that figure by another 400 teenagers) and 372 to non-U.S. countries outside of Europe, while 179 preferred European exchanges. I was one of them in 1972/72, living with a family in Danville, California.[36]

Again, the personal testimonials tell us how deeply a year in the U.S. at an impressionable young age affected these teenagers. The experience of the American way of life and American tolerance changed many a young Austrian for good. Others were impressed by American optimism and open-hearted friendliness. Others, like myself, experienced a brave new world beyond hidebound Austrian authoritarian education and stultifying Catholic morality. The study of how Americans came to terms with the Vietnam War taught me how Austrians ought to come to terms with World War II. Among the leading scholars in the Austrian and German American Studies movement, many (perhaps most) first experienced the U.S. through the AFS and never abandoned their desire to get to understand this complex society even better.[37]

Since the end of the Cold War, a debate over whether sending AFSers to the United States is still "timely" has gathered speed. Some denounce the arrogance of the United States. Others say Western Europe has become too much like the U.S. and youngsters have little to learn in America other than improved English. Patrick Worms argues that with the onset of the U.S.

global hegemony, complete immersion in the heartland of "empire" is more necessary than ever: "This maybe necessary for purely selfish reasons (to better succeed in a race whose terms the 'Empire' dictates) or for altruistic ones (to exploit its weaknesses to better oppose the new ways, say)."[38] According to this latter view, familiarization with American values is needed to know "the enemy" rather than deepen one's friendship with like-minded, friendly people, which raises the question of whether AFS exchanges ought to *counter* the Americanization process.

Since Austrian universities began internationalizing in the 1980s, a growing number of institutions of higher learning have begun bilateral exchanges with American universities. Most Austrian universities have partner institutions in the United States. An outstanding example of such a model partnership is the friendship treaty initialed between the universities of Innsbruck and New Orleans (UNO) in 1983. A growing number of exchanges has brought over 1,000 Austrians to UNO. Two hundred Austrian students have spent an entire year studying in New Orleans since 1979 (I happened to be the first one). In 2003/04 there are almost as many Austrians studying at UNO through this bilateral program (30) as there are Fulbright grantees coming to the U.S. from Austria (35). More than 800 Austrians have studied at UNO for a month on a short-term program. And since 1976 some 7,000 Americans have studied in Innsbruck at the UNO International Summer School.[39]

No other institution had as profound an impact on the Americanization of European—and Austrian—intellectuals and the formation of American Studies on the continent as the famous Salzburg Seminar, initiated by a group of Harvard students in 1947. Ninety young Europeans and 20 Americans met in the gorgeous Rococo Castle Leopoldskron—amidst a Central Europe destroyed as a result of Hitler's war of aggression—to participate in "the first experiment in international education in postwar Europe." The famous Harvard American Studies scholar F. O. Matthiesen, in a highly thoughtful opening address, set the tone for the seminar and, in a way, for the genesis of the entire American Studies movement in postwar Europe. He noted that the Americans were the Romans of the modern world. He added, however, "none of our group come as imperialists of the pax Americana to impose our values upon you. All of us come nonetheless with a strong conviction of the values of American democracy" and also "with what I take to be the saving characteristics of American civilization: a sharp sense of both excess and its limitations." Oliver Schmidt, in his brilliant archeology of the Salzburg Seminar's genesis, rejects the thesis that it was driven by "American cultural imperialism": "Instead, I take the origins of the seminar to be an apt case study of American cultural diplomacy competing for cultural hegemony in Western Europe."[40]

The story of Clemens Heller is highly symbolic of the serendipity of the exploding intellectual Cold War in Europe.[41] A refugee from Vienna (his father had been Freud's publisher) and a graduate student in history at Harvard University, Heller was one of the seminar's founders. Brimming with missionary enthusiasm, the young Austrian strove to make the seminar in his native Austria into a young people's meeting ground between East and West to counter the growing Cold War division of Europe. Instead of bridging the Cold War divisions in Europe, the fellow Austrian Fritz Molden, an OSS collaborator and CIA mole who had attended the first session, denounced Heller's "certain 'leftist' tendencies." U.S. Army officials in the Educational Division suspected Heller of being a communist and branded Matthiesen's socialist humanist ideals as un-American. The U.S. Army did not give Heller a visa to return to his native Austria for the second session in the summer of 1948 and even went so far as to bar Matthiesen from returning to Salzburg. In 1950 a personally distraught Matthiesen committed suicide.[42] In the turmoil of the exploding Cold War in Europe, the politics of American anticommunism reared its ugly head early in the Salzburg Seminar and might have set it on a track of preaching American exceptionalism more than the likes of Matthiesen had envisioned.

In spite of these early discontents among the "100 percent Americanism" crowd, it is a fitting comparison to call the Salzburg Seminar "a cultural and intellectual Marshall Plan" for Europe.[43] During that fateful summer of 1947 American leaders initiated the Cold War with their dual policy of containing the Soviets and reconstructing the war-torn Western European economy with economic aid. In the same summer, private American students and educators such as Scott Elledge and Matthiesen also sensed that the European mind, ravaged by wartime destruction and totalitarian mind control, needed as careful a nurturing as the economy. To date some 17,000 participants from more than 120 countries have participated in some 400 sessions, among them an average of twenty Austrians annually over the past twenty years. While Heller's vision of tearing down the Iron Curtain and East meeting West was quickly stopped by the U.S. Army's rigid Cold War mindset, starting during the détente period in the 1960s a growing number of Eastern Europeans came to Salzburg. Still, in Schmidt's apt phrase, "cultural diplomacy did not prove to be the avant-garde of détente." In the 1980s the sessions on every conceivable subject matter attracted an increasingly global audience and became less and less American Studies seminars.[44]

Yet the Salzburg Seminar was not only one of "the world's foremost centers for intellectual exchange" but also doubled as a hub of the burgeoning American Studies movement in Europe.[45] Neutral Austria became the central meeting ground, revolving door, and transmission belt of American studies in Europe. Ever since 1947 young Europeans have learned about American intellectual life and American institutions (such as democracy) in the Salzburg Seminar. At the same time "the *Schloss*" was a powerful force in beginning an organized American Studies movement. The European Association of

American Studies (EAAS) had its inaugural meeting at Leopoldskron in 1954 with thirty-eight Americanists attending. The Norwegian Americanist Sigmund Skard, one of the founders of the movement and an attendee at the EAAS meeting in 1954, noted "that the influence of the Salzburg seminar can hardly be overestimated."[46] The hundreds of Austrians who participated in the sessions of the Salzburg Seminar were no doubt internationalized, Americanized, and Westernized while meeting their peers from around the world.

"The *Schloss*" was also the meeting place that saw the genesis of the Austrian Association for American Studies (AAAS) in 1972. The AAAS met numerous times at Leopoldskron with Americanists from all over the world regularly attending.[47] This Americanist has been fortunate enough to attend such meetings off and on since 1981. The Salzburg Seminar and the EAAS and AAAS meetings have probably provided American Studies with its most important networking opportunities in Europe. In other words, not only was Austria Americanized in the process, but the Americanization of Western Europe—especially of West Germany, which boasted numerous fellows—proceeded via *Schloß Leopoldskron* in Salzburg as the grand central station of the intellectual Americanization of Europe.[48]

The founding of the Institute for Advanced Studies (*Institut für höhere Studien,* or IHS) in Vienna with an endowment from the Ford Foundation constituted another crucial initiative in the "Americanization" of Austrian academics and intellectuals. As was the case with Clemens Heller and the Salzburg Seminar, the driving force and crucial transmitters behind this private American initiative were two Austrian prewar émigrés to the U.S.—the famous social scientist Paul Lazarsfeld and the economist Oskar Morgenstern. Their goal was to begin serious social science studies in nonexistent fields such as political science, or improve them towards international standards in the case of both economics and sociology, by confronting young Austrian graduates with eminent American scholars. The purges of Jewish academics from Austrian universities after 1934 and the politicization of Austrian academe during the Nazi era had left Austrian academic life totally impoverished by 1945. Moreover, unlike Germany, Austria did not invite its eminent émigrés to return after the war. Anton Pelinka has shown how the IHS introduced American-style political science to Austria in the 1960s. An entire generation of young scholars like him were trained in up-to-date social science methodology. To this day, the elite of Austrian political scientists are IHS graduates. Up until the early 1960s, the only politics taught at Austrian universities was positivistic public law (*Staatswissenschaften*) in the law schools. The IHS changed all that. The extent of the Americanization of Austrian political science, however, may be an unusual case in Austrian academia.[49]

Under another exchange program that has been studied with regard to West German visitors but not Austrian grantees, the armed forces brought officers and soldiers to American military facilities. West Germany, a NATO alliance member, sent hundreds of officers to American bases every year for training and indoctrination.[50] Such officer exchanges helped "contain" the remilitarized West Germany and make it a reliable ally and friend. Compared to this flood, the trickle from neutral Austria was minimal. Yet ever since the U.S. Army helped rearm and train the secret Austrian armed police forces (before 1955) and the fledgling army (after the Austrian state treaty was signed), Austrian staff officers have gone regularly to American command and staff colleges. These elite exchanges helped "de-Germanize" and "Westernize" the Austrian army, while the Americanization of the German armed forces "de-Prussianized" and "de-nazified" it.[51]

Behind the various exchange programs and the Salzburg Seminar was the expectation that such consummate networking by "citizen-diplomats" would have infinite multiplier effects. Journalists would presumably report more fairly and evenly about America; politicians might have more sympathy for American decisions and join in fighting the Cold War against the Soviet Union; businessmen would bring back American management methods and introduce "the politics of productivity" in the European factories; and educators an all levels would spread the American gospel in their lectures and classrooms. Washington's cultural diplomacy aimed to improve the U.S. image abroad and hoped Germans (and Austrians) would understand liberal democracy as practiced in the United States. Studies of the immediate impact of teenager exchanges found that upon return they served as "spokesmen" for the American way of life, and that they spread what they had learned in the U.S. Estimates had it that every exchangee spoke with 150 compatriots after his return home.[52] What American control commissioner John J. McCloy said of Germany regarding the fruits of the visitors' programs rings true for Austria as well: "They sense that we are aiming our program at broad democratization *and not (repeat not) at a narrow Americanization* [emphasis in original]."[53]

Adding up the numbers of "future leaders," *ÖPZ* visitors, Fulbrighters, and AFSers that visited the United States in the postwar period (not counting the numerous bilateral university exchanges and the Salzburg Seminar), we arrive at rough figure of some 7,000 Austrians who took the trip across the Atlantic. With a multiplier of 150 contacts back home per person, this would make for a minimum audience of roughly 1 million Austrians (in a population of 7 million). Obviously, the exchange programs were more important in the first three Cold War decades, when Austria was poor and less than democratic in its statist ("Josephinian") government structure, than later, after it had become prosperous and begun to resemble a normal Western European democracy.[54] These numbers speak for themselves. Clearly, even though their influence in "Americanizing" Austria after 1945 cannot be quantified, individual testimonials tell us again and again that it was enormous.

While among the young generation the acceptance of American popular culture spread like wildfire (see below), the condescending Austrian elites wallowed in rejecting American high culture. For the champions of Austria as a cultural superpower, all American culture was *"Unkultur."* The American occupiers may have been successful in spreading the *Pax Americana* politically in the democratization of postwar Austria, but high culture was "the last refuge" of the superiority of the defeated elites. During the first half (1945–50) of the occupation decade, the Theater & Music Section of the Information Services Branch (ISB), and then the United States Information Services (USIS/USIA), fought valiantly to bring American high culture to Austria (in spite of the "low culture" prejudices vis-à-vis jazz held by some the American culture officers). As Wagnleitner has shown, the ISB controlled 17 theaters, 1 opera house, the Salzburg festival house, 24 concert halls, and 46 variety theaters in the American zone and tried to schedule American high culture in all of them. In Salzburg alone, twenty-one plays by U.S. authors were staged during the occupation decade representing 12 percent of all plays staged. Thornton Wilder, William Saroyan, and Tennessee Williams were favored by the American culture officers since their plays proffered "American values." These stage productions were usually dismissed by critics as being *"typisch amerikanisch,"* which meant of inferior quality. E. Wilder Spaulding reported back from the Embassy in Vienna that large numbers of American plays were appearing in Austria but many of them brought "only the drab side of American life to the Austrians." He concluded with resignation that "These plays tend to confirm the impression which American motion pictures give to so many Austrian that America is a land of degeneracy and gangsterism."[55]

If Wilder and Williams had a hard time making it on the Danube and Salzach in spite of massive support from the American cultural officers, U.S.–produced "serious music" by the likes of Samuel Barber and Aaron Copland had no chance with audiences in the homeland of Haydn and Mozart. It did not help either that the fabled Salzburg Festival House was renamed "Roxy's," or that the composer Anton von Webern was shot by a GI in the little Salzburg village of Mittersill. The ISB spared no expense in bringing famous American conductors such as George Szell, Eugene Ormandy, and Leonard Bernstein to the Vienna concert halls and the Salzburg Festival, as well as soloists of the stature of Yehudi Menhuin. The audience "went deaf" (Wagnleitner) when they played "modern" American music (including works by the well-known Austrian émigré to Hollywood Ernst Krenek) and cheered when they played Beethoven and Mahler. The audiences and critics in Austria, "the land of music," never managed to overcome their cultural hubris. Only *Porgy and Bess,* George Gershwin's famous jazzy opera, was received "triumphantly" in Vienna in the fall of 1952. (I remember *Porgy and Bess* productions at the summer Bregenz Lake Festival in the 1970s; by the 1990s they had become perennial favorites). Once again, it was the Austrian remigré music critics and producers Ernst Haeussermann and Marcel Prawy who, as part of the ISB's Theater & Music Section, introduced Austria to the American musical, which "conquered Vienna in a whirlwind." After the occupation the Viennese operetta had to accept an uneasy coexistence with the popular American musicals.[56]

The story was even more complicated in the promotion of the visual arts by the State Department. Like jazz, abstract expressionism was considered too controversial to be sent abroad as representative of the American tradition. But Europeans wanted to see American abstract expressionism. To the rescue came the Museum of Modern Art (MOMA) and its Austrian-born director Rene D'Harnoncourt, with the financial support of the Rockefeller Foundation. Starting with the 1956 exhibition "Modern Art in the United States," older artists such as Lyonel Feininger and the realist Edward Hopper were exhibited next to abstract moderns such as Jackson Pollock and Mark Rothko. In addition, design and architecture were shown along with prints, sculptures by Alexander Calder, and the work of leading photographers such as Ansel Adams, Alfred Stieglitz, and Walker Evans was shown in Vienna and Linz. Subsequent MOMA shows concentrated on photography, household design, woodcuts, skyscrapers, and posters. While hungry young artists—starving to break away from the stultifying restorative cultural climate in a land of hidebound traditions—flocked to these shows, the critics remained skeptical vis-à-vis abstract expressionism seemingly operating without "formal principles."[57] Austria, with its rich cultural tradition, thought that the modern world did not have much to offer to its refined tastes.

Austrian Anti-Americanism

Austrian anti-Americanism is too complex a subject matter to investigate here in great detail.[58] Austria's is not much different from the anti-Americanism of its Western European neighbors.[59] Anti-Americanism in Austria as elsewhere is part fiction, part fact. Ever since the discovery of the new continent, every positive European image of America as a free, enlightened paradise has sparked corresponding images of America as hell, an overly materialistic and degenerated land of barbarians without culture. The reverse side of "America as a dream" is "America as nightmare."[60]

The growing presence of the "hyperpower" United States in the world and the establishment of American hegemony and empire along with the popularity of American popular culture in the Cold War and beyond,[61] have spurred a growing critique and rejection of American "imperialism." "The American empire of fun"—notions of "coca-colonization" and "sili-colonization," "Hollywoodization" and "Disneyfication," "Microsoftification," "McDonaldization," and "Starbucksification"—are part and parcel of critiques of a globalized American "turbo-capitalism" that brings its products into world markets with firm government support and reckless marketing techniques, as well as superior and more efficient capital outlays creating attractive products that beat the competition and subvert local tastes.[62] Every globally successful American product thus reproduces the endless cycle of growing anti-Americanisms. The American "militarization of the world" has spawned passionate critiques at home[63] and pacifist anti-American outbursts abroad; American "fast food" has produced a "slow food" movement; a perceived U.S. capital–driven global market has sparked violent anti-globalist campaigns.[64]

The anti-American views of nineteenth-century Austrian romantic poets and writers such as Lenau and Kürnberger had a profound effect, both on all of German-speaking Europe at the time and on subsequent generations. They also helped "metastasize" America as a concrete place and country one visited and studied to the abstractions "Americanism," "Americanization," and "American-ness"—"America was entering the realm of the spirit," as political scientist James W. Caesar has observed.[65] In other words, these "German" romantics hailing from Austria prepared the ground for America as a *projection* that eventually came to contain all the negative images Central European intellectuals and observers managed to construe.[66] Historian Thomas Fröschl has shown how these persistent anti-American sentiments have been very deeply rooted in Europe ever since the discovery of the "New World."[67]

During the post–World War II occupation the Americanization of Austria produced corresponding projections against America along the usual lines. It is noted above that the American GIs were frequently perceived as lacking in culture and refinement by the local Austrian population.[68] Dependency on American economic aid produced resentment in Austria and elsewhere: "There is much evidence that the Europeans find continued American economic aid psychologically galling." Deliveries of military aid were considered less offensive since they contributed to the common defense against communism.[69] The mushrooming presence of American pop culture produced the usual protests against "barbarian" Americans lacking culture from the traditional elites, many of whom had also been deeply implicated in the triumph of Nazism in Austria. Austrian historian Reinhold Wagnleitner, one of the leading European authorities on "Americanization," has amply demonstrated that the triumph of American popular culture in postwar America was also a form of generational rebellion: "The major attraction of an opposition to American popular culture for young people lies in the fact that it always contains an element of rebellion: a rebellion against the tastes of politicians, priests, the military, and teachers"[70]—as well as their (Nazi?) parents, one might add.

During the anticommunist hysteria of the early 1950s, McCarthyism was lambasted by the European left as a form of American "fascism." The Eisenhower administration was sufficiently worried about the U.S.'s declining prestige around the world to embark on a global study of America's failing popularity and tarnished image abroad. It did not help when McCarthy sent his "junketeering gumshoes" Shine and Cohn abroad to engage in purging the America House libraries of suspected communist literature. In Vienna, as elsewhere, this was seen as the American version of "book burning."[71]

The British Americanist Marcus Cunliffe has observed that in the nineteenth century the professional and upper classes were traditionally anti-American (see Archduke Francis Ferdinand and Sigmund Freud above) given their fear of modernism, mass culture, and democratic ideology, whereas in the twentieth century they tended to be increasingly pro-American. For the laboring classes and the left, the trend was the reverse: in the nineteenth century, America represented an opportunity to leave the class struggle behind, while after World War II the left came to see the U.S. increasingly through the simplistic Marxist lens as a monopolistic, oligarchic, and hegemonic empire, and more recently as the much-too-powerful globalizing Moloch.[72] Richard Pells refines the picture for the postwar era with the variable of culture: "upper-class Europeans were more apt to be anti-American, on cultural grounds, than were those on the lower rungs of the social and economic ladder," and adds that America increasingly became the scapegoat "for everything that had gone wrong in modern Europe."[73] These classifications bring us into the midst of postwar Austrian anti-Americanism on the old right and the new left.

A case study of selected issues from the 1950s, 1960s, and late 1990s of the unabashedly pro-German and anti-American right-wing Austrian nationalist fraternity weekly *Die Aula* gives us a sense of the principal themes of Austrian old nationalist right anti-Americanism. Like French Gaullism, it blasted American hegemony in the geostrategic and nuclear arena, degrading Western Europe into a mere *Vorfeld* ("front") of Western defense planning. The widespread apprehension of the 1980s that Hamburg would be sacrificed for New York in a nuclear war in Central Europe had emerged in the early 1960s in nationalist right-wing circles. The French author Jean Jacques Servan-Schreiber's *Die Amerikanische Herausforderung*—which propagated his notion that Europe was becoming a "franchise colony" owing to America's global hegemony and the "brain drain" of European intellectuals to American universities—was eagerly discussed as well in the same circles in Austria. American popular low culture, and above all the triumph of jazz, was seen as a great threat to European high culture (meanwhile, the European left was more crazy about jazz than most Americans). The Nazis had already banned American jazz—along with the late 1920s' "jazz opera" *Jonny spielt auf,* by the Austrian composer Ernst Krenek—as "degenerate" music.[74]

The post-Nazi nationalist right in Austria would have followed suit, had they been in a position to do so. The "mere noise" that was "negro jazz" featured no order, harmony, or melody. Jazz was the "revenge" of American ne-groes against the white elite that had enslaved them (*"Rache durch Rythmus"*). American jazz was degenerating the European peoples (*"volktumszersetzender Einfluss"*) and needed to be stopped. The American cultural assault on the European value system was ruining an old civilization. The gloomy "conser-vative revolutionary" Spenglerian *"Untergang des Abendlandes,"* as well as the Heideggerian America-as-catastrophic-modernizer mood, which had con-tributed to the rise of National Socialism, clearly had a long afterlife in Cen-tral Europe's nationalist right.[75]

The sharpest turn taken by right-wing nationalist anti-Americanism in Austria was its historical revisionism in interpreting National Socialism's fail-ure and the Anglo-American victory during World War II. The Austrian right never could accept the defeat of the imperialist, racist, and genocidal Hitler regime that they had so eagerly served until the final day. In the mental land-scape of these post-Nazis, Germany's problems started with Woodrow Wil-son's betrayal in the waning days of World War I and the postwar "unjust Versailles dictate." These reactionary nationalists also deny the German *"Allein-schuld"* (exclusive responsibility) for the origins of World War II and blame Churchill and the British for being determined to dismember Germany be-fore it became too powerful again. Like the recent bestseller in Germany by Jörg Friedrich, this old right denounced the murderous Anglo-American bombing war on Germany and demanded to know when the Allies would be put on trial for "genocide and war crimes" in Katyn, Hiroshima, Nagasaki, Berlin, and Dresden, and for the expulsion and liquidation of millions of Germans from Eastern Europe. *Die Aula* gleefully tore the "veil of lies" from the Anglo-American "unmastered past." The editors and writers of *Die Aula* condemned Churchill's terror bombing and Roosevelt's Morgenthau Plan, doing more than the Nazis ever had to fatally weaken Germany and allow So-viet communism to conquer one half of Europe.[76]

While anti-Americanism on the right was shrill and persistent in the 1960s and beyond, on the left it ran through a spectrum of gradations. On the far left, the Communist Party was predictable in its "gut" anti-Americanism, reg-ularly denouncing monopoly capitalism and American imperialism in Viet-nam. The communist daily *Volksstimme* blasted away at "naked American aggression" and "U.S. massacres of civilians" in Vietnam (and other Third World countries) and demonstrated its "solidarity" with the Vietnamese lib-eration struggle.[77] The Austrian Socialist Party (SPÖ) had been part of the governing grand coalition from 1945 to 1966. During this time they regu-larly were more pro-American than the conservative People's Party (ÖVP), whose right wing blended into nationalist Right thinking. Gratitude for the Marshall Plan, indeed, was profound among the "founding fathers" of the post–World War II Second Republic on both sides of the political spectrum.

Bruno Kreisky, Austria's leading postwar Socialist and longest-serving chancellor (1970–83), maintained a solid positive public memory of the Marshall Plan far into the 1980s.

Sampling the socialist theoretical journal *Die Zukunft*, one is struck by the absence of anti-Americanism. Critiques of America during the Vietnam War were usually obliquely proffered to their readership through American critiques of America, such as Fulbright's "arrogance of American power." While *Die Aula* lamented that violence, sex, and trash in Hollywood movies was leading to the demise of Western civilization, *Die Zukunft* featured long reviews of popular "wild West" movies and their archetypal celebration of the American frontier spirit and its romantic way of life.[78]

While the older middle-of-the-road Socialist left was remarkably free of anti-Americanism, the young new left in the SPÖ tended to be tamer than the German and American new left. Yet its rhetoric was in tune with the international 1968 movement. The young Socialists (along with some "revolutionary Socialists" from the 1930s) were situated on the left margin of the SPÖ. During the height of the Vietnam War they organized the "Social Democratic Indochina Committee" and in 1972 published a pamphlet that offers us a glimpse of how they profiled their critique of Kreisky's party leadership. The young Turks in the Socialist Party harkened back to the famous left-wing 1926 Linz Party program and blasted American exploitative capitalism and imperialism in the Third World and the profiteering of the military industrial complex in Vietnam, as well as the "brutal cynicism" of America's power elite and their destructive "counter-revolutionary aggression" in Vietnam. They severely criticized the "blind anti-communism" in the SPÖ party leadership and its eager dismissal of the "national revolutionary independence movement" in Vietnam as "communist." It was a "mistake" among the party elders to be forever grateful for the Marshall Plan and in the process ignore the "imperialist adventurism" in American foreign policy in Indochina. Citing "progressive" American critics of the war, the new left insisted that taking a stand on the "brutal aggression of U.S.-imperialism in Indochina," "had nothing at all to do with anti-Americanism."[79]

European critics of American foreign policy have a long tradition of referencing their views back to a better, "other America." Much as today's adversaries of "cowboy Bush's war in Iraq" on the left like to quote Michael Moore's irreverent work, the new left's Generation of '68 insisted on lambasting "the ruling power elite and their representative in the White House" and not the American people themselves. The only mass protest in Austria against American Vietnam policy came in March 1972, when Nixon visited Salzburg. Chancellor Bruno Kreisky's son Peter was one of the most visible protestors; he was also on the steering committee of the Indochina Committee and one of the authors of its pamphlet.[80]

In spite of their Vietnam protests, the new left was remarkably sedate in 1968 in Austria.[81] Maybe the Austrian students were preoccupied more with the war crimes of their Nazi fathers than American hegemony. While their fathers fought a rearguard action to save tradition, their children, as a form of protest against their parents' staunch conservatism or Nazi involvement, swallowed American lifestyles and popular culture hook, line, and sinker. In Richard Kuisel's turn of phrase, they "delighted in the loss of tradition." It has been noted that the student protests against the Vietnam War in Austria were mild, not on the level of violence exercised by their brethren in Berkeley, Paris, and Berlin. Clearly, Austrian neutrality and the lack of NATO propaganda in the country was producing an increasingly pacifist generation. Intellectually, their critique of American "imperialism" in Vietnam, as stated in the university arena, ran along the lines of the arguments of the American Cold War revisionist historians (W. A. Williams' Wisconsin School and the Kolkos). By the late 1970s this increasingly pacifist new left was moving more into the camp of opposing civilian nuclear power plants: here lies the taproot of the neutralist, anti–military defense Austrian Green Party. In the 1980s those who protested against the "dual track" decision and the stationing of American medium-range nuclear missiles in Western Europe joined the massive "anti-nukes" movement on West German streets.[82]

There was hardly a noticeable open protest in Austria against Reagan's second Cold War. Yet after the end of the Cold War, Austrian anti-Americanism grew steadily. A vast majority of pacifist youngsters opposed Austria joining NATO in the changing security environment of the post–Cold War era. Anti-Americanism can now be found in *all* political camps, particularly expressed in a growing chorus by commentators blasting American global hegemony and interventionism in the Balkans and the Middle East; Peter Pilz, one of the leaders of the Austrian Green Party, is representative of such views.[83] Anti-Americanism is on the rise again on the left in the strictly anti-NATO Socialist and Green camps and has stayed consistently strong on the right.[84]

The Austrian conservatives are still smarting under the Reagan-era decision to put the "former Nazi" President Kurt Waldheim on the "watch list" and prevent him from entering the U.S. Jörg Haider's Freedom Party is fickle about America. Haider studied recent American campaigning strategies intimately and successfully applied them to the Austrian arena; like Newt Gingrich, he formulated a ten-point "contract with Austria." He even attended Harvard summer school and regularly visited American politicians. When he visited Saddam Hussein on the eve of the 2003 U.S. attack on Iraq, his enthusiasm for America had cooled visibly.[85] In an interview on Austrian television after Saddam's dramatic apprehension by the Americans, he called Israel a "dictatorship," denounced the American "bad comedy" of Saddam's capture (*"Schmierenkomödie"*), and even went so far as to compare the fallen Iraqi dictator with Bush: "Both were on a warpath with international law, both violated human rights. One of them was lucky enough to command a world power, strong enough to write the rules of engagement, while the other was a weak dictator." Here the populist Haider was appealing to Austrian anti-Americanism and anti-Semitism. The day after the television interview he defended his verbal gaffe on the radio by noting that he had merely expressed what many Austrians were thinking.[86]

But people's and parties' views of America can quickly change both with the political season and along with American behavior in the world, and one has to follow the tergiversations of observers' views in response to geopolitical crises carefully. George W. Bush's post-9/11 policies and his precipitated war against Iraq have brought America's image to the lowest point since the end of World War II. Following international trends, 62 percent of Austrians think that the U.S. plays a "negative" role in creating world peace, while only 17 percent say the U.S. role is positive.[87]

Like other places in Europe, Austria is witnessing further swells of anti-Americanism—or is it merely "anti-Bushism"?[88] Two voices from the principal political camps, probably not unrepresentative of the larger public, must suffice to indicate this new mood. On the right, Gerd Bacher, a self-proclaimed Austrian "Atlanticist" (a rare breed among neutralist Austrians) and former chief of Österreichischer Rundfunk (ORF), attacked the "mass psychosis" and patriotism of the American mass media in the pages of the leading conservative newspaper in Vienna *Die Presse*. Bacher opines that the warmongers in Washington come across as John Wayne's heirs in a Hollywood B-movie, acting to rule the world. "The daily high noon coming from the White House is unbearable and laughable." The combative conservative Bacher characterizes George W. Bush's Washington as "an amalgamation of hypocritical puritanism, shameless business practices, fearful ignorance of the world, besotten with power [*"Machtbesoffenheit"*], and claiming for itself to decree what is good and what is bad." Bacher calls upon Europe to learn a new role not as vassal but as a partner of the world's lone superpower.[89]

On the left, a self-appointed America expert (there are few genuine ones in Austria), the media artist Peter Weibel, offers an even more strident, old-fashioned conspiracist critique of America in an interview with the leading liberal Vienna newspaper *Der Standard*. Weibel argues that the American "rogue economy" is deeply embedded in the system and has acted as a motor of U.S. foreign policy "in projecting domestic conflicts and deficits abroad." Similar to the Third Reich, the American "rogue economy" constructs enemies abroad in order to divert attention from domestic problems. America's economic problems are corrected again and again, he insists, by a "war economy." The militarization of American foreign policy thus is based on purely economic considerations. Paranoia defines the U.S. economy, and 9/11 has further infused the American "culture of fear," inflating it into a sort of "psychosis of destiny" (*"Schicksalspsychose"*).[90]

An odd mixture of conspiracist Chomsky and pop Freud seems to drive Weibel's neo-Marxist analysis and its revival of the "military-industrial complex" critique. Paranoia seems to hold sway over European critics of America like Weibel, or the bestselling French author who has asserted that the U.S. government staged the 9/11 attacks and no jetliner ever crashed into the Pentagon, or the large number of young Germans who believe these conspiracist versions of the 9/11 attacks. Opinion leaders and a growing number of the European public increasingly buy into such conspiracy history. These views suggest that the recent upsurge in irrational anti-Americanism goes beyond mere rational criticism of Bush's foreign policy. Passing the demarcation line between rational critiques of American policy and irrational denunciation of all things American, however, constitutes the crucial divide between analysis and emotional anti-Americanism.[91] Among anti-Americanists we can distinguish between the "murderous" and the "lite" sort. Bin Laden's fundamentalist, Islamicist-inspired attacks on American embassies and warships, and on the twin towers on 11 September 2001, represent the murderous variant, whereas the knee-jerk anti-Americanism of people like Pilz, Bacher, and Weibel in Austria is of the "lite" sort.[92]

Conclusion

In spite of the profound influence of the American occupation regime, Austria did not become a "special case"[93] in the trajectory of the Americanization of Europe. While an avalanche of American occupiers descended upon "defeated" (West) Germany to "reeducate" it, no such regime was ever officially launched in "liberated" Austria. Even though the presence of the American cultural affairs division was ubiquitous and their obvious political *Hintergedanken* (ulterior motives) often made them appear heavy-handed, the American cultural "blitz" was short-lived. The culturally arrogant Austrian elites pooh-poohed American high culture and rejected popular culture as degenerate, just as the "Austrian" Romantics had denounced the American way of life. Unlike Germany, Austria remained intact during the Cold War and paid the price of neutralization for its political unity. It never joined NATO, and it became a member of the European Economic Community and European Union only after the end of the Cold War in 1995.

The close Euro-Atlantic partnership steadily helped Americanize West Germany, not least via a steady presence of up to half a million U.S. soldiers on German soil, practicing a policy of "dual containment" (containing both Germans and Soviets). Neutral Austria meanwhile tried to build bridges between East and West and practiced a growing neutralist equidistance in the Cold War. Moving closer to the West was not tolerated by the Soviets—too much American influence had to be kept at bay. On the one hand, since Austria was not a NATO partner, the impact of the "1968" generational rebellion in Austria was not as profound as in Germany. On the other hand, the country experienced hardly a ripple of protest against the "dual track" decision and the stationing of nuclear weapons in Western Europe during the "second Cold War." Since the 1970s, the energy of the Green movement in Austria has been concentrated on successfully stopping the civilian use of atomic power. Only after the end of the Cold War did they begin to strongly criticize NATO and the American militarization of international conflicts.

Austrian anti-Americanism may be a bit more "special." "German" Romantic poets hailing from old Habsburg "Austria" have given the world the notion of America as a degenerate place without any roots (*"bodenlos"*). This projection of America figured heavily in the early twentieth-century views of the "revolutionary conservatives" (or "reactionary modernists," as they were also called) that prepared the ground for the "Third Reich."[94] In this sense Austrians may have played a fateful role in the construction of a strain of European anti-Americanism. The epigones of the reactionary right in Austria, even after Hitler, continue this projection of America as a rootless society without culture to this day (Haider remains in their tradition, despite having been impressed by American campaign strategies). Given the broad front of rejection of American high culture in postwar Austria, the right fringe may have extended into the core of traditional Austrian elites (and the middle class). After Hitler's failed bid for power over Europe, the hidebound Austrians refused to accept a world under American hegemony, even the benevolent sort. Meanwhile, their kids imbibed American pop culture at home or went on exchange programs to the U.S. to experience the American way of life and value system. They made the profound turn toward Americanization and eagerly embraced democratic society. People increasingly watched American-produced television programs on Austrian TV and flooded the cinemas to "inhale" the Hollywood movies.

After two centuries of scapegoating America for the Old World's troubles, Europe had lost its place to the United States in the world arena.[95] During the Cold War the U.S. spared no effort to "Americanize" occupied Germany and Austria by democratizing them and making them more prosperous with American economic aid. Most of the new German and Austrian postwar elites in power were brought to America on generous grants provided through numerous visitors' programs. During the Cold War it seemed that the Americanization of Europe could not be stopped.

Yet with the gathering speed of European integration in the post–Cold War era, the recent resurgence of anti-Americanism as a result of a paradigm shift from consensual relations with allies towards unilateral interventionism and empire-building makes one wonder how deeply this Cold War Americanization has taken root in Germany and Austria. The famous "Atlantic spirit" seems to have been battered, in Austria as elsewhere, by Bush's intervention in Iraq. The popularity and bestseller status of Michael Moore's critical books on the "toxic Texan" in Germany and Austria provide a simplistic lens for understanding a complex American polity. Like American critics of the Vietnam War, Moore represents the "other America" that affirms facile German and Austrian stereotypes and prejudices of the U.S.[96] In such times the *traditional* stereotypes about the United States ("America") resurface and can be politically instrumentalized quickly. They have always been there—Americanization after World War II has not managed to wipe them out. In the contest over Americanization, the struggle will continue between those who want to save tradition (resisting Americanization) and those who delight in casting it over board (welcoming Americanization).

Notes

Acknowledgements
The author would like to thank Lonnie Johnson, Karen Schmidt-Gerlich, and Timothy Ryback for providing me with updated data on the Austrian Fulbright exchange programs, the State Department's Visitors Program, and the Salzburg Seminar. Berndt Ostendorf, Reinhold Wagnleitner and Thomas Fröschl have been congenial critics of my work on these issues. Konrad Jarausch let me use an unpublished essay and Georg Rigele portions of an unpublished edition of Archduke Franz Ferdinand's Travel Diaries. Oliver Schmidt's unpublished Harvard dissertation has been enormously helpful in crystallizing my thinking on the impact of exchange programs. Alexander Stephan has been a gentle and thoughtful editor.

1. James W. Caesar, *Reconstructing America: The Symbol of America in Modern Thought* (New Haven: Yale University Press, 1997), 16. The major exception is Alexis de Tocqueville.
2. C. Van Woodward, *The Old World's New World* (New York: Oxford University Press, 1991), xxif.
3. On the background of the former priest and adventurer Sealsfield, see Heinrich Drimmel, *Die Antipoden: Die Neue Welt in den USA und das Österreich vor 1918* (Vienna: Amalthea, 1984), 79–89.
4. Dan Diner, *America in the Eyes of the Germans: An Essay on Anti-Americanism* (Princeton: Marcus Wiener, 1996), 31–51; on Lenau and Hülsemann, see also Drimmel, *Die Antipoden,* 89–92, 98ff. The famous sociologist Max Weber, influenced by Kürnberger's novel, coined the notion that he "paraphrased" Lenau. See Caesar, *Reconstructing America,* 184.

5. Diner, *America in the Eyes of the Germans*, 42, 43. Caesar sees the same profound impact of the "German romantics'" projection of America on subsequent European projections of America.

6. Caesar is as confused as Diner when he pigeonholes Lenau as the foremost representative of "German romantic thinking," yet at the same time has him wanting to "escape the dreary despotism of Austria." Later on, he calls Kürnberger a "fellow Austrian" of Lenau's: see *Reconstructing America*, 165, 169, 170. Admittedly, the confusion emerges from the fact that these authors speak of Lenau and these Romantic authors as representatives of German literary history, which traditionally includes Austrian and Swiss authors since they write in German too. Also, in the prenational *Vormärz* period the Austrian empire was still very much part of the German *Bund*—though the first stirrings of nationalism were felt in the Habsburg empire too.

7. Caesar, *Reconstructing America*, 169.

8. Robert Hoffmann, *Erzherzog Ferdinand und der Fortschritt* (Vienna: Böhlau, 1997).

9. Prejudices about America were not necessarily class-based. Arthur Schnitzler's friend Eugen Deimel, a commoner who emigrated to the U.S. in 1882 and began as a dishwasher, kept up a long correspondence with Schnitzler. He expressed all the usual stereotypes about American "materialism," "show-off money-bags," and the *"Land der Gleichheitsflegel."* Missing the cultured city of Vienna, he observed: "Vienna is to New York, what a grain exchange is to a temple of Apoll, what an accounting sheet is to a symphony of Beethoven." Heinz P. Adamek, ed., *In die Neue Welt ... : Arthur Schnitzler—Eugen Deimel Briefwechsel* (Vienna: Holzhausen, 2003); see also the review of this exchange of letters by Konstanze Fliedl in *Die Presse/Spectrum*, 26 July 2003, VI.

10. Justin Stagl, Ulrich Graf Arco-Zinneberg, Verena Winiwarter, and Georg Rigele, eds., Draft of the Final Report of the research project "Eine Reise um die Erde ... Adelige Weltanschauung und Naturbild um 1900: Das 'Tagebuch meiner Reise um die Erde 1892-1893' von Erzherzog Franz Ferdinand." In this research report the original text of the diary is juxtaposed with the published one. In the published version Francis Ferdinand's outspoken observations were censored and toned down by his editor, Count Beck. I am grateful to Georg Rigele for providing me with a copy of the research report.

11. Peter Gay, *Freud: A Life for Our Time* (New York: Doubleday, 1988), 211f., 497f., 560–70 (quotations).

12. Kurt Albert Mayer, "A Massachusetts Yankee in Emperor Franz Joseph's Court: Charles Francis Adams, Jr., Sojourning in Austria, 1873," in Thomas Fröschl, Margarethe Grandner, and Birgitta Bader-Zaar, eds., *Nordamerikastudien: Historische und literaturwissenschaftliche Forschungen aus österreichischen Universitäten zu den Vereinigten Staaten und Kanada*, Wiener Beiträge zur Geschichte der Neuzeit, Series 24 (Vienna: Verlag für Geschichte und Politik, 2000), 175–91.

13. Richard Kuisel, "Americanization for Historians," commentary on Jessica C. W. Gienow-Hecht's *"Shame on US?* Academics, Cultural Transfer, and the Cold War—A Critical Review," *Diplomatic History* 24 (summer 2000), 466–515 (quotation on 509).

14. Helmut Lackner, "Travel Accounts from the United States and Their Influences on Taylorism, Fordism and Productivity in Austria," in Günter Bischof and Anton Pelinka, eds., *The Americanization/Westernization of Austria*, Contemporary Austrian Studies [CAS], Series 12 (New Brunswick: Transaction, 2004), 38–60.

15. Ibid., 42–50.

16. André Pfoertner, "The Americanization of Austrian Business Culture," in Bischof and Pelinka, *The Americanization/Westernization of Austria*, 61–73.

17. Matthias Fuchs and Klaus Weiermaier, "The Impact of U.S. Management on Austrian Management Cultures in Tourism," in ibid., 74–96.

18. Peter Eppel, "Exiled Austrians in the USA 1938 to 1945: Immigration, Exile, Remigration, no Invitation to Return," in Walter Hölbling and Reinhold Wagnleitner, eds., *The European Emigrant Experience in the U.S.A.* (Tübingen: Gunter Narr Verlag, 1992), 25–50.

19. Adi Wimmer, "'Expelled and Banished': The Exile Experience of Austrian 'Anschluss' Victims in Personal Histories and Literary Documents," in Hölbling and Wagnleitner, *The European Emigrant Experience in the U.S.A.*, 51–72. The Austrian legation in Washington faced a great challenge answering all the émigrés' "letter to the editor" denouncing Austria for complicity in Hitler's war crimes. See Günter Bischof, *Austria in the First Cold War, 1945—55: The Leverage of the Weak* (New York: St. Martin's, 1999), 66.

20. Günter Bischof, "Einige Thesen zu einer Mentalitätsgeschichte deutscher Kriegsgefangenschaft in amerikanischer Gewahrsam," in Günter Bischof and Rüdiger Overmans, eds., *Kriegsgefangenschaft im Zweiten Weltkrieg: Eine vergleichende Perspektive* (Ternitz-Pottschach: Höller, 1999), 175–212.

21. Heinrich Treichl, *Fast ein Jahrhundert: Erinnerungen* (Vienna: Zsolnay, 2003), 171–77.

22. Arnold Krammer, *Nazi Prisoners of War in America* (New York: Stein and Day, 1979), 197; Matthias Reiß, *"Die Schwarzen waren unsere Freunde": Deutsche Kriegsgefangene in der amerikanischen Gesellschaft 1942–1946*, Krieg und Geschichte Series, Series 11 (Paderborn: Schöningh, 2002). For a keen analysis of the American reeducation efforts among German POWs in the U.S., see Oliver M. A. Schmidt, *A Civil Empire by Co-optation: German-American Exchange Programs as Cultural Diplomacy, 1945–1961* (Ph.D. diss., Harvard University 1999), 109–19 (quotation on 118).

23. See the classic study by Reinhold Wagnleitner, *Coca-Colonisation und Kalter Kreig: Die Kulturmission der USA in Österreich nach dem Zweiten Weltkrieg* (Vienna: Verlag für Gesellschaftskritik, 1991); English version: *Coca-Colonization and the Cold War: The Cultural Mission of the United States in Austria after the Second World War* (Chapel Hill: University of North Carolina Press, 1994); on the Marshall Plan see Günter Bischof, Anton Pelinka, and Dieter Stiefel, eds., *The Marshall Plan in Austria*, CAS, Series 8 (New Brunswick: Transaction, 2000). Gerhard H. Weiss makes the point that the American occupiers had only modest success in reforming the Austrian education system. There were too many obstacles of tradition and also a hidebound educational bureaucracy. See his "Das österreichische Erziehungswesen nach 1945 im Einfluss der USA," in Peter Pabisch, ed., *From Wilson to Waldheim: Proceedings of a Workshop on Austrian-American Relations 1917–1987* (Riverside: Ariadne, 1989), 228–38.

24. Ingrid Bauer, *Welcome Ami Go Home: Die amerikanische Besatzung in Salzburg 1945–1955: Erinnerungslandschaft aus einem Oral-History-Projekt* (Salzburg: Pustet, 1998), citation 214.

25. Wagnleitner, *Coca-Colonisation und Kalter Krieg*, 195. The peak of the German program came in the midst of the Korean War in 1952, when 4,000 German leaders visited the U.S.

26. Ibid., 195; the raw estimate of 800 Austrian leaders comes from Karin Schmidt-Gerlich, an employee of the U.S. Embassy in Vienna, who is involved in organizing the program today. On Gruber's October 1946 visit, see Günter Bischof, "Where May Meets Lazarsfeld: American Public Opinion toward Austria in the Early Cold War," in Akira Iriye, ed., *Rethinking International Relations: Ernest R. May and the Study of World Affairs* (Chicago: Imprint Publications, 1998), 313f.

27. Hermann-Josef Rupieper, *Die Wurzeln der Westdeutschen Nachkriegsdemokratie: Der Amerikanische Beitrag 1945–1952* (Opladen: Westdeutscher Verlag, 1993), 403.

28. Kurt K. Tweraser, "The Politics of Productivity and Corporatism: The Late Marshall Plan in Austria, 1950–54," in Günter Bischof, Anton Pelinka, and Rolf Steininger, eds., *Austria in the Nineteen Fifties*, CAS, Series 3 (New Brunswick: Transaction, 1995), 91–115 (quotation on 104f).

29. See the essays by Wilfried Fluck and Volker Berghahn in Alexander Stephan, ed., *Americanization and Anti-Americanism: The German Encounter with American Culture after 1945* (New York: Berghahn, 2004); for Fritz Plasser's essay, see Bischof and Pelinka, eds., *Americanization and Westernization of Austria* (New Brunswick: Transaction, 2004). The 1990s' "post-cultural imperialism" and "poststructural" agency, where acceptance and resistance of receiving societies is stressed in the "cultural transmission" process, is the also the subject of analysis of Gienow-Hecht, *"Shame on US?,"* 479–94 and the sophisticated responses by Richard Pells, Bruce Kuklick, Richard Kuisel, and John W. Dower, 495–528.

30. Cited in Wagnleitner, *Coca-Colonisation,* 195.

31. Cited in Schmidt, *Civil Empire by Co-optation,* 251. On Stone's central role in the cultural and intellectual cold wars in Europe, see the outstanding biography by Volker R. Berghahn, *America and the Intellectual Cold Wars in Europe* (Princeton: Princeton University Press, 2001).

32. In the post-9/11 world, the U.S. government is obviously trying to influence the Middle East and Asia, like it did Western Europe after World War I. Fourteen Pakistani and Indian students, chosen carefully by the U.S. embassies from hundreds of applicants, were deepening their knowledge of American Studies during the summer of 2003 at Washington College in Chestertown, Maryland, in the tongue-in-cheek commentary by Nick Paumgarten—"for an immersion in the American way of life (small-town variety): rigorous study, Dunkin' Donuts, Single-A ball." See Nick Paumgarten, "Leaders of Tomorrow: Salaam New York," *The New Yorker,* 11 August 2003, 24f. On 9 December 2003, three upper administrators from a Vietnamese university visited the University of New Orleans to discuss American Studies programming as part of their tour through the U.S., facilitated through the State Department Visitors Program.

33. The complete numbers are in the anniversary brochure, Lonnie Johnson and Karin Riegler, eds., *Fulbright at Fifty: Austrian-American Educational Exchange 1950–2000* (Vienna: Austrian-American Educational Commission, Fulbright Commission, 2000), 54. I am grateful to Dr. Lonnie Johnson, the Executive Secretary of the Austrian Fulbright Commission, for kindly providing me with the updated set of figures.

34. Arno Heller, "'I will never forget the lecture he gave on ...'" in Johnson and Riegler, *Fulbright at Fifty,* 29.

35. Thomas Chorherr, *Wir Täterkinder: Junges Leben zwischen Hakenkreuz, Bomben und Freiheit* (Vienna: Molden, 2001), 287–96 (citation on 297).

36. For a brochure with the complete statistical breakdown of Austrian AFSers up to 1993, see AFS Austauschprogramme für Interkulturelles Lernen, ed., *AFS Jahresprogramm 1950–1993* (Vienna, 1993).

37. See the testimonials by Ruth Feldgrill-Zankel, Gerda Frey, and Günter Bischof in the fiftieth anniversary brochure "50 Jahre AFS-Österreich: Forever young!" *Intercultura* 3 (May, 1999): 14, 15, 30.

38. See the commentaries by Patrick Worms and Julia Häusler in "Diversion in AFS oder: Ist Austausch mit den USA noch zeitgemäss?" *Intercultura* 4 (September, 2001): 4.

39. See the brochure Günter Bischof and Franz Mathis, *Friends and Partners in Education 1976–2003* (Innsbruck, 2003), 35f. (statistics of exchange programs), 25–32 (personal testimonials).

40. Oliver Schmidt, "No Innocents Abroad: The Salzburg Impetus and American Studies in Europe," in Reinhold Wagnleitner and Elaine Tyler May, eds., *"Here, There and Everywhere": The Foreign Politics of American Popular Culture* (Hanover: University of New England Press, 2000), 64–78 (citations on 64f.). This essay is based on his much more

detailed dissertation chapter "Of Passionate Pilgrims and Innocents Abroad"; see *Civil Empire by Co-optation,* 302–418. On Matthiesen and his Salzburg experience in 1947, see his *From the Heart of Europe* (New York: Oxford University Press, 1948), 3–66.

41. The larger story is told in Berghahn, *America and the Intellectual Cold Wars in Europe.*

42. On the U.S. Army's politics of anticommunism, led by the Education Chief Dr. Samuel H. Williams, see Schmidt, *Civil Empire by Co-optation,* 334–62 (Molden's denunciation on 344ff.).

43. Schmidt, citing Sigmund Skard, *American Studies in Europe,* 2 vols (Philadelphia, 1958), in "No Innocents Abroad," 65.

44. Schmidt, "No Innocents Abroad," 71–74 (citation on 73). No exact number of Austrians attending the Salzburg Seminar since 1948 is available. Marie-Louise Ryback of the Salzburg Seminar has provided the estimate of 20 Austrians annually over the past twenty years. In 2002, for example, a total of 1,158 people participated in Salzburg Seminar sessions, among them 26 Austrians. Personal e-mail, Ryback to Bischof, 15 October 2003. I am grateful to Mrs. Ryback for providing these numbers.

45. Timothy Ryback, "Encounters at the Schloss," *Harvard Magazine* (November-December 1987): 67–72 (citation on 67).

46. Skard also added: "In a period when American studies were being organized all over Europe, under great difficulties and sometimes against resistance, the Seminar served as a spearhead by offering unobtrusively to the postwar generation of European scholarship a brief and informal, but solid introduction to the field." Quoted in Schmidt, "No Innocents Abroad," 64f.

47. On the slow, uneven, and spotty development of American Studies in Austria before World War II, see Margarete Grandner and Birgitta Bader-Zaar, "Lehre und Forschung über Nordamerika an Österreichs Universitäten vom Beginn des 19. Jahrhunderts bis 1955," in: Fröschl, Grandner, and Bader-Zaar, *Nordamerikastudien,* 108–73.

48. Schmidt argues that the Salzburg Seminar was crucial for the development of American Studies in and the Americanization of West Germany, ever since four Germans were invited to attend the first session in 1947. The list of German Salzburg fellows reads like a who's who of German academia in general and American Studies in particular; see *Civil Empire of Co-optation,* 453–62 (list on 454). For a highly informative analysis of the development of American studies in Germany, see Philipp Gassert, "Between Political Reconnaissance Work and Democratizing Science: American Studies in Germany, 1917–1953," *Bulletin of the German Historical Institute* [Washington] 32 (spring 2003): 33–50; see also the testimonials in the interviews by Astrid M. Eckert of four prominent German historians of America, in "American History in Germany: The View of the Practitioners," ibid., 51–84.

49. Anton Pelinka, "The Impact of American Scholarship on Austrian Political Science: The Making of a Discipline," in Bischof and Pelinka, eds., *Americanization/Westernization of Austria,* 226–34.

50. Klaus Naumann, "Der Beginn einer wunderbaren Freundschaft. Beobachtungen aus der Frühzeit der deutsch-amerikanischen Militärbeziehungen," in Heinz Bude and Bernd Greiner, eds., *Westbindungen: Amerika in der Bundesrepublik* (Hamburg: Hamburger Edition, 1999), 138–80.

51. Günter Bischof and Martin Kolfer, "Austria's Postwar Occupation, the Marshall Plan, and Secret Rearmament as 'Westernizing Agents' 1945–1968," in Bischof and Pelinka, *Americanization/Westernization of Austria,* 199–225.

52. Schmidt, *Civil Empire by Co-optation,* 419–33 (for the 150 multiplier, 433). For an extensive evaluation of the German visitors programs, see also Rupieper, *Wurzeln,* 403–20.

53. McCloy quoted in Schmidt, *Civil Empire by Co-optation,* 420.

54. This trajectory is analyzed in Günter Bischof, "Restoration, Not Renewal: From Nazi to Four-Power Occupation—The Difficult Transition to Democracy in Austria after 1945," *Hungarian Studies* 14, no. 2 (2000): 207–31.

55. For more information, see the informative chapter by Wagnleitner, *Coca-Kolonisation und Kalter Krieg*, 207–24 (numbers and quotations on 209, 215, 221, 224). He concludes in his typical tongue-in-cheek style that the ISB helped establish a "beachhead" for American drama in Austria and made it *"hof- oder besser: burg-fähig"* (220), which is to say that some American plays eventually made it onto the stage of Vienna's venerable old *Burgtheater.*

56. Ibid., 224–34 (quotations on 230, 234).

57. Christina Hainzl, "American Painting: The New York Museum of Modern Art's International Program in Austria," in Bischof and Pelinka, *Americanization/Westernization of Austria,* 139–52. Robert Fleck suggests that the "young Turks" of the postwar Austrian art scene looked to Paris rather than New York for inspiration: see "Kunst in einer Zeit der Restauration: Die Rekonstruktion einer Szene moderner Kunst in der österreichischen Nachkriegszeit," in Wolfgang Kos and Georg Rigele, eds., *Inventur 45/55: Österreich im ersten Jahrzehnt der Zweiten Republik* (Vienna: Sonderzahl, 1996), 441–71.

58. For more detail, see Günter Bischof, "Is There a Specific Austrian Anti-Americanism after World War?" in Michael Daxlbauer, Astrid Fellner, and Thomas Fröschl, eds., *Austrian (Anti-)Americanisms* (Tübingen: Lit Verlag, 2004).

59. David W. Ellwood, *Anti-Americanism in Western Europe: A Comparative Perspective* (Occasional Paper, European Seminar Studies Series, no. 3), The John Hopkins University Bologna Center, April 1999.

60. See the opening chapters of Wagnleitner, *Coca-Colonization;* Caesar, *Reconstructing America;* Berndt Ostendorf, "Americanization and Anti-Americanism in the Age of Globalization," copy of unpublished paper in possession of the author.

61. Berndt Ostendorf, "Why is American Popular Culture so Popular? A View from Europe," *Amerikastudien/American Studies* 56, no. 3 (2001): 339–66.

62. For one of the premier analyses of these trends, see Reinhold Wagnleitner, "The Empire of Fun, or Talkin' Soviet Union Blues: The Sound of Freedom and U.S. Cultural Hegemony in Europe," *Diplomatic History* 23 (summer 1999): 499–524, repr. in Michael J. Hogan, ed. *The Ambiguous Legacy: U.S. Foreign Policy in the American Century* (Cambridge: Cambridge University Press, 1999), 463–99; idem, " 'No Commodity Is Quite So Strange As This Thing Called Cultural Exchange': The Foreign Politics of American Pop Culture Hegemony," *Amerikastudien/American Studies* 46, no. 3 (2001): 443–70 (for a complete listing of his "Americanization" *oeuvre,* see 468–70); idem, "I'm Made for American from Head to Toe (The Project for a New American Century)," in Bischof and Pelinka, *Americanization/Westernization of Austria,* 18–28.

63. See the analysis by Andrew J. Bacevich, *American Empire: The Realities & Consequences of U.S. Diplomacy* (Cambridge: Harvard University Press, 2002). Paul Hollander's study of anti-Americanism makes the basic argument that most of anti-Americanism around the world starts at home in the U.S. in his *Anti-Americanism: Rational & Irrational,* expanded ed. (New Brunswick, N.J.: Transaction, 1995), see also the updated version, Paul Hollander, ed., *Understanding Anti-Americanism: Its Origins and Impact at Home and Abroad* (Chicago: Ivan R. Dee, 2004). As a case in point see the extensive discussion on Noam Chomsky's role in critiquing American foreign policy on the H-Diplo discussion network during the summer of 2003.

64. "Throughout the world, global markets are bitterly perceived as reinforcing American wealth and dominance," says Yale law professor Amy Chua, adding: "At the same time, global populist and democratic movements give strength, legitimacy, and voice to the

impoverished, frustrated, excluded masses of the world—in other words, precisely the people most susceptible to anti-American demagoguery." See Chua, "A World on the Edge," *Wilson Quarterly* 26 (autumn 2002): 62–77 (citation on 67).

65. Caesar, *Reconstructing America*, 163.

66. The situation is no different in Great Britain, where nineteenth-century stock negative images of America have been reproduced to these days; see Simon Schama's essay "The Unloved American," *The New Yorker*, 10 March 2003, 34–39.

67. Thomas Fröschl sees these roots as far back as the early sixteenth century during the discovery of America, see his "Antiamerkanismus in Europa und Lateinamerika: Sieben historische Dimensionen," in idem, ed., *Atlantische Geschichte: Wiener Zeitschrift zur Geschichte der Neuzeit* 3, no. 2 (2003): 82–97.

68. Bauer, *Welcome Ami Go Home*.

69. Merchant to Dulles, 24 August 1953, with attached Draft Memorandum from the Bureau of European Affairs, in U.S. Department of State, ed., *Foreign Relations of the United States 1952–1954*, vol. 1, part 2: *General: Economic and Political Matters* (Washington, D.C.: Government Printing Office, 1983), 1475 [hereinafter cited as FRUS].

70. "No Commodity is Quite so Strange," 447.

71. Eisenhower's prestige project is analyzed in Günter Bischof, "The Politics of Anti-Communism in the Executive Branch during the Early Cold War: Truman, Eisenhower and McCarthy(ism)," in André Kaenel, ed., *Anti-Communism and McCarthyism in the United States (1946–1954): Essays on the Politics and Culture of the Cold War* (Paris: Messene, 1995), 69–71; for Cohn and Shine's one-day rampage through Vienna and the negative press it produced, see Bischof, "Is There A Specific Austrian Anti-Americanism?"

72. Marcus Cunliffe, "The Anatomy of Anti-Americanism," in Rob Kroes and Maarten van Rossem, eds., *Anti-Americanism in Europe* (Amsterdam: Free University Press, 1986), 20–36; Konrad H. Jarausch, "Missverständnis Amerika: Antiamerikanismus als Projektion," unpublished paper read at the 2003 German Studies Association meeting in New Orleans.

73. Richard Pells, *Not Like US: How Europeans have loved, hated, and transformed American Culture since World War II* (New York: Basic Books, 1997), 160, 162.

74. Austrian Nazis protested the first performance of *Jonny* in Vienna in October 1929 and attacked it as the "outrageous introduction of Jewish-Nigger filth" by the "half-Jewish Czech" Krenek (in fact, Krenek was neither a Jew nor a Czech). See Kurt Drexel, "American Jazz in Ernst Krenek's Opera *Jonny spielt auf*," in Bischof and Pelinka, *Americanization/Westernization of Austria*, 102–11.

75. Max Merz, "Unsere Zeit und der Jazz," *Die Aula*, 14 October 1963, 6–8; for more detail see Bischof, "Is There a Specific Austrian Anti-Americanism?"; Heidegger's, Spengler's, and Jünger's analyses of the clash of American mass culture and traditional European civilization, namely America's "catastrophic" influence on Western civilization, is analyzed in Caesar, *Reconstructing America*, 187–213.

76. For a sampling of *Die Aula*'s historical revisionism, see W. W. Von Wolmar, "Erste Teilung Deutschlands," *Die Aula*, 11 May 1961, 3f.; Karl Hanns, "Der wahre Grund für die entscheidende Rolle Washingtons bei der Einkreisung und Vernichtung Deutschlands," ibid., 13 February 1963; Edmund Marheska, "Forschung und Propaganda zur Kriegsschuldfrage," ibid., 16 December 1966; 12f.; Karl Hans, "Die Wahrheit ist auf dem Wege," ibid., 12 November 1961, 9–11; Silesius, "Die Sünden wider den Geist," ibid., 12 October 1961; "Krieg und Kriegsschuldfrage," ibid. September 1999, 23–30. The bestseller is Jörg Friedrich, *Der Brand: Deutschland im Bombenkrieg 1940–1945* (Munich: Propyläen, 2002); a sample of critiques and reviews (including British) of the book is reprinted in Lothar Kettenacker, ed., *Ein Volk von Opfern: Die neue Debatte um den*

Bombenkrieg 1940–45 (Berlin: Rowohlt, 2003). The popularity of this book and the recent debate in Germany seem to suggest that the view of the murderous bombing of German civilians as an "Allied war crime" has broad support in Germany (and Austria too) as well as within the minority of the nationalist right.

77. I took a sampling of the *Volksstimme* in February 1968; see, for example, 8, 10, 12, 17 February 1968.

78. Walter Hollenstein, "Die Furchtlosen: Bemerkungen zum Wildwestfilm," *Die Zunkunft*, 11 January 1965; for further discussion and evidence, see Bischof, "Is there a Specific Anti-Americanism in Austria?" On Kreisky, see Wolfgang Petritsch, "Die österreichisch-amerikanischen Beziehungen in der Ära Kreisky (1970–1983)," in Pabisch, *From Wilson to Waldheim,* 239–56.

79. Sozialdemokratisches Indochinakomitee, ed., *Vietnam und die Sozialisten: Materialien zum Konflikt in Indochina, zu Imperialismus, Kolonialismus und Sozialdemokratie* (Vienna, 1972), 30f., 52f.

80. On the tradition of invoking the "other America," see Jackson Janes, "Michael Moore and the Parameters of the German-American Dialogue," American Institute of Contemporary Germany *At Issue* Report, http://www.aicgs.org/at-issue/ai-jj (last accessed: 10 December 2003). On Peter Kreisky and the "first" protest against the Vietnam War, see Helfried Bauer, *Vietnam und die Sozialisten: Materialien zum Konflikt in Indochina, zu Imperialismus, Kolonialismus und Sozialdemokratie* (Vienna: Sozialdemokratisches Indochina-Komitee, 1972), 61; and Heinz Fischer, *Reflexionen* (Vienna: Kremayr and Scheriau, 1998), 197f.

81. On the tameness of 1968 in Austria, see Alexandra Friedrich, "1968 in Austria," in Günter Bischof, Anton Pelinka, and Michael Gehler, eds., *Austria in the European Union,* CAS, Series 10 (New Brunswick: Transaction, 2002), 324–33. Salzburg, in fact, may have been a bit more lively than Vienna in 1968; see Ewald Hiebl, "Kein ruhiges Plätzchen: Studentenbewegung in Salzburg 1965–1975," MA Thesis, University of Salzburg, 1991.

82. This is a summary of Bischof, "Is there a Specific Anti-Americanism in Austria?"

83. Another of the more prominent critics is Günter Nenning, who used to write for the CIA-financed *Forum,* but has increasingly moved to the right. His *Profil* columns during the first Gulf War were filled with tirades decrying American "egoism and hypocrisy" and the fighting of the war for Kuwait's independence with the "typical thin veneer of the moralistic cover of crusaders." Similarly, Nenning engaged in the age-old cultural critique of American mass products ("This melting down and stamping into uniformity— this McDonaldization … this is not the 'multicultural society' but inhumanity itself, utterly desolate." See *Profil,* 12 and 21 January, 4 February 1991. Nenning quoted in Ellwood, *Anti-Americanism in Western Europe,* 21f.

84. Peter Pilz, one of the leaders of the Austrian Green Party, has provided us with a *summa* of the burgeoning anti-Americanism in the Austrian Green Party; see his *Mit Gott Gegen Alle: Amerikas Kampf um die Weltherrschaft* (Stuttgart: Deutsche Verlags-Anstalt, 2003).

85. Lothar Höbelt, *Defiant Populist: Jörg Haider and the Politics of Austria* (West Lafayette: Purdue University Press, 2002), esp. the chapter "The First American-Style Austrian Politician," 143–63.

86. The conservative Foreign Minister blasted Haider's comparison as "absurd," while the opposition political parties denounced it as "intolerable," demanding an apology from Haider and a clarification from the governing parties (among them Haider's FPÖ); see "Haider vergleicht Bush mit Saddam," and "Opposition fordert Distanzierung," *Die Presse,* 17 December 2003, http://www.diepresse/at/Artikel.aspx?channel=p&ressort=&id=394923 and http://www.diepresse/at/Artikel.aspx?channel=p&ressort=i&id=394924

(both last accessed: 17 December 2003). Ernst Sittinger column "Schadensbregenzung bei einem Weiderholungstäter," *Die Presse*, 19 December 2003, http://www.diepresse.at/ Artikel.aspx?channel-p&ressort=pk&id=3 (last accessed: 19 December 2003).

87. "Image der USA in Österreich am Tiefpunkt," *Die Presse*, 23 July 2003, 1.

88. See commentary by Burkhard Bischof, "Böser Uncle Sam," *Die Presse*, 23 July 2003, 1. A vast amount of public opinion evidence seems to indicate that anti-Americanism may be on the rise worldwide. But there is also an important trend indicating that most people have no problem with American values but do distinguish between America and George W. Bush's aggressive policies; see Reinhold Wagnleitner, "Back to the Future Revisted; Changing European Attitudes toward the United States of America between Utopia an Dystopia," *Diplomatische Akademie Occasional Paper* (forthcoming). In analyzing the dissonance between the similarity of public opinion on foreign policy issues in Europe and the U.S. on the one hand, and on the other the vast gulf that has opened between the elites on both sides of the Atlantic, Gert Krell makes the same point; see "Arroganz der Macht, Arrroganz der Ohnmacht," *Aus Politik und Zeitgeschichte*, B 31–32 (2003), 23–30. See also David W. Ellwood's updated study of European anti-Americanism, "A Brief History of European Anti-Americanism," copy of paper delivered at the Organization of American Historians' annual meeting in Memphis, Tenn., April 2003, in possession of author, now also available online as "Anti-Americanism: Why Do Europeans Resent Us?" at the History News Network's http://hnn.us/articles/1426.html (last accessed: 3 March 2005).

89. Gerd Bacher, "Gross-Texas," *Die Presse*, 31 January 2003, 2; idem, "Jeden Staat wegräumen, der im Wege steht?" ibid., 14 March 2003.

90. See the two-part interview with Peter Weibel, "Die USA—der grösste Räuber des Globus," *Der Standard*, 10/11 May 2003, and "Amerika und seine Schicksalspsychose," ibid., 12 May 2003.

91. This is the theme of Hollander's study of *Anti-Americanism*.

92. Moisés Naím, the editor of *Foreign Policy*, reminds us that European anti-Americanism "lite" has its hidden costs too: "But lite anti-Americans are equally wrong when they assume there is no cost to their broad denunciations, especially when strident attacks against U.S. policy help stoke far deeper and more pervasive animosities and suspicions against the United States, its government, and its people. Unfortunately it has become all too easy for those who disagree with specific U.S. policies to believe and disseminate the worst possible assumptions about the malicious nature, dark motivations, and hidden agendas of the United States—including horrible falsehoods." See his "The Perils of Lite Anti-Americanism," *Foreign Policy* (May/June 2003): 95f.

93. The classic study of proclaiming Austria a "special case" in the early Cold War is Manfried Rauchensteiner, *Der Sonderfall: Die Besatzugnszeit in Österreich 1945 bis 1955* (Graz: Styria, 1979).

94. Caesar devotes two chapters to the intellectual pedigree of this fateful German conservatism (Nietzsche, van den Bruck, Spengler, Jünger), ending in Heidegger's notion of America as a "catastrophe" for Western civilization: *Reconstructing America*, 162–213.

95. Günter Bischof, "Das amerikanische Jahrhundert: Europas Niedergang—Amerikas Aufstieg, *Zeitgeschichte* 28, no. 2 (March/April 2001), 75-95.

96. Janes, "Michael Moore and the Parameters of the German-American Dialogue."

Part III

USSR/RUSSIA, POLAND

FROM COLD WAR TO WARY PEACE: AMERICAN CULTURE IN THE USSR AND RUSSIA

◆　　◆　　◆

Marsha Siefert

"Their starting-point is different, and their courses are not the same; yet each of them seems to be marked out by the will of Heaven to sway the destinies of half the globe."[1] Alexis de Tocqueville's 1835 prediction about the United States and Russia seemed to come true after 1945. In 1941 both had put aside their ideological enmity sufficiently to defeat Germany and, as immortalized in the familiar 1944 photographs of Stalin first with Roosevelt and then Truman, discussed their destinies as equals. The rapid dissolution of the wartime alliance and Churchill's 6 March 1946 "iron curtain" speech christened the "superpowers" as rivals for the rest of the globe. Thus to discuss American culture in the Soviet Union after 1945 is to invoke the major rhetorical frame of the second half of the twentieth century—the Cold War.

Few subjects escaped that rhetorical frame, and each side developed formulaic condemnations of the other, upping the "anti-" in times of political tension. At the same time each developed policies and practices, covert and overt, whereby they pursued their goals. International cultural events, whether film festivals, trade fairs, or Olympic competitions, were sites where not just countries but political systems were pitted against each other. Cultural products, along with missiles and microbes, became a test of what each system could produce, in quality and content.

Since each side proclaimed itself an egalitarian political and social system, domestic critiques of the other were as important as positive cultural projection abroad. Each side ferreted out traitors, whether denouncing communist spies or exiling "cosmopolitan wreckers." In such a tense environment, espe-

---

Notes for this section begin on page 209.

cially in the first two decades after World War II, it is not surprising that the Soviet Union would actively seek to regulate what was in other countries called "Americanization."

Several contexts inform any analysis of American culture in the Soviet Union. The first is World War II, or as it is known in the USSR, the Great Patriotic War. The Soviet Union was a victor, but as compared to the United States it sustained huge losses of over 26 million people and devastating damages to its cities, collective farms, and infrastructure. The housing shortage alone was formidable, and the remaining population was exhausted. The Soviet government saw the Marshall Plan as a pretext to "Americanize" Europe; its extension to the former enemy, Germany, drew the line in the sand. The country's choices to invest in heavy industry, weaponry, and science took a toll on the population and, given the resulting consumer shortages, left it vulnerable to the seductions of American images.

The image of world communism is a significant factor in interpreting American cultural efforts. After the October Revolution, which was the most significant temporal demarcation between Russia and "the West," the Soviet "experiment" was of interest to Europe, and the USSR a place to which curious Americans ventured. But officially, even after American diplomatic recognition in 1933,[2] the U.S. continued to be the most overtly anticommunist of all the Western powers. The Soviet control of communist parties continued to foster fears of world revolution even after the dissolution of the Comintern in 1943. In the wake of World War II the activities of communist parties in several European countries outside the reach of the Red Army, like France, Greece, and Italy, energized the U.S. anticommunist effort, especially given the effectiveness of the "iron curtain" around Eastern Europe. The 1948 formation of a new international communist organization, the Cominform, appeared to confirm America's worst suspicions. In American rhetoric all communism—whether Asian, Latin American, African, or European—emanated from Moscow. Thus American metaphors for Soviet influence—"captive nations," "Soviet satellites," and puppet governments—fueled the rhetoric of American cultural diplomacy.

The Soviet position toward American culture historically takes strength from the longer debate among Russian intellectuals about "the West." So-called "Westernizers" and "Slavophiles" experienced alternations and altercations in their influence arising from external threats and internal tensions. Even when most positively tilted toward the West, the Russian elites tend to pick and choose which Western innovations they prefer to adopt, from constitutions to fashions. Russia's statesmen have forged alliances and fought wars with other European powers, and its performers and writers have created a vogue for Russian culture in European capitals, but "the West" is always suspect, always a visitor. For their part, even the most fervent Westernizers have never doubted the uniqueness of Russian culture.[3] So while the Soviet Cold War formulation of antipathy and aspiration toward the West, coupled with a belief in the strength of Russian culture, is not new, the active inclusion of the U.S. in "the West" seems a particular Cold War formulation, whereby the label "American" was singled out as representing individual cultural items or specific political actions.

Claims of Russian uniqueness were, as with most other national ideologies, often combined with messianic ideas, as in works by Berdyaev and Dostoevsky. The 1945 war victory reinforced the Soviet Union's belief in its historic destiny and claim to Great Power status. The vehemence of the Russian response to what was called American imperialism was in part a demand to be treated as equal in all negotiations, and cultural agreements were no exception. American culture was accepted into the USSR on the formal principle of exact exchange: one performer for another, ten students for another ten. Still, of course, each desired the better of the balance and each attempted to play upon the other's inconsistencies between ideology and practice. The Americans' most critical weakness was their treatment of race relations.

Both sides recognized that "the Negro" was a target of international communism in the 1920s and 1930s,[4] which underlay infinite complexities in Americans' attempt to control their image abroad. Too, recognition of the African-American contribution to American popular culture was not unproblematic at home, where cover songs, easily excised film sequences, and segregated audiences allowed for it to be mediated or made invisible well into the postwar period. Soviet commentators magnified racial unrest, and Soviet artists did not shy away from including downtrodden black characters in anti-American dramatizations on canvas, stage, and screen. American politicians recognized this vulnerability and countered it both in cultural diplomacy and, eventually, in domestic policy.[5]

The Soviet Union, on the other hand, was vulnerable in several areas of domestic policy and outlook. The tenet of atheism in communist ideology and the intermittent state persecution of various churches made their citizens a target for American exports with a religious theme. Concomitantly, their so-called "Puritanism" gave American cultural representations of intimate and private life a particular appeal. State support for anti-Semitism, particularly virulent during the last years of Stalinism, never wholly disappeared. Support for Jewish emigration from the USSR entered U.S. law in 1974 when Congress passed the Jackson-Vanik Amendment to the Trade Act, which prohibited extending "most favored nation" trading status to countries that, among other things, restricted the right to emigrate.[6]

Thus, American culture reached the Soviet Union under tightly controlled circumstances, whether through official exchanges or other negotiated agreements. Once selected, American cultural items were screened frame by frame, reviewed word by word. Texts for print, stage, or screen were edited to eliminate what was considered harmful, for example political discourse or excessive sex and violence. New introductions for translated books and careful reviews published guidelines for interpreting movies and novels, and instructions to this end were provided to youth leaders in the Komsomol (communist youth league) or at "culture houses." The America presented to the bulk of the Soviet population represented what the authorities deemed consistent with the negative images of American capitalism or otherwise "harmless." Of course there were limits to Soviet control. Popular responses to cultural products that seemed to match ideological criteria sometimes backfired. Also, American cultural products appeared in many "unofficial" ways in the Soviet Union. These contraband items, sometimes paid for, sometimes appropriated, sometimes smuggled, sometimes bartered, sometimes broadcast, sometimes given as gifts, were a critical part of the American cultural presence in the Soviet Union, and their illegality made them more desirable and perhaps more influential. The Soviet Union may offer literally a "controlled" experiment of a country attempting to prevent Americanization.

For a land as large as the Soviet Union, it is impossible to generalize about the interpretation and reception of American culture. While many Western reports of American cultural influence by necessity concentrated on Moscow—and indeed, influential audiences were certainly located there—the varied contexts of reception from the Caucasus to Siberia, from the Baltic republics to Central Asia, made a difference in terms of what items circulated and to whom they appealed. At times the peripheries proved safe havens for imports during repressive state campaigns. Seaports provided active trading centers, while border locations benefited from permeable frontiers. East European "satellites," with much less stringent censorship, were important gateways for Western ideas and products. The extent to which the Soviet press identified jazz clubs in Ivanovo or jeans made in Tblisi or film preferences in Taganrog, therefore, suggests the penetration and spread of American culture beyond the Moscow and Leningrad intelligentsia and their offspring. Ultimately the flavor of American cultural influence must depend upon individual items and individual audiences, and further must be situated in the whole of Soviet foreign imports, which in almost all areas were more numerous from Europe and the rest of the world than from America. This essay will sample the official and remembered response to American culture with these caveats.

The drama of the Soviet collapse has contributed to the victor's history, giving a not-insignificant role to American popular culture.[7] This essay must also cover a second postwar period—the post–Cold War. Fifty years behind Europe, the Russian Federation is subject to a new round of what might be recognized as classic Americanization. In this story too the continuity and legacy of the Cold War period helps to provide an interpretative frame for the American model and the Russian idea.

American Cold War Cultural Diplomacy

Anticommunism was a cornerstone of American cultural as well as conventional diplomacy. The Cold Warriors close to the Truman White House, warming to containment policy, passed legislation to enable its overt and covert pursuit to the farthest regions. After armed conflict in Korea and the "loss" of China, Eisenhower's administration, especially through the ministrations of the Dulles brothers, made the disintegration of the Soviet Union and the liberation of the "captive nations" a central goal.[8] Key to their psychological warfare was a direct appeal to the "Soviet hearts and minds" via radio.

The Voice of America (VOA), which had begun as a U.S. government broadcaster in 1942, was revitalized in 1947 by broadcasts in Russian to the Soviet Union. In 1953 it was divorced from the U.S. State Department and put under the aegis of the newly formed U.S. Information Agency (USIS abroad). Encouraged by Western émigré organizations as well as hard-liners in the administration, VOA alternated its programming of news, features, and entertainment, including rebroadcasts of American radio shows containing strident anticommunist propaganda. Predictable themes were framed in apocalyptic language, depicting the USSR as a "power of evil" and proclaiming "the inevitability of the [U.S.'s] ultimate triumph." Even sympathetic analysts feared that Soviet listeners might experience "propaganda fatigue." After being targeted by the McCarthy hearings for potential communist infiltration, VOA adopted the C. D. Jackson Committee's recommendation that in future they avoid the propaganda line in favor of straight news and entertainment to enhance their credibility.[9] In 1957, for example, a VOA Russian broadcaster was able to write that VOA's mission was "to tell the world the truth about the United States and its people," and show "the distinctiveness of American culture" because it was "so far from the Old World."[10]

Instead of abandoning radio's propaganda aims, however, the Cold Warriors privatized them. A new radio station called Radio Free Europe (RFE) was organized to be "a free-wheeling, free-speaking ally in the propaganda war," according to *Time*,[11] and its sister station, Radio Liberty, began broadcasting to the Soviet Union a few days before Stalin's death. An extensive U.S. fundraising campaign, "Crusade for Freedom," provided the cover story for covert CIA support and allowed its government association to be "plausibly denied."[12] At both radio stations, which maintained separate administrations in Munich,[13] news was gathered using high-level monitoring of Soviet and East European publications and broadcasts, reformulated according to "objective" standards, and broadcast back into communist lands via transmitters located in Munich, at the permission and sometimes sufferance of the West German government, and later Spain. Supervised by Americans who were sometimes but not always knowledgeable about broadcasting, Radio Liberty's émigré staff, which transmitted in eighteen languages, represented a mini-USSR in exile without the space to contain the tension among the various peoples.[14] The stress was on cultural programming, and the hope was to encourage "anti-Sovietism" among intellectual and cultural elites. In addition to high-level interviews with political and cultural figures, the broadcasts carried religion as a continuing theme.

Unsurprisingly, the Soviet government consistently and vehemently denounced both these stations. Putting their money behind their words, they began jamming broadcasts in 1948 and by 1958 had expended more resources on jamming than on their own domestic and international broadcasting. Paradoxically, after the war the Soviet government had provided their citizenry with 5 million new short-wave radio receivers, enlarging the potential audience for Radio Liberty.[15] The Soviet government (and many others) never believed the government-private distinction between the "voices" of America, and the 1967 revelation of Radio Liberty's CIA funding was mined for future Soviet press attacks, themselves notable for explosive and creative invective. Nonetheless, though listening to the radios was discouraged, it was never made illegal, and the English-language stations were never jammed—presumably because Soviet elites who understood English were ideologically equipped to decode it appropriately.

As the policy of the Eisenhower administration shifted to a more gradual approach and Stalin's death loosened the zealous anticosmopolitan yoke, both countries moved toward the establishment of cultural exchange, which began in "the spirit of Geneva" after 1955. The general agreement, legalized in the Lacey-Zarubin bill of 1958, provided for a range of exchanges, from performing arts groups to students, professors, and business professionals. Cooperation was initiated in several fields, including biology, medicine, science, and aeronautics. All through the well-publicized cancellations of performance tours, Olympic boycotts, and other political crises, the student exchanges and most of the scientific exchanges were never halted.

During negotiations the Soviet side was adamant about including personnel exchanges in technological fields, an area in which Russia and other European countries had long recognized American achievement.[16] Because both Soviet and American negotiators recognized technological knowledge as a potential carrier of military secrets, it was also the area in which American politicians most often assaulted the exchange program.[17] In return the Americans demanded onsite exhibitions and open distribution of information about America. For the Americans it was a bargain well made.[18] The 1959 American National Exhibition in Moscow's Sokolniki Park was a major diplomatic coup for the U.S. From the cheerful and fluent young American guides to the glossy technological exhibits, the crowds responded enthusiastically. Symbolic locations of Cold War geography always include the exhibition's model kitchen, in which Khrushchev debated Nixon; consumer goods seemed to win a clear victory for capitalist production.[19] To bring home the contrast, the exchange agreement revived the wartime Russian-language monthly *Amerika* in 50,000 copies in exchange for equivalent copies of *Soviet Life.* Some *Amerika* articles were reprinted from U.S. photo magazines about everyday life, from fashion to automobiles and other "polite propaganda." But too few Americans were buying *Soviet Life,* so the Soviets in turn limited *Amerika*'s distribution. The USIA, which published the magazine, began printing it on stronger paper with better binding, hoping it would be "passed around."[20]

The most visible aspects of American culture in the Soviet Union were the exchange programs in the performing arts. Precedents, such as the 1949 meeting of liberal-leaning American writers and musicians like Arthur Miller and Aaron Copland with their Soviet counterparts at the Waldorf-Astoria in New York City, ended in ideological impasse. So the next jousts took place by proxy, in locations outside the USSR and the U.S. For example, in 1952 the Congress of Culture Freedom (CCF) chose Paris, a "hotbed of communist intellectuals" and the "soft underbelly of the North Atlantic Treaty Alliance,"[21] as the site of a major arts festival to canonize the "Masterpieces of the Twentieth Century." The CCF, though ostensibly a transatlantic culture alliance, was known to be essentially American-funded; it was not only anticommunist, but also antineutralist.[22] As with other cultural efforts of the time,[23] the goal was to showcase the American culture as both equal to the European and superior to the results of Soviet socialist realism. Any art form, whether serialism in music or abstract expressionism in art, that was branded as "modern," "decadent," or forbidden by the Soviets was by definition a demonstration of freedom and anticommunism. The Paris musical program included several "modern" American composers as well as several compositions by Russian émigrés like Stravinsky, and "cosmopolitan" works by Shostakovich and Prokofiev no longer heard in the Soviet Union. The program notes and attendant publicity made it clear that only communists, not Russians, were excluded from twentieth-century artistic "products of free minds in a free world."[24]

The Paris festival exhibits several characteristics of American cultural diplomacy toward the Soviet Union. First, American CCF officials privately saw "the traditional European misconception of the United States as a country lacking in culture [as] a misconception consistently exploited by Communist propaganda."[25] Second, the anticommunist left, which had once been acquainted with, if not enamored of, "the God that Failed," was heavily involved in both the American CCF and the critique of American mass culture. As a consequence many began "to see anti-communism and the defense of high culture as two aspects of the same struggle."[26] In sum, the Paris festival established a formula for high culture in the Cold War that came to be instrumental in populating arts exchanges during the Thaw and afterwards. From the Soviet point of view the American emphasis on high culture, while demonstrably less successful in Western Europe, fit precisely the cultural preferences of the Soviet Union. Although they differed in method and highlighted those differences rhetorically, both America and the Soviet Union had traditions of cultural enlightenment vis-à-vis culture. Both saw themselves as latecomers to the European center, and both had highly evolved systems of education that were geared to incorporate their large populations into the "history of civilization." Thus both countries hoped to win the cultural contest in terms of achievement in European high culture.

One U.S. touring group sent throughout Europe and the rest of the world demonstrates the complexities of this contest. In late 1955 the Soviet Union had issued to the Everyman Opera an invitation for December 1955–January 1956 performances of *Porgy and Bess* in Leningrad and Moscow. They offered to provide transportation, lodging, and a guaranteed sum in return for the performances that made the trip feasible.[27] In spite of the conflicting American views of the opera, seen either as high culture or as a representation of "Negro" life,[28] the U.S. State Department believed in its propaganda value. Eisenhower's special assistant C. D. Jackson argued that the Negro cast, through the elegance of their clothes and their freedom from fear "offstage," would counter Soviet propaganda about racial injustice. And in any case, the opportunities for the cast to talk to individual Russians would be "very limited."[29] Certainly the U.S. State Department briefed the cast to avoid discussing the race issue. Before the first performance in Leningrad, the Soviet hosts countered their own propaganda vulnerability by providing transportation to Baptist and Catholic church services for the cast members. Khrushchev, Molotov, and Bulganin attended the Moscow performance and were reported on in the Soviet press. The American director explained in a Leningrad periodical that *Porgy and Bess* was about "undying love" and "affirms our belief in the essential goodness which is in everyone."[30] Still, the violence of the murder, the venality of all the white characters, and the drug use and heightened sexuality of the rape scene on stage[31] confirmed some Soviet preconceptions about the degradation of American society in spite of the well-dressed Negro cast. As a Soviet reviewer noted, "the spectator leaves the theatre with the full assurance that Porgy will find his wife and that happiness will once again be established in his miserable hut."[32] There was something for every interpretation.

Whether the exchange visits of American performers after 1958 were perceived as demonstrating specifically American culture is highlighted by the Soviet response to classical musicians on the exchange. When van Cliburn won the Tchaikovsky piano competition in Moscow in May 1958 he became an American hero, but Russians, well aware that his Juilliard teacher was the Russian émigré Rosina Lhévinne, called him "Vanushka," and he called Russians "my people."[33] Metropolitan Opera tenor Jan Peerce revisited his father's homeland and was engaged for a recital in Moscow. Encouraged by the Israeli Ambassador at intermission, he added a Yiddish-Hebrew song, "A Plea to God" dealing with Jewish oppression, as an encore. Soviet officials indirectly suggested he continue this practice, although his future visits were more proscribed.[34] Paul Robeson, whose passport was revoked by the U.S. State Department in 1950, was granted a visa to sing at the 100th anniversary of the birth of Sholom Aleichem. But when he sang encores of Yiddish songs in Russian, he unexpectedly proclaimed solidarity between the black and Jewish peoples.[35] Aaron Copland, appreciated by the Soviets for his wartime support, his hosting of the Soviet Waldorf delegation in 1949, and his ordeal at the McCarthy hearings, visited for the first time in 1960 and was considered a friend of Soviet music.[36] But he too angered the Soviet editors of *Sovietskaia Muzyka* in 1972 in his postscript to the new addition of *The New Music* (1968) by writing that "musical creativity in the U.S.S.R. has been stultified."[37] Violinist Isaac Stern provided a light-hearted summation of the exchanges: "We send them our Jewish violinists from Odessa, and they send us their Jewish violinists from Odessa."[38] This difficulty in "Americanizing" through musical performers is illustrated by the way in which other affiliations become more important than their American-ness as their cultural ambassadorship is monitored from both sides of the Cold War divide.

The exchanges among dance companies provide the most vivid illustration. The first Soviet visit by the American Ballet Theatre, with the "very American work" of *Rodeo*, music by Aaron Copland, was received better than the U.S. had expected.[39] But the Soviet Union, in return for a Bolshoi ballet tour, demanded a visit by George Balanchine, the innovative New York City Ballet choreographer originally from the USSR's Georgian Republic. He boldly programmed abstract ballets danced to "decadent dodecaphony" by Webern and Schoenberg along with Prokofiev's *Prodigal Son*, a biblical story not yet seen in the Soviet Union.[40] He also featured an African-American male dancer whose dance, though heavily applauded, was described the next morning as "a Negro slave's submission to the tyranny of an ardent white mistress."[41]

Ballet came to symbolize another crisis important to the Cold War competition—the importance of defections.[42] Russian ballet star Rudolf Nureyev was one of the first to vote with his feet, defecting to England in 1961, with others like Mikhail Barishnikov in 1974 and Alexander Godunov in 1979 following suit. Because substantial privileges were given to top Soviet performers, these defections appeared to demonstrate the lure of American life, however the Soviet authorities tried to portray it. A summing up of all these themes at the darkest moments of the "evil empire" emerges—with the help of Hollywood—in the film *White Nights* (1985). Ballet dancer and Russian defector Mikhail Barishnikov stars as a ballet dancer and Russian defector whose plane is forced to land on Soviet territory. To "convince him" to return to the Bolshoi, the KGB places him in the care of an American who has defected to Russia—a black tap dancer played by black tap dancer Gregory Hines. Who persuades whom, with calculated rapprochement—between ballet and tap, black and white, Russian and American, high and pop—is Hollywood's gloss on what was projected as the persuasive power of American culture.

The Crucible: Ideology and "High Culture"

The importation, translation, study, critique, and performance of American literature and drama were indeed a "crucible" for the influence and reception of American culture in the Soviet era. Writers had always been regarded as "the conscience of the nation," and among the intelligentsia being well-read was a necessity.[43] "Progressive" American authors who seemed sympathetic to socialist ideals or portrayed capitalism at its worst were translated into Russian; complete sets of Jack London and Theodore Dreiser in Russian sold out immediately. All books, especially the expensive or hard-to-obtain translations of foreign fiction, were valued household goods.[44]

Beginning in 1955 American literature entered the USSR through the monthly magazine *Inostrannaia literatura*. Continuing earlier publications devoted to "foreign literature," this magazine, which included translations of short stories, serialized novels, and criticism, was an immediate success. Heavily subscribed among the intelligentsia, copies were also shared or "borrowed" (sometimes permanently) from local libraries. The magazine's frequency allowed publishers to respond quickly when an author was "suddenly" deemed in favor so that books could be published to "capitalize" on the demand. "Modern" authors were always introduced carefully into the Soviet publishing world, accompanied by volumes of criticism, essays about interpretation, and a selective translation, censored along ideological lines. This practice accounts for the seemingly sudden emergence of William Faulkner's works in the 1950s[45] and the republication of authors who had been neglected during the darkest days of Stalin.

Writers critical of America were warmly welcomed in translation and in person, but the relationship did not always last. John Steinbeck, who toured the USSR in 1937 and again in 1948, provides a good example of how literature was intertwined with Cold War politics. *The Grapes of Wrath* was translated in 1940 and with 300,000 copies was the largest single printing of any American author up to that time. After 1956, large editions of other early works like *The Pearl* (350,000), *Tortilla Flat* (100,000), and a dramatization *Of Mice and Men* were also published and reviewed. *The Winter of Our Discontent* was translated and published within a year of its English-language appearance in 1961, with a half million copies, a reprint, and a serialization in *Inostrannaia literatura* (nos. 1, 2, and 3, 1962). However, after Steinbeck published "an open letter to the [Soviet] poet Yevtushenko" in support of the Vietnam War in 1966,[46] he was "nullified as a citizen and a writer" by *Pravda* for "service to an antihuman cause."[47]

The American literature that reached Soviet readers often "lost" in translation those elements that were judged by Soviet authorities to be excessive in sexuality, violence, profanity, and of course the usual political suspects. The extent to which this practice was monitored by those literary critics who could read the original is suggested by a long article in *Novy Mir* about the "shockingly poor" translation of *From Here to Eternity* and the "bowdlerized" *Catch-22*. The critic charges that in the latter, because "the author's thought … fail[s] to please the translators … they take it upon themselves to function as editors, eliminating whole paragraphs or even whole pages."[48] While such comments drawing attention to patterns of editorial censorship are unusual, they do demonstrate the extent to which the Soviet censors attempted to shape the America that reached the readers.[49]

A final example illustrates the combination of sympathy and censorship that was often to prove the undoing of Soviet attempts to make friends through the celebration of selected American literature. Arthur Miller, also in attendance at the Waldorf meeting, had already been translated in 1948 with his first play, *All My Sons* (1947). Subsequent plays were translated almost as soon as they appeared. Not surprisingly, following his appearance at the McCarthy hearings, his related play *The Crucible* (1953) was translated as *The Trial of Salem* and "somewhat abridged" for the Soviet stage in 1955. He later reported, after visiting the USSR in 1969, that the abridgement not only changed dialogue but also deleted the author's commentary, which condemned any "witch-hunts" for nonconformists in both Western and Communist countries.[50] And so his plays disappeared from the major Soviet stages.

Miller represents a second way in which American writers participated in cultural diplomacy when he became president of International PEN (Poets, Essayists and Novelists) by supporting, circulating, and publishing dissident writing. Beginning in the early 1950s, when Boris Pasternak's *Doctor Zhivago* was published outside the USSR, *tamizdat* (foreign publishing) of non-approved Soviet authors irritated the authorities as much as the *samizdat* works by dissidents that circulated via manuscript at home.[51] Cynics say that the Soviet Union joined the international copyright convention in 1973 to protest the foreign publication of their authors. In difficult times, summits of American and Soviet authors aired grievances and showcased literary values about their respective literatures.[52] Soviet writers complained that while they translated numerous modern works by American writers, the Americans translated only dissident writers.[53] American writers protested the fate of these writers, often directly to the Soviet Writers' Union.[54] Arthur Miller recalled the ultimate value of the writers' summits. After one in 1986, Miller found himself standing in the offices of the Communist Party Central Committee "looking down into the witty eyes of Mikhail Gorbachev," who said, "I know all your plays."[55] In literature, at least, American authors did seem to contribute to shaping the conscience of the intelligentsia.

"Some Like It Hot"—Hollywood and the USSR

Film, Lenin's "most important medium," was a critical component of the "propaganda state,"[56] but like most other nations, the Soviet Union had imported many American films during the 1920s. They cut back drastically for both financial and ideological reasons in the mid 1930s and then again, in the liberalization that obtained during the Soviet-American alliance in World War II, imported several more American films. *Sun Valley Serenade* (1943) brought the warmth of its Glenn Miller swing musical score to both the lush ski resort setting and the chill of the Cold War with "Chattanooga Choo Choo," a local hit.[57] Stalin's fondness for Deanna Durbin films, indulged during the wartime film purchase agreement, gave her long-lived Soviet fame.[58] A new agreement for importing American films was negotiated with the U.S. Motion Picture Export Agency in 1948[59] to help fill empty screens (only nine Soviet films were produced in 1951). Each side remained selective: the U.S. State Department and the USIA had to approve American films for export throughout the early days of the Cold War.[60] Scandals surrounding the early 1950s Soviet release of some American films, called "trophy films," which had been captured during the war but never officially purchased, suggest how these purloined and parsed movies found their way to the general public. Soviet critics described *Stagecoach* (1939), retitled *The Journey Will Be Dangerous,* as "an epic about the struggle of Indians against the White imperialists on the frontier." The lingering sound from Stalin's last days is young men imitating Johnny Weismuller's call from *Tarzan's New York Adventure* (1942), released in the Soviet Union in 1951/52.[61] Still, Soviet censors took heart that Tarzan had doffed his loincloth and donned a zoot-suit, and that the villains were not African tribesmen but New York City gangsters.

The high cost of Hollywood films and the scarcity of the foreign currency needed to acquire them meant that American imports numbered only four or five a year. After Stalin's death Soviet purchases of American films continued to favor those genres that either were deemed "safe" or offered a critical portrayal of life in the United States. *Marty* (1955), in spite of its "humane message," portrayed America as a "land of little culture, boredom, and purposeless existence."[62] Four American films, imported in 1968 and then, after immense popularity, withdrawn, illustrate the difficulty Soviet officials faced in circumscribing content and interpretation. According to *Sovetskaia Rossiia*[63] a "high culture" biopic on Francisco Goya too much resembled its title, *The Naked Maja* (1959). *Some Like It Hot* (1959), a critique of how "Diamonds Are a Girl's Best Friend," was more erotic than satiric. *Spartacus* (1960), another biopic on the leader of a slave revolt and the namesake of the Soviet games, the Spartakiads, turned out to be too "biblical." And when *The Magnificent Seven* (1960) rode (briefly) into Moscow, they created a Soviet craze for western style from Odessa to Sverdlovsk. Paradoxically, Soviet film policy reinforced the extended showing of American blockbusters because theater managers had to show "hits" at least half the month in order to gain enough revenue to support the domestic film industry.

These popular films also represent the last burst of cinematic dominance before the widespread availability of television. The USSR continued to purchase five or six American films a year.[64] Because older films cost much less, images of "contemporary" America on Soviet screens were often twenty years out of date. For example, older films dealing with racial strife like *A Raisin in the Sun* (1961) and *If He Hollers, Let Him Go* (1968), based on Chester Himes's 1945 novel, were shown in 1977. Viewers remembered working-class portraits like *White Line Fever* (1975) for the high-speed truck chases. The rare costume drama *Cleopatra* (1962), imported in 1979, did claim the big screen over both its homemade rivals, but American films remained in the minority of foreign imports.[65] After relations worsened when the Americans condemned the 1979 Soviet invasion of Afghanistan, Soviet critics used their positions to attack American films that were not imported, providing more fuel for anti-American sentiments. When *The Deerhunter* was shown at the Belgrade Film Festival in 1979, both the Soviet and Yugoslav delegations lambasted the film for showing the "Vietnamese people from essentially slanderous and openly racial positions."[66] Hollywood's most direct offensive, *Red Dawn* (1984), showed midwestern high school students organizing themselves as a guerilla force to defend against invading Soviet forces at the outbreak of World War III. That Reagan and Gorbachev would meet the next year might have surprised American viewers as well as the Soviet critics who charged that the film was "doing [the] utmost to hasten a Walpurgis Night of malicious anti-Soviet hysteria."[67] But American youth culture had already proved a guerilla force in Soviet lands.

"Back in the USSR"— Youth, *Dzhaz,* and *Dzhins*

Youth culture emerged in the Soviet Union, as elsewhere in the postwar world, with musical energy and "in your face" lifestyles. Its models were American, but Soviet criticism was rhetorically generalized to the West, since European youth seemed equally susceptible. A 1958 NATO journal article that advocated using Western popular music to woo Soviet youth from communism was cited by Soviet authorities for the next thirty years as evidence of subversive Western intentions.[68] The Soviet leadership tried to use the youth organization's newspaper *Komsomolskaia Pravda* to counter "foreign influence," sometimes through outright condemnation and other times through attempts to create an alternative culture that would be attractive to the young. As one critic charged, "every ounce of energy used on the dance floor was energy which could, and should, have been invested in building a hydroelectric plant."[69]

American jazz fever inspired the first devotees of a Soviet subculture in the postwar era, the 1950s hip *stiliagi* (from *stil* [style]).[70] *Stiliagi* sported homemade copies of big jackets, narrow pants, wide colorful ties, and the slicked-back Tarzan hairstyle, turned up in the back with a curling iron.[71] They danced "non-recommended dances" like the foxtrot, lindy hop, and jitterbug to the big-band swing of Glenn Miller and the older jazz of Ellington, Basie, and Armstrong, and they adopted slang from the Jimmy Cagney movie *The Roaring Twenties* (1939).[72] Beginning in 1955, the weekly VOA program "Music USA" broadcast music and English-language commentary that was valued by jazz fans and Russian musicians who wrote their own.[73] The 1950s *stiliagi* were isolated from each other and limited to small groups in Leningrad, Moscow, Lviv, and the western-oriented cities of the Baltic republics. Among their numbers were the "golden youth," children of the *nomenklatura* who enjoyed great social prestige owing to their access to foreign records and magazines throughout the Soviet period.[74]

Among the Thaw generation of the late 1950s and early 1960s, Hemingway was a cult hero. In Moscow they wore *kovboyki* (cowboy-style plaid shirts) under their sweaters, grew bush beards, and called each other "old man," after Hemingway's *The Sun Also Rises*.[75] A Hemingway portrait was a favorite decoration in the student dormitory. While the men fashioned themselves after his heroes, women recalled the chaste descriptions—"That night they loved each other"—that included sex as a feature of love, absent in Russian and Soviet literature. Bebop and cool jazz accompanied the nights of the *shtatniki* (from *shtat* [state], referring to fans of the U.S.). But the thaw did not last.

After walking out of a Benny Goodman exchange tour in 1962, Khrushchev's indigestion of a second jazz band performance—like "gas on the stomach"—launched a new crackdown against jazz in 1963.[76] Unfortunately, he had already made two miscalculations. Khrushchev's increased drive for more consumer goods had made available more tape recorders and blank tapes at the very time that Radio Liberty initiated "This Is Jazz" to broadcast jazz composed by Russians.[77] Furthermore, he did not realize that jazz was already on its way out, in large part because the Seventh International Festival of Youth and Students in Moscow had brought the first rock bands to the Soviet Union in May 1957. Here and there *beatniki*, wearing jeans, sweaters, and sneakers, listened to Bill Haley on "ribs" of rock, pirate recordings reproduced on x-ray plates cheaply obtained from hospitals.[78] But American rock was not as attractive as the music of the Beatles, who became an all-Union phenomenon and prompted the translation of regional styles into variations on their look and sound.[79] Russian preferences for more melodic songs accounted for the popularity of American crooners like Pat Boone, Andy Williams, and the otherwise unknown American Dean Reed. By 1975 Reed's guitar-accompanied love ballads and mild protest songs denouncing capitalism had been issued on four labels by USSR state record producer Melodiia. His political stature was such that when Reed was imprisoned in the U.S., President Carter received a letter of protest signed by the head of the Soviet Composers Union and three of its most prominent "high culture" composers.[80]

The Soviet authorities tried many schemes to wean Soviet youth from their appetite for rock.[81] An early campaign spearheaded by Igor Moiseev, a famed Soviet choreographer and visitor to the West, attempted to introduce "new Russian dances" to compete with the twist, whose popularity persisted till the 1970s. *Sovetskaia Kultura* mounted attacks on the Beatles in 1966 and 1968, one written by the most famous Soviet jazzman, Alexander Tsfasman, and the other exposing the capitalist exploitation of "some good songs with folk roots."[82] They also tried to control rock music's means of production— and reproduction. In a move not unlike the tactics of the late 1940s' "cosmopolitan" campaign, which confiscated all saxophones ("that American instrument"), Soviet industry "neglected" to produce electric guitars, an instrument too "easy" to play without professional mastery.[83] Meanwhile, Fender guitars were smuggled in from Iran via Black Sea ports, and homemade amplifiers were plugged in at youth clubs. Even on Siberian beaches, tape recorders and transistor radios were playing Western popular music.[84]

By the late 1970s Soviet authorities had put a better face on what seemed to be uncontrollable, continuing to reproach the West even as they tried to find acceptable American bands to invite on exchange. They supported "country music," such as the tour of the Roy Clark Band in 1976, as more compatible with Soviet values. The 1979 Elton John tour was used as an occasion to condemn the West for not inviting Soviet popular groups to tour or publishing their music, as was stipulated in the Soviet interpretation of the Helsinki accords.[85] Youth groups and clubs were the site of the strongest Soviet interventions. On the one hand, in 1978 *Komsomolskaia Pravda* introduced a pop music hit parade and proposed an ideologically correct "Soviet discotheque." On the other, youth groups were used to enforce censorship. For example, a 1985 memo, circulated by the Nikolaevskii Regional Committee of the Komsomol in Ukraine, listed thirty-eight Anglo-American rock

groups and singers whose repertoire contained "ideologically harmful productions." The Sex Pistols and B-52s led the list for unacceptable punk and
violence. Other singers were condemned for eroticism (Donna Summer), sex
(Tina Turner), neofascism (Julio Iglesias), and anti-Soviet propaganda (Van
Halen). That the music of these thirty-eight bands might be available for such
analysis—as well as airplay at discos—documents the penetration of rock and
punk before *perestroika*.[86]

A view of "bourgeois" American influence would be incomplete without
the story of "jeans."[87] As elsewhere, jeans became a symbol of youth culture
to be obtained at any cost; even the name, *dzhins,* was a neologism that reflected its American origins. While jeans made in Poland or the GDR were
acceptable, those that were *leiblom* [labeled] Lee, Levi-Strauss, and Wrangler
were the most desirable. Back-pocket symbols like American flags, buttons,
and other accoutrements allowed black-market counterfeiting. Under Brezhnev efforts were made to cope with the jeans phenomenon by the usual
methods: out and out condemnation, criminalization, and attempted coop-
tation. In 1975, after a series of published letters and exchanges, the Ministry
of Light Industry announced that it would manufacture Soviet denim and
Soviet jeans. The first batch in 1976 was predictably criticized for poor quality in design, construction, and fabric, but as efforts continued over the next
years, the Soviet magazine *Nedielia* joked that jeans were so popular that they
were now being claimed as a Soviet invention.

The seriousness of the failed efforts is demonstrated by the Soviet interest
in negotiating with all three major U.S. manufacturers of jeans to build a
plant in the USSR in the late 1970s. But any such talks were doomed by the
1980 boycott of the Russian Olympics, when the Levi-Strauss director said,
"No U.S. team, no jeans." Subsequent anti-jeans campaigns chastised indul-
gent parents ("prosperity without culture") and a "predatory consumerism"
that led to "jeans crimes," a term applied by law-enforcement officials to "law
violations prompted by a desire to use any means to obtain articles made of
denim."[88] Lax customs officials, visiting tourists, and inefficient industry
were all blamed for the persistence of jeans culture, but jeans themselves were
never made illegal. Instead they were lumped together with other artifacts of
bourgeois culture as targeting vulnerable Soviet youth with the aim of Western cultural infiltration.

"We will bury you!": Anti-Americanism

Anti-Americanism was of course a central tenet of Soviet ideology. The rhetoric was sensitive to foreign-policy crises, however, and was moderated during
Soviet leaders' visits to the U.S. and demonstrations of "peaceful co-existence"

or "détente." Domestic politics and internal power plays within the USSR could also call forth a round of anti-Americanism. Although analysts attempted to interpret linguistic shifts and variations, no simple formula existed. Still, a few techniques of culturally representing anti-Americanism were common.

First, parody brought anti-Americanism to a level beyond crude communist boilerplate. The most consistent representation was the magazine *Krokodil,* which satirized capitalism, Uncle Sam, and American cultural problems. Political cartoons were also a regular feature of the daily press, and "the radio voices" in particular were a frequent target of attack. But such satires proved a double-edged sword, as American and Western positions could be explicated while being denounced. Also, the film *Mr. MacKinley's Flight* (1975) used its anti-American theme to slip a number of songs by the forbidden Soviet bard Vladimir Vysotskii into the soundtrack.

Second, Soviet novels, plays, and films regularly featured American characters whose negative qualities varied with the political atmosphere. For example, Grigorii Aleksandrov's depiction of a venal American spy in his famous Stalinist film, *Meeting on the Elbe* (1949), was softened by a rapprochement between Americans, other Europeans, and Russians on an odyssey through Siberia in his *Russian Souvenir* (1960), where problems in relations resulted from prejudice rather than politics. Soviet spy films (e.g., *Game Without Rules,* 1965), nuclear war films (*Doctor Ivens's Silence,* 1973), and Vietnam films (*Night on the 14th Parallel,* 1971) had credible American villains. Some films were recognizable responses to particular U.S. anti-Soviet films, and others were barely disguised commentaries on current events, like the search for oil in *On Rich Red Islands* (1981).[89]

Third, when Soviet authorities imported films, books, and music that criticized America, they attempted to give them a spin that reinforced preferred interpretations. The idea and ideal of social criticism were touted by both societies but meant different things. Western writers charged that American artistic freedom accounted for the existence and availability of criticism, whereby Soviet writers countered that the tradition of "self-criticism" of artistic works within artistic unions and by the press was a more rigorous standard. The critique of America could even be of bestseller quality, as when Soviet television made two miniseries in the early 1980s based on "popular" American novels— Irwin Shaw's *Rich Man, Poor Man* and Irving Wallace's *The R Document* (1979), about a conspiracy to undercut the U.S. Bill of Rights.[90] Neither side could enforce interpretations, however. Viewers noticed that Joads in *The Grapes of Wrath* had their own car, and one woman was impressed that in *The Apartment* a man (Jack Lemmon) warmed up a TV dinner and lit the oven with a match.[91]

Fourth, set pieces of Soviet rhetoric embodied sentiments that often softened in the interpersonal settings of informal diplomacy, like the Dartmouth and Pugwash conferences. As early as the late 1950s "unofficial" delegations of cultural and intellectual figures, usually briefed and debriefed by their governments, began meeting together over time. Few officials would risk bold public statements, so Americans too came to "read between the lines" to interpret signs of change in the Kremlin. For example, Khrushchev's famous phrase, translated "We will bury you," was the subject of a long debate at the 1961 Dartmouth conference.[92] In Russian the phrase means "we shall be present at your funeral," implying "victory in the peaceful competition with capitalism" (a title of collected and translated Khrushchev speeches), not a literal threat.

Finally, public opinion surveys begun in the 1970s and other evidence suggest that the Soviet public overall, when they attended to foreign policy, followed the Soviet line but did not extend that judgement to the American people or their culture. They believed that the U.S. was a committed adversary, and they would defend their country if unexpectedly they met a foreigner.[93] However, according to Soviet ideology, American people were in fact "victims" of capitalism, so the enemies had to be defined as particular groups— Wall Street capitalists, Texas oil magnates, gangsters, and Pentagon militarists. Since these were the same villains of literature and film, these enemy images allowed for a positive appreciation of America's "soft power." Too, as the intelligentsia and nomenklatura began to merge into a middle class and meet more Americans, they became more open to American values.[94] In the words of one young man interviewed at a disco in 1984, after he had publicly imitated John Travolta in *Saturday Night Fever:* "America is a very bad country. Not the people. I think they want peace just like the Soviet Union does. It's their government that is to blame." He added, "and the United States forces Europe to do what it wants because it has so many weapons."[95] This was anti-Americanism on the verge of *perestroika.*

The "American Model" and the "Russian Idea"

Perestroika, the Russian word for restructuring that named the era following the Gorbachev-Reagan rapprochement, also rehabilitated American culture and encouraged joint initiatives. "Space bridges" linked Phil Donahue's American audiences to Russian television studios. American universities toasted cooperative agreements with Soviet institutions, and American cities "twinned" with Soviet cities then unknown. *Some Like it Hot, Spartacus,* and *The Magnificent Seven* were reissued in 1985. The Esalen Institute sponsored a 1989 U.S.-Soviet exchange to mark the fiftieth anniversary of *The Grapes of Wrath.* Dave Brubeck performed at a 1988 summit honoring the Gorbachevs, and in 1989 the first McDonalds opened on Moscow's Pushkin Square. Leading Soviet scholars, musicians, scientists, and others found themselves in demand in the West as institutions vied to have a visiting scholar or performer among their constituency. Dissidents in particular were valued prizes for Western display, and many would be feted as heroes as first the Wall fell and later the union disintegrated.

The former enemy was welcomed in part because Soviet cultural figures felt that the liberalization of censorship and bureaucratic oversight would allow Soviet artists and musicians to become financially viable in the Western marketplace. Initially this seemed possible. In 1989 CBS Records released the first Soviet rock album on an international label, Boris Grebenshchikov's *Radio Silence,* and Paul McCartney released an album of oldies exclusively on Melodiia.[96] Novels like *Children of the Arbat* and art films like *Repentance* were well received in the West. But the novelty soon wore off. The competitiveness of the global cultural marketplace, not fully grasped even by the elites who had had access to most foreign cultural products, was a still greater shock to the Soviet system of cultural production. Without state funds and in an environment of consumer choice, domestic cultural production plummeted and urban populations gravitated to what had earlier been controlled through limited access and heavy criticism—American entertainment. Rushing to fill the gap were retro festivals of Tarzan movies and the well-publicized Soviet premiere of *Gone with the Wind.*[97]

The abundance of the West, earlier known to some, was now experienced by few but seen by all in the flood of photos, advertisements, and other visualized riches that appeared on the nightly news. In short, when the communist system disintegrated from within, the opening of demand and the possibility of choice created a cultural vacuum. Along came entrepreneurs, who translated and published popular Western novels, imported *Playboy,* and pirated the latest Western music and video hits.[98] The "Wild, Wild East" became a catchword for the new Russian Federation and Yeltsin "rocked the vote" for his first presidential campaign. The opportunity or chaos, depending upon the viewpoint, saw the rise of the oligarchs who were able to profit from providing circuses even as bread periodically went in short supply. The optimism was perhaps most pronounced among the young, who flocked to the new capitalist professions like marketing and public relations, multiplying their English-language skills by heading outposts in the new offices of multinational corporations. The "new Russians," so called because their new wealth was gaudily and ostentatiously displayed, came to symbolize the acquisition mode of the West.[99]

Was this the start of "Americanization?" In the initial years Soviet (later Russian) public figures lauded the "American model" of economic and technical practices, and Western experts flocked to assist in the transition to some form of "democratic capitalism." American advice was coupled with an increase and broadening of Russian elite visits to law firms, business schools, the U.S. Congress, and U.S. banks. At the height of optimism the numbers in these programs—12,000 traveling to the U.S. in 1994 and 10,000 projected for 1995—fostered comparisons with the 24,000 Europeans brought by the Marshall Plan after 1945. As time wore on, such comparisons were increasingly avoided because "Washington didn't drown these programs in funds." Among all the Eastern European nations, Russia ranked about the lowest in per capita U.S. assistance, receiving only about 5 percent of the per capita foreign investment in East Germany.[100]

The manner in which America aided Russia was also subject to interpretation. Perhaps the most widespread symbols of American aid in the 1990s were the chicken drumsticks, known as "Bush legs" (*nozhki Busha*), that were exported during the first Bush administration to the far reaches of the federation. "Like so many other foreign products in Russia, they provoke a combination of intrigue, contempt and envy. They are said to be unhealthy, tainted with preservatives and growth hormones; they are said to be flavorless, ersatz, unsanitary—people tell stories of Russians dying from eating these chicken legs. At the same time, they are a common item in many households." For the American exporter, meanwhile, Russia became the largest market for chicken legs because Americans preferred white meat.[101]

In the end, the American model of "democratic capitalism" did not take root easily or broadly. Take for example the goal of American advisers to revive the jury trial and parliamentary elections. The importance of these "democratic mechanisms" was widely publicized, but their reception and interpretation among the Russian population showed a mix of American and Russian referents. In Nizhny Novgorod participants in a 1997 focus group explained the new legal culture by referring to an American film where a woman was acquitted for lack of evidence and to the O. J. Simpson case, obvious American media influences. But more typical was a St. Petersburg journalist who quoted Pushkin: "The harshness of Russian laws is softened by their nonenforcement."[102] In 1999 the jury system had functioned in only 422 Russian cases and by 2002 in only 9 of 89 administrative regions.[103]

These examples illustrate how the "American model" has come to be critically interpreted within the larger framework of "the Russian idea." In its broadest sense it is the "conviction that Russia has its own independent, self-sufficient, and eminently worthy cultural and historical tradition that both sets it apart from the West and guarantees its future flourishing."[104] Searching for an acceptable definition of the Russian idea was the purpose of a commission set up by Boris Yeltsin in his second term, and Putin has picked up on the theme. "The experience of the 1990s demonstrates vividly that merely experimenting with abstract models and schemes taken from foreign textbooks cannot assure that our country will achieve genuine renewal without excessive costs," wrote Putin. "[E]very country, Russia included, has to search for its own path to renewal."[105]

It would be inaccurate to ascribe this sentiment only to ardent nationalists, to nostalgia for lost "greatness," or to another version of national exceptionalism.[106] The Russian reaction must also be seen in the context of the response of many nation-states to globalization, intensified in Russia by the demise of the Soviet version of the Russian idea. In fact, the widespread emergence of the discourse on globalization coincided in part with the collapse of the bi-polar world.[107] Therefore it is not surprising that in Russia globalization has been interpreted as a political, or "ideological," project led by the West. The global community has been considered to be a Western idea, world culture equated with the Americanization of peripheral national cultures, and economic and political globalization interpreted as a means of subordinating Russia (and the East) to the interests of the West, above all the United States. Equally important, "Russia does not position itself as a 'peripheral receiver' of Western cultural messages but rather as the embodiment of alternative cultural values."[108] In the second decade of the Russian Federation, then, the Russian response to American culture, both institutionally and among the population, has to be understood as a relation between the national and the global. The Putin government understands that it is neither possible nor desirable to be outside globalization, nor to eliminate pluralism, while at the same time the state intends to project a strong national Russian identity. The government's approach to cultural imports might be characterized by the concept of "managed pluralism"—being rhetorically open, keeping diversity within limits, and retaining state control of the most important institutions.[109]

Cinema provides an excellent case. In 1991 Soviet studios decided to import just a few Hollywood films and use the profits to finance their own films. But what they could afford, in the words of the director of Soveksportfilm, was the "refuse" of Western civilization—*Hot Target, The Beach Girls, The Nine Deaths of the Ninja.*[110] By 1994, including the "refuse" bought for a "fistful of dollars," 73 percent of the films on Moscow screens were American.[111] But the impression is misleading. Tickets to the few first-run films were too expensive; many empty theaters were converted into "auto salons" or casinos. By 2000 Moscow ticket prices ranged from USD 4 (an average monthly salary was around USD 50) to as much as USD 25 to experience a new American-style theater and its blockbusters.[112] Too, moviegoers now viewed American movies more critically, complaining that Hollywood stereotyped Russians as mafiosi, gangsters, spies, wealthy villains, or well-meaning idiots,[113] very much like Soviet characterizations of Americans in the "old days." Still, affordable American imports continued. In July 2003 a member of the Russian Duma proposed to copy France and institute quotas on American film imports in a stepwise fashion. Putin addressed the issue directly at a State Council session, saying that in effect bans on American movies would not change preferences and publicly opposing quotas.[114]

Putin's position demonstrated his understanding of the international market for cultural goods and also takes into account the partial recovery of the domestic media market for Russian film production. In 1996 the independent television networks owned by Vladimir Guzinsky and Boris Berezovsky entered the film production business with the private film studio NTV-Profit and ORT. Although both oligarchs had fallen by 2001, the five years of financing films plus a renewed government investment in three major, now private, studios (Mosfilm, Lenfilm, and Gorky Studio) helped to bring Russian production to over 50 films in 1997. This trend has continued through 2003, with many of the films made for the more dependable television market. Still, the lack of Russian entertainment movies, the gigantic illicit video market, and the superiority of the American distribution system suggest that Hollywood's America is likely to remain highly visible in the near future.[115]

But another reason that film imports pose less of a threat to Russia is that politically television is the important domestic market—the young and wealthy might attend *Matrix Reloaded,* but the voters watch state television.[116] Thus, January 2003 saw the fall of TVS, the last private national television station, NTV and TV6 having been closed in 2001 and 2002.[117] The political implications of this development emerged in the 2003 parliamentary elections, but the independent TV networks had already set the film diet. From 1994 through 2003, on average about half of the films shown on television were Russian, with the majority being from Soviet times—and it is these that are rated the most popular. In 1994 American televised films accounted for only 27 percent, European 18 percent, and Latin American 11 percent.[118] The most popular imported television program was a low-budget 1970s Mexican soap opera, *The Rich Also Cry (Bogatye tozhe plachut)*; the U.S. soap opera *Santa Barbara* was much less popular.[119] After the collapse of the ruble in 1998, which made most U.S. imports too expensive, Russian television studios increased their output of television miniseries, detective series, and other genres.[120] In Russian critical discourse, these series are seen as beginning to define a "national idea," perhaps "capitalist in form" but "national in content."[121]

One American import has drastically increased in importance since *perestroika*—the American tourist. Given the value attributed to "high culture" sites by this rich source of revenue, government funds and some international monies have been used to refurbish and maintain national cultural institutions, such as the Bolshoi Theatre and the Hermitage Museum.[122] Many American chain clothing stores and restaurants have opened in the capital, with prices denominated in U.S. currency. On the other hand, famous Russian singers and dancers, authors with English facility, and promising artists have toured abroad and often emigrated, melding into the decreasing market for high culture worldwide. Serious writers, meanwhile, fear the politicization of literature and the "economic censorship" that favors the mass market.[123] The "best-seller," condemned by the Soviets as in bad taste and identified with the West,[124] took over the market in the 1990s with translations of the usual Americans—Stephen King, John Grisham, Sidney Sheldon, Danielle Steele, and Tom Clancy.[125] In the meantime, the intelligentsia, as the prime supporters of a positive view of America under perestroika, had their own crisis of confidence and purpose.[126] The publishing industry best illustrates the realization of these fears of Americanization. At the 1995 Frankfurt Book Fair, the Russian publishers' booth featured a coffee table book on Soviet ballet that the publisher hoped to have translated into English. However, the most successful publisher, who treated the rest to dinner, had succeeded with an American diet book translated into Russian. "I had hoped to publish the collected works of Arthur Koestler," he said, "but my next book will be a translation of an American book on how to stop smoking."

Youth culture is the area in which the most visible Americanization might be expected. Again, however, the reception and valorization of American culture is demonstrably selective and varied.[127] A five-year sociological study of youth media and of different age groups in three cities—Moscow, Ul'ianovsk, and Samara—during the late 1990s supports a "mix and match" consumption strategy.[128] For example, although several television programs specifically devoted to youth issues had been produced since *perestroika,* their popularity among young people, with the exception of pure music programs, was very low. Youth-oriented magazines were more popular. Although some adopted the format and style of Western magazines, the late 1990s saw a new phase in which openly sensational or pornographic magazines were displaced by specifically targeted publications for rich youth or various "subcultures," and by the rise of amateur "fanzines." Magazines devoted to progressive or alternative lifestyles presented America as a dominant reference point, often in opposition to Europe, and often in a negative light. Fashion "authority"—from clothing to cosmetics—was shown to reside in European (usually British) high street fashion, even though the market was dominated by mass-produced clothing from Poland and Turkey. Teen fashion demonstrated another interesting "glocalization": as a carryover from times of Soviet shortage, quality designer fashions for women were still portrayed as desirable even as Western feminism was perceived as giving Western women a freedom in their choice of dress. Unisex and combinatory styles, especially in the alternative magazines, opened up a broader range of expression for both men and women.

Music preferences turned out to be central to understanding young Russian responses to American culture. Simplifying a complex set of relations, those young people who saw themselves as progressive, as in Soviet times, were highly knowledgeable about Western music forms and used this knowledge for self-definition. Their magazines centered the music scene in Britain, even though they acknowledged American market dominance. However, for progressive youth the increased accessibility of Western music to everyone meant that new genres of music—including Russian music—were required to demonstrate taste. They labeled Western pop as "commercial." Other young people, who used music as a background for peer group activities, seemed to attach little significance to whether or not the music came from "the West." It was just "normal." Probably the most interesting continuity from the Soviet period was that almost all young people differentiated Western dance music and pop as meaning*less* "music for the body" and Russian rock, bard music, and pop as meaning*ful* "music for the soul."

Overall, even though America was the most frequent referent, young Russians expressed many European stereotypes about America—materialism, fragmentation, artificiality, and lack of culture.[129] In fact, "those young people who appeared to be most attuned to Western ways of life were actually the most critical of them." The Russian understanding of the global marketplace may be best illustrated by the success of the Russian pop female duo, Tatu. Their electro-pop music video, "All the Things She Said," became a hit in both England and America. It featured the teenage stars, dressed in school uniforms, kissing and singing in the rain. In 2003 a British producer recorded their million-selling album, *200 km/h in the Wrong Lane,* in English, and their "improvised smooch" generated more publicity on Jay Leno's *Tonight Show.* Lena Katina, whom *USA Today* described as reading Dostoevsky and Chekhov when not on camera, has said that "America should be more open, especially about love."[130]

In sum, the Russian Federation presents a complex and ever changing portrait of American culture in Europe. As in Soviet times, politics influences opinions on America; the expansion of NATO, the Kosovo crisis, the U.S. response to the Chechnya conflict, and the Iraq war have all fueled critical views of America.[131] As contemporary public opinion has spread from the elites in the capitals throughout the country via national television news, a moderate anti-Americanism remains consistent in spite of "soul talks" between the two nations' leaders. The Russian idea, with its strong state and communitarian values, is a wellspring of enthusiasm for national transformations of global genres and the strengthening of national institutions to support the production of domestic culture. But leaders from Gorbachev to Putin also believe that Russian culture is more akin to European than American culture, even though Russia does not belong to any all-European institutions and Europe has shown little sign of wanting it.

The Russian dilemma might be expressed by comparing two recent bids for "blockbuster" status in the Russian film industry. *The Barber of Siberia,* directed by Nikita Mikhalkov, known to Western audiences for *Burnt by the Sun,* invokes a heroic eighteenth-century past as a model for the future. Its title and frame story about American soldiers' hostility to Mozart valorizes European high culture and its production was supported by European money. It was widely panned and has yet to find a U.S. distributor. In contrast, *Brother-2*, directed by Aleksei Balabanov, is also about a soldier, this one on a mission to contemporary America to rescue Russian hostages from an evil global empire run by American entrepreneurs, and in the process emerge a Russian hero. Its website and the responses to it suggest that the film's popularity is due in part to its anti-Americanism.[132] As elsewhere, American culture will continue to provide the model for its own critique, and ironically, anti-Americanization rhetoric and a belief in state support for culture may provide Russia with something to hold in common with Europe.

Notes

Acknowledgements
The author would like to thank Elena Androunas, Sergei Dobrynin, Vitaly Ivanov, Olga Kudriashova, Zsuzsa Macht, Alexei Miller, and Alfred J. Rieber for sharing their memories of American culture in Russia during the Cold War and beyond. Special appreciation goes to Yassen N. Zassoursky, Dean of the Moscow State University School of Journalism and Mass Communication and an important critic and translator of American literature, for his comments and for his generosity over the years. Sue Curry Jansen has provided her customary insightful discussion of cultural diplomacy via e-mail. Thanks to Katalin Dobo and the staff of the Open Society Archives (formerly the RFE/RL Research Archives) for exceptional cooperation and to the professional staff of the Central European University Library, especially Richard Kartonoso and Emilia Berenyi. A CEU Faculty Research grant provided financial support.

1. Russians were fond of quoting *Democracy in America* in late perestroika. Eric Shiraev and Vladislav M. Zubok, *Anti-Americanism in Russia: From Stalin to Putin* (New York: Palgrave, 2000). Americans reclaimed Tocqueville in the early 1950s, seeking affirmation of shared values in opposition to the Soviet model; the book had been out of print since the 1920s. Michael Kammen, "Alexis de Tocqueville Revisited," *Library of Congress Information Bulletin* (December, 1997).
2. Peter G. Filene, *Americans and the Soviet Experiment, 1917–1933* (Cambridge: Harvard University Press, 1967).
3. On Westernizers and Slavophiles and their relation to Russian culture, see James H. Billington, *The Icon and the Axe: An Interpretive History of Russian Culture* (New York: Vintage, 1970 [1966]), Orlando Figes, *Natasha's Dance: A Cultural History of Russia* (New York: Metropolitan, 2002), and Shiraev and Zubok, *Anti-Americanism*, 9–10.
4. See contemporary works such as Wilson Record, "The Development of the Communist Position on the Negro Question in the United States," *Phylon Quarterly* 19, no. 3 (1958): 306–36 and William A. Nolan, *Communism versus the Negro* (Chicago: Regnery, 1951).

5. Of the recent books addressing U.S. racial attitudes in an international context, none have dealt directly with studies of the Soviet Union, which I am pursuing in a separate project. Some establish a rhetorical link drawn by architects of Cold War policy between U.S. vulnerability on racial inequalities and choices in cultural diplomacy. See Thomas Bostelmann, *The Cold War and the Color Line: American Race Relations in the Global Arena* (Cambridge: Harvard University Press, 2002); Mary L. Dudziak, *Cold War Civil Rights: Race and the Image of American Democracy* (Princeton: Princeton University Press, 2000); Penny M. von Eschen, *Race Against Empire: Black Americans and Anticolonialism, 1937–1957* (Ithaca: Cornell University Press, 2001).

6. Geoffrey Hosking, *The First Socialist Society: A History of the Soviet Union from Within*, enlarged ed., (Cambridge: Harvard University Press, 1990), 436–47.

7. See, for example, Scott Shane, *Dismantling Utopia: How Information Ended the Soviet Union* (Chicago: Dee, 1994).

8. Walter L. Hixson, *Parting the Curtain: Propaganda, Culture, and the Cold War* (New York: St. Martin's, 1996), chap. 1; Scott Lucas, *Freedom's War: The US Crusade Against the Soviet Union, 1945–56* (New York: New York University Press, 1999).

9. Hixson, *Parting the Curtain*, chap. 2; Donald Browne, *International Broadcasting: The Limits of a Limitless Medium* (Westport: Praeger, 1982); K. R. M. Short, ed., *Western Broadcasting over the Iron Curtain* (London: Croom Helm, 1986). Greater credibility was given the BBC World Service in most opinion surveys during the Cold War.

10. Alexander Rapoport, "The Russian Broadcasts of the Voice of America," *Russian Review* 16, no. 3 (1957): 3–14.

11. Cited in Hixson, *Parting the Curtain*, 61.

12. Stacey Cone, "Presuming a Right to Deceive: Radio Free Europe, Radio Liberty, the CIA and the News Media," *Journalism History* 24, no. 4 (1998/99): 148–57; Shawn Parry-Giles, *The Rhetorical Presidency, Propaganda and the Cold War* (Westport: Praeger, 2001).

13. After Congressional hearings, they were merged into RFE/RL in 1976.

14. Michael Nelson, *War of the Black Heavens: The Battles of Western Broadcasting in the Cold War* (London: Brassey's, 1997); Arch Puddington, *Broadcasting Freedom: The Cold War Triumph of Radio Free Europe and Radio Liberty* (Lexington: University Press of Kentucky, 2000). For a review, see Marsha Siefert, "Radio Diplomacy and the Cold War," *Journal of Communication* 53, no. 2 (2003): 363–73.

15. Nelson, *War*, 91; Hixson, *Parting the Curtain*, 33.

16. J. D. Parks, "The USSR and American Technology," chap. 3 in *Culture, Conflict and Coexistence: American-Soviet Cultural Relations, 1917–1958* (Jefferson: McFarland, 1983), 33–46 and, more recently, Alan M. Ball, *Imagining America: Influence and Images in Twentieth-Century Russia* (Lanham: Rowman and Littlefield, 2003), chaps. 1 and 4.

17. For a spirited defense of the scientific and technological exchange and cooperation, especially against Richard N. Perle's charge that exchanges were "Like Putting the KGB in the Pentagon" (*New York Times*, 30 June 1987, A-31), see chap. 24 by Yale Richmond in *Cultural Exchange and the Cold War: Raising the Iron Curtain* (University Park: Pennsylvania State University Press, 2003), 210–25. A Deputy Director of the CIA and Director of the NSA testified to the U.S. Senate in 1982 that 70 percent of the Soviet technological knowledge came through its intelligence services, another 20 to 30 percent through legal purchases and published materials, and only a very small percentage from direct technical exchange (219).

18. For opposition to this agreement see Frederick C. Barghoorn, "Patterns of Soviet-American Exchange," *The Soviet Cultural Offensive: The Role of Cultural Diplomacy in Soviet Foreign Policy* (Westport: Greenwood Press, 1976 [1960]), 268–335.

19. Hixson, *Parting the Curtain*, chaps. 6 and 7.

20. Richmond, *Cultural Exchange*, 148–51; Hixson, *Parting the Curtain*, 117–19.
21. Mark Carroll, *Music and Ideology in Cold War Europe* (New York: Cambridge University Press, 2003), 8.
22. The major works on the CCF are Peter Coleman's sympathetic account, *The Liberal Conspiracy: The Congress for Cultural Freedom and the Struggle for the Mind of Postwar Europe* (New York: Free Press, 1989), and the more critical and controversial Frances Stonor Saunders, *Who Paid the Piper? The Cultural Cold War: The CIA and the World of Arts and Letters* (New York: New Press, 1999).
23. For example, the international program of the Museum of Modern Art was described as overtly political: "to let it be known especially in Europe that America was not the cultural backwater that the Russians, during that tense period called 'the cold war' were trying to demonstrate that it was." Russell Lynes, cited in Eva Cockcroft, "Abstract Expressionism, Weapon of the Cold War," *Artforum* 12, no. 10 (1974): 39–41. Reprinted in Francis Frascina, ed., *Pollock and After: The Critical Debate* (New York: Harper and Row, 1985), 127.
24. Ian Wellens, *Music on the Frontline: Nicholas Nabokov's Struggle against Communism and Middlebrow Culture* (London: Ashgate, 2002).
25. Cited in Wellens, *Music on the Frontline*, 50.
26. Wellens, *Music on the Frontline*, 90.
27. Negative interpretations of the deal are often attributed to the revenues expected by the Soviet government, but the government provided the orchestra and paid for the hundreds of staff members required to keep the theaters open. Hollis Alpert, *The Life and Times of Porgy and Bess: The Story of an American Classic* (New York: Knopf, 1990), 217.
28. David Monod, "Disguise, Containment and the *Porgy and Bess* Revival of 1952–1956," *Journal of American Studies* 35, no. 2 (2001): 297–98.
29. C. D. Jackson Papers, 1951–56, Box 91, Rockefeller, Nelson A., Eisenhower Library, cited in Ellen Noonan, "Representing Race, Representing America: *Porgy and Bess* Abroad and At Home, 1952–1956," paper presented at the American Studies Association, Detroit, October 2000, 4.
30. Robert Breen, *Neva* (4 January 1956), cited in Monod, "Disguise," 292.
31. Histories of this production affirm that the director heightened the explicitness of the rape scene beyond what would have been acceptable on Broadway. Monod, "Disguise," 299, 300–303.
32. U. Kovalyev, "Porgy and Bess," *Smema* (29 December 1955), cited in Monod, "Disguise," 307.
33. Harlow Robinson, *Last Impresario: The Life, Times, and Legacy of Sol Hurok* (New York: Penguin, 1995), 358–59. *Time* Magazine (18 May 1958) also used the occasion to compare more favorably the quantity and youth of America's talent to Europe's. To compliment the Americans, the 1959 Soviet Exhibition in New York displayed boxes of candy featuring van Cliburn's photograph. Barghoorn, *Soviet Cultural Offensive*, 302.
34. Robinson, *Last Impressario*, 350–51; Alan Levy, *The Bluebird of Happiness: The Memoirs of Jan Peerce* (New York: HarperCollins, 1976), 238–39, 240–42.
35. Alison Blakely, *Russia and the Negro: Blacks in Russian History and Thought* (Washington: Howard University Press, 1986), 152–54.
36. Copland had also been frank in conversations at the Moscow Conservatory in 1960, complaining that Russian composers "knew *too* well what style to write in." Howard Pollack, *Aaron Copland: The Life and Work of an Uncommon Man* (New York: Faber and Faber, 2001), 464.
37. Boris Schwarz, *Music and Musical Life in Soviet Russia, 1917–1981*, enlarged ed. (Bloomington: Indiana University Press, 1983), 447.

38. Robinson, *Last Impresario,* 337.
39. Naima Prevots, *Dance for Export: Cultural Diplomacy and the Cold War* (Hanover: Wesleyan University Press, 1999), esp. 69–91.
40. Schwartz, *Music,* 358.
41. Prevots, *Dance,* quotations on 82, 87. The warm reception is all the more remarkable for occurring at the height of the Cuban missile crisis.
42. Thus the significance of David Caute's recent title, *The Dancer Defects: The Struggle for Cultural Supremacy during the Cold War* (Oxford: Oxford University Press, 2003).
43. Jeffrey Brooks, *When Russia Learned to Read: Literacy and Popular Literature, 1861–1917* (Princeton: Princeton University Press, 1988).
44. Stephen Lovell, "Publishing and the Book Trade in the Post-Stalin Era: A Case-Study of the Commodification of Culture," *Europe-Asia Studies* 50, no. 4 (1998): 679–99.
45. Maurice Friedberg, *A Decade of Euphoria: Western Literature in Post-Stalinist Russia, 1954–64* (Bloomington: Indiana University Press, 1977), 194–96.
46. "An Open Letter to the Poet Yevtushenko," *Newsday* 26 (11 July 1966): 1.
47. Friedberg, *Decade,* 191–93 and Deming Brown, *Soviet Attitudes towards American Writing* (Princeton: Princeton University Press, 1962), 74–80.
48. N. Anastasyev and A. Zyverev, "Marginal Notes on Translated Prose," *Novy Mir* 9 (September 1972): 242–53 [*Current Digest of the Soviet Press* (hereafter *CDSP*) 25, no. 1, 14].
49. Friedberg offers numerous dissections of translation practice in chapter 1 of *Decade of Euphoria.*
50. Friedberg, *Decade,* 48–50, 196–97.
51. The Soviet press complained bitterly about the choice of exiled Soviet writers, like Joseph Brodsky and Vasily Aksyonov, who were translated and published in English, and about the "book fairs," such as the one held in New York, to showcase them. A. Nikolayev, "Riffraff Fair," *Literaturnaya gazeta* (30 September 1981): 14 [*CDSP* 33, no. 43, 13].
52. For an American report see Richmond, *Cultural Exchange,* 157–61, and for a Soviet report see Iona Andronov, "Writers' Dialogue in New York," *Literaturnaya gazeta* (10 May 1978): 15 [*CDSP* 30, no. 19, 1–9].
53. In an interesting clash of hierarchical judgements, at one Moscow event the Soviet delegation suggested that Arthur Hailey be asked to sit on the stage, a request that horrified the American delegates, who prevented it. According to Soviet criticism, Hailey's novels treat "the major junctions of modern society's nerve cells—the passenger airplane, the airport, the hospital, the automotive plant—and heroes with 'manly courage,'" in contrast to Mailer or Updike. Vsevolod Revich, "Automatic Pilot Cannot Land a Plane," *Literaturnoye obozreniye* 4 (April 1979): 67–70 [*CDSP* 31, no. 27, 15].
54. See the issue of "Metropol," a literary anthology published in New York by Ardis Press that engaged major American writers—Albee, Miller, Styron, Updike, Vonnegut—in international controversy. The Soviet view is "What's All the Noise About?" *Literaturnaya gazeta* (19 September 1979): 9 [*CDSP* 31, no. 38, 1–4].
55. Arthur Miller, *Timebends: A Life* (New York: Penguin, 1995), 559.
56. Peter Kenez, *Birth of the Propaganda State: Soviet Methods of Mass Mobilization, 1917–1929* (Cambridge: Cambridge University Press, 1985), 8–11.
57. Richard Stites, *Russian Popular Culture: Entertainment and Society Since 1900* (Cambridge: Cambridge University Press, 1992), 126. Marek Korczynski explains "Why 'Chattanooga Choo-Choo' rather than 'The International' became the song to unite the human race" for the British and American working classes as well, becoming the first record ever to sell a million copies. *Labour History Review* 68, no. 1 (2003): 129–38, here footnote 2.
58. Peter Kenez, *Cinema and Soviet Society, 1907–1953,* 2nd ed. (London: Tauris, 2001).

59. Ian Jarvie, *Hollywood's Overseas Campaign: The North Atlantic Movie Trade, 1920–1950* (Cambridge: Cambridge University Press, 1992), chaps. 9–11; Marsha Siefert, "Allies on Film: US-USSR Filmmakers and the *Battle of Russia,*" in Marsha Siefert, ed. *Extending the Borders of Russian History: Essays in Honor of Alfred J. Rieber* (Budapest: Central European University Press, 2003), 373–400.

60. George Kennan also sent a telegram alerting the U.S. to be wary of the films they sold the Soviets. John Paton Davies, "Motion Picture Program for SSR," Memorandum to Secretary of State, 18 February 1946, no. 2449, 861.4061, Record Group 9, U.S. Dept. of State, National Archives, Washington D.C., reprinted in David Culbert, ed., *Mission to Moscow* (Madison: University of Wisconsin Press, 1980), 262–64; Richmond, *Cultural Exchange,* 129.

61. Stites, *Russian Popular Culture,* 125–26. This film, despite its "animalistic-sexual basis of the plot," was also shown on horsecarts outdoors in villages. S. Frederick Starr, *Red and Hot: The Fate of Jazz in the Soviet Union, 1917–1980* (New York: Oxford University Press, 1983), 126.

62. Friedberg, *Decade,* 192–94.

63. I. Leshchevsky, "Face to Face with the Screen," *Sovetskaya Rossiya* (17 April 1968). The article summarized a discussion that was held on "Western Films: What Do They Bring Us and What Do They Teach Us?" at the Palace of Culture in the Krasnoe Sormovo factory in Gorky province, demonstrating the wide dissemination and discussion of films. Excerpts in English appeared as "Another Opinion: Down with Western Movies," in the *New York Times* (21 April 1968): E13.

64. As film attendance declined, film managers gave more prominence to imported films in their schedules. Sofya Dyak, "Cinemas between Cultural Enlightenment and Entertainment: Case Study of Lviv during the Brezhnev Era," unpublished MA thesis, History Department, Central European University, Budapest, 2002.

65. Ellen Propper Mickiewicz, "The Audience for Movies, Theater and Music," chap. 6 in *Media and the Russian Public* (New York: Praeger, 1981).

66. V. Gavilevsky, "Principle and Reality," *Sovetskaya kultura* (20 February 1979), 7 [*CDSP* 31, no. 10, 5]. Warren Beatty's film *Reds,* however, was praised highly because "a grain of truth about the country of the victorious revolution has reached the American screen," and the reviewer hints that political reasons cost it the 1981 Oscar for best picture. A. Repin, "Reds," *Trud* (31 January 1982), 4, and V. Chernyshev, "Oscar Surprises," *Sovetskaya kultura* (6 April 1982), 7 [*CDSP* 34, no. 14, 19–20].

67. G. Vasiliev, "Sowers of Hatred: The Latest Anti-Soviet Film Concoction on American Screens," *Pravda* (18 September 1984), 5 [*CDSP* 36, no. 38, 21].

68. Stites, *Russian Popular Culture,* 143.

69. Hilary Pilkington, *Russia's Youth and Its Culture: A Nation's Constructors and Constructed* (London: Routledge, 1995), 68.

70. S. Frederick Starr's classic, *Red and Hot: The Fate of Jazz in the Soviet Union, 1917–1980* describes these periods along with the local groups who played American jazz as well as their own.

71. Memory of Alexander Kozlov, founding member of the Soviet punk/new wave band Arsenal, in Artemy Troitsky, *Back in the USSR: The True Story of Rock in Russia* (Boston: Faber and Faber, 1988), 13–14.

72. Starr, *Red and Hot,* 238.

73. In spite of press celebrations linking the music programs and the fall of communism, they were not popular with everyone. In a 1985 survey about VOA, 40 percent of Soviet emigrants disliked the Conover program on jazz and one half disliked the popular music concerts. Twenty-nine out of 32 respondents wanted less music and more airtime on dissidents. Admittedly a small and self-selected sample, nonetheless it suggests that pop-

ular music may have "turned off" the intelligentsia of a certain age. "The Differential Approach and Communications Appeal Among East Europeans (Study II)," Radio Free Europe, Audience and Public Opinion Research Department, RL Library.

74. Troitsky, *Back in the USSR*, 16.

75. *For Whom the Bell Tolls* had been censored before its translation could be published because of objections to Hemingway's portrayal of Soviet advisers as "manipulative cynics" and of the Republican slaughter of prisoners. The translation finished during the war was circulating in manuscript form by 1956 and was finally published in 1976. Ludmilla Alexeyeva and Paul Goldberg, *The Thaw Generation: Coming of Age in the Post-Stalin Era* (Boston: Little, Brown, 1990), 7, 99; Friedberg, *Decade of Euphoria*, 43–45.

76. Stalin liked opera and tolerated some jazz, as evidenced by his grudging approval of the 1934 Russian film *The Happy Guys*, which profiles a local band who eventually play jazz at the Bolshoi. Starr, *Red and Hot*, 126–27. Brezhnev, however, aside from a ritual attendance at Swan Lake, preferred ice hockey. Anatoly Smeliansky, *The Russian Theatre after Stalin* (Cambridge: Cambridge University Press, 1999), 87.

77. George T. Simon, "Radio Liberty to Broadcast Jazz Composed by Russians," *New York Herald Tribune* (25 June 1963), [HU-OSA-300-80-1, Box 574, Folder 3]. The article ends by quoting an American musician who attributes the paucity of U.S. State department sponsorship of jazz tours to the fact that "most Americans still look down on jazz."

78. Gene Sosin, "Magnitizdat: Uncensored Songs of Dissent," in R. Tokes, ed., *Dissent in the USSR: Politics Ideology, and People* (Baltimore: Johns Hopkins University Press, 1975), 276–309 and Irina Orlova, "Notes from the Underground: The Emergence of Rock Music Culture," in Marsha Siefert, ed., *Mass Culture and Perestroika in the Soviet Union* (New York: Oxford University Press, 1991), 66–71.

79. Troitsky, *Back in the USSR*, 23; Timothy W. Ryback, *Rock Around the Bloc: A History of Rock Music in Eastern Europe and the Soviet Union* (New York: Oxford University Press, 1990), 62–65.

80. Nick Hayes, "The Dean Reed Story," in Sabrina Petra Ramet, ed., *Rocking the State: Rock Music and Politics in Eastern Europe and Russia* (Boulder: Westview Press, 1994), 165–78; Soviet letter published in *Izvestiya* (11 November 1978), 3 [*CDSP* 30, no. 45, 17].

81. Ryback, *Rock*, esp. chaps. 6, 7, 10, and 14.

82. Ryback, *Rock*, 54.

83. Stites, *Russian Popular Culture*, 119; Vladislav Chachin, "In the Grip of a Musical Fad," *Izvestiya* (17 September 1981), 6 [*CDSP* 33, no. 37, 19].

84. Mikhail Melnikov, "The Cares of the Ninth Muse," *Nash sovremennik*, no. 12 (1980): 157–65 [*CDSP* 33, no. 8, 24].

85. Yaroslav Khabarov, "Truth and Falsity about Cultural Exchanges," *Sovetskaya kultura* (29 May 1979), 8 [*CDSP* 31, no. 22, 12].

86. Thanks to Miglena Ivanova for providing this document.

87. Larissa Flint, "Unzipping the USSR: Jeans as a Symbol of the Struggle between Consumerism and Consumption in the Brezhnev Era," unpublished MA thesis, Department of History, Central European University, 1997.

88. I. Inoveli, "Jeans Crimes," *Zarya Vostoka* (10 Sept. 1978), 2 [*CDSP* 30, no. 37, 18].

89. This tradition began as early as 1924 with *The Extraordinary Adventures of Mr. West in the Land of the Bolsheviks*, which used American film techniques to mock American ignorance and innocence. See "Arrogance & Envy: Anti-American Cinema Under Communism and After," http://www.rusfilm.pitt.edu/2003/ (last accessed: 8 June 2003).

90. Vladimir Prosorov, "The Ills of Limitation and the Evils of Disorientation: Perceptions of Post–WWII American Literature in the USSR/Russia," *American Studies International* 39, no. 3 (2001): 41–50, here 45.

91. Shiraev and Zubok, *Anti-Americanism,* 14; Richmond, *Cultural Exchange,* 128.

92. Richmond, *Cultural Exchange,* 103–4; Maureen R. Berman and Joseph E. Johnson, eds., *Unofficial Diplomats* (New York: Columbia University Press, 1977); Marian Anderson papers, Annenberg Rare Book and Manuscript Library, University of Pennsylvania, Folder 7984.

93. Vladimir Shlapentokh, "Soviet People and the West," chap. 5 in his *Public and Private Life of the Soviet People: Changing Values in Post-Stalin Russia* (New York: Oxford University Press, 1989), 139–52; here 139–42.

94. Shiraev and Zubok, *Anti-Americanism,* 14, 19.

95. Louise Branson, "Soviet Kids Say the West Is a Bad Place with Great Music," UPI, B-Wire, FF021, 21 January 1984 [HU-OSA-300-80-1, box 575, folder 1].

96. Ryback, *Rock,* 249.

97. This most famous Southern novel circulated only in typescript, however; because *Gone With the Wind* was deemed to show slaves preferring the plantation to liberation, the film had been forbidden.

98. See Ellen Mickiewicz, "Piracy, Policy, and Russia's Emerging Media Market," *Press/Politics* 6, no. 2 (2001): 30–51.

99. William G. Rosenberg, "The Democratic Experience in Transitional Russia," in Marsha Siefert, ed., *Extending the Borders of Russian History,* 509–32.

100. Ball, *Imagining America,* 216, 218, 270, 224.

101. Nelson Hancock, "Televisions and Computers: Giving New Names to Old Tools in the Political Economy of Central Kamchatka," *Anthropology of East Europe Review* 16, no. 2 (1998): 1; Ball, *Imagining America,* 226.

102. Anatole Shub, "Why Russians Miss the Rule of Law: 12 Focus Groups in Four Cities," U.S. Information Agency Office of Research and Media Reaction Report R-2-97 (Washington: USIA, 1997), 4–5; Ball, *Imagining America,* 270.

103. American critics cite vested interests in market exploitation as more potent than democratic reform. David Lempert, "The Colonization of the Russian Political and Legal System," in Mike-Frank G. Epitropoulos and Victor Rodometof, eds., *American Culture in Europe* (New York: Praeger, 1998), 91–118.

104. Tim McDaniel, *The Agony of the Russian Idea* (Princeton: Princeton University Press, 1996), 11.

105. Vladimir Putin, *First Person* (New York: Public Affairs Press, 2000), 212.

106. See, e.g., Vladimir Shlapentokh, "Is the 'Greatness Syndrome' Eroding?" *Washington Quarterly* 25, no. 1 (2002): 131–46.

107. Roland Robertson, *Globalization: Social Theory and Global Culture* (Beverly Hills: Sage, 1992), 50.

108. Hilary Pilkington, Elena Omel'chenko, Moya Flynn, Ul'iana Bliudina, and Elena Starkova, *Looking West? Cultural Globalization and Russian Youth Cultures* (University Park: Pennsylvania State University Press, 2002), xiv, 13, chap. 2.

109. Harley Balzer, "Managed Pluralism: Vladimir Putin's Emerging Regime," *Post-Soviet Affairs* 19, no. 3 (2003): 189–227, here 195.

110. Denise J. Youngblood, "Americanitis: The Amerikanshchina in Soviet Cinema," *Journal of Popular Film and Television* 19, no. 4 (1992): 148–56, here 153.

111. Brigit Beumers, "Cinemarket, or the Russian Film Industry in 'Mission Possible,'" *Europe-Asia Studies* 51, no. 5 (1999): 871–96; here 886, Table 5B.

112. Anna Lawton, "Russian Cinema in Troubled Times," *New Cinema: Journal of Contemporary Film* 1, no. 2 (2002): 99–100.

113. Shiraev and Zubok, *Anti-Americanism,* 82.

114. "Russian Deputies Protest Against American Films," pravda.ru (18 June 2003), Johnson's Russia List [hereafter JRL] 7256 , #16 and Anatoli Korolev, "Kremlin against Foreign Movies Quotas," RIA Novosti (17 July 2003) [JRL 7256, #15].

115. Olga Sobolevskaya, "Russian Cinema more than ready for Action," RIA Novosti (25 August 2003) [JRL 7300, #10].

116. Meanwhile, the Internet is the least restricted of the Russian media. Putin has rejected a technology that would allow the government to monitor content. Balzer, "Managed Pluralism," 203.

117. Vladimir Kovalev, "Media Notes: NTV RIP, Again," *Transitions Online* (24 February 2003). Private television channels were a symbol of media freedom during the first half of the 1990s, and their increasing concentration in the hands of the oligarchs simultaneously has put them often in opposition to the government. Terhi Rantanen, *The Global and the National: Media and Communications in Post-Communist Russia* (Lanham: Rowman and Littlefield, 2002); Ellen Propper Mickiewicz, *Changing Channels: Television and the Struggle for Power in Russia,* rev. and exp. ed. (Durham: Duke University Press, 1999); Kaarle Nordenstreng, Elena Vartanova, and Yassen Zassoursky, eds., *Russian Media Challenge* (Helsinki: Kikimora, 2001).

118. The same pattern emerged in the recording industry, which had always recycled classical music but now was issuing "the best of communism" as a large part of the market. Marsha Siefert, "Re-Mastering the Past: Musical Heritage, Sound Recording, and the Nation in Hungary and Russia," in Mihály Szegedy-Maszák, ed., *National Heritage— National Canon* (Budapest: Collegium Budapest, 2002), 251–80.

119. Frank G. Ellis, "The Media as Social Engineer," in Catriona Kelly and David Shepherd, eds., *Russian Cultural Studies: An Introduction* (Oxford: Oxford University Press, 1998), 219–20.

120. Natalya A. Avseenko, "American Programs and their Effectiveness on Russian Television," *American Studies International* 41, nos. 1–2 (2003): 203–19; Elena Prokhorova, "Can the Meeting Place Be Changed? Crime and Identity Discourse in Russian Television Series of the 1990s," *Slavic Review* 62, no. 3 (2003): 512–24.

121. Stephen Hutchings argues that Russia's dominant literary canon, an emblem of "culturedness" (*kul'turnost'*), provides a "translation code" for its reception and reshaping of Western television genres. "Ghosts in the Machine: Literature as Translation Mechanism in Post-Soviet Television Representations of Western-ness," *International Journal of Cultural Studies* 5, no. 3 (2002): 291–315.

122. *Cultural Policy in the Russian Federation* (Strasbourg: Council of Europe, 1997), 155–56, 179, 252–53.

123. Rosalind Marsh, "The Death of Soviet Literature: Can Russian Literature Survive?" *Europe-Asia Studies* 45, no. 1 (1993): 115–29.

124. Yassen N. Zassoursky, "Mass Culture as Market Culture," in Siefert, *Mass Culture and Perestroika,* 13–18.

125. Prosorov, "Ills of Limitation," 49.

126. Boris Firsov, "Intelligentsia, Intellectuals, and Elites in Transition: A Critical Discourse at the Beginning of the Twenty-First Century," in Marsha Siefert, ed., *Extending the Borders of Russian History,* 443–56.

127. As of the 2001 budget, the Kremlin has recognized the importance of spending on youth programs, directly and indirectly. The most "notorious" of the GONGOs (Government-Organized Non-Government Organizations) is the youth group Idushchiye Vmeste, translated as Moving Together, whose 2001 membership hit 45,000. Dubbed the Putsomol for their support of Putin, the group offers a conduct code to revitalize Russian youth, from "saying no to drunkenness, drugs, and swearing" to saying "yes to patriotism, physical

fitness, and respect for one's elders." Although some fear its occasional excess, the group has been pro-Russian without specifically being anti-American. Balzer, "Managed Pluralism," 208–9; Guy Chazan, "Efforts to Indoctrinate Russian Youths with Love for Putin has Mixed Results," *Wall Street Journal* (29 May 2001) [JRL 5275, #5].

128. The next paragraphs are based on Pilkington et al., *Looking West?* unless otherwise noted.

129. Pilkington cites these characteristics from David W. Ellwood, "Comparative Anti-Americanism in Western Europe," in H. Fehrenbach and U. Poiger, eds., *Transactions, Transgressions, Transformations: American Culture in Western Europe and Japan* (New York: Berghahn, 2000). *Looking West,* 164.

130. Hugh Porter, *Time Europe* 161, no. 6 (2003); Elysa Gardner, "From Russia with Love Comes Naughty T.A.T.U.," *USA Today* (5 March 2003); "Channel One: Eurovision is Political Contest," http://www.rosbaltnews.com/print/print?cn=62753 (last accessed: 10 March 2003).

131. Walter D. Connor, "Anti-Americanism in Post-Communist Russia," in Paul Hollander, ed., *Understanding Anti-Americanism: Its Origins and Impact at Home and Abroad* (Chicago: Dee, 2004), 214–35. One critic of American policy charges that widespread anti-Americanism is a direct reaction to American policies of the 1990s, not a legacy of communism. Stephen F. Cohen, *Failed Crusade: America and the Tragedy of Post-Communist Russia* (New York: Norton, 2000), 192.

132. Sue Larsen, "National Identity, Cultural Authority, and the Post-Soviet Blockbuster: Nikita Mikhalkov and Aleksei Balabanov," *Slavic Review* 62, no. 3 (2003): 491–511, provides the basis for this discussion.

POLAND: TRANSMISSIONS AND TRANSLATIONS

◆   ◆   ◆

Andrzej Antoszek
Kate Delaney

Introduction

The period under discussion in this book—1945–2004—can be divided into Cold War and post–Cold-War eras, and for Poland the story of "Americanization" breaks sharply along that divide. Poland, which once lent the name of its capital to the Warsaw Pact, was among the first group of new NATO members in 1999 and became part of the "coalition of the willing" in the 2003 Iraq war. Bearing in mind this temporal divide, the issue of Americanization also needs to be examined from the perspectives of transmission and reception, from the viewpoint of the sender as well as that of the receiver. We are presenting this chapter in two distinct voices to reflect this double vision and dialogue. The section headed "Transmissions"—representing the voice of the "sender"—presents a largely chronological account of U.S. efforts to exert cultural influence on Poland. "Translations"—representing the voice of a Polish "receiver"—presents a more subjective view, giving Polish responses to American cultural imports. Finally, we take a look at anti-Americanism in Poland.

Transmissions

U.S. cultural policy toward Poland must be seen in the broader context of U.S.-Polish diplomatic relations, a context that has always been greatly influenced by the large and vocal Polish-American community. Estimated to exceed

---

10 million in number, backed by the Roman Catholic hierarchy, and concentrated in several key states, the Polish-American community has closely monitored U.S. foreign policy toward their homeland and willingly exerted pressure on presidents and members of Congress to assist Polish resistance to communist rule during the Cold War and support the transition to democracy and a market economy in the post–Cold-War era. The export of U.S. culture can be seen as playing a role in both those endeavors.

In the immediate post–World War II years cultural relations between the two countries were limited, and they remained so until after Stalin's death. One visible sign of this cultural freeze was a drastic curtailment of the teaching of English at Polish universities. After the 1947 elections, through which the Communists consolidated their control in Poland, English departments that had recently been opened at the new universities in Łódź and Wrocław and reopened in Poznań and at Jagiellonian University in Kraków were closed. This left only two English departments open at Polish universities: one in Warsaw, which was intended to train interpreters and translators to fulfill government needs, and the other at the Catholic University in Lublin, which maintained resistance to ideological pressures. The formalization of censorship[1] and other restrictions on publication meant that American literature in this period was largely represented by translations of the works of Howard Fast and other proletarian writers as well as reissues of works by John Steinbeck, Jack London, Theodore Dreiser, Sinclair Lewis, and Mark Twain.[2] Polish authorities in turn accused the U.S. of also implementing cultural restrictions. A 1952 illustration entitled "Culture Bearer" by Polish artist Jerzy Flisak depicts a fat cowboy wearing American stripes carrying to a bonfire books by Howard Fast, Lenin, Gorky, Mayakovsky, and Marx. Howard Fast was not the only U.S. cultural figure officially admired in Poland in the early 1950s. Paul Robeson was honored by a larger-than-life 1952 sculpture by Danuta Tomaszewska-Kolarska that identified him as a "winner of the Lenin Peace Prize."

With many other channels of cultural communication between Poland and the U.S. blocked during these early postwar years, international broadcasting played an important role in disseminating American culture. In 1952 Radio Free Europe (RFE) was established in Munich with a Polish section headed by Jan Nowak-Jeziorański, who had been a courier for the Polish underground in World War II. The initial Polish broadcast began precisely at 11:00 A.M. on 3 May 1952, the anniversary of the Polish Constitution. Polish listeners heard: "This is Radio Free Europe speaking—the Voice of a Free Poland.... Poles speaking to Poles." The Polish program, like those of its sister stations broadcasting to other Eastern European countries, was to serve as a surrogate home service staffed with émigré broadcasters providing news and opinion about developments in Poland as well as broader cultural and information programs. Publicly RFE was not a government-funded station but a private organization under the National Committee for a Free Europe that solicited donations from the public through the Crusade for Freedom, an organization especially incorporated for this purpose. In fact the stations were funded by Congress through the CIA until 1971. The Polish government reacted to RFE not only by jamming its broadcasts but also by conducting a publicity campaign against it. A 1955 poster by Ignacy Witz depicts a funnel going into the head of an RFE broadcaster. Into this funnel two figures—one a Nazi identified by swastika signs, the second an American, identified by a red-striped bow-tie decorated with $$ and a blue-starred shirt—are pouring such toxic ingredients as lies, gossip, blackmail, and libel. Polish authorities would use the Munich location of RFE to link this station in the public mind with the hated Germans.

The Voice of America Polish service, begun in 1942, was the open, public, government foreign broadcast service. In addition to news bulletins and editorials supporting U.S. government policy and attacking communism, VOA carried various cultural features. One of the most popular VOA programs was Willis Conover's *Music, USA Jazz Hour,* broadcast six nights a week starting on 6 January 1955. When Conover died in 1996, the *New York Times* noted that "at the peak of the cold war it was estimated that Conover had 30 million regular listeners in Eastern Europe and the Soviet Union."[3] Polish pianist Adam Makowicz has credited Conover with inspiring his jazz career: "In the mid-fifties I discovered Willis Conover's program *Music USA Jazz Hour,* broadcast every night by the Voice of America. It changed my life forever. I chose a new life of freedom and improvisation considered by the authorities to be 'decadent' over the career of a classical pianist my parents and teachers envisioned for me."[4] Countless Polish jazz fans have expressed their appreciation for Conover's program, which kept them connected to current developments in jazz ("America's classical music") throughout the Cold War. Indeed, it is almost impossible to find a memoir by a Polish jazz artist or fan that does not begin with a tribute to the influence of Willis Conover and VOA and an account of the excitement of huddling around a short-wave radio to catch the broadcasts. When Conover first visited Poland in 1959, he was exuberantly welcomed as a hero by cheering crowds, young girls bearing flowers, and a band. The VOA and RFE Polish service both introduced programs of pop and rock and roll music in the 1960s, and Polish state radio responded by broadcasting its own rock music program on a short-wave band close to that of RFE.[5] Popular music thus entered Poland with little official resistance after 1956 and was readily adopted and adapted by Polish listeners. The story of the reception and translation of the various forms of popular music will be told in the "Translations" section below.

The "thaw" in U.S.-Polish relations can be dated from the Polish October of 1956, when after the workers' demonstrations in Poznań in June of that year, Władysław Gomułka became First Secretary of the Party and initiated a policy of increased liberalization. Cardinal Wyszyński was released, restrictions on the church were eased, censorship was relaxed in comparison to the Stalinist period, emigration policy was loosened, the jamming of foreign broadcasts ceased, and in general contacts with the West increased. Indeed, contacts grew so rapidly in the three years following Gomułka's assumption of power that Jan Błoński could even refer to the "invasion of Americans."[6] The U.S. government had identified Poland as "a model for other regimes to emulate in pursuing independence from Moscow" and elaborated a program of cultural contacts, including the distribution of U.S. publications, films, and exhibits; the establishment of a USIS library; and the funding of exchange programs to bring Polish scholars, technical experts, and cultural leaders to the U.S. and send their American counterparts to Poland.[7]

Implementation of this program of increased contacts was tied directly to Poland's need for economic aid. Starting in 1957 the Polish government was allowed to purchase U.S. agricultural commodities (wheat and cotton) under Public Law 480. Payment was made in zlotys, which the U.S. government would use to finance (among other things) cultural and educational exchange programs.[8] Under the Information Media Guarantee Program, Poland was given the right to buy in zlotys U.S. media products including films, books, authors' rights, stage-production rights, musical recordings, newspapers and periodicals, and TV series.[9] The spread of U.S. cultural products in Poland was thus directly related to the policy of economic aid ("peaceful engagement") instituted after 1956. The U.S. also signed agreements providing loans and credits to the new Polish government, and in 1957 sent to Poznań a trade fair exhibit housed in a Buckminster Fuller dome. The American Pavilion displayed to the Poles not only machinery but also the latest examples of American consumer culture including cars, a model home, and women's fashions, all of which attracted eager crowds of Polish fair-goers.[10] Jeans were the hit of the 1958 Poznań fair,[11] and as elsewhere in the Eastern bloc, they became the symbol of the West. The "thaw" also meant that restrictions on music and popular culture were eased. Jazz, which had been suppressed during Stalin's lifetime, flourished. Jazz festivals were organized in Sopot in 1956 and 1957. In 1958 Warsaw created the Jazz Jamboree, a festival that over the years attracted to Poland many of the top names in American jazz, including Duke Ellington, Miles Davis, Dizzy Gillespie, Thelonious Monk, Charlie Mingus, Sarah Vaughan, Herbie Hancock, Ray Charles, and Keith Jarrett.

Political relations also entered a new era. In 1959 Vice President Nixon visited Warsaw from 2 to 5 August, and on 29 August of that year the United States reopened its consulate in Poznań. Poland also saw the beginnings of its Fulbright program in 1959. Under this program young Polish scholars traveled to the U.S. to conduct research, and American Fulbright professors came to teach at Polish universities, mostly in American Literature and American Studies in the early years of the program. However, the selection of the Polish participants in the Fulbright program, as in other scholarship programs such as those administered by the Ford Foundation, was controlled by Polish authorities. This governmental control of the selection of scholarship recipients would lead the Ford Foundation to suspend in 1967 the program that it had financed since 1957 to bring Polish scholars to U.S. universities.[12]

English departments were restored at the universities that had had them prior to the 1947 closures, and a new department was opened at the Maria Curie-Skłodowska University in Lublin. At Warsaw University, Margaret Schlauch, an American expatriate who had become head of the university's English department, helped promote the teaching of American Literature.[13] With the relaxation in censorship more American authors appeared in Polish translation, including William Faulkner, Ernest Hemingway, Thomas Wolfe, and Norman Mailer. Best-sellers in this period included *The Snows of Kilimanjaro, For Whom the Bell Tolls, The Grapes of Wrath, East of Eden, Absalom, Absalom!,* and *Light in August.*[14] Books by Hemingway, Faulkner, and Thorton Wilder took the top three places in a 1959 survey of Polish writers, who were asked to name the new novels they had read that year that had most impressed them. In a similar survey in 1960 works by Faulkner, Wilder, and Steinbeck topped the poll.[15] Seeking to account for the enduring popularity of these writers, Błoński remarks, "Polish readers see Hemingway as a marvelous upholder of human liberty."[16] He also notes parallels between Faulkner's South and Polish society: "The Polish South died in the Warsaw insurrection of 1944. But the vanquished are not always defeated, as Faulkner's work testifies."[17]

Over the 1960s the Polish government reasserted some of the censorship controls that had been loosened after 1956. *New York Times* correspondent David Halberstam was ordered out of Poland in December 1965 for writing "slanderous articles about Poland." Reporting on the Vietnam War in the Polish press was also censored. One Polish newspaper was accused by the censorship bureau of an ill-considered selection of information when it described the case of a U.S. marine corporal sentenced to life imprisonment by a U.S. military tribunal in Chalai for killing a Vietnamese peasant-housewife in cold blood. Readers in Poland were not to be given the impression that the U.S. would actually prosecute war crimes.[18] The 1968 repression of universities and trials of dissidents subdued much of the freedom of expression that had been gained in 1956.[19] However, cultural exchange was allowed to continue. Under the President's Special International Program for Cultural Presentations, the U.S. State Department sent American performing artists, among them major ballet companies and symphony orchestras as well as jazz groups, college and university bands, and vocal groups, on tour to Poland. Arts exhibits accompanied by Polish-speaking guides were also sent. The touring

Family of Man photography exhibition attracted a quarter of a million Polish visitors. The monthly Polish-language magazine *Ameryka* (circulation 30,000), produced and distributed by the United States Information Agency, provided stories about U.S. society, culture, and technology.[20] Arthur Miller, Saul Bellow, and John Steinbeck were among the American writers who visited Poland in the 1960s, a decade in which Miller's plays were staged in Poland, as were those by Tennessee Williams and Edward Albee. Translations appeared of works by a new generation of American authors: John Updike, J. D. Salinger, Truman Capote, James Baldwin, Phillip Roth, Bernard Malamud.[21]

A new warming in U.S.-Polish relations in 1972 was accelerated by the broader East-West thaw known as *détente*. In May 1972 Richard Nixon returned to Poland, this time as the first U.S. president to visit that country. This visit was followed by an agreement to establish a U.S. consulate in Kraków and by the signing of a science and technology agreement. Subsequently, Presidents Ford and Carter also visited Poland, and Poland's leader Edward Gierek went to the U.S. In 1976 policy changed at Radio Free Europe, and new guidelines were issued in keeping with the new era of *détente*. In May 1976 Jan Nowak retired under what George Urban, RFE's director in the 1980s, has termed "the result of pressure from the State Department."[22]

This increasing warmth in political relations was matched by greater cultural contact. The major American Bicentennial Exhibition "The World of Franklin and Jefferson" was shown in Warsaw in 1975. However, the information about the American Bicentennial itself was subject to censorship guidelines and could only be reported through the intermediary of the official Polish news agency Polska Agencja Prasowa (PAP), although "mentions of and references to the anniversary are also permissible in publications popularizing the role of Poles in the revolution, history and modern life in the United States and in historical articles that contrast the progressive nature of these past events with current U.S. socioeconomic problems."[23] In 1974 the censorship office also denied permission for a student production of Allen Ginsberg's *Howl* at Warsaw University because the work "presented the fundamentals of hippie ideology."[24]

In 1976, however, after three years of negotiations, an agreement was signed by Warsaw University and Indiana University to create reciprocal centers— an American Studies center in Warsaw and a Polish Studies center in Bloomington, Indiana. The American Studies center in Warsaw housed a research library, hosted American students and professors, organized seminars and lectures, and published the journal *American Studies*. The American Studies center and journal were the first of their kind among the Warsaw Pact countries, benefiting not only from the relatively relaxed restrictions on Polish academic freedom but also from the support of the Polish-American community, who endorsed such efforts in their homeland. Seminars organized by the American Studies Center and by English departments at Polish universities brought noted American writers such as Robert Coover, Susan Sontag, John Ashbery, and Joyce Carol Oates to Poland.

Polish journals such as *Literatura na Świecie* (Literature Throughout the World, established in 1971) and *Przekrój* (Profile) published Polish translations of American fiction, poetry, and essays. Among the writers whose works appeared in Polish translation in the 1970s were Robert Coover, Thomas Pynchon, Ken Kesey, John Barth, Sylvia Plath, Kurt Vonnegut, Donald Barthelme, and Joseph Heller. One critic attributes the runaway success of Heller's *Catch-22* to the resonance many Polish readers found between their own situation in 1975 and that of the novel's protagonist Yossarian. "As someone who rebelled against authority and tried to fight a senseless system, he was particularly attractive to Poles, many of whom were involved with their own private struggle with an absurd system they could not accept." This book, along with Vonnegut's *Slaughterhouse Five*, opened a generation gap as older reviewers condemned the mocking of World War II and younger reviewers and readers championed these novels.[25] An anthology of American short stories of the 1960s and 1970s was published in 1980: *Gabinet luster: krótka proza amerykańska 1961–1977* (Room of Mirrors: Short American Prose 1961–1977). Postmodern and experimental writing enjoyed particular acceptance among Polish scholars and critics.[26]

Works of American literature, once translated into Polish, circulated beyond Poland's borders into other Slavic-language countries. Readers in Warsaw Pact countries with stricter censorship than Poland often first encountered many American authors in Polish translation. Joseph Brodsky said he taught himself Polish in order to read *Literatura na Świecie*.[27] "In those days [the 1960s] the bulk of Western literature, and of news about cultural events in the West, was not available in the Soviet Union. Poland was even at that point the happiest and most cheerful barrack in the Soviet camp. People there were much better informed and they were publishing all sorts of magazines and translating everything into Polish."[28] Lithuanian poet Tomas Venclova had a similar experience: "I was one of a large number of people in the USSR who learned Polish for obtaining information on the West and Western culture. We had no access to Western books and newspapers, yet we could subscribe to Polish newspapers and magazines, which from 1956 on became appreciably more informative than Soviet publications."[29] Thus Poland served as both a translator and transmitter of American culture, making American works accessible to others in the Eastern bloc.

American films were also more available in Poland than in neighboring countries through most of this period. From 1945 to 1967, 336 American films were imported for exhibition in Poland.[30] Polish authorities tried to keep an ideological balance by importing equal numbers of films from the

West and from the Eastern bloc, and by giving greater and more enthusiastic press coverage to films from the East, but American films ran longer and played to larger audiences than did those from the East. For example, "although only 5 per cent of the (old and new) films shown in 1960 were American, they accounted for 16 per cent of the total cinema-audience." In that year 29 U.S. and 64 Russian films were imported into Poland.[31] Polish audiences became very familiar with Western "myth-setters," including John Ford's *Stagecoach* (*Dyliżans*) (1939) starring John Wayne as the Ringo Kid, *High Noon* (*W samo południe*) (1952) directed by Fred Zinnemann with Gary Cooper and Grace Kelly, Howard Hawks' *Rio Bravo* (1959) with John Wayne, Dean Martin, Ricky Nelson, and Angie Dickinson, and John Sturges' *Last Train from Gun Hill* (*Ostatni pociąg z Gun Hill*) (1959) with Kirk Douglas and Anthony Quinn. Although the popularity of westerns declined towards the end of the 1980s, there are very few people in Poland unfamiliar with the figure of the lonely cowboy, the saloon, or the "red-skins."

Another group of movies enjoyed by Polish cinema-goers was what today would probably be labeled (light) entertainment; however, many of the actors in those films became household names in Poland. Such movies included films with Marilyn Monroe, from *Niagara* to *Gentlemen Prefer Blondes* (*Mężczyźni wolą blondynki*), *How to Marry a Millionaire* (*Jak poślubić milionera*) (all 1953), and *Some Like It Hot* (*Pół-żartem, pół-serio*) (1959). Polish audiences also enjoyed *The Barefoot Contessa* (*Bosonoga kontesa*) (1954) with Ava Gardner, Humphrey Bogart, and Edmond O'Brien, as well as musicals like *An American in Paris* with the superstars Gene Kelly and Leslie Caron.

The more serious productions included Orson Welles' *Citizen Kane* (*Obywatel Kane*) (1941) with Welles and Joseph Cotton, Frank Capra's *Mr. Smith Goes to Washington* (*Mr. Smith jedzie do Waszyngtonu*) (1939), Nicholas Ray's *Rebel without a Cause* (*Buntownik bez powodu*) (1955), and Billy Wilder's *Witness for the Prosecution* (*Świadek oskarżenia*) (1957) with Tyrone Power and Marlene Dietrich. There were also movies that Polish fans instantly recognized as absolute blockbusters, including Fleming, Cukor, and Wood's *Gone with the Wind* (*Przeminęło z wiatrem*) (1939) with Vivien Leigh and Clark Gable, Fred Zinnemann's *From Here to Eternity* (*Stąd do wieczności*) (1953) with Burt Lancaster, Montgomery Clift, Deborah Kerr, and Frank Sinatra, and *Casablanca* with Humphrey Bogart and Ingrid Bergman. More recent hits included movies such as John Badham's *Saturday Night Fever* (*Gorączka sobotniej nocy*) (1977) with John Travolta and Karen Lynn and *Dirty Dancing* (*Wirujący seks*) (1987) with Patrick Swayze and Jennifer Grey. Due to the scarcity of funds available to Polish state distributors, the release dates of American films in Poland almost never coincided with their release dates in the West. This, however, did not prevent Polish cinema-goers from enjoying movies made even before World War II.

The most popular American film in Poland before 1989 (third in the overall rankings) was Bruce Lee's martial arts film *Enter the Dragon* (*Wejście Smoka*). Steven Spielberg's *Raiders of the Lost Ark* (*Poszukiwacze zaginionej arki*) ranked nineteenth on the list of most popular films in the 1951–1988 era.[32] Not all major American films were allowed into Poland before 1989. Films considered anti-Soviet or biased against other communist governments were prohibited. As Gierek sought more economic aid and trade ties from the West, he wanted to reassure the Russians of Poland's continuing ideological reliability. Thus, *Doctor Zhivago* was not shown in Polish cinemas before 1989,[33] nor were James Bond films, Ken Russell's *The Devils,* or Fred Zinnemann's *The Men (Battle Stripe).* However, the total number of films—both foreign and Polish—that were prohibited or removed from distribution was relatively small, confirming the observations that Poland enjoyed greater cultural freedom than other countries of the Soviet Bloc. In 1970, for example, censors watched 859 feature films, 247 medium-length films, and 205 shorts, out of which only 6 were held back (compared to 21 in 1969, which, according to Pawlicki, was an exceptionally high number).[34] Decisions regarding the exhibition and prohibition of films treating the Vietnam War show the nuances of Polish censorship. *Apocalypse Now* (*Czas Apokalipsy*), with its portrayal of drugged, violent Americans, was publicly exhibited in Poland, but both *Rambo* (an American hero killing "evil" Vietnamese) and *The Deerhunter* (*Łowca jeleni*) ("evil" Vietnamese torturing Americans) were not, although the latter circulated in underground film clubs. *Apocalypse Now* was playing when martial law was declared in December 1981, and Chris Niedenthal's unforgettable photograph of the period shows a tank in front of Warsaw's Moskwa (!) cinema with the words *Czas Apokalipsy*—The Time of Apocalypse—on the marquee.

The history of motion pictures in Poland would not be complete without a brief historical sketch showing the development of television, which in addition to serving its political "mission" turned many of the American actors and titles mentioned above into household names. The beginnings of Polish state television go back to the late 1930s, when the first regular broadcasts began in Warsaw. As Tadeusz Pikulski writes in his book *Prywatna historia telewizji publicznej* (A Private History of Public Television), after the war it was mainly the voices of Polish émigrés in the U.S. that contributed to the growing interest in the medium, making the authorities realize that not having television in Poland proved Poland's cultural inferiority to America.[35] American entertainment—both feature films and TV series—was popular on Polish state television. Premiers of the movies *The Great Escape* and *The Graduate* as well as the *Dynasty* TV series attracted millions of television viewers. The country held its breath watching Alexis's merciless assaults on Krystle and also copied their hairstyles and ways of dressing.

Dynasty's popularity matched the reverence with which Poles had earlier treated the *Rich Man, Poor Man* series, adapted from Irwin Shaw's novel and extremely popular in Poland owing to its novelty and "reality" in presenting the Land of Dreams. Halina Frąckowiak, a popular music icon of the 1980s, turned the Polish title of the series *Pogoda dla bogaczy* (*Weather for the Rich*) into a hit song still played by Polonia stations all over the world.[36] The popular American series *Roots* was shown in Poland, not for its portrayal of social changes but for its critique of slavery and inequality in the Land of the Free. Probably each person born in Poland in the early 1970s or earlier remembers Kunta Kinte, but few realize that Nyo Boto was played by Maya Angelou, whose poetry Polish students read now as part of the American literature canon. Walt Disney's *Zorro*, Westerns like *Bonanza*, and family entertainment like *Disneyland* also played on Polish state TV.

The imposition of martial law in December 1981 reversed the "thaw" in bilateral relations and provoked a sharp and immediate response from the Reagan administration. Economic sanctions were placed on Poland, and President Reagan proclaimed 30 January as "A Day of Solidarity with the Polish People." Well-wishers throughout the U.S. attended union rallies and church meetings, excerpts of which were included in "Let Poland be Poland," a 90-minute television program broadcast on 31 January. This show, which was organized by Charles Z. Wick, the director of the International Communication Agency (the successor to the USIA, which had been reorganized and renamed in the Carter years), also included world political leaders' messages of support for Solidarity and a free Poland as well as statements and readings by cultural figures such as Bob Hope, Charlton Heston, Kirk Douglas, Henry Fonda, Joan Baez,[37] and Frank Sinatra. "Ever Homeward," a Polish-language song sung by Sinatra in the 1948 film *Miracle of the Bells*, was accompanied by a "video-over with current scenes from Poland that," according to Wick, "will hopefully be symbolic of the anguish involved with tanks and that sort of thing."[38] The show was beamed by satellite to more than fifty countries, but of course it was not shown by Polish television. "Let Poland Be Poland" was not the only action Wick took in support of Solidarity. According to Peter Schweizer, in violation of the VOA charter, Wick allowed VOA to be used to send coded messages to the Solidarity underground in Poland. "A special song might be played; a carefully crafted broadcast could pass along information about an impending crackdown, a special shipment, or a meeting time and place."[39] Radio Free Europe reversed its détente-era policy and was now collecting and broadcasting Polish *samizdat*.

In spite of the economic sanctions imposed by the U.S. against Poland, and notwithstanding the tight surveillance kept on the U.S. Embassy and its diplomats during the martial law period, other academic and cultural exchanges were able to continue to operate. American lecturers and scholars came to

Poland under the Fulbright program and other exchange programs such as the International Research and Exchanges Board (IREX, founded in 1968 to conduct academic exchange programs with the Soviet Union and Eastern Europe). Polish scholars still had access to American books and periodicals at the American Studies Center in Warsaw,[40] and in Poznań foreigners who could enter the library at the American Consulate checked out books on behalf of Polish students and scholars who were prevented from entering.[41] The teaching of American literature continued at the universities, as did the publication of *Literatura na Świecie.* A major study of American literature, *Historia literatury Stanów Zjednoczonych w zarysie* (an outline history of the literature of the United States) was published in 1982/83 by Andrzej Kopcewicz and Marta Sienicka.

The 1980s also saw the creation of several new foundations, public and private, that operated in the international cultural field. In 1983 the National Endowment for Democracy was founded by an act of Congress. It channeled support funds to Solidarity and supported various publications, both *samizdat* and open. In 1988 George Soros funded the establishment of the Stefan Batory Foundation, an organization that makes grants to various groups and individuals developing civic society in Poland. In 1984 the Trust for Mutual Understanding was established by an anonymous American philanthropist as a private, grant-making organization funding cultural exchanges between the U.S. and the countries of the Eastern bloc. This trust has provided American performing and visual artists with the support they needed for them to participate in festivals, stage exhibits of their work, or performances in Poland. For example, it has regularly supported an American season of dance and art at the Center for Contemporary Art in Warsaw's Ujazdowski Castle. Leading dance companies and artists have thus been able to make their work known to the Polish public. The impact of American influence on modern dance in Poland has been pronounced. Like jazz, modern dance is largely identified with the U.S., and American companies have been prominent in all the Polish dance festivals. Polish dancers maintain active contacts with the U.S. and many have trained there.

After the Round Table talks, the Solidarity election victory, and the installation of Tadeusz Mazowiecki as prime minister, the U.S. Congress passed legislation establishing SEED (Support for East European Democracy) in November 1989. The Marshall Plan was not to be repeated; Poland and other Eastern European countries would instead be the beneficiaries of SEED, which promoted the development of a free market economic system by establishing "enterprise funds" to finance private enterprise activities, by providing agricultural and technical assistance, and by providing currency stabilization loans. This act also specifically included support for expansion of educational and cultural exchange activities in Poland. It called for the establishment of a binational Fulbright commission in Poland and the creation of a cultural center. In March 1990 an agreement signed by the U.S. Government and the Government of Poland established the Office of Polish-U.S. Educational Exchanges, the first independent binational Fulbright office set up in a former Warsaw Pact country.

The early years of the post–Cold War era were marked by a burst of activity in cultural exchanges funded by Congress as well as by private sources. The U.S. Embassy opened a cultural center in a palace near Warsaw's Old Town in 1993. It featured a spacious library, an active English-teaching program, and exhibit space where U.S. art could be shown to the Polish public. Lectures and performances were also held there. However, the initial Congressional euphoria over the downfall of the communist system could not be sustained, and budget cuts led to the closure of this center in 1996. The U.S. Embassy would continue to sponsor cultural exhibits and performances in Poland but would do so in cooperation with local institutions or by renting halls. Exhibits by James Turrell, Tony Oursler, David Hammons, and Jenny Holtzer were among the visual arts projects supported by the embassy, and Steve Reich's orchestra, Trisha Brown's dance group, and the Pilobolus Dance company were among the entertainers receiving embassy support for performances in Poland in the 1990s.

Corporate sponsorship of culture became an increasingly common feature in Poland in the 1990s—as it had done earlier in the West, for largely the same reason: government support for the arts was no longer sufficient to maintain the arts institutions and programs. A major exhibition of works by Andy Warhol and concerts by the Philadelphia Orchestra were among the prestigious cultural events that were largely underwritten by corporate sponsorship. Many other American performers, especially musicians playing jazz, rock, or various forms of popular music, toured Poland under purely commercial auspices. In the 1990s the roles of both the Polish and U.S. governments in the cultural field in Poland declined in relation to the growing importance of corporate sponsorship, private foundations, and commercial activities.

U.S. culture found new channels by which to enter Poland. Among the changes introduced by the postcommunist government was the establishment of teacher training colleges, three-year postsecondary institutions designed to prepare English teachers for a new curriculum in which English would replace Russian as the principal second language to be studied by Polish schoolchildren. The American, British, and Canadian governments supported this effort, providing materials, training workshops, and scholarships for study abroad, and posting ESL specialists at the new institutions. U.S. Peace Corps volunteers were also assigned to these colleges, as well as to high schools, to give instruction in English. The teaching of English carried a cultural component that added works by American authors, American documents such as the Declaration of Independence, and American music and films to the curriculum. And the Polish Association for American Studies, which among other activities organizes annual conferences on American culture attended both by Polish and international American Studies scholars, was founded in 1990.

The lifting of censorship after 1989 unleashed an outpouring of new publications. Between 1979 and 1987 an average of 20 American novels were published in Polish translation each year. In 1990 this figure zoomed to 116. It eventually peaked at 530 titles in 1994 before returning to 250 in 1997.[42] Previously banned works of American literature became available, both in the original English and in Polish translation. American periodicals became ubiquitous on Polish newsstands, including Polish editions of *Time, Newsweek, Playboy, Cosmopolitan,* and *National Geographic.*

Among scholars and critics, American ethnic fiction by African-American, Asian-American, Native American, and Latina/Latino authors received increasing attention. Toni Morrison was the leading subject for masters' theses in American literature in this decade. In 1996 the number of M.A. degrees granted in American Literature/American Studies—200—by Polish universities surpassed those granted in British subjects by the same universities that year.[43] At the end of the decade (and of the century), a team of senior Polish literary scholars under the leadership of Professor Agnieszka Salska produced a monumental study of twentieth-century American literature.[44]

The 1990s also saw American dominance of mass-market fiction. American "popular" writers like Stephen King, Robert Ludlum, Tom Clancy, Danielle Steele, and John Grisham were translated into Polish, as were endless numbers of formulaic romance novels. The particular phenomenon of William Wharton deserves mention. This American writer is so popular in Poland that the term "whartonomania" has been coined to describe the fervor he incites, and his fans are known as "whartoniowcy."[45] Eight titles by this author came out in Polish in 1996 alone, placing him ahead of Stephen King (six titles).[46]

The importation of American films also accelerated after 1989—over 200 U.S. films are now distributed in Poland each year.[47] Spielberg's *Jurassic Park (Park Jurajski)* (1993), the most popular film in the 1990–1995 period, was accompanied by elaborate merchandising of T-shirts, toys, and other tie-in products.[48] In addition to the mass influx of commercial films in the 1990s we can point to examples of more ambitious cinema, probably best illustrated by David Lynch's movies, whose resonance remains very high in Poland. Lynch, a representative of postmodern cinema, won his fans in Poland with his first, "underground" productions—*Elephant Man (Człowiek słoń)* (1980) and *Eraserhead (Głowa do wycierania)* (1984)—and "swept" predominantly highbrow audiences with *Blue Velvet* (1986) and *Wild at Heart (Dzikość serca)* (1990). It was *Twin Peaks* that introduced Lynch to a wider audience in Poland, making viewers ponder the mystery of Laura Palmer's death. In 1991 an entire issue of the magazine *Film na świecie* (*Film in the World*) was dedicated to Lynch with contributions from Henry Welsh, Jacques Valot, and Mateusz Werner. Another director who became an icon among a relatively narrow circle of devotees was Jim Jarmusch, whose *Stranger than Paradise* (*Inaczej niż w raju*) (1984), *Down by Law* (*Poza prawem*) (1986), and *Mystery Train* (1989) soon acquired the status of cult movies due to their "undecidability," openness of form, and intriguing message. While in the post-1989 context such movies were unconnected to any "anti-system" or "freedom" impulses, they can be labeled as alternative or niche cinema. In time, they generated quite a wide response among their Polish fans; the "candy-colored clown they call the sandman," from Roy Orbison's *In Dreams* in Lynch's *Blue Velvet*, brought back people's interest in music of the 1960s. The popular Polish rock group T. Love released a song called *Dzikość serca*, and Tom Waits became an icon of the alternative music scene in Poland. In 2003, Kazik Staszewski, leader of the legendary Polish group Kult, recorded an album with his own versions of Waits's 19 songs called *Piosenki Toma Waitsa*.

The year 1989 also marks the end of Polish state television's monopoly and the beginning of various cable "televisions," where the enthusiasm of their founders sometimes exceeded their professionalism and compliance with the law: by the mid 1990s, most of the private stations had been taken over by foreign companies with abundant capital. Polish cable television, profit-oriented from the outset, tried to meet its market targets by catering to less demanding, more entertainment-seeking audiences with the "safest available option"— broadcasting many American programs and movies that had already enjoyed success in the U.S. and Western Europe. As a result, subscribers of cable programs could watch not only NBA playoff games and American wrestling, but also the "future" episodes of *Beverly Hills 90210*, which "wired" aficionados of the series followed on German RTL, getting well ahead of those who were only able to watch the "current" episodes on Program II of state television.

The development of Poland's biggest cable television network, Polska Telewizja Kablowa, illustrates the trajectory that the more important players on the market followed. Set up in 1989 by David Chase, a businessman with Polish roots, it managed to persuade Lech Wałęsa to become its first customer. In 1999 it was taken over for half a billion dollars by United Pan-Europe Communications (UPC); currently it has over 1.2 million customers. Its offerings include HBO, which broadcasts predominantly American and relatively recent movie hits and original series. The latest premieres include *The Lord of the Rings, Ocean's Eleven*, and *Pearl Harbor*. The 1997 campaign to launch HBO in Poland played explicitly on the Polish desire to have the latest American products: "To co kocha Ameryka teraz w Polsce. HBO 1997" ("Now you can get in Poland what America loves: HBO 1997").[49]

American culture in Poland is expressed not only in the visual and performing arts and in language and literature but also in the ways of organizing political campaigns, in business and media practices, and in the creation of NGOs. American multinational companies operating in Poland have become, in the decade or so since the fall of communism, the most desired employers for young people leaving universities. Job fairs organized by AIESEC (Association Internationale des Etudiants en Sciences Economiques et Commerciales, an organization of students in economics and management) at Warsaw University have drawn such companies as Arthur Andersen, Price Waterhouse, Procter and Gamble, and Mars Masterfoods Polska.[50] A survey carried out by AIESEC in 2002 revealed that the top ten "most desirable" employers on the Polish market included PricewaterhouseCoopers (the winner), Masterfoods Polska (2), Ernst & Young (6), and Procter and Gamble (10). According to the survey the promise that American corporate culture holds for Polish students is twofold: they can work in a highly professional environment and earn a lot of money. Academic programs granting MBAs and diplomas in public relations have sprung up, often under the auspices of a U.S. university.[51] New academic programs in gender and queer studies have also grown out of links with their American counterparts. Since 1991 the Network of East-West Women has been active in supporting the growth of women's movements in Poland and other Eastern European countries. In 1998 Polish universities established a university accreditation commission (UAC) that drew on American practice.

In 1999 Poland became a member of NATO and was on the way to joining the European Union.[52] By the year 2000 Poland had "graduated" from the SEED program, the Peace Corps was bringing its Polish program to an end, RFE had moved to Prague and was no longer broadcasting in Polish, and the VOA Polish Service was greatly reduced. The U.S. Consulate in Poznań closed at the end of 1995. The libraries of the U.S. Embassy in Warsaw and the U.S. Consulate in Kraków were converted into "Information Resource Centers" and their collections donated to local universities. Official U.S. cultural activities in Poland became comparable to those in other EU countries: modest grants in support of exhibits and performances, educational and cultural exchange visits, and support for American Studies conferences. The transmission of U.S. culture to Poland, carried out increasingly through commercial channels, resembled the transmission to other European markets. However, the reception of that culture was marked by its Polish translations and adaptations as will be developed below in the voice of the "receiver."

Translations

The story of American culture in Poland is also the history of decoding and encoding messages, of interpreting and, eventually, appropriating various

American voices for people's own purposes in order to oppose, undermine, and maybe even shake off the shackles of the system—the history of a people turning American productions into their own, indigenous fictions.

Tracing the resonance and the actual incorporation of such narratives into Polish culture is sometimes problematic, as is tracking American influences in Poland after 1945 in an orderly and sequential manner. The following points should help the reader understand what limitations might be encountered in trying to investigate the roots and development of Americanization in Poland.

First of all, there is the problem of sources, which were scanty until the early 1990s. In the official culture, for four decades or so, America represented "rotten imperialism," to use the phrase coined and spread by ardent believers in communism. Since the U.S. represented the other end of the political and ideological spectrum, one must not be surprised to find many officially biased voices on America. Then there were the "poetics of silence," the authorities' strategy of simply refusing to acknowledge things that were otherwise obvious to everyone, for instance, the official channels' ignoring America's various successes and achievements. Such a strategy was supposed to prevent people from finding out about America's superiority in practically every field, a ploy that fooled no sane citizen of Poland (including those in power).

Therefore, when studying American influences in Poland after 1945 one must oftentimes resort to evidence that few courts would treat as conclusive. This evidence includes the *Polish Film Chronicles* (*Polskie kroniki filmowe*), newsreels about ten minutes long that played in Polish cinemas before feature films until the late 1980s. Watching them can probably be compared to listening to the English anthem played in UK cinemas before and *after* films, yet they provide the viewer with a unique mixture of sociorealist perspectives on more or less important events taking place in Poland after 1945, including official reactions to various American "utterances."

The most relevant printed sources include old newspapers (*Trybuna Ludu* or *Sztandar Ludu*) and magazines (*Polityka*) as well as memoirs, biographies, and other books published by people of various political stripes, including Leopold Tyrmand's *Dziennik 1954* (Diary 1954), Stefan Kisielewski's *Dzienniki* (Diaries), Zygmunt Kałużyński's *Podróż na zachód* (A Trip to the West) and *Pożegnanie Molocha* (Good-bye to Moloch), Michał Głowiński's *Peereliada* (PRL's Carnival) and *Końcówka* (Endgame), Jerzy Urban's *Alfabet Urbana* (Urban's Alphabet), and others. One has to use these sources very skillfully to avoid getting lost in misinterpretations and "mistranslations." Studying these books requires the reader to engage in the meticulous process of reading between the lines and decoding information, in picking up allusions and references and translating them into coherent pieces of information. In the years between 1945 and 1989 this strategy was not unfamiliar to members of Polish society, a group used to re-creating or even making up wholes out of the little pieces that were available.

Another important source in helping to restore the multifaceted construct of Polish-American relations after 1945 was word of mouth, a medium that can hardly aspire to be either truthful or objective, but may prove quite useful in researching areas that were never included in other, more formal records. Thus the authors profited from conversations with many Poles who lived through these decades. Given the breadth of the topic, the reader should realize that although this part of the chapter tries to group various American influences in Poland between 1945 and 2004, it does not, by any means, exhaust all the possible exchanges, themes, and directions that might have existed during those years.

In the period between 1945 and 1989 one can distinguish two dimensions to the reception of American culture in Poland: when times were good, reactions to American cultural production had mainly an "aesthetic" character, and when times were bad American cultural products served as tools with which to fight the regime. The deep ideological and political roots of this second dimension made people perceive American products as symbols of anti-communism, which destined them for success. It also meant, however, that even very poor "voices" were likely to have a great influence on Polish culture.

Another important issue that scholars need to consider in their reconstructions of Americanization in Poland after 1945 is the fact that Polish people—and most likely the majority of Czechoslovak, Russian, and Romanian citizens—did not always distinguish between particular Western countries, which were often grouped under one common denomination as "the West." In other words, treating France, England, and the United States as an almost identical triad was common practice in Poland, representing people's desire for that which was absent and unattainable, but also their very vague notion of what the West really was.

The vision of the West—including the U.S.—that was created and sustained in Poland for many years was to some extent idealized and false. Therefore, Americanization in Poland should not be treated as an "official" and sequential process whose frames and mechanisms can be precisely defined. "Americanization" in Poland between 1945 and 1990 involved idolizing, iconizing, mythologizing, and even politicizing many U.S. cultural products. The "real"—or perhaps more precisely, "traditional"—Americanization started in the early 1990s, after the fall of communism, when people's hunger for consumer goods was insatiable.

This section will show particular Polish voices born of Americanization. The five categories into which American influences have been grouped—movies, music, sports, books, and business practices—are by no means definitive and offer only snapshots of the whole process. In addition, we will examine several published accounts of the U.S. and impressions of American life written by those who traveled there, often under official U.S. sponsorship. The Polish "translations" of "America" demonstrate what interesting and sometimes comic hybrids resulted from such exchanges over almost six decades. While Poland was, among the Eastern bloc countries, particularly susceptible to American culture—partly because it was the country with the least censorship and most intellectual freedom, a circumstance recognized by the U.S. and reflected in its cultural policy—the U.S. still could not predict that the results of this freedom would sometimes acquire a somewhat simulacral character.

Several Polish films of the 1990s, Władysław Pasikowski's *Psy* (Dogs) (1992), Janusz Zaorski's *Szczęśliwego Nowego Jorku* (Happy New York) (1997), and Juliusz Machulski's *Kiler* (Killer) (1997) can be considered the best embodiments of both growing Americanization and anti-Americanism. According to reviewer Tadeusz Miczka, *Psy,* a movie "more American than Polish," tells the story of a retired Urząd Bezpieczeństwa (UB, internal security office) agent who goes on to work in the police force and has to solve a case of weapons smuggling in which his former colleagues are involved.[53] Full of obscenities, shooting, and blood, the movie turned Bogusław Linda into the chief "thug" of Polish cinema. In the final scene of the movie Franz—"much like Clint Eastwood's Dirty Harry"—promises to "be *fucking* back," and indeed, like Stallone's Rambo or Schwarzenegger's Terminator, back he was in the sequel to the movie, *Psy II.*[54]

A second movie, *Szczęśliwego Nowego Jorku,* portrays the lives of six Poles living in Greenpoint, New York, brought to this "earthly paradise" by the promise of the American Dream. From having been "someone" in Poland, each of the characters goes to the dogs in America, forced to participate in a cruel rat race in pursuit of the almighty dollar. Blessed with an excellent cast, including Janusz Gajos, Bogusław Linda, and Zbigniew Zamachowski, the movie becomes a *memento mori* to thousands of Poles seeking their (financial) happiness across the Big Pond. In a "footnote" to the movie, Edward Redliński, the author of the novel on which the film is based who had himself spent a decade or so working as an illegal emigrant in New York, gives a very negative picture of the majority of Poles who come to the U.S. in search of work and better opportunities, calling them "ham" or "jeep" emigrants who, unlike citizens of Mexico, Pakistan, Haiti, or the Philippines, never suffered from real poverty.[55]

Kiler, a production of the "Polish Hollywood" (a Hollywood film lacking in means, glamour, and, obviously, power, hence only one 'l' in the film's title!) is a fast-moving crime comedy—and a parody of many American movies as well—whose major characters are played by the biggest stars of Polish cinema, including Cezary Pazura, Jerzy Stuhr, and Katarzyna Figura.[56] The soundtrack's music, performed by Elektryczne Gitary, turns the film into a "super-production," meant to top all the charts, which indeed it did. A self-reflexive metanarrative that is somewhat shameless about borrowing (or stealing) from various American films—from *Some Like it Hot* to *Midnight Run* to *Pulp Fiction*—*Kiler* marks the beginning of a purely commercial Polish cinema, where profit margins are far more important than "ambitious marginality."

Another major cultural field in which America has exerted considerable influence on Poland has been music. The 2002 collection *Jazz in Poland—Anthology*, which traces the development of jazz in Poland between 1950 and 2000, demonstrates how close the links between American and Polish jazz have been and how the progress of the genre in Poland corresponded to the state of Polish-U.S. relationships. In the booklet accompanying the anthology, particular sections are titled "1950–1960: The Beginnings," "1961–1970: The Great Opening," "1971–1980: Normalization," "1981–1990: Young Lions," and "1991–2000: Professionals."[57] The anthology presents contributions by many artists and propagators of jazz in Poland, including Glenn Miller, Louis Armstrong, Duke Ellington, John Coltrane, and, of course, Willis Conover. Polish and American artists have produced music together in many exchanges between the two cultures, such as those carried out by the sax player Michał Urbaniak and singer Urszula Dudziak, who have worked with Lester Bowie, Bobby McFerrin, and Lauren Newton. Other American musicians popular in Poland have included Ella Fitzgerald, Count Basie, Elvis Presley, Bill Haley, Bing Crosby, Perry Como, Doris Day, Connie Francis, Rosemary Clooney, Bob Dylan, and Joan Baez.

Obviously one must not omit the whole gamut of American pop and rock groups—from older groups like the Beach Boys or the Supremes to the more recent phenomena of Nirvana or the Red Hot Chili Peppers—who found ardent followers and inspired imitators in Poland. In this regard we can cite famous Polish musicians and performers like the legendary Czesław Niemen,[58] rock groups like Niebiesko-Czarni or Czerwone Guitary, and more contemporary and still active groups like Kult, Lady Pank, Budka Suflera, and others who have transformed Anglo-American popular music into Polish rock/punk culture.[59] In fact, in his fascinating study on Anglo-American rock and roll music, *To tylko rock 'n' roll* (It's only rock 'n' roll), Jerzy Wertenstein-Żuławski claims that "the huge development of rock music in our country [Poland], due to the specific character of social conditions in Poland, demonstrates which part of Anglo-American music has turned out to be important for the world and which was only *depeche mode*."[60] Wertenstein-Żuławski's list of influential musicians includes Elvis Presley, Bob Dylan, the Doors,[61] and Frank Zappa, among others. The point that one should bear in mind when considering the scale and nature of these influences is that their main source should be labeled Western rather than American, English, or even Australian. In the pre–hip-hop era Western popular culture was viewed as homogenous by the Poles, just as the Soviet-bloc countries resembled one another in the minds of many Westerners.

The genre that will receive the most attention in this text has very little to do with jazz improvisation or instrumental acrobatics. Polish hip-hop—a "phat" example of both Americanization and anti-Americanization—is all about verbal acrobatics. Perceived as anarchic and therefore appealing to the contesters of the new market economy, American rap—the father of Polish hip-hop—was rapidly "domesticated" to produce the Polish rapper, at first glance a very weird hybrid. Such African-American notions as "brothers," "'hood," or "black pride" were translated into indigenous forms, adapting the black heritage to the local, yet remained still very discernable. The influence of American rap music is evident in the clothing styles adopted by various Polish groups (baggy trousers, oversized shirts, baseball caps worn backwards), the themes they touch upon in their music (for example, the loneliness of poor project dwellers or long-distance school commuters), and in the vocabulary used to express these problems. A great number of words and phrases used by American rappers in their productions, including "the yard," "homies," "yo," and "bitches" were translated into Polish, creating some rather comic borrowings: *podwórko, kolesie, trzym się, foki.*

The most important hip-hop groups of the mid and late 1990s included Wzgórze Yapa 3, Kaliber 44, and the verbal acrobat Fisz. Yet the "real hip-hop" soon fell prey to numerous imitations, "dissed" by Polish rappers as *Xerocopies,* whose sole aim was to capitalize on the genre's growing popularity, a process that developed in a similar way in the U.S. "Old school" Polish rappers like DJ Volt and Peja accused many "new kids on the block" of propagating the new American hip-hop, which comes down to sporting cool clothes, pimping and rapping about fucking the police.[62] Even the godfather of Polish hip-hop—Liroy, who records with Lords of Brooklyn (yes, *the* Lords of Brooklyn)—is scorned by the "independent" scene for giving in to Mammon. The latest edition of Poland's most prestigious and commercial festival, and the one most "dissed" by independent musicians, Opole 2004, was won by Sistars, an R&B/soul/hip-hop duet performing excellent but hardly original replicas of recordings by the first ladies of American soul as well as songs by Lauryn Hill, Erykah Badu, and Alicia Keys. Their victory corroborates that Polish show business is "going hip-hop" in an attempt to cash in on the popularity of the once marginal genre.

In the world of sports, many American legends have enjoyed huge popularity in Poland: Jesse Owens, the sprinter and football star Bob Hayes, Harold Connolly, who won three gold medals in three consecutive Olympic games, and the professional boxers Joe Frazier, Rocky Marciano, Jake la Motta, Floyd Peterson, and of course, Cassius Clay, a.k.a. Muhammad Ali.[63] The Carl Lewis vs. Ben Jonson feud kept fans glued to the boxes in Poland, whereas the USSR's boycott of the 1984 Olympic Games in Los Angeles made people hate the Soviet Union even more and admire the Romanian authorities who said "No" to Big Brother. Yet it was basketball and the best league in the world, the NBA, that, having won the hearts of American fans, went on to cross the Iron Curtain. Little known and appreciated in Europe and still less so in the Soviet bloc countries because of the simple fact that no games were broadcast there, the NBA secretly "videotaped" itself to Poland in the 1980s, and the 1984/85 playoff games between the Los Angeles Lakers and Boston Celtics were played back for friends by the lucky owners of the first VCR machines. The Larry Bird vs. Magic Johnson college and then big-league rivalry was quintessentially about America. When live transmissions began in the early 1990s, the popularity of the game rose considerably. No kid playing street-ball these days wears the jersey of a player other than Bryant, O'Neal, or Iverson, the latter embodying the rapper and athlete. Listing "cool" things to do in Poland, *Gazeta Wyborcza,* the leading opinion-making daily, mentioned playing street-ball in front of Warsaw's Pałac Kultury, Nauki i Sztuki (Palace of Culture, Sciences and Arts), if not the greatest than at least the tallest remnant of communism in Poland.[64]

In any discussion of Polish reception of American literature, it must be stressed that until the early 1990s, when new opportunities became overwhelming, Poles were great readers of books—either because there was nothing else to do, as some say, or because books offered a free pass to worlds that could not be reached otherwise. In addition to the authors and titles discussed earlier, one could also mention the Beat Generation, whose appeal, like that of Janis Joplin, Jim Morrison, or Jimi Hendrix, seems never to subside among certain age groups. Marek Hłasko, the *enfant terrible* of Polish literature, is often compared to Jack Kerouac, but it is Waldemar Łysiak who, in his *Asfaltowy Saloon* (Asphalt Saloon), appears more American than many Americans: a pair of Levi's jeans, a Coke in his hand, and an old "junk" auto going hell-for-leather on the endless highways are the attributes of the new conqueror of America. Original he is not, since his book very much resembles Jack Kerouac's *On the Road;* Łysiak and his companion take an "exemplary trip" to twenty-three states, and the account of the trip is a series of literary snapshots taken in various places. Much as they are mawkish, conventional, and cliché-ridden—since Łysiak assumes the stance of a new Walt Whitman, believing that whatever he infers the reader too will take for granted—they are a thought-provoking foreword to the immigrant vision of America.

The depiction of the community of emigrants in Edward Redliński's *Szczuropolacy* (Ratpolacks) calls into question the advantages of the Land of Plenty. The delineation of this group is rarely present in the official media; its story is hideous and tragic and does not promise well for the future. It seems that the process of assimilation costs much more than the lucky winners of the green card estimated at first. Despite the fact that they hail from different walks of life and social strata in Poland, the new environment merges them into a socially and economically deprived minority possessing a number of common features. Employing a language that parodies English by substituting *dżus* (juice), *kokrocz* (cockroach), *gastrajter* (ghostwriter), *erkondyszner* (air conditioner), and *klinować* (clean) for their Polish equivalents, the "ratpolacks" assume names reflecting their position in the new hierarchy, such as *Azbest* (Asbestos), *Pank* (Punk), *Profesor* (Professor), and *Lojer* (Lawyer), and lead lives of humiliation and hopelessness. This is not the American the reader knows from the narratives Crevecoeur or Łysiak.

An important contemporary novel where the thin line between the imported and the "domesticated" suddenly starts to blur is Dorota Masłowska's *Wojna polsko ruska pod flagą biało czerwoną* (*Snow White and Russian Red*). Written in "a rotten literary language," as Marcin Świetlicki put it in the cover blurb, the book may be called the first Polish hip-hop or maybe *blokowisko* (urban housing project) novel. Since she was only eighteen years of age when she wrote the book, Masłowska could not possibly have read many of the African-American accounts labeled eventually as predecessors of hip-hop novels, or even hip-hop novels proper: Claude Brown's *Manchild in the Promised Land*, Paul Beatty's *Tuff*, or Nathan McCall's *Makes me Wanna Holler*. Masłowska's method is rather like that of Whitman; it consists of ingesting cultural vibrations present "in the air" and then "spitting" them back to the reader, which probably means that most of the things she is writing about are "out there," in the housing project "culture" that, like Compton or Harlem in the U.S., can be labeled a Polish "ghetto" in that few people want to explore it and even fewer escape.

In language that cuts deeply, bloodily, into the syntax and beauty of the Polish tongue, but also in language that—to quote Toni Morrison—"may be the meaning of life and may be the measure of our lives,"[65] Masłowska tells the story of a group of poor young project dwellers, so-called *blokersi*, whose lives of hassling, gang fights, and drug and sex abuse seem to lead inevitably to either a prison cell or a fatal drug overdose. Masłowska explores the "slums" of the new Polish democracy in a painfully up-to-the-minute manner, forcing readers to confront the whole picture of the new "culture" that they normally try to dodge. When one of the characters says that "Tylko ja wolę jak mężczyźni śpiewają. Na przykład hip hop, piosenki angielskie o tym, że dzieje się terror, że żyjemy tu w getto, no" ("But I prefer when men sing. For instance hip-hop, English songs about terror going on here, about our living in the ghetto, yeah"),[66] the reader realizes that the Polish ghetto exists *for real*, and that it has much in common with the places that Public Enemy and 2Pac rap about.

It was not only in fiction that Poles could read about America. Accounts by various Polish writers and scholars about visits to the U.S. were available even before 1989. Some of these introductions to the "real" America written by Polish "writers" (read: members of the communist regime encouraged by the authorities in Poland to "destroy" the enemy system from inside) look naively banal, one-sided, and biased.[67] An early example of such a narrative is Jerzy Putrament's *Dwa łyki Ameryki* (*Two Swallows of America*), published in 1956, in which he describes his "neophyte" trip to the States by focusing mainly on the negative aspects of what he saw. Thus Ellis Island reminds him of a con-centration camp, supermarkets are symbols of "customer care resulting from merciless competition," and automobile companies seem to be more interested in laying off employees than making cars.[68] However, Putrament also notices the absurdity of criticizing drinking Coke—"the potion of imperialism"—in Poland, where people guzzle gallons of vodka, and postulates that literary achievements of various Polish emigrant poets and writers (Lechoń, Kunce-wiczowa, Wierzyński) should not be diminished by the fact that they are liv-ing in America at the moment.

Another diary from an encounter with the American Moloch, "a unique occa-sion to observe [an] America different from the colorful propaganda,"[69] was published in 1964 by Mieczysław F. Rakowski, editor-in-chief of the opinion-making magazine *Polityka* from 1958 to 1982, later Polish prime minister in 1988/89 and the Party's (PZPR's) last secretary until 1989. Although he had been invited by the U.S. government, Rakowski used this opportunity to write a clearly anti-American journal, although one not devoid of some interesting observations and conclusions. Apart from his general critique of the issues America cannot be proud of—including the terror of the McCarthy era, seg-regation in the South and racist riots in Mississippi, as well as the inadequa-cies in the provision of health services, Rakowski makes a number of comments pertaining to less infamous but nevertheless sensitive areas: "the reactionaries from the John Birch Society forcing shop owners to discontinue selling Pol-ish ham" in Urbana, Illinois,[70] Europeans' perception of America as a coun-try of neighbors but not friends, and California "being full of the putrid smell of weapons of mass destruction produced there."[71] In a postscript to his book, written after the assassination of Kennedy, Rakowski concludes that he "does not see in America real social and political forces which could support [Ken-nedy's] fight against everything which plunges the country into anarchy and conservatism, and which causes the astonishment, reluctance and disgust of other people."[72]

It is interesting to compare Putrament's or Rakowski's accounts with the impressions of Polish scholars[73] who visited America for different periods of time and who offer in their books answers to questions posed at a symposium reported on in *Przegląd Kulturalny* in February 1964: "Does the popular Pol-ish image of America reflect American reality?" (no) and "Is the number of false concepts about the United States increasing or decreasing as a result of expanding contacts and the growing number of publications on the subject?" (decreasing).[74] They also conclude that "the biggest mistake Poles make is to try to fit the facts about the United States ... to 'our own Polish notions,'" that "the level of consumption determines a man's social status in America," that the "prevailing ideology of success determines the common hierarchy of values based on the belief that 'good is what leads up'," and that "the intensity of cultural activities at the American universities is startling."[75]

The discussion of various American "translations" in Poland would not be complete without looking at how certain corporate patterns and practices have been adopted by Polish employers and employees. In a recent insightful study based on the empirical data she collected for her Ph.D. thesis, *Sukces: Amerykańskie wzory—polskie realia* (Success: American Patterns—Polish Realities), Ewa Grzeszczyk presents an analysis of the development of U.S. business and corporate practices in Poland, drawing the reader's attention to the fact that many of them have become so "Polonized" that the previously sharp border between American and Polish practices has blurred. In the first part of her book Grzeszczyk cites some American notions of success, including Benjamin Franklin's recipe for success, Lee Iacocca's corporate self-made man, and the new lifestyles of yuppies, guppies, milkies, and bobos, as well as the critique of the culture of success offered by such thinkers as Thoreau or Christopher Lasch.[76]

The second part of the book, entitled "Made in Poland," discusses the "transfer" of many of these concepts onto Polish ground. Grzeszczyk observes that whereas in the past going to America and working there was the ultimate goal, since the early 1990s it is a job with a big American company in Poland that has become a symbol of professional success.[77] The image projected by employees of such companies is that of a young, dynamic professional, or a "cool dude," or a member of a happy corporate family.[78] Grzeszczyk cites numerous examples of English vocabulary being used in the professional environment despite the fact that their Polish equivalents would not be very hard to find. The examples include "*prawdziwy* off-take," (real off-take), "*launche*," (launches), "*stepy w zonie*" (steps in zone), and many others.[79] The author then goes on to describe some of the stops on the road to success in American companies in Poland: personality-changing courses and training, career manuals, various "brainwashing" techniques used by companies including Amway. Grzeszczyk concludes *Sukces: Amerykańskie wzory—polskie realia* with a chapter on accepting and rejecting American patterns of success, presenting the respondents' ideas about how the media creates reality and demonstrating their lack of faith in actually achieving such success, but also sharing their opinion on the role of the TV series *Dynasty* in forming people's aspirations.[80]

Grzeszczyk's study, published in 2003, validates the results of a much smaller project pursued a decade earlier by Irmina Wawrzyczek and Zbigniew Mazur of Maria Curie-Skłodowska University in Lublin, who studied the attitude of Polish youth toward Americans and the American Dream. Wawrzyczek's and Mazur's conclusion was that "America is perceived as the country of great economic opportunities, mainly due to good government, sound policies, capitalist economy and liberalism, [that] the Americans are viewed as strongly materialistic and hedonistic in their pursuits, and that they acknowledged American superiority in many areas, yet do not see it as an excuse for the Americans to be megalomaniac, assertive, arrogant and patronizing."[81]

The reception, therefore, of American culture in Poland, when examined at the micro-level in surveys, interviews, and diaries, appears to have been a nuanced mixture of acceptance and rejection, and to have produced many cultural hybrids.

Anti-Americanism

In the early 1950s the Polish government carried out a program of crude anti-American propaganda, displayed in banners, posters, and other art forms. The U.S. was typically represented by a wild, gun-toting cowboy or a fat, greedy banker clad in stars and stripes along with dollar signs. American products such as Coca-Cola were demonized (one banner proclaimed "The enemy is tempting you with Coca-Cola"), and even an infestation of potato beetles was blamed on the U.S. In a social-realist painting by Wojciech Fangor, healthy, tanned Polish workers and peasants were depicted scorning an "Americanized" Pole wearing oversized sun glasses, bright red nail polish, and lipstick, and a dress imprinted with the words "New York," "Wall Street," and "Coca-Cola."[82] During the 1960s and 1970s the Polish government's official policy was often in open opposition to the U.S., adhering to the Moscow line during the Bay of Pigs operation, the Berlin crisis, and the Vietnam war, and criticizing race relations, poverty, and violence in the U.S. Opponents of the regime, on the other hand, tended to idealize the West, on the principle that "the enemy of my enemy is my friend."

The "normalization" of U.S.-Polish relations after 1989 was followed by an initial period of uncritical acclaim and insatiable consumption of anything "made in the USA." Soon, however, voices in Poland warned of the "McDonaldization" of the country and "a loss of economic independence because the share of foreign capital in Polish market was too large" and expressed fears of "the degradation of Polish culture due to widespread and uncritical imitating of Western patterns."[83] Similar concerns were raised by respondents in Ewa Grzeszczyk's study *Sukces* (Success) who saw the "dark side" of adopting American patterns: "They are flooding us with everything. Our whole business was learning from whom, from Americans, Cartoon Network, marketing..., all these schools and training programs coming to Poland. Also, films, a flood of American pop culture, music ... America is pushing its way in here."[84] One character in Edward Redliński's play *Cud na Greenpoincie* (*A Miracle in Greenpoint*), complains that "Poland is already America. A worse America. American prices, Polish salaries."[85] Redliński himself said that "America was flooding the whole world. This is an irreversible process: whoever does not give in to Americanization, will feel like strangers in their own country."[86] This painful "myth-breaking session" was necessary to shift the relations between the countries from the realm of dreams to that of reality.

Many of the outbursts of anti-Americanism in post–Cold War Poland can be grouped (as is true for many of the other countries in this study) under the heading "reaction against modernity." Such antimodern statements are exemplified by "Rynek bez Big Maca" (*Rynek*–Market Square–without Big Mac), a letter from a group of Kraków intellectuals to Polish authorities in 1994, asking them to prevent McDonalds from building a restaurant in the heart of Poland's "cultural capital," and by the Polish Roman Catholic hierarchy's criticism of "American postmodernism" (a term used to denote moral relativism, feminism, and homosexuality), a reaction that parallels the "moral panic" cited in other chapters of this volume. Nationalist groups have been gaining force in Poland in recent years. The publications and broadcasts of the right-wing Catholic radio station Radio Maryja (founded in 1991) are marked by xenophobia within which is an anti-American strain. The League of Polish Families (Liga Polskich Rodzin—LPR), a political party founded in 2001 by elements connected to Radio Maryja, came in second in the 2004 European parliamentary elections after running on a nationalist, anti-American/ anti-EU platform. The antiglobalization forces exemplified by Andrzej Lepper's Samoobrona party have also made a strong showing in recent elections. Together these populist/nationalist political forces reflect a rejection of an "America" that is seen as a force for globalization, modernization, secularization, and commercialization and thus a threat to Polish culture. These parties also blame "America" for growth in crime and insecurity and a decline in moral values in Poland.

Frequent complaints about U.S. visa policies can be found in the Polish press. Newspaper editorials have urged the authorities to introduce visas for Americans as a direct response to the U.S. policy of charging Poles high fees for their visa applications, regardless of whether the visa is ever issued. Since Poland has been a loyal member of the "coalition of the willing," there have been many calls in the press for Poland to be added to the list of countries in the "visa waiver" program—and many expressions of resentment that in this respect Poland is treated less favorably than countries that did not participate in the Iraq war. Expectations of "rewards" for participation in the second Iraq war were high, and the actual returns have been disappointing.

In spite of such complaints, however, overall relations between the two countries remain close, so close that French President Chirac has even accused Poland of being a lackey of the U.S.[87] Indeed, in any comparative study of European anti-Americanism Poland would rank at the bottom, i.e. among the least anti-American countries in Europe. In response to a survey conducted for the German Marshall Fund, only 34 percent of Poles polled (as compared with 38 percent of Britons, 50 percent of Germans and Italians, and 70 percent of French) said they found it "undesirable" for the U.S. to exert strong leadership in world affairs.[88] Not only was Poland a member of the "coalition of the willing" during the Iraq war, but its forces have assumed responsibility for a region of the occupied country.[89]

In a comparative trends survey carried out by the Pew Research Center for the People and the Press, those holding positive views of the United States represented a greater proportion of the respondents in Poland than in any other European country, although this percentage declined from 86 percent in 1999/2000 to 79 percent in 2002 and again to 50 percent in March 2003, the decline in 2003 traceable to opposition to U.S. foreign policy, particularly concerning Iraq.[90] But that 50 percent score put the Poles well ahead of the Germans (25 percent), the French (31 percent), the Italians (34 percent), and even the British (48 percent) in their favorable views of the U.S. In admiration of U.S. popular culture Poland was outranked only by Great Britain. In a 2002 survey 76 percent of Britons and 70 percent of Poles agreed they liked American popular culture. Only 22 percent of Poles professed not to like it,[91] confirming their status as the least anti-American in both the political and cultural realms. Adam Michnik used a medical metaphor to compare the anti-Americanism in Poland with that prevalent in Western Europe. Calling anti-Americanism a "European illness," Michnik diagnosed the Polish variety as having only "the severity of a light head cold," compared to the "very dangerous illness" infecting other parts of Europe.[92]

Conclusion

As the above dialogue between the sender and receiver demonstrates, the paths of Americanization in Poland have been varied and tangled, with what is received often no longer recognizable to the sender. In studying the influence of American culture beyond its borders, translations as well as transmissions have to be taken into account. During the Cold War American culture was appropriated in Poland as an emblem of resistance to the Polska Rzeczypospolita Ludowa (Polish People's Republic, PRL). In the post–Cold War era American culture has often come to symbolize the greater social and economic changes taking place in Polish society and is therefore resisted and attacked by those who feel threatened by the new system.

In contrast to most of the countries surveyed in this volume, Poland continues to send a significant number of immigrants to the U.S. each year, continually renewing the ties between the two countries and making the border between transmissions and translations, the sender and the receiver, and even "them" and "us" much less visible and divisive. An important cultural event organized in June–July 2004 by the U.S. Embassy in Warsaw, "New New Yorkers and their Friends," "the biggest cultural exchange in the history of Polish-American relations" according to representatives of the embassy, illustrates this point.[93] The title indicates that the former period of cultural transmissions and translations is now entering an era of "trans-nations," where the "trans"—meaning "beyond," "crossing," and "on the other side"—is accompanied by "nativization," i.e., blending the "foreign" with the "native," or to put it differently, a "domestication" of foreign influences. Most of the artists participating in the New New Yorkers event—among others, Janusz Głowacki (literature), Michał Urbaniak and Urszula Dudziak (jazz), Rafał Olbiński (poster art), Maria Przybysz and Ryszard Horowitz (photography), and Andrzej Dudziński (painting)—have emigrated to the U.S. and achieved success there but have also, more recently, re-established their ties with Poland. They consider success in their home country an important part of their artistic fulfillment, and through their work they have blurred the lines between Polish and American culture. To paraphrase the title of Jerzy Durczak's book on ethnic literature,[94] these artists have become transcultural selves rather than selves between cultures, and are able to be both American artists in Poland and Polish artists in the U.S.

Notes

1. Although the Główny Urząd Kontroli Prasy, Publikacji i Widowisk (Main Bureau of Press, Publications and Shows Control) was *officially* established by the decree of the Krajowa Rada Narodowa (National State Council) on 5 July 1946, censorship had existed in Poland since 1944, when a special Censorship Unit was set up in the Public Safety Department of the Polski Komitet Wyzwolenia Narodowego (Polish Committee for National Liberation, PKWN). This action violated the provisions of the March 1921 Constitution, whose article 105 prohibited the introduction of censorship and licensing regulations for publishers. The censor's interventions in newspapers, books, and other printed materials were usually marked by special codes, informing the reader that the text

had been censored. In the case of films, movies considered "ideologically improper" or "dangerous" were stopped from being distributed at all, or "shelved" by censorship officers for many years, something that happened to Kieślowski's *Przypadek* (made in 1981 and officially released in 1987) or Bugajski's *Przesłuchanie* (of 1982, released in 1989). Censorship in Poland was finally abolished in 1990 by the Press Law Bill. For more information on censorship, sometimes referred to as "the greatest poet of People's Republic of Poland," see Jane Leftwich, ed., *Czarna Księga Cenzury PRL* (PRL's Black Book of Censorship) (London: Aneks, 1977) or Aleksander Pawlicki's *Kompletna szarość: Cenzura w latach 1965–1972: Instytucje i ludzie.* (Complete Grayness: Censorship 1965–1972: Institutions and people.) (Warsaw: Wydawnictwo TRIO, 2001). For censorship in the 1980s, see Alexander Remmer, "A Note of Post-Publication Censorship in Poland 1980–1987," *Soviet Studies* 41, no. 3 (July 1989): 415–25.

2. Elżbieta Foeller-Pituch, "Catching Up: The Polish Critical Response to American Literature," in Huck Gutman, eds., *As Others Read Us: International Perspectives on American Literature* (Amherst: University of Massachusetts Press, 1991), 206.

3. Robert McG. Thomas, Jr., "Willis Conover, 75, Voice of America Disc Jockey," *New York Times,* 19 May 1966, A35.

4. http://www.west.net/~jazz/bio.html (last accessed: 3 March 2005).

5. Timothy W. Ryback, *Rock around the Bloc: A History of Rock Music in Eastern Europe and the Soviet Union* (New York: Oxford University Press, 1990), 867–87.

6. Jan Błoński, "Americans in Poland," *The Kenyon Review* 23, no. 1 (Winter 1961): 39. This "invasion of Americans" was balanced by the more than 1,500 Poles who traveled to the U.S. on cultural and scientific exchange programs between 1 January 1958 and 30 June 1962. See Emilia Wilder, "America as Seen by Polish Exchange Scholars," *The Public Opinion Quarterly* 28, no. 2 (Summer 1964): 243–56.

7. Walter L. Hixson, *Parting the Curtain: Propaganda, Culture and the Cold War: 1945–1961* (New York: St. Martin's, 1997), 111.

8. Stephen S. Kaplan, "Aid to Poland, 1957–1964: Concerns, Objections and Obstacles," *The Western Political Quarterly* 28, no. 2 (1975): 155.

9. Hansjakob Stehle, *The Independent Satellite: Society and Politics in Poland since 1945* (London: Pall Mall, 1965), 239.

10. Robert H. Haddow, *Pavilions of Plenty: Exhibiting American Culture Abroad in the 1950s* (Washington: Smithsonian Institution Press, 1997), 63.

11. Ibid., 147.

12. Tadeusz N. Cieplak, *Poland since 1956* (New York: Twayne, 1972), 413.

13. Yale Richmond, "Margaret Schlauch and American Studies in Poland," *The Polish Review* 44, no. 1 (1999): 54–55.

14. Jerzy Durczak, "Mixed Blessings of Freedom: American Literature in Poland Under and After Communism," *American Studies* 40, no. 2 (1999): 140.

15. Błoński, "Americans in Poland," 32.

16. Ibid., 45

17. Ibid., 48.

18. Pawlicki, *Kompletna szarość,* 57–58. Pawlicki goes on to say that the information was in fact an example of "an attempt to compromise the American army, where the emotionally laden statement 'in cold blood' was to be authenticated by making reference to Washington's UPI."

19. Pawlicki offers other interesting and surprising examples of censors' intervention in Poland at that time, including removing any positive references to the hippie movement in the U.S. from newspapers, magazines, and books and presenting the movement as an excellent illustration of the collapse of moral values in the West.

20. Stehle, *Independent Satellite*, 239.
21. Durczak, "Mixed Blessings of Freedom," 140.
22. George R. Urban, *Radio Free Europe and the Pursuit of Democracy: My War Within the Cold War* (New Haven: Yale University Press, 1997), 297.
23. Jane Leftwich, ed., *The Black Book of Polish Censorship* (New York: Random House, 1984), 135.
24. Ibid., 399–400.
25. Durczak, "Mixed Blessings of Freedom," 142.
26. Foeller-Pituch, "Catching Up," 214.
27. Wojciech Liponski, "Western Teachers and East European Students," *Polish–Anglo Saxon Studies* 6–7 (1997): 35.
28. Joseph Brodsky, in Anna Husarska, "A Talk with Joseph Brodsky," *New Leader*, 14 December 1987, 9.
29. Tomas Venclova in Yale Richmond, *Cultural Exchange and the Cold War: Raising the Iron Curtain*, (University Park: Pennsylvania State University Press, 2003), 201.
30. Agnieszka Gadomska, "The Theatrical Distribution of American Films in Poland After 1989," in Cynthia Dominik, ed., *Is Poland Being Americanized?* (Warsaw: American Studies Center Warsaw University, 1998), 18.
31. Stehle, *Independent Satellite*, 209–10.
32. Gadomska, "The Theatrical Distribution of American Films in Poland After 1989," 18–19.
33. The book was also prohibited.
34. Pawlicki, *Kompletna szarość*, 104.
35. Tadeusz Pikulski, *Prywatna historia telewizji publicznej* (Warsaw: Muza, 2002). The whole interesting study is also available online at http://ww2.tvp.pl/tvppl/12,2003111268480 .strona (last accessed: 3 March 2005).
36. http://renma.w.interia.pl/playlista.htm (last accessed: 3 March 2005).
37. Joan Baez, well known for her support for Polish dissidents, first came to Poland in 1970 and then in 1985 with her fellow activist, Ginetta Sagan. During her visit she met Lech Wałęsa.
38. Wick quoted by Bernard Gwertzman, "Now, the Star of the Show: Poland," *New York Times*, 20 January 1982, A24.
39. Peter Schweizer, *Victory: The Reagan Administration's Secret Strategy that Hastened the Collapse of the Soviet Union* (New York: Atlantic Monthly Press, 1994), 89.
40. Leonard J. Bałdyga, "The 20th Anniversary of the American Studies Center at the University of Warsaw: An Historic Overview," in Andrzej Bartnicki and Zbigniew Kwiecień, eds., *Pochwała Historii Powszechnej* (Warsaw, Instytut Historyczny Uniwersytetu Warszawskiego, 1996), 571.
41. Liponski, "Western Teachers and East European Students," 42.
42. Franciszek Lyra, "Is Poland being Americanized? American Literature in Poland, 1989–1997," in Dominik, *Is Poland Being Americanized?* 32.
43. Ronnie D. Carter, "Paradigm Shifts in Polish Academic Writing on American Literature, Arts and Culture," Paper presented at Warsaw University, 14 June 1997.
44. Agnieszka Salska, ed., *Historia Literatury Amerykańskiej XX Wieku*, 2 vols. (Kraków: Universitas, 2003).
45. Lyra, "Is Poland being Americanized?" 33.
46. Ibid., 38–39.
47. Gadomska, "The Theatrical Distribution of American Films in Poland After 1989," 18.
48. Ibid., 22.
49. Ibid., 25.
50. Ewa Grzeszczyk, *Sukces: amerykańskie wzory—polskie realia.* (Warsaw: Wydawnictwo Instytutu Filozofii i Socjologii, Polska Akademia Nauk, 2003), 131.

51. Among the oldest and most prestigious of such programs are the Executive MBA Program run by Warsaw University's International Management Center and School of Management and the University of Illinois at Urbana-Champagne, and the Warsaw Executive MBA offered by the Szkoła Główna Handlowa (School of Economics) in Warsaw and the University of Minnesota.
52. Poland became a member of the EU on 1 May 2004.
53. http://www.arts.uwaterloo.ca/FINE/juhde/micz952.htm (last accessed: 24 July 2004).
54. http://www.warsawvoice.pl/old/v520/Buzz00.html (last accessed: 24 July 2004).
55. Wiesław Kot, "Za szynką;" rozmowa z Edwardem Redlińskim" (Interview with Edward Redliński), *Wprost,* 10.03, no. 10 (1996): 83–84.
56. Figura is an interesting *figure* herself and an example of transmissions and translations merging into one. She starred in Radosław Piwowarski's *Pociąg do Hollywood* (Train to Hollywood), a comedy about a girl living in a train car and working in a buffet but dreaming, at the same time, of making a career like that of Marilyn Monroe in Hollywood. The girl keeps writing letters to American director Billy Wilder, hoping against hope that she may get an invitation from him one day. The *real* Figura actually did go to Hollywood and played a minor role in Robert Altman's *Prêt-a-Porter.*
57. Jan Borkowski, "Jazz in Poland—Anthology" (Warsaw: Polskie Radio S.A., 2002).
58. During the 1969 Sopot Festival Niemen met the famous Radio Luxembourg DJ Alan Freeman, who then played Niemen's "Przyjdź w taką noc" on the radio.
59. As far as Polish rock music is concerned, the word "transform" stands dangerously close to the word "plagiarize." In the case of many groups it is not difficult to recognize their musical "fascinations"—Lady Pank being in love with The Police, TSA with AC/DC, and RSC with Kansas.
60. Jerzy Wertenstein-Żuławski, *To tylko rock 'n' roll* (It's only Rock'n'Roll) (Warsaw: Związek Polskich Autorów i Kompozytorów, ZAKR, 1990), 5.
61. During student strikes at Warsaw University in the Solidarity era, music by The Doors was omnipresent.
62. Bartek Chaciński, "Hymny biedy i wkurwienia wykrzykuje Peja, nowa nadzieja polskiego rapu." *Przekrój,* Nr 32/33 (10 sierpnia, 2003): 65.
63. Discussing boxing one should not forget, of course, about Poland's hero in America, Andrzej Gołota, or Andreeeeeeeeeeeeeeeeeeeeeeeew, Gooooooooooooooolota!!! Wanted by the Polish judiciary for a minor offense, he escaped to America, where, promoted by Ziggy Rozalsky and eventually Don King, he was transformed from the "rag" he had been in Poland into the "white men's hope against the black," as many Polish newspapers put it, clearly unaware of the racist connotations of the expression. The stardom of the former illegal immigrant and truck driver reached its peak when he fought against Riddick Bowe, Lennox Lewis, and Mike Tyson, in matches broadcast by HBO and state television in Poland.
64. Wojciech Staszewski, "Spoko Alfabet," *Gazeta Wyborcza: Duży format,* 31 July 2003, 26.
65. http://www.literature-awards.com/nobelprize_winners/toni_morrison_nobel_lecture .htm (last accessed: 5 March 2005).
66. Dorota Masłowska, *Wojna polsko ruska pod flagą biało-czerwoną* (Warsaw: Lampa i Iskra Boża, 2002), 107.
67. One should not forget that until the early 1990s Poles were not allowed to keep their passports at home but had to apply for them at the Internal Affairs Offices each time they wanted to travel. In practice, most of the dissidents were not allowed passports, which meant they had no chance to go abroad.
68. Jerzy Putrament, *Dwa łyki Ameryki* (Two Swallows of America) (Warsaw: Czytelnik, 1956), 88–106.

69. Mieczysław F. Rakowski, *Ameryka wielopiętrowa* (Multi-storied America) (Warsaw: Czytelnik, 1964), 5.

70. Ibid., 83. Urbana-Champagne is an important place in the discourse on translation as the University of Illinois at Urbana-Champagne was one of the first American universities to establish commercial cooperation with Polish institutions after 1989. Offering courses on human resource development, marketing, logistics, and strategic planning, first in cooperation with OIC Poland and then with Polish universities (Warsaw University, Politechnika Lubelska), it has contributed to the development of business, particularly small-medium enterprises, the target group for which most of the courses were designed. Currently, in addition to the courses mentioned above, the University of Illinois runs two MBA programs for business executives in Lublin and Warsaw. For more details visit http://hre.ed.uiuc.edu/poland.htm (last accessed: 5 March 2005).

71. Rakowski, *Ameryka wielopiętrowa*, 117.

72. Ibid. postcriptum.

73. These books include: Józef Chałasiński, *Kultura Amerykańska: Formowanie się kultury narodowej w Stanach Zjednoczonych Ameryki* (American Culture: The Formative Development of a National Culture in the United States of America) (Warsaw: Ludowa Spółdzielnia Wydawnicza, 1970); Stanisław Ehrlich, *Władza i interesy: studium struktury politycznej kapitalizmu* (Power and Interests: A Study of Capitalism's Political Structure) (Warsaw: Państwowe Wydawnictwo Naukowe, 1974); Stanisław Ehrlich, *Grupy nacisku w strukturze politycznej kapitalizmu* (Pressure Groups in the Political Structure of Capitalism) (Warsaw: Państwowe Wydawnictwo Naukowe, 1962); Aleksander Matejko, *Socjologia przemysłu w Stanach Zjednoczonych Ameryki* (Industrial Sociology in the United States of America) (Warsaw: Państwowe Wydawnictwo Naukowe, 1962); Edmund J. Osmańczyk, *Spółczesna Ameryka: Stany Zjednoczone Ameryki* (Contemporary America: The United States of America) (Warsaw: Ludowa Współdzielnia Wydawnicza, 1961); Jan Strzelecki, *Niepokoje amerykańskie* (American Anxieties) (Warsaw: Wydawnictwo Instytutu Filozofii i Socjologii Polska Akademia Nauk, 2004); Włodzimierz Wesołowski, *Studia z socjologii klas i warstw społecznych* (Studies in Sociology of Social Classes and Strata) (Warsaw: Książka i wiedza, 1962); Jerzy J. Wiatr, *Amerykańskie wybory* (American Choices) (Warsaw: Książka i wiedza, 1962); Janusz G. Zieliński, *Big Business: Z problematyki nowych technik zarządzania* (Big Business: Problems of New Management Techniques) (Warsaw: Książka i Wiedza, 1962).

74. Emilia Wilder, "America as Seen by Polish Exchange Scholars," *The Public Opinion Quarterly* 28, no. 2 (1964): 243–56.

75. Ibid., 253–55.

76. Grzeszczyk, *Sukces,* 131.

77. Grzeszczyk rightly observes that few accounts of "successful" trips to America do more than mention the places and conditions in which many Poles have traditionally worked in the U.S.: slaughterhouses, cleaning jobs, removing asbestos insulation, etc.

78. Ibid., 133.

79. Ibid., 134.

80. Ibid., 263.

81. Irmina Wawrzyczek and Zbigniew Mazur, "Do Polish Youth Dream American? The Penetration of American Cultural Values in Poland," in Agnieszka Salska and Paul Wilson, eds., *The American Dream, Past and Present. Polish Association for American Studies, Proceedings of the Second Annual Conference, Skierniewice, November 26–28, 1992* (Łódź: Wydawnictwo Uniwersytetu Łódzkiego, 1994), 21.

82. The image actually represented the figure of the so-called "*bikiniarz*" (from Louis Réard's chic bikini costumes), someone dressing in a flashy and caricaturedly "fashionable" manner, a loafer and hooligan imitating American gilded youth and not contributing to the building of socialism. Jacek Kuroń, one of Poland's dissidents, who before spending many years in prison was one of the builders of socialism, describes "*bikiniarzí*" in the following way: "they wear colorful checked shirts with a colorful striped t-shirt. The colors may not have matched, although different sets of colors were fashionable; chives on the scrambled eggs, which was green on yellow. The neckerchief was also very American, very colorful too, or a tie, very wide, hand-painted. Ties with an island and a palm were particularly fashionable, a naked girl under the palm and a little mushroom above it, because it was supposed to represent the Bikini atoll. Girls wore long skirts with long slits on the side. '*Bikiniarze*' liked jazz, danced boogie-woogie. There were few real believers in the American lifestyle among them, although some of them may have realized they were for the United States and against the Soviet Union or maybe for the colorful West against the drabness of life in Poland." Jacek Kuroń, "Trzeba wierzyć partii" (One has to trust the Party"), *Gazeta Reporterów* (*Gazeta Wyborcza*), *Duży Format*, 21 June 2004, 4–5.

83. Karolina Zawieska, in *Poland in Europe; SWOT Anlayses.* http://info.wizytowka.pl (last accessed: 3 March 2005).

84. Grzeszczyk, *Sukces,* 263.

85. Kot, "Za szynką;" 83.

86. Ibid., 83.

87. Wiesław Godzic, *Oglądanie i inne przyjemności kultury popularnej* (Kraków: Universitas, 1996), 168.

88. Thomas Crampton, "Europeans' doubt over U.S. policy rises," *International Herald Tribune,* 4 September 2003, 8.

89. The scale of the changes in the Polish-U.S. relationship may also be illustrated by a somewhat comic situation. The Polish premiere of Michael Moore's *Fahrenheit 9/11* (originally scheduled for 16 July 2004) was postponed, giving rise to speculation that political pressure had been brought to bear because of the film's questioning of the foreign policy of Poland's ally, the U.S., and by extension the policies of President Kwaśniewski regarding Iraq. It seemed as if Poland was now using censorship to placate the U.S., just as previously it had aimed to placate the USSR. However, when Marcin Piasecki, director of Kino Świat International, the Polish distributor of the movie, later announced that the film would open on 23 July, one week later than originally scheduled, his announcement provoked suspicions that the postponement and talk of political influence had been a means to increase public interest in the film—in other words, censorship in the interest of increasing profits. http://film.onet.pl/ (last accessed: 3 March 2005)

90. Support for the Iraq war continues to decline among the Polish public, while opposition to the war grows. In April 2004 an opinion poll found only 29 percent of Poles supported the role (down 7 percent from the preceding November), while opposition had increased to 66 percent (up 6 percent). http://www.cbos.com.pl/SPISKOM.POL/2004/K_076_04.PDF (last accessed: 3 March 2005).

91. Pew Research Center for People and the Press, "What the World Thinks in 2002." http://people-press-org/reports/display.php3?ReportID=165 (last accessed: 3 March 2005).

92. Adam Michnik, "What Europe Means for Poland," *Journal of Democracy* 14, no. 4 (2003): 133–34.

93. http://www.newnewyorkers.pl/docs/prconf.htm (last accessed: 3 March 2005).

94. Jerzy Durczak, *Selves Between Cultures: Contemporary American Bicultural Autobiography* (San Francisco: International Scholars Publications, 1997).

– Part IV –

ITALY, GREECE, SPAIN

CONTAINING MODERNITY, DOMESTICATING AMERICA IN ITALY

◆　◆　◆

David W. Ellwood

Introduction

The Italian story begins with a series of crucial, wrenching episodes and then settles down into a complex but fairly stable pattern in which America plays a significant but not dominant role in Italy's search for a modernity of its own. It could even be argued that the evolution of Italian modernity has been distinguished by the success of efforts to *prevent* the American version from becoming predominant, but this too is only a part of the picture. Since the end of the Cold War and the subsequent attempts by every European nation—and America itself—to redefine its own ideas of modernity, identity, and sovereignty in the new world situation, it has become clear that Italy's experience of this challenge is all tied up with questions from its past. These are questions that have remained unresolved owing to the creation, almost from scratch over fifty years, of a prosperous consumer society. The legacies of Catholicism, Fascism, and Communism, not America, come first in today's intense debates on what it means to be Italy or Italian. Where, then, to locate the American challenge in the rise to global status of the land of pizza, pasta, and cappuccino, of Armani and Benetton, of Alfa Romeo and Ferrari, of Fo, Eco, Benigni, and all the other miraculous products of the world's sixth-largest industrial power?

Today's Italian historians are aware that they do not search for answers to this question in a vacuum. For more than twenty years, along with colleagues from the rest of Europe and from the U.S. itself, they have been self-consciously trying to define how the workings of American power in all its manifestations have interacted with the disorderly local processes of modernization, "devoid

Notes for this section begin on page 273.

of a formalised national ethos," in Federico Romero's phrase, to produce the results we see before us on the restless contemporary scene. Everywhere, says Romero, local protagonists of adaptation "adjusted in various ways to opportunities and difficulties flowing out of technological changes that were not solely or uniquely American, and would probably have taken place—albeit with different shape and timing—even without U.S. influence." Every group, generation, locality, productive or cultural sector made its own deal with whatever America was offering, suggests Romero, just as they did with all the other sources of innovation: the economy, science and technology, mass communications, social developments, ideas of progress, "Europe." The result is a scholarly consensus against "Americanization," a generalized rejection of any idea of widespread emulation, of the uncritical application of American solutions to the problems of development in whatever form they might take. Instead there is broad agreement about the selective adaptation or appropriation of the American inspiration, of a filtering and domestication procedure, "a segmented process, pervasive and yet limited," in Romero's words.[1]

At the same time Italy has—since the disaster of World War II—always remained a nation-state profoundly conscious of its vulnerability in the world of the superpowers. Repeated crises of financial, geopolitical, or trade security have bred an extreme sensitivity to shifts in international power as conventionally understood. For the first thirty years of its existence the precarious new republic addressed its desire for support and assurance almost obsessively to the United States, since the discovery that the Cold War would develop inside Italy, as well as all around it, provoked among its early postwar governments the deepest sense of exposure and helplessness. The realization that dependence on the U.S. came at a price—a form of permanent ideological mobilization that was alien to the political culture of the new republic—simply added to the tension provoked at the same time by the compelling nature of America's modernity. As a leading local scholar of American culture has written:

> ... the same forces which were turning Italy into a political satellite of the United States, were also vociferously worried about the invasion of American cultural artifacts, undermining our humanistic civilisation and our classical culture—as well as our rural, Catholic way of life.[2]

But political currents with this sort of outlook on the world were convinced that taking a stand against any manifestation of America would seem to open the floodgates to Soviet-style communism or at the least mean "objectively" playing the communist game. Wasn't anti-Americanism a basic tenet of communist civic religion? Since the war the country had indeed bred the largest Communist Party in the West, a force whose electoral strength grew in fits and starts from the end of the war all the way through the "economic miracle," down to the late 1970s. In reality the Partito Comunista Italiano (Communist Party, PCI) developed over time an ever more complex relationship with what America stood for and produced, not least as its electoral base became more articulated and mature, and prosperity spread its effects across the ideological barriers. Against America the formal political and ideological power of the PCI was armed and prepared to do battle, along the lines the Cominform had laid down in 1947. But the force of America's cultural radiance, in Italy as elsewhere so much more appealing to the working masses than to any other section of society, found the party largely unprepared. Its intellectual sympathizers rediscovered the cultural anti-Americanism that had united conservatives of various colors across Europe between the wars, based on a nostalgic humanism and a rejection of machine-made modernity. But when new generations of rebellious young people began to arise from the 1960s onwards, the PCI's stock response could not begin to answer the questions they raised. The defiant energies of the youth movements (with their own idea of America) had run their course by 1977, but the PCI never recovered from its confrontation with them, and its decline was almost continuous from then on.[3]

The decade from 1967 to 1977 then, was the turning point. It had been preceded by the "classical" era of reconstruction, the Cold War, and democratic stabilization (three right-wing coups d'état were attempted but failed in the 1970s, years that also saw the rise and defeat of the ultra-left terrorist phenomenon). After 1977 came a general reconsideration of the postwar settlement, with its paralyzing deal between official left and right that accepted, albeit reluctantly, limited sovereignty and constant supervision by the American superpower. Now that a more stable, mature, and detached attitude to the workings of American influence could be contemplated, the 1980s were the decade of the "rediscovery" of America, and thus of the first reflections on "Americanization" and the function of American myth and model in Italy's tumultuous postwar development experience.

This does not mean that there was a clear succession of phases; simply, new themes were superimposed on the old ones. The Cold War never went away, even after 1989 and the collapse of the postwar political order. Il Cavaliere Berlusconi uses its rhetoric constantly to this day. And on every major anniversary even the experience of the war, of resistance and liberation, has been rehashed yet again in a public debate that has begun to look more and more like a morbid hangover from the past, having little to do with a healthy collective renewal of values and aspirations. But no matter how inward-looking and self-referential these confrontations have been, there is no escaping the American theme. Ever since the first wave of America's invading armies swept over Sicily in July 1943, Italy's place on the "periphery of the empire" (an Umberto Eco phrase) was assured. The secret then was to make this place as

convenient and profitable as possible, to make sure that whatever the inequalities of power might be, domination and dependence would be organized on "our" terms, politically, economically, and culturally.

War and Cold War

During World War II the American army spent more time liberating Italy
than any other enemy-occupied territory. The campaign dragged on far longer
than expected, and although it had become a scaled-down sideshow by the
end (May 1945), the experience made a deep impression on every level of
society and left a lasting legacy of images, symbols, memories, legends, and
controversies. A southern writer recalled how "modern civilization cheerfully
and noisily penetrated cities and towns ... the fabulous and far away America, country dear to the dreams and labors of the fathers, had come among
us."[4] Although most of the time the British were very firmly in charge of the
joint Anglo-American war effort, militarily and politically, it was the Americans who were seen to hold the keys to the future, and who went on to provide most of the aid, money, and propaganda, including a grand backlog of
Hollywood films.

But the net result of all their activities was profoundly ambiguous, and has
continued to generate argument ever since. The American army differed from
the others in the lavishness of its facilities, its relatively lax discipline, and its
detached attitude to the Italian people and their politics. It was also the army
of a power with—until this time—an extremely small stake in the country it
was fighting over. The result was that in many areas, the drawn-out process
of liberation gradually turned into a kind of occupation.[5] In the second of
Rossellini's neorealist classics, *Paisà* of 1946, the stages of this evolution are
vividly depicted, with the effects of the black market, poverty, and rife prostitution in Rome and the south particularly in evidence. An Afro-American
soldier is brought to realize that there are people in Naples much worse off
materially than he is, people who consider him a conquering hero.

As recalled today, the war is thought to have brought liberation for the
north, occupation for the south; liberation for the young, occupation for the
old; liberation for women, occupation for men; liberation for the Right, occupation for the Left, and so on (although any of these stereotypes can easily be
turned on its head by referring to facts). Everyone agrees that the British were
the occupiers, the Americans the liberators, and the longer the campaign
went on the more this conviction turned into enduring legend. A 1995 celebration of the liberation of Bologna, published by the press of the former
Communist Party, dwelt on the music and dancing the Americans had brought,
the baseball and Camel cigarettes, the color-filled images of a renewed way

of life and an undreamt-of prosperity. Leading Bolognese poets, filmmakers, and singers such as Pupi Avati and Francesco Guccini have recalled here how the Germans were capable of removing everything a people could possess; the Americans instead brought things, tons of them, and expressed their own idea of democracy in the heroes of their comics and the appeal of their big bands.[6]

Although some writers at first saw a subterranean psychic connection linking the arrival of the Americans in wartime to the great internal migrations that would transform Italy into an industrial power during the 1950s,[7] it is hard now to discern any revolution of rising expectations at work in the desolate peninsula of those years, where the battle for survival meant so much to so many. Instead a different kind of aspiration began to emerge. The total discrediting of fascism and the inability of Italy's own forces to destroy Nazi-Fascism unaided meant that a nation that had once vaunted its national pride and great power ambitions was now in a state of humiliating dependence on the victorious armies of Britain and the United States. Yet only the Americans possessed a future for the world worth the name, and only they—unlike the British, the Russians, the French, and all the others who had outstanding accounts to settle with fascism's successors—seemed willing to imagine that the Italians might one day be part of it. If only the Americans could be brought to see their responsibilities in this direction, then the old Fascist hope for an Italian place in the sun might be revived in a new form.

The last remnants of the wartime American army pulled out, along with all the others, on 31 December 1947 under the terms of the Peace Treaty of 1946. They left behind a small aid program, an even smaller information program based on libraries attached to the U.S. Embassy and local consulates (a complete novelty for Italy), and a growing controversy over the presence of Hollywood. Well aware that the distinguished Italian film industry lay in tatters, the big American studios sent over 600 films in 1946, and even more in following years: by 1948 the figure was 668.[8] In the middle of this crucial formative moment for the two political and social cultures emerging as dominant in postwar Italy—the Catholic and the Communist—here was an outside force of well-nigh irresistible charisma and penetrative power, bringing messages of individualism and consumerism that were antithetical to almost everything those two mass movements stood for. As elsewhere in Europe, they mobilized to fight the threat. The Church talked directly to the heads of the studios and American diplomats, and kept firm control of the state censorship mechanisms. The PCI demanded cultural protectionism and exalted the national cinema heritage, especially now that it had invented neorealism.[9]

But Cold War politics soon forced the Catholic Church to consider its alliances afresh, and a rapid convergence took place between the interests of the U.S. government and the Vatican as they faced the rising popular force of the PCI. Although this alliance was not one of the specific actions that flowed from the Truman Doctrine, promulgated in March 1947, the overall message of that pronouncement was obviously welcome to official and conservative Italy. The announcement of the Marshall initiative that June brought the country fully into the radius of American action to save Europe from its own past and the risk of a communist future, and it was made clear that there would be no help for the country should the Communist Party come back to power by any means.[10]

But what if the PCI were restored to power by democratic means, by winning a regular parliamentary election? As the first general election approached under the new Republican constitution, in April 1948, the likelihood of such an outcome began to look more and more probable, the only such case in the Western world. The result was the first great pitched political battle of the Cold War, in which both of the main parties were heavily backed by their superpower sponsors, with an unprecedented mobilization of propaganda weapons of every type. Vividly remembered, celebrated, and excoriated to this day, 18 April 1948 inaugurated the long era of Christian Democratic rule in Italy, and the country was said to have "chosen sides" once and for all.

American experts in "counterinsurgency" ten years later characterized the Italian campaign of 1948 as opening a new era of "psychological warfare." They made clear that for their part, no overall propaganda strategy existed: whatever it took to stop the Left was allowed. A pattern of action emerged based on "explanation, terror, and reassurance." Covert funding of the main governing parties began, and great effort was made to supply the forces of law and order with the equipment needed to face down an insurrection. Even the use of military force was "never completely ruled out," writes James Miller in the most detailed study of the campaign based on American sources.[11] The private campaign set in motion by the Italian-American community was even more remarkable, not least for its originality. It was the most intense, large-scale private mobilization to support a government policy in the entire Cold War period, involving letter-writing campaigns, celebrity endorsements, fund-raising, and other eye-catching initiatives.

To avoid continuing dependence on America and to provide a new legitimacy for democracy based on the hope of a better life under its rules were among the key ambitions of the Marshall Plan in Italy when it finally got under way in June 1948. American myth promised to turn into American model under the Marshall Plan, because under its provisions the U.S. showed not only what could be done but *how* it could be done. "You Too Can Be Like Us" was the message of the Economic Recovery Plan (ERP). And the vast propaganda operation that accompanied the Plan in Italy, the largest in any of the sixteen participating countries, set out to ensure that every Italian citizen, at every level of society, understood the nature of what it was the Americans were offering.

As a result the Italian experience of the Marshall Plan was never just an abstract affair of economic numbers—loans, grants, investment, production, productivity, etc.—even if these were its key operating tools. Nor was it merely another weapon in America's Cold War anticommunist crusade, though all concerned were well aware that in operating as an "indigenous group," the Italian communists had an immense psychological and political advantage over the trans-Atlantic superpower. The ERP "information" effort aimed to get as close as possible to the people it was benefiting, at all levels of society, and was intended particularly to affect the relations between the citizen and the state. The challenge was to channel attitudes, mentalities, and expectations in the direction Americans understood as the key to stability under mid-twentieth-century democracy: ever-greater prosperity for an ever-greater majority.

In 1990, at a post–Cold War conference held to discuss the impact of American culture in all its forms on the ideologically radicalized Italy of the 1950s, the veteran left-wing intellectual Enzo Forcella proclaimed: "The American myths kept their promises and won through!" Forcella was referring specifically to the images purveyed by the documentaries of the American way of life that accompanied the Marshall Plan, particularly those showing workers arriving at factories at the wheel of their own cars, an unthinkable notion in the Italy of 1949.[12] "Americanization and modernization were put over (and greeted) as synonymous," wrote the conference organizer Pier Paolo D'Attorre afterwards in a seminal essay:

> In the long term the ideology of growth, sustained by productivity and mass consumption, and spread by new political organs which were both public (the European Cooperation Administration, USIS etc.) and private (trade union missions, foundations), set in motion productive and commercial energies between countries which were far more effective than anything seen in the trans-Atlantic financial maneuvers of the 1920s.[13]

D'Attorre went on to cite the attention given to intellectuals and other opinion-leaders including: special missions, conferences, and film programs, expanded efforts by Embassy information services, new libraries and publications. But it was the support given to the mass effort by its Italian allies that probably counted most, suggested D'Attorre. The Italian edition of *Readers' Digest* (ERP-supported) reached 500,000 families monthly and prompted similar initiatives by emerging publishing companies who would become household names. The firm Mondadori, then as now the country's leading publisher, imported new rotary presses with ERP help and soon spread Disney products everywhere. As an entirely new children's comic industry took off, the first Italian newsweekly, *Epoca,* also appeared from the Mondadori presses.[14] As to the general effects of all the projections of American cultural power in postwar Italy, Umberto Eco has written:

America as model, as a universe and system of products, as political influence, as an image channeled by the mass media, invaded Italy. Before it had been something you read about in books or saw in the cinema. Now it was a presence in the life of the average Italian, from chewing gum to records, all the way to the development of car-ownership and television.[15]

But there was deep, structural diffidence about all this in many influential quarters. The Italian governments of the day made no secret of how alien and bewildering the entire Piano Marshall idea was to them, and an enormous effort was set in motion up and down the state structure to contain its effects, politically and especially economically, as new studies have confirmed.[16] The ERP agents also found an unlikely adversary in the influential figure of Angelo Costa, head of the principal industrialists association. Costa was implicitly opposed to the spread of large-scale industry and urbanization, and now expressed all his skepticism concerning the culture of productivity and high wages. No matter how cheap synthetic fibers became, he insisted, Italian women would always prefer clothes made in the home with natural materials; tinned food might be sold very cheaply, but Italian traditions of cooking would always be preferred. Small firms and traditional artisan skills would be central to Italy's future just as they had been in the past.[17]

The Church of Rome provided yet another source of difficulty. Catholic doubts about American values and lifestyles, dating back to the end of the nineteenth century, now took on more urgent form. Like many conservative thinkers in the 1930s, Pius XII was inclined to see common defects in Soviet communism and Americanism: an obsession with material output, technical progress, and consumption; a standard of life defined economically. But only in America were individualism and secularization so openly proclaimed and encouraged, only there was licentiousness commercialized and godlessness so flaunted. The example of the U.S. demonstrated the ways in which mass media held such awful responsibilities. The Marshall Plan propaganda was purveying a vision of life that was economic, private, consumerist, limitless, and available for emulation, but all the while the Vatican and Christian Democrat politicians were encouraging the emergence of a strong state that was socially oriented, collective, and welfarist. The Marshall Plan eventually found itself obliged to make a serious effort to adapt to this reality. Meanwhile, the right-wing Catholic Edilio Rusconi, editor of what turned out to be the best selling new newsweekly of all, *Oggi*, kept up a solid campaign of denunciation of the American "liberation" effort of wartime, the meretricious values it had imported, and the opening of Europe to Soviet communism that it had allowed.[18]

The PCI's uncontestable, uncontested obedience to the new Soviet line laid down at the birth of the Cominform meant that total opposition to the Marshall Plan was obligatory for the party. This quickly became part of a comprehensive form of official anti-Americanism that embraced NATO, the Korean war effort, and the politics of productivity. There was an endless and ever more intense denunciation of American actions in the party's press, meetings, and demonstrations, where the message varied in form and content only according to the location and the level of education of the audience. But the battle was a losing one. The Marshall Plan delivered the goods, and American economic and cultural power was able to deploy an ever wider range of communication methods to inform, educate, and convince its allies. The PCI failed to learn the importance of mass audiovisual media from its defeat in the 1948 elections, and had no useful response to the triple onslaught of ERP propaganda, Hollywood, and the shift to a new kind of America-inspired prosperity that began to appear from 1952/53 onwards. Only with its anti-war stand after the Korean outbreak in 1950 did the PCI see a major, enduring propaganda impact.[19]

The Boom Years

The outcome of the Italian "economic miracle," so called because it was in reality so unexpected, has led some historians to include the nation among the most Americanized of all the Western European countries in these years.[20] Certainly its need for a strong development model was more deeply felt as expectations rose and the technological possibilities of fulfilling them became more readily available. Urbanization (7–8 million moved to the cities in the 1950s), the expansion of welfare, the development projects, and Washington's system for spreading its influence by distributing public money all pushed consumption upwards. Wages grew more slowly than productivity, but still consumption increased 5 to 6 percent per year on average. In no country was the impact of the motor car revolution more tremendous. The leading company, Fiat, had been a privileged beneficiary of ERP aid and made no secret of its admiration for American methods of production, distribution and selling. Yet the car that put the Italians on wheels, the Fiat 600 of 1955, was a small utility model, in no way resembling the Detroit product. As a functional source of inspiration and methods, what America offered was always adopted as far as it was useful and no further.

In a long and interesting analysis of European attitudes to America that was supplied to the U.S. intelligence services by an anonymous Bolognese observer just after the elections of June 1953, particular importance was attached to the crucial role of the cinema in the filtering and appropriation process: "95 percent of all Europeans—friends and enemies of America—judge American society by what they see at the cinema." Hollywood's products had given many a dreadful impression of the country, of its crime and corruption, and of the venality and brutality of its ruling groups in particular. But the medium "was useful above all in reinforcing the European admiration for the American standard of living, for American technique.... Undoubtedly film has given the U.S. a propaganda triumph, to the extent that it has reminded Europeans of their traditionally optimistic vision of the 'American paradise.'"[21]

Whilst the concepts of productivity and growth had furnished the key modernizing concept on the supply side of the transformations under way, a force like the cinema worked on the demand side of the same social and economic changes, accelerating and channeling the evolutions of mentality and behavior. But even here the local culture found ways to mediate these effects. Together with popular music, Italian cinema itself became one of the most successful mechanisms of all for the purpose of adapting, filtering, and domesticating the American challenge, and the celebrated *commedia all'italiana* showed it off with pride. Alberto Sordi's Christmas 1954 film, *Un americano a Roma*, remains to this day the classic example, a milestone in the evolution of Italian self-identification.

The story is of a Roman working-class youth infatuated with everything American. Nando Mericoni's sole ambition—misunderstood as he is at home—is a ticket to the land of his dreams, evidently a location fabricated by Hollywood. After a series of humiliations, Nando threatens to commit suicide from the top of the Coliseum unless he is allowed to emigrate. The dénouement, involving a scuffle with the U.S. Ambassador himself, lands Nando in hospital, but to the dismay of all around him, his infatuation with the U.S. remains as strong as ever. Sordi, Italy's most celebrated and best loved screen comic, was an actor who liked to give his career its full historical significance, making clear over the years that his *comédie humaine* was a way of using irony to reconcile Italians to the changes going on all around them. In the case of *Un americano a Roma*, he told a critic that by including episodes that pilloried behavior such as Marlon Brando's in *The Wild One* of 1953, he would save Italian youth from the temptation of imitating him. In this way the film's essentially defensive nature was revealed, showing how the bombardment of novelties from America could be demystified and dealt with on terms that left the locals much preferring their own traditions.[22]

The most significant of the *commedia* films all reflect this anxiety over control, an apprehension about how, in a situation of continuous and painful upheaval, society could continue to invent means for maintaining some sort of order in the balance between tradition and innovation, between the inheritance of the past and the modernity of technology, mass consumption, and ever-expanding mobility. An eloquent expression of the tension this outlook provoked is visible in official attitudes toward the new medium of television, which began transmission in 1954. Controlled formally and exclusively by the state, and materially by one of the more conservative elements of the ruling Christian Democrat party, its guiding principles seemed to have been taken directly from the instructions handed down to the cinema industry by the Roman Curia in 1941, writes Silvio Lanaro. In its light entertainment programs, a measured adaptation of familiar American television formats might be allowed, but in the transmissions that counted most, especially the evening news bulletins, no concession was to be made to the notion of entertainment that pervaded every American offering. Even the on-screen advertising—produced almost exclusively at first by the Italian branches of the big American agencies—was rigorously regulated to make sure its commercial and persuasive effects were strictly contained.[23]

This sort of attitude was not held by Christian Democrat conservatives alone. The denunciation of consumption as an end in itself was a key theme in the work of Pier Paolo Pasolini, a critic who combined elements of Catholic ethics and communist propaganda in a highly personalized rhetoric directed against the era's new conjunction of cosmic fear and hedonistic individualism. Pasolini's contribution to the 1963 television documentary *Anger*, on the fear of atomic war, declaimed at one point—against a background of the finale of the 1956 Republican convention—"When the classical world has finally been worn out, when all the artisans and peasants have died out, when industry has set up an unstoppable cycle of production and consumption, then history will have ended for us." In a mirror-like contribution from the far right to the same film, Giovanni Guareschi, author of the *Don Camillo* comedies, developed his own condemnation of the "lonely crowd" and the "live now, pay later" mentality. In response to pictures of violence at a rock concert in France, Guareschi concluded that "[t]he frantic search for material goods, the lack of faith in the future, the disintegration of the family, these are the roots of our discontent and anguish."[24]

The Americans themselves had already started to take notice of the disquiet. In 1955 the *New York Times* had celebrated the spread of American-style consumer culture to Italy, with jeans, T-shirts, TV quiz shows, and a yearning for homes fitted with modern conveniences prominently cited. In Naples twenty years of mingling with American servicemen had brought a new sense of "hurry and urgency" to that sleepy old city, said the report.[25] In contrast, 1960 saw the release of *It Started in Naples*, a Clark Gable classic with a memorable scene of a rich Philadelphia lawyer (Gable) teaching a local street urchin the joys of the hamburger, and how to eat it. But the visitor's well-meaning efforts to convert the little boy to the American dream and save him from what looks like poverty are rebuffed by the boy, his flamboyant folk-mother (Sophia Loren), and all the indignant local community.

The Death and Rebirth of the American Myth

The Bolognese historian of popular culture Franco Minganti has written:

> The 1950s were crucial for redefining the status of youth in Italy, particularly in the
> social climate of pervasive cultural eclecticism. Italian adolescents developed a distinct
> lifestyle and became a distinct social group. They mixed American, British and French
> imports with a revolutionary outcome ... youth as a world apart, a world of its own,
> almost a class in itself. Youths tended to slip out from under the control of traditional
> institutions, with their own meeting points and sites of empowerment (jukebox bars),
> their own time (the night), their own uniforms (jeans and highly stylized fashions).

As the analysis implies, the relationship with whatever America was offering
was not a straightforward one:

> In spite of criticisms by cultural conservatives, these adolescent styles did not repre-
> sent a passive integration into alien—namely American—music and fashion. Rather
> adolescents used these styles to mark their difference from previous generations of Ital-
> ians and from Italian tradition.[26]

The 1960s confrontations spawned by this search for difference ended, as was
the case everywhere else in Europe, when the role of America had been repositioned in the clash of youth versus authority. Umberto Eco noted afterwards
that "when the '68 generation launched its challenge ... America as Power
was the enemy, the world sheriff, the adversary to overcome in Vietnam as in
Latin America. But that generation fought a four-front war: the enemies were
capitalist America, the Soviet Union which had betrayed Lenin, the Communist Party which had betrayed the revolution and—lastly [in Italy's case]—
the Christian Democrat Establishment."

Because anti-authoritarianism was in fact more important to this struggle
than anti-Americanism, the internal conflicts that now simmered within the
United States over war, values, and lifestyles ended up creating new forms of
trans-Atlantic understanding and solidarity. The reason was that as soon as
the Generation of '68 discovered the "counter-culture," the movement began
to adapt it and mythologize it for use against its domestic enemies.[27] As one
of the era's ex-combatants put it: "The idea of 'the other America' enabled us
to absorb America in ourselves without having to shoulder the political responsibilities of ... 'official' America."[28] After the end of the Vietnam disaster
gave way to the Watergate crisis, while the devalued dollar fought to counter
the effects of hyperinflation and soaring energy prices, it seemed easy indeed
to announce the death of the myths of official America. Commentators were
united in perceiving the failure of U.S. society to renew inherited symbols
such as "the melting pot," to reinvent the politics of the New Deal coalition,
to reestablish the old ideological certainties and restart growth. The American Dream, in this view, was already headed for its own Sunset Boulevard.[29]

But as Alessandro Portelli points out, Italian opposition culture was permeated with the spirit of that "Puritan ideological and rhetorical ritual whereby the denunciation of existing evils, of America's declension, becomes the occasion and means for a renewal of the myth of America, 'invariably joining lament and celebration in reaffirming America's mission.'"[30]

When Italian youth opposition finally stopped projecting its own concerns on America's counterculture and discovered the difference between an *antagonistic* and an *alternative* outlook on the existing system, says Portelli, then it became possible to appreciate what was truly novel in the American scene and start to learn from it constructively. It was by this route that such cultural and social innovations as contemporary feminism and environmentalism, the importance of private life, and gender relations arrived in Italy during the latter part of the nation's unsteady 1970s.[31]

Nothing, of course, could be more alien to the culture of the traditional opposition in Italy. The communist view of the world had always adopted a simple and puritanical approach to questions of personal life, and dealt "awkwardly (with) such issues as divorce and abortion," says Stephen Gundle.[32] The PCI's long-established deference to the Catholic Church's preferences in these areas was profoundly shaken by the struggle over divorce that led to the referendum of 1975 (won by the pro-divorce lobby), but this was only the beginning of a confrontation that in the long term proved fatal to Italy's Communist Party. Feminism, reports Gundle, "was seen as an imported phenomenon of American origin that was of concern to middle-class women with no experience of the world of work."[33] Understanding nothing of the trends of the "me-decade" (Tom Wolfe), and prejudicially opposed to all forms of "subjectivism," the Party soon found itself on the defensive.

Meanwhile, the shift from a society dominated by the forces of production to one conditioned supremely by consumption and its markets was gathering pace, in Italy as everywhere else. The service industry of the imagination suddenly swelled into view, pushed by an ever accelerating revolution in communications technology. "The vanishing working class, related to material production, is replaced by the processes of immaterial production: electronics, advertising, television," wrote Portelli. "Of course all this radiated mainly from America."[34] Parliamentary action opened Italy's airwaves for the first time to private commercial broadcasting channels in television and radio. Uninterested, at least in the short term, in investing in production, they were immediately swamped with cheap imported American materials. The leisure press was quick to capitalize on the success of new commercialized electronic media, which coincided with the rise and triumph of Ronald Reagan in presidential politics.

"A myth is not a myth unless it can regenerate itself," wrote the glossy women's weekly *Annabella* in November 1981, "so John Travolta is back, more terrific than ever in *Urban Cowboy* … Urbanised, in other words a bit cleaner than the cowboys of the real Far West, Travolta makes us dream again because he for sure is virile and strong, but also honest and generous." A list of clothes, food, music, TV series, and films buttressed the article's claim to show that the myth of the West was reborn. Reagan himself was nothing if not a true Western hero. But what had all this got to do with Europe? Were America's myths inevitably ours? "They've got to do with us because here too there is a great desire for a new climate of moral reconstruction, but also because John Wayne is practically a family member … the cowboy belongs to everyone's culture because now he's come to town…"[35]

On the periphery of the empire, across the political spectrum, it was always considered inevitable that in some part of America, Italy's future too was being shaped. The trick then was to be the first to see it coming and to be prepared for its arrival. *Lei*, the Italian edition of *Glamour*, declared in October 1980 that New York was the "in" place of the moment, the preferred destination of intellectuals, actors, photographers, artists, designers and businessmen, but also of young people from all over the world." TV programs instead preferred California. Whatever the location, declared *Tam-Tam*, a current affairs program run on the main state channel in January 1981, if young people wanted to know where they were going to find their life's work, they need look no further than America, where the service sector was already well in the lead: "That's the direction we will be going in, that's the destiny waiting for us."[36]

Throughout the 1980's political and intellectual culture began to catch up with the resurgence of American power in all its forms, and to take stock of the significance of this development for its future. The Communist Party organized in spring 1981, through its research and discussion branch the Istituto Gramsci, the movement's first-ever high-level scholarly debate on the contemporary U.S., in the presence of the American cultural attaché among other luminaries. Here it was agreed that America as a complex of powers had lost prestige in the 1970's and appeared at that time as an ailing giant. But America as myth was something else. History showed how it needed to die or be killed off from time to time, in order to be reborn, Phoenix-like, stronger than ever. In this way the myth of the myth had come into existence. Although not present at this Bologna event, Umberto Eco's musings on America's place in the emerging post-industrial society were often in the air, particularly his toying with the notion that "Americanization" might be simply a process which occurred wherever mental imagery and the decision to consume met each other.

In 1984 Eco announced, with two other literary critics, the "Rediscovery of America," and three years later the Rome-based scholar of American literature Ugo Rubeo published a long series of interviews with prominent personalities on their relationships with everything the United States had stood for and done, entitled "Mal d'America," (American Longings).[37] Leading intellectuals such as Antonioni, Calvino, and Moravia confirmed here that for them the voyage to America had been a crucial rite of passage, if only as an escape from provincialism and a discovery of a world of perpetual self-criticism and renewal, some of whose charisma would, they hoped, rub off on themselves. But they tended to be pessimistic about Italy's experience of American culture in all its forms, the novelist Moravia in particular deploring the form of backward, vulgar Americanization that he felt had sprung up in the land of the Renaissance.[38] For better or for worse this pronouncement came—as elsewhere in continental Europe—just as the first explicit scholarly discussions and research projects on the concepts of "Americanization" and "anti-Americanism" began to arrive, all of which mercilessly attacked the "Americanization" notion as backward, vulgar, and useless as a tool of analysis.[39] Within a very few years, though, this verdict had to be reassessed.

After the Cold War

As the old connections based on security and Atlanticism faded in significance after the end of the Cold War, America's role as creator and seller of uniquely appealing models and myths became more prominent. The U.S. was no longer held up as a model society, but American products, fashions, stars, icons, and languages (including the computer versions) remained ubiquitous and compelling, available for appropriation and adaptation—and rejection— by everyone. As conflicts over communal, national, and supranational loyalties now become ever more significant in European politics, so the debate over the new American challenge encountered a rising wave of anxiety about the future of identities in the Old World, be they individual or collective.

In a country like Italy this development could never be entirely separated from the general context of international politics, and there were repeated flurries of traditional anti-Americanism whenever the U.S. launched a military campaign and called for support from its allies. Nevertheless an edition of the review of geopolitics *liMes* (sic) dedicated to America and its relationship with Italy, which appeared to coincide with the U.S. presidential election of 1996, concluded on the basis of opinion polling, that "our relationship with the United States is more cynical than many suspected. To Coca-Cola we prefer the Sixth Fleet."[40] The full significance of this remark quickly became evident elsewhere in the journal. In a personal contribution, Deputy Prime Minister Walter Veltroni emphasised his absolute belief in the continuing role of NATO and Atlanticism in general. What gave Veltroni's remarks their piquancy was the fact that the he had been a lifelong member of the PCI, until its post–Cold War conversion into the Democratic Party of the left, and at the same time a fervent admirer and consumer of American popular culture.[41] Having acclaimed President Clinton's 1992 victory as editor of the PCI daily *Unità*, Veltroni now insisted that Europe's renewed social democracy and Clinton's liberalism—"in the noblest sense of the word"—were one and the same thing.[42]

Not for the first time, Veltroni made much of the cultural heritage that bound him to the U.S. Citing a long list of books and films that inspired his American fascination, Veltroni said that for his generation of the 1960s the mental equation was "America = movement = discovery = conquest of new frontiers." Obsessed with the search for novelty, this generation inevitably looked to Kennedy and then to the "other America" of the opposition to the war in Vietnam. Caught now between Europe and America, he felt closer to the U.S. Paradoxically, however, he claimed to be as worried as the French over U.S. cultural colonialism.[43]

The density and relentlessness of the United States' impulse to project the power of its mass culture into Italy (as elsewhere), in an endlessly changing variety of forms and directions, represented a challenge that Italians could never ignore and were compelled always come to some sort of terms with. Renewing old arguments about "Americanization" reflected an awareness—and very often a resentment—that America's demotic culture expressed creative energies more dynamic, innovative, and involving than those generated by the Italian versions of either neocapitalism or the welfare state, with their shared clienteles, moral ambiguities, and dim sense of accountability. Yet by contrast with other European nations caught in the identity crises of the times, the Italians appeared more open and relaxed, preferring to dispute in the 1990s whether Fascism, Catholicism, or Communism had done more to condition their national identity and their lack of what they saw as a healthy sense of collective existence and national pride. Their problems were thought to be entirely historical and internal: America attracted little or no blame.[44]

When the soccer and media tycoon Berlusconi appeared on the political scene, he made no secret of the roots of his success: young people, who had voted for him thanks to the values his television empire had introduced to them:

> I know the young generation well. They grew up seeing America through the television shows that I brought to Europe. They have come to believe in the meritocratic philosophy that will help us develop a more liberal and free-market society without losing our cultural roots or traditions ... Young people everywhere now share the same political values.[45]

Whether this was true or not, the *fear* of its being true seemed as likely to reawaken old currents of anti-Americanism in some camps as the *hope* that it had enhanced the legitimacy of America's cultural hegemony in so many others. As elsewhere in Europe, far from encouraging the Italians to find their unity in creating an imaginary American "other," the American cultural challenge was once more reinforcing their divisions.

From 9/11 to the Iraq War

The attacks on the Twin Towers arrived at a very delicate time in Italian political life. A new government led by the increasingly controversial figure of Silvio Berlusconi had won a bitterly contested election campaign less than five months previously, taking over from a shifting coalition of center-left forces. The aftermath of the Balkan wars, and the NATO bombing campaign in Kosovo of 1999, largely staged from U.S. airbases in Italy, continued to weigh heavily on attitudes toward war and peace, and American foreign policy in particular.[46] The extreme violence of the police forces used to control protesters at the Genoa meeting of the G-8 in July 2001, thought to be at least condoned by the new government (or parts of it), had the effect of galvanizing the Italian "no-global" movement and stiffening other parts of the opposition. Sentiments towards George W. Bush were rarely enthusiastic in any part of the political spectrum, given the controversial nature of his election and his clear lack of interest or experience in European politics. In the Vatican Pope John Paul II expressed an obvious dislike for American geostrategic behavior as demonstrated in the Balkans and the Middle East, for the materialistic values that were most clearly on display in the United States, and for the controversies that swirled in the rising scandals around the activities and personalities of the American Catholic Church.

All this guaranteed, from the very first moment, that responses to the new, post-9/11 situation would be highly politicized, but also that much of the political energy generated by the disaster and the challenges flowing from it would be directed inwards, discharged into the never-ending battle between left and right for the soul of local public opinion. In other nations the new situation was said to have catalyzed the expression of underlying attitudes to what the U.S. stood for, as well as what the U.S. did in the world as a superpower. This may well have been in the case in a country like the UK that is little disposed in normal times to think outside the confines of the military-diplomatic "Special Relationship." But in Italy the inheritance of the Cold War, carried over into the era of globalization, meant that public attention could never forget the strength of the mechanisms that bound together all the forms of American power, soft as well as hard. Globalization itself, as an idea, was digested without too much difficulty, and the new "no-global" movement had taken up a normally noncontroversial place in the variegated Italian political spectrum. But the exaltation of the market mechanism that globalization implied, bringing ever less controllable shifts of people as well as capital, goods, and information—that was something else. The immigration question loomed large in Italian politics in the 1990s, much larger than the conflicts over McDonald's, Hollywood, or the English language that so disturbed cultivated minds elsewhere in Europe.

The attacks on the Twin Towers and the Pentagon wiped out ten years of globalization debate in the space of a European afternoon, and immediately brought the Italian nation face to face again with the choice it has always found most disagreeable of all: war or peace? Asked by an opinion poll ten days after the attacks whether Italy should take part in armed action against any country harboring the terrorists, 47 percent agreed. But 36 percent said "no," while a further 8.5 percent insisted on complete neutrality. Fully 15 percent of those interviewed felt that the U.S. should bear part of the responsibility for the attacks, "because [it was] too strongly aligned with Israel against the Islamic world."[47] While a second poll found that only 23 percent of the population could be classified as more or less anti-American, a third reported 26 percent (36 percent among voters on the left) agreeing with Bin Laden's alleged view that the U.S. was historically guilty of world-class crimes against peoples in various parts of the globe, including on occasion Arabs.[48]

From the start the Berlusconi cabinet spared no efforts to declare its solidarity with the American government and people. One of its more prominent supporters, the television personality and newspaper editor Giuliano Ferraro, organized a "U.S.-Day" in Rome on 9 November 2001 as a demonstration to counter a "no-global" mass gathering organized on the same occasion. However, as the question began to loom of taking the "war on terror" directly to Sadam Hussein's regime in Iraq, the government changed tack. While maintaining and even increasing the rhetoric for America and against the opposition—"the left has once more demonstrated its eternal attraction to dictators and dictatorships," said the prime minister in early April 2003[49]—Berlusconi started to make clear that whatever assistance Italy might lend to the cause would be humanitarian, and furnished only after hostilities had ceased. This had been the practice in the Balkans, and in Afghanistan, and corresponded to the historic mission of the Italian armed forces, went the argument: did the Constitution of the Republic itself not limit Italy's military forces to purely defensive purposes?

In reality no Italian government has ever been strong enough politically to order the armed forces into combat. Even the participation of an air force unit in the first Gulf War of 1991 under the UN mandate was a very limited affair indeed, conducted against a background of intense internal conflict. The overwhelming reality facing governments in this sort of situation is the force of Italian pacifism, an amorphous but vast and emotional movement that in times of crisis rises and falls according to a now well-established pattern, independent of cause, context, or consequence. Reflecting the deep sense of vulnerability that has always accompanied the history of the Republic, as already seen, Italian pacifism expresses a profound sense of sympathy with the underdog, an equally deep suspicion of the righteousness of the strong, and a conviction that all conflicts can somehow be "mediated" by political means— and indeed ought to be, no matter the cost in terms outside those of the conflict itself. This is not neutralism; as a nation Italy has always joined whatever strategic alliance might be on offer in the West, and has officially and staunchly defended the rights and duties of such commitments. But if ever there was a movement that confirms Robert Kagan's judgements on the difference between "Americans" and "Europeans" in attitudes to security questions, it must surely be Italian pacifism. Kagan wrote:

> On the all-important question of power—the efficacy of power, the morality of power, the desirability of power—American and European perspectives are diverging. Europe is turning away from power, or to put it a little differently, it is moving beyond power into a self-contained world of laws and rules and transnational negotiation and cooperation.[50]

There is of course nothing new about this outlook in Italy, or about its Spanish, Greek, or other equivalents. Nor should it be confused with the institutionalized program of any political party or group. Instead it is an underlying group of sentiments that immediately surface under the threat of armed conflict, only to disappear when the crisis passes. These produce movements, from the streets and to the parliament, strong enough to condition governments and limit their freedom of action, even to undermine the credibility of Italy's armed forces, in the eyes of the influential former diplomat and commentator Sergio Romano.[51] They offer little to those attempting to find a constructive solution, political or otherwise, to the problems that any particular crisis expresses. Faced, however, with the Bush administration's "war on terror," they have spurred a new debate on the meaning of American power in the world, combined for the first time with a reflection on the history and status of Italian anti-Americanism.

As in France it is the anti–anti-Americans who have had the best of the confrontation. Distinguished commentators from the left, center, and right of the political spectrum have united to defend not U.S. foreign policy as such (though the more pro-government voices have also done that), but the right to express a judgement on the workings of American society and its politics that is not ideological, not based on conspiracy theories, not Manichaean, yet is capable of appreciating the greatness of America's contributions to progress in the West without illusions as to the price paid. While commentators from the left have worried over the apparent paradox of democratic imperialism, and some on the right have shared the widespread concern over the perceived "unilateralism" and aggressivity of the Bush administration's foreign policies, all have insisted that the U.S. itself has been seriously hurt, is divided, and demands a more serious effort of understanding than it usually enjoys.[52]

But over the months and even years that have passed since the "war on terror" was declared, it has proven impossible to avoid the subjugation of the debate to the exigencies of Italy's unending left-right battles, especially in the form they have taken since leadership on the right has fallen into the hands of the media tycoon Silvio Berlusconi. Examples are not hard to find. Historical science and contemporary politics were conflated without restraint in the major conference at Naples in April 2002 on "Anti-Americanism in Italy and Europe in the post Second World War period," opened by President of the Senate Marcello Pera, an outspoken defender of the U.S. government's policies. The sixtieth anniversary of the Italian surrender in World War II, in September 2003, was another occasion for the two sides to argue over the rights and wrongs of America's place in Italian history and politics. New contributions, purportedly aspiring to inform discussion on anti-Americanism with the aid of historical evidence, have proved in reality to be political pamphlets denouncing Left, Right, and the Catholic church *en bloc* for attacking America in all its forms over many years, thereby betraying the fundamentally antidemocratic, antiliberal nature of all concerned and giving comfort to the Soviet enemy. A major work of detached historical research such as that produced by Philippe Roger in France was nowhere to be seen.[53]

Beyond the confines of the daily political struggle, the old patterns of attraction and repulsion, of challenge and response, of projection and selective appropriation continued to evolve, just as they did elsewhere in the Old World. Possibly a new awareness of the stakes of the game emerged after 9/11 and the Iraq war. One Bologna-bred lecturer in Political Theory at Princeton, Maurizio Viroli, told his compatriots that while Europe had remained substantially unchanged through the drama, Americans had rediscovered their idea of liberty as a form of civic religion: true Americanism *was* the political religion of liberty. Others among the intellectuals, all formed in the most classic of classic traditions, wondered whether Athens or Rome would be the true reference point for the fate of the United States.[54] Reformers who admired America's 1990s dynamism were grateful for the degree of modernizing "Americanization" that had been evident in Italy over the decade: the dismantling of the old state industries, the liberalizing of capital markets, the updating of corporate governance. Doubters deplored the creeping privatization of health, education, and scientific research, as well as the emerging tyranny of the market in energy and environmental policies. Could the nation that had invented all this and refused to sign the Kyoto protocol really be considered the supreme bulwark of the free world? asked the philosopher Gianni Vattimo.[55]

Italy, then, never found her comfortable place under the sun of the American superpower because the balance between external commitments and internal arrangements could never be considered self-supporting and stable. While some hankered through the years for the bargain the nation had struck with the U.S. at the start of the Cold War, others looked to a mystically-defined "Europe" for inspiration. The majority meanwhile seemed to prefer a self-referential, even autarchic definition of Italian identity, counting on the intuitive genius of *il belpaese*, and its allegedly infinite capacity for adaptation and survival to see it through. In December 2002 the U.S. State Department's information services distributed through a multitude of states a specially commissioned anthology entitled "Writers on America." In the piece translated for the front page of Italy's premier daily newspaper, *Corriere della Sera*, Richard Ford explained that at the heart of his writing was an effort to understand the most basic American question of all: "How could we be so different, and yet so similar?"[56] In Italy the question looked different: "How can we be so ideologically opposed and yet coexist so peacefully in the same place, even—at a pinch—under the same flag?" On balance, decades of containing and domesticating the American challenge, in all its fluid variety of forms, was probably an experience that helped to unite Italians more than it divided them.

Notes

1. Federico Romero, "Americanization and National Identity: The Case of Postwar Italy," in Luciano Tosi, ed., *Europe, Its Borders and the Others* (Napoli: Edizioni scientifiche italiane, 2000), 263–77.
2. Alessandro Portelli, "The Transatlantic Jeremiad: American Mass Culture and Counterculture and Opposition Culture in Italy," in Rob Kroes, et. al., eds., *Cultural Transmissions and Receptions: American Mass Culture in Europe* (Amsterdam: VU University Press, 1993), 129.
3. Simon Parker, "Political Identities," in Stephen Gundle and Simon Parker, eds., *Italian Cultural Studies: An Introduction* (Oxford: Oxford University Press, 1996), 111–12; this is not to say that the youth movements caused the decline of the PCI directly; many factors hastened the decay of the postwar political settlement in the 1980s. The Christian Democrats' electoral weakening paralleled that of the PCI.
4. Giuseppe Galasso cited in Stephen Gundle, *Between Hollywood and Moscow: The Italian Communists and the Challenge of Mass Culture, 1943–1991* (Durham: Duke University Press, 2000), 32.
5. I have explored this process in detail in *Italy 1943–1945: The Politics of Liberation* (Leicester: Leicester University Press, 1985).
6. 'C'era una volta l'America', supplement to *L'Unità*, Emilia-Romagna edition, 21 April 1995.
7. Eugenio Scalfari, *L'autunno della Repubblica* (Milan: Etas Kompass, 1969), 95–96.
8. Gundle, *Between Hollywood and Moscow*, 33; on the U.S. film industry's campaign to rebuild its European markets; Paul Swann, "The Little State Department: Washington and

Hollywood's Rhetoric of the Postwar Audience," in David W. Ellwood and Rob Kroes, eds., *Hollywood in Europe: Experiences of a Cultural Hegemony* (Amsterdam: VU University Press, 1995), 176–95.

9. On the Papal audience of a Hollywood producers' group, Ellwood, "Il Rapporto Harmon (Rapporto di un gruppo di dirigenti dell'industria cinematografica americana, 1945)," *Mezzosecolo* 3 (1979); Bruno P. F. Wanrooij, "Dollars and Decency: Italian Catholics and Hollywood, 1945–1960," in Ellwood and Kroes, *Hollywood in Europe*, 247–65; on the PCI reaction, Gundle, *Between Hollywood and Moscow*, 66.

10. Cf. Ellwood, "Italy, Europe and the Cold War: The Politics and Economics of Limited Sovereignty," in Christopher Duggan and Christopher Wagstaff, eds., *Italy in the Cold War: Politics, Culture and Society, 1948–58* (Oxford: Berg, 1995); Italian perspectives in Mario Del Pero, *L'alleato scomodo: Gli Usa e la DC negli anni del centrismo* (Rome: Carocci, 2001).

11. James Edward Miller, "Taking Off the Gloves: The United States and the Italian Elections of 1948," *Diplomatic History* 7, no. 1 (1983): 35–56; David W. Ellwood, "The 1948 Elections in Italy: A Cold War Propaganda Battle," in I. Tocci, ed., *Ripensare il 1948: Politica, economia, società, cultura* (Ancona: Il lavoro editoriale, 2000).

12. Proceedings of the conference of Bologna, January 1990, in Pierre Paolo D'Attorre, ed., *Nemici per la pelle: Sogno americano e mito sovietico nell'Italia contemporanea* (Milan: Angeli, 1991); Forcella's intervention is conserved on audio tape at the Istituto Gramsci, Bologna.

13. Pierre Paolo D'Attorre, "Sogno americano e mito sovietico nell'Italia contemporanea," in D'Attorre, *Nemici per la pelle*, 15–34; in the field of children's comics, D'Attorre points out, Catholic, Communist, and above all the patriotic *Corriere dei piccoli* were at least as successful as the Disney products, ibid., 33.

14. Ibid., 29.

15. Cited in ibid.

16. Carlo Spagnolo, *La stabilizzazione incompiuta: Il piano Marshall in Italia (1947–1952)* (Rome: Carocci, 2001).

17. David W. Ellwood, *Rebuilding Europe: Western Europe, America and Postwar Reconstruction* (London: Longmans, 1992), 196.

18. Ibid., 165–66; on Rusconi and *Oggi*, Marco Mariano, "L'America in Italia: La seconda guerra mondiale e l'occupazione secondo *Oggi*, 1950–1955," paper presented at the conference at Vercelli, "Comunicare il passato," Università del Piemonte orientale (June 2003); the views of Rusconi and his collaborators continue to be staple ingredients of right-wing attitudes to Italy's experience in World War II.

19. David W. Ellwood, "The Propaganda of the Marshall Plan in a Cold War Context," *Intelligence and National Security* 18, no. 2 (2003): 230–32.

20. Stephen Gundle, "L'americanizazione del quotidiano: Televisione e consumismo nell'Italia degli anni '50." *Quaderni storici* 62 (1986): 563; cf. Silvio Lanaro, *Storia dell'Italia repubblicana* (Venice: Marsilio, 1994).

21. Report "European Attitudes Toward the U.S.," sent 10 June 1953, in National Archives, Washington, D.C., Record Group 469, ECA Mission to Italy, Office of Director, Subject Files (Central Files) 1948–57, "Public Relations" subfile.

22. Detailed treatment in Ellwood, "*Un americano a Roma*: A 1950's satire of Americanization," *Modern Italy* 2, no. 1 (1996): 93–102; the Italian "covers" of famous American rock songs of the era very often served an identical function, reports Franco Minganti in "Jukebox Boys: Postwar Italian Music and the Culture of Covering," in Heide Fehrenbach and Uta Poiger, eds., *Transactions, Transgressions, Transformations: American Mass Culture in Western Europe and Japan* (New York: Berghahn, 2000), 150–51.

23. Lanaro, *Storia dell'Italia repubblicana,* 200–202, 256–58.
24. Pier Paolo Pasolini and Giovanni Guareschi, dirs., *La Rabbia,* (Rome: Opus Film, 1963); *Anger* was retransmitted by RAI 3, 29 May 1992.
25. "Italians Take to Jukeboxes," *New York Times,* 21 August 1955:76.
26. Minganti, "Jukebox Boys," 154.
27. Umberto Eco, "Il mito americano di tre generazioni anti-americane," in Carlo Chiarenza and William L. Vance, eds., *Immaginari a confronto. I rapporti culturali tra Italia e Stati Uniti: la percezione della realtà fra stereotipo e mito* (Venice: Marsilio, 1993), 27.
28. Portelli, "The Transatlantic Jeremiad," 130.
29. Massimo Teodori, *La fine del mito americano* (Milan: Rizzoli, 1975); Luciana Castellina, "Fine del mito americano," in Saveria Chemotti, ed., *Il mito americano: Origine e crisi di un modello culturale* (Padua: Cleup, 1980), 35–57.
30. Portelli, "The Transatlantic Jeremiad," 131; Portelli is quoting Sacvan Bercovitch's *The American Jeremiad* (Madison: University of Wisconsin Press, 1978).
31. Portelli, "The Transatlantic Jeremiad," 133; "Feminism," in *Routledge Encyclopedia of Contemporary Italian Culture* (London: Routledge, 2000), 219.
32. Gundle, *Between Hollywood and Moscow,* 150–51.
33. Ibid.
34. Portelli, "The Transatlantic Jeremiad," 134.
35. *Annabella* (November 1981).
36. *Lei* (October 1980); *Tam-Tam,* TG1, 16 January 1981.
37. Umberto Eco, Gian Paolo Ceserani, and Beniamino Placido, *La riscoperta dell'America* (Bari: Laterza, 1984); Ugo Rubeo, *Mal d'America* (Rome: Editori Riuniti, 1987).
38. Rubeo, *Mal d'America,* "Introduzione" and 166–74.
39. *Quando l'America arriva in Italia,* special issue of *Quaderni storici* 20, no. 1 (1985); "Anti-Américanisme en Europe," European University Institute, Florence, April 1984, October 1985; this view of Americanization has since beeen revised, particularly in the work of German scholars, e.g. the U.S.-based Volker Berghahn, *America and the Intellectual Cold Wars in Europe* (Princeton: Princeton University Press, 2001).
40. "Un impero senza territorio?" *liMes* 96, no. 4 (1996): 7–10.
41. He was also Minister of Culture in the government of the day.
42. Walter Veltroni, "Vogliamo gli Stati Uniti d'Europa," *liMes* 96, no. 4 (1996): 23–29.
43. Ibid., 29.
44. Cf. Gian Enrico Rusconi, "Che nazione siamo," and other articles in *Il Mulino* 96, no. 3 (1996); cf. Ernesto Galli della Loggia, *L'identità italiana* (Bologna: Il Mulino, 1998); for a comparative treatment concentrating on France, Germany, and Britain, David W. Ellwood, "The American Challenge Renewed: U.S. Cultural Power and Europe's Identity Debates," in *Brown Journal of World Affairs* 4, no. 1 (1997): 271–83.
45. *International Herald Tribune,* 30 May 1994.
46. The legacy of the Cermis disaster of February 1998 might also be mentioned. After slicing through an Alpine cable car and causing the deaths of twenty people, the U.S. air force pilots responsible, on an unauthorized flight at the time, were given the lightest possible sentences by military courts back in the U.S. Congress then cut back the monetary damages apparently promised by the U.S. authorities soon after the incident. The episode caused a flurry of comments on the many meanings of the strategic link between the U.S. and Italy, and an emollient press intervention by the U.S. Ambassador: *Il Resto del Carlino,* 19 March 1999.
47. Cited in Massimo Teodori, *Maledetti americani: Destra, sinistra e cattolici: storia del pregiudizio antimericano* (Milan: Mondadori, 2002), 9.
48. Ibid., 10.

49. *La Repubblica,* 9 April 2003.

50. Robert Kagan, "Power and Weakness," *Policy Review* 113 (2002): 3.

51. "Prefazione," in Teodori, *Maledetti americani,* x.

52. See contributions in "America," special issue of *Parolachiave* 29 (2003); also Michela Nacci, "America: non solo 'anti,'" in *Rivista dei Libri* (July/August 2003): 34–35; Gian-franco Pasquino, "Ideologie italiane e antiamericanismo," in *Rivista dei Libri* (November 2002): 26–28; Umberto Eco, "Amare l'America e marciare per la pace," in *La Repubblica,* 14 February 2003, available on: http://www.repubblica.it/online/politica/noguerra/eco/eco.html (last accessed: 3 March 2005).

53. Massimo Teodori, *Benedetti americani: Dall'Alleanza Atlantica alla guerra al terrorismo* (Milan: Mondadori, 2003). Teodori's outspoken work as a Professor of American History has the curious feature of documenting with quotations the anti-Americanist attitudes of significant components of the Berlusconi government that he himself has militantly sup-ported. Philippe Roger, *L'ennemi américain: Généalogie de l'anti-américanisme français* (Paris: Seuil, 2002).

54. Maurizio Viroli, "L'America e la religione della libertà," in *Specchio,* supplement to *La Stampa,* 24 May 2003; Giorgio Ruffolo, "La forza e la fragilità dell'impero Americano," in *La Repubblica,* 14 April 2003.

55. Sergio Romano, "Americanization," ix; but cf. Sergei Romano, *Il rischio Americano: L'america imperiale, l'Europa irrelevante* (Milan: Longanesi, 2003); in this book Romano, a former ambassador and prominent conservative commentator on international affairs, expresses concern over the risks of an imperial turn in U.S. policy; Gianni Vattimo, "Ma quale America amiamo," *Unità,* 22 February 2003.

56. *Corriere della Sera,* 13 December 2002.

THE INTERFACE BETWEEN POLITICS
AND CULTURE IN GREECE

❖ ❖ ❖

Konstantina E. Botsiou

"... that hangs together with our form of government and our method of
doing international business. We simply lack the techniques by which you
intervene successfully in the internal political affairs of other countries.
Our propaganda instrument is rudimentary and pathetically weak. The
educated classes from one end of Europe to the other have already been
affected to some extent by Soviet propaganda. They are cynical about our
motives and skeptical as to our reliability. We have no political movements
in Europe working on our behalf. Our purposes in Europe are basically
defensive. It would be hard to develop them into the basis of a militant
political movement which might successfully oppose communism."[1]

Introduction

When, in late 1947, the U.S. Policy Planning Staff and Harry S. Truman's
executive team were thus pondering the inherent weaknesses of American[2]
involvement in postwar European affairs, their reasoning relied heavily on their
disheartening interference in the first year of the Greek civil war (1946–1949).[3]
Following the officially notified withdrawal of British financial and military
support in early 1947, the promulgation of the Truman Doctrine[4] had introduced Washington in lieu of London as the chief protector and guarantor of
the country's Western orientation. Torn apart by a bloody civil war between
communists and anticommunists, Greece easily became one of the first test-
ing grounds for U.S.-Soviet strategic antagonism and a political laboratory
for George F. Kennan's symmetric containment policies.[5]

What the Truman presidency started as an urgent intervention in the struggle soon became an unintentionally heavy and long-term American commit-

ment in Greek domestic affairs to guarantee the country's economic and political survival within the Western orbit. In the extensive body of social sciences studies on Greek Western policies after World War II, the idea of imposed unilateral U.S. interventionism has grown into a classic argument for explicating the anomalies in Greece's postwar political course, notably the institutionalization of emergency civil war legislature in the postwar years (the so-called "parastate" system)[6] and the military dictatorship of 1967–1974. Only in recent, or recently noticed academic work, is the Greek government's chronic reluctance to see the American tutelage replaced by more assertive liberal options, without compromising the country's Western profile, introduced into the Athens-Washington equation.[7] Apparently, the *strategy of dependency* on external aid, a salient feature of early postwar governments, has to be taken seriously into consideration. This does not contradict the hypothesis that the early postwar patron-client relationship between the United States and Greece eventually had to evolve into more balanced Euro-Atlantic policies at the end of the 1950s and, definitively, after the junta.

For our discussion about American cultural influences in Greece, though, it is important to note that the transition from a period of overt American interference to an increasingly hands-off "vigilance" at the end of the 1950s marked a turning point for the style and implementation of cultural diplomacy as well. The drastic reduction of direct financial support to Greece in 1957/58, in conjunction with the changing power diplomacy of the incoming Kennedy administration, also brought cultural containment policies to the fore. The aim was, obviously, twofold: first, to secure long-term American influence after the sharp cuts in aid and personnel; and second, to continue to cultivate the concept of a shared Euro-Atlantic culture based on a common value system in an age of détente, when the call for reform, liberalization, and revision of Cold War politics was shaking up both sides of the Atlantic.

To a great extent, the establishment of the military dictatorship in 1967 demonstrated the failure of the Greek political system to sustain its dual mission of safeguarding democracy and Western orientation without massive foreign aid and interference. For Greek-American relations, the junta constituted a milestone. Above all, it inaugurated a period of fierce anti-Americanism in Greek society. Indeed, Washington's cooperation with the military regime opened a Pandora's box, resulting in what has perhaps been, among the countries of Western Europe, a uniquely negative perception of American political culture ever since. In retrospect, the Greeks' perception of their overall postwar history runs through this channel of anti-American bias, even under conditions of unquestioned pro-Western orientation.

Yet, and perhaps not surprisingly, the popular inclination to reject the *Pax Americana* failed to produce fanatic objections to everything American in cultural terms. Falling by default within the mainstream Western European paradigm, Greek cultural identity took a rather highbrow approach to American cultural "imports," but in the end it showed no genuine willingness to avert the powerful trend of Americanization, especially that of the globalization variety. This emotional dualism toward the U.S. image after 1945 emanates largely from the specific historical conditions under which the American presence took root in Greece.

Civil war,[8] dependence on American aid—USD 2.56 million between May 1947 and June 1956, the highest per capita U.S. assistance received until then by any underdeveloped country[9]—and domestic antagonisms between political parties and non–democratically accountable but powerful structures, such as the monarchy and the military, had rendered Greece, since the 1940s, all but a mainstream Marshall aid recipient.[10] Unlike most European Recovery Program (ERP) countries, Greece failed to decontrol and liberalize in time. This loss of time was realized at a high cost when the Korean War exploded. Determined to limit its commitments to immediate defense priorities, Washington quit ambitious liberalization and democratization projects.[11] The guardians of Greece's security apparatus, in effect the monarchy and the army, became indispensable players in the restructuring of U.S. priorities. Yet, as resolute advocates of victimization of the "defeated" of the civil war, they were also *a priori* unfit to merge the culture of democratization with security objectives under ebbing U.S. presence. Deprived of time and resources, American interference became also more blatant in moments of crisis.[12]

Anti-Americanism, nourished by the notion of "satellitization," turned thus into the spirit of the day. It attacked Washington's control over the Greek monetary policy through U.S.-manipulated organizations like the Nomismatiki Epitropi (Currency Committee, NE), and the Diikisi Exoterikou Emporiou (Foreign Trade Agency, DEE),[13] the extensive American interference in social security agencies (Idryma Kinonikon Asfaliseon [Institute of Social Security], IKA) and labor unions (Geniki Synomospondia Ergaton Elladas [General Workers' Federation of Greece], GSEE),[14] the wide-ranging extraterritorial rights recognized to almost all American personnel stationed in Greece, and the steady drastic cuts in U.S. aid after 1952.

These issues became more explosive under the impact of the Cyprus imbroglio. The volatile manifestation of Greek anti-Americanism over the thorny Cyprus question released a deep-seated resentment of foreign interference.[15] Undeniably, the balancing acts of Washington in the Cyprus question struck a sensitive chord among Greek nationalists. American officials were quick to notice that under the escalation "American prestige and influence has taken sharp downward turn in Greece ... Behind this is a real feeling of abandonment and isolation ..."[16] Prime Minister Constantine Karamanlis indicated that even moderate newspapers stigmatized him as an "American lackey"[17] and "quisling for not adopting neutralist policies for Greece and for not withdrawing completely from NATO."[18] Again, neither the settlement of the Cyprus issue by the Zurich and London Agreements (1959/60), nor the continuance of discreet U.S. funding "to offset the harassment and failures … in foreign affairs,"[19] nor the association with the European Economic Community (EEC) in 1961/62 could absorb the emerging culture of protest.

In the mid 1950s, a mix of nationalism and anti-American protest became the driving force behind the social calls for genuine consensus-liberalism. At the same time, national fundamentalism and anti-American populism flared among marginalized leftists, especially after the Eniea Dimokratiki Aristera (United Democratic Left, EDA), the facade party of the since 1947 outlawed Kommounistiko Komma Elladas (Communist Party of Greece, KKE), became the major opposition party for three quite "cold" years in trans-Atlantic relations (1958–1961).[20] These developments not only guided—with American advice—the reshuffle of local political parties into an Anglo-Saxon–style two-party system after the formation of the Enosi Kentrou (Center Union, EK) party in 1961,[21] but they also introduced the agenda that mobilized many Western societies in the same period (e.g., democratization of the Cold War state; liberalization of labor, educational, and cultural mechanisms). Anti-Americanism had already become a national, unifying "cult idea." However, the local rebellious zeitgeist made enthusiastic use of American-inspired means of expression. The setting seemed ripe for a political and ideological breakthrough that could make a way from the gloomy post–civil war underdevelopment to all-out modernization. But this prospect would soon prove stillborn, insofar as the coup d'état of 21 April 1967 put a violent stop to both political agitation and cultural reform.[22]

The brutal seven-year rule of the colonels had lasting consequences for Greek-American relations. In large segments of Greek society, the junta has ever since been conceptualized as an American-inspired "solution" to the dramatic domestic crisis that preceded the dictatorship, in which the call for democratization had held a key position. The authentic ideological effects of the American "velvet" pressure on the colonels[23] were felt in the aftermath of July 1974, when the junta collapsed as a result of its adventurism towards Turkish aggression on Cyprus. As George Th. Mavrogordatos vividly pointed out: "the junta swept away with it all ideas it had exploited or, in any way, associated with. Therefore, it nullified the post-war narrative of the so-called victors of the civil war and the ideological foundation on which pre-dictatorial governments rested."[24] Apparently, the perception of Greece's "belonging to the West," a condition that had been considered tantamount to American influence and protection alike, fell among the first victims discredited along with the *ancien régime*. It was at this juncture that the European dimension of Greece's Western policies acquired prestige equal to, if not more than, that of the alliance with the United States and NATO and was promoted the alter ego of the post-1974 democratization process. Although in practice Europe and the United States were mutually reinforcing and complementary players, thereafter they were often viewed as alternative options of Greece's Western identity.[25]

Greek-American relations entered a phase of institutional normalization in the beginning of the 1980s. Nonetheless, the return to mainstream Atlantic policies took place in an atmosphere of virulent anti-American rhetoric. This was largely a byproduct of the October 1981 rise to power of the socialist Panellinio Sosialistiko Kinima (Panhellenic Socialist Movement, PASOK) party, where it would remain almost uninterruptedly for over twenty years (except for the period 1989–2003). Headed by Andreas Papandreou, the socialists sought a bridge between their leader's pre-1967 rebellious initiatives and a new brand of anti-Western populism and Third World neutralism, an approach that successfully garnered electoral support in a change-thirsty society.[26]

The Politics of Culture

"… those who have taken a permanent residence in the larger metropolitan areas have found themselves living in overcrowded conditions, often lacking employment: on the other [hand], those ones exposed to urban conditions are dissatisfied with a return to truly primitive rural conditions. In both cases, traditionally conservative elements have tended to become disorientated, and to listen with some attention to the blandishments of the neo-communists."[27]

The Truman Doctrine was presented as an opportunity for nations to choose between "two alternative ways of life."[28] Initial U.S. planning in Greece had self-confidently relied on the hypothesis that "dollar diplomacy" would not solely end internal bloodshed, but would also metamorphose Greece from a conservative agricultural nation, suffering from ideological anachronisms and an almost "physical fear" for its national existence, into an open, modern society, as well as a touchstone for the superiority of American power and values.[29]

However, if one compares Washington's extraordinary impact on political developments with its involvement in cultural policies, only very few analogies can be drawn. This is particularly true for the period in which governmental planning was subject to American scrutiny across the board, namely the decade 1947–1957. In reality, American cultural influence was first channeled through official diplomatic and institutional structures in the late 1950s, that is, *after* political interventionism began to subside in favor of a "normal" diplomatic presence. In other words, American policy began to emphasize cultural convergence as soon as financial assistance ceased to act as a leverage for political control. At the same time, it seems that proactive cultural initiatives entailed a defensive dimension: the United States had to promote its cultural values the moment it diagnosed a clear "psychological dis-association of Greece from American policy."[30] Americanization had hitherto been pursued through the general, transnational impact of U.S. economic, political, and cultural power. Postwar cultural consensus was expected to pour naturally from the multifaceted interaction of American agencies and Greek postwar politics.

Various reasons might explain this restrained attitude. The American interest turned originally to the efficient use of U.S. funds so that the domestic organizational model could converge with the rest of the Organization of European Economic Co-operation (OEEC) area.[31] Initial Marshall Plan ideas for a New Deal–like industrial democracy in Greece were undermined, at the dawn of the 1950s, by the change in the hierarchy of American priorities toward short-term modernization projects and, predominantly, monetary stability. In the meantime, the transfer of normative orientations from the American patron had actually facilitated a certain degree of compatibility with Western European institutions; also, a pervasive type of "Americanization" held sway in terms of long-term economic planning, free enterprise, acquisitive individualism, and basic welfare state–politics until the late 1960s, when the state sector began to expand rapidly.[32]

The urgency of socioeconomic issues offers one sound explanation for the discreet American involvement in Greek cultural affairs until 1957/58. Answers could be detected also in the dynamics of Greek ideology and culture. Owing to the nature of the Greek security doctrine, which pointed chiefly to the internal communist threat, the Athens governments enjoyed considerable freedom in defining postwar social and cultural reconstruction. In this context, for instance the military, as the guarantor of peace and stability, was assigned with a cultural and "educational" role inversely related to its actual mission and abilities. In fact it was the great contributor to the central cultural ideology of the state, the so-called *ethnikofrosyni* (i.e., national conviction, the ideology of the nationally minded as opposed to the soldiers of subversive ideologies and foreign—read, Soviet—masters), which demanded absolute devotion to the nationalistic objectives of the country. *Ethnikofrosyni* was originally tolerated by the Americans, because it was a concept not only compatible with the Cold War rhetoric, particularly in the McCarthyist period, but also more easily understood and accepted by the average noncommunist Greek. But whereas McCarthyism fell into decline, Greece's domestic version of Cold War tenets blocked any serious efforts at cultural modernization for years.

Ethnikofrosyni was devised during the civil war as the legitimate "response" of the state against communist aggression. Its primary aim had been to neutralize permanently the influence of the communists by adding ideological and social isolation to military defeat. Thereafter, it was sustained for polemic purposes in order to discredit all that reminded Greeks of the left and its role in recent Greek history. On the ideological level, communism represented the opposite of national unity and sovereignty. Communists, who had advocated the autonomy of Macedonia during the civil war, presupposing the self-determination of Slav-Macedonians in Northern Greece, were not plainly the dissident pawns of an international crusade against the Western values of freedom and democracy; they were essentially traitors, enemies of the motherland, "viruses" in the inviolable national body. *Ethnikofrosyni* was meant to serve the self-contradictory notion of "Hellenic-Christian" civilization, which had hitherto inspired the most conservative segments of the sociopolitical sphere and was worshipped by military dictators (e.g. the colonels' "mystifying" motto was "Greece of the Hellenic Christians").[33]

It was not so much the general trans-Atlantic consensus on the threats posed by international communism and Soviet-led aggression, but rather the Greek interpretation of it that forged the quintessence of postwar policies. Furthermore, the nationalistic credo urged vigilance at all times towards external influences, both non-Western *and* Western. Limitation of exposure was put forward as the best shield for safeguarding Greek culture. In the early postwar years, this peculiar isolationism contrasted sharply even with the canon of Western orientation. The mostly conservative elites and the communists continued to look down on cultural styles associated with American modernity—much more than was the case for standard European styles—while at the same time they appropriated selected American cultural expressions to employ as Cold War weapons.

By allowing Greece's domestic culture to roll under the auspices of the "nationally minded," the United States largely compromised its overall investment in the political and cultural recovery of the country. Instead of exploiting the advantages of Western liberalism and European convergence, the Greeks were confined within a conservative paternalistic order: the everyday hero was the "unpretentious" man of the land, now become the new lower middle class that seized the urban centers; also lionized were the people who "minded their own business" and translated liberal capitalism into chances to promote private interests with no social limitations. Loyalty to national and religious ideals had to be proven by compliance with the traditional gender roles, blind identification of "old age" with "authority," and admiration of "charismatic" political figures. Just as the older generation dominated the young, so the military hierarchy took the stage as superior to the political and civil order. Blind faith in the historical unity of the Greek nation, from the ancient times up to the present, was the *conditio sine qua non* for being accepted into the official culture of the state.[34] The preservation of the Slav-communist *feindbild* constituted an integral part of the same process.

Nowhere was this mentality reflected so clearly as in the educational order, which continued to depend on the state for teaching and administrative staff, ideological screening, and the preparation of educational material.[35] Illiteracy remained high, affecting almost one out of four Greeks in 1951. Access to tertiary (post-secondary) education continued to be "reserved" for the privileged offspring of established upper and upcoming urban-middle classes that could afford the "economic time" entailed in the long road to higher education. Until 1974, university studies also remained beyond the reach of many "suspected" communists and sympathizers, who did not present the necessary "record of social convictions" for their enrollment.[36] Moreover, Greek education suffered from the predominance in secondary and college education of the pure national language (*katharevousa*), which, after 1945, was also presented as the flagship of the nationally-minded. Other facets of educational underdevelopment were the great deficit in technical and vocational education and the inadequate resources devoted to educational purposes altogether (only 6–7 percent of the regular budget in the 1950s or 1.5 percent of GDP).[37]

It was little wonder that postwar Greek education aimed at "the creation of honest citizens within the framework of the Hellenic-Christian civilization."[38] The American missions, in their effort to minimize financial commitments to Greece, failed to realize that the domestic educational problem was a barrier to the policies of bilateral cultural convergence. Only so late as 1958 did American officials suitably note that

> The role of the intelligentsia is a subject which has been insufficiently studied. The Greek educational system, based upon that of France, is malformed to produce a fairly high cadre of those dissatisfied intellectuals who traditionally, in Asia as in Russia, have turned to extremist solutions. The ranks of the … neo-communists contain a strikingly high proportion of doctors, lawyers, and other professionals for whom Greece offers pathetically little opportunity for economic success … they are the product of a social system in which their skills are not marketable or indeed needed.[39]

Under these circumstances, the Athens U.S. Embassy was now mobilized to grant more substantial help and guidance in the field of education, with emphasis on the tertiary level and on programs of postgraduate professional training. The political aim was to alleviate, without jeopardizing political stability, the growing anti-American sentiment that was related "more to the sense of social, economic and political injustice … than to a complete endorsement of communist tactics."[40]

The new approach became evident in the case of the University of Patras, which was finally founded in 1968 after many years of deliberations since the inception of the project in the mid 60s. American support was instrumental in Greece's search for appropriate loans from the World Bank and the design of the various departments and curricula. The departments of the new university distanced themselves from the rigid classicism of other Greek institutions. They were built almost exclusively upon technology-oriented disciplines (mathematics, physics, engineering, etc.) and engaged mostly academics who had studied and worked in the United States. For some,[41] the Patras project belonged to the broader U.S. effort to promote technological studies across the Western bloc under the negative impact of "Sputnik" psychology.

American expertise was also to be found behind the establishment, in 1957, of the Anotati Viomichaniki Scholi Thessalonikis (Higher Industrial School of Thessaloniki, AVSTH), the forerunner of the University of Macedonia. American funds, and American economic diplomacy in international institutions (banks, institutes, donors, etc.), were involved in the establishment of technological institutes (Kentra Anotatis Technikis Ekpedefsis [KATE], later Technologika Ekpedeftika Idrymata [TEI]), technical and vocational schools (Kentra Epaggelmatikis kai Technikis Ekpedefsis [KETE]), and research institutes, such as the Center for Social Research (KKE; today the Ethniko Kentro Kinonikon Erevnon [National Center for National Research], EKKE), and the Greek Center of Natural Sciences "Democritus."

"Americanization" worked effectively through private U.S. foundations after the 1957/58 reform. The Ford Foundation, active in Greece since 1959, financially supported the Doxiadis Technology Organization—which was later absorbed by the public sector—and the Vasiliko Idryma Erevnon (Royal Institute for Research; now the Ethniko Idryma Erevnon [National Hellenic Research Foundation], EIE), which had been founded by Marshall aid grants in 1958. Also the Kentro Programmatismou kai Erevnas (Center for Economic Planning and Development, KEPE), which started its operations in 1959 under the direction of the later Prime Minister Andreas Papandreou,[42] was set up on the basis of a generous grant by the Rockefeller Foundation. All these institutes became magnets for researchers and academics in political economy, physics, humanities, and social sciences who had studied or were about to study in the United States.

Apart from the operation of new universities and research institutes, the American cultural diplomacy sought to convince the Greek authorities of the need to open all levels of education to all classes and social groups, encourage students' associations—which became a factor in academic and political affairs only in the 1960s—invest in human capital, and change the content of primary and secondary education.

In the period of piecemeal liberalization, bilateral Greek-American agreements facilitated systematic mutual academic exchanges. The Fulbright program alone brought more than 1,000 researchers, professionals, undergraduates, and graduate students to the United States and 800 Americans to Greece between 1949 and 1969.[43] The majority of the Greek Fulbright applicants were channeled to natural sciences, engineering, architecture, and economics. Parallel efforts were undertaken in Washington to arrange for Greece bilateral agreements for academic, scientific, and technical cooperation with the countries of Western Europe. U.S. mediation, at times pressure, in favor of the Greek application for association with the European Economic Community (EEC) (negotiated from 1959 until 1961) resulted *inter alia* in bilateral agreements with Germany (1958) and France (1961) for technical and vocational training of Greeks abroad.[44]

In 1959, the UN Social Fund started financing and supporting, with visiting American experts, applied academic research and vocational—especially teachers'—training offered by special institutes (Scholi Ekpedeftikon Litourgon Epaggelmatikis Technikis Ekpedefsis, SELETE) that continued the work of the Marshall Plan and the OECD. In response to American concerns about economic planning after U.S. assistance ended, American state agencies cooperated with the European Center of Productivity to establish a Greek branch in 1953, the Elliniko Kentro Paragogikotitas (ELKEPA), which promoted American models of accounting, management, and marketing. The Athens U.S. Information Agency (USIA) enhanced its program for visits by about twenty young Greek academics and professionals to the United States annually.

In 1957/58 more emphasis was put on the popularization of American schools and institutions in big cities, notably Athens and Thessaloniki. The Ellinoamerikaniki Enosi (Hellenic American Union, EAE) was established in 1957. With its broad collections on economics, political science, sociology, education, art, linguistics, literature, management, marketing, and applied sciences, the EAE filled a painful vacuum in the domestic educational landscape and boosted awareness of international affairs. The EAE became also an exquisite meeting point for young Greeks who were learning English—available in Greek schools systematically only after 1976. Because of the relatively small number and the high cost of translated American books, American literature was circulated mainly through the EAE.

The American schools and colleges that had operated in Greece since the nineteenth century (Athens College/Hellenic American Educational Foundation [HAEF]; Pierce College-Junior College-Deree College in Athens; the Anatolia College in Thessaloniki) sought to rebalance the large numbers of their elitist clients with scholarships and special educational programs for poorer gifted students. Another important asset of American cultural influence in Greek educational affairs was the work of the American School of Classical Studies in Athens (ASCSA, established in 1881) and the outstanding adjunct Gennadius Library. A leading teaching and research institution, the ASCSA was first and foremost a teaching institution, introducing North American students to Greek history and civilization from Antiquity to contemporary times. It also attracted an international array of scholars and cooperated systematically with Greek academics in the school's principal fields of study: archaeology, history, language, and literature. At the end of the 50s and 60s, the ASCSA expanded its capacity to foster Greeks' contact with the researchers from over 100 colleges and universities in North America and other parts of the world who joined the activities of the school every year.

In sum, since the second half of the 1950s American involvement in the Greek educational structures has been inversely related to the amount of the overall direct financial assistance granted to Greece by Washington. State-sponsored and private development credits came to address the notion that

> U.S. information and cultural programs should seek to convince the Greek people that Greece's alliance with the West represents the best means of maintaining political and economic independence. The programs should seek to promote confidence in the U.S. and in NATO by publicizing their military and economic strength and promote understanding of special aspects of U.S. policy of particular interest to Greece. The programs should seek to promote confidence in U.S. leadership by publicizing U.S. achievements in scientific, cultural and social fields. The programs should emphasize the mutuality of Greek-American security interests and political ideals and give recognition to American heritage of Greek culture. At the same time, in view of the increasing respectability of the Soviets in Greece, the programs should publicize events and writings which expose Soviet strategy and those which emphasize the dangers inherent in the communist economic, political and cultural overtures designed to maneuver the country toward neutralism. The principal effort should be directed to Greek media officials and opinion-molders in the political, military, professional and educational field, who are in turn capable of reaching large segments of the population.[45]

Until the end of the Cold War, these policies would prove quite fruitful. American influence was kept alive not merely because a great number of Greek academics, in all fields of study, had fully or partially acquired an American academic background, but also because constant communication tied the Greek community to the leading ideological currents blossoming overseas, from the New Left to social constructivism.

A prominent exception to the rule of Greek-American mutuality was the underdevelopment of American studies in Greece. American studies as a discipline has only recently—since the late 1970s—been introduced in English departments through courses in language and literature. Similarly, American history courses were not developed inside history or political science departments until the end of the Cold War. The causes might be sought on various fronts: the persistence of Greek historians preferring more familiar and "classical" Greek and European subjects, the delayed development of the history of international relations in Greece (visible only as of the 1970s), and the overall lack of "area studies," the still strongly nation-centered curricula of Greek universities. Other reasons include the focus on European studies since Greece's accession to the EEC in 1981, but also the tacit preference of Greek and American authorities that the old negative feelings towards the United States not be revived—to this day, students' anti-Americanism keeps responding suspiciously to official American cultural services that aim to spread an idealistic vision of American politics. The first institutionalized American Studies Seminar in Greece was held only as late as 1993, along the lines of similar seminars around the world.

The Greek "anticommunist state"[46] of the early postwar decades disagreed intensely with the American style of cultural democracy. The United States was not spared blame, however, for tolerating domestic archaic structures in the name of anticommunist solidarity. Still, rebels and reformers of the 1960s did not fail to realize that the American model of open cultural frontiers was a major source of inspiration and pressure on the Greek governments to reform, framed as "a choice between isolation and integration in the international community."[47] This generally admitted fact is reflected most in the trends of Greek literary production of the 60s. Literary journals then took up, for the first time, the international discussions on styles and social critique to apply them to the domestic situation. Against the dogmatic beliefs of the rigid civil war camps, Greek writers from all domestic "blocs" began to look more carefully on the dialectics between their society and other societies. Their subjects reflected the challenges and internal clashes of modernity. The struggle between individual interests and collective aspirations, and the efforts of modern men—and women—to conciliate them, became a recurrent theme, clearly reminiscent of contemporary American writings (e.g., Tatiana Gritsi-Milliex, Antonis Samarakis, Kiki Dimoula, Dinos Christianopoulos, Katerina Aggelaki-Rouk, Olga Votsi).[48]

The retreat of the interwar pessimistic language of poetry and prose works entailed a strong affinity for the more familiar American theater language of the 50s. Unlike theatrical productions, though, literature proved a slower medium for communication with contemporaries about developments that transformed, or promised to transform, their lives beyond the war experience. Only when faced with mass cultural inflows from abroad and the demands of modern transnational and transcultural contacts did major Greek authors make the leap from monotonous national recipes to more complex modern techniques.

As the readers became more numerous in the 1960s, the issues addressed became more elaborate. As a rule, themes moved away from wartime reminiscences, which tended to insist on bitter, uncompromising views of the "other," and away from the disruption of harmony between man and nature, a theme that pervaded the lion's share of interwar Greek literature. Attention now turned to the typical human example of a society struggling to survive between the Scylla of political conservatism and the Charybdis of leftist antiliberalism. Both seemed to block the way to what most Greeks deemed to be their natural right to enjoy consumerism, education, professional security, and economic and social mobility—in a word, the tangible products of peace and democracy and the antidote to the languishing of the Western democratic project. Conventional interpretations of organic intellectuals and political writers of the left were reexamined in literary journals (e.g., *Nea Estia, English-Greek Review, Kochlias, Elefthera Grammata, Pali, Diagonios, Kritiki, Epoches, Oi Dromoi tis Eirinis*). To be sure, the common political experience could not be totally eliminated as a background for projecting literary narratives. Hence, the general public associated works on the oppressive character of totalitarian states (e.g., those of Antonis Samarakis) more strongly with right-wing dictatorships than with communist regimes. For similar reasons, literary attacks on conflicts as the main source of social dislocation and individual misery identified "war" with Western containment policies rather than bipolar antagonism. Hymns to peace appeared often as an alternate revival of leftist angst (e.g., in the poetry of Yannis Ritsos).[49]

Later on in Cold War Greece's brief cultural renaissance of the 1960s, literature became more accessible to the average—increasingly literate and educated—Greek and adopted a more compatible cultural outlook. Many authors sought not only to study modern Greek society, but also to discuss their findings with their contemporaries in the most direct possible way; theater plays attracted their pens more than classical novels. Especially poetry, long a bastion of literary work due to its fluency in the cryptic language required by state order and readers, became widely available. It tailored its verses to classical Greek musical themes (Mikis Theodorakis, Manos Chadjidakis, Stavros Xarchakos, and Manos Loizos are believed to set typical "modern" examples of the Greek "cultural psyche"), which were the chosen entertainment of the expanding *petit* middle class. Radio stations, and later television, proliferated the new mix of high and popular culture by presenting exhaustively the "pristine" musical and theater works, singers, actors, composers, directors. Not surprisingly, the generation of the 60s, the first to profit from this openness as well as from practices directly imported from Hollywood, has been glorified ever since as the pioneer of the modern Greek cultural identity.

When literature began to seek contact with contemporary currents, the theatrical record of the previous decade had already offered significant thematic and stylistic inputs. Since the end of the 50s, Greek modern theater had undergone major transformations, mainly as a result of its exposure to American influences. This process, which broke the monopoly of light bourgeois vaudeville and sterile classicism in Greek theatrical affairs, owed much to the work of the director Karolos Koun (1908–1987). Widely known and recognized as the "master," Koun introduced the Greek theater to the school of "poetic realism," which he identified with modern American theater. His brainchild, the Theatro Technis (Art Theater), first established in 1942,[50] constituted a point of reference for postwar generations: it was celebrated as an oasis of liberalism, multiculturalism, optimism, and modernity for Greeks who longed for a glimpse into the "outer" world.

A typical diaspora cosmopolitan, Koun perceived modern Greece as a "front-line state" between two different "worlds": the mystic, "underdeveloped" world of the East and the rational, developed West, a twilight merge of Dionysian and Apollonian elements. Koun's interpretations of ancient Greek drama—the third major category of his plays, after American and modern Greek plays—were catalytic.[51] The "frontline psychology" appeared to run through Greek history in his major performances, from Aeschylus' *Persians* to the works of his "students," whose ranks included gifted modern writers like Iakovos Kambanellis, Dimitris Kechaidis, Loula Anagnostaki, Notis Pergialis, and Georgios Skourtis. Thus did national identity in the Cold War become synchronized with the deeper historical destiny of a nation at the crossroads of East and West.

Having worked in the 1920s and 1930s as a teacher of English language and literature at the American College of Athens, where he directed his first plays in the 30s, and later as cofounder of the Laiki Skini (Popular Scene, 1933), Koun distinguished himself in the 1950s as the channel of communication between Greek norms and American modern realism. Both at his own theater and from 1950 to 1954 as Acting Director of the National Theater, the oldest, most conservative and upper-class–oriented state-sponsored theatrical institution in Athens, he successfully challenged the dated themes and methods of his Greek and European contemporaries. While retaining the most advanced elements of Greek dramaturgy, he invested extensively in modern American works that were performed in Athens a few months after their premiere in the United States. Between 1946 and 1950 Tennessee Williams' *The Glass Menagerie* and *A Streetcar Named Desire,* and Arthur Miller's *All My Sons,* had already made headlines in Athens newspapers and journals. John Steinbeck's *Of Mice and Men* was performed in the National Theater in 1950, together with classical plays by Chekhov, Pirandello, and Shakespeare.[52] In 1954, Theatro Technis opened its doors again with Wilder's *Our Town.*

Tennessee Williams, Eugene O'Neill, Arthur Miller, John Steinbeck, Thornton Wilder, William Inge: such playwrights were deliberately chosen for a public that flooded Athens after ten years of war in search of a better *vita urbana.* This "transitional" flock secured the theater growing attendance and a broader basis for social influence. As a school of drama, Theatro Technis baptized the most acknowledged cultural generation of postwar Greece in the waters of American modernity (Manos Chadjidakis and Melina Merkouri numbered among the associates of the school).

Kambanellis, Kechaidis, Anagnostaki, and Skourtis, "brought up" in the Theatro Technis, were among the most prominent writers of the 60s, 70s, and 80s. The American vogue is detectable in the themes played out in their studies on modern Greek society: the middle-class need for optimism, the shared anxieties and dreams of the common man everywhere in the world, the role of personal will in shaping one's destiny, which also defied the fatalistic belief in the omnipotence of big powers over the small and weak. Thus, Kambanellis' *The Seventh Day of Creation* (1956), *Courtyard of Miracles* (1957) and *The Age of Night* (1959) examine people who have recently moved from villages to the capital and their everyday struggle to maintain their dignity and dispel their nostalgia for the depressing past and present, in a way strongly reminiscent of Wilder's melancholic comments on the psychological condition of the individual within the community. Similarly, Kechaidis' *Games in the Salt Marshes* (1956/57), *Distant Song Sorrow* (1957), *Suburb of Neo Faliro* (1959), and *The Great Walk* (1960) swarm with accomplishments that reveal Tennessee Williams as a source of inspiration. Anagnostaki's trilogy *The City* (1965), which attacks the violence and brutality of society against the individual, echoes the contemporary avant-garde American writers. Skourtis' *The Musicians* (1972) and *Karagioz almost vizir* (1976), published some ten years later, focus again on the antiheroic protagonists of modern life, a theme that had dominated American theater plays in the early Cold War. These late works were historically timely for the additional reason that they heralded a new antiheroic period following the epic downfall of the junta. All the avant-garde work of Koun's team exposes the promises and pitfalls of the "Greek dream" in ways that sympathize clearly with the parallel fate of the American dream in classical Cold War writings from the United States.

Theatro Technis, the biggest and oldest non-state theatrical institution in Athens, became more conventional in the 70s. Economic problems (partially solved by a generous grant from the Ford Foundation during the dictatorship), as well as the rapid pace of Greek social and political life toward postmodernity after 1974, rendered it less "revolutionary" for the increasing number of theatergoers. Nevertheless, it remained an incontestable symbol of the cultural regeneration of the 60s. Koun's insistence on the search for the "new men and women" who would be in a position to convey the common fears and hopes of the modern individual to the demoralized Greek society was popularized and internationalized through the various Greek festivals that were organized starting in the late 50s.[53] The merging of modern text with popular expressionism—wide use of *rebetico* music,[54] popular art, scenes and costumes from everyday life (the famous painter Yannis Tsarouchis was a close associate)—rendered this art understandable and acceptable even to those who had only partial contact with it through music and songs, or radio and televised performances.

The Art of Mass Entertainment

As one of the most easily accessible information and entertainment fields, given the economic plight of most Greeks and the high rate of illiteracy even in the urban centers, the Greek cinema consistently served the ultraconservative state ideology, particularly in the austere 1950s. Under American advice, state agencies sought to illustrate through the seventh art the shared fears and threats of the Western community, together with the power of the Greek nation against internal and external foes. This policy was built upon old and new practices. The former included the presentation of political documentaries in the form of "educational" film journals (*Epikera*), which were prepared and distributed by the state Press and Information Office in order to provide information about the most important national and international developments. If the theater owners neglected to play these fifteen-minute films for three consecutive days, the operation of the theater could be suspended for up to fifteen days.[55]

These documentaries, a tradition dating back to the interwar years, now stated the official view of the government and the foreign missions in the country, notably the American and NATO officials, on major events. Regarding international themes, priority was given to the triumphs of the Western Allies in World War II, the victories against communist forces (e.g., in the Korean War), and the operations of NATO. High-ranking information also included the successful Western recovery from war and the affluence of the Western lifestyle as antithetical to the barren landscape behind the iron curtain, as well as the Western technological advances that facilitated communication, entertainment, productivity, and the liberation of women from the most laborious of household tasks, which allowed them to join the workforce. Regarding national themes, the recipe was long established, presenting first the royal family, then the work of the Greek government, and finally, local news (celebrations, inauguration of infrastructure works, charity, and tourism activities). Although Law 4208/1961 revised their function, the *Epikera* remained a compulsory component of the information and entertainment business until 1974.

Apart from the film journals and the selective promotion of politically "correct" American films, powerful mechanisms were set up to control indigenous film production. The networks of censorship were put under the direct control of the Deputy Minister of Press, following basically the legal framework of the prewar dictatorial Metaxas regime and the civil-war legislation. Censorship lay in the hands of the Movies Control Committee, which comprised not only field professionals (state-sponsored writers, directors, actors, etc.) but also officers of the Security Ministry and its enforcement agency, the Elliniki Stratiotiki Astynomia (Greek Military Police, ESA), which was a very familiar visitor to the U.S. missions, too. Apart from the detailed screening of new productions, writers, directors, and actors, the committee relied heavily on "blacklists" of "unwelcome" professionals.

Compelled to practice self-censorship and confine themselves to selective truths, most Greek film directors ended up in the massive production of "safe" movies. The rapid development in the 50s and 60s of the indigenous industry, which used to bring out almost sixty films a year, coincided with a dominance of melodramas and spy movies. Pompous acting and psychological "neutrality" towards history glorified the suffering of the protagonists in isolation from social and political collective experience. Certain subjects derived from World War II, or the civil war, remained taboo for decades. A marked exception was provided by the movie *Oi Germanoi xanarxontai* (The Germans Come Again, 1947/48), which criticized postwar national discord while sending hints of optimism and excitement with modern life; meanwhile external—U.S.—support promised pacification and recovery.

Works that are usually classified as Greek variations of the postwar Italian neorealist school—more on the basis of their focus on social critique than on the espousal of the Italian technical and aesthetic tools—were but sparsely promoted in Greece in the early postwar years. Among them, the films *Bitter Bread* (1951) by Grigoris Grigoriou, *Black Soil* (1952) by Stelios Tatasopoulos, and the internationally acclaimed *Barefoot Battalion* (1954) by Greg Talas stand out. All three movies converged with parallel European reports on the cruel effects of war and the problems of recovery, especially the social reintegration of marginalized and handicapped people (resistance fighters, refugees, orphans, widows, the unemployed). The neorealists gained more publicity after 1955. Films like *Magic City* (1956) by Nikos Koundouros and *The Dream Neighborhood* (1961) by Alekos Alexandrakis, a film often compared with Nicholas Ray's *Rebel Without A Cause* (1955), made wise use of symbolic film language to display the poverty, social discrimination, and struggle for survival in the oppressive urban environments beneath the familiar surface of prosperity and a carefree Western lifestyle.[56]

Joint European and American postwar impressions also became evident in internationally recognizable films like *Stella* (1955) and *Never on Sunday* (1960) by Jules Dassin, featuring Melina Merkouri, a future Socialist Minister of Culture (1981–1989, 1993–1994) and Dassin's wife, in the leading female roles. As in the cult film *The Ogre of Athens* (1956) by Nikos Koundouros, the plot unraveled in neighborhoods teeming with impoverished inhabitants and hoodlums, both suffering from the social disasters caused by war and political repression. The U.S.-born director Jules Dassin had actually exemplified these in his earlier works in the United States and France, works that had interrupted his American career after he was "blacklisted" by Senator McCarthy's House Un-American Activities Committee (HUAC).

The apolitical stance of directors and producers was concomitant with the tacit ban on political films. With rare exceptions (such as *The Outlaws*, 1958, by Nikos Koundouros), only in the 60s did Greek cinema begin to reflect the general relaxation of Cold War austerity as well as the growing contact with American studios and producers. This trend contributed to the improvement of artistic techniques and screenplays. Films like *The Red Lanterns* (1963) and

Blood on the Land (1965), both directed by Vassilis Georgiadis and nominated for the Oscar award for best foreign film, bore clearer political messages. To the critical eye, the former, describing the evacuation of the red light district in Piraeus after the limitation of visits by the Sixth Fleet, mixed, the exploitation of the country by its allies with the challenges that more independence should entail for the Greeks. The latter movie centered on the Greek agrarian movement of the early twentieth century, a "banned" subject, and searched for parallels with the socioeconomic inequalities of present-day Greece. The case of Georgiadis becomes all the more interesting if one takes account of his pioneer work in movies that blended the American genre of the movie Western with domestic patriotic drama (*Krystallo* [1959]; *Shepherd's Pipe and Blood* [1961]; *The Mother's Curse* [1961]). The emergence of a movie like *The Aegean Tragedy* (1961) by Vassilis Maros signaled a clear break with the established censorship against war documentaries. A politically "correct" movie, praising the nation and its victories against external and internal enemies, this film nonetheless presented valuable historical material and found the courage to use its subject—the Greek-Turkish war of 1919–1922 in Asia Minor—to "attack" the elimination of the war experience from the public vocabulary.

Belated responses to the rebellious spirit of pieces like *The Catcher in the Rye* (J. D. Salinger, 1951) appeared in Greek letters and movies in the same period. The "young generation" was then studied as a distinct social group. Film scenarios, often adaptations of Greek and foreign novels, addressed the generation gap, the antisocial behavior of youth, gender discrimination, and the rigidity of traditional family values in *Law 4000* (1962), *Rage* (1962), *Vertigo* (1963), *Downhill Course* (1961), and *Stefania* (1966). Unavoidably, the American film industry became a standard point of reference for Greek musical films. Apart from the still-prevalent classical subjects of Greek postwar movies—family life, love stories, the promising economic prospects of the country—the natural beauty of Greece and the quality of Greek entertainment composed a new stereotypical theme for such movies. The development of tourism became the common denominator of most folklore images of Greece and the Greeks, which swung—against all odds—from the glory of the sun and the deep blue of the sea to an endless optimism danced to the rhythm of *syrtaki* as hands are joined with international friends.

The American genre of the musical did not manage to enter the theatrical stage until the 70s. One of its tremendous opponents was the indigenous musical theater (*Epitheorisi*), which combined influences from the Parisian revue, the German cabaret, and American variety shows. Frequently political, this sort of popular theater competed successfully with prose plays to garner the broad audiences, while the musical surrounding of the improvising actors consumed the space that otherwise might have called for the development of fancy musical performances in the American style.[57]

In general, the deeper Greek producers and directors slid into the 60s, the more freely they seemed to experiment with national and international forms of expression and cinematographic techniques. The United States, together with European influences, was now more obvious in the form of expression rather than the thematic orientation (or the scarcity thereof). Naturally, the military coup d'état of 1967 put an abrupt end to this trend. During the dictatorship, American Westerns swamped television screens, while bombastic military films presented productions concerning military operations from ancient times to the Korean War.

Overall, Greek film production between 1947 and 1967 was shaped by the same postwar and Cold War doctrines that formed Greek political and cultural life as a whole. Naturally, wartime resistance as a grass-roots movement appeared nowhere, so that no reference could be made to its leftist side. The issue of the Greek resistance was for the first time openly addressed for national and international audiences through an expensive Hollywood production, *The Guns of Navarone* (1961), a film promoted systematically by American agencies both in Greece and the United States as the "real story" of the Greek resistance. In this case the resistance was presented as a branch of British and American planning, which conflated the royal Greek military forces in the Middle East with the "Westerners" at home who had exclusively borne the burden of fighting inside occupied Greece.[58]

The fall of the dictatorship in 1974 granted unprecedented freedom to the Greek film industry. Now, unhindered by outside pressure, neglected topics flourished: war (e.g., *La troupe* [1975] and *The Hunters* [1977] by Theodore Aggelopoulos, and *1922* by Nikos Koundouros [1978]), the communist-led resistance (*Aris Velouchiotis—The Dilemma* by Fotis Labrinos [1981]), the civil war (*Civil Word* by D. Leventakos [1978]), the Greek left and rightist witch-hunting (*The Man with the Carnation* by Nikos Tzimas [1980]), the repressive postwar mechanisms (*Stone Years* by Pantelis Voulgaris [1986]). The legalization of the Communist Party of Greece (KKE) in 1974 and the official recognition of the KKE-led resistance by the first socialist government in the 80s rebalanced the outlook of all artistic production in the country, including the expected extreme narratives on the part of those long oppressed, or their political patrons.

However, Greek cinema was allowed to recover only after it was already handicapped by the invasion of television. Since 1966, when TV was officially introduced in Greece, it had won over the Greek family. In ironic fashion, the dictatorship had not only convinced people to seek home entertainment instead of risky socializing in public places, but had also taken maximum advantage of television as a propaganda instrument, *inter alia* by establishing its own channel, the Ypiresia Enimeroseos Enoplon Dynameon (Information Agency of the Armed Forces, YENED). The Greek television "culture" then tended to imitate the path of post-1945 Greek cinema. American movies, most preferably Westerns, which were in keeping with the views of the junta on racial purity and military solutions, and series celebrating most conservative views on gender roles (*I Love Lucy*), traditional moral qualities (*Lassie, Little House on the Prairie*) and the technological achievements of the West (especially space-related technology: *Lost in Space, Space 1999*) went hand in hand with local gangster-movie productions focusing on visible and invisible threats (*The Unknown War*) and the decency of workers and peasants (*Frontier Station, Luna Park*). Greek cinema "classics" from the 50s and 60s continued to reach the wide public via the highly watched Saturday night zone of national television. The establishment of private television stations in 1989/90 did not imperil this dominant position. Since 1974, however, more mainstream television programs, including numerous U.S. productions, have updated the ideological and cultural outlook of the new media.

Social change in the 60s set the local conditions under which foreign cultural transfers could meet with broader success. U.S.-style consumption and production transcended social and class borders, especially through the channel of youth culture. The general positive image of America in theater, literature, and film, as well as in technology, education, and social progress, created a unified cultural disposition toward cultural expressions from the United States. This trend further weakened boundaries between high and popular culture. Although politically willing but culturally recalcitrant elites and leftist intellectuals continued to take for granted the naïveté and anti-intellectualism of American culture, the majority of Greeks did not seem to identify commercialism with low cultural quality. Thus did the deep-rooted prejudice of the traditionalists come into conflict with the restless modernism of the young generation, particularly during the presidency of John F. Kennedy.

As in most European countries, Kennedy became an icon in Greece, symbolizing new chances for democratization, social freedom, and the replacement of the Cold War generation by the champions of détente and the Popperian open society—at a time when General Charles de Gaulle was also idolized as a symbol of political independence from the United States.[59] New Left theories were then taken up by Greek leftist intellectuals in an effort to engage their contemporaries in a provocative political language. During the dictatorship such influences remained strong among academics, writers, and journalists. One of the most influential and often anti-American political journals, *Anti*, which was first published in 1972, emulated the New Left U.S. journal *Ramparts* in setting up its style and thematic orientation.[60]

Cultural interactions promoted hitherto irreconcilable mixed preferences: Ernest Hemingway along with the French existentialists, American jazz together with Greek popular music, Hollywood and French critique or Cinecittà dominated elite and middle-class interests. The rediscovery of the state-sponsored musical wealth (from *rebetico* to folk dances) did not detract from the radio broadcasting of the "Voice of America," which kept the multiplied fans of jazz, swing, and rock n' roll music up to date across ages and social milieus. After Kennedy's assassination, though, political criticism of America flared up again, joining forces with the internal discontent over foreign and social policy issues that was later fueled by the Vietnam War. Antiroyal demonstrations filled the streets at the peak of the 1965 domestic crisis (the downfall of the elected government following a clash between the prime minister and the king), chanting anti-American slogans to heighten public rage. Self-Americanization did go ahead, though, even during the dictatorship, which took a dubious position toward cultural transfers from the outside world: a characteristic act was the unenforceable decision to deny entry into the country to men with long beards and women wearing mini skirts, despite the regime's dependence on tourism to sustain economic growth and counterbalance its own international isolation.[61]

The ambivalence of old elites, torn between reasserting traditional "national" cultural norms and embracing Westernization, "helped" the younger generation to effect "Americanization from below." As consumerism permeated the bourgeois culture and provided it with new legitimacy and political power, the adaptation of American cultural styles by the lower classes resulted in the reconfiguration of social boundaries. This major contribution to the democratization of habits and the reinforcement of Westernization became obvious under the democratization policies of the 70s and 80s. Still, although popular culture was used by the underprivileged to legitimate their values, it could do little to challenge the social hierarchy, since it depended on the consumer demands of capitalism. Thus, demonstrations of political anti-Americanism using American cultural instruments of expression were not as odd as they might appear at first sight.

But such political expression becomes more unexplainable in present-day situations, which see the light of day in a greatly transformed and democratized political and cultural environment in Greece. For instance, the application of a double standard reached a climax during the Kosovo war in 1999, when the Athens government complied with the NATO policies of intervention while almost 99.5 percent of the population was estimated to oppose the military campaign[62] and big antiwar demonstrations blocked the streets for weeks. Even more striking, though, was the schism within the government itself in the case of the 2003 war in Iraq, when 94 percent of Greeks were reported to oppose the American attack:[63] whereas the government kept a very cautious stance towards the United States, from day one some of its most prominent members and *enfants terribles* of the 60s and 70s led huge anti-American demonstrations.

Anti-Americanism

Was Greece a typical case of cultural Americanization and political anti-Americanism during the Cold War? If one looks at the considerable, expressed popular resentment of American influence in Greek politics, the answer is an unreserved yes. Solid majorities condemned the equidistant U.S. policy toward Greeks and Turks in the Cyprus issue, loathed Washington's cooperation with the military dictatorship, and were constantly suspicious of America's unrivaled power in the trans-Atlantic community. The "defeated" of the civil war never forgave the United States for its intervention in favor of the anti-communist forces; in their view, Greece's recent struggle with political coercion and underdevelopment had sprung from that fateful turn of fortune. The painful course to democratization and prosperity concerned also the "winners" of the civil war, who saw no way of containing the communists and preserving national unity other than depending on foreign, for decades predominantly American, aid. In the postdictatorial years, the dismal image of the United States frequently metastasized into a holistic rejection of American political culture.

The widespread anti-American sentiment contradicted the much warmer, albeit not universal,[64] endorsement of Westernization through Europeanization. In psychological terms, after joining the European Community (EC) in 1981, Greeks deviated further from trans-Atlantic orthodoxy by regarding Greece's European identity as alternative, not complementary, to its Atlantic policies. Although an essential trait of the socialists' rhetoric for radical change, which held domestic politics hostage until the end of the Cold War, this view took hold of numerous groups across the party spectrum and had a strong impact on the public discourse. The ardent advocacy of Third World neutralism by Andreas Papandreou was fanned by populist anti-American tirades of all political stripes. Although it was practically harmless for official Greek-American relations, the angry socialist rhetoric did little to wash away the impression that anti-Americanism was legitimized by state sponsorship of U.S. aims.

Yet if one scratches the surface of conventional wisdom about Greek anti-Americanism, the origins and evolution of the phenomenon are not as clear-cut as we have assumed. The communist-anticommunist divide, the association of the United States with democratically non-accountable institutions like the crown and the army in the early postwar years, the junta and the Cyprus tragedy, and the expected underdog mentality of weak dependent states do not tell us the full story, especially if we examine incoming archival evidence. As we uncover more information about Greek-American relations over a longer period of time, the esoteric confrontation between U.S.-connected internationalism and the sharp national reflex that answers to the need for coherence or, at times, isolationist conformity, turns our attention to political and cultural dynamics that exist beyond the Cold War. Neither cultural Americanization nor political anti-Americanism can be taken for granted, in this context.

Apart from the expected communist polemic, anti-American perceptions have fed, for instance, the conservative press since the beginning of the 50s. Depending on the situation, the idea of American violations of Greek national sovereignty was broadly disseminated by royalist newspapers hoping to thwart U.S. efforts to limit the crown's "prerogative" to manipulate the political parties (e.g., in the case of U.S. support for General Plastiras in 1950–1952, or Papagos after 1952).[65] The conservative Athens government's discontent with the gradual reduction of direct U.S. assistance was also barely concealed in the editorials and news coverage of "friendly" media from the right and the center throughout the 50s. Military and religious circles had been pioneers in anti-American campaigns ever since the Cyprus problem enhanced the belief in the nation's exploitation by the Great Powers. As more and more analogies were drawn between British colonialist policies and American strategies in the Mediterranean and the Middle East, the Athens U.S. Embassy clearly understood that "the psychological impact of the reductions in American aid and believed American hostility on the question of Cyprus, have combined to push the Greek back to its own channels of thought. The average foreign observer is now used to hearing many Greeks explain their present alignment with the U.S. as being essential in view of American control of the Mediterranean sea lanes."[66]

In the 60s and 70s, dependency theorists[67] examined the problem of foreign intervention and underdevelopment selectively, neglecting the indigenous pious hope for continuous dependence that characterized most postwar governments. Whereas this strengthened collective memories of the detrimental effects of foreign "penetration," such recollections remain detached from the vicious circle of dependency-based strategies for democratization and welfare economics. In working from the top down, the analysts that shaped the post-1974 political self-image of Greece often overlooked the Greeks' quest for security in dependence structures: the worse the state failed to invent a more liberal relation with Western capitalism, the more the citizens sought shelter from the "imported" market economy under the roof of the expanding democratic state.

Connoisseurs of Greece's postwar political development have not ignored the significant political and economic changes American influence left behind. U.S. hegemony in the early Cold War included successful attempts to stabilize the electoral laws, organize the fragmented and discredited political parties into a two-party system that could sustain consensus-liberalism, activate mass participation in politics, cut down the hierarchical educational system, integrate the young generation into activist and political institutions, change the conservative views on gender issues, and lessen isolationist trends. With regard to the implementation of liberalization and welfare state rules,

American missions institutionalized centralized annual planning of development projects, encouraged the disarming of the protectionist trade policies, sought to bridge the center-periphery gap by emphasizing infrastructure and communications, and made tourism the gateway to capital and cultural contacts, trying to intensify Greece's interdependence with Western Europe and pointing to the European integration process as the natural environment for "Western" and "European" Greece. On the other hand, of course, imprudent failures in the realm of social democratization and political freedom overshadowed the fixed importations.

As in many European countries, except during the McCarthyist period, America was portrayed as a Janus face: politically, it was identified with power; culturally, with questioning authority and cultural diversity. Greeks found it increasingly hard to fuse their political weakness and the postulate of ethnic-national uniformity with this "foreign" contribution. Elites were dubious about the impact of American popular culture on social hierarchies and the moral outlook of the young. Selective anti-Americanism periodically attacked the "made-in-the-USA" consumerist and materialist habits that endangered the unity of the "plain" Greek families and communities. Concern about the cultural likings of children and adolescents was also intense: in tirades against media ranging from comic books and cartoons to "trash" novels and "superficial" Hollywood products, conservatives declared the superiority of the Greek culture and warned that it might be destroyed if foreign influence were left free to pollute Greece's linguistic and moral foundation with cultural "junk food." Not surprisingly, European cultural imports were more openly welcomed by the sophisticated anti-American critics, and were often compared favorably to "crude" American products (for instance, Disney cartoons and Marvel comic books were thought to belong with more primitive readers than Asterix, Rantaplan, or Lucky Luke, just as U.S. gangster and political movies or books of the 60s ranked beneath their French counterparts).

While American educational standards were rapidly winning the admiration of wealthy and middle-class groups, the adaptation of social and political behaviors *à l'americaine* was discouraged as a danger to young people's social integration at home. Still, American cultural expressions and political "loans" were highly visible when the domestic movements of the 1960s questioned the status quo. For the lower and middle classes, the nonconformity and informality of American culture was attractive and self-reassuring. The flexibility of the American lifestyle, studied through mass culture and the experience of immigrants to the United States, who provided almost every Greek family regular first-hand information about the higher standards of living, better job and educational opportunities, and unlimited chances for social mobility overseas, was sharply contrasted with domestic conditions in the 60s and 70s—much as the industrialization miracle of the Soviet world had been a source of Greek frustration in the early 50s.[68] The association of American life with violence, profit, and the absence of social safety nets did not subside, though. It was the permanent basis for a more general conviction about America's cruel pursuit of individual interest and disregard of humanistic and community values. The systematic mass anti-American demonstrations of the 70s against policies in other "underdeveloped" and "dependent" countries, from Chile and Nicaragua to Palestine, summoned both young and old, working- and middle-class protesters. The junta radicalized the political mentalities to such a critical degree that, in 1974, only rapid democratization and the official expression of resentment and disassociation from the United States could turn the tide away from anarchy, or war with Turkey. While Greece's withdrawal from NATO's military planning (1974–1981) had little practical effect on American politics for Cyprus, it did have an explicit pacifying impact inside Greece.

The young Greek democracy was firmly established in the subsequent years. Europeanization helped blur the postwar political animosities and allay concerns over Greece's economic course. Greek-American relations, despite socialist criticism, were also normalized after several bilateral issues (e.g., U.S. military facilities and military assistance, terrorism) were settled via negotiations. Anti-Americanism remained a diehard, recognizable force in the domestic political culture. Following the post–Cold War international upsurge in anti-American protests in "old Europe," it regained an international visibility fairly incompatible with Greece's present economic and political position within the "privileged" zone of the most democratic and prosperous countries in the world. A clear difference from the Cold War, however, lies in the fact that Greek anti-Americanism has now become "integrated," and assimilated, into the general unfavorable view of American unilateralism. Back in the 50s, 60s, and 70s, anti-Americanism enticed Greeks to question altogether the country's option for the Western camp. Neutrality, nonalignment, and isolation were then the ideological counterparts to today's safe outrage from an unquestionably stable Euro-Atlantic standpoint.

Conclusion

The process of Americanization and the creed of anti-Americanism in postwar Greece cannot be separated from the country's deep dependency on the United States for its political and economic survival within the Western bloc for many years after the end of World War II and the civil war. Since 1947, Greece has undergone a gradual, though not unopposed, Americanization. Political, economic, and military affairs were the first to be influenced by the all-pervasive American missions in Greece. Issues of culture and identity were addressed in a subterranean manner as long as strategic priorities absorbed the bulk of aid and attention. In this period, U.S. influence was detected in the full range of public policy. The "American way" spread through the inter-action of U.S. agencies and Greek postwar politics in the fields of economic reconstruction, institutional order, security policy, and social restructuring. It also effected changes, in the organization of society and in the way of life, that adopted institutions, practices, and symbols from the "protecting power" with an eye to the progress of Greece's fellow partners in the ERP. In this re-spect, Americanization was the pivot of Europeanization from an early stage in the country's postwar history.[69]

Transition from subtle cultural policies to dynamic engagement was sought by Washington in the late 50s, as soon as its political representation in Greece began to acquire standard characteristics. This shift in political-cultural em-phasis took place within an atmosphere of all-embracing social protest against both the conservative Greek social order and Greece's Western allies as a re-sult of the Cyprus problem. The United States bore the brunt of the attacks, which generated an enduring challenge to conventional wisdom regarding the local operation of the trans-Atlantic system of norms and values. Through-out the Cold War, many Greeks continued to harbor ambivalent, if not openly hostile, feelings toward American political styles. For those who took up anti-Americanism as an eye-opening posture toward Greece's political and social underdevelopment, Washington's "fellow-traveling" with the military dicta-torship only confirmed the detrimental essence of America's disrespect for the trans-Atlantic community it so adamantly claimed to defend.

Rejection of U.S. political control, but not necessarily U.S. protection, did not mean, however, that American cultural imports were excluded from the evolution of domestic popular and high-brow culture. With the constant ex-ception of both right- and left-wing zealots, the Greeks proved receptive to cultural transfers from overseas, which enabled a growing relativism in the def-inition of upper and lower middle-class tastes. Impressively enough, steady exposure to U.S. cultural production enhanced local demands for democra-tization of the largely archaic social, economic, and political mechanisms, which kept together the polarized postwar state. In the mass social rebellion against established political codes and alliances, American forms of expres-sion were widely in vogue; the New Left theories made this trend inclusive also of youths, intellectuals, and politicians who stood against the concept of Westernization altogether.

For the active involvement of the United States in Greek cultural affairs, the years 1957/58 constitute a watershed. It was after that time that Ameri-can impact became decisive in matters of education, training, social policies, the media, and entertainment. By replacing the ubiquitous German and French approach in educational affairs, all the while fostering contact with American academic norms, Washington sought to participate at an unprecedented tempo in the process of cultural modernization. At the same time, it promoted the massive inflow of popular culture and commercial styles, many of which were adopted by the insurgents of the 60s and the 70s to flout the cultural conservatism that prevailed until the fall of the dictatorship.

Cultural Americanization enveloped the Greek society in the post-junta and particularly in the post–Cold War years. International education, cinema, television, media, and, after accession to the EC, the trans-Atlantic creed of globalization allowed the American "way of life" to make impressive headway against an obdurate nostalgia of conventional anti-Americanism that is still to be found among older and younger generations alike. This peculiar postmodern ideological muddling, however, derives equally from deep-seated historical perceptions and the broader challenges imposed upon the Euro-Atlantic community by the end of the Cold War.

Notes

1. National Security Council (hereafter NSC) to the White House, 17 December 1947, United States National Archives, Washington, D.C. Record Group (hereafter RG) 59, Records of the Policy Planning Staff 1947–53, Box 17.
2. In this paper, the terms "America," "American," "Americanization," and "anti-Americanism" refer to the United States of America.
3. From the rich bibliography on the Greek civil war see John O. Iatrides, ed., *Greece in the 1940's: A Nation in Crisis* (Hanover: University Press of New England, 1981); Lars Baerentzen, John Iatrides, and Ole Smith, eds., *Studies in the History of the Greek Civil War, 1945–1949* (Copenhagen: Museum Tusculanum Press, 1987).
4. On the Truman Doctrine in Greece, see Michael Mark Amen, *American Foreign Policy in Greece 1944–1949* (Frankfurt: Lang, 1978); Lawrence S. Wittner, *American Intervention in Greece 1943–1949* (New York: Columbia University Press, 1982).
5. John Lewis Gaddis, *Strategies of Containment: A Critical Appraisal of Postwar American National Policy* (New York: Oxford University Press, 1982).
6. This system is analyzed by Theodore Couloumbis, John A. Petropulos, and Harry Psomiades, *Foreign Interference in Greek Politics: An Historical Perspective* (New York: Pella, 1976), 103ff.; Nicos C. Alivizatos, "The Emergency Regime and Civil Liberties," in Iatrides, *Greece in the 1940's*, 220–28.
7. Stefanidis, Ioannis, *From the Civil to the Cold War: Greece and the Allied Factor 1949–1952* (Athens: Proskinio, 1999) (in Greek); George Stathakis, *The Truman Doctrine and the Marshall Plan: The History of US Assistance to Greece* (Athens: Vivliorama, 2004) (in Greek); Van Coufoudakis, "Greek Foreign Policy, 1945–1985: Seeking Independence in an Interdependent World—Problems and Prospects," in Kevin Featherstone and Dimitrios K. Katsoudas, eds., *Political Change in Greece Before and After the Colonels* (London: Croom Helm, 1987), 230–52.

8. American Embassy Athens to Department of the Army, 30 September 1950, National Archives, Washington, D.C., RG 59 781.(W)/9–3050; William McNeill, *Greece: American Aid in Action 1947–1956* (New York: Twentieth Century Fund, 1957), 95–146; John V. Kofas, *Intervention and Underdevelopment: Greece during the Cold War* (University Park: Pennsylvania State University Press, 1989), 122–35.

9. American Embassy Athens to Department of State, 18 September 1951, National Archives, Washington, D.C., RG 59 881.00/10–1751; Wray O. Candilis, *The Economy of Greece 1944–1966: Efforts for Stability and Development* (New York: Praeger, 1968), 53–67.

10. Grady to Marshall, 30 November 1948, National Archives, Washington, D.C., RG 59 1946–1950 868.1950/11–2478; American Embassy Athens to Department of State, 14 August 1950, National Archives, Washington, D.C., RG 59 881.00/8–1450, Box 5401.

11. Konstantina Botsiou, *Griechenlands Weg nach Europa: Von der Truman-Doktrin bis zur Assozierung mit der Europaischen Wirtschaftsgemeinschaft, 1947–1961* (Frankfurt: Lang, 1999), 123–42; Stefanidis, *From the Civil to the Cold War,* 196–226.

12. Striking cases of this kind were the interventions of the U.S. Ambassador Henry F. Grady in early 1950 and John Peurifoy in 1952 to determine the timing of elections and the electoral law, respectively; Cavendish Cannon (Ambassador to Greece) to Department of State, 14 February 1955, National Archives, Washington, D.C., RG 59, 781.00/2–1455 CS/MD; *Ethnikos Kyrix,* 7 May 1950, Benakios Library, M 2112.

13. Kofas, *Intervention and Underdevelopment,* 112–17.

14. Adamantia Pollis, "US Intervention in Greek Labor Unions, 1947–1950," in Iatrides, *Greece in the 1940s,* 259–74.

15. See Theodore Couloumbis, *Greek Political Reaction to American and NATO Influences* (New Haven: Yale University Press, 1966).

16. Telegram from the Embassy in Greece to the Department of State, 13 September 1955, *Foreign Relations of the United States* (hereafter *FRUS*) XXIV (1955–1957): 289.

17. Despatch from the Embassy in Greece to the Department of State, 4 January 1957, ibid., 599.

18. Telegram from the Army Attaché in Greece (Strange) to the Department of the Army, 13 October 1955, ibid., 547.

19. Memorandum from the Director of Central Intelligence (Allen Dulles) to the Secretary of State, 26 May 1956, ibid., 563.

20. See Eckart Conze, *Die gaullistische Herausforderung: Die deutsch-französischen Beziehungen in der amerikanischen Europapolitik 1958–1963* (Munich: Oldenbourg, 1995); Max Beloff, *The United States and the Unity of Europe* (Washington: Brookings Institution, 1963).

21. American Embassy Athens to the Department of State, 22 September 1958, National Archives, Washington, D.C., RG 59, 781.00/9–2258.

22. Andrew Galbraith Carey and Jane Perry Carey, *The Web of Modern Greek Politics* (New York: Columbia University Press, 1968), 58–184; Keith Legg, *Politics in Modern Greece* (Stanford: Stanford University Press, 1969), 154–58.

23. Evangelos Averoff-Tosizza, *Lost Opportunities: The Cyprus Question, 1950–1963* (New York: Caratzas, 1986).

24. George Th. Mavrogordatos, "The Problematic Relation with the Past," *Liberal Emphasis* 3 (2004): 85–89 (in Greek).

25. Konstantina E. Botsiou, "In Search of Lost Time: The European Course of Democratization," in Dimitri Constas and Marilena Koppa, eds., *30 Years of Greek Foreign Policy, 1974–2004* (Athens: Livanis, 2005, 99–121) (in Greek).

26. On PASOK's ideology and rise to power, see George Th. Mavrogordatos, *Rise of the Green Sun: The Greek Election of 1981* (King's College, Occasional Paper 1, London: Centre of Contemporary Greek Studies, 1983).

27. American Embassy Athens to Department of State, 22 September 1958, National Archives, Washington, D.C., RG 59, 781.00/9–2258.

28. US House of Representatives, *Assistance to Greece and Turkey: Hearings Before the Committee on Foreign Affairs,* House of Representatives, 80th Congress, 1st Session on H.R. 2616 (Washington: U.S. Government Printing Office, 1947).

29. NEA to Department of State, 1 October 1951, National Archives, Washington, D.C., RG 59 881.00/10–151, Box 5401; Constantine Svolopoulos, *History of the Greek Foreign Policy, 1900–1981,* 2 vols. (Athens: Estia, 2002), vol. 2, 100–106, 207–26 (in Greek).

30. Despatch from the Embassy in Greece to the Department of State, 4 January 1957, *FRUS* XXIV (1955–1957), 599.

31. Paul Porter to Harry S Truman, 1 April 1947, National Archives, Washington, D.C., RG 59 Records of Greek, Turkish and Iranian Affairs, Greece, Lot 54 D 363.

32. Panos Kazakos, *Between State and Market: Economy and Economic Policy in Postwar Greece 1944–2000* (Athens: Patakis, 2001), 246–350 (in Greek).

33. Constantine Tsoucalas, "Ideological Impact of the Civil War," in Iatrides, *Greece in the 1940's,* 321–43.

34. Efi Avdela, "The Teaching of History in Greece," *Journal of Modern Greek Studies* 18, no. 2 (2000): 239–52.

35. For a good discussion of Greek education see Pantelis Kyprianos, *Comparative History of Greek Education* (Athens: Vivliorama, 2004) (in Greek); Christos Katsikas and Costas N. Therianos, eds., *History of Modern Greek Education* (Athens: Savvalas, 2004) (in Greek); Theofanis D. Hadjistefanidis, *History of Modern Greek Education (1821–1980)* (Athens: Papadimas², 1986) (in Greek).

36. Carey and Carey, *The Web of Modern Greek Politics,* 163.

37. For public investments in human capital as the safest way to sustainable prosperity for all social strata, see Andy Green, *Education and State Formation: The Rise of Educational Systems in England, France and the USA* (London: Macmillan Press, 1990).

38. According to the words of George Papandreou, Minister of Education in 1951; see Tsoucalas, "Ideological Impact of the Civil War," 336.

39. American Embassy Athens to the Department of State, 22 September 1958, National Archives, Washington, D.C., RG 59, 781.00/9–2258.

40. Ibid.

41. Kyprianos, *Greek Education,* 262.

42. American Embassy Athens to Department of State, 18 November 1958, National Archives, Washington, D.C., RG 59, 469 Deputy Director of Operations, Office of Near East and South Asian Operations, Subject Files 1953–1959, Box 5.

43. Stephanos Pesmazoglou, "Technical Assistance and Educational Exchanges," in Sakis Karagiorgas Foundation, ed., *The Greek Society in the Early Postwar Period,* 2 vols. (Athens: Sakis Karagiorgas Foundation, 1993), vol. 1, 457–70, here 462.

44. EWG/EURATOM, 28 September 1959, Archives of the European Communities/Florence, EWG-Ministerrat Akten, Kassette CM 2 1959/94, R/708/59; Constantine Svolopoulos, "La perspective européenne de la politique extérieure grecque et le général de Gaulle (1959–1963)," in Institute Charles de Gaulle, *De Gaulle et son siècle, t. V* (Paris: La Documentation française—Plon, 1992), 247–55.

45. Operations Coordinating Board, 21 April 1958, *FRUS* X (1958–60), 623–24.

46. The term used by Stavros B. Thomadakis in "Deadlocks of Reconstruction and Economic Institutions of the Postwar State," in Sakis Karagiorgas Foundation, *The Greek Society in the Early Postwar Period,* 34–40, here 38; cf. Ilias Nikolakopoulos, *The Sickly Democracy: Parties and Elections 1946–1967* (Athens: Patakis, 2001) (in Greek).

47. According to the Prime Minister George Papandreou; see Alexander-Andreas Kyrtsis, "Cultural-Ideological Expressions of Post–Civil War Modernity," in Sakis Karagiorgas Foundation, *The Greek Society in the Early Postwar Period,* 399–413.
48. See the voluminous section "Postwar Literature from the End of the War Until the Dictatorship of 1967," in *Postwar Literature,* vols. 1–8 (Athens: Sokolis, 1988) (in Greek).
49. See Roula Kaklamanaki, *Yannis Ritsos—His Life and His Work* (Athens: Patakis, 1999) (in Greek).
50. For a detailed account see Michael Mayar, *Karolos Koun and Theatro Technis* (Athens: ELIA, 1993) (in Greek; original Ph.D. thesis submitted at New York University).
51. Ibid., 88, 115.
52. See, for example, M. Karagatsis' comments in the conservative newspaper *Vradini* on 12 January 1951, 13 April 1951, and 10 May 1951.
53. American Embassy Athens to Department of State, 31 August 1958, National Archives, Washington, D.C., RG 469 NEA subject files 1953–1959, Box 5.
54. *Rebetico* is the popular music that originally represented the culture of uprooted Greeks: refugees, immigrants to urban centers, outlaws, etc. After 1945, expressions and social behaviors connected with *rebetico* were endorsed by the middle class, as opposed to the Western European conventional tones and ethics preferred by the elites.
55. This subject is discussed for the 1960s by D. Pantavos, "The 'Enlightenment' of the Public: Cinema Journals about Greece's Relations with NATO," *Greek Review of Political Science* 1 (2003): 70–91 (in Greek).
56. Maria Paradisi, "Neorealism in Greek Cinema," *Istorika* 20 (1994) (in Greek).
57. Alexis Solomos, *People and Issues from the World Theater* (Athens: Kedros, 1989), 124–25 (in Greek).
58. American Embassy Athens to Department of State, 13 November 1959, National Archives, Washington, D.C., RG 59 881.00/11–1359, Box 4895; Greek Ministry of Press, Film Archives, Epikera nr. 196123, 1961.
59. Botsiou, *Griechenlands Weg nach Europa,* 363–94.
60. Speech of the publisher of *Anti,* Christos G. Papoutsakis, at the symposium *Dissenting Journalism: Greece, the CIA and USA,* Columbia University, 1 February 2001.
61. Richard Clogg, *A Short History of Modern Greece* (Cambridge: Cambridge University Press, 1979), 273 (in Greek).
62. *Ta Nea,* 26 April 1999.
63. Anthee Karassava, "Anti-Americanism in Greece Reinvigorated by War," *New York Times,* 7 April 2003.
64. See Panos Kazakos, "Socialist Attitudes toward European Integration in the Eighties," in Theodore Kariotis, ed., *The Greek Socialist Experiment* (New York: Pella, 1992), 257–78.
65. Peurifoy to Acheson, 1 April 1952, National Archives, Washington, D.C., RG 59 881.00/3–3152; American Embassy Athens to William O. Baxter (GTI), 8 April 1955, National Archives, Washington, D.C., RG 59 781.00/4–855.
66. American Embassy Athens to the Department of State, 22 September 1958, National Archives, Washington, D.C., RG 59, 781.00/9–2258.
67. See Kostas Ifantis, "State Interests, Dependency Trajectories and 'Europe': Greece," in Wolffram Kaiser and Jürgen Elvert, eds., *European Union Enlargement: A Comparative History* (London: Routledge, 2004), 70–89.
68. American Embassy Athens to Department of State, 14 January 1949, National Archives, Washington, D.C., RG 59 868.017/1–1449, M 98, reel 35; William Hardy McNeill, *The Metamorphosis of Greece Since World War II* (Chicago: University of Chicago Press, 1978), 86–93.
69. Botsiou, *Griechenlands Weg nach Europa,* 12–19, 438–52.

WAITING FOR MR. MARSHALL: SPANISH AMERICAN DREAMS

◆   ◆   ◆

Dorothy Noyes

Is Spain different? The tourist slogan said so, and Spain's history of relations with the U.S. is marked by obvious differences from that of either Western or Eastern Europe. The symbolic turning points in Spanish-American cultural relations were not 1945 and 1989 but 1898, when Spain lost its last remaining colonies after being defeated by the U.S., and 1953, the date of the Madrid Pact establishing U.S. military bases on Spanish soil. Once an imperial rival, Spain became less an ally than a client state of the U.S. during the Franco regime. As Spaniards frequently point out, Spain was the only country in Europe to be left out of the Marshall Plan, and the two concerns driving U.S. cultural policy in the rest of Europe did not apply to Spain: it was not in the U.S. national interest that Spain democratize, and Franco himself was taking care of anticommunism. U.S. culture entered Spain by commercial more than political channels.

For Spaniards too, *América* and *americano* mean something more complex than they do for many other Europeans, as the politically correct terms *las Américas* and *norteamericano* indicate. Spain had, and lost, its America, and continues to strive to regain its influence there. Latin America (*Iberoamérica*), the principal site of Spanish emigration, furnishes the Spanish cultural imagination with a different outlet for fantasies of expansion, primitivism, wealth, and so on. The U.S. was never a paradise-in-waiting for poor Spaniards, nor (with the exception of the Basques in the West) was there much of a Spanish-American community in the U.S. to sustain more personal ties.

Spain's symbolic position in Europe has been problematic since the seventeenth century, when its decline as a world power and the rise of France gave rise to the famous slur "Africa begins at the Pyrenees." Spanish elites have

---

Notes for this section begin on page 330.

been sensitive to the perceptions of Europeans ever since, seeking recognition by attempting to undermine the stereotypes and, failing that, by performing them. The U.S. is thus not Spain's only significant other: France still matters more to many intellectuals, and even now Spain's European identity is not taken for granted. In Spanish conceptual geography, moreover, there have long been two sites of modernity. Since the eighteenth century, *Europa* has stood for cultural and political modernity; since 1898 the discourse of technological and economic modernity has centered on *el yanqui*. Progressives and conservatives of various stripes have long differed on whether they want one, both, or neither of these, but their geography is shared.[1]

"American culture," then, remains something of an oxymoron in Spanish discourse. Americanization is understood to apply to mass culture and lifestyle: its principal referents are film and, more recently, fast food. Viewed more globally, "American culture" is neither the expression of the spirit of a people nor the realm of individual cultivation, as European folk and high cultures are respectively understood, but a *techne* of domination. In the language of anxious masculinity that continues to inform Spanish identity debates, mass culture is the "Vaseline"™ that eases American penetration.[2] By the same token, American countercultures, widely appropriated, are understood as technologies of resistance.

In the metacultural realm of explicit cultural policy and commentary, this kind of analysis is almost universal. American culture is understood as a top-down creation of commercial and government interests, fostering the naïveté and rootless vulgarity of the well-meaning American masses, while selected American countercultures and elites are singled out for celebration precisely for their ability to withstand this overwhelming force. Through the international reach of these American influences, the Spanish public is understood as vulnerable to this same process. "American culture" is, indeed, almost always a proxy for cultural tendencies within Spain. The internal diversity of Spain, an explosive subject, can more safely be projected onto its external relations. In Spanish national identity debates, the U.S. is one of four competing compass points, along with Europe, *la Hispanidad,* and the Mediterranean. To be sure, even symbolically it is rather more equal than the others.

Rejected in theory, in practice American influence is highly visible in the media and genres that the word "culture" most commonly denotes, that is, arts and leisure. This influence increases as a market model of cultural production gains political currency and spreads from popular to elite culture. Culture increasingly assumes the commodity forms received from U.S. and global sources, and emulates American production values. Cultural content appears to move in the opposite direction, often becoming more localized and "Spanish," especially when intended for an international market: the globalization of consumerism necessitates the creation of a differential product identity. Here, however, the spirit of empire has revived: though not a world power, Spain has a world language, and a renewed sense of rivalry with the U.S. is evident.

It is at the level of what we might call infraculture (unhappily beyond the scope of this essay) that the struggle is greatest. Sociability, family life, the disciplines of the body, the ordering of time and space, and the categories of personal identity present deep inertias. At the same time, they are vulnerable to the effects of a changed economic life. The Americanization of working conditions, with greater demands for residential mobility and flexibility, and the Americanization of incentives, with a greater possibility of social mobility than ever before, present the possibility of change at this deepest level. In so reflexive a society as the Spanish, where the political staging of everyday identities dates at least from the first "clash of civilizations" with France in the eighteenth century, the signs of change have not gone unnoticed, provoking both vigorous cultural criticism and active resistance at the level of folk culture. They have also been welcomed for their promise of individual liberation from the intense constraints of traditional communal life.

All generalizations are overgeneralizations, and as an ethnographer of the Catalan mountains, I am the more reluctant to speak of so dubious a unity as "Spain." However, this entity, created by both domestic imposition and foreign ascription, has acquired a complex discursive reality, shored up by increasingly general participation in shared institutions and media—a development fostered by both the Franco regime and U.S. commercial culture. If Spain lacks a unitary identity, it possesses a common field of debate. To be sure, limited education, political repression, concentrations of ownership, and something of a star system have operated in historical succession to constrain the national public sphere so that it does not express the full range of regional and ideological variation within the country. I explore here, in roughly chronological order of their emergence, the most widespread Spanish discourses on America, showing their relationship to actual transactions between the two countries. The U.S. is variously personified as a rival, a friend, or a lover.

The Empire of the Dollar

La Libertad, ¡tu Libertad! a oscuras
su lumbre antigua, su primer prestigio,
prostituida, mercenaria, inútil,
baja a vender su sombra por los puertos.
   Tu diplomacia del horror quisiera
la intervención armada hasta en los astros;
zonas de sangre, donde sólo ahora
ruedan minas celestes, lluvias vírgenes.

Liberty, your Liberty! in darkness now
her former light, her old prestige
prostituted, mercenary, without use,
descends to sell her shadow in the ports.
   Your diplomacy of horror wants to see
armed intervention even in the stars;
zones of blood, where now alone
wheel heavenly mines and virgin rains.

Mas aún por América arde el pulso
de agónicas naciones que me gritan
con mi mismo lenguaje entre la niebla,
tramando tu mortal sacudimiento.
   Así un día tus trece horizontales
y tus cuarenta y ocho estrellas blancas
verán desvanecerse en una justa,
libertadora llama de petróleo.
	Still more across America burns the pulse
	of nations in their agony shouting to me
	in my own language through the fog,
	plotting your fatal shakeup.
	   Thus one day your thirteen horizontals
	and your forty-eight white stars
	will see themselves vanish in a righteous
	and liberating flame—of oil.

The unexpected configuration of the flag tells us that this is not a contemporary Spanish protest against the second Bush administration, though it does uncannily prefigure everything from the missile defense shield to the Iraq war. This is the work of the communist poet Rafael Alberti, criticizing U.S. policy in the Caribbean in 1935. The language of Spanish anti-Americanism across the political spectrum has been remarkably consistent from 1898 to the present. Alberti's poem employs several of its recurrent themes: general resentment of American economic imperialism, particular resentment of American interference in Spain's historical zone of influence, the rising up of the oppressed, America as a statuesque woman who is nonetheless sexually available for money, and America as a seller of superficially attractive shoddy goods.

Spanish rhetoric had its counterpart in the U.S. After the First Columbian Exhibition of 1893, during which polite parallels were drawn between American and Spanish imperial projects, the romantic nostalgia that had previously dominated American representations of Spain shifted radically as the Hearst and Pulitzer newspapers resurrected the Elizabethan Black Legend to galvanize support for the war. Spain was now a nation of still-medieval conquistadors fleeing the poverty of their own land to impose Inquisition and terror on helpless indigenous people, in contrast to the American imperialists and their enlightened paternalism. Much anti-Francoist propaganda in the 30s and 40s revived the images of medieval fanaticism; the romanticism of Franco's U.S. defenders was no better. The *leyenda negra* and the U.S. role in propagating it continue to preoccupy some Spanish intellectuals even today, and its impact on Spanish historiography and literary scholarship, given the prestige of American Hispanism, has been a matter of continuing concern among scholars.[3] The continuity of the anti-Catholic *leyenda negra* from the time of the Armada to 1898 has caused "*yanqui*" and "*anglosajón*" to be closely linked in Spanish political discourse, opposed either to autochthonous tradition or to European civilization. The equation of the U.S. and Britain is frequently revived, as during the 1980s when the Reagan-Thatcher alliance created pressure on European socialists to revise their economic policies, or more recently as the Spanish public criticized the foreign policy of the Bush-Blair team.

Propaganda on the two sides of the Spanish-American War was equally intemperate: for every drawing of an undergrown Spanish bully flagellating a frail weeping Cuba, there was a ravenous Uncle Sam wading towards Havana with dollars bursting from his pockets, a saber in one hand and a bottle of rum in the other, or a Spanish lion tearing out the belly of an American pig with dollars spilling from its entrails. The Spanish press impugned the masculinity of its opponent:

Tienen los yankees orgullo	The Yankees have pride,
y también tienen milliones,	and they also have millions,
mas no tienen . . . ¡una cosa	but they don't have . . . one thing
que tienen los españoles!	that Spaniards do!

The omitted word, of course, is *cojones*. In the bullfighting reviews of the period, meek bulls that failed to perform in the arena were referred to as "*yankiformes*."[4]

After such posturing, the defeat was still more humiliating, and the well-known "Generation of 1898" turned inward to consider the problems of Spain itself—all the more urgent given that already powerful social tensions were exacerbated by economic stress and the trauma of the war for its working-class combatants. In these debates, the U.S. stood as a great civilizational Other, its liberal modernity contrasted to France's Jacobin model. Spanish writers drew, as Lily Litvak has shown, from a broader European debate over the superiority of the Latin or the Anglo-Saxon race.[5] The racial discouse continued through early Francoism (notably in the 1941 epic film scripted by the dictator himself, *Raza*), and in particular in Spain's attempts to recover its influence in Latin America. Spain answered the U.S. cooption of Columbus by proclaiming 12 October the "Día de la Raza" or "Día de la Hispanidad." Ortega y Gasset's 1929 essay *La rebelión de las masas* describes America as vital and primitive, a mass society in which prosperity conceals immaturity, inaugurating a continuing discourse on Americans as *un pueblo joven*.

Nostalgia for Cuba has persisted to the present: it is a popular vacation site for Spaniards. Cuba is the underside of the U.S. in the poetry of the 1930s: Alberti's denunciation of American petroleum-driven imperialism includes a nostalgic lyric about an Andalusia redolent of cigar smoke and swaying to Havana rhythms, a sleepy world of childhood indulgence supported by Cuban labor that died when "they turned the *Sí* into *Yes*."[6] The mix of nostalgia and denunciation persists in popular culture, minus Alberti's irony toward the mother country. One of the most characteristic collective activities along the Costa Brava, once an important site of emigration, is the singing of *havaneres* by male quartets. The best-loved, most emblematic *havanera* today is not from the 30s, but 1968: a composition by a former Army officer, "El meu avi se'n va anar a Cuba" (My grandfather went away to Cuba). The song celebrates the nationalist camaraderie of the fishermen turned soldiers—its refrain is

"Long live Catalonia!"—and rather than recall the ferocious antigovernment violence with which the Catalan masses reacted to conscription at the turn of the century, the song ends clearly: "It was the fault of the Americans." Given its author and its composition under the Franco regime, the song could hardly say otherwise. In historical fact anti-Spanish Catalanism received an enormous boost from the 1898 disaster, but in a convivial atmosphere in which the goal was to create local fellowship; the enemy is better placed at a distance. This rhetorical strategy of overcoming internal quarrels through the invocation of a foreign enemy has a long history in Spain.

The critique of the native bourgeoisie—many of them in fact "*americanos*" who had made their fortunes in Cuba before the war, then returned to invest them at home—had begun even before the defeat, and here there was slippage in the referent of "American." As early as 1896 the conservative Ángel Ganivet protested the "*americanismo*" of the city of Granada,[7] tracing its new rectilinear avenues and utilitarian public spaces to the influence of Minneapolis and Chicago, "extended railway stations" rather than cities.[8] "The 'habanera' alone is worth the entire production of the United States, not excluding sewing machines and telephones," insisted Ganivet.[9] The commercial bourgeoisie of the period did indeed aspire to the influence of their U.S. counterparts, emulating the display modes of American new money. This pro-Americanism of the business class continued quietly through the twentieth century and, as that class swelled in power and numbers, has had a greater influence on government policy than the noisier anti-Americanism of either right or left.

Federico García Lorca's *Poeta en New York* of 1930 anticipates Alberti's opposition of sensual Cuba to soulless New York. Here, though, they are part of the same society. The city crushes nature and feeling under the grids of business and finance: "beneath the arithmetic, a river of tender blood." Looking at Harlem as a site of tropical vestiges, "your great king prisoner in a doorman's uniform," the poet imagines a vengeful apocalypse in which the city is buried beneath a southern nature, choked in vines, the domain of iguanas and serpents. In the last poem of the sequence he depicts himself fleeing to Cuba. More than Alberti, he engages with the particulars of North American culture, and here his understanding of America as containing its own sources of resistance has a long afterlife in Spanish culture, which repeatedly calls on American countercultures to criticize local modernities. His Harlem is echoed again and again, from the jazz clubs of 1960s Barcelona to the Basque-language hip-hop of the 1990s.[10] His love poem to Walt Whitman, "who in mountains of coal, advertisements and railroads/dreamed of being a river," foreshadows an important later line of criticism using homosexuality as a site of distancing from normative national imaginaries. His references to the landscape beyond New York are echoed in later poems and essays using America's settling of the west as a metaphor of emotional repression.[11]

Like the European democracies, the U.S. government did not intervene in the Spanish Civil War. At the end of World War II, contrary to the expectation of exiled Republicans who had fought with the French Resistance and in the Allied armies, collaborated with American intelligence, and been interned in Nazi camps, the U.S. did not feel it necessary to liberate Spain from Fascism.[12] While the participation of the Lincoln Brigades in the Civil War has long been honored by the Spanish left, the overall attitude to the United States has been shaped by these larger governmental decisions. U.S. and European relations with Spain continued to balance ideology and pragmatism through the 1940s. Military and then economic considerations promoted quiet international cooperation without diplomatic fanfare: for the U.S., the stability of the Franco regime meant the security of Gibraltar and therefore control of access to the Mediterranean during the war.[13] But public opinion demanded the isolation of the regime, and European pressures as well as the refusal of the Truman administration meant that Spain was the sole country in Western Europe to be excluded from the Marshall Plan. From 1945 to 1948 it was excluded from the UN as well (as later from NATO and the Council of Europe), and Western ambassadors withdrew, arguing that this was the maximum gesture permitted by the principle of noninterventionism and that increasing economic stress would incite the masses to revolt. In fact, repression and exhaustion kept the masses in check, and many argue that isolation consolidated elite support for the regime.[14]

Making a virtue of necessity, the regime celebrated its diplomatic isolation, in its most extreme moments identifying every rejected tendency with the American enemy. Said Antonio Castro Villacañas, a leading journalist of the Falange, in 1948: "We don't want progress, that romantic and liberal, capitalist and bourgeois, Jewish, Protestant, atheist and Masonic Yankee progress. We prefer the backwardness of Spain, our backwardness."[15] The regime's anti-Americanism was not only a continuation of prewar discourses from very different political sources, but drew on them directly: in 1948 *La Hora,* the official student newspaper, published an analysis of American racism by a Soviet commentator. Insofar as the regime's own ideological diversity permitted, it attempted to position itself as the spiritual "reservoir" of Europe, caught between "two materialisms, face to face." An article with this title in *La Hora* displayed two photographs, one of Soviet masses lined up on a beach in identical bathing suits, as if they were troops to be reviewed, and another of an American girl doing the "*bugui*" with her boyfriend, hair and skirt flying. "Oriental" materialism reduced man to statistics; American materialism left him "the puppet of instinct."[16]

Already the regime was dependent on American genres to convey anti-American messages. Film had had a great early success in Spain, insofar as the general poverty permitted its diffusion, and in the brief period between the advent of sound film and the invention of dubbing many Spanish actors and writers worked in Hollywood, producing Spanish-language remakes for the Latin American market. Recognizing the importance of film as a propaganda tool and as a "culture of evasion,"[17] the regime promoted the production of films that would unite the public but also help it to forget the hunger and squalor of the present. Producers made the films that would most easily and cheaply pass the censors in order to get licenses for the distribution of the Hollywood films that the public wanted. Compañía Industrial Film Español, SA (CIFESA), the company most closely allied to the regime, produced a series of historical epics on the Hollywood model, featuring Spanish military triumphs. Antonio Román's *Los últimos de Filipinas,* from 1945, featured the last stand of a battalion in the Philippines after the defeat of 1898: ecstatic in martyrdom, they sanctified the isolation of the regime from the materialist success of Western imperialism. The 1951 *Alba de América,* intended as a Catholic corrective to a Hollywood Columbus epic, had a script from the Institute for Hispanic Culture, the personal support of Franco's second-in-command Carrero Blanco (who, as an admiral, felt a personal identification), and strong budgetary support from the government; it was a commercial disaster and the last of these epics.[18]

In the hungry 1940s, pulp fiction still reached far more people than film, and though subject to the censor, these subliterary works did not receive much attention from the authorities; they were often written by ex-Republican writers unable to publish elsewhere.[19] In the 1930s most pulps had been translations of American originals; now, with the difficulties of communication under autarky, Spanish authors wrote their own American-style thrillers, romances, horror novels, science fiction, and above all Westerns.[20] Many Spanish scholars have argued that the popularity of this theme in Spain depends on its compatibility with the Spanish epic and *romancero* traditions, each of which emphasizes male honor, the multicultural frontier, and the problem of imposing order.[21]

The most popular pulp hero—indeed, one scholar argues, the most celebrated Spanish literary character of the twentieth century, with a long afterlife in comics and film—was José Mallorquí's *El Coyote,* a reworking of the American Zorro.[22] Mallorquí transforms the politics by updating the setting: it is no longer Los Angeles under Spanish rule, but Los Angeles shortly after its incorporation into the U.S. In the first and most celebrated tale, the hero is shown defending the lands of the Spanish against "rapacious Yankees." To be sure, El Coyote takes justice into his own hands against the state, and this is the period in which the ex-Republican Mallorquí's native Catalonia was full of *maquis* fighters. But Mallorquí was not writing anything so simple as pure political allegory: genuinely fascinated with the history of the American West, he drew on a large personal library and prided himself on his verisimilitude. Dating from 1944 to the emblematic year of 1953, the 192 episodes of *El Coyote* deal with the interactions of Spaniards, Anglos, and Native Americans in great local detail, rework many U.S. myths of the West (e.g. the Alamo) from new viewpoints, and enter into such ethnographic exotica as the proper construction of a mint julep, prepared for the bemused Californian hero by a visiting southerner.[23] In *El Coyote* as well as in the hugely popular hard-boiled thrillers, the Spanish working class found unexpected political leeway and became familiar with heterogeneous aspects of U.S. culture and history that undermined the more monolithic representations of the official media. When the accommodation between the U.S. and the regime took place in 1953, both the educated and the general population already had complex expectations of the encounter.

El amigo americano

In spring 2003, Spanish bookstores gave prominent place to an essay by Carlos Elordi, a leading columnist of *El País*, the socialist-sympathizing Spanish daily of record. Its title, *The American Friend*, recalls the Wim Wenders film, an allusion by which the left frequently ironizes the diplomatic relationship between the U.S. and Spain. On the front cover, an atypically relaxed José María Aznar sits smoking a cigar on a sofa next to George W. Bush. Both men are smiling and have their feet up. On the back, a delighted Franco embraces an unenthusiastic Eisenhower. Elordi argues for a substantive continuity between the 1950s of the military pact and the new millennium of the Atlantic alliance, claiming that in each case the government's desire to be a player on equal terms led in fact to a new servility.

Eager not to be left further behind a recovering Europe, the regime made overtures to the U.S. throughout the 1940s, attempting both to claim a right to Marshall Plan reconstruction funds and, when that proved a diplomatic impossibility, to work out a bilateral arrangement through the offer of military cooperation.[24] The outbreak of the Korean War increased Spain's strategic value to the U.S., and the Madrid Pact was negotiated shortly afterwards and crowned by Eisenhower's visit in 1953, the first personal recognition of Franco by any international figure other than the Argentine dictator Perón. "Now I really can say I won the war," he is reported to have said afterwards.[25] Spain's strategic importance to the U.S. has only increased since the end of the Cold War: as the nexus between operations in Europe, Africa, the Atlantic, and the Mediterranean, Spanish bases are in constant expansion and at this writing are, with those in Germany, the U.S.'s most active.[26] The U.S. has therefore interfered little with Spanish internal affairs, keeping the relationship largely on a business footing rather than a political one.[27] Various

Latin American and Middle Eastern issues have, however, brought Spain into greater prominence as a U.S. ally since the 1990s, and the Aznar government was repaid for its support of the Iraq war with reciprocal U.S. support for its the campaign against ETA terrorism. But overwhelming public disapproval of American foreign policy has changed things at the government level. Since the Madrid bombings and the change of government in March 2004, with the subsequent withdrawal of Spanish troops from Iraq, the alliance has become more problematic and the political pendulum has swung back to Europe. Moreover, Spain's diplomatic importance to the U.S. as a secondary bridge to the European Union has diminished in view of the EU's recent enlargement. It is likely, therefore, that the next several years will see a more discreet, pragmatic working relationship.

A film of 1952, directed by Luís García Berlanga and scripted in part by the clandestine Communist Juan Antonio Bardem, offers a remarkable summation of the Spanish-American cultural imaginary at the moment of the military pact. *¡Bienvenido, Mr. Marshall!* is set in the present, at the moment when Spain is lobbying for inclusion in the Marshall Plan, and filmed in newsreel style with a voice-over narrator. A Castilian town receives a visit from the local authorities announcing that American emissaries will be coming through in order to assess local needs. "Be sure to show them your industries," says the official, an apostle of Francoist progress. Lacking any industries to display, the local notables assemble to discuss a strategy. The manager of a singer who happens to be on tour there has worked in the U.S. and knows all about it. Forget industry: they must give the Americans local color, and that means Andalusia. In haste, the villagers cover their stone façades with white plaster and their balconies with geraniums; the men take bullfighting lessons and the women learn how to dress from the visiting *folklórica*.

Having turned the town into a film set of Seville, the notables prepare the villagers to make appropriate requests from the Americans. Each lines up for a dress rehearsal before the authorities, as if on a visit to a department-store Santa Claus.[28] "What do they expect from this *piñata?*" asks the narrator. They ask: a new cow, a sewing machine, *un carro*—A Ford, you mean? asks the mayor. No, a cart for my mule, explains the farmer. The townspeople go to sleep and dream of the great day, each in a different film genre. The mayor dreams he is in a Western shootout. The aristocrat dreams he is a conquistador in a CIFESA epic, but the plot goes awry and he is cooked by American cannibals. The peasant (whose political sympathies are more complex) dreams in Soviet social-realist style of an American plane carrying the Three Kings (givers of gifts on Twelfth Night), who drop a new tractor on his field. In a sequence cut by the censor, the unmarried schoolteacher dreams of being sexually assaulted by a pair of American football players. The priest dreams of an Inquisition procession that mutates into a Klan rally; he is then taken to a film-noir police interrogation and ultimately appears before the "Committee on Un-American Activities." The following morning, with the villagers assembled to greet them, the Americans drive through without stopping.

¡*Bienvenido!* made it past the censor because it was comic, and because its satire of America was more obvious than its deeper critique of the Franco regime. It had more trouble with Americans. Although it received the Special Jury Prize at Cannes, Edward G. Robinson, chairman of the jury, protested its anti-Americanism, and a final scene of an American flag floating away in a ditch as the villagers clean up after the fracas had to be cut. More delicate was the moment when the new American ambassador who would negotiate the military pact arrived in Madrid: When his car was driven under banners on the Gran Vía reading "¡Bienvenido, Mister Marshall!" he panicked and was not easily reassured that this was only publicity for a film.[29]

In fact, the film's assessment of the American presence proved prophetic. For many years, aid was largely limited to military assistance and to American surplus agricultural products (many remember the importance of American powdered milk, associated in the cultural imaginary with the bosomy stars of the period's films). Spanish commentators tend to emphasize how cheaply the U.S. bought its bases. Overtly described as a pact between equals—Franco pointed out that the Americans had at last come round to his early recognition of the Communist threat, thus validating his regime's existence[30]—the agreement in fact featured secret provisions that ceded Spanish sovereignty.[31] And Spain was treated more like a client than an ally, ranked not with Europe but with its own former colonies and their "friendly tyrants." With the military pact came U.S. demands for economic reforms, but there was never any American call for political reform. Indeed, U.S. officials remarked on the convenience of having a population that did not have to be kept informed of, for example, the flying of planes carrying nuclear missiles over populated areas.[32] This became an international embarrassment in 1966 when four missiles fell from a plane onto the territory of Palomares in Almería province: the zone where three fell is still contaminated and the fourth, which fell over water, eluded the efforts of American search teams and was eventually recovered with the advice of a local fisherman. Though massive local protest met with silence from the media, eventually, in response to both it and the concerns of European tourists and fruit importers, the U.S. Ambassador and Spain's Minister of Information had to be photographed together in bathing suits to prove that the water was safe. Spain was a staging ground for the cultural Cold War: Radio Liberty, the American channel aimed at the Soviet republics, broadcast from the Costa Brava. But Spain itself was hardly a target for American public relations.

The record of American government cultural initiatives in Spain is ambiguous, and hardly visible in Spanish public memory. Viewed cynically, there was no need for cultural diplomacy. Public opinion on foreign policy was of minimal importance in a dictatorship, and the U.S. had no interest in destabilizing the Franco regime; moreover Franco could be trusted to counter communist propaganda on his own. Practically, there was the matter of finding local collaborators or even an audience. Until the liberalizations of the mid 1960s, both the universities and the Consejo Superior de Investigaciones Científicas were controlled by the National-Catholic faction of the regime, which was eager to stamp out all foreign intellectual influences.[33] Under censorship, there was no autonomous public sphere in which contact could be cultivated with the intellectual opposition to the regime, a situation exacerbated by the high levels of illiteracy and relative poverty of resources in Spain. Moreover, this opposition looked elsewhere. The communists were culturally internationalist; the socialists were oriented toward Europe, with a strong investment in French cultural models; and the liberals, sympathetic to Anglo-American ideas and interlocutors, took by definition no activist interest in culture.

As bilateral cooperation between Spain and the U.S. increased, Spain was, of course, incorporated into the Fulbright program, becoming indeed one of its most important beneficiaries.[34] Cultural cooperation, with a focus on academic exchanges, has been mentioned in all renewals of the 1953 pact.[35] American influence on Spanish academia has been far greater than one might guess from the discourse of public intellectuals, though technical and administrative fields, including the more applied social sciences, are less shy of acknowledging the fact.

U.S. power continues to be associated with the long stability of the Franco regime, and with the conversion of the *dictadura* into a *dictablanda* with consumer comforts to mitigate its political frustrations. After the press liberalizations of 1966, when international news was no longer censored, young Spaniards often protested U.S. policy both in itself and as a proxy for that of the regime. Spaniards looking to U.S. influence to open up their own government were strongly disillusioned by the Vietnam War and still more so by the never-forgotten CIA-backed coup in Chile. The students' embrace of the U.S. counterculture in this period indicates simultaneously a real international solidarity, a desire to participate in Europe by participating in "1968," and the oblique beginning of what became eventually open revolt against their own government.[36] The political left of the 80s, rising out of these earlier student movements, celebrated Europe, not America, as the future of Spain: a practical enough stance given Spain's need to enter and then consolidate its place in the European Community.

In course, the interests of state fostered political convergence between right and left, as with the Socialist reconciliation to NATO membership and the eventual embrace of the euro by the post-Francoist Partido Popular. Broader public opinion has generally been more skeptical of American intentions: the

NATO referendum, for example, was tense, with the populations of Catalonia and Madrid voting No. Moreover, there has been substantial steady opposition to the American bases, with the annual marches at Rota and Torrejón now almost a festive tradition.[37] The balance of conscious anti-Americanism and structural Americanization can be summed up by a Catalan protest song that is rapidly losing its irony as the young forget its origins: "Americans, foteu el camp" (Americans, get the fuck out of here), sung to the tune of "When the Saints Go Marching In."

From Imaginary Friends to Imagined Communities

In 1975, during the tense months of Franco's long final illness, the Catalan *cantautor* Jaume Sisa released an album called *Qualsevol nit pot sortir el sol* (Any night now the sun might come out). The title song is narrated by a man having a party in order to "send our sadnesses up in smoke." In a subdued melody he invites the guests in, calling each by name: they are figures from Catalan children's folklore and, to a greater extent, from mostly American mass culture: Donald Duck, Frankenstein, King Kong, Superman, Tarzan's chimp Cheetah, and fairy tale heroines known through Disney versions, as well as Astérix and such Spanish characters as "Taxi Key," an American detective in a popular radio serial. The refrain offers all these foreign guests a traditional hospitable formula with a doubtful coda: "My house is your house—that is, if houses belong to anybody." Later in the song we hear the discreet popping of champagne corks and recall that Barcelona ran out of champagne on the day Franco died.

The song records the infantilization of postwar Spaniards and their forced refuge in the fantasy world of popular consumer culture. The friends who kept them company during the years of isolation were fictional heroes, not real foreigners and not serious makers of art or ideas. It recalls a key theme of popular song in the postwar period: the loved one who is abroad, either an exile or a foreigner. In multiple verses, the narrator crams figure after figure into the house, frantic for contact in that surreal period of waiting for an event as improbable as the sun emerging in darkness.[38]

Figures from American mass culture provide emotional support for the protagonists of several Spanish films of the Transition. Pilar Miró's *Gary Cooper que estás en los cielos* (Gary Cooper Who Art in Heaven, 1980) traces a day in the life of a television producer—evocatively, in Spanish, a *realizadora*—who is waiting for a cancer diagnosis. Throughout the day she clutches as her talisman a crumpled photo of the actor cut out from a magazine in her childhood. Better-known and more complex is Victor Érice's *The Spirit of the Beehive* (1973), set in a Castilian village in 1941. The child protagonist sees the film *Frankenstein* when a traveling cinema truck visits the village. Fascinated by the monster and too young to understand either fiction or mortality, she identifies him with a Republican maquis fighter she finds in the woods; she brings him food and her father's clothes until the villagers capture and kill him. The film plays with the emotional absence of Ana's real parents, each absorbed in the prewar past, and her greater communion with the imaginary monster, created by a man whose name recalls "Franco."[39]

Another variant on the theme comes in Francisco Regueiro's film of 1993, *Madregilda,* set in 1947 when the Madrid screening of *Gilda* caused a Falangist street demonstration, while those who went to see it were threatened from the pulpits with excommunication. The film's epoch-marking impact in Spain was conditioned not only by the Spanish sense of sexual exclusion—rumors circulated that the censors had cut a scene in which Rita Hayworth danced naked and drank champagne from a shoe[40]—but by the common knowledge of Hayworth's Spanish ethnicity, disguised by a studio name change. *Madregilda* shows Franco plotting to bring Hayworth back to Madrid to make propaganda films, and another Falangist denouncing her as one of the deported communists responsible for stealing the famous Spanish gold supposedly lying in Moscow vaults: she is the focus of all manner of imagined abundances. The protagonist is once more a child, whose mother is dead—murdered, as it turns out, by his father. He sneaks in to see the film, and thereafter Gilda appears to him as his mother. At the end, she comes back to life to assassinate Franco, but nothing changes: the generals install a double in office, and life and the regime go on.[41]

The critic José María Castellet theorized the postwar relationship to mass culture in a celebrated 1970 anthology of young poets: this, he said, was the first generation of intellectuals in Spain to have grown up without literature as their primary cultural input. At that date he could not spell out the equally important point that they had grown up without much by way of realities either. Rather, as Manuel Vázquez Montalbán's *Crónica sentimental de España* records in detail, the primary source of rich emotional experience was mass culture, between the offerings of Hollywood and the melancholy or boisterous mass "folklore" produced at home. The poets anthologized by Castellet, reacting to the grim neorealism of literature in the 1940s and 50s,[42] return to the "filmic writing" and collage techniques of the 1920s avant-garde[43]—the last period in which Spanish culture participated in a peaceful world community. This poetry is almost hysterically intertextual: like Sisa's partygiver, it shoves through the door everyone that it can. Castellet's introduction itself exemplifies a tendency that can be seen in much subsequent Spanish humanistic scholarship, to cite every single one of the best international theoretical authorities. One can see both the poets and the critics weaving a virtual social network for themselves, a safety net they hope will hold them up in the cosmopolitan world of the avant-garde despite the precariousness of their national position. Castellet himself aptly characterizes his native Barcelona—in the 1960s the cultural capital of the country—as "pequeño vanguardista." Furthermore, Catalan culture since the nineteenth century has urgently sought to claim participation in European modernity, with an anxiety that Pierre Bourdieu did indeed characterize as petit-bourgeois.[44] The appropriations from foreign high culture or alternative American popular culture were strategies of distinction and of belonging—of rejecting one milieu and claiming another—but here had clear political as well as class resonances.[45]

A more optimistic vision emerges from the end of Sisa's 1975 song, which any *pequeño-vanguardista* Catalan of the period can still sing by heart. The lyrics suggest that the imagined community of mass culture could foster the real thing. At the end, as the champagne is opened, the speaker looks around, reassured, and says, "Now no one is missing—or perhaps yes...." and he invites the listener in.

The "Cine-Clubs" and other cultural organizations of the period did indeed shelter emergent political communities, fostering sociability in times when public assembly was tightly controlled and, eventually, providing a cover for clandestine activity. Choral singing, particularly important in Catalonia, cultivated a sense of collective force, and when Catalan political songs were outlawed, songs from the American folksong revival, learned from records, were substituted. Pete Seeger, and later Bob Dylan, provided models for the *nova cançó* that emerged in the 1960s, and today any nostalgic dinner of old student militants ends with the singing of such authentic Catalan classics as "Puf, el drac màgic" over the cognac.[46]

In the broader Spanish context, American mass culture may well have eased the difficult process of national reconciliation by providing a neutral ground on which at least the younger generation could meet.[47] Very little space at home was free of divisive regional, class, and ideological resonances, and when the consensus was that only a "pact of forgetting" would permit democratic transition, mutual imaginary friends could facilitate introductions across face-to-face social boundaries:

També pots venir si vols	You can come too, if you like
T'esperem, hi ha lloc per a tots.	We're waiting for you, there's room for everyone.
El temps no compta ni l'espai	Time doesn't matter, nor space
Qualsevol nit pot sortir el sol.	Any night now the sun might come out.

Recognition and Seduction

Amigos para siempre
Means you'll always be my friend

Amics per sempre
Means a love that cannot end
Friends for life
Not just a summer or a spring
Amigos para siempre…[48]

Here is Barcelona fusion: a trilingual slogan on a ground of English in a song of vaguely Latinate rhythm from the leading composer on Broadway, sung in stanzas exchanged between an Iberian opera singer and an Anglo-American pop star. Not least, it offers the promise of eternal love.

The tourist romance of Franco's Spain, like the defense pact, was based on a fiction of equality. The economic superiority of the tourist was balanced by Spain's abundant natural resources of wine, women, and song. Vázquez Montalbán cites a macaronic pop song of the early 60s that satirizes the two parallel fictions.[49] A male American tourist is wandering through the capital:

Americano: Hello, hello,
ya ni la atómica ni el radar ni el Efe Be I
han de servir contra el fuego concentrado
de la mirada de una chica de Madrid.

American: Hello, hello,
now neither the Bomb nor radar nor the FBI
can hold out against the concentrated fire
of the eyes of a girl from Madrid.

But no one brought up under the repressions of the regime could believe in Spain's hedonistic capabilities any more than in its military capabilities, and Spanish narrations of the tourist romance exhibit simultaneous hopefulness and skepticism. In films with titles such as *Un beso en el puerto* (A Kiss in the Port), a rich American woman is swept away by a macho "Latin lover" and his country. A real-life equivalent, much celebrated in the *prensa del cor*,[50] was the 1950 affair of Ava Gardner with bullfighter/film star Mario Cabré, for whom she left Frank Sinatra. Cabré, who had "exportable good looks" and stood 15 centimeters above the average height of Spanish males in the period, according to Vázquez Montalbán, was the nation's greatest hope of competing in a Technicolor world—at least until Sinatra reasserted himself. "The triumphs of Mario Cabré were the triumphs of all Spaniards," and set the pattern by which famous Spanish men tend to marry American starlets,[51] most recently instanced in Antonio Banderas's desertion of his Spanish wife for Melanie Griffith. In real life, male fantasies focused on the more visible Swedish tourist, but the fictions intensified the geopolitical implications of sexual encounter, with deprived Spanish manhood finding both abundance and validation in the voluptuous figure of the American woman. Today a bronze statue of a near-naked Ava overlooks the port of Tossa de Mar, in enduring municipal gratitude for the effect of her film *Pandora and the Flying Dutchman* on the local tourist industry. As Franco said in his speech explaining the 1953 defense pact to the public: "If we have to dance, let's dance with the prettiest and richest girl there."[52]

A comic novel from 1969 by Ramon Sender, a war exile then teaching at a U.S. university, plays with the theme. *La tesis de Nancy* deals with a California ex-cheerleader who comes to Andalusia to write a dissertation on the Romanies, has an affair with one and is led by her linguistic and cultural naïveté into various misadventures out of which she rises completely unaffected, a Daisy Miller who triumphs.[53] The other literary model is, of course, Mérimée's "Carmen," another story of an archaeologist who discovers that the Andalusian past is not past after all. Now, however, the metropolitan evaluation is given not by a French male but by an American female, and the balance of power has shifted entirely. Nancy's lover's machismo is as comically ineffectual as Don José's is tragic. Misinterpreting her as having declared her infidelity, he determines to kill her and himself. Discovering his error just in time, he scratches his head, once more bewildered Spanish manhood in the face of imperturbable American femininity. Much recent anthropological literature on the cult of male honor has noticed its prevalence in socially marginal populations; here we see it wholly deflated as a mere object of antiquarian and erotic curiosity, no threat to the men or even the women of the West.

An attempt to get out of this gendered geopolitical dynamic is one of the points of the famous Spanish *destape* (uncovering): the sexual revolution of the transition to democracy. While it was certainly sex for its own sake, the "mobile sexuality" of the Transition[54] was also the first step out of several Francoist straitjackets, including the relationship with America. Transvestism—a key Transition symbol of emergence into modern freedoms[55]—became a way of evading the preoccupation with a less than adequate national virility. But many male intellectuals on the Spanish left did not escape it, and the more explicitly political films, novels, and songs of the period draw frequently on rape as a metaphor, preferring revenge to freedom and relieving general frustrations through vividly imagined particular acts of sadism. Juan Goytisolo's 1970 novel *La Reivindicación del Conde Don Julián* (The Vindication of Count Julian) proposes a violently sexualized reorientation of the national identity. The Spanish protagonist, whose name, Don Julian, is that of the "traitor" held responsible for the medieval Muslim conquest of Spain, finds his cultural roots and his sexuality in Morocco.[56] But he is always looking back across the Straits of Gibraltar, where Don Álvaro, a regime intellectual and proxy for Franco, drones about the national glories unheeded by Spaniards caught in the delights of the American-led "consumer society." This figure of Spanish male impotence is countered in Morocco by that of "Mrs. Putifar," a middle-aged, full-bosomed, ghastly American tourist: Rita/Ava/Nancy gone to seed. She is assaulted in the marketplace by the phallic creature of an Orientalized snake-charmer, then grotesquely defiled by all present: a subaltern, atavistic revenge anticipating the apocalyptic fate Goytisolo wishes upon "stepmother" Spain and her bastard sons at the hands of Muslim manhood.[57]

After the transition to democracy and the international success of the Madrid *movida*, and with the approach of 1992 as the Year of Spain, uniting the Barcelona Olympics, the Seville Expo, Madrid as Cultural Capital of Europe, and the Columbus Quincentenary, it became possible to imagine a happier and more egalitarian trans-Atlantic encounter, at least in the cultural sphere. Antoni Miralda, one of a large number of artists who divided their time between New York and Spain in the 1980s, dreamed up an embodiment of the new relationship, harking back to the symbolism of a hundred years before: a marriage between the Statue of Liberty and the Columbus statue in the port of Barcelona, intended to celebrate "cultural fusion."[58] Miralda organized a global, multi-year series of *happenings*[59] beginning with the Statue of Liberty's centennial celebration in 1986 and culminating in a Vegas wedding on Valentine's Day, 1992. The betrothal ceremony in New York featured the two mayors as fathers; but in the engagement announcements, true to Francoist tradition, the majestic American bride had to be photographed carefully so as not to embarrass her undergrown Iberian fiancé.

The American reception of these performances was bemused at best,[60] and the main event of the "Honeymoon Project" fizzled, as have so many trans-Atlantic romances, over logistical and financial difficulties. Nevertheless, the endeavor bespoke the eternal optimism of a particular segment of the Spanish and especially Catalan cultural community. Miralda has brought Mediterranean festival exuberance to unlikely places, parading giant steers and sheaves of wheat in Nebraska and organizing a Tea Cod Party in Boston, and in performances in Miami has done his best to sweeten the conquest of the Americas by celebrating its culinary consequences. His latest endeavor, Barcelona's "Food Culture Museum,"[61] synthesizes all his previous work in presenting traditional and fast food, communion and consumption, as not merely compatible but capable of fusing into global multicultural bliss.

Both Catalonia and the Basque Country have been especially tempted by the have-it-all ethos of postmodernism as the cultural salve to globalization. Each has had an industrial economy to rescue; each has a small culture to defend and promote; each continues, with some reason, to distrust Madrid; and each has therefore been especially eager for American economic investment and American cultural recognition, two sides of the same coin in this framework. The globalization guru Manuel Castells has singled out his native Catalonia as a model for small cultures in the new "information society": it has become a purely cultural nation that requires no state and participates eagerly in every available political and economic network.[62] Bill Clinton, in a post-9/11 speech given at the invitation of multinational consulting firms installed in Barcelona, spoke with still greater enthusiasm of Catalonia's open society and eclectic culture, concluding with a soundbite to send his audience into ecstasies: "The future will be Catalan or Taliban."[63]

Intellectuals, however, continue to mistrust so very unequal a love affair, seeing recognition as insufficient compensation for lost autonomy. In a ferocious chronicle of the creation of the Guggenheim Museum in Bilbao (1996), Joseba Zulaika develops the metaphor of seduction, defining globalization as the promise that is forgotten once the fruits of union are enjoyed.[64] Zulaika shows how the Basque government was led to believe that it had to compete against multiple European cities for the Guggenheim franchise, inducing it to come up with a huge sum of public money that in fact was desperately needed to shore up the overstretched Guggenheim operation in New York.[65] Both Thomas Krens, the Guggenheim director, and Frank Gehry, architect of the museum's now celebrated titanium silhouette, spoke with fervor of the love at first sight that Bilbao inspired in them, and the Partido Nacionalista Vasco, delighted to see the adjective "Basque" coupled in the world press with any substantive other than "terrorism," was easy prey for their blandishments.[66] The Guggenheim has, of course, been a great success and the centerpiece of a large-scale architectural revitalization of this decayed industrial capital; but there may be some bitterness in the fact that while billowing titanium look-a-likes by Gehry are now popping up all over the United States, the Bilbao building is already exhibiting structural problems.

Market Imperialism: Spain as a Cultural Great Power?

The market seduces both ways. Spaniards are drawn in to desire new things, and so one sees the gradual "Americanization" of consumption, from tastes in alcohol to domestic architecture. But the rule of the market also forces Spain to seduce, to cultivate distinctive attractions—to brand itself.

Two hundred years as a tourist destination has made this move easier for Spain than for some countries, although most Spaniards are weary of playing Carmen. *¡Bienvenido, Mr. Marshall!* had already remarked upon Spain's self-folklorization in relation to American expectations. There is plenty of paella and flamenco still on offer, at levels of sophistication calculated for each taste segment of the tourist market. But accommodations to foreign tastes have diversified. Facing competition from cheaper Mediterranean beaches, democratic Spain has had to develop its inland attractions for more specialized audiences: adventure sports, cultural patrimony, arts festivals, ecotourism, etc. One notable example of this has been Spain's extensive rediscovery of its Jewish heritage, for which the 1992 quincentary of the expulsions provided the historical excuse, but the potential of the American Jewish tourist market virtually all the incentive.

Spanish cultural exports have changed along with the tourist attractions. As elsewhere in southern Europe, "folk" and medieval music are being repositioned for the benefit of a global/American audience as "world" (sexier, more African, as in the band Radio Tarifa), New Age (the bestselling "Chant" album of the monks of Santo Domingo de Silos), or rock fusion (as with the Gypsy Kings, who furnished the song for a Burger King commercial in the early 1990s). Spain is even producing blockbuster novelists, such as the much-translated Arturo Pérez-Reverte, who draws on esoterica of the Spanish artistic and religious past to produce thrillers suitable for airplane reading by a cosmopolitan audience.

An alternative strategy for the prestige market has been not to exoticize but to Europeanize Spanish cultural exports through an emphasis on pure design: this has been strongly driven by both the desire to move upmarket and, domestically, the need to avoid divisive historical resonances. Examples of such exports include the works of the architects Ricardo Bofill, Rafael Moneo, and Santiago Calatrava (who has built a museum revitalizing old industrial Milwaukee to balance Gehry's revitalization of old industrial Bilbao). The work of these, according to Manuel Castells, exemplifies the new architecture of nodes and flows that will replace the defined spaces of the prenetwork society.[67]

Haute cuisine was the greatest success of the 1990s. Basque and Catalan chefs, notably Ferran Adrià of El Bulli on the Costa Brava, have for several years provided the inspiration for the "deconstructionist" avant-garde in the U.S.: chefs such as Charlie Trotter declare that Spanish cooks lead the world in culinary innovation. Adrià notes that his work is not a continuation of traditional Catalan cuisine, but rather the revision of the great European tradition stemming from Escoffier; specifically, a post–nouvelle cuisine.[68] This *cocina de autor,* consecrated in 2003 by a profusely illustrated cover story in the *New York Times Magazine* proclaiming Spain "the new France," is in continual motion.[69] Extrapolating from cuisine to film, architecture, nightlife, business taxation, and foreign policy, the author draws a dramatic contrast between France as Old Europe—stodgy, blasé, exhausted—and Spain as the Young Europe of passion, hard work, and unbridled invention. The *Times* article noted that Barcelona now provides the scenario for films about Americans abroad, as Paris used to—Whit Stilman and Susan Seidelman have both created examples of the genre—and now the French themselves are going to Barcelona to lose their inhibitions, as seen in the 2003 hit movie *L'Auberge Espagnole.*

The day after the article came out, *La Vanguardia* ran a story both ironic and grateful: "The prestigious newspaper itself undoes itself in praise of Barcelona and Catalan cuisine."[70] The Barcelona paper noted that the apparent shift in the longstanding Francophilia of the American elite provided an odd contrast to a recent sense of discouragement locally, citing a conference of Catalan businessmen at Harvard to discuss the city's image problem. This inferiority complex is longstanding in Catalonia, and in fact has generated astonishing cultural wealth: a tradition of hypermodernity extending from Gaudí to the Barcelona Olympics, which set the standard at which all subsequent games have aimed (both Atlanta and Salt Lake City brought in consultants from Barcelona). Any American who spends time in Barcelona has had the experience of being taken on an all-night crawl through the *bars de disseny* (designer bars), each higher-concept than the last and none with anything so mundane as a bathroom identifiable as such—and, as bewilderment mounts, being asked at the last, hopefully, "It's like New York, isn't it?"

Beneath the boom of auteur cuisine lies a deeper and broader penetration of the American market, inaugurated by the Catalan wine industry in the 1980s. Casa Torres has been especially savvy in promoting both its wines and Catalan cuisine to American food writers. Several influential cookbooks were published in the same years that Torres expanded its production to California, and Freixenet and Codorniu became the best-selling brands of sparkling wine in the U.S. Traditional Catalan cuisine is much appreciated by the Slow Food movement, but the real Spanish success has been the more readily identifiable formula of *tapas*, assimilable into American "grazing" habits and facilitated by the now general availability in the U.S. of manchego cheese, sherry vinegar, Ribera del Duero wines, and so on.

Although the Socialist government of the 1980s was strongly attracted to the French ministry-of-culture model, it is unhappily clear that the future of Spanish culture lies in market competition. The Partido Popular government of 1996–2004 embraced this proposition unabashedly, providing increasingly limited subventions to those projects already seen as commercially viable. But the successes of the 80s fostered the market ambitions of the 90s. In international politics Aznar may have aspired to be no more than Bush's favorite dance partner, but in the cultural sphere the language of imperial rivalry was returning. Spain once provided the raw materials to foreign cultural manufacturers (as in the nineteenth century, when local cultural products could not compete with the *Don Carlos* of Schiller and Verdi, much less the *Carmen* of Mérimée and Bizet). Today Spain is a global cultural producer.

A recent conference asked "Is Spain a cultural power?" and concluded that, indeed, it is at least a *potencia en potencia*.[71] Spain has a major world language, as most of the participants noted, one that is rapidly gaining ground in the United States itself, to say nothing of the demographic and economic promise of Latin America. The Real Academia Española has been active in the global promotion of Spanish and especially interested in securing its official status in Puerto Rico.[72] By 1987 Spain was the fourth-largest producer of books in the world,[73] and not just for *la Hispanidad*: 44 percent of Spanish book exports go to Europe.[74] Spanish publishers are setting up multinational operations and, notes the head of the Spanish publishers' guild, Spain is better positioned in Latin America than is the U.S., having maintained its presence and offered credit to distributors through periods of crisis when U.S. publishers moved out.[75] By contrast, the Spanish music industry is not well-integrated with the five dominant multinationals; but, they insist, there is potential here as Spanish music integrates itself into the exploding global "Latin music" market, now consolidated through the creation of the "Latin Grammys," for which the Spanish Sociedad General de Autores y Editores was a major lobbyist.[76]

To be sure, a major point of the conference was to lobby the Aznar government for greater support in promoting Spanish culture abroad and fostering its development at home: Spain is not there yet.[77] But the conclusion of the conference was that "the Spanish language is our petroleum:"[78] Spain, as mother of the language and a more developed cultural purveyor than Latin America, is in a position to dominate not just the production but, more importantly, the distribution of Spanish-language world culture.

Other Spanish entrepreneurs have concluded that language need not limit them, and that it is not the revival of empire but the "glocal" model that can serve them best: here the Catalans, as usual, are quick to embrace America as an escape from Spain.[79] One notable success is a franchise called "Pans & Company," founded in 1991, which by 1999 controlled 51 percent of the Spanish fast food market. Its secret: "to apply the marketing models of U.S. ... chains to a product offering much closer to the customer."[80] The assembly-line versions of traditional Catalan sandwiches are now enjoyed in Portugal and Italy, and the company obviously looks to move farther: the name, with its strategic ampersand, can be read in Catalan as meaning "Breads and Friends," but it works in English as well. Perhaps prophetic is that the menu has been internationalizing itself over the years and the Catalan language is disappearing from their publicity; my Catalan friends pronounce the name in English.

One prominent Spanish cultural export does not bode well for a new Spanish empire: the movie star. Antonio Banderas "arrived" when he was declared "the sexiest man alive" by Madonna in the film *Truth or Dare;* shortly afterward, he moved to Hollywood. Next came Penelope Cruz; likely to follow are Sergi López and Javier Bardem. Critics have noted that Banderas brought his omnisexual appeal—the aura of the *movida*—into his first American films, but is now being reduced to the macho Latin lover stereotype; Cruz is likewise being disciplined into a normative Mediterranean femininity.[81] Their triumph in the U.S. has won an ambivalent response in Spain. Their every success is celebrated in the media as a triumph of superior Spanish sex appeal, but there is both concern that individual success means abandoning the national project and a rueful sense that culturally Spain will continue to be known only for the quality of its raw materials.

Pedro Almodóvar's appeal is another matter, and perhaps the best indicator for the future. More than anyone else he has created a Spanish brand in film and design,[82] which incorporates American pop culture, stereotypical Spanish passions, and the frivolous hypermodernity of the 1980s into a distinctively local synthesis. Almodóvar's look has been imitated in the U.S., but the "libertarian sexuality" central to his work means that he can neither be fully coopted by the conservative American market nor ever achieve a mass success in it. Almodóvar will stay Spanish, enjoying a substantial *succès d'estime* and a certain commercial success internationally. His followers—the more vulgar Bigas Luna, the more orthodox Fernando Trueba, rewarded with an Oscar for *Belle Epoque*—will do well, if not splendidly. He has founded not an empire, but a secure niche in the global market.

Conclusion: Is Spain Different?

Spain looks much like the rest of Europe now, with respect to Americanization among other things. Like the rest of the wealthy world, including the U.S. itself, Spain is moving toward a split-level globalization.

At the highest socioeconomic level, an elite with no incentive to resist economic globalization will produce a distinctive, high-quality high culture, both eclectic and locally marked, and consume a thoroughly cosmopolitan high culture, all increasingly within a market framework rather than one of government subsidies—which means that Spanish cuisine and design will do better than literature and possibly film.

For the majority, changes in the organization of work will continue to foster the Americanization of everyday life (e.g., in eating habits) and therefore also the cultural path of least resistance: the consumption of American/multinational mass culture. Those aspects of local culture that are not already museified will become so. Cultures of resistance will also continue to globalize, drawing both on "world" cultures and U.S. subcultures.

Does the different history make any difference then, or not?

One Spanish argument is that it happened there first. Spain was globalized *avant la lettre* because of the Francoist special relationship with U.S. capital[83] and its exclusion from the EEC. Spain has been in certain respects a Wild West economy since 1953, and capital has had comparatively free rein in the cultural sphere. Spain did not participate in the postwar development of the "European" model now seen as under threat, although in the Socialist decade much of the apparatus of European cultural policy and the European welfare state was quickly acquired. Given the overall Americanizing trajectory from Franco to Aznar, the surprise is not that the European model is being lost in Spain, but that it became so quickly and deeply rooted in the structure of (some) institutions and in the hearts of (some of) the public. The electoral change of 2004 confirms this attachment, but is unlikely to bring radical reorientation.

By the same token, Spain became postmodern *avant la lettre* because the consumer society preceded political liberalization,[84] meaning that freedom was experienced as consumer choice and political identities had to be shaped through the manipulation of cultural imagery. Long before Daniel Bell and Francis Fukuyama, Francoist intellectuals were prophesying that the liberal consumer economy would bring about the end of ideology and history.[85] Moreover, because of its history as Europe's internal Other, Spain began packaging its national identity for both native and foreign consumption as early as the 1760s and has done so without interruption ever since;[86] this and dictatorship have made Spaniards long accustomed to the simulacrum as a way of life.[87] And the demands of Spain's lively minority cultures have further provoked the center's tolerance for global mass cultures in lieu of the fissile precedent set by the "cultural exception." The divisive potential of culture identified with a social location and a form of life has long fostered the trivialization of culture and (as in the U.S.) its identification with leisure and consumption. Franco's "culture of evasion" proved still more useful during the delicate transition to democracy, and today the market model exacerbates this long-nurtured preference for hedonistic, undemanding cultural products: "cultura *light.*" Berlanga, director of *¡Bienvenido!*, declared in his old age that not so much had changed.[88] Once, he said, the regime censored Spanish creators. Now they censor themselves for the market.

Notes

Acknowledgements
Many thanks for suggestions and assistance to the Oxford conference attendants, Lorda Brichs, Cristina Sánchez Carretero, Josep Maria Solé i Sabaté, and especially Lluís Calvo i Calvo. All translations are mine unless otherwise noted.

1. It is important to insist that this is a discursive isolation from modernity, though political isolation has been real as well. Revisionist historians of Spain insist that the country participated in general European historical processes throughout the modern and contemporary periods—though, to be sure, their work emerged in the post-transition moment of intense discursive Europeanization. See for example David Ringrose, *Europe, and the "Spanish Miracle" 1700–1900* (Cambridge: Cambridge University Press, 1996) and José Álvarez Junco and Adrian Shubert, eds., *Spanish History Since 1808* (London: Arnold, 2000).
2. Manuel Vázquez Montalbán, *La penetración americana en España* (Madrid: Cuadernos para el Diálogo, 1974), 365.
3. José Álvarez Junco, a leading revisionist historian, gives an excellent summary of the *leyenda* and its romantic but equally reductionist antitheses of anarchist and/or traditionalist Spain in the introduction to Álvarez Junco and Shubert, *Spanish History Since 1808*, 1–17.

See also his account of the impact of 1898 on Spanish national identity in Juan Pan-Montojo, José Alvarez Junco, Manuel Pérez Ledesma, Juan Pro Ruiz, Christopher Schmidt-Nowara, and Carlos Serrano, *Más se perdió en Cuba: España, 1898 y la crisis de fin de siglo* (Madrid: Alianza, 1998), 405–75.

4.   Pan-Montojo et al., *Más se perdió en Cuba,* 336, 405.

5.   Lily Litvak, "Latinos y anglosajones: Una polémica de la España de fin de siglo," in Lily Litvak, ed., *España 1900: Modernismo, anarquismo y fin de siglo* (Barcelona: Anthropos, 1990), 155–99.

6.   Rafael Alberti, *13 bandas y 48 estrellas* (Madrid: Espasa-Calpe, 1985 [1935]), 64.

7.   The word *americanismo,* meaning enthusiasm for things American, dates from 1845 in Spain; by Ganivet's time it refers to the U.S. specifically. *Americanización* and the grammatically related forms, also referring to the U.S. rather than to the Americas in general, are documented from 1903. See Real Academia Española, *Diccionario de la lengua española* (Madrid: Real Academia Española, 1999), vol.1, 818–19.

8.   Ángel Ganivet, cited in Juan Carlos Rodríguez, "A Sad Diagnosis of a Sad Town: Granada and the Dream of the Recumbent Woman," in Joan Ramon Resina, ed., *Iberian Cities* (New York: Routledge, 2001), 123.

9.   Cited in Jesús Torrecilla, *La imitación colectiva: Modernidad versus autenticidad en la literatura española* (Madrid: Gredos, 1996), 134.

10.   See Jacqueline Urla, "'We are all Malcolm X!' Negu Gorriak, Hip-Hop and the Basque Political Imaginary," in Tony Mitchell, ed., *Global Noise: Rap and Hip-Hop Outside the U.S.A.* (Middletown: Wesleyan University Press, 2001).

11.   E.g. José María Castellet, ed., *Nueve novísimos poetas españoles* (Barcelona: Barral Editores, 1970); Miguel Morey, *Deseo de ser piel roja: Novela familiar* (Barcelona: Editorial Anagrama, 1994).

12.   The most famous Spanish camp survivor is the novelist Jorge Semprún, later Minister of Culture in the González government and a chief proponent of the French model. The sense of betrayal is particularly strong in Catalonia and the Basque Country. Of the 5,000 Spanish Republicans who died in Mauthausen, a third were Catalan exiles deported by the Pétain government. The Partido Nacionalista Vasco, still today the dominant party in the Basque Country, collaborated in exile with American intelligence during World War II and through the 1950s. See Carlos Elordi, *El amigo americano. De Franco a Aznar: Una adhesión inquebrantable* (Madrid: Temas de Hoy, 2003), 17–19.

13.   Carlton J. H. Hayes, *The United States and Spain: An Interpretation* (New York: Sheed and Ward, 1951); Arthur P. Whitaker, *Spain and Defense of the West: Ally and Liability* (New York: Harper, 1961); Fernando Guirao, *Spain and the Reconstruction of Western Europe, 1945–57: Challenge and Response* (Basingstoke: St. Martin's, 1998), 4.

14.   Whitaker, *Spain and Defense of the West,* 26–27.

15.   Quoted in Carmen Martín Gaite, *Usos amorosos de la postguerra española* (Barcelona: Anagrama, 1987), 29.

16.   "Dos materialismos frente a frente," *La Hora, semanario de los estudiantes españoles* 2, no. 1 (1948): 5.

17.   Raymond Carr, *Spain 1808–1975,* 2nd ed. (New York: Clarendon, 1982), 766.

18.   Rob Stone, *Spanish Cinema* (Harlow: Longman, Essex, 2002), 38–39.

19.   Fernando Martínez de la Hidalga, ed., *La novela popular en España* (Madrid: Ediciones Robel, 2000), 34. Compare blacklisted authors of McCarthyism such as Howard Fast, who also found an outlet writing genre fiction.

20.   Ibid.

21.   José Francisco Álvarez Macías, *La novela popular en España: José Mallorquí* (Seville: University of Seville, 1972); Álvarez Junco and Shubert, *Spanish History Since 1808,* 6.

22. Martínez de la Hidalga, *La novela popular en España,* 37. The *El Coyote* stories were translated into fourteen languages, an international success almost unparallelled in Francoist Spain and hardly equaled by any Spanish writer since Cervantes and Lope. (Only the romance novels of Corín Tellado, another product of the 1940s, have outsold both *El Coyote* and Cervantes; ibid., 37). The most recent remake is the 1998 *La Vuelta del Coyote,* from the director Mario Camus; perhaps a commentary on the pro-business, pro-American, ecologically dubious turn of Spain in the 1990s?

23. Álvarez Macías, *La novela popular en España,* 183–96.

24. Whitaker, *Spain and Defense of the West,* 1961. European resistance to undermining the democratizing intent of the Plan was more important than American unwillingness in determining Spain's final exclusion, but Spanish memory is rather inclined to assume that the Americans would not pay for anything they didn't have to. See Guirao, *Spain and the Reconstruction of Western Europe,* 195, and Hayes, *The United States and Spain.*

25. Elordi, *El amigo americano,* 15

26. Felipe Sahagún, "Spain and the United States: Military Primacy," in Richard Gillespie and Richard Youngs, eds., *Spain: The European and International Challenges* (London: Cass, 2001), 157–61.

27. Ibid.; Elordi, *El amigo americano,* 51–55.

28. Virginia Higginbotham, *Spanish Film Under Franco* (Austin: University of Texas Press, 1988), 45–46.

29. For useful discussions of this much-loved film, see ibid., 44–46; Tatjana Pavlovic', "';Bienvenido, Mr. Marshall!' and the Renewal of Spanish Cinema," in G. Cabello-Castellet, J. Martí-Olivella, and G. H. Wood, eds., *Cine-Lit II: Essays on Hispanic Film and Fiction* (Portland: Oregon State University Press, 1991), 169–74; Kathleen M. Vernon, "Reading Hollywood in/and Spanish Cinema: From Trade Wars to Transculturation," in Marsha Kinder, ed., *Refiguring Spain: Cinema/Media/Representation* (Durham: Duke University Press, 1997), 35–64; Stone, *Spanish Cinema,* 44–56; Antonio Elorza, "De 'Bienvenido Mister Marshall' au 11 septembre 2001: Les sources de l'anti-américanisme espagnol," *Cahiers d'histoire sociale* 21 (2002–2003): 43–56. The fiftieth anniversary of the film's release was celebrated in December 2002 with lectures and extensive press attention to its continued timeliness.

30. Whitaker, *Spain and Defense of the West,* 2

31. Ángel Viñas, *Los pactos secretos de Franco con Estados Unidos: bases, ayuda económica, recortes de soberanía* (Barcelona: Grijalbo, 1981).

32. Elordi, *El amigo americano,* 25.

33. Carr, *Spain 1808–1975,* 763–64.

34. Sahagún, "Spain and the United States," 166–68.

35. Ibid.; Vázquez Montalbán, *La penetración americana,* 14–15.

36. Elordi, *El amigo americano,* 42–43.

37. Lluís Calvo i Calvo, personal communication.

38. My interpretation follows that of Teresa Vilarós, *El mono del desencanto: Una crítica cultural de la transición española (1973–1993)* (Madrid: Siglo, 1998), 205–10.

39. Higginbotham, *Spanish Film Under Franco,* 119.

40. Manuel Vázquez Montalbán, *Cronica sentimental de España,* 2nd ed. (Barcelona: Grijalbo, 1998 [1971]), 109.

41. For *Madregilda* and a larger argument on the place of U.S. film in the "alternative imaginary" of Francoism, see Vernon, "Reading Hollywood."

42. After the U.S., Italy was the world's major source of cultural imports in the 1940s and 50s, and its pop songs and films, closer to Spanish realities, mediated U.S. consumer culture for Spaniards. See Vázquez Montalbán, *Crónica sentimental.*

43. Franz-Josef Albersmeier, *Theater, Film, Literatur in Spanien: Literaturgeschichte als integrierte Mediengeschichte* (Berlin: Schmidt, 2001).

44. Castellet, *Nueve novísimos poetas*, 22; Pierre Bourdieu, *Distinction: A Social Critique of the Judgment of Taste* (Cambridge: Harvard University Press, 1984).

45. This is not to say that some Spaniards did not participate as recognized players in the international avant-garde: Antoni Tàpies, Eduardo Chillida, Ricardo Bofill, and others continued the development of Spanish modernism in an internationalist context. This has always been easier in the visual arts and architecture, where questions of censorship and translation are more easily negotiated. All in all, though, the cultural confidence of these few was not the general tone of the Francoist period.

46. By the same token, a person who has spent a little too long in the Boy Scouts is known as a *kumba*, from "Kumbayah."

47. Cf. Kroes, this volume.

48. Theme song of the Barcelona Olympics, lyrics: Don Black, music: Andrew Lloyd Webber, 1992.

49. *Crónica sentimental*, 129–30.

50. "Press of the heart," or gossip magazines, still the best-selling periodicals in Spain. Indeed, Spain is a world leader in this cultural field, with its *¡Hola!* magazine spun off internationally as, for example, the British *Hello!*

51. *Crónica sentimental*, 91.

52. Pavlovic', "'¡Bienvenido, Mr. Marshall!'" 170.

53. I was strongly encouraged to read this book on my arrival in a small Catalan city to do dissertation fieldwork.

54. Marsha Kinder, "Refiguring Socialist Spain: An Introduction," in Kinder, *Refiguring Spain*, 3.

55. Paul Julian Smith, "Pornography, Masculinity, Homosexuality: Almodovar's *Matador* and *La ley del deseo*," in Kinder, *Refiguring Spain*, 193.

56. Later Spanish activists would explicitly celebrate this model as a "Mediterranean sexuality" of acts, as distinct from an American "gay identity." Alberto Mira, "Laws of Silence: Homosexual Identity and Visibility in Contemporary Spanish Culture," in B. Jordan and R. Morgan-Tamosunas, eds., *Contemporary Spanish Cultural Studies* (London: Oxford University Press, 2000), 247.

57. After the Madrid bombings of March 2004 one might credit Goytisolo with uncanny geopolitical intuition.

58. *Miralda. Obras 1965-1995* (Barcelona and Valencia: Fundació "La Caixa," 1995). Cf. the German-American critic Werner Sollors on the mixed marriage as a key symbol of America's "identity of consent" in *Beyond Ethnicity: Consent and Descent in American Culture* (Oxford: Oxford University Press, 1986).

59. A word ensconced in the Spanish artistic lexicon since the 1960s.

60. Stephen J. Summerhill and John Alexander Williams, *Sinking Columbus: Contested History, Cultural Politics, and Mythmaking during the Quincentenary* (Gainesville: University Press of Florida, 2000), 29–31, 179–80.

61. *Sic*, in English.

62. Manuel Castells, *The Information Age: Economy, Society, and Culture*, 3 vols. (Oxford: Blackwell, 1997), vol. 2, 50.

63. Dorothy Noyes, *Fire in the Plaça: Catalan Festival Politics After Franco* (Philadelphia: University of Pennsylvania Press, 2003), 272–73.

64. *Crónica de una seducción: El museo Guggenheim Bilbao* (Madrid: Nerea, 1997); a summary article in English is Joseba Zulaika, "Krens's Taj Mahal: The Guggenheim's Global Love Museum," *Discourse* 23 (2001): 100–118.

65. The first payment was equivalent to USD 100 per Basque (Zulaika, "Krens' Taj Mahal," 110). Zulaika emphasizes the pioneering Guggenheim strategy of applying the franchise model to cultural institutions—in effect, McGuggenheim.

66. Zulaika, *Crónica de una seducción.*

67. Castells, *The Information Age,* vol. 1, 420–23.

68. Ferran Adrià, "La cocina moderna española," *Anuario El País 1998* (Madrid: El País, 1999): 306.

69. Arthur Lubow, "El Bulli: A Laboratory of Taste," *The New York Times Magazine,* 10 August 2003.

70. *La Vanguardia,* 11 August 2003.

71. Eduardo Bautista, Antonio Cordón, Miguel Ángel Cortés et al., *España, ¿potencia cultural?* (Madrid: Biblioteca nueva, 2001).

72. An attitude in telling contrast with its hostility towards peninsular minority languages, according to defenders of the latter.

73. Jo Labanyi, "Narrative in Culture, 1975–1996," in D.T. Gies, ed., *The Cambridge Companion to Modern Spanish Culture* (Cambridge: Cambridge University Press,1999), 148.

74. Bautista, *España, ¿potencia cultural?,* 22.

75. Ibid., 23.

76. Ibid., 27–31.

77. Here again the Socialist-dominated Spanish cultural establishment prefers the French to the American model and would like to become "the new France" in this respect. One author notes that François Mitterrand, before dying, remarked that Spanish culture was the only one "capable of talking on a first-name basis to the Anglo-Saxon empire." Jacques Chirac urged Aznar to join him in the fight for the "cultural exception" against the U.S. push for free trade, but Aznar repeatedly insisted that market competition would be viable for Spain (ibid., 83).

78. Ibid., 62.

79. In fact, according to Franco's old principle: if you have to dance, dance with the richest girl at the party.

80. Félix Martínez, "El bocadillo más suculento," *El Mundo,* 16 May 1999.

81. Kinder, "Refiguring Socialist Spain," 5–7; Stone, *Spanish Cinema.*

82. Edward F. Stanton, *Handbook of Spanish Popular Culture* (Westport: Greenwood, 1999).

83. Gregorio Morán, *El precio de la transición* (Madrid: Planeta, 1991), 26; Vázquez Montalbán, *La penetración americana.*

84. Vilarós, *El mono del desencanto,* 78; Guillermo Martínez, ed., *Almanaque Franquismo pop* (Barcelona: Mondadori, 2001).

85. Carr, *Spain 1808–1975,* 725.

86. Dorothy Noyes, "*La maja vestida:* Dress as Resistance to Enlightenment in Late 18th-Century Madrid," *Journal of American Folklore* 111 (1998): 197–218.

87. Such arguments can be made for much of peripheral Europe, but the continuity, focus, and breadth of social participation in the construction of national images performed at the interpersonal level is surely exceptional in Spain.

88. Stanton, *Handbook of Spanish Popular Culture,* 164.

CONCLUSION

IMAGINARY AMERICAS IN EUROPE'S PUBLIC SPACE

◆　　◆　　◆

Rob Kroes

Needed: An Archeology of Europe as Remembered Space

In my education as a European—a haphazard trajectory at best, never consistently planned or pursued—I remember one formative moment. I had the good fortune, as an undergraduate in political science, to find a book on the required reading list—Edward Atiyah's *The Arabs*[1]—that shook my established views of the history of Western civilization.

I had had the privilege to attend an old-style Dutch *gymnasium* and had read some of the classics from antiquity, such as Homer in Greek and Virgil in Latin, in addition to some of the great works in four modern languages, German, French, English, and of course Dutch. It had left me with a mistaken sense of unilineal evolution from Greek and Roman times to modern European civilization. Thus I had an etymological sense of the modern languages at my command, including those of Germanic origin, as resonant with ancient Greek and Latin. I saw Goethe, Shakespeare, and Racine as inspired by the masters of antiquity. Words like Renaissance and Enlightenment only confirmed my reading of Western civilization as repeatedly reinvigorating itself by returning to its intellectual and artistic origins. Everything in my high-school education had worked to instill in me this sense of history as a transformational process, continuing in one unbroken line, for all its inner hybridity and the admixtures from other sources. My sense, and that of many others, was the unquestioned latter-day version of the old myth of the Westward Course of Empire and Civilization, or as it was known in the days when Europe's common language was still Latin, the *Translatio Studii et Imperii*. Taken up by Bishop Berkeley in the eighteenth century and projected onto the can-

---

Notes for this section begin on page 358.

vas of America, his poem would be eagerly adopted by Americans in the nineteenth century as one of the historical justifications for their westward expansion in what they saw as their manifest destiny.[2] From Virgil to Berkeley there was this sense of an unbroken line of Western civilization evolving over time, while it traveled ever farther westward. Nothing had prepared me for the reading of Atiyah's book.

He presents Arab civilization at the time of its greatest flowering, not as something out there, beyond the self-enclosed sphere of a European world immersed in its own process of civilization, but as critically linked to it, in dialogue, in cultural encounters and clashes, nurturing and further enriching a classical heritage, appropriating it before Europeans claimed it as exclusively theirs. Not only does Atiyah interweave the story of Arab civilization with that of European civilization, offering a larger cosmopolitan perspective; he also explodes current conceptual habits that see Arabs as a homogeneous "Them" versus an equally homogeneous "Us." At the time of its greatest geographical reach the Arab empire held a population teeming with immense religious, ethnic, and linguistic variety, yet freely intermingling, and fully partaking of the intellectual and cultural ferment in its urban centers. Atiyah forever changed my mental map of the history of what we now call Western civilization, of its locale as much as of its agency. Europe as an organizing idea, conflating a geological land mass with the stage on which Western civilization unfolded, would henceforth be a blur rather than offer a clear focus.

Much the same story could be told about the Ottoman Empire, successor to the Arab era of cultural and political predominance. Centered in one of the great European cities, which under the name of Constantinople had for a thousand years been a cultural haven in the history of Christendom, in addition to being a cosmopolitan crossroads, the Ottomans confusingly and tellingly invaded it from Europe, entering the city through its West gate, and renamed it Istanbul. They appropriated its rich cultural landscape rather than razing it to the ground, in marked contrast to the pillage and desecration of a then Orthodox Christian Constantinople at the hands of Frankish crusaders in 1204. Under the Ottomans Christian iconography was plastered over, not iconoclastically smashed to pieces. In the cultural sedimentation of history a new layer was added, like a new coat of paint. In cultural syncretism mosques were built emulating the grand structure of the Aya Sophia. Again, artisans, artists, and intellectuals from inside the realm as well as from outside, in fact from all over the larger Mediterranean world, flocked there to contribute to Ottoman civilization. Ironically, with the Ataturk turning toward a radical Western secularism and nationalism, seeking to Westernize Turkish society following the breakup of the Ottoman Empire, the Aya Sophia was decommissioned as a mosque and restored to its former Christian symbolism. Frescoes and mosaics have been uncovered, and now sit alongside the later Muslim iconography honoring Mahomet and the first four Khalifs. It is a lasting memento to the history of related, though rival, civilizations washing across each other in an ongoing ebb and flow.

As happens so often, rivals locked in combat in the end turn out to resemble each other. Within the Christian world the mirror image of the two great Muslim empires is without a doubt the Austro-Hungarian Empire, deriving its cultural sense of itself from its long-time struggle against the expansionist Ottomans as its cultural Other. Yet the resemblance is striking in terms of the multiethnic cultural vibrancy, centered in the Austrian case on its seat of empire, Vienna. Nor was the dividing line ever very neat in religious terms. Muslims and Christians lived next to each other on either side of the line, although tolerance of religious diversity may have been greater under the Ottomans. If tolerance is a virtue claimed on behalf of European civilization, which of the two empires then was more European?

The question is meant to be more than merely flippant. Christianity's defense against two successful Muslim empires was always fueled by an exclusionist reading of its cause, a driving sense of religious purity. It fired the fervor of the Crusades; it was behind the Spanish riconquista, as much as it inspired later religious wars on European soil. Compared to the religious live-and-let-live attitude in the Muslim empires, what a sorry sight is presented by the successful Christian reconquest of the Iberian Peninsula, which seamlessly blended into the expulsion of the Jews. Nor were the Spaniards alone in this endeavor. In a letter to the French king the Dutch humanist Erasmus, trying to flatter him, complimented him on making France free of Jews. Elsewhere as well anti-Semitism served the purpose of creating the necessary Other for cementing cultural homogeneity, around versions of Christianity first, and notions of the nation later. Slowly but surely much of Europe began to harden around lines of social and cultural exclusion. Alien communities were hounded out, their places of worship demolished, their graveyards plowed under.

Amazingly, after all these years, Europeans still could not believe their eyes when this same logic of ethnic cleansing attended the breakup of yet another multiethnic state on European soil, Yugoslavia. It was the latest frantic attempt to cleanse the map of Europe of the vestiges of earlier forms of communal and cultural life. Photographs and television footage of Sarajevo, showing a multiethnic and cosmopolitan hub styled in the grand Austro-Hungarian tradition being shelled by surrounding Serb artillery, left European viewers speechless and powerless. Pictures of concentration camps, their emaciated inmates clutching the fence that held them captive, evoked instant associations with Nazi atrocities that Europeans might have hoped were forever in the past. The pictures and the associations they called forth triggered collective memories and provided a ready historical context for the interpretation of what was going on in Bosnia.

Yet it took unconscionably long for the West to actively intervene. Impotent anger was the first response. As Barbie Zelizer points out, there is a paradox in this conflation of atrocities remembered and atrocities recently perpetrated. "The insistence on remembering earlier atrocities may not necessarily promote active responses to new instances of brutality. (I have) argued that the opposite, in fact, may be true: we may remember earlier atrocities so as to forget the contemporary ones."[3] I am not sure whether I agree with her last point. As I remember it, it was precisely the fact that associations with Nazi atrocities were triggered that led contemporary witnesses to sense the enormity of what was going on, and created a large popular pressure in Europe and the United States not to stand by idly but to intercede and stop the brutality. Other, more shameful memories came back. After all, nothing had been done during World War II to stop or hinder the Holocaust. The photographs that bore ample witness to the atrocities that had taken place were all taken after the fact. Now, in Bosnia, photographs showed atrocities as they were under way. Now was the time to act. In the end, things were brought to a halt before they had had a chance to run their full dismal course.

The shocking dimensions of the Balkan tragedies of the 1990s may make them seem a fluke, a throwback to a past we mistakenly thought we had forever put behind us, yet the sorting out of European populations along lines of ethnic and cultural purity proceeds apace across the map of Europe, with greater or lesser violence. It ranges from the Basque Country, Ulster, Corsica, and Brittany all the way to the successor states of the former Soviet empire. There is much unfinished business on the agenda of cultural purity and homogeneity.

The logic inherent in all this may be of European vintage, centering for the last two centuries on the purity of the nation or of subnational entities like cultural regions. But it has proved contagious. Thus, in the course of a mere hundred years following the breakup of the Ottoman Empire, Turkey as one of its successor nation-states lost much of its cosmopolitan diversity through the forced expulsion of Greeks, whose settlement in fact predated the advent of the Turks on the peninsula, or through the voluntary emigration of people who had given Istanbul its cosmopolitan flavor. Internal migration from the countryside in Anatolia to the industrial labor market of Istanbul exploded its population while making it, demographically and culturally speaking, ever more Asian (its population at the turn of the twenty-first century was about 25–30 percent Kurdish). As a result, Turkey's most European city has seen its Westernized Turkish bourgeoisie and its international community become an ever smaller minority.

Given this reordering of the map of Europe over the last centuries, the willful erasing of remnants and markers of earlier social arrangements, it is small wonder that most people living in Europe see the current map as the natural one. To them, this is how things are and how they have always been. As I mentioned before, I managed to rid myself of this habit of mind as a student by reading a book about Arab civilization. The book, for me, served the purpose of an archeological exercise in recovering older memories of European space, suppressed and willfully forgotten, yet of great value for current debates concerning what Europe is and isn't. High-school textbooks across Europe need to be rewritten with a view to unsettling the pernicious presentism of people's ideas about Europe. This ideal new textbook would offer a tour across European space, forgetting about borders and current lines on the map and turning it into one, big memory space, a *lieu de mémoire,* evoking the sense of space that emerges from W. G. Sebald's journeys across time and space, stumbling upon triggers of memory, bringing back voices long gone silent, conjuring shimmering faces from mists before these envelop them once again.

We need to construct Europe as its own underworld, with ghosts wandering about, demanding to be heard. We need museums, of Jewish history, of colonial history, of regional history, of maps of past Europes smaller than its present landmass or extending far beyond it, museums of population movements, forced or voluntary, of diasporic communities, like people of Turkish descent in Germany and the Netherlands, who find a new sense of self. We need film and photographs, documenting Europes long since vanished. We need interviews with people who now live where others lived before them, in the ruthless succession of populations across the map of Europe, asking them what, if anything, they remember. We need to look at Europe from its liminal points, following a perimeter of contested terrain; more often than not the liminal points are located inside Europe, rather than relegated to its perimeter as gate-keeping devices for the cultural and civic exclusion of those considered outsiders. We need a map of Europe showing only cultural islands, its "pure" cultural regions as people see them, and then showing what larger cultural currents wash across these outposts of insulation. We need to turn present-day Europeans into a new audience beholding the pageant of earlier Europes that they should, but often do not, remember.

These would all be necessary exercises in what I called the archeology of remembered space. Yet we need not recover only the past while peeling back Europe's layered history. Layers are being added right before our eyes, affecting, as they should and for millions actually do, the collective sense of European space, or rather of the many Europes as people now construct them in the wake of the Cold War. In films and writing many creative minds have set out to explore the debris left by the receding tide of Soviet power.

At the end of Anne Applebaum's journey *Between East and West: Across the Borderlands of Europe,*[4] from Kaliningrad on the Baltic through Lithuania, Belarus, Ukraine, Bukovina, Moldova, and Transdniestria to Odessa, she crosses the Black Sea. Arriving in the Bosphorus at dawn, she is struck by the color, energy, and prosperity after months of an ex-socialist drabness of brown and grey: "Ahead of us gleamed the minarets of Istanbul. I was back in the West." As Moray McGowan astutely comments,[5] this exemplifies unusually clearly how meaning and identity are relative and constituted through oppositions. Istanbul is usually invoked in Western discourse as a bridge between East and West or as a quintessentially Oriental city. But Applebaum, by viewing it as part of a bright, affluent West in contrast to a physically drab and psychologically depressed ex-communist East, locates it, surely with conscious irony, within another, familiar, but very different polarity, that of the Cold War. In Cold War terms, Turkey, NATO's key southeastern flank, belonged to "Europe" as defined by Western powers. Walter Hallstein, as president of the European Commission at the time of Turkey's Treaty of Association in 1964, had declared emphatically that "Turkey is part of Europe."[6] This same Hallstein had given his name, as McGowan reminds us,[7] to the West German "Doctrine" of 1955 that, in a microcosm of Western Cold War positions, sought to isolate the German Democratic Republic (GDR) by threatening to sever relations with any third state that recognized it. In certain circumstances, then, Turkey was more Western, more "European," than East Germany.

Switching to film, a masterpiece by the young Swedish director Lukas Moodysson, entitled *Lilya 4-ever,* depicts the bleak and devastatingly powerful story of Lilya, a poverty-stricken teenage girl in a crumbling Russian town in an unspecified Baltic state. The girl is abandoned by her mother, who leaves, apparently for the United States, with a man she has met through a dating agency. In her wretchedness Lilya finds a friend in a lonely 11-year-old boy, Volodya, but then duplicates her mother's betrayal by casting her lot with a smooth-talking young guy who says he can take her away to Sweden, like "America" another beckoning refuge from her pauperized and hopeless life. As it turns out, Sweden offers captivity and slavery rather than liberation. Visually, the director shows us a Sweden that is not all that different from the wasteland of the former Soviet empire. Blocks of apartment high-rises may be in a better state of repair, but otherwise look as grim and forbidding as anything in the East. On arriving in Sweden, Lilya finds that the promised job was a trick. Imprisoned and forced into prostitution, the girl is repeatedly raped, day after day after day, in ways that Moodysson pitilessly shows us from her perspective. Forced prostitution is exposed as a horrible reality, one that links the impoverished post-Soviet states to the sex industry in the moneyed West.

If this film conflates "Europe" and "America" as paradises of freedom and riches, the connection comes out still more strongly in a 1994 film by Italian director Gianni Amelio, *L'America.* It depicts another post-Soviet state, Albania, as a place of unspeakable horror where anarchy, brutality, and corruption are rampant. The film offers a frightening view of a world devoid of the least trace of civil protection as we value it in the West, a world where every civil institution has collapsed. The final images, of an escape from this nightmarish landscape by ship, present it in the light of a crossing to "America," although in fact the ship only crosses the Adriatic to Italy. Yet the images are visually reminiscent of ships entering New York harbor, their steerage passengers crowded *en masse* on the decks to behold the land of promise.

But we need not enter the fringe of the former Soviet empire to get a glimpse of the threats to civil life in Europe. A 1999 film by Spanish director Helena Taberna, *Yoyes*, takes a sobering look at the Leninism and terrorism that characterize the movement for Basque national emancipation. Much as the movement's early appeal lay in its use of a language of cultural rights and ethnic self-determination rooted in the larger liberationist enthusiasms of the 1960s, the means it now uses in pursuit of its goals are a travesty of the rules of the democratic game. Since democracy came to Spain, the ETA has lived a life of denial of its changed environment and has withdrawn into the conspiratorial worldview of its small band of hardened activists. The film tells the true story of a woman member of ETA, a participant in many of its violent actions, who after a period of exile in Paris wants to return to the Basque Country and resume a normal civilian life. In retaliation for her defection and denunciation of ETA's totalitarianism, ETA activists track her down; while taking a walk with friends she hears someone call her name, turns around, and is shot straight in the face, executed in cold blood. It took courage to make this film in the Basque Country, given the climate of fear and intimidation that effectively silences the voice of dissent and obscures the plurality of views among the Basque population. If film allows its audience to widen its view and look beyond Europe's borders, a movie like *Yoyes* deserves far wider distribution than it actually got. And if one of Europe's problems is the creation of truly European audiences, Europe's film and television industries need all the support they can get for the visual representation of Europe's many faces for European audiences.

One further contemporary film by Russian director Alexander Sokurrow, *Russian Ark,* is an example of such a transnational collaborative effort, in terms of its financing and distribution. Ironically, it may have had a greater *succes d'estime* in the United States than in Europe: as almost a cult film it has run for months in art houses in New York and other big American cities, and although it was acclaimed by the European press, its public exposure there cannot compare with that in the United States.[8] The film takes us back to the archeology of Europe as remembered space. Loosely based on Astolphe de Custine's classic *La Russie en 1839,* it brings the French nobleman back to life as a ghost from the nineteenth century wandering about the premises of the Saint Petersburg Hermitage, but wandering through time as well. At times rooms are filled with present-day Russians, whom the Frenchman engages in conversation, on occasion scolding them for their lack of historical appreciation of paintings that collectively represent European culture. At other moments, in other rooms, we are taken back in time to the days of Catherine the Great, or of the last Czar and his family on the eve of the revolution.

The final scenes are of a ball in the main ballroom, where the upper crust dances to music by Glinka, a Russian composer of music in a European vein. With apparent gusto Valery Gergiev, a cosmopolitan star in the world of music, conducts the costumed orchestra. Then, in ominous foreboding of an era coming to its end, we see the hundreds of guests descending the stairs in a seemingly endless procession. The final shot takes our gaze outside the building, through an open door, into a bleak and nebulous night, a stark reminder of the dark times ahead, an era in which Russia's infatuation with a bourgeois Europe would be only a distant memory. The film is one astounding, uninterrupted take. The director turns his camera into yet another character in the film, invisible to all except the French nobleman. They engage in conversation, with the Frenchman going through raptures at the European culture on display, or mimicked in the lavish architecture and interior design of the Hermitage. He tends to disparage Russian culture. It makes his skin itch. Yet in the end he joins the dance, satisfied with the Russian version of the good life in Europe. When all the others leave, he refuses to go along. He would rather continue his ghostly existence as a perennial nostalgic. He takes a little bow to his camera friend and says: "Goodbye, Europe."

Custine's *La Russie en 1839* came out at about the same time as Alexis de Tocqueville's *De la démocratie en Amérique*. The one French nobleman had measured Russia by the standards of European high taste and high culture; the other had gone to America to try and fathom what democracy in America, as the wave of a future coming to Europe later, would mean for Europe's cultural landscape. Tocqueville's view was typically ambivalent. He marvelled at the vitality of democratic life in the American Republic. Aware of the old wisdoms concerning the life cycle of republics, from early vigor to decline and eventual demise, he wondered about the secrets of the apparent stability of America's republic. His insights all concerned the forms of social, or "associative," life in America rather than the intricacy of its constitutional apparatus. Its political stability was anchored in its social pluralism. Tocqueville was among the first to explore "civil society," the social sphere beyond the reach of government control or surveillance, and critically dependent on democratic freedoms. Only they allowed the citizenry to be the agent of its manifold associative activities, ranging from political parties to churches, schools, and the many other forms of group activities in pursuit of collective interests.

If Tocqueville's grasp of the voluntarism characteristic of democratic life makes him one of the fathers of modern sociology, his exploration of the impact of mass democracy on culture makes him a precursor in a long line of critics of mass culture. Here his views are much more sobering. They held out a warning to Europeans and their more aristocratic views of taste hierarchies and the role of cultural elites. He was keenly aware of the leveling effects of cultural production under democratic conditions, aiming as it did at the lowest common denominator of public taste rather than catering to the tastes of social elites. Culture followed the dictates of majority conformism rather than the intricate games of cultural distinction characteristic of Europe's stratified societies. Both his views of the self-sustaining forces of democracy in America and his views of cultural life under democratic conditions were informed by his sense that what he observed in America was a prefiguration of Europe's future. If Custine's book explored European culture as it was appropriated beyond its eastern frontier, Tocqueville foresaw the advent of mass society as a force undermining European culture from within. As it happened, later cultural critics would see much of this erosion not as indigenous but as a process of Europeans appropriating forms of American mass culture. Whereas Bishop Berkeley had envisioned a westward course of empire and civilization, the twentieth century, also known as the American century, would see a reverse course. The empire, once it had reached American shores, would strike back, Americanizing Europe in its turn.

Many have been the discussions in Europe as to what exactly it was that America, regarded as the harbinger of Europe's future, held in store. Germany had its *Amerikanismus* debate in the 1920s; France looked on in fascination and trepidation for over two centuries as modernity in its American guise unfolded. Intellectuals in many other countries contributed their views as they observed the American scene.[9] Many traveled there and reported back to their various home audiences; others stayed home trying to grasp the forms of reception and appropriation of the American model in culture, in economics, and in politics. More often than not the form of these critical exchanges was one of triangulation. Parties engaged in debate on how to structure the future in Europe's various nation-states used America as a reference point to define their positions, either rejecting the American model or promoting it for adoption. I have written extensively on these processes of triangulation.[10] Here I propose to take a different approach. I will look at iconographic representations of America across Europe, exploring the ways in which their presence may have affected the sense of European space among Europeans.

American Iconography in Europe's Public Space

I must have been twelve or thirteen when in the early 1950s, in my home town of Haarlem in the Netherlands, I stood outside on the sidewalk looking in, enthralled at a huge picture displayed along the entire rear wall of a garage. As I remember it now, it was my first trance-like glimpse of a world unlike anything I had known so far. Not surprisingly, for this garage sold American cars, the picture was of a 1950s American car gleaming in its full iconographic force as a carrier of dreams rather than as a mere means of transportation. Cars in general, let alone their gigantic American versions, were a distant dream to most Dutch people at the time. Yet what held my gaze was not so much the car as the image of a boy, younger than I was at the time, who came rushing from behind the car, his motion stopped, his contagious joy continuing. He wore sneakers, blue jeans rolled up at the ankles, a T-shirt. His hairdo was different from that of any of my friends, and so was his facial expression. Come to think of it, there must have been a ball. The boy's rush is imagined as the exhilarating dash across a football field or a basketball court, surging ahead of others. The very body language, although frozen into a still picture, bespoke a boisterous freedom. Everything about the boy radiated signals from a distant but enticing world.

This may have been my first confrontation with a wide-screen display of the good life in America, of its energy, its exhilaration, its typical pursuits and satisfactions. As I now think back on the moment, I am aware that in my distant exposure to America's dreamscape I was not unlike an astronomer, catching light emitted aeons ago by distant stars. Metaphorically speaking America was aeons away from Europe at the time, feverishly engaged as it was in the construction of the consumers' republic and the pursuit of happiness that it incited. Beholding a picture of America in a garage in Haarlem, I was exposed to a representation of life in America in a rare reflection of public imagery that was already ubiquitous in the U.S. itself, and not all that recent. Even at the depth of the Great Depression, the National Association of Manufacturers (NAM) in typical boosterism had pasted similar images across the nation, advertising "The American Way" in displays of happy families riding in their cars. Much of the jarring dissonance between these public displays and the miseries of collective life in 1930s America still applied to Europe, where the early 1950s were still lean years. Yet in Haarlem I was enthralled by an image that, despite having no visual referent in real life anywhere in Europe, may have been equally seductive for Europeans as for Americans. Consumerism may have been a distant dream in postwar Europe, but it was eagerly anticipated once Europeans were exposed to its American version through advertising, photojournalism, and Hollywood films.

As images of America's culture of consumption began to fill Europe's public space, they exposed Europeans to views of the good life that Americans themselves were exposed to. To that extent such images may have Americanized European dreams and longings. But might there also be a way to argue that Europe's exposure to American imagery may have worked to Europeanize Europe at the same time? There are several ways of going about answering this question. It has been said in jest that the only culture Europeans had in common in the late twentieth century was American culture. Their exposure to forms of American mass culture transcended national borders in ways that no national varieties were ever able to rival. True, the occasional Italian or German hit song ran up the charts in other European countries. Audiences across Europe still paid to see films made in one or another European country. And there were the 1960s, when England contributed to international youth culture in areas such as music and fashion, often giving its own characteristic twist to the American mass culture that had reached England in the years before. But the one continuing line throughout the latter half of the twentieth century traces the exposure of European publics to American mass culture.

The points of exposure were not necessarily in public space. Much of the consumption of American mass culture took place in private settings when people watched television in their living rooms, or Hollywood movies in the quasi-private space of the darkened movie theater. American popular music reached Europeans via the radio or on records and once again made for a practice of audiences assembling in private places, such as homes or dance clubs. This private, or peer-group, consumption of American mass culture did not rule out the emergence of larger virtual audiences across Europe. Far from it. Repertoires, tastes, and cultural memories held in common would give rise to quick and easy cultural exchange across national borders among Europe's younger generations. They could more readily compare notes on shared cultural preferences by using American examples instead of those drawn from varieties of mass culture produced in national settings.

Yet this is not what I intend to explore here. There is an area, properly called public space, outside private homes, outside gathering places for cultural consumption, that has served across Europe as a site of exposure to American mass culture. Much as it is true that forms of American mass culture, transmitted via the entertainment industry, travel under commercial auspices— that is, they are always economic commodities in addition to being cultural goods, to be sold before they are consumed—public space is the area where American mass culture has most openly advertised itself, creating the demand, if not the desire, for its consumption. In public space, including the press, we find the film posters advertising the latest Hollywood movies, or the dream-like representations of an America where people smoke certain cigarettes, buy certain cars, cosmetics, clothes. They are literally advertisements, creating economic demand while conveying imaginary Americas at the same time. They thus have contributed to a European repertoire of an invented America: a realm for reverie, filled with iconic heroes, setting standards of physical beauty, of taste, of proper behavior. If Europe to a certain extent has become "other-directed," much like America itself under the impact of its own commercial culture, Europe's significant Other has become America, as commercially constructed through advertising.

If we may conceive of this redirection of Europe's gaze toward America as a sign of Europe's Americanization, it betokens an appropriation of American standards and tastes in addition to whatever cultural habits were already in place to direct people's individual quest for identity. Americanization is never a simple zero-sum game where people trade in their European clothes for every pair of blue jeans they acquire. It is more a matter of cultural syncretism, an interweaving of bits of American culture into European cultural habits, where every borrowing of American cultural ingredients creatively changes their meaning and context. Certainly, Europe's cultural landscape has changed, but never in ways that would lead visiting Americans to mistake Europe for a simple replica of their own culture.

My larger point, though, is to pursue a paradox. Henry James at one point astutely perceived that it is for Americans rather than Europeans to conceive of Europe as a whole, and to transcend Europe's patterns of cultural particularism. He meant to conceive of it as one cultural canvas of a scale commensurate with that of America—as one large continental culture. His aphoristic insight certainly highlights a recurring rationale in the way that Americans have approached Europe, whether they are businessmen seeing Europe as one large market for their products, or post–World War II politicians pursuing a vision of European cooperation transcending Europe's divisive nationalisms. If we may rephrase James's remark as referring to Americans' inclination to project their mental scale of thought onto the map of Europe, then Europe may in turn have experienced the cultural impact of that inclination as an eye-opening revision of their mental compass, inspiring a literal re-vision.

Whatever the precise message, owing to the fact that American advertising has for decades appeared across European countries, traveling Europeans are exposed to commercial communication proliferating across national borders, addressing Europeans wherever they live. More specifically, though, there is a genre of advertising that precisely confronts Europeans with the fantasy image of America as one, open space. It may be that all American advertising conjures up fantasy versions of life in America, but the particular fantasy of America as unbounded space, free of the confining limits set by European cultures on dreams of individual freedom, may well have activated the dream of a Europe as wide and open as America.

The particular genre of advertising I am thinking of finds its perfect illustration in the myth of Marlboro Country and the Marlboro Man. The idea of tying the image of this particular brand of cigarette to the mythical lure of the American West goes back to the early 1960s and has inspired an advertising iconography that retains its appeal up to the present day (at least in those countries that have not banned cigarette advertising). Over time the photographic representation of the imaginary space of Marlboro Country has expanded in size, filling Europe's public space with wide-screen images of

Western landscapes lit by a setting sun, rock formations glowing in deep red color as horses descend to their watering hole and rugged-faced cowboys light up after the day's work is done. This is a space for fantasy to roam, offering a transient escape into dreams of unbounded freedom, of being one's own free agent. It is hard not to see these images. They are often obtrusively placed, hanging over the crowds in railway stations or adding gorgeous color to some of Europe's grey public squares. I remember one prominent advertisement on the left of the steps leading up to Budapest's great, grey Museum of Art. The show opened right there. One couldn't miss it.

The formula has been widely imitated. Other cigarette brands came up with their own variations on the theme using different iconography, showing young couples in leisure time pursuits, or depicting a jet-set lifestyle that one might vicariously share in the time it took to smoke a cigarette. An ad on a roadside poster in post–Cold War Poland showed a young couple, radiating joy; the text invited the audience "to have a taste of freedom." The advertisement was for an American cigarette, but European cigarette makers as well adopted the approach, as in a French Gauloises campaign that used Parisian settings. The young, attractive males in the photographs emanate a casual informality, with jackets flung over their shoulders or their feet up on the table of a sidewalk cafe, that is vaguely resonant of American styles of public behavior. The overall impression is summarily captured in the advertisements' affirmative statement: "La liberté, toujours."

Peter Stuyvesant cigarettes in the Netherlands used a more postmodern collage technique to convey a similar message. The images reduce the explicit markers of European dreams of America as open space, so central to the Marlboro approach, to mere echoes that still trigger the same repertoire of fantasies. They show young couples in the gathering places of an international leisure class, captioned in each case by the name of a hotel in Miami Beach, San Francisco, or another such rendezvous. The central slogan, giving meaning to the jumble of text and visuals, reads: "There are no borders." That the campaign was set up by a Dutch advertising agency is further testimony to the adoption by Europeans of American dreams and messages of unbounded space. The use of English in a campaign addressing a Dutch audience is increasingly common, and purports to give an international flavor to the message. Indeed, there are no borders.

In fact, the commodified lure of open space has by now become so familiar that advertisers have begun to ironize their messages with an implied wink to an audience of initiates. One example of such an ironic twist is a commercial for an Italian travel agency that calls itself Marlboro Country Travels. Playing on the escapism of much modern tourism, where one is to lose oneself in the hope of finding oneself, it arranges travel to the United States while casting the destination in the image of Marlboro Country's fictional space. A large color photograph, actually a montage, shows a 1950s gas pump, a nostalgic reminder of the romanticism of Route 66 ("Get your kicks on Route 66"), of Jack Kerouac's *On the Road,* of the exhilaration of road movies. As a backdrop the photograph offers a view of the American West, a little cloud of dust at its center trailing a diminutive SUV rolling off into the distance. The central slogan tells us to "Fai il vuoto" ("Go for the void"). It plays on the standard request at gas stations to "fill'er up" (*fai il pieno*). It beautifully captures the desire of modern travelers to purge themselves of their concerns and preoccupations, to leave all their worries behind and take off into empty space.

A similar punning approach to advertising can be found all over Europe's public space nowadays. Freedom still is the central idea in these games, although it is given many ironic twists. A poster for Levi's 508 jeans that was pasted all over the Netherlands in the mid 1990s jumps to mind.[11] The photograph showed a male torso, naked from the neck down to the pair of blue jeans. The iconography has a high degree of intertextuality, at least to an audience steeped in American mass culture. It is reminiscent of the cover of Bruce Springsteen's album "Born in the USA," or of Andy Warhol's design for the Rolling Stones' "Sticky Fingers" album cover. Again, the poster uses a collage technique, offering a jumble of visual and textual ingredients. Surprisingly, given that this was an advertisement designed by a Dutch agency, in the lower left-hand corner we see a variation on Roosevelt's famous four freedoms. The first two sound pretty Rooseveltian, evoking the Freedoms of Speech and Expression, followed by the Freedom of Choice (not among Roosevelt's foursome, and itself forbearing to choose whether to see people as political citizens or as individual consumers). In fourth place, following the words "Levi's 508" in boldface, is the Freedom of Movement. Again there is the political ring, expressive of a political longing that many in Eastern Europe may have felt during the years of the Cold War. Yet a pun is intended. The freedom of movement in this context is meant to refer to the greater movement offered by the baggier cut of the 508, a point visually illustrated by the unmistakable bulge of a male member in full erection, touched casually at the tip by the right hand of its master.

The list of further examples is endless. Advertising across Europe's public space has assumed common forms of address, common routines, and common themes (with many variations). Originating in America, it has now been appropriated by European advertising agencies and may be put in the service of American as well as European products. That in itself is a sign of a transnational integration of Europe's public space. But as I suggested before, the point of many of the stories advertisements tell refers precisely to space, to openness, to a dreamscape transcending Europe's checkered map. An international commercial culture has laid itself across public space in Europe, using an international language, often literally in snippets of English, and instilling cravings and desires now shared internationally. Has all this gone on without voices of protest and resistance rising in these same public spaces?

In fact there are many instances of such contestation, turning Europe's public space into yet another showcase of liminal Europes. Right at the heart of Europe, in its public space, we can see battle lines running as so many indications of groups pitting themselves against forces of globalization and its appropriation. If appropriation, however playfully and creatively done, is a form of acceptance, we can see many signs of rejection at the same time. On a highway outside Warsaw I saw a poster for ladies' lingerie, using the familiar techniques of drawing the spectator's gaze. It used the female body, shown here from the back, in reference (if not deference) to international ideals of female beauty. If such pictures are apt to draw the male gaze, they do so indirectly, through the male gaze as internalized by women: this is what they would like to look like in the eyes of men. The poster further used the appeal of English. The brand of lingerie was called "Italian Fashion," throwing in the appeal of Italian fashion design for good measure. But evidently, such public display of the female body was not to everyone's taste in Poland. Someone had gotten out his or her spray-paint to write the Polish word "Dość" (meaning "enough" or "stop it") across the poster. The perpetrator may have been a devout Catholic protesting against the desecration of public space, but is just as likely to have been a feminist objecting to the commodification of the female body. In another instance, in the Northern Italian city of Turin, my gaze was drawn to the base of an equestrian statue. On all four sides, another spray can artist had left such public messages as "McDonald bastardi," "Boycotta McDonald," and more such. If the square had been turned into a liminal Europe where Europeans resisted what they saw as foreign encroachments, it happened in a rather ironic, if not self-defeating way. The point of the protest may have been to rise in defense of the European cultural heritage, but it did not shrink from turning one emblem of that heritage, an equestrian statue, into a mere blackboard for messages of protest, desecrating what it meant to elevate.

In Europe's lasting encounter with American mass culture, the voices expressing concern about its negative impact have been many. Cultural guardians in Europe saw European standards of taste and cultural appreciation eroded by an American way with culture that aimed at a mass market, elevating the lowest common denominator of mass preferences to the main vector of cultural production. This history of cultural anti-Americanism in Europe has a long pedigree. In its earlier manifestations the critique of American mass culture was highly explicit and had to be. Many ominous trends of an evolving mass culture in Europe had to be shown to have originated in America, reaching Europe under clear American agency. An intellectual repertoire of Americanism and Americanization evolved in a continuing attempt at cultural resistance against the lures of a culture of consumption. Never mind that such cultural forms might have come to Europe autonomously, even in the absence of an American model. America served to give a name and a face to forces of cultural change that would otherwise have been anonymous and seemingly beyond control.

Today this European repertoire is alive and kicking. Yet, ironically, as a repertoire that has become common currency to the point of being an intellectual stereotype rather than an informed opinion, America nowadays is often a subtext, unspoken in European forms of cultural resistance. A recent example may serve to illustrate this. A political poster for the Socialist Party in Salzburg, in the run up to municipal elections in the city, shows us the determined face and the clenched fist of the party's candidate. He asks the voting public whether the younger generation will be losers, and calls on the electorate to "fight, fight, and fight." What for? "In order to avoid that young people would get fed up with the future." ("Damit unsere Jugend die Zukunft nicht satt wird.") In a visual pun, at the poster's dead center, the getting fed up is illustrated by the blurred image of a hamburger flying by at high speed. Fast food indeed. The call to action is now clear: Austrians should try to fend off a future cast in an American vein. American culture is condensed into the single image of the hamburger, as a culture centered on consumption rather than consummation. It is enough to trigger the larger repertoire of cultural anti-Americanism.

We may choose to see this poster as only a recent version of cultural guardianship that has always looked at the younger generation as a stalking horse, if not a Trojan horse, for American culture. In fact, historically, it has always been younger generations who, in rebellion against parental authority and cultural imposition, opted for the liberating potential of American mass culture. Yet interesting changes may have occurred in this pattern. Today young people as well, in their concern about forces of globalization, may target America as the central agency behind these global trends. They might smash the windows of a nearby McDonald's (and there is always a McDonald's nearby), deface equestrian statues in Turin, or choose more creative and subtle forms of protest. Yet again America tends to be a mere subtext in their resistance against global cultural icons.

One more example may serve to illustrate this. I have a music video, a few years old, of a Basque group. The video is an act of cultural emancipation in its own right. The lyrics are in the Basque language and the station broadcasting the video had all-Basque programming. While this may suggest localism, if not cultural provincialism, nothing would be farther from the truth. What we have here is a perfect example of "glocalisation," to use Roland Robertson's neologism.[12] The music is ska, an ingredient of "world music" hailing from the Caribbean and popularized through the British music industry. The music video itself, as a format, is part of global musical entertainment.

Yet the message is local. What the video shows is a confusing blend of the traditional and the modern. In the opening shot, a man is using a scythe to cut grass. The camera moves up to show a modern, international-style office block. A mobile phone rings, and the grass cutter answers the call. More images show modern life. We see an old man talking into a microphone strapped to his head, as if he were talking to himself. A group of young men moves through traffic on a flatbed lorry. They are working out on treadmill machines in tandem, yet in complete isolation, a transported glimpse of an American gym. Then the protagonists of the video appear, in a rickety van, getting ready to sell the local variety of Basque fast food, a sausage on a roll. The smell of their "own" food breaks the isolation of people caught in the alienating life of modernity. They all flock to the sausage stand to get a taste of true Basqueness, and having done so, they come to life, spurred by an alleged authenticity of Basque tradition. The lyrics repeat the refrain: Down with Big Mac, Long live (follows the name of the Basque delicacy).

This video makes a claim on behalf of the authenticity of regional cultures struggling to survive in a world threatened by the homogenizing forces of globalization. Yet the medium of communication testifies to the impact of those very forces as much as it protests against them. There is much irony in all this, but most important is the fact that the ways the video depicts modernity truly revive a long repertoire of European cultural anti-Americanism. America *is* modernity, and the long history of European resistance to America is truly a story of resisting the onslaught of modernity on Europe's checkered map of regional and/or national cultures.

To watch this ambiguous proclamation of a regional culture's superiority and authenticity, for its adherents, is to be reminded again of the irony of life in today's many liminal Europes, literally at the *limes,* the edge, of Europe's cultural sway. As one visit to Bilbao, the industrial hub of the Basque Country, will make clear, the Basqueness of the place is, if anything, an imposed and unduly homogenized reading. Under the impact of industrialization Bilbao, like so many other industrial centers, has drawn its work force from an expansive hinterland, forgetful of the integrity of local culture. If capitalism, as Joseph Schumpeter reminded us long ago, is a force of creative destruction, Bilbao testifies to the truth of this statement. People have migrated there from all over Spain to live for several generations, giving the place a multicultural tone and eroding Basqueness from within its own territory.

Following years of decline, the city has now revived. In addition to restoring its residential and industrial architectural heritage, redolent of its past prowess, it has also sought to reconnect itself to the contemporary modernity of cutting-edge architecture. By the river that runs through the city now stands one of Europe's great modern structures, a museum of art designed by the American architect Frank Gehry and financed by Guggenheim money. With its wavy lines it evokes the local seafaring history and seems to mirror the river that connected Bilbao to the wider world. It is a modern rendition of a local history that lives on as collective memory. It seems to have sprouted from that store of memories, much as the creative genius who shaped it arose across the ocean waves that wash the Basque coast at their eastern reach. If Bilbao seeks to reconnect itself to a cosmopolitanism it once reflected, its strivings stand at loggerheads with the efforts at freezing Basqueness in time. Whatever the peculiarities of this tension, its inherent logic makes Bilbao a microcosm of Europe's many internal contradictions.

Europe's Inner Contradictions: Nationalism versus Cosmopolitanism

In current reflections on the ways in which Europe is changing, if not evolving, two pairs of buzzwords emphasize the contradictory forces affecting Europe's changes. One pair, cosmopolitanism and transnationalism, focuses our attention on the many ways in which the political affiliations and cultural affinities of Europeans have transcended their conventional frames of reference, away from the nation and the nation-state. The other pair, nationalism and localism, stresses the enduring power of precisely such conventional forms of affiliation and self-identification. At the present point in time, with Europe engaged in the Promethean venture of framing a Constitution for the European Union on the eve of a dramatic expansion of its scale, a hidebound nationalism and localism is gaining strength. Public opinion in the EU member states is increasingly skeptical of the whole project, seeing it as a cultural and economic threat rather than a promise of a better life for all involved.

This may be temporary and transient, a moment's hesitation in the face of a daring leap into a future whose costs may outweigh its benefits. The current economic malaise in much of Europe may in fact lead many to look back ruefully at the days of national sovereignty and the sense of collective control of the national destiny, which is now a nostalgic memory. A feeling of loss of direction has led people in many member states to reflect anew on national identity and national culture. Even in countries like the Netherlands, where Dutchness has most of the time been more of a "given"—to use Daniel Boorstin's turn of phrase to describe the consensual nature of America's political culture[13]—and therefore hardly ever openly contested or argued, these national topics have recently become the focus of lively intellectual discussion. The triggers are as much domestic, to do with the increased multicultural nature of Dutch society, as they are European. Yet in the eyes of many, they are interrelated, and the increased porousness of national borders is attributed to the superimposition of a "Europe without borders."

This hidebound view of what is wrong with Europe stands in opposition to views of European developments in the light of cosmopolitanism and transnationalism. German sociologist Ulrich Beck is among those who see transnationalism as the outcome of long-term processes ushering in a stage of Second Modernity; they are processes that have worked to erode the logic of the historical stage of First Modernity, centered on the bonding and bounding force of nationalism in the historical formation of the nation-state.[14] Nationalism, as a historical project, aimed at molding nations conceived in terms of cultural and political homogeneity, speaking one national language, sharing one cultural identity. Its logic was inherently binary. At the same time that it defined insiders, it defined outsiders. These could be strangers in the midst of the "imagined community" of the nation, subject to a range of forms of exclusion, or they could literally be outsiders, members of other nations, and therefore cultural "others."

Our age of globalization has relentlessly chipped away at this binary logic. Exposed to a worldwide flow of cultural expression, people everywhere have appropriated cultural codes alien to their homogenized national cultures. They have developed multiple identities, allowing them to move across a range of cultural affinities and affiliations. The communications revolution, most recently in the form of the World Wide Web, has made for freedom of movement among a multitude of self-styled communities of taste and opinion, transcending national borders. A person's national identity is now only one among many options for meaningful affiliation with fellow human beings, triggered at some moments while remaining dormant, or latent, at others. One's local roots are now only one of the many signifiers of a person's sense of self. Beck calls this rooted cosmopolitanism, noting that there is no cosmopolitanism without localism.[15]

As Beck also points out, much of this new cosmopolitanism is relatively unconsidered, "banal."[16] Teenagers affiliating with a transnational youth culture, sharing cultural appetites with untold others dispersed across the globe, are simply consumers of mass culture, unaware of the existential joy of their transnational venture. Banal nationalism is being constantly eroded by the torrent of banal cosmopolitanism in the forms of mass culture that wash across the globe. It is banal because it is unreflected, never leading the new cosmopolitans to pause and ponder: What happened to their sense of self? Yet, unaware as they may be of the intricate pattern of cultural vectors that guide their cultural consumption, collectively they have worked to cosmopolitanize the nation-state from within. Countries like France, Germany, the UK, and the Netherlands are no longer nation-states but transnational states.

To be sure, mass culture is only one of the forces of change. International migration, the formation of diasporic communities across the map of Europe, and the attendant rise of multiculturalism have also changed the conventional paradigm of the nation-state. There is nothing banal here, in the sense of an unreflected cosmopolitanism taking root. Quite the contrary; the anguished consideration of the changed contours of the citizenry is a clear reflection of the concern, shared by many, about what has happened to the idea of the nation. Then again, as Beck argues in *Dissent*, the only way for the European project to go forward is for Europe to become a transnational state, a more defined and complex variant of what its component nations are already becoming.

Much as I agree with this vision of Europe's future, I am struck by the historical myopia in Beck's argument. As he presents his case, Europe's Second Modernity, its age of transnationalism and cosmopolitanism, evolves from Europe's First Modernity, an age whose central logic was that of the nation-state. This seems to deny the long historical experience of cosmopolitanism in Europe, of a view of the civilized life centering on what can only be described as European culture. This was no banal cosmopolitanism, but rather the high-minded version, that of cultural elites producing and consuming a culture that was truly cosmopolitan, transcending the borders and bounds of the nation-state. It was always a rooted cosmopolitanism, with European trends and styles in the arts always being refracted through local appropriations, reflecting local tastes and manners.

As Kant defined cosmopolitanism, it was always a way of combining the universal and the particular, *Nation und Weltbürger*, nation and world citizenship. This is the lasting and exhilarating promise of European history, in spite of the atrocities committed on European soil in the name of the homogenized nation, marching in lock-step, purging itself of unwanted "others." The vision of world citizenship, the transcending idea of humanity, has always had to be defended against the other half of Kant's dialectical pair, against the claims on behalf of the nation. In an astute discussion of the Nuremberg tribunal and the new legal principle of "crimes against humanity" that it introduced, Beck makes the following observation, worth quoting in full:

> It is at this point that cosmopolitan Europe generates a genuinely European inner contradiction, legally, morally, and politically. The traditions from which colonial, nationalist, and genocidal horror originated were clearly European. But so were the new legal standards against which these acts were condemned and tried in the spotlight of world publicity. At this formative moment in its history, Europe mobilized its traditions to produce something historically new. It took the idea of recognition of the humanity of the Other and made it the foundation of an historically new counter-logic. It specifically designed this logic to counteract the ethnic perversion of the European tradition to which the nation-based form of European modernity had just shown itself so horribly liable. It was an attempt to distill a European antidote to Europe.[17]

This is truly what the post–World War II project of building a new Europe has been all about: to draw on a long European tradition of high-minded cosmopolitanism, inclusive of cultural variety and cultural Others, and internalized by its citizens as a plurality of individual selves.

It is truly a daunting project. If it succeeds it may well serve as a model to the world, a rival to the American ideal of transnationalism, of constituting a nation of nations. If they are rival models, they are at the same time of the same make. They represent variations on larger ideals inspiring the idea of Western civilization and find their roots in truly European formative moments in history: the Renaissance, the Reformation, the Enlightenment.

So went the first trans-Atlantic reading of the significance of the terrorist attack of 9/11, which was seen as an onslaught on the core values of a shared civilization. How ironic, if not tragic, then, that before long the United States and Europe had parted ways in finding the proper response to the new threat of international terrorism. As for the United States, the first signs of its farewell to internationalism in foreign policy—to its Wilsonianism, if you wish—and to its pioneering role in designing the institutional and legal framework for peaceful interstate relations in the world, had actually preceded 9/11. No longer did the Bush administration conceive of the United States as a "first among equals," setting the guidelines for collective action while seeking legitimacy for action through treaties and United Nations resolutions. As the one hegemon on the world stage it felt free to pursue its national interest through policies that justly can be described as unilateralist. Many observers label it a throwback to the time of nation-state sovereignty, a stage in history that Europe is struggling to transcend.

In the vitriolic vituperation that now sets the tone of trans-Atlantic exchanges Americans discard as the "Old Europe" those countries that criticize the drift of American foreign policy, while hailing as the "New Europe" those countries that are willing to follow in America's footsteps. Robert Kagan contributed to this rising anti-Europeanism in the United States when he paraphrased the dictum that men are from Mars, women from Venus. As he chose to present the two poles, Americans now are the new Martians, while Europeans are the new Venutians. Never mind the gendering implied in his view that Europeans are collectively engaged in a feminine endeavor when they pursue the new, transnational and cosmopolitan Europe; he does make an astute point when he describes the European quest as Kantian, as an attempt to create a transnational space where laws and civility rule. As Kagan sees it, though, the Europeans are so self-immersed that they are forgetful of a larger world that is Hobbesian, and is a threat to them as much as to the United States. The European involvement that does occur in the larger world, he points out, tends to emphasize peacekeeping operations rather than preemptive military strikes.[18]

Kagan and many others tend to forget that it took the United States about a hundred years to find and test its institutional forms and build a nation of

Americans from people flooding to its shores from all over the world. And what made it possible for the U.S. to turn its back to the world, in self-chosen isolationism, was the protective umbrella of the Pax Britannica. Europe had only some forty years to turn its gaze inward so as to engage in shaping the contours of a new Europe. During those years it enjoyed in its turn the protection of an umbrella, provided this time by the Pax Americana.

This constellation came to an end along with the Cold War. Only now could the European construction fully come into its own, conceiving of the new Europe on the scale of the entire continent—a tremendous challenge that Europe needs time to cope with. Should it succeed, though—and this means the inclusion of Turkey—Europe would offer a model to the world, particularly the world of Islam or for that matter the state of Israel, of a civil and democratic order far more tempting than the imposition of democracy through preemptive military invasion. Those who support what the United States is pursuing in Iraq blithely call it a neo-Wilsonianism. I beg to differ. If there is a neo-Wilsonian promise, it is held by the new Europe, not the current Bush administration.

Notes

1. Edward Atiyah, *The Arabs* (Harmondsworth: Penguin Books, 1955).
2. On the history of this myth, see Jan Willem Schulte Nordholt, *The Myth of the West: America as the Last Empire* (Grand Rapids: Eerdmans, 1995).
3. Barbie Zelizer, *Remembering to Forget: Holocaust Memory Through the Camera's Eye* (Chicago: University of Chicago Press, 1998), 227.
4. Anne Applebaum, *Between East and West: Across the Borderlands of Europe* (London: Papermac, 1995), 305.
5. Moray McGowan, "'The Bridge of the Golden Horn': Istanbul, Europe and the 'Fractured Gaze from the West' in Turkish writing in Germany," *Yearbook of European Studies* 15 (2000): 53–69.
6. Quoted in Udo Steinbach, "Die Turkei zwischen Vergangenheit und Gegenwart," *Informationen zur politischen Bildung* 223, no. 2 (1989):43.
7. McGowan, "Bridge," 54.
8. This is true more generally, it is my impression, for European films shown in the United States. When in the United States, in places like Boston, New York, or even a small university town like Bloomington, I found it easier to keep up with recent European films than in my home town of Amsterdam. Important films reached those places, and ran in numerous cases for many weeks in the various art houses in the area.
9. For a survey of these European debates I refer the reader to my *If You've Seen One, You've Seen the Mall: Europeans and American Mass Culture* (Urbana: University of Illinois Press, 1996). For a survey of French views of American modernity, see my chapter on the subject in Rob Kroes, *Them and Us: Questions of Citizenship in a Globalizing World* (Urbana: University of Illinois Press, 2000).
10. See, e.g., Rob Kroes, "America and the European Sense of History," in Kroes, *Them and Us*.

11. I would like to thank Kate Delaney for calling this poster to my attention one rainy night in Amsterdam.

12. Roland Robertson, "Globalisation or Glocalisation?" *Journal of International Communication*, 1, no. 1 (1994): 33–52.

13. Daniel Boorstin, *The Genius of American Politics* (Chicago: University of Chicago Press, 1953).

14. Ulrich Beck, "Rooted Cosmopolitanism: Emerging from a Rivalry of Distinctions," in Ulrich Beck, Nathan Sznaider, and Rainer Winter, eds., *Global America? The Cultural Consequences of Globalization* (Liverpool: Liverpool University Press, 2003), 15–30. Also see Ulrich Beck, "Understanding the Real Europe," *Dissent* 50, no. 3 (2003): 32–39.

15. Beck, "Rooted Cosmopolitanism," 17.

16. Beck, "Rooted Cosmopolitanism," 21.

17. Beck, "Understanding the Real Europe," 35.

18. Robert Kagan, *Of Paradise and Power: America and Europe in the New World Order* (New York: Knopf, 2003).

SELECTED BIBLIOGRAPHIES

BIBLIOGRAPHIES

General Bibliography

Appadurai, Arjun. *Modernity at Large: Cultural Dimensions of Globalization.* Minneapolis: University of Minnesota Press, 1996.

Arndt, Richard T. *The First Resort of Kings: American Cultural Diplomacy in the Twentieth Century.* Dulles: Brassey's, 2005.

Ash, Timothy Garton. *Free World: America, Europe, and the Surprising Future of the West.* New York: Random House: 2004.

Bacevich, Andrew, ed. *Imperial Tense: Prospects and Problems of American Empire.* Chicago: Ivan R. Dee, 2003.

———. *American Empire: The Realities and Consequences of U.S. Diplomacy.* Cambridge: Harvard University Press, 2002.

Bach, Gerhard, Sabine Broeck, and Ulf Schulenberg, eds. *Americanization—Globalization—Education.* Heidelberg: Winter, 2003.

Barber, Benjamin R. *Fear's Empire: War, Terrorism, and Democracy.* New York: Norton, 2003.

———. *Jihad vs. McWorld.* New York: Times Books, 1995.

Beck, Ulrich, Natan Sznaider, and Rainer Winter, eds. *Global America? The Cultural Consequences of Globalization.* Liverpool: Liverpool University Press, 2003.

Bender, Peter. *Weltmacht Amerika: Das neue Rom.* Stuttgart: Klett-Cotta, 2003.

Berghahn, Volker R. *America and the Intellectual Cold Wars in Europe: Shepard Stone between Philanthropy, Academy, and Diplomacy.* Princeton: Princeton University Press, 2001.

Berghahn, Volker R., Anselm Doering-Manteuffel, and Christof Mauch, eds. 1999. "The American Impact on Western Europe: Americanization and Westernization in Transatlantic Perspective." Available at http://www.ghi-dc.org/conpotweb/westernpapers (last accessed: 21 November 2003).

Berman, Russell A. *Anti-Americanism in Europe: A Cultural Problem.* Stanford: Hoover Institution Press, 2004.

Beyme, Klaus von. *Vorbild Amerika? Der Einfluß der amerikanischen Demokratie in der Welt.* Munich: Piper, 1986.

Bigsby, C. W. E., ed. *Superculture: American Popular Culture and Europe.* Bowling Green: Bowling Green University Popular Press, 1975.

Blair, John G., and Reinhold Wagnleitner, eds. *Empire: American Studies. Selected Papers from the Bi-National Conference of the Swiss and Austrian Associations for American Studies at the Salzburg Seminar, November 1996.* Tübingen: Narr, 1997.

Bogart, Leo. *Cool Words, Cold War: A New Look at USIA's Premises for Propaganda.* Washington: American University Press, 1995.

Bromark, Stian, and Dag Herbjørnsrud. *Frykten for Amerika: En europeisk historie.* Oslo: Tiden Norsk, 2003.

Brzezinski, Zbigniew. *The Grand Chessboard: American Primacy and Its Geostrategic Imperatives.* New York: Basic Books, 1997.

Busse, Sabine. *Europa blickt auf Amerika—und umgekehrt? Die neue transatlantische Agenda als Grundlage einer effektiven Partnerschaft.* Bonn: Europa Union, 2003.

Campbell, Neil. *Landscapes of Americanisation.* Derby: University of Derby, 2003.

Campbell, Neil, Jude Davies, and George McKay. *Issues in Americanisation and Culture.* Edinburgh: Edinburgh University Press, 2004.

Caute, David. *The Dancer Defects: The Struggle for Cultural Supremacy during the Cold War.* New York: Oxford University Press, 2003.

Ceasar, James W. *Reconstructing America: The Symbol of America in Modern Thought.* New Haven: Yale University Press, 1997.

Chargaff, Erwin. *Armes Amerika-Arme Welt: Ein Essay.* Stuttgart: Klett-Cotta, 1994.

Chiesa, Giulietto. *Das Zeitalter des Imperiums: Europas Rolle im Kampf um die Weltherrschaft.* Hamburg: Europäische Verlagsanstalt, 2003.

Chomsky, Noam. *Hegemony or Survival: America's Quest for Global Dominance.* New York: Metropolitan Books, 2003.

Cohen, Jean-Louis. *Scenes of the World to Come: European Architecture and the American Challenge, 1893–1960.* Paris: Flammarion, 1995.

Coleman, Peter. *The Liberal Conspiracy: The Congress for Cultural Freedom and the Struggle for the Mind of Postwar Europe.* New York: Free Press, 1989.

Coleman, Vernon. *Rogue Nation: Why America Is the Most Dangerous State on Earth.* Barnstaple: Blue Books, 2003.

Crockatt, Richard. *America Embattled: September 11, Anti-Americanism, and the Global Order.* London: Routledge, 2003.

Czempiel, Ernst-Otto. *Weltpolitik im Umbruch: Die Pax Americana, der Terrorismus und die Zukunft der internationalen Beziehungen.* Munich: Beck, 2002.

Dallek, Robert. *The American Style of Foreign Policy: Cultural Politics and Foreign Affairs.* New York: Knopf, 1983.

Dean, John, and Jean-Paul Gabilliet, eds. *European Readings of American Popular Culture.* Westport: Greenwood Press, 1996.

DeFleur, Melvin L., and Margaret H. DeFleur. *Learning to Hate Americans: How U.S. Media Shape Negative Attitudes among Teenagers in Twelve Countries.* Spokane: Marquette Books, 2003.

Dizard, Wilson P. *Inventing Public Diplomacy: The Story of the U.S. Information Agency.* Boulder: Lynne Rienner, 2004.

Djelic, Marie-Laure. *Exporting the American Model: The Postwar Transformation of European Business.* Oxford: University Press, 1998.

Draxlbauer, Michael, Astrid M. Fellner, and Thomas Fröschl, eds. *(Anti-) Americanisms.* Vienna: Lit, 2004.

Dudden, Arthur Power, and Russell R. Dynes, eds. *The Fulbright Experience, 1946–1986: Encounters and Transformations.* New Brunswick: Transaction Books, 1987.

Duignan, Peter, and L. H. Gann. *The Rebirth of the West: The Americanization of the Democratic World, 1945–1958.* Cambridge: Blackwell, 1992.

Ellwood, David W. *Anti-Americanism in Western Europe: A Comparative Perspective.* Bologna: Johns Hopkins University Bologna Center, 1999.

———. *Rebuilding Europe: Western Europe, America, and Postwar Reconstruction.* London: Longman, 1992.

Ellwood, David W., and Rob Kroes, eds. *Hollywood in Europe: Experiences of a Cultural Hegemony.* Amsterdam: VU University Press, 1994.

Epitropoulos, Mike-Frank G., and Victor Routometof, eds. *American Culture in Europe: Interdisciplinary Perspectives.* Westport: Praeger, 1998.

"Europa oder Amerika: Zur Zukunft des Westens." *Merkur* Sonderheft 9-10 (2000).

Faath, Sigrid, ed. *Antiamerikanismus in Nordafrika, Nah- und Mittelost: Formen, Dimensionen und Folgen für Europa und Deutschland.* Hamburg: Deutsches Orient-Institut, 2003.

Fehrenbach, Heide, and Uta G. Poiger. *Transactions, Transgressions, Transformations: American Culture in Western Europe and Japan.* New York: Berghahn, 2000.

Ferguson, Niall. *Colossus: The Price of America's Empire.* New York: Penguin, 2004.

Fink, Hermann, and Liane Fijas. *America and her Influence upon the Language and Culture of Post-Socialist Countries.* Frankfurt: Lang, 1998.

Flynn, Daniel J. *Why the Left Hates America: Exposing the Lies that Have Obscured Our Nation's Greatness*. New York: Three Rivers Press, 2004.

Frankel, Charles. *The Neglected Aspect of Foreign Affairs: American Educational and Cultural Policy Abroad*. Washington: Brookings Institution, 1965.

Frascina, Francis. *Pollock and After: The Critical Debate*. New York: Harper and Row, 1985.

Funke, Hajo. *Der amerikanische Weg: Hegemonialer Nationalismus in der US-Administration*. Berlin: Schiler, 2003.

Gellner, Winand, ed. *Europäisches Fernsehen—American Blend? Fernsehmedien zwischen Amerikanisierung und Europäisierung*. Berlin: Vistas, 1989.

German Historical Institute. "The American Impact on Western Europe: Americanization and Westernization in Transatlantic Perspective." http://www.ghi-dc.org/conpotweb/westernpapers/ (last accessed: 24 February 2005).

Gibson, John. *Hating America: The New World Sport*. New York: Regan Books, 2004.

Gienow-Hecht, Jessica C. E. "Shame on US? Academics, Cultural Transfer, and the Cold War—A Critical Review." *Diplomatic History* 24 (summer 2000): 466–515.

Gienow-Hecht, Jessica C. E., and Frank Schumacher, eds. *Culture and International History*. New York: Berghahn, 2003.

Giorcelli, Cristina, Rob Kroes, and Peter G. Boyle. *Living with America, 1946–1996*. Amsterdam: VU University Press, 1997.

Glaser, Elisabeth, and Hermann Wellenreuther, eds. *Bridging the Atlantic: The Question of American Exceptionalism in Perspective*. Washington: Cambridge University Press, 2002.

Haddow, Robert H. *Pavilions of Plenty: Exhibiting American Culture Abroad in the 1950s*. Washington: Smithsonian Institution Press, 1997.

Haller, Gret. *Die Grenzen der Solidarität: Europa und die USA im Umgang mit Staat, Nation und Religion*. Berlin: Aufbau, 2002.

Hanson, Victor Davis. *Between War and Peace: Lessons from Afghanistan to Iraq*. New York: Random House, 2004.

Hardt, Michael, and Antonio Negri. *Empire*. Cambridge: Harvard University Press, 2000.

Haskell, Barbara, and Lisa Phillips. *The American Century: Art and Culture, 1900–2000*. 2 vols. New York: Whitney Museum of American Art, 1999.

Hebel, Udo, and Karl Ortseifen. *Transatlantic Encounters: Studies in European-American Relations*. Trier: Wissenschaftlicher Verlag, 1995.

Herm, Gerhard. *Amerika ist an allem schuld: Die Amerikanisierung der Alten Welt*. Munich: Heyne, 1980.

———. *Amerika erobert Europa*. Duesseldorf: Econ, 1964.

Hertsgaard, Mark. *The Eagle's Shadow: Why America Fascinates and Infuriates the World.* New York: Farrar, Straus, and Giroux, 2002.

Higson, Andrew, and Richard Maltby, eds. *"Film Europe" and "Film America:" Cinema, Commerce, and Cultural Exchange 1920–1939.* Exeter: University of Exeter Press, 1999.

Himmelfarb, Gertrude. *Roads to Modernity: The British, French, and American Enlightenments.* New York: Knopf, 2004.

Hirsh, Michael. *At War with Ourselves: Why Is America Squandering its Chance to Build a Better World.* New York: Oxford University Press, 2003.

Hixson, Walter L. *Parting the Curtain: Propaganda, Culture, and the Cold War, 1945–1961.* New York: St. Martin's Press, 1997.

Hogan, Michael J., ed. *The Ambiguous Legacy: US Foreign Policy in the American Century.* Cambridge: Cambridge University Press, 1999.

———. *The Marshall Plan: America, Britain, and the Reconstruction of Western Europe, 1947–1952.* Cambridge: Cambridge University Press, 1987.

Hollander, Paul, ed. *Understanding Anti-Americanism: Its Origins and Impact at Home and Abroad.* Chicago: Dee, 2004.

———. *Anti-Americanism: Rational and Irrational.* New Brunswick: Transaction, 1995.

Horwitz, Richard P., ed. *Exporting America: Essays on American Studies Abroad.* New York: Garland, 1993.

Houe, Poul, and Sven Hakon Rossel, eds. *Images of America in Scandinavia.* Amsterdam: Rodopi, 1998.

Hudson, Cheryl, ed. "Americanisation and Anti-Americanism: Global Views of the USA." *European Journal of American Culture.* Special Issue 23, no. 2 (2004).

Huntington, Samuel. *The Clash of Civilizations and the Remaking of World Order.* New York: Simon and Schuster, 1996.

Hutton, Will. *A Declaration of Interdependence: Why America Should Join the World.* New York: Norton, 2003.

———. *The World We're In.* Boston: Little, Brown, 2002.

Iriye, Akira. *Cultural Internationalism and World Order.* Baltimore: Johns Hopkins University Press, 1997.

Jarvie, Ian. *Hollywood's Overseas Campaign: The North Atlantic Movie Trade, 1920–1950.* Cambridge: Cambridge University Press, 1992.

Johansson, Johny K. *In Your Face: How American Marketing Excess Fuels Anti-Americanism.* Upper Saddle River: Financial Times Prentice Hall, 2004.

Johnson, Chalmers. *The Sorrows of Empire: Militarism, Secrecy, and the End of the Republic.* New York: Metropolitan, 2004.

———. *Blowback: The Costs and Consequences of American Empire.* New York: Metropolitan, 2000.

Kagan, Robert. *Of Paradise and Power: America and Europe in the New World Order.* New York: Knopf, 2003.

Kaiser, Karl, and Hans-Peter Schwarz, eds. *America and Western Europe: Problems and Prospects.* Lexington: Lexington Books, 1978.

Kamalipour, Yahya R. *Images of the U.S. around the World: A Multicultural Perspective.* Albany: State University of New York Press, 1999.

Kamps, Klaus, ed. *Trans–Atlantik–Trans–Portabel? Die Amerikanisierungsthese in der politischen Kommunikation.* Wiesbaden: Westdeutscher Verlag, 2000.

Katzarov, Georgy, ed. *Regards sur l'antiaméricanisme: Une histoire culturelle.* Paris: Harmattan, 2004.

Kipping, Matthias, and Ove Bjarnar. *The Americanisation of European Business: The Marshall Plan and the Transfer of US Management Models.* London: Routledge, 1998.

Kissinger, Henry. *Does America Need a Foreign Policy? Toward a Diplomacy for the 21st Century.* New York: Simon and Schuster, 2001.

Krabbendam, Hans, J. Verheul, and Hans Bak, eds. *Through the Cultural Looking Glass: American Studies in Transcultural Perspective.* Amsterdam: VU University Press, 1999.

Kraus, Elisabeth, and Carolin Auer. *Simulacrum America: The USA and the Popular Media.* Rochester: Camden House, 2000.

Kroes, Rob, ed. *Predecessors: Intellectual Lineages in American Studies.* Amsterdam: VU University Press, 1999.

———. *If You've Seen One, You've Seen the Mall: Europeans and American Mass Culture.* Urbana: University of Illinois Press, 1996.

———. *Within the US Orbit: Small National Cultures Vis-à-vis the United States.* Amsterdam: VU University Press, 1991.

———, ed. *High Brow Meets Low Brow: American Culture as an Intellectual Concern.* Amsterdam: VU University Press, 1988.

Kroes, Rob, and Maarten van Rossem, eds. *Anti-Americanism in Europe.* Amsterdam: VU University Press, 1986.

Kroes, Rob, Robert W. Rydell, D. F. J. Bosscher, and John F. Sears, eds. *Cultural Transmissions and Receptions: American Mass Culture in Europe.* Amsterdam: VU University Press, 1993.

Kupchan, Charles A. *The End of the American Era: U.S. Foreign Policy and the Geopolitics of the Twenty-First Century.* New York: Knopf, 2002.

Kurtz, Jonathan D. *Fixing the Transatlantic Relationship: Improving U.S.-European Relations.* Carlisle Barracks: U.S. Army War College, 2004.

Lehmann, Hartmut. *Alte und neue Welt in wechselseitiger Sicht: Studien zu den transatlantischen Beziehungen im 19. und 20. Jahrhundert.* Göttingen: Vandenhook and Ruprecht, 1995.

Lerda, Valeria Gennaro, ed. *Which "Global Village?" Societies, Cultures, and Political-Economic Systems in a Euro-Atlantic Perspective.* Westport: Praeger, 2002.

Lipset, Seymour. *American Exceptionalism: A Double-Edged Sword.* New York: Norton, 1996.

Lorenz, Sebastian, and Marcel Machill, eds. *Transatlantik: Transfer von Politik, Wirtschaft und Kultur.* Opladen: Westdeutscher Verlag, 1999.

Markovits, Andrei S. *Amerika, dich haßt sichs besser: Antiamerikanismus und Antisemitismus in Europa.* Hamburg: KVV Konkret, 2004.

McKay, George, ed. *Yankee Go Home (& Take Me With U): Americanisation and Popular Culture.* Sheffield: Sheffield Academic Press, 1997.

Meier-Walser, Reinhard. *Transatlantische Partnerschaft: Perspektiven der amerikanisch-europäischen Beziehungen.* Landsberg: Olzog, 1997.

Melling, Philip H., and Jon Roper. *Americanisation and the Transformation of World Cultures: Melting Pot or Cultural Chernobyl?* Lewiston: Edwin Mellen Press, 1996.

Mitchell, Tony. *Global Noise: Rap and Hip-Hop Outside the USA.* Middletown: Wesleyan University Press, 2001.

———. *Popular Music and Local Identity: Rock, Pop, and Rap in Europe and Oceania.* London: Leicester University Press, 1996.

Moore, R. Laurence, and Maurizio Vaudagna, eds. *The American Century in Europe.* Ithaca: Cornell University Press, 2003.

Müller-Hofstede, Christoph. *Die Zukunft der transatlantischen Beziehungen im Kontext der Globalisierung: Eine deutsch-amerikanische Konferenz.* Brühl: Ost-West-Kolleg der Bundeszentrale für politische Bildung, 2001.

Nakaya, Andrea C. *Does the World Hate the United States?* Detroit: Greenhaven Press, 2005.

Ney, John. *The European Surrender: A Descriptive Study of the American Social and Economic Conquest.* Boston: Little and Brown, 1970.

Ninkovich, Frank A. *The Diplomacy of Ideas: U.S. Foreign Policy and Cultural Relations, 1938–1950.* Chicago: Imprint Publications, 1995.

Nowell-Smith, Geoffrey, and Steven Ricci, eds. *Hollywood and Europe: Economics, Culture, National Identity, 1945–95.* London: British Film Institute, 1998.

Nye, Joseph S., Jr. *The Paradox of American Power: Why the World's Only Superpower Can't Go It Alone.* New York: Oxford University Press, 2002.

Ostendorf, Berndt, ed. *Transnational America: The Fading of Borders in the Western Hemisphere.* Heidelberg: Winter, 2002.

———. "Why is American Popular Culture so Popular? A View from Europe." *Amerikastudien/American Studies* 56, no. 3 (2001): 339–66.

Packer, George. *The Fight for Democracy: Winning the War of Ideas in America and the World.* New York: Perennial, 2003.

Panfilow, A. *Der USA-Rundfunk im psychologischen Krieg.* Potsdam-Babelsberg: Deutsche Akademie für Staats- und Rechtswissenschaft, 1969.

Passerini, Luisa, ed. *Across the Atlantic: Cultural Exchanges between Europe and the United States.* Brussels: Lang, 2000.

Pells, Richard. *Not Like US: How Europeans Have Loved, Hated, and Transformed American Culture Since World War II.* New York: Basic Books, 1997.

Peterson, Peter G., Kathy F. Bloomgarden, Henry A. Grunswald, David E. Morey, Shibley Telhami, Jennifer Seig, and Sharon Herbstman. *Finding America's Voice: A Strategy for Reinvigorating U.S. Public Diplomacy: Report of an Independent Task Force Sponsored by the Council on Foreign Relations.* Washington, D.C.: Brookings Institution Press, 2003.

Pilz, Peter. *Mit Gott gegen alle: Amerikas Kampf um die Weltherrschaft.* Stuttgart: Deutsche Verlags-Anstalt, 2003.

Polster, Bernd, ed. *Westwind: Die Amerikanisierung Europas.* Cologne: Dumont, 1995.

Prestowitz, Clyde. *Rogue Nation: American Unilateralism and the Failure of Good Intentions.* New York: Basic Books, 2003.

Puddington, Arch. *Broadcasting Freedom: The Cold War Triumph of Radio Free Europe and Radio Liberty.* Lexington: University Press of Kentucky, 2000.

Ramet, Sabrina Petra, ed. *Rocking the State: Rock Music and Politics in Eastern Europe and Russia.* Boulder: Westview Press, 1994.

Ramet, Sabrina Petra, and Gordana P. Crnković, eds. *Kazaaam! Splat! Ploof! The American Impact on European Popular Culture since 1945.* Lanham: Rowman and Littlefield, 2003.

Ramet, Sabrina Petra, and Christine Ingebritsen, eds. *Coming In from the Cold War: Changes in U.S.-European Interaction since 1980.* Lanham: Rowman and Littlefield, 2002.

Reid, T. R. *The United States of Europe: The New Superpower and the End of American Supremacy.* New York: Penguin, 2004.

Revel, Jean-François. *Anti-Americanism.* San Francisco: Encounter Books, 2003.

Richmond, Yale. *Cultural Exchange and the Cold War: Raising the Iron Curtain.* University Park: Pennsylvania State University Press, 2003.

Rifkin, Jeremy. *The European Dream: How Europe's Vision of the Future Is Quietly Eclipsing the American Dream.* New York: Penguin, 2004.

Rittberger, Volker, and Fariborz Zelli. *Europa in der Weltpolitik: Juniorpartner der USA oder antihegemoniale Alternative?* Tübingen: Institut für Politikwissenschaft, 2003.

Rollin, Roger, ed. *The Americanization of the Global Village: Essays in Comparative Popular Culture.* Bowling Green: Bowling Green University Popular Press, 1989.

Ross, Andrew, and Kristin Ross, eds. *Anti-Americanism.* New York: New York University Press, 2004.

Rubin, Barry, and Judith Colp Rubin. *Hating America: A History.* New York: Oxford University Press, 2004.

Russell, Bertrand, ed. *The Impact of America on European Culture.* Boston: Beacon, 1951.

Ryback, Timothy W. *Rock Around the Bloc: A History of Rock Music in Eastern Europe and the Soviet Union.* New York: Oxford University Press, 1990.

Rydell, Robert W., and Rob Kroes. *Buffalo Bill in Bologna: The Americanization of the World, 1869–1922.* Chicago: University of Chicago Press, 2005.

Sardar, Ziauddin, and Merryl Wyn Davies. *Why Do People Hate America?* New York: Disinformation, 2002.

Saunders, Frances Stonor. *The Cultural Cold War: The CIA and the World of Arts and Letters.* New York: New Press, 2000.

Schwartz, Richard A. *Cold War Culture: Media and the Arts, 1945–1990.* New York: Facts on File, 1998.

Scott-Smith, Giles. *The Politics of Apolitical Culture: The Congress for Cultural Freedom, the CIA, and Post-War American Hegemony.* London: Routledge, 2002.

Scott-Smith, Giles, and Hans Krabbendam, eds. *The Cultural Cold War in Western Europe. 1945–1960.* London: Cass, 2003.

Scowen, Peter. *Rogue Nation: The America the Rest of the World Knows.* Toronto: M&S, 2003.

Shafer, Byron E., ed. *Is America Different? A New Look at American Exceptionalism.* New York: Oxford University Press, 1991.

Shlapentokh, Vladimir, Joshua Woods, and Eric Shiraev, eds. *America: Sovereign Defender or Cowboy Nation?* Aldershot: Ashgate, 2005.

Skard, Sigmund. *American Studies in Europe: Their History and Present Organization.* Philadelphia: University of Pennsylvania Press, 1958.

Slater, David, and Peter J. Taylor. *The American Century: Consensus and Coercion in the Projection of American Power.* Oxford: Blackwell, 1999.

Speck, Ulrich, and Natan Sznaider, eds. *Empire Amerika: Perspektiven einer neuen Weltordnung.* Munich: Deutsche Verlags-Anstalt, 2003.

Stearn, Gerald Emanuel, ed. *Broken Image: Foreign Critiques of America.* New York: Random House, 1972.

Stich, Sidra. *Made in the U.S.A.: An Americanization in Modern Art, the '50s & '60s.* Berkeley: University of California Press, 1987.

Thomsen, Christian W., ed. *Cultural Transfer or Electronic Imperialism? The Impact of American Television Programs on European Television.* Heidelberg: Winter, 1989.

Thorton, Thomas Perry, ed. "Anti-Americanism: Origins and Context." *The Annals of the American Academy of Political and Social Science.* London: Sage, 1998.

Todd, Emmanuel. *After the Empire: The Breakdown of the American Order.* New York: Columbia University Press, 2003.

Tomlinson, John. *Globalization and Culture.* Chicago: University of Chicago Press, 1999.

———. *Cultural Imperialism: A Critical Introduction.* Baltimore: Johns Hopkins University Press, 1991.

Trumpbour, John. *Selling Hollywood to the World: U.S. and European Struggles for Mastery of the Global Film Industry, 1920–1950.* Cambridge: Cambridge University Press, 2001.

Tuch, Hans. *Communicating with the World: U.S. Public Diplomacy Overseas.* New York: St. Martin's Press, 1990.

Urban, George R. *Radio Free Europe and the Pursuit of Democracy: My War within the Cold War.* New Haven: Yale University Press, 1997.

Uwer, Thomas, Thomas von der Osten-Sacken, and Andrea Woeldike, eds. *Amerika: Der "War on Terror" und der Aufstand der Alten Welt.* Freiburg: ça ira, 2003.

Vries, Tity de, Hans Bak, and F. L. van Holthoon. *Dynamics of Modernization: European-American Comparisons and Perceptions.* Amsterdam: VU University Press, 1998.

Wagner, Bernd, ed. *Kulturelle Globalisierung: Zwischen Weltkultur und kultureller Fragmentierung.* Frankfurt: Klartext, 2001.

Wagnleitner, Reinhold, and Elaine Tyler May, eds. *"Here, There, and Everywhere:" The Foreign Politics of American Popular Culture.* Hanover: University of New England Press, 2000.

Walker, Robert H., ed. *American Studies Abroad.* Westport: Greenwood, 1975.

Wallerstein, Immanuel. *The Decline of American Power: The U.S. in a Chaotic World.* New York: New Press, 2003.

Weidenfeld, Werner. *America and Europe: Is the Break Inevitable?* Gütersloh: Bertelsmann, 1996.

White, Donald W. *The American Century: The Rise and Decline of the United States as a World Power.* New Haven: Yale University Press, 1996.

Woodward, C. Vann. *The Old World's New World.* New York: Oxford University Press, 1991.

Zunz, Oliver. *Why the American Century?* Chicago: University of Chicago Press, 1998.

Austria

Adamek, Heinz P., ed. *In die Neue Welt...: Arthur Schnitzler—Eugen Deimel Briefwechsel.* Vienna: Holzhausen, 2003.

AFS Austauschprogramme für Interkulturelles Lernen, ed. *AFS Jahresprogramm 1950–1993.* Vienna: AFS, 1993.

Bauer, Ingrid. *Welcome Ami Go Home: Die amerikanische Besatzung in Salzburg 1945–1955: Erinnerungslandschaft aus einem Oral-History-Projekt.* Salzburg: Pustet, 1998.

Bischof, Günter. *Austria in the First Cold War, 1945–55: The Leverage of the Weak.* New York: St. Martin's, 1999.

Bischof, Günter and Anton Pelinka, eds. *The Americanization/Westernization of Austria.* New Brunswick: Transaction, 2004.

Bischof, Günter, Anton Pelinka, and Dieter Stiefel, eds. *The Marshall Plan in Austria.* New Brunswick: Transaction, 2000.

Bischof, Günter and Rüdiger Overmans, eds. *Kriegsgefangenschaft im Zweiten Weltkrieg: Eine vergleichende Perspektive.* Ternitz-Pottschach: Höller, 1999.

Bischof, Günter, Anton Pelinka, and Rolf Steininger, eds. *Austria in the Nineteen Fifties.* New Brunswick: Transaction, 1995.

Friends and Partners in Education 1976–2003. Innsbruck: Center Austria, University of New Orleans, 2003.

Chorherr, Thomas. *Wir Täterkinder: Junges Leben zwischen Hakenkreuz, Bomben und Freiheit.* Vienna: Molden Verlag, 2001.

Daxlbauer, Michael, Astrid Fellner, and Tomas Fröschl, eds. *Austrian (Anti-) Americanisms.* Tübingen: Lit Verlag, 2004.

Drimmel, Heinrich. *Die Antipoden: Die Neue Welt in den USA und das Österreich vor 1918.* Vienna: Amalthea, 1984.

Fröschl, Thomas, Margarethe Grandner, and Birgitta Bader-Zaar, eds. *Nordamerikastudien: Historische und literaturwissenschaftliche Forschungen aus österreichischen Universitäten zu den Vereinigten Staaten und Kanada.* Vienna: Verlag für Geschichte und Politik, 2000.

Hölbling, Walter, and Reinhold Wagnleitner, eds. *The European Emigrant Experience in the U.S.A.* Tübingen: Narr, 1992.

Johnson, Lonnie and Karin Riegler, eds. *Fulbright at Fifty: Austrian-American Educational Exchange 1950–2000.* Vienna: Austrian-American Educational Commission (Fulbright Commission), 2000.

Kos, Wolfgang, and Georg Rigele, eds. *Inventur 45/55: Österreich im ersten Jahrzehnt der Zweiten Republik.* Vienna: Sonderzahl, 1996.

Krammer, Arnold. *Nazi Prisoners of War in America.* New York: Stein and Day, 1979.

Matthiesen, Francis Otto. *From the Heart of Europe.* New York: Oxford University Press, 1948.

Pabisch, Peter, ed. *From Wilson to Waldheim: Proceedings of a Workshop on Austrian-American Relations 1917–1987.* Riverside: Ariadne Press, 1989.

Reiß, Matthias. *"Die Schwarzen waren unsere Freunde:" Deutsche Kriegsgefangene in der amerikanischen Gesellschaft 1942–1946.* Paderborn: Schöningh, 2002.

Schama, Simon. "The Unloved American." *The New Yorker,* 10 March 2003, 34–39.

Schmidt, Oliver M. A. *A Civil Empire by Co-optation: German-American Exchange Programs as Cultural Diplomacy, 1945–1961.* Ph.D. diss., Harvard University, 1999.

Treichl, Heinrich. *Fast ein Jahrhundert: Erinnerungen.* Vienna: Zsolnay, 2003.

Wagnleitner, Reinhold. *Coca-Colonization and the Cold War: The Cultural Mission of the United States in Austria after the Second World War.* Chapel Hill: University of North Carolina Press, 1994.

Denmark

Bech-Petersen, Ole. *Encounters: Danish Literary Travel in the United States.* Ph.D. diss., University of Southern Denmark, 2000.

Christensen, Peter Knoop, ed. *USA og os. En antologi om det danske samfunds påvirkning af impulser fra USA efter 1945.* Herning: Systime, 1984.

————, ed. *Amerikanisering af det danske kulturliv i perioden 1945–58.* Ålborg: Ålborg University Press, 1983.

Hertel, Hans. "Kulturens kolde krig. Polarisering, antikommunisme og antiamerikanisme i dansk kulturliv 1946–60." *Kritik* 135, no. 158 (August 2002): 9–23.

————. *Vor tids Reitzel. En pionerforlægger og hans samtid 1949–1999.* Copenhagen: Hans Reitzels, 1999.

Jensen, Klaus Bruhn, ed. *Dansk mediehistorie,* vols. 1–3. Copenhagen: Samleren, 1997.

Jacobsen, Henrik Galberg. *Dansk sprogrøgtslitteratur 1900–1955.* Copenhagen: Dansk Sprognævns Skrifter, 1974.

Mariager, Rasmus. *I tillid og varm sympati: Dansk-britiske forbindelser og USA 1945–1959–1965.* Ph.D. diss., University of Copenhagen, 2003.

Nelleman, George, ed. *Dagligliv i Danmark i vor tid,* vols. 1–2. Copenhagen: Nyt Nordisk, 1989.

Nielsen, Niels Jul. *Mellem uskyld & A-bomber: Koldkrigens København i 1950'erne.* Copenhagen: Bymuseet, 2003.

Petersen, Klaus, and Nils Arne Sørensen. *Den kolde krig på hjemmefronten.* Odense: Syddansk University Press, forthcoming.

Petersen, Pia Riber. *Nye ord i dansk 1955–1975.* Copenhagen: Gyldendal, 1984.

Philipsen, Ingeborg. "Selskabet for Kultur og Frihed: Congress for Cultural Freedom i Danmark 1953–60." *Kritik* 135, no. 158 (2002): 38–51.

Sevaldsen, Jørgen, ed. *Britain and Denmark: Political, Economic and Cultural Relations in the 19th and 20th Century.* Copenhagen: Museum Tusculanum Press, 2003.

Toft Hansen, Søren. *Rationaliseringsdebatten i Danmark 1918–1947: Industriledelse, Produktivitet og Social Fred. Jern- og Metalsektoren som eksempel.* Ph.D. diss., University of Aalborg, 2001.

Villaume, Poul. *Allieret med forbehold: Danmark, Nato og den kolde krig: En studie i dansk sikkerhedspolitik 1949–1961.* Copenhagen: Eirene, 1995.

France

Agamben, Giorgio. *Etat d'Exception.* Paris: Seuil, 2003.

"Anti-américanisme heir et aujourd'hui." *Les Cahiers d'Histoire Sociale* 21 (2002–2003).

Arnavon, Cyrille. *L'américanisme et nous.* Paris: Del Duca, 1958.

Astier, Henri. "La maladie française: When Trouble Comes, First Blame the Americans." *Times Literary Supplement,* 10 January 2003, 3–4.

Balibar, Etienne. *L'Europe, L'Amérique, La guerre: Réflections sur la médiation européenne.* Paris: La Découverte, 2003.

———. *Droit de cité: Culture et politique en démocratie.* Paris: L'Aube, 1998.

Baudrillard, Jean. *Paroxysm: Interviews with Philippe Petit.* London: Verso, 1998.

———. *La guerre du Golfe n'a pas eu lieu.* Paris: Galilée, 1991.

———. *America.* London: Verso, 1988.

Beauvior, Simone de. *America Day by Day.* London: Duckworth, 1952.

Brinton, Crane. *The Americans and the French.* Cambridge: Harvard University Press, 1968.

Bruckner, Pascal. *Misère de la prospérité: La religion marchande et ses ennemis.* Paris: Grasset, 2002.

Bumiller, Elisabeth. "US, Angry at French Stance on War Considers Punishment." *The New York Times,* 24 April 2003, A20.

Chesnoff, Richard Z. *The Arrogance of the French: Why They Can't Stand Us and Why the Feeling Is Mutual.* New York: Sentinel, 2005.

Colombani, Jean-Marie. *Tous Américains? Le monde après le 11 septembre 2001.* Paris: Fayard, 2002.

Colombani, Jean-Marie, and Walter Wells. *Dangerous De-liaisons: What's Really Behind the War Between France and the U.S.* Hoboken: Melville House, 2004.

Conan, Eric. "L'antiaméricanisme: Un mal français." *L'Express* 10 April 2003, 45–50.

Costigliola, Frank. *France and the United States: The Cold Alliance since World War II.* New York: Twayne, 1992.

Daniel, Jean. *Lettres de France: Après le 11 septembre.* Mesnil-sur-l'Estrée: Saint-Simon, 2002.

Debouzy, Marianne. "Does Mickey Mouse Threaten French Culture? The French Debate over Eurodisneyland." In Sabrina P. Ramet and Gordana P. Crnković, eds., *Kazaam! Splat! Ploof! The American Impact on European Popular Culture since 1945.* Lanham: Rowman and Littlefield, 2003.

Dupuy, Jean-Pierre. *Avions-nous oublié le mal? Penser la politique après le 11 septembre.* Paris: Bayard, 2002.

Ferro, Maurice. *De Gaulle et l'Amérique: Une amitié tumultueuse.* Paris: Plon, 1973.

Finkielkraut, Alain. *L'imparfait du présent.* Paris: Gallimard, 2002.

Glucksmann, André. *Ouest contre Ouest.* Paris: Plon, 2003.

Grantham, Bill. *"Some Big Bourgeois Brother:" Contexts for France's Culture Wars with Hollywood.* Luton: University of Luton Press, 2000.

Grewe, Astrid. *Das Amerikabild der französischen Schriftsteller zwischen den beiden Weltkriegen.* Heidelberg: Winter, 1985.

Hanson, Victor, Anatol Lieven, and Felix Rohatyn. "Où vont les Etats-Unis?" *Le Débat* 123 (Jan/Feb. 2003): 4–30.

Hassner, Pierre. *La terreur et l'empire: la violence et la paix II.* Paris: Seuil, 2003.

Hétu, Richard. *Lettre ouverte aux antiaméricains.* Montreal: VLB, 2003.

Hoffmann, Stanley. "La nouvelle version de l'exceptionnalisme américain." *Esprit* (February 2003): 6–20.

Khilnani, Sunil. *Arguing Revolution: The Intellectual Left in Postwar France.* New Haven: Yale University Press, 1993.

Kuisel, Richard. "The Fernandel Factor: The Rivalry between the French and American Cinema in the 1950's." *Yale French Studies* 98 (2000): 119–134.

———. "Learning to Love McDonald's, Coca-Cola, and Disneyland Paris." *La revue Tocqueville/The Tocqueville Review* 21 no. 1 (2000): 129–134.

———. *Seducing the French: The Dilemma of Americanization.* Berkeley: University of California Press, 1993.

Kuisel, Richard, and Tony Judt. "Deteriorating US-French Relations." *The Chronicle of Higher Education* 49, no. 25 (2003): B4.

Lacorne, Denis, and Jacques Rupnik, eds. *The Rise and Fall of Anti-Americanism: A Century of French Perception.* New York: St. Martin's Press, 1990.

Laughland, John. *The Death of Politics: France under Mitterrand*. London: Michael Joseph, 1994.

Launay, Stephen. *La guerre sans la guerre: essai sur une querelle occidentale*. Paris: Descartes and Cie, 2003.

"Linguists Urge French over English." *The New York Times,* 8 April 2003, A9.

Lukic, Reneo, and Michael Brint, eds. *Culture, Politics, and Nationalism in the Age of Globalization*. Aldershot: Ashgate, 2001.

Mahan, Erin R. *Kennedy, de Gaulle, and Western Europe*. New York: Palgrave Macmillan, 2002.

Mathy, Jean-Philippe. *French Resistance: The French-American Culture Wars*. Minneapolis: University of Minneapolis Press, 2000.

———. *Extrême Occident: French Intellectuals and America*. Chicago: University of Chicago Press, 1993.

Miller, John J., and Mark Molesky. *Our Oldest Enemy: A History of America's Disastrous Relationship with France*. New York: Doubleday, 2004.

Nora, Pierre. "America and the French Intellectuals." *Daedalus* 107, no. 1 (1978): 325–37.

Pagedas, Constantine, A. *Anglo-American Strategic Relations and the French Problem 1960–1963: A Troubled Partnership*. London: Frank Cass, 2000.

Paxton, Robert O., and Nicholas Wahl, eds. *De Gaulle and the United States: A Centennial Reappraisal*. Oxford: Berg, 1994.

Peer, Shanny. "Marketing Mickey: Disney Goes to France." *La revue Tocqueville/The Tocqueville Review* 13, no. 2 (1992): 130–34.

Revel, Jean-François. *Anti-Americanism*. San Franciso: Encounter Books, 2003.

Rigoulet, Pierre. *L'antiaméricanisme: Critique d'un prêt-à-penser retrograde et chauvin*. Paris: Laffont, 2004.

Roger, Philippe. *L'ennemi américain: Généalogie de l'antiaméricanisme français*. Paris: Seuil, 2002.

Ross, Kristin. *Fast Cars, Clean Bodies: Decolonization and the Reordering of French Culture*. Cambridge: MIT Press, 1995.

Rupnik, Jacques. "Anti-Americanism and the Modern: The Image of the United States in French Public Opinion." In John Gaffney, ed. *France and Modernisation*. London: Gowers, 1988.

Strauss, David. *Menace in the West: The Rise of French Anti-Americanism in Modern Times*. Westport: Greenwood, 1978.

Thibau, Jacques. *La France colonisée*. Paris: Flammarion, 1980.

Timmerman, Kenneth R. *The French Betrayal of America*. New York: Crown Forum, 2004.

Todorov, Tzvetan. *Le nouveau désordre mondial: réflexions d'un Européen*. Paris: Laffont, 2003.

———. *L'Homme dépaysé*. Paris: Seuil, 1996.

Ulff-Møller, Jens. *Hollywood's Film Wars with France: Film-Trade Diplomacy and the Emergence of the French Film Quota Policy.* Rochester: University of Rochester Press, 2001.

Védrine, Hubert. *L'hyperpuissance américaine.* Paris: Fondation Jean-Jaures, 2000.

Wall, Irwin M. *The United States and the Making of Postwar France, 1945–1954.* Cambridge: Cambridge University Press, 1991.

Winock, Michel. *Le siècle des intellectuels.* Paris: Seuil,1997.

Germany

Abelshauset, Werner. *Kulturkampf: Der deutsche Weg in die Neue Wirtschaft und die amerikanische Herausforderung.* Berlin: Kulturverlag Kadmos, 2003.

Adams, Willi Paul, and Knud Krakau, eds. *Deutschland und Amerika: Perzeption und historische Realität.* Berlin: Colloquium, 1985.

Aguilar, Manuela. *Cultural Diplomacy and Foreign Policy: German-American Relations, 1955–1968.* New York: Lang, 1996.

Alfred Herrhausen Gesellschaft für internationalen Dialog. *Pax Americana?* Munich: Piper, 1998.

"The American Occupation of Germany in Cultural Perspective." *Diplomatic History* 23, no. 1 (1999): 1–77.

"Amerika und seine Kritiker: Politik des Verdachts." *Literaturen* (October 2003): 13–39.

Angster, Julia. *Konsenskapitalismus und Sozialdemokratie: Die Westernisierung von SPD und DGB.* Munich: Oldenbourg, 2003.

Bach, Gerhard, Sabine Broeck, and Ulf Schulenberg, eds. *Americanization—Globalization—Education.* Heidelberg: Winter, 2003.

Barclay, David E., and Elisabeth Glaser-Schmidt, eds. *Transatlantic Images and Perceptions: Germany and America since 1776.* Cambridge: Cambridge University Press, 1997.

Barry, Dave. *David Barry Hits Below the Beltway.* New York: Random House, 2001.

Bauschinger, Sigrid, Horst Denkler, and Wilfried Malsch, eds. *Amerika in der deutschen Literatur: Neue Welt—Nordamerika—USA.* Stuttgart: Reclam, 1975.

Beck, Earl R. *Germany Rediscovers America.* Tallahassee: Florida State University Press, 1968.

Behrens, Michael, and Robert von Rimscha. *Der kleine Bruder: Deutschland und das Modell USA.* Bonn: Bouvier, 1997.

Berg, Manfred, and Philipp Gassert, eds. *Deutschland und die USA in der internationalen Geschichte des 20. Jahrhunderts: Festschrift für Detlef Junker.* Stuttgart: Steiner, 2004.

Berghahn, Volker R. *The Americanisation of West German Industry, 1945–1973.* Cambridge: Cambridge University Press, 1986.

Bergsdorf, Wolfgang, Dietmar Herz, Hans Hoffmeister, and Wolf Wagner. *Amerika—Fremder Freund. 11 Vorlesungen.* Weimar: Rhino Verlag, 2003.

Bredella, Lothar, and Dietmar Haack, eds. *Perceptions and Misperceptions: The United States and Germany. Studies in Cultural Understanding.* Tübingen: Narr, 1988.

Breitenkamp, Edward C. *The U.S. Information Control Division and Its Effect on German Publishers and Writers, 1945–1949.* Grand Forks: University Station, 1953.

Broder, Henryk M. *Kein Krieg, Nirgends: Die Deutschen und der Terror.* Berlin: Berlin Verlag, 2002.

Bude, Heinz, and Bernd Greiner, eds. *Westbindungen: Amerika in der Bundesrepublik.* Hamburg: Hamburger Edition, 1999.

Bundeszentrale für politische Bildung. *Die Zukunft der transatlantischen Beziehungen im Kontext der Globalisierung: Eine deutsch-amerikanische Konferenz.* Bonn: Ost-West-Kolleg der Bundeszentrale für politische Bildung, 2001.

Bungenstab, Karl-Ernst. *Umerziehung zur Demokratie! Re-education-Politik im Bildungswesen der US-Zone 1945–1949.* Dusseldorf: Bertelsmann, 1970.

Clemens, Gabriele, ed. *Kulturpolitik im besetzten Deutschland 1945–1949.* Stuttgart: Steiner, 1994.

Corbin, Anne-Marie. *L'image de l'Europe à l'ombre de la guerre froide: La revue* Forum *de Friedrich Torberg à Vienne (1954–1961).* Paris: L'Harmattan, 2001.

"Cultural Transfer or Cultural Imperialism?" *Diplomatic History* 24, no. 3 (2000): 465–528.

Danuser, Hermann, and Hermann Gottschewski, eds. *Amerikanismus, Americanism, Weill: Die Suche nach kultureller Identität in der Moderne.* Schliengen: Edition Argus, 2003.

Dettke, Dieter, ed. *America's Image in Germany and Europe: Papers of a Seminar on "Anti-Americanism in Germany: Slogan or Reality?"* Washington: Friedrich-Ebert-Stiftung, 1985.

Diefendorf, Jeffry M., Axel Frohn, and Hermann-Josef Rupieper, eds. *American Policy and the Reconstruction of West Germany, 1945–1955.* Cambridge: Cambridge University Press, 1993.

Dienstag 11. September 2001. Hamburg: Rowohlt, 2001.

Diner, Dan. *America in the Eyes of the Germans: An Essay on Anti-Americanism.* Princeton: Markus Wiener, 1996.

Divers, Gregory. *The Image and Influence of America in German Poetry since 1945.* Rochester: Camden House, 2002.

Dobbins, James F. "America's Role in Nation-building: From Germany to Iraq." *Survival* 45, no. 4 (2003-2004): 87–110.

Doering-Manteuffel, Anselm. *Wie westlich sind die Deutschen? Amerikanisierung und Westernisierung im 20. Jahrhundert.* Göttingen: Vandenhoeck and Ruprecht, 1999.

Domentat, Tamara. *Coca-Cola, Jazz & AFN: Berlin und die Amerikaner.* Berlin: Schwarzkopf and Schwarzkopf, 1995.

Durzak, Manfred. *Das Amerika-Bild in der deutschen Gegenwartsliteratur: Historische Voraussetzungen und aktuelle Beispiele.* Stuttgart: Kohlhammer, 1979.

Engelbrecht, Lloyd C. "*Bauhäusler:* A Case Study of Two-Way Traffic across the Atlantic." *Yearbook of German-American Studies* 22 (1987): 149–72.

Ermarth, Michael, ed. *America and the Shaping of German Society, 1945–1955.* Providence: Berg, 1993.

Fehrenbach, Heide. *Cinema in Democratizing Germany: Reconstructing National Identity after Hitler.* Chapel Hill: University of North Carolina Press, 1995.

Fink, Hermann. *Amerikanisierung in der deutschen Wirtschaft: Sprache, Handel, Güter und Dienstleistungen.* Frankfurt: Lang, 1995.

Finzsch, Norbert, and Ursula Lehmkuhl, eds. *Atlantic Communications: The Media in American and German History from the Seventeenth to the Twentieth Century.* Oxford: Berg, 2004.

Fluck, Winfried. "The 'Americanization' of History in New Historicism." *Monatshefte* 84, no. 2 (1992): 220–28.

Frei, Norbert. *Amerikanische Lizenzpolitik und deutsche Pressetradition: Die Geschichte der Nachkriegszeitung 'Südost-Kurier.'* Munich: Oldenbourg, 1986.

Frenz, Horst, and Hans-Joachim Lang, eds. *Nordamerikanische Literatur im deutschen Sprachraum seit 1945: Beiträge zu ihrer Rezeption.* Munich: Winkler, 1973.

Gaida, Burton C. *USA-DDR: Politische, kulturelle und wirtschaftliche Beziehungen seit 1974.* Bochum: Brockmeyer, 1989.

Garten, Jeffrey E. *A Cold Peace: America, Japan, Germany, and the Struggle for Supremacy.* New York: Times Books, 1992.

Gassert, Philip. "Amerikanismus, Antiamerikanismus, Amerikanisierung: Neue Literatur zur Sozial-, Wirtschaft- und Kulturgeschichte des amerikanischen Einflusses in Deutschland und Europa." *Archiv für Sozialgeschichte* 39 (1999): 531–61.

Gehring, Hansjörg. *Amerikanische Literaturpolitik in Deutschland 1945–1953: Ein Aspekt des Re-Education-Programms.* Stuttgart: Deutsche Verlags-Anstalt, 1976.

Gelfert, Hans-Dieter. *Typisch amerikanisch: Wie die Amerikaner wurden, was sie sind.* Munich: Beck, 2002.

Gemünden, Gerd. *Framed Visions: Popular Culture, Americanization, and the Contemporary German and Austrian Imagination.* Ann Arbor: University of Michigan Press, 1998.

Gerhards, Jürgen, ed. *Die Vermessung kultureller Unterschiede: USA und Deutschland im Vergleich.* Wiesbaden: Westdeutscher Verlag, 2000.

German-American Cultural Relations: A Summary Record of a Conference Held at Harrison House, Glen Cove, L.I., New York, January 16–18, 1975. Washington: U.S. Government Printing Office, 1976.

Gersemann, Olaf. *Amerikanische Verhältnisse: Die falsche Furcht der Deutschen vor dem Cowboy-Kapitalismus.* Munich: FinanzBuch, 2003.

Gienow-Hecht, Jessica C. E. *Transmission Impossible: American Journalism as Cultural Diplomacy in Postwar Germany, 1945–1955.* Baton Rouge: Louisiana State University Press, 1999.

Giovanopoulos, Anna-Christina. *Die amerikanische Literatur in der DDR: Die Institutionalisierung von Sinn zwischen Affirmation und Subversion.* Essen: Die Blaue Eule, 2000.

Goedde, Petra. *GIs and Germans: Culture, Gender, and Foreign Relations, 1945–1949.* New Haven: Yale University Press, 2003.

Grabbe, Hans-Jürgen. "Das Amerikabild Konrad Adenauers." *Amerikastudien* 31, no. 3 (1986): 315–23.

Große, Jürgen. *Amerikapolitik und Amerikabild in der DDR 1974–1989.* Bonn: Bouvier, 1999.

Gutzen, Dieter, Winfried Herget, and Hans-Adolf Jacobsen, eds. *Transatlantische Partnerschaft: Kulturelle Aspekte der deutsch-amerikanischen Beziehungen.* Bonn: Bouvier, 1992.

Hahn, Michael, ed. *Nichts gegen Amerika: Linker Antiamerikanismus und seine lange Geschichte.* Hamburg: Konkret Literatur, 2003.

Hanuschek, Sven, Therese Hörnigk, and Christine Malende. *Schriftsteller als Intellektuelle: Politik und Literatur im Kalten Krieg.* Tübingen: Niemeyer, 2000.

Hardt, Ursula. *From Caligari to California: Erich Pommer's Life in the International Film Wars.* Providence: Berghahn, 1996.

Harpprecht, Klaus. *Der fremde Freund: Amerika, eine innere Geschichte.* Stuttgart: Deutsche Verlags-Anstalt, 1982.

Hauler, Anton, Werner Kremp, and Susanne Popp, eds. *Die USA als historisch-politische und kulturelle Herausforderung: Vermittlungsversuche.* Trier: Wissenschaftlicher Verlag, 2003.

Hein-Kremer, Maritta. *Die amerikanische Kulturoffensive: Gründung und Entwicklung der amerikanischen Information Centers in Westdeutschland und West-Berlin 1945–1955.* Weimar: Böhlau, 1996.

Heinemann, Manfred, ed. *Umerziehung und Wiederaufbau: Die Bildungspolitik der Besatzungsmächte in Deutschland und Österreich.* Stuttgart: Klett-Cotta, 1981.

Herzinger, Richard, and Hannes Stein. *Endzeit-Propheten oder Die Offensive der Antiwestler: Fundamentalismus, Antiamerikanismus und neue Rechte.* Hamburg: Rowohlt, 1995.

Hess, Jürgen C., Hartmut Lehmann, and Volker Sellin. *Heidelberg 1945.* Stuttgart: Steiner, 1996.

Hinz, Hans-Martin, ed. *Die vier Besatzungsmächte und die Kultur in Berlin 1945–1949.* Leipzig: Leipzig University Press, 1999.

Hochgeschwender, Michael. *Freiheit in der Offensive? Der Kongreß für kulturelle Freiheit und die Deutschen.* Munich: Oldenbourg, 1998.

Hoenisch, Michael, Klaus Kämpfe, and Karl-Heinz Pütz. *USA und Deutschland: Amerikanische Kulturpolitik 1942–1949. Bibliographie—Materialien—Dokumente.* Berlin: John F. Kennedy Institut, 1980.

Höhn, Maria. *GIs and Fräuleins: The German-American Encounter in 1950's West Germany.* Chapel Hill: University of North Carolina Press, 2002.

Holler, Manfred J. "Artists, Secrets, and CIA's Cultural Policy." In Birger Priddat and Horst Hegmann, eds. *Finanzpolitik in der Informationsgesellschaft: Festschrift für Gunther Engelhardt.* Marburg: Metropolis, 2002.

Horkheimer, Max, and Theodor W. Adorno. "Kulturindustrie: Aufklärung als Massenbetrug." In Max Horkheimer and Theodor W. Adorno. *Dialektik der Aufklärung: Philosophische Fragmente.* Frankfurt: Fischer, 2000 [1944].

Hörnigk, Therese, and Alexander Stephan, eds. *Jeans, Rock und Vietnam: Amerikanische Kultur in der DDR.* Berlin: Theater der Zeit, 2002.

Hurwitz, Harold. *Die Stunde Null der deutschen Presse: Die amerikanische Pressepolitik in Deutschland 1945–1949.* Cologne: Verlag Wissenschaft und Politik, 1972.

Huyssen, Andreas. *After the Great Divide: Modernism, Mass Culture, Postmodernism.* Bloomington: Indiana University Press, 1986.

Huyssen, Andreas, and Klaus R. Scherpe, eds. *Postmoderne: Zeichen eines kulturellen Wandels.* Hamburg: Rowohlt, 1986.

Jarausch, Konrad, and Hannes Siegrist, eds. *Amerikanisierung und Sowjetisierung in Deutschland 1945–1970.* Frankfurt: Campus, 1997.

Junker, Detlef. *Power and Mission: Was Amerika antreibt.* Breisgau: Herder, 2003.

———, ed. 2001. *Die USA und Deutschland im Zeitalter des Kalten Krieges 1945–1990: Ein Handbuch.* 2 vols. Stuttgart: Deutsche Verlags-Anstalt.

Engl. transl. *The United States and Germany in the Era of the Cold War, 1945–1990: A Handbook.* Cambridge: Cambridge University Press, 2004.

Kellermann, Henry J. *Cultural Relations as an Instrument of U.S. Foreign Policy: The Educational Exchange Program between the United States and Germany, 1945–1954.* Washington: U.S. Department of State, 1978.

Kleinschmidt, Johannes. *"Do not fraternize:" Die schwierigen Anfänge deutsch-amerikanischer Freundschaft 1944–1949.* Trier: Wissenschaftlicher Verlag, 1997.

Klepper, Martin, and Joseph C. Schöpp, eds. *Transatlantic Modernism.* Heidelberg: Winter, 2001.

Klöckner, Thomas. *Public Diplomacy—Auswärtige Informations- und Kulturpolitik der USA: Strukturanalyse der Organisation und Strategien der United States Information Agency und des United States Information Service in Deutschland.* Baden-Baden: Nomos, 1993.

Krakau, Knud, and Franz Streng, eds. *Konflikt der Rechtskulturen? Die USA und Deutschland im Vergleich/American and German Legal Cultures: Contrast, Conflict, Convergence?* Heidelberg: Winter, 2003.

Krampikowski, Frank, ed. *Amerikanisches Deutschlandbild und deutsches Amerikabild in Medien und Erziehung.* Baltmannsweiler: Pädagogischer Verlag Burgbücherei Schneider, 1990.

Krätzer, Anita. *Studien zum Amerikabild in der neueren deutschen Literatur: Max Frisch—Uwe Johnson—Hans Magnus Enzensberger und das 'Kursbuch.'* Bern: Lang, 1982.

Krewson, Margrit B. *German-American Relations: A Selective Bibliography.* Washington: Library of Congress, 1995.

Krohn, Claus-Dieter, Erwin Rotermund, Lutz Winkler, Irmtrud Wojak, and Wulf Koepke, eds. *Rückkehr und Aufbau nach 1945: Deutsche Remigranten im öffentlichen Leben Nachkriegsdeutschlands.* Marburg: Metropolis, 1997.

———, eds. "Exil und Remigration." *Exilforschung,* vol. 9. Munich: edition text + kritik, 1991.

Krohn, Claus-Dieter, and Axel Schildt, eds. *Zwischen den Stühlen? Remigranten und Remigration in der deutschen Medienöffentlichkeit der Nachkriegszeit.* Hamburg: Christians, 2002.

Lange, Wigand. *Theater in Deutschland nach 1945: Zur Theaterpolitik der amerikanischen Besatzungsbehörden.* Frankfurt: Lang, 1980.

Langthaler, Wilhelm, and Werner Pirker. *Ami go home: Zwölf gute Gründe für einen Antiamerikanismus.* Vienna: Promedia, 2003.

Larres, Klaus, and Torsten Oppelland, eds. *Deutschland und die USA im 20. Jahrhundert: Geschichte der politischen Beziehungen.* Darmstadt: Wissenschaftliche Buchgesellschaft, 1997.

Leggewie, Claus. *Amerikas Welt: Die USA in unseren Köpfen.* Hamburg: Hoffmann und Campe, 2000.

Lenz, Günter H., and Klaus J. Milich, eds. *American Studies in Germany: European Contexts and Intercultural Relations.* Frankfurt: Campus, 1995.

Lindemann, Beate, ed. *Amerika in uns: Deutsch-amerikanische Erfahrungen und Visionen.* Mainz: Hase and Koehler, 1995.

Ludes, Peter. *Kulturtransfer und transkulturelle Prozesse: Amerikanisierung und Europäisierung des Fernsehprogramms in der Bundesrepublik.* Heidelberg: Winter, 1991.

Lüdtke, Alf, Inge Marßolek, and Adelheid von Saldern, eds. *Amerikanisierung: Traum und Alptraum im Deutschland des 20. Jahrhunderts.* Stuttgart: Steiner, 1996.

Maase, Kaspar. *Grenzenloses Vergnügen: Der Aufstieg der Massenkultur 1850–1970.* Frankfurt: Fischer, 1997.

———. *Bravo Amerika: Erkundungen zur Jugendkultur der Bundesrepublik in den fünfziger Jahren.* Hamburg: Junius, 1992.

Maase, Kaspar, Gerd Hallenberger, and Mel van Elteren. *Amerikanisierung der Alltagskultur? Zur Rezeption US-amerikanischer Populärkultur in der Bundesrepublik und in den Niederlanden.* Hamburg: Hamburger Institut für Sozialforschung, 1990.

Milich, Klaus J. *Die frühe Postmoderne: Geschichte eines europäisch-amerikanischen Kulturkonflikts.* Frankfurt: Campus, 1998.

Milich, Klaus J., and Jeffrey M. Peck, eds. *Multiculturalism in Transit: A German-American Exchange.* New York: Berghahn, 1998.

Moeller, Robert G., ed. *West Germany under Construction: Politics, Society, and Culture in the Adenauer Era.* Ann Arbor: University of Michigan Press, 1997.

Mueller, Agnes C., ed. *German Pop Culture: How American Is It?* Ann Arbor: University of Michigan Press, 2004.

———. *Lyrik 'Made in USA': Vermittlung und Rezeption in der Bundesrepublik.* Amsterdam: Rodopi, 1999.

Müller, Emil-Peter. *Antiamerikanismus in Deutschland: Zwischen Care-Paket und Cruise Missile.* Cologne: Deutscher Instituts-Verlag, 1986.

Müller, Harald. *Amerika schlägt zurück: Die Weltordnung nach dem 11. September.* Frankfurt: Fischer, 2003.

Müller, Winfried. *Schulpolitik in Bayern im Spannungsfeld von Kultusbürokratie und Besatzungsmacht, 1945–1949.* Munich: Oldenbourg, 1995.

Osterle, Heinz D., ed. *Amerika! New Images in German Literature.* New York: Lang, 1989.

———, ed. *Bilder von Amerika: Gespräche mit deutschen Schriftstellern.* Münster: Englisch Amerikanische Studien, 1987.

Paul, Heike, and Katja Kanzler, eds. *Amerikanische Populärkultur in Deutschland.* Leipzig: Leipziger Universitätsverlag, 2002.

Paulsen, Wolfgang, ed. *Die USA und Deutschland: Wechselseitige Spiegelungen in der Literatur der Gegenwart.* Bern: Francke, 1976.

Piltz, Thomas, ed. *1776–1976: Zweihundert Jahre deutsch-amerikanische Beziehungen.* Munich: Moos, 1975.

Poiger, Uta G. *Jazz, Rock and Rebels: Cold War Politics and American Culture in a Divided Germany.* Berkeley: University of California Press, 2000.

Pommerin, Reiner, ed. *The American Impact on Postwar Germany.* Providence: Berghahn, 1995 [rev. ed. 1997].

Prätorius, Rainer. *In God We Trust: Religion und Politik in den USA.* Munich: Beck, 2003.

Preuß, Ulrich K. *Krieg, Verbrechen, Blasphemie: Gedanken aus dem alten Europa.* Berlin: Wagenbach, 2003.

Probst, Alfred. *Amideutsch: Ein kritisch-polemisches Wörterbuch der anglo-deutschen Sprache.* Frankfurt: Fischer, 1989.

Rauhut, Michael. *Beat in der Grauzone: DDR-Rock 1964 bis 1972—Politik und Alltag.* Berlin: BasisDruck, 1993.

Rentschler, Eric. "How American Is It: The U.S. as Image and Imaginary in German Film." In Terri Ginsberg and Kirsten Moana Thompson, eds., *Perspectives on German Cinema.* New York: G. K. Hall, 1996.

Ritter, Alexander, ed. *Deutschlands literarisches Amerikabild: Neuere Forschungen zur Amerikarezeption der deutschen Literatur.* Hildesheim: Olms, 1977.

Rosellini, Jay. *Literary Skinheads? Writing from the Right in Reunified Germany.* West Lafayette: Purdue University Press, 2000.

Rupieper, Hermann-Josef. *Die Wurzeln der westdeutschen Nachkriegsdemokratie: Der amerikanische Beitrag 1945–1952.* Opladen: Westdeutscher Verlag, 1993.

Rutschky, Michael. *Wie wir Amerikaner wurden: Eine deutsche Entwicklungsgeschichte.* Munich: Ullstein, 2004.

Sammons, Jeffrey. "Zu den Grundlagen des Antiamerikanismus in der deutschen Literatur." In Michael S. Batts, ed. *Alte Welten—neue Welten. Akten des IX. Kongresses der Internationalen Vereinigung für Germanische Sprach- und Literaturwissenschaften,* vol. 1. Tübingen: Niemeyer, 1996.

Sauermann, Ekkehard. *Neue Welt Kriegs Ordnung: Die Polarisierung nach dem 11. September 2001.* Bremen: Atlantik, 2002.

Scharnholz, Theodor. *Heidelberg und die Besatzungmacht: Zur Entwicklung der Beziehungen zwischen einer deutschen Kommune und ihrer amerikanischen Garnison.* Heidelberg: Regionalkultur, 2002.

Schildt, Axel. *Ankunft im Westen: Ein Essay zur Erfolgsgeschichte der Bundesrepublik.* Frankfurt: Fischer, 1999.

————. *Zwischen Abendland und Amerika: Studien zur westdeutschen Ideen-landschaft der 50er Jahre.* Munich: Oldenbourg, 1999.

————. *Moderne Zeiten. Freizeit, Massenmedien und "Zeitgeist" in der Bundesrepublik der 50er Jahre.* Hamburg: Christians, 1995.

Schildt, Axel, and Arnold Sywottek, eds. *Modernisierung im Wiederaufbau: Die westdeutsche Gesellschaft der 50er Jahre.* Bonn: Dietz, 1993.

Schildt, Axel, Detlef Siegfried, and Karl Christian Lammers, eds. *Dynamische Zeiten: Die 60er Jahre in den beiden deutschen Gesellschaften.* Hamburg: Christians, 2000.

Schissler, Hanna, ed. *The Miracle Years: A Cultural History of West Germany, 1949–1968.* Princeton: Princeton University Press, 2001.

Schivelbusch, Wolfgang. *In a Cold Crater: Cultural and Intellectual Life in Berlin, 1945–1948.* Berkeley: University of California Press, 1998.

Schmiese, Wulf. *Fremde Freunde: Deutschland und die USA zwischen Mauerfall und Golfkrieg.* Paderborn: Schöningh, 2000.

Schneider, Irmela, ed. *Amerikanische Einstellung: Deutsches Fernsehen und US-amerikanische Produktionen.* Heidelberg: Winter, 1992.

Schneider, Irmela, Christian Werner Thomsen, and Andreas Nowak, eds. *Lexikon der britischen und amerikanischen Serien, Fernsehfilme und Mehrteiler in den Fernsehprogrammen der Bundesrepublik Deutschland, 1953–1985.* 3 vols. Berlin: Spiess, 1991.

Schnoor, Rainer, ed. *Amerikanistik in der DDR: Geschichte—Analysen—Zeitzeugenberichte.* Berlin: Trafo, 1999.

Schrenck-Notzing, Caspar. *Charakterwäsche: Die amerikanische Besatzung in Deutschland und ihre Folgen.* Stuttgart: Seewald, 1965.

Schumacher, Frank. *Kalter Krieg und Propaganda: Die USA, der Kampf um die Weltmeinung und die ideelle Westbindung der Bundesrepublik Deutschland, 1945–1955.* Trier: Wissenschaftlicher Verlag, 2000.

Schwaabe, Christian. *Antiamerikanismus: Wandlungen eines Feindbildes.* Munich: Fink, 2003.

Schwan, Gesine. *Antikommunismus und Antiamerikanismus in Deutschland: Kontinuität und Wandel nach 1945.* Baden-Baden: Nomos, 1999.

Seliger, Helfried W. *Das Amerikabild Bertolt Brechts.* Bonn: Bouvier, 1974.

Sichelschmidt, Gustav. *Deutschland—eine amerikanische Provinz: Der große Seelenmord.* Berg: VGB-Verlagsgesellschaft, 1996.

————. *Amerikanismus: Der Weltfeind Nr. 1.* Berg: Türmer, 1990.

Siebald, Manfred, and Horst Immel, eds. *Amerikanisierung des Dramas und Dramatisierung Amerikas.* Frankfurt: Lang, 1985.

Spevack, Edmund. *Allied Control and German Freedom: American Political and Ideological Influences on the Framing of the West German Basic Law (Grundgesetz).* Munster: Lit, 2001.

Stephan, Alexander, ed. *Americanization and Anti-Americanism: The German Encounter with American Culture after 1945.* New York: Berghahn, 2005.

———. "The Historical Context of the German Reaction to 9-11." In Vladimir Shlapentokh, Joshua Woods, and Eric Shiraev, eds. *America: Sovereign Defender or Cowboy Nation?* Aldershot: Ashgate, 2005, 15–27.

———. "Culture Clash: Notes on a Debate between American, German, and Saudi Intellectuals about the Concept of a 'Just War'." In *America and the Orient.* Heidelberg: Winter, forthcoming 2005.

———. "Der wiedererwachte Systemkonflikt. Der 'neue' Bruch zwischen den USA und Deutschland ist eigentlich ein 'alter.'" In Hermann Strasser and Gerd Nollman, eds. *Endstation Amerika? Sozialwissenschaftliche Innen- und Außenansichten,* forthcoming 2005.

Stephan, Alexander, and Jochen Vogt, eds. *Das Amerika der Autoren: Deutsche Ansichten von Kafka bis 9/11.* Munich: Fink, forthcoming 2005.

———, eds. *Die Amerikanisierung der (west-) deutschen Kultur seit 1945.* Munich: Fink, forthcoming, 2006.

Szabo, Stephen F. *Parting Ways: The Crisis in German-American Relations.* Washington: Brookings Institution, 2004.

Tent, James F., ed. *Academic Proconsul: Harvard Sociologist Edward Y. Hartshorne and the Reopening of German Universities 1945–1946: His Personal Account.* Trier: Wissenschaftlicher Verlag, 1998.

———. *The Free University of Berlin: A Political History.* Bloomington: Indiana University Press, 1988.

———. *Mission on the Rhine: Reeducation and Denazification in American-Occupied Germany.* Chicago: University of Chicago Press, 1982.

Trommler, Frank, and Joseph McVeigh, eds. *America and the Germans: An Assessment of a Three-Hundred-Year History.* Philadelphia: University of Pennsylvania Press, 1985.

Trommler, Frank, and Elliott Shore, eds. *The German-American Encounter: Conflict and Cooperation between Two Cultures 1800–2000.* New York: Berghahn, 2001.

Tüngel, Richard, and Rudolph van Wehrt. *Auf dem Bauche sollst du kriechen…: Deutschland unter den Besatzungsmächten.* Hamburg: Wegner, 1958.

von Dirke, Sabine. *"All Power to the Imagination!" The West German Counterculture from the Student Movement to the Greens.* Lincoln: University of Nebraska Press, 1997.

Weigelt, Klaus, ed. *Das Deutschland- und Amerikabild: Beiträge zum gegenseitigen Verständnis beider Völker.* Melle: Knoth, 1986.

Weissman, William J. *Kultur- und Informationsaktivitäten der USA in der Bundesrepublik Deutschland während der Amtszeiten Carter und Reagan:*

Eine Fallstudie über Alliierten-Öffentlichkeitsarbeit. Pfaffenweiler: Centaurus, 1990.

Weisz, Christoph. *OMGUS Handbuch: Die amerikanische Militärregierung in Deutschland, 1945–1949.* Munich: Oldenbourg, 1994.

Wenzel, Harald, ed. *Die Amerikanisierung des Medienalltags.* New York: Campus, 1998.

Weßel, Daisy. *Bild und Gegenbild: Die USA in der Belletristik der SBZ und der DDR (bis 1987).* Opladen: Leske and Budrich, 1989.

Wettberg, Gabriela. *Das Amerika-Bild und seine negativen Konstanten in der deutschen Nachkriegsliteratur.* Heidelberg: Winter, 1987.

Wierlemann, Sabine. *Political Correctness in den USA und in Deutschland.* Berlin: Schmidt, 2002.

Willett, Ralph. *The Americanization of Germany, 1945–1949.* London: Routledge, 1989.

Winter, Rolf. *Little America: Die Amerikanisierung der Deutschen Republik.* Hamburg: Rasch und Röhring, 1995.

Zimmer, Dieter E. *Deutsch und anders—die Sprache im Modernisierungsfieber.* Hamburg: Rowohlt, 1997.

Great Britain

Bradbury, Malcolm. *Dangerous Pilgrimages: Trans-Atlantic Mythologies and the Novel.* London: Secker and Warburg, 1995.

———. "How I Invented America." *Journal of American Studies* 14, no. 1 (1980): 115–35.

Campbell, Neil. *Landscapes of Americanisation.* Derby: University of Derby Press, 2003.

Cooper, Laura E., and B. Lee Cooper. "The Pendulum of Cultural Imperialism: Popular Music Interchanges Between the United States and Britain, 1943–67." *Journal of Popular Culture* 27, no. 3 (1993): 61–78.

Fisher, Ali, and Scott Lucas. "Master and Servant? The U.S. Government and the Founding of the British Association for American Studies." *European Journal of American Culture* 21, no. 1 (2002): 16–25.

Hebdige, Dick. "Towards a Cartography of Taste, 1935–62." In Dick Hebdige, ed., *Hiding in the Light: On Images and Things.* London: Routledge, 1988.

Hoggart, Richard. *The Uses of Literacy: Aspects of Working Class Life with Special Reference to Publications and Entertainments.* London: Chatto and Windus, 1957.

Marling, Susan. *American Affair: The Americanisation of Britain.* London: Boxtree, 1993.

Shaw, Tony. *British Cinema and the Cold War: The State, Propaganda and Consensus.* London: I. B. Tauris, 2001.

Sinfield, Alan. *Literature, Politics and Culture in Postwar Britain.* Oxford: Blackwell, 1989.

Snowman, Daniel. *Britain and America: An Interpretation of Their Culture, 1945–75.* New York: New York University Press, 1977.

Stacey, Jacky. *Star-Gazing: Hollywood Cinema and Female Spectatorship.* London: Routledge, 1994.

Swann, Paul. *The Hollywood Feature Film in Postwar Britain.* London: Croom Helm, 1987.

Vidal, John. *McLibel: Burger Culture on Trial.* London: Pan Books, 1997.

Walker, John A. *Cultural Offensive: America's Impact on British Art Since 1945.* London: Pluto, 1998.

Webster, Duncan. *Looka Yonder! The Imaginary America of Populist Culture.* London: Routledge, 1988.

Wilford, Hugh. *The CIA, the British Left and the Cold War: Calling the Tune?* London: Frank Cass, 2003.

Greece

Amen, Michael Mark. *American Foreign Policy in Greece 1944–1949.* Frankfurt: Lang, 1978.

Botsiou, Konstantina E. *Griechenlands Weg nach Europa: Von der Truman-Doktrin bis zur Assoziierung mit der Europäischen Wirtschaftsgemeinschaft, 1947–1961.* Frankfurt: Lang, 1999.

Clogg, Richard, ed., *Greece in the 1980's.* London: St. Martin's Press, 1983.

Couloumbis, Theodore. *Greek Political Reaction to American and NATO Influences.* New Haven: Yale University Press, 1966.

Couloumbis, Theodore, John A. Petropulos, and Harry Psomiades. *Foreign Interference in Greek Politics: An Historical Perspective.* New York: Pella, 1976.

Featherstone, Kevin, and Dimitrios Katsoudas (eds.). *Political Change in Greece: Before and After the Colonels.* London: Croom Helm, 1987.

Katsikas, Christos, and Costas N. Therianos. *History of Modern Greek Education.* Athens: Savvalas, 2004 (in Greek).

Kofas, John V. *Intervention and Underdevelopment: Greece during the Cold War.* University Park: Pennsylvania State University Press, 1989.

Mavrogordatos, George Th. *Rise of the Green Sun. The Greek Election of 1981.* King's College, Occasional Paper 1, London: Centre of Contemporary Greek Studies, 1983.

McNeill, William Hardy. *The Metamorphosis of Greece since World War II.* London: Blackwell, 1978.

Mouzelis, Nicos P. *Modern Greece: Facets of Underdevelopment.* London: Macmillan, 1978.

Papadantonakis, Constantin Spyros. *Greece: The Structure of Dependence.* Ph.D. diss., Cornell University, 1981.

Roubatis, Yannis P. *Tangled Webs: The U.S. in Greece 1947–1967.* New York: Pella, 1987.

Rousseas, Stephen. *The Death of Democracy: Greece and the American Conscience.* New York: Grove Press, 1967.

Stathakis, George. *The Truman Doctrine and the Marshall Plan: The History of US Assistance to Greece.* Athens: Vivliorama, 2004 (in Greek).

The Greek Society in the Early Postwar Period. 2 vols. Athens: Sakis Karagiorgas Foundation, 1993.

Tsoucalas, Constantine. *The Greek Tragedy.* Baltimore: Penguin, 1969.

Wittner, Lawrence S. *American Intervention in Greece 1943–1949.* New York: Columbia University Press, 1982.

Italy

Bobbio, Norberto, Renzo De Felice, and Gian Enrico Rusconi. *Italiani, amici nemici.* Milano: Reset, 1996.

Brunetta, Gian Piero. *Storia del cinema italiano: Dal neorealismo al miracolo economico 1945–1959.* Rome: Editori Riuniti, 1993.

Chemotti, Saveria, ed. *Il mito americano: Origine e crisi di un modello culturale.* Padua: Cleup, 1980.

Chiarenza, Carlo, and William L. Vance, eds. *Immaginari a confronto: I rapporti culturali tra Italia e Stati Uniti: la percezione della realtà fra stereotipo e mito.* Venice: Marsilio, 1993.

Craveri, Peiro, and Gaetano Quagliariello. *L'antiamericanismo in Italia e in Europa nel secondo dopoguerra.* Soveria Mannelli: Rubbettino, 2004.

D'Attorre, Pierre Paolo, ed. *Nemici per la pelle: Sogno americano e mito sovietico nell'Italia contemporanea.* Milan: F. Angeli, 1991.

Di Nolfo, Ennio. *Le paure e le speranze degli italian (1943–1953).* Milan: Mondadori, 1986.

Eco, Umberto. *Dalla periferia dell'impero.* Milan: Bompiani, 1977.

Eco, Umberto, Gian Paolo Ceserani, and Beniamino Placido. *La riscoperta dell'America.* Bari: Laterza, 1984.

Ellwood, David W. "Italian Modernisation and the Propaganda of the Marshall Plan." In Luciano Cheles and Lucio Sponza, eds. *The Art of Persuasion: Political Communication in Italy from 1945 to the 1990's.* Manchester: Manchester University Press, 2001.

————. "The 1948 Elections in Italy: A Cold War Propaganda Battle." In I.Tocci, ed. *Ripensare il 1948: Politica, economia, società, cultura.* Ancona: Il lavoro editoriale, 2000.

————. "The American Challenge Renewed: U.S. Cultural Power and Europe's Identity Debates." *Brown Journal of World Affairs* 4, no. 1 (1997): 271–83.

————. "*'Un americano a Roma'*: A 1950's satire of Americanization." *Modern Italy* 2, no. 1 (1996): 93–102.

————. "Italy, Europe and the Cold War: The Politics and Economics of Limited Sovereignty." In Christopher Duggan and Christopher Wagstaff, eds. *Italy in the Cold War: Politics, Culture and Society, 1948–58.* Oxford: Berg, 1995.

————. *Italy 1943–1945: The Politics of Liberation.* Leicester: Leicester University Press, 1985.

————. "Il Rapporto Harmon (Rapporto di un gruppo di dirigenti dell' industria cinematografica americana, 1945)." *Mezzosecolo* 3 (1979): 305–35.

Ellwood, David W., and Adrian Lyttelton, eds. "Quando l'America arriva in Italia." Special edition of *Quaderni storici* (1985), 1.

Fabbrini, Sergio. "L'antiamericanismo che molti unisce." *Il Mulino* 3 (2003): 345–57.

Forgacs, David, and Robert Lumley, eds. *Italian Cultural Studies: An Introduction.* Oxford: Oxford University Press, 1996.

Galli della Loggia, Ernesto. *La morte della patria: la crisi dell'idea di nazione tra Resistenza, antifascismo e Repubblica.* Bari: Laterza, 1999.

————. *L'identità italiana.* Bologna: Il Mulino, 1998.

Gundle, Stephen. *Stolen Bicycles: Mass Culture and National Identity in Italy, 1936–54.* (with David Forgacs and Marcella Filippa) Berkeley: University of California Press, 2003.

————. "Hollywood Glamour and Mass Consumption in Postwar Italy." *Journal of Cold War Studies* 4, no. 3 (2002): 95–118.

————. *Between Hollywood and Moscow: The Italian Communists and the Challenge of Mass Culture, 1943–1991.* Durham: Duke University Press, 2000.

————. "The Americanization of Daily Life: Television and Consumerism in Italy in the 1950s." *Italian History and Culture* 2 (1996): 11–39.

Gundle, Stephen, and Simon Parker, eds. *The New Italian Republic: From the Fall of the Berlin Wall to Berlusconi,* London: Routledge, 1996.

Miller, James E. *The United States and Italy 1940–1950: The Politics and Diplomacy of Stabilization.* Chapel Hill: University of North Carolina Press, 1986.

————. "Taking Off the Gloves: The United States and the Italian Elections of 1948." *Diplomatic History* 7, no. 1 (1983): 35–56.

Morsi, Gamal. *"Amerika ist immer woanders:" Die Rezeption des American Dream in Italien.* Marburg: Tectum-Verlag, 2001.

Romano, Sergio. *Lo scambio ineguale: Italia e Stai Uniti da Wilson a Clinton.* Bari: Laterza, 1995.

Romano, Sergio, ed. *Gli americani e l'Italia.* Milan: Libri Scheiwiller per Banco Ambrosiano Veneto, 1993.

Romero, Federico. "Americanization and National Identity: The Case of Postwar Italy." In Luciano Tosi, ed., *Europe, Its Borders and the Others.* Napoli: ESI, 2000.

————. "Gli Stati Uniti in Italia: Piano Marshall e Patto Atlantico." In Franco Barbagallo, ed., *Storia dell'Italia Repubblicana,* vol. 1. Torino: Einaudi, 1994.

————. *The United States and the European Trade Union Movement 1944–1951.* Chapel Hill: University of North Carolina Press, 1993.

————. "Americanizzazione e modernizzazione nell' Europa postbellica." A discussion with Michael Hogan, Leonardo Paggi, Vibeke Sorensen. *Passato e presente* 7, no. 23 (1990): 19–48.

Romero, Federico and Luciano Segreto, eds. *Italia, Europa, America: L'integrazione internazionale dell'economia italiana (1945–1963).* Special issue of *Studi storici* 37, no. 1 (1996).

Routledge Encyclopedia of Contemporary Italian Culture. London: Routledge, 2000.

Rubeo, Ugo. *Mal d'America.* Rome: Editori Riuniti, 1987.

Rusconi, Gian Enrico. *Patria e repubblica.* Bologna: Il Mulino, 1997.

Teodori, Massimo. *Maledetti americani: Destra, sinistra e cattolici: storia del pregiudizio antimericano.* Milan: Mondadori, 2002.

————. *La fine del mito americano.* Milan: Rizzoli, 1975.

Torriglia, Anna M. *Broken Time, Fragmented Space: A Cultural Map for Postwar Italy.* Toronto: University of Toronto Press, 2002.

Poland

Globalization, Transnationalism, and the End of the American Century. Special Issue. *American Studies* 41, no. 2/3 (2000).

Bałdyga, Leonard J. "The 20th Anniversary of the American Studies Center at the University of Warsaw: An Historic Overview." In Z. Kwiecień, K. Michalek, L. Mularska-Andziak, and H. Parafianowicz, eds., *Pochwala historii powszechnej.* Warsaw: Instytut Historyczny Uniwersytu Warszawskiego, 1996.

Błoński, Jan. "Americans in Poland." *The Kenyon Review* 23, no. 1 (1961): 32–51.

Borkowski, Jan. "Jazz in Poland—Anthology." Warsaw: Polskie Radio S.A., 2002.

Brzezinski, Zbigniew. *Alternative to Partition: For a Broader Conception of America's Role in Europe.* New York: McGraw-Hill, 1965.

Centralny Osrodek Badania Opinii Spolecznej. 2004. http://www.cbos.com .pl/SPISKOM.POL/2004/K_076_04.PDF (last accessed: 24 July 2004.)

Chaciński, Bartek. "Hymny biedy i wkurwienia wykrzykuje Peja, nowa nadzieja polskiego rapu." *Przekrój* 10, no. 32/33, (2003): 62–65.

Cieplak, Tadeusz, N. *Poland since 1945.* New York: Twayne, 1972.

Connelly, John. *Captive University: The Sovietization of East German, Czech, and Polish Higher Education 1945–1956.* Chapel Hill: University of North Carolina Press, 2000.

Crevecoeur, Michel-Guillaume-Jean. *Letters from an American Farmer; Letter III: What Is an American?* In George McMichael, ed., *Anthology of American Literature, Volume I.* New York: Macmillan, 1985.

Curry, Jane Leftwich, ed. *The Black Book of Polish Censorship.* New York: Random House, 1984.

Czarnik, Oskar Stanislaw. "Control of Literary Communication in the 1945–1956 Period in Poland." *Libraries & Culture* 36, no. 1 (2001): 104–15.

Dominik, Cynthia, ed. *Is Poland Being Americanized?* Warsaw: American Studies Center, Warsaw University, 1998.

Durczak, Jerzy. "Mixed Blessings of Freedom: American Literature in Poland Under and After Communism." *American Studies* 40, no. 2 (1999): 137–50.

———. *Selves Between Cultures: Contemporary American Bicultural Autobiography.* San Francisco: International Scholars Publications, 1997.

Film na świecie. no. 382 (May–June, 1991).

Foeller-Pituch, Elżbieta. "Catching Up: The Polish Critical Response to American Literature." In Huck Gutman, ed., *As Others Read Us: International Perspectives on American Literature.* Amherst: University of Massachusetts Press, 1991.

Godzic, Wiesław. *Oglądanie i inne przyjemności kultury popularnej.* Cracow: Universitas, 1996.

Grose, Peter. *Operation Rollback: America's Secret War behind the Iron Curtain.* Boston: Houghton Mifflin, 2000.

Grzeszczyk, Ewa. *Sukces: Amerykańskie wzory—polskie realia.* Warsaw: Wydawnictwo Instytutu Filozofii i Socjologii PAN, 2003.

Jedlicki, Jerzy. "The Image of America in Poland, 1776-1945." *Reviews in American History* 14, no. 4 (1986): 669–86.

Kaplan, Stephen S. "Aid to Poland, 1957–1964: Concerns, Objections and Obstacles." *The Western Political Quarterly* 28, no. 2 (1975): 155.

Liponski, Wojciech. "Western Teachers and East European Students." *Polish–Anglo Saxon Studies* nos. 6-7 (1997): 5–56.

Łysiak, Waldemar. *Asfaltowy saloon.* Warsaw: Polonia, 1986.

Masłowska, Dorota. *Wojna polsko ruska pod flagą biało-czerwoną.* Warsaw: Lampa i Iskra Boża, 2002.

Miczka, Tadeusz. "Cinema Under Political Pressure: A Brief Outline of Authorial Roles in Polish Post-War Feature-Film 1945–1995." http://www.arts.uwaterloo.ca/FINE/juhde/micz952.htm (last accessed: 3 March 2005).

Michnik, Adam. "What Europe Means for Poland." *Journal of Democracy* 14, no. 4 (2003): 128–36.

Mulroy, Kevin, ed. *Western Amerykański: Polish Poster Art and the Western.* Seattle: University of Washington, 1999.

Polish Association for American Studies (PAAS) publications:

1. Salska, Agnieszka, and Paul Wilson, eds. *The American Dream, Past and Present: The Proceedings of the Second Annual Conference of the Polish Association for American Studies.* Łódź: Łódź University Press, 1992.

2. Oleksy, Elżbieta, ed. *American Cultures: Assimilation and Multiculturalism.* San Francisco: International Scholars Publications, 1995.

3. Durczak, Jerzy, and Joanna Durczak, eds. *Polish-American Literary Confrontations: The Proceedings of the International Conference of the Polish Association for American Studies.* Lublin: Maria Curie-Skłodowska University Press, 1994.

4. Kutnik, Jerzy, and Cezar Ornatowski, eds. *Re-Visioning Democracy in Central Europe and America: The Proceedings of the International Conference of the Polish Association for American Studies.* Lublin: Maria Curie-Skłodowska University Press, 1994.

5. Wilczyński, Marek, and Marcin Turski, eds. *Canons, Revision, Supplements in American Literature and Culture: The Proceedings of the 5th International Conference of the Polish Association for American Studies.* Poznań: Adam Mickiewicz University Press, 1995.

6. Preis-Smith, Agata, and Piotr Skurowski, eds. *Cultural Policy, or the Politics of Culture? The Proceedings of the 7th International Conference of the Polish Association for American Studies.* Warsaw: Warsaw University Press, 1999.

7. Pyzik, Teresa, ed. *Reflections on Ethical Values in Post(?)Modern American Literature: The Proceedings of the International Conference of the Polish Association for American Studies.* Katowice: Uniwersytet Śląski Press, 2000.

8. Pyzik, Teresa, and Tomasz Sikora, eds. *New Shape of Ethics? Reflections on Ethical Values in Post(?)Modern American Literature.* Katowice: Uniwersytet Śląski Press, 2000.
9. Salska, Agnieszka, and Zbigniew Maszewski, eds. *Apocalypse Now: Prophecy and Fulfillment: The Proceedings of the 1999 International Conference of the Polish Association for American Studies.* Łódź: Łódź University Press, 2001.
10. Wiszniowska, Maria, ed. *Local Colors of the Stars and Stripes: The Proceedings of the International Conference of the Polish Association for American Studies.* Torun: Mikołaj Kopernik University Press, 2001.
11. Durczak, Jerzy, and Paweł Frelik, eds. *American Portraits and Self-Portraits: The Proceedings of the International Conference of the Polish Association for American Studies.* Lublin: Maria Curie-Skłodowska University Press, 2002.

Pawlicki, Aleksander. *Kompletna szarość: Cenzura w latach 1965–1972. Instytucje i ludzie.* Warsaw: Trio, 2001.

Pew Research Center for People and the Press. 2002. "What the World Thinks in 2002." Available on http://people-press.org/reports/display.php3?ReportID=165 (last accessed: 3 March 2005).

Pikulski, Tadeusz. *Prywatna historia telewizji publicznej.* Warsaw: Muza, 2002.

Plasser, Fritz. "American Campaign Techniques Worldwide." *Press/Politics* 5, no. 4 (2000): 33–54.

"Polish Hip-Hop Scene," http://hip-hop.pl/english.php (last accessed: 3 March 2004).

Putrament, Jerzy. *Dwa łyki Ameryki.* Warsaw: Czytelnik, 1956.

Rakowski, Mieczysław. *Ameryka wielopiętrowa.* Warsaw: Czytelnik, 1964.

Redliński, Edward. *Szczuropolacy.* Warsaw: Polska Oficyna Wydawnicza "BGW," 1994.

Remmer, Alexander. "A Note of Post-Publication Censorship in Poland 1980–1987." *Soviet Studies* 41, no. 3 (1989): 415–25.

Richmond, Yale. "Margaret Schlauch and American Studies in Poland." *The Polish Review* 44, no. 1 (1999): 53–57.

Salska, Agnieszka, ed. *Historia literatury amerykańskiej XX wieku,* 2 vols. Cracow: Universitas, 2003.

Schweizer, Peter. *Victory: The Reagan Administration's Secret Strategy that Hastened the Collapse of the Soviet Union.* New York: Atlantic Monthly Press, 1994.

Staszewski, Wojciech. "Spoko Alfabet." *Gazeta Wyborcza* 31, no. 542 (2003): 10–14.

Stehle, Hansjakob. *The Independent Satellite: Society and Politics in Poland since 1945.* London: Pall Mall Press, 1965.

Thomas, Lawrence L. "Polish Literature and the 'Thaw'." *American Slavic and East European Review* 18, no. 3 (1959): 394–416.

Thomas, Robert McG., Jr. "Willis Conover, 75, Voice of America Disc Jockey." *New York Times,* 19 May 1966, 35.

Tyrmand, Leopold. *Dziennik 1954.* Warsaw: Prószyński i S-ka, 1999.

Urban, Jerzy. *Alfabet Urbana.* Warsaw: Polska Oficyna Wydawnicza "BGW," 1990.

Wedel, Janine R. *Collision and Collusion: The Strange Case of Western Aid to Eastern Europe 1989–1998.* New York: St. Martin's Press. 1998.

Wertenstein-Żuławski, Jerzy. *To tylko rock'n roll* (It's only Rock'n'Roll). Warsaw: ZAKR, 1990.

Wilder, Emilia, "America as Seen by Polish Exchange Scholars." *Public Opinion Quarterly* 28, no. 2 (1964): 243–56.

Spain

Bautista, Eduardo, Antonio Cordón, and Miguel Ángel Cortés et al. *España, ¿potencia cultural?* Madrid: INCIPE (Instituto de Cuestiones Internacionales y Política Exterior), 2001.

Elordi, Carlos. *El amigo americano: De Franco a Aznar: Una adhesión inquebrantable.* Madrid: Temas de Hoy, 2003.

Elorza, Antonio. "De 'Bienvenido Mister Marshall' au 11 septembre 2001: Les sources de l'anti-américanisme espagnol." *Cahiers d'histoire sociale* 21 (2002–2003): 43–56.

Hayes, Carlton J. H. *The United States and Spain: An Interpretation.* New York: Sheed and Ward, 1951.

Liedtke, Boris N. *Embracing a Dictatorship: U.S. Relations with Spain, 1945–53.* London: Macmillan, 1998.

Pan-Montojo, Juan, José Alvarez Junco, Manuel Pérez Ledesma, Juan Pro Ruiz, Christopher Schmidt-Nowara, and Carlos Serrano. *Más se perdió en Cuba: España, 1898 y la crisis de fin de siglo.* Madrid: Alianza, 1998.

Sahagún, Felipe. "Spain and the United States: Military Primacy." In Richard Gillespie and Richard Youngs, eds., *Spain: The European and International Challenges.* London: Frank Cass, 2001.

Summerhill, Stephen J., and John Alexander Williams. *Sinking Columbus: Contested History, Cultural Politics, and Mythmaking during the Quincentenary.* Gainesville: University Press of Florida, 2000.

Urla, Jacqueline. "'We are all Malcolm X!' Negu Gorriak, Hip-Hop and the Basque Political Imaginary." In Tony Mitchell, ed., *Global Noise: Rap and Hip-Hop Outside the U.S.A.* Middletown: Wesleyan University Press. 2001.

Vázquez Montalban, Manuel. *Cronica sentimental de España.* 2nd ed. Barcelona: Grijalbo, 1998 [1971].
————. *La penetración americana en España.* Madrid: Cuadernos para el diálogo, 1974.
Verdú, Vicente. *El planeta americano.* Barcelona: Anagrama, 1996.
Vernon, Kathleen M. "Reading Hollywood in/and Spanish Cinema: From Trade Wars to Transculturation." In Marsha Kinder, ed., *Refiguring Spain: Cinema/Media/Representation.* Durham: Duke University Press, 1997.
Viñas, Ángel. *Los pactos secretos de Franco con Estados Unidos: bases, ayuda económica, recortes de soberanía.* Barcelona: Grijalbo, 1981.
Whitaker, Arthur P. *Spain and Defense of the West: Ally and Liability.* New York: Council on Foreign Relations, 1961.
Zulaika, Joseba. "Krens's Taj Mahal: The Guggenheim's Global Love Museum." *Discourse* 23, no. 1 (2001): 100–118.
————. *Crónica de una seducción: El museo Guggenheim Bilbao.* Madrid: Nerea, 1997.

Sweden

Åhnebrink, Lars, ed. *Amerika och Norden.* Stockholm: Almqvist and Wiksell, 1964.
Alm, Martin. *Americanitis: Amerika som sjukdom eller läkemedel: Svenska berättelser om USA åren 1900–1939.* Lund: Studia Historica Lundensia, 2002.
Anderson, Carl L. *The Swedish Acceptance of American Literature.* Philadelphia: University of Pennsylvania Press, 1957.
Åsard, Erik, and Rolf Lundén, eds. *Networks of Americanization: Aspects of the American Influence in Sweden.* Uppsala: Almqvist and Wiksell, 1992.
Barton, H. Arnold. "The New Deal and the People's Home: American and Swedish Perspectives from the 1930s." In Dag Blanck et al., eds., *Migration och mångfald: Essäer om kulturkontakt och minoritetsfrågor tillägnade Harald Runblom.* Uppsala: Centrum för multietnisk forskning, 1999.
Eidevall, Gunnar. *Amerika i svensk 1900-talslitteratur: Från Gustaf Hellström till Lars Gustafsson.* Stockholm: Almqvist and Wiksell International, 1983.
Elovson, Harald. *Amerika i svensk litteratur 1750–1820: En studie i komparativ litteraturhistoria.* Lund: Ohlssons, 1930.
Erickson, Scott. *American Religious Influences in Sweden.* Uppsala: Svenska kyrkans forskningsråd, 1997.
Leifland, Leif. *Frostens år: Om USA's diplomatiska utfrysning av Sverige.* Stockholm: Nerenius och Santérus, 1997.

Lundén, Rolf, and Erik Åsard, eds. *Networks of Americanization: Aspects of the American Influence in Sweden.* Uppsala: Almqvist and Wiksell, 1992.

Myrdal, Gunnar, and Alva Myrdal. 1941. *Kontakt med Amerika.* Stockholm: Bonnier.

O'Dell, Tom. *Culture Unbound: Americanization and Everyday Life in Sweden.* Lund: Nordic Academic Press, 1997.

Runeby, Nils. *Den nya världen och den gamla: Amerikabild och emigrationsuppfattning i Sverige 1820–1860.* Stockholm: Läromedelsförlaget, 1969.

Scott, Franklin. *The American Experience of Swedish Students: Retrospect and Aftermath.* Minneapolis: University of Minneapolis Press, 1956.

Shands, Kerstin W., Rolf Lundén, and Dag Blanck. *Notions of America: Swedish Perspectives.* Huddinge: Almqvist and Wiksell, 2004.

Steene, Birgitta. "The Swedish Image of America." In Poul Houe and Sven Haakon Rossel, eds., *Images of America in Scandinavia.* Amsterdam: Rodopi, 1998.

USSR/Russia

Aksenov, Vassily. *In Search of Melancholy Baby.* New York: Random House, 1987.

Alexeyeva, Ludmilla. *U.S. Broadcasting to the Soviet Union.* New York: Helsinki Watch Committee, 1986.

Alexeyeva, Ludmilla, and Paul Goldberg. *The Thaw Generation: Coming of Age in the Post-Stalin Era.* Boston: Little, Brown, 1990.

Ball, Alan M. *Imagining America: Influence and Images in Twentieth-Century Russia.* Lanham: Rowman and Littlefield, 2003.

Barghoorn, Frederick Charles. *The Soviet Cultural Offensive: The Role of Cultural Diplomacy in Soviet Foreign Policy.* Westport: Greenwood Press, 1976 [1960].

———. *The Soviet Image of the United States: A Study in Distortion.* New York: Harcourt Brace, 1950.

Barker, Adele Marie, ed. *Consuming Russia: Popular Culture, Sex, and Society since Gorbachev.* Durham: Duke University Press, 1999.

Becker, Jonathan A. *Soviet and Russian Press Coverage of the United States: Press, Politics and Identity in Transition.* London: Palgrave Macmillan, 1999.

Berman, Maureen R., and Joseph E. Johnson, eds. *Unofficial Diplomats.* New York: Columbia University Press, 1977.

Berry, Ellen E., and Mikhail N. Epstein. *Transcultural Experiments: Russian and American Models of Creative Communication.* New York: St. Martin's Press, 1999.

Brown, Deming. *Soviet Attitudes towards American Writing*. Princeton: Princeton University Press, 1962.

Carroll, Mark. *Music and Ideology in Cold War Europe*. New York: Cambridge University Press, 2003.

Cohon, George. *To Russia with Fries*. Toronto: McClelland and Stewart, 1997.

Cushman, Thomas. *Notes from Underground: Rock Music Counterculture in Russia*. Albany: State University of New York Press, 1995.

Dennis, Everette E., George Gerbner, and Yassen N. Zassoursky, eds. *Beyond the Cold War: Soviet and American Media Images*. Newbury Park: Sage, 1991.

Friedberg, Maurice. *A Decade of Euphoria: Western Literature in Post-Stalin Russia 1954–64*. Bloomington: Indiana University Press, 1977.

Ganley, Gladys D. *Unglued Empire: The Soviet Experience with Communications Technologies*. Norwood: Ablex, 1996.

Gibert, Stephen P., ed. *Soviet Images of America*. New York: Crane, Russak, 1978.

Johnson, Priscilla, and Leopold Labedz, eds. *Khrushchev and the Arts: The Politics of Soviet Culture, 1962–1964*. Cambridge: MIT Press, 1965.

Kalashnikov, Maksim, and Iurii Krupnov. *Osedlai molniiu! Amerika protiv Rossii*. Moscow: Astrel', 2003.

Lewin, Moshe. *The Gorbachev Phenomenon: A Historical Interpretation*. Berkeley: University of California Press, 1988.

Lucas, Scott. *Freedom's War: The US Crusade Against the Soviet Union, 1945–56*. New York: New York University Press, 1999.

Mehnert, Klaus. *Russians and their Favorite Books*. Stanford: Stanford University Press, 1983.

Mickiewicz, Ellen Propper. *Changing Channels: Television and the Struggle for Power in Russia*. Durham: Duke University Press, 1999.

———. *Split Signals: Television and Politics in the Soviet Union*. New York: Oxford University Press, 1988.

———. *Media and the Russian Public*. New York: Praeger, 1981.

Nelson, Michael. *War of the Black Heavens: The Battles of Western Broadcasting in the Cold War*. Syracuse: Syracuse University Press, 1997.

Nordenstreng, Kaarle, Elena Vartanova, and Yassen Zassoursky, eds. *Russian Media Challenge*. Helsinki: Kikimora, 2001.

Parks, J. D. *Culture, Conflict and Coexistence: American-Soviet Cultural Relations, 1917–1958*. Jefferson: McFarland, 1983.

Parshev, A. P. *Pochemu Rossiia ne Amerika: Kniga dlia tekh, kto ostaetsia zdes'*. Moscow: Krymskii Most-9D, 2003.

Pilkington, Hilary. *Russia's Youth and its Culture: A Nation's Constructors and Constructed*. London: Routledge, 1995.

Pilkington, Hilary, et al. *Looking West? Cultural Globalization and Russian Youth Cultures.* University Park: Pennsylvania State University Press, 2002.

Prevots, Naima. *Dance for Export: Cultural Diplomacy and the Cold War.* Hanover: Wesleyan University Press, 1999.

Puddington, Arch. *Broadcasting Freedom: The Cold War Triumph of Radio Free Europe and Radio.* Lexington: University Press of Kentucky, 2000.

Rantanen, Terhi. *The Global and the National: Media and Communications in Post-Communist Russia.* Lanham: Rowman and Littlefield, 2002.

Richmond, Yale. *U.S.-Soviet Cultural Exchanges, 1958–1986: Who Wins?* Boulder: Westview Press, 1987.

Riordan, Jim, ed. *Soviet Youth Culture.* Bloomington: Indiana University Press, 1989.

Schwarz, Boris. *Music and Musicians in Soviet Russia, 1917–1981.* Bloomington: Indiana University Press, 1983.

Shiraev, Eric, and Vladislav M. Zubok. *Anti-Americanism in Russia: From Stalin to Putin.* New York: Palgrave, 2000.

Shlapentokh, Vladimir. "Soviet People and the West." In Vladimir Shlapentokh, ed., *Public and Private Life of the Soviet People: Changing Values in Post-Stalin Russia.* New York: Oxford University Press, 1989.

Short, K. R. M., ed. *Western Broadcasting over the Iron Curtain.* London: Croom Helm, 1986.

Siefert, Marsha, ed. *Mass Culture and Perestroika in the Soviet Union.* New York: Oxford University Press, 1991.

Sosin, Gene. *Sparks of Liberty: An Insider's Memoir of Radio Liberty.* State College: Pennsylvania State University Press, 1999.

Starr, S. Frederick. *Red and Hot: The Fate of Jazz in the Soviet Union, 1917–1980.* New York: Oxford University Press, 1983.

Stites, Richard. *Russian Popular Culture: Entertainment and Society Since 1900.* Cambridge: Cambridge University Press, 1992.

Troitsky, Artemy. *Back in the USSR: The True Story of Rock in Russia.* Boston: Faber and Faber, 1988.

Wellens, Ian. *Music on the Frontline: Nicholas Nabokov's Struggle against Communism and Middlebrow Culture.* London: Ashgate, 2002.

CONTRIBUTORS

Andrzej Antoszek is Lecturer in American Literature and American Studies at the Catholic University of Lublin, Poland. He has contributed articles to such journals as *Counter-Art Revue, Literatura na Świecie,* and *American Studies in Europe,* as well as *Art Magazine* and *Akcent,* for which he edited volumes dedicated to contemporary American culture and black culture. His chapters on contemporary American and Polish culture have appeared in various books, including *PASE PAPERS in Literature, Language and Culture* and *Internet 2000.* He is a member of several American Studies organizations, including Collegium for African American Research and the Polish Association for American Studies. His Ph.D. dissertation was on "Don DeLillo's Evolving Picture of Contemporary America." Currently he is working on a special volume of *Art Magazine* dedicated to the problems of African-American culture. antoszek@kul.lublin.pl

Günter Bischof is Professor of History, Director of the Center for Austrian Culture and Commerce, and the Interim Director of the Eisenhower Center for American Studies at the University of New Orleans. He has studied American Studies and History at Austrian and American institutions and holds a Ph.D. from Harvard University. He taught for two years at the Amerika-Institut of the University of Munich and also was a guest Professor of History at the Universities of Salzburg, Innsbruck, and Vienna. His primary research interests are Cold War studies, history and memory, World War II prisoners of war, and contemporary Austrian history. He has authored *Austria in the First Cold War, 1945–55: Leverage of the Weak* (Basingstoke, 1999) and co-edited *The Marshall Plan and Germany* (Oxford, 1991), *Facts Against Falsehood: Eisenhower and the German POWs* (Baton Rouge, 1992), *Eisenhower: A Centenary Assessment* (Baton Rouge, 1995), *The Pacific War Revisited* (Baton Rouge, 1997), *Cold War Respite: The Geneva Summit of 1955* (Baton Rouge 2000), and 13 volumes in the *Contemporary Austrian Studies* series.

Activities related to the topic of this book are a conference organized in 2002 on the "Americanization/Westernization of Austria" (the conference volume

was published in 2004 in the *Contemporary Austrian Studies* series), a paper on "Anti-Americanism on post-World War II Austria" delivered at the Austrian Association for American Studies' annual conference in Vienna in 2002 (published in the conference volume *Austrian (Anti-)Americanisms* [Vienna, 2004]), a panel on "European Anti-Americanism: Past and Present" organized for the Organization of American Historians' 2003 annual meeting in Memphis, and the essay "Das amerikanische Jahrhundert: Europas Niedergang—Amerikas Aufstieg," published in the Austrian journal for contemporary history *Zeitgeschichte* 28 (March/April 2001).
gjbhi@mobiletel.com

Dag Blanck is University Lecturer at the Centre for Multiethnic Research at Uppsala University, Sweden, and the Director of the Swenson Swedish Immigration Research Center at Augustana College in Rock Island, Illinois. He was educated in the United States and Sweden and holds a Ph.D. in History from Uppsala University. He is the former president of the Swedish Association for American Studies. His research has focused on the history of Swedish immigration to the U.S., issues relating to multicultural societies, and most recently, the transcultural processes through which American influences have entered Swedish society.

Some of his publications include: "'We Have a Lot to Learn from America': The Myrdals and the Question of American Influences in Sweden," in Clara Juncker and Russell Duncan, eds., *Angles on the English-Speaking World: Trading Cultures: Nationalism and Globalization in American Studies,* vol. 2 (Copenhagen, 2002); *Swedes in the Twin Cities: Immigrant Life and Minnesota's Urban Frontier* (St. Paul and Uppsala, 2001) [co-editor]; "Academic migration: Sweden and the United States," *Swedish American Genealogist* 18, no. 2–3 (1999); *Becoming Swedish-American: The Construction of an Ethnic Identity in the Augustana Synod, 1860–1917* (Uppsala, 1997); "Inte bara McDonald's: Amerika i Europa- och i Sverige," in Gunilla Gren-Eklund, ed., *Att förstå Europa- mångfald och sammanhang: Humanistdagarna vid Uppsala universitet 1994* (Uppsala, 1996); "The Impact of the American Academy in Sweden," in Rolf Lundén and Erik Åsard, eds., *Networks of Americanization: Aspects of the American Influence in Sweden* (Uppsala, 1992); *American Immigrants and Their Generations: Studies and Commentaries on the Hansen Thesis After Fifty Years* (Urbana, 1990) [co-editor].
dag.blanck@multietn.uu.se
http://www.multietn.uu.se/staff/blanck.htm.

Konstantina Botsiou is a Lecturer in Modern European History at the National and Capodistrian University of Athens. She studied History at the Universities of Athens and Tübingen and holds a Ph.D. in Modern and Contemporary History from the University of Tübingen. Her research interests focus on the history of European integration, Cold War studies, modern Greek history, and contemporary Southeast European history. She has previously worked at the Jean Monnet Chair in the History of European Integration, University of Tübingen, and has been a research fellow at the Constantinos G. Karamanlis Foundation and the Jean Monnet Centre in European Policy, University of Athens. Since 2001 she is Director for Publications and Research Programs at the Constantinos Karamanlis Institute for Democracy. Her publications include: *Griechenlands Weg nach Europa: Von der Truman-Doktrin bis zur Assoziierung mit der Europäischen Wirtschaftsgemeinschaft, 1947–1961* (Frankfurt, 1999) [co-authored with Yannis Valinakis]; *International Affairs and Strategy in the Atomic Era* (Athens, 2000); *Between NATO and the EEC: Europe in Search of a Defense and Political Union, 1949–1957* (Athens, 2003) [co-editor with C. Arvanitopoulos and B. Lammers]; *EU Integration and the Future of Southeastern Europe* (Athens, Berlin, 2003); "In Search of Lost Time: the European Course of Democratization," in *30 Years of Greek Foreign Policy, 1974–2004* (Athens, 2005); "Greek–Turkish Relations since 1974: Efforts for Rapprochement and Co-operation," *Mésogeios* 22–23 (2004); "Greece in the European Union: A Historical Account," in *Greece and the European Union: The New Role and the New Agenda* (Athens, 2002); "Karamanlis' European Policies and the Association of Greece with the European Economic Community," *De Gaulle et Karamanlis: La Nation, L'Etat, L'Europe* (Athens/Paris, 2001). kpetro@otenet.gr

Kate Delaney is a Lecturer in American Literature at the Massachusetts Institute of Technology. She has been a Fulbright lecturer in American Civilization at the Université de Caen, France and has given numerous guest lectures at other universities in Europe, Africa, and Asia. A member of the editorial board of *American Studies,* she contributes regularly to the series *European Contributions in American Studies* and to the Polish cultural quarterly *Akcent.* Selected publications: "America Perceived" and "America Perceived after 9/11" in the *Encyclopedia of American Studies* (Danbury, 2001); "The Debate over the National Endowment for the Arts: Bellwether for U.S. Cultural Politics," in Agata Preis-Smith and Piotr Skurowski, eds., *Cultural Policy, or the Politics of Culture* (Warsaw, 1999); "What We Talk About When We Talk About Family Values," in Teresa Pyzik and Tomasz Sikora, eds., *New Shape of Ethics? Reflections on Ethical Values in Post (?) Modern American Cultures and Societies* (Katowice, 2000). From 1991 to 1995 she served as Cultural Attaché at the U.S. Embassy in The Hague and from 1996 to 2000 as U.S. Cultural Attaché in Warsaw. kdelaney@MtHolyoke.edu

David W. Ellwood is Associate Professor in International History, University of Bologna, and Professorial Lecturer in European-American relations, Johns Hopkins University, School of Advanced International Studies, Bologna Center. After a Ph.D. thesis on "Allied Occupation Policy in Italy 1943–1946" (University of Reading, UK, 1977), and the production of books and articles on this theme (particularly *Italy 1943–1945: The Politics of Liberation*, Leicester, 1985), research interests expanded to the postwar period, and the Marshall Plan in particular. A Fellowship at the European University Institute facilitated the production of *Rebuilding Europe: Western Europe, America and Postwar Reconstruction* (London, 1992), centered on the European Recovery Program. The fundamental theme of the research—the working of American power in contemporary European history—was expanded to include cultural power, particularly that of the American cinema industry, hence two edited books on the theme *Hollywood in Europe* (Florence, 1991; Amsterdam, 1995). Other themes treated include the U.S. and European integration, Americanization and anti-Americanism, and the Anglo-American "Special Relationship." Currently in production is a large-scale survey on *America and the Politics of Modernization in Europe* for Oxford University Press.

He was awarded a Senior Associate Membership of St. Antony's College, Oxford, 1989/90, and is currently a member of the European Science Foundation/Netherlands American Studies Association research project on "Post Cold War Europe, Post Cold War America," coordinated by Rob Kroes, University of Amsterdam. He was President of IAMHIST, the International Association for Media and History, from 1995 to 1999.
ellwood@spbo.unibo.it

Richard Joseph Golsan is Professor of French and editor of the *South Central Review* at Texas A&M University, and has been the codirector of several National Endowment for the Humanities' seminars in France. Previously he taught at Université Paris III-Sorbonne Nouvelle and Case Western Reserve University, Cleveland, Ohio. Major book publications: *Vichy's Afterlife: History and Counterhistory in Postwar France* (Lincoln, 2000), *René Girard and Myth: An Introduction* (New York, 2001), *Service inutile: A Study of the Tragic in the Theatre of Henry de Montherlant* (University, 1988); edited books: *The Papon Affair: Memory and Justice on Trial* (New York, 2000), *Fascism's Return: Scandal, Revision and Ideology since 1980* (Lincoln, 1998), *Gender and Fascism in Modern France* (Hanover, spring 1997, co-edited with Melanie Hawthorne), *Memory, the Holocaust, and French Justice: The Bousquet and Touvier Affairs* (Hanover, 1996), *Epic and Epoch: Essays on the Interpretation and History of a Genre* (Lubbock, 1994, co-edited with Stephen Oberhelman and Van Kelly), *Fascism, Aesthetics and Culture* (Hanover, 1992), *German and International Perspectives on the Spanish Civil War: The Aesthetics of Partisanship* (Columbia,

1992, co-edited with Wulf Koepke, Richard Critchfield, and Luis Costa); anno-
tated editions and translations: *A French Tragedy* by Tzvetan Todorov, translated
by Mary Byrd Kelly (Hanover, 1996), *The Future if a Negation: Reflections on
the Question of Genocide* by Alain Finkielkraut, translated by Mary Byrd Kelly
(Lincoln, 1998), *Dispatches from the Balkan War* by Alain Finkielkraut, translated with Peter S. Rogers (Lincoln, 1999), *Fascism and Communism* by Francois
Furet and Ernst Nolte, translated by Katherine Golsan (Lincoln, 2001), *Stalinism and Nazism: History and Memory Compared*, edited by Henry Rousso
(Lincoln, 2004).

He has recently completed a book entitled *French Writers and the Politics
of Complicity: Crises of Democracy in the 1940s and 1990s* that deals with, among
other things, the 9/11 attacks.
Rjgolsan@aol.com

Rob Kroes is the Chair of American Studies at the University of Amsterdam.
He is a past President of the European Association for American Studies (1992–
1996) and the author, co-author, or editor of thirty-one books, including *The
Persistence of Ethnicity: Dutch Calvinist Pioneers in Amsterdam, Montana* (Urbana, 1992), *If You've Seen One, You've Seen the Mall* (Urbana, 1996), *Predecessors: Intellectual Lineages in American Studies* (Amsterdam, 1999), *Them and
Us: Questions of Citizenship in a Globalizing World* (Urbana, 2000) and (with
Robert W. Rydell) *Buffalo Bill in Bologna: The Americanization of the World,
1850–1920* (Chicago, 2005). As a 2003 fellow of NYU's International Center
for Advanced Studies, he completed a book, entitled *Photographic Memories:
Private Pictures, Public Images and American History* (forthcoming 2006).
r.kroes@uva.nl

Dorothy Noyes is Associate Professor of Folklore in the Departments of English, Comparative Studies, and Anthropology at Ohio State University. She
is the author of *Fire in the Plaça: Catalan Festival Politics After Franco* (Philadelphia, 2003) and co-editor, with Cristina Sánchez-Carretero, of *Performance,
arte verbal y comunicacion: Nuevas perspectivas en los estudios de folklore y cultura popular en USA* (Oiartzun, Spain, 2000). In addition, she has published
numerous articles on the politics of popular culture in Spain and Europe generally. Her current project is entitled *Voicing Redemption: Industrial Feudal-
ism and the Folk in Modern Europe*.
noyes.10@osu.edu

Klaus Petersen is Associate Professor in Contemporary History at the University of Southern Denmark. He has previously taught at the University of
Copenhagen. Most important book publications: *Legitimität und Krise: Die
politische Geschichte des dänischen Wohlfahrtsstaates 1945–1973* (Berlin, 1998),

Socialdemokratisk Samfund 1966–1973: De loyales ungdomsoprør (Copenhagen, 2001). He has co-edited *The Nordic Welfare States 1900–2000,* with Neils Finn Christiansen (*Scandinavian Journal of History,* vol. 26, 2001) and is currently working on contributions to *The Nordic Model—A Historical Re-Appraisal: Studies in Nordic Welfare Policy,* with Niels Finn Christiansen and Nils Edling (Copenhagen, forthcoming), and *13 historier om den dansk velfærdsstaten* (Odense, 2003). He is also co-editor of the journals *Arbejderhistorie* and *Den Jyske Historiker* as well as the discussion list H-Skand.
Klaus.Petersen@hist.sdu.dk
http://www.humaniora.sdu.dk/scripts/template_inst.html?vis=2&niveau=institut&id=2

Marsha Siefert teaches in the history department at Central European University in Budapest. For many years she was Editor of the *Journal of Communication* and the co-editor of two book series. Among her own edited books are *Mass Communication and Perestroika in the Soviet Union* (Oxford University Press, 1991) and *Extending the Borders of Russian History* (Central European University Press, 2003). She has lectured widely in Russia and Eastern Europe and has published several journal articles and book chapters on music, communication, sound recording, film, and history.
siefertm@ceu.hu

Nils Arne Sørensen is Senior Lecturer in Modern European History at Syddansk University, Odense, Denmark. He studied at the University of Aarhus, Denmark, and at the European University Institute in Florence. He previously taught at the University of Aarhus and at Millikin University, Illinois. He is the co-author of *Fascismen i Italien* (Århus, 1984, 2nd. ed. 1986), *Verdens historie 1750–1945* (Copenhagen, 1989), *European Identities* (editor, Odenske, 1995), *Briterne og Europa* (Copenhagen, 1997), *Verdens historie: Tiden siden 1945* (Copenhagen, 1998), and *Gads historieleksikon* (Copenhagen, 2001, 2nd ed., 2003), and has published numerous articles on Danish and European history. He also comments on contemporary British and Italian politics on Danish radio and television.
nils@hist.sdu.dk

Alexander Stephan is Professor of German, Ohio Eminent Scholar, and Senior Fellow of the Mershon Center for the Study of International Security at Ohio State University. Previously he taught at Princeton University, at the University of California at Los Angeles, and in Florida. Book publications related to the topic of this volume: *Americanization and Anti-Americanism: The German Encounter with American Culture after 1945* (New York, 2005), *Jeans, Rock und Vietnam: Amerikanische Kultur in der DDR* (Berlin, 2002), co-edited

with Therese Hörnigk. Future publications include: *Die Amerikanisierung der (west-) deutschen Kultur seit 1945* (Munich, forthcoming, 2006), co-edited with Jochen Vogt, and *Das Amerika der Autoren: Deutsche Ansichten von Kafka bis 9/11* (Munich: forthcoming, 2005. Other book publications: *Im Visier des FBI: Deutsche Exilschriftsteller in den Akten amerikanischer Geheimdienste* (Stuttgart, 1995, paperback edition, Berlin, 1998, published in English as *"Communazis:" FBI Surveillance of German Emigré Writers,* New Haven, 2000), *Christa Wolf* (Munich, 4th, enl. and rev. ed., 1991), *Die deutsche Exilliteratur* (Munich, 1979), *Max Frisch* (Munich, 1983), *Anna Seghers im Exil* (Bonn, 1993), *Anna Seghers: 'Das siebte Kreuz'. Welt und Wirkung eines Romans* (Berlin, 1997); edited books: *Peter Weiss: Die Ästhetik des Widerstands* (Frankfurt, 3rd ed., 1990), *Schreiben im Exil* (Bonn, 1985), co-edited with Hans Wagner, *Exil: Literatur und die Künste nach 1933* (Bonn, 1990), *Christa Wolf: The Author's Dimension* (New York, 1993; London, 1993; Chicago, 1995), *The New Sufferings of Young W. and Other Short Stories from the German Democratic Republic* (New York, 1997), co-edited with Therese Hörnigk, *Uwe Johnson: Speculations About Jakob and Other Writings* (New York, 2000), *"Rot=Braun?" Brecht Dialog 2000: Nationalsozialismus und Stalinismus bei Brecht und Zeitgenossen* (Berlin, 2000), co-edited with Therese Hörnigk, *A. Döblin, L. Feuchtwanger, A. Seghers, A. Zweig: Early Twentieth Century German Fiction* (New York, 2003), *Anna Seghers: Die Entscheidung. Roman* (Berlin, 2003). Stephan is editor of the book series *Exil-Studien/Exile Studies* and has made numerous contributions to radio and television in Germany and the U.S. on Bertolt Brecht, Marlene Dietrich, Anna Seghers, Thomas Mann, and other topics, also producing for German television a documentary film titled *Im Visier des FBI: Deutsche Autoren im US-Exil* (ARD, 1995).
stephan.30@osu.edu
http://people.cohums.ohio-state.edu/stephan30

Hugh Wilford is a Senior Lecturer in American History at the University of Sheffield. He is author of two books, *The New York Intellectuals: From Vanguard to Institution* (Manchester, 1995) and *The CIA, the British Left and the Cold War: Calling the Tune?* (London, 2003). He has also contributed articles to such journals as *Diplomatic History,* the *Journal of Contemporary History,* and the *Journal of American Studies.* Currently he is working on two projects: a study of CIA sponsorship of American citizen groups during the early Cold War era, and a collaborative investigation into Americanization, globalization, and American team sports.
h.wilford@sheffield.ac.uk

INDEX

Natlogi betalt (1957), 132
NATO (North Atlantic Treaty Organization), 2, 9, 13, 45, 51, 110, 117, 134, 162, 169, 171, 172, 198, 208, 261, 269, 292, 297, 301, 342
    French involvement with, 55, 56, 62–63
    Greek involvement with, 280–81, 297
    Italy's involvement with, 267
    Poland's membership in, 218, 232
    Spain's membership in, 313, 318–19
Natt och Dag, Otto, 94
Nea Estia, 289
NE (Currency Committee), 279
Negro in the USA, The, 118
Nelson, Ricky, 225
Nerman, Ture, 94
Never on Sunday (1960), 293
New Critics, 28
New Deal, 107, 264
New Music, The, 193
Newsweek, 230
Newton, Lauren, 236
New World Order, 7
New Yorker, 48
New York Intellectuals, 77
New York Times, 3, 66, 220, 222, 263
New York Times Magazine, 326
NFFC (National Film Finance Corporation), 37, 38
NGOs (nongovernmental organizations), 232
Niagara (1953), 225
Nicaragua, 301
Niebiesko-Czarni, 236
Niedenthal, Chris, 226
Nielsen, Harald, 116
Night on the 14th Parallel (1971), 201
9/11, 59
    image of US after, 1, 13
    terrorist attacks on, 171, 270, 357
    US foreign policy after, 5, 7, 14, 18, 46, 48, 84, 109, 170, 171, 357
Nine Deaths of the Ninja (1998), 205
Nirvana, 236

Nisser, Peter, 107
Nixon, Richard M., 168, 191, 221, 222, 223
No Logo (Klein), 81
Nora, Pierre, 58
Nord (Céline), 50
North Korea, 65
Novy Mir, 195
Nowak, Jan, 223
Nowak-Jeziorański, Jan, 219
Nureyev, Rudolf, 193

O

Oasis, 34
Oates, Joyce Carol, 95, 224
O'Brien, Edmond, 225
Obsession anti-américaine, L' (Revel), 45, 56
Ocean's Eleven (2001), 231
October Revolution, 186
OEEC (Organization for European Economic Cooperation), 117, 282
Office of Strategic Services, 71
Of Mice and Men (Steinbeck), 290
Of Paradise and Power (Todd), 65
Oggi, 260
Ogre of Athens, The (1956), 293
Olbiński, Rafał, 245
Old World's New World, The (Woodward), 147
Olsen, Ernst Bruun, 138
Olympics, 190, 238
OMGUS (Office of Military Government United States), 72, 74, 76
O'Neill, Eugene, 7, 95, 290
On Rich Red Islands (1981), 201
On the Road (Kerouac), 123, 238, 350
Operational Plan for Germany, 71
ÖPZ (Österreichisches Produktivitätszentrum), 155–56, 158, 162
Orbison, Roy, 231
ORF (Österreichischer Rundfunk), 170
Orgmandy, Eugene, 163
Orr, Charles A., 120
Ortega y Gasset, José, 311
Orwell, George, 31–32
Osborne, John, 29
Öste, Sven, 104
Ottoman Empire, 338, 340

Printed in the United States
201815BV00001B/1-36/P

9 781845 450854